LOTTE MEITNER-GRAF
LONDON

THE AGE OF THE ENLIGHTENMENT

Studies presented to Theodore Besterman

Edited by
W. H. BARBER, J. H. BRUMFITT, R. A. LEIGH,
R. SHACKLETON and S. S. B. TAYLOR

Published for the
University Court of the University of St Andrews

OLIVER AND BOYD
EDINBURGH : TWEEDDALE COURT
LONDON : 39a WELBECK STREET
1967

First published 1967

Printed in Great Britain for Oliver & Boyd Ltd.
by R. & R. Clark, Ltd., Edinburgh

Foreword

It was a group of English eighteenth-century scholars who made the first moves towards a volume to honour Theodore Besterman's achievement in eighteenth-century studies. With the completion of his edition of Voltaire's *Correspondence*, the unbelievable has been accomplished; we now have 98 volumes of text, over 20,000 letters, four volumes of bibliographical and reference material, and finally a five-volume index. The whole will enrich research on all aspects of the period and demand a reconsideration of many of the basic assumptions of scholarship in this field. The warmth of the response by scholars in France, Italy, Britain, Belgium, the United States, Germany and Switzerland is in itself sufficient evidence of his reputation. Indeed, the Committee was confronted with an embarrassing task in limiting contributions to a manageable number.

This volume reflects the gratitude of scholars for Theodore Besterman's work in one field alone and it ignores others in which he has equal standing, a fact evident from even the most cursory glance at Sir Frank Francis's concluding article. Bibliographers, psychical research workers, art collectors and iconographers, humanists and bibliophiles regard him as a specialist in their particular disciplines. It is clear that so versatile a mind cannot be satisfactorily reflected in a single volume, and it is primarily as a tribute to the Voltaire scholar and admirer of the Enlightenment that this volume is envisaged. It has been published with the generous help of the Publications Committee of the University of St Andrews, a University of which Theodore Besterman holds the honorary doctorate. We wish to express our gratitude to the University of St Andrews, to Messrs. Oliver & Boyd, and also to those colleagues and friends who gave their warm support although themselves prevented from contributing.

As a result of Besterman's work, Voltaire studies have been rejuvenated, and research material made available which it will require many years to assimilate. In addition, Voltaire himself and the period of the Enlightenment have been re-opened as fields of study, and an international community of scholars has come into being through the First International Congress on the Enlightenment of which he was prime mover and president. Out of this community there is to emerge an international society for eighteenth-century studies which will associate all students of this period in man's intellectual history, whether historians, scientists, economists, literary historians, musicologists, art historians or philosophers.

The techniques of research and the editing of primary source materials themselves have been revolutionised by his rigorous respect for scientific accuracy, and his documentary researches. For the *Correspondence* of Voltaire itself manuscript material was found in his own large collection and elsewhere for practically all the texts published, and photocopies or originals have been made available to scholars at the *Institut et musée Voltaire*, of which he is founder-director. Over twenty different countries were searched for manuscripts, and over 500 printed sources utilised for letters in print. As his wife said: 'If Theodore had lived centuries ago he would have been a Benedictine monk'. So many other enterprises, even of smaller scale, have been attempted only with an ample team of collaborators and research assistants, not to mention grants. It appears incredible that this—which must surely rank as one of the largest scholarly tasks ever accomplished—was undertaken alone and without the support of foundations, governments or universities. It was only when a considerable part of the text had been established and with the early volumes already published that he was joined by an assistant to help in the completion of the work and by an indexer. A measure of financial assistance also became available from Swiss sources. Yet for all this the burden fell principally upon Theodore Besterman himself and every aspect of it bears his personal stamp—a truly magnificent achievement.

It is this total dedication to his work which has characterised all of Theodore Besterman's activities, whether it be the production of the *World Bibliography of Bibliographies*, or that of Voltaire's *Correspondence*. It may even be seen in his first published work written when he was not yet twenty years of age. It is still evident late in a life which rivals that of Voltaire himself for sheer intensity of labour. The comparison is not idle: 'For 40 years', Besterman once said, 'I have been a Voltaire admirer. I have spent the last twenty in his company, lived in his house for the last six years, slept in his room, read his letters and opened his mail in his own study, been the intimate of his secrets: I have become Voltaire himself, if you wish *longo intervallo*. In these circumstances it would be wrong and hypocritical to speak of this great man in an impersonal, detached manner.'

Like Voltaire himself, Theodore Besterman has become not merely a man or a writer, but an example of what may be achieved in a lifetime, and achieved with an intellectual integrity of the highest order. And with this he has remained a man, a man of ideals, radical sympathies and refined tastes; with a strong love for England, and yet the most cosmopolitan of outlooks.

The editorial committee are pleased to take this opportunity of recording their respect for him and of offering him this volume, on behalf of all who have actively contributed or expressed their encouragement and approval.

Contents

CONTEMPORARIES AND FRIENDS

CONTENTS

Bibliographical Abbreviations

AT. *Œuvres complètes de Diderot*, edd. J. Assézat [and M. Tourneaux] (Paris 1875–1877)

Best. *Voltaire's Correspondence*, ed. Theodore Besterman (Genève, Institut et Musée Voltaire, 1953–1965)

DP. *Correspondance générale de J.-J. Rousseau*, edd. Théophile Dufour [and Pierre-Paul Plan] (Paris 1924–1934)

Leigh *Correspondanee complète de Jean Jacques Rousseau*, ed. R. A. Leigh (Genève, Institut et Musée Voltaire, 1965–)

M. *Œuvres complètes de Voltaire*, [ed. Louis Moland] (Paris, Garnier frères, 1877–1885)

Pléiade Jean-Jacques Rousseau, *Œuvres complètes*, edd. Bernard Gagnebin and Marcel Raymond etc. (Paris, Bibliothèque de la Pléiade, 1959–)

Roth. Denis Diderot, *Correspondance*, ed. Georges Roth (Paris, Editions de minuit, 1955–)

SM. Georges Streckeisen-Moultou, *Œuvres et Correspondance inédites de J.-J. Rousseau* (Paris 1861)

Studies on Voltaire: Studies on Voltaire and the eighteenth century, ed. Theodore Besterman (Genève, Institut et Musée Voltaire, 1955–)

Voltaire's apprenticeship as a Historian: La Henriade

O. R. Taylor

Voltaire's interest in history may have been kindled in school, at the Collège Louis-le-Grand.[1] From the Jesuit order had issued a number of distinguished historians (Petau, Labbe, Sirmond), the latest of whom was Father Gabriel Daniel (1649–1728), royal historiographer and author of a famous *Histoire de France* (1696; 1713). It seems unlikely that, as a schoolboy, Arouet came into contact with him, but the Collège Louis-le-Grand was in its way a centre of historical studies. In Arouet's time there were resident there François Catrou (1659–1737) who was to be part author of a highly esteemed *Histoire romaine* (1725–37), Jean Hardouin (1646–1729) who for long was sceptical about the authenticity of surviving Greek and Latin texts, René-Joseph de Tournemine (1661–1739) who was less paradoxical, but adventurous in his historical and chronological speculations[2] and Claude Buffier (1661–1737) in whom Voltaire was later to appreciate the disciple of Locke as well as the historian. Buffier's preoccupation with history was such that, with the support of colleagues like Charles Porée (1667–1741), he engineered a minor revolution in the curriculum of the school into which he managed to introduce a small amount of modern history. Some idea of the course Arouet may have followed can be gathered from Buffier's school textbook, his frequently reprinted *Éléments* or *Nouveaux éléments d'histoire et de géographie* [?1702],

[1] For a discussion of Voltaire's early interest in history and the historical documentation of *La Ligue* and *La Henriade* see O. R. Taylor, 'Voltaire, La Henriade. Édition critique', *Studies on Voltaire* (1965), xxxviii-xl. 161-178, henceforth referred to as 'Taylor'.

[2] H. Beaune, *Voltaire au collège* (Paris 1867), p. xcix.

or from a longer version of the same work, his *Pratique de la mémoire artificielle* (1701 etc.), highly praised by Voltaire in the *Siècle de Louis XIV* (M. xiv. 48). Year by year the rudiments of ancient and modern 'universal', European and French history (in 5e) were inculcated through a series of questions and answers and consolidated in the pupil's memory in mnemonic doggerel. The printed evidence suggests that the course was, basically, a dull, chronological list of important events with a pitifully thin commentary; unless good teaching clothed the bones with flesh, it can hardly, it would seem, have kindled a vocational flame among the students of Louis-le-Grand.

More excitement may have been generated by another of Buffier's innovations, the extracurricular 'exercices publics'.[3] These, it would appear from such programmes as have survived, were occasional public lectures in which answers were provided to historical problems likely to interest an eighteenth-century audience. Arouet may have been present at one of them, an *Exercice de chronologie historique et géographique* organised on 6 May 1709 by François-Emmanuel de Crussol-Florensac. We do not know whether these 'exercices' involved debate or critical treatment. It seems unlikely.

These public occasions, like the formal history courses, probably provided little nourishment for Arouet's restless mind. If he became interested in history at school, he was in all likelihood first attracted by the historical excursions which at the Collège Louis-le-Grand became a feature of the teaching of the humanities. History tended to intrude into the syllabus wherever and whenever a pretext could be found. Porée, for instance, would seize upon a Latin or Greek text as an excuse to extol the régime of Louis XIV and to emphasise its advantages when compared with the republics of antiquity, the Polish elective monarchy or the British constitution. He was given to commenting on the civil wars of the sixteenth century and to composing panegyrics of great French heroes such as du Guesclin. It is possible that the themes treated in the classroom led to the discussion of contemporary problems during the recreations which Arouet spent in conversation with his teachers, Porée and Tournemine. There may be a measure of truth in Duvernet's hagiographical account of Arouet's interests at school (*La Vie de Voltaire*, Genève

[3] G. Dupont-Ferrier, *Du Collège de Clermont au lycée Louis-le-Grand* (1563–1920) (Paris 1921–25), i. 147-149.

1786). 'Deux sortes d'études, & communément étrangères à celles des collèges, occupaient fortement Voltaire,' says the biographer. 'L'une était l'histoire des grands hommes contemporains, l'autre du gouvernement actuel. . . . Le gouvernement était pour lui un sujet habituel d'étude & de méditation: il se montrait attentif aux diverses révolutions du ministère, aimant à savoir ce qui se passait dans l'état, & à raisonner sur l'événement du jour. C'était la matière la plus ordinaire de ses entretiens, soit avec ses professeurs, soit avec ses condisciples. Il aimait, disait le P. Porée, à peser dans ses petites balances les grands intérêts de l'Europe.' Arouet was perhaps more sensitive than most of his fellow-pupils to the problems of the day, to the internal and external problems created by the War of the Spanish Succession. His curiosity was being drawn towards history by the momentous times in which he lived.

In retrospect, the ungrateful Voltaire thought that he had derived little profit either from his formal or from his informal education at the Collège Louis-le-Grand. Discussing Jesuit teaching in the article 'Éducation' in his *Questions sur l'Encyclopédie* (1771), he made his Counsellor observe: 'Lorsque j'entrai dans le monde . . . le pays même où je suis né était ignoré de moi; je ne connaissais ni les lois principales, ni les intérêts de ma patrie; . . . je savais du latin et des sottises' (M. xviii. 471). And it is fair to assume that in 1711 he was much better acquainted with ancient history and ancient historians than with modern historical writing. According to Jouvancy, a pupil at a Jesuit school might have read (no doubt for the most part in extracts) before he left: Caesar, Quintus Curtius, Eutropius, Florus, Herodianus, Justin, Livy, Valerius Maximus, Velleius Paterculus, Plutarch, Sallust, Suetonius, Tacitus, Thucydides and Aurelius Victor.[4] Of these, if we are to judge by later evidence, Voltaire developed a taste for Quintus Curtius,[5] Plutarch, Tacitus, Suetonius, Thucydides, Livy and Sallust. At the same time, he must have been taught the platitudes of humanist history. It is unlikely that he was otherwise introduced to the problems of historiography. History, as written by Jesuits like Maimbourg and Daniel, was informed by a Catholic, providentialist and monarchist orthodoxy

[4] A. Schimberg, *L'Éducation morale dans les collèges de la Compagnie de Jésus sous l'ancien régime* (Paris 1913), pp. 133-134.

[5] He had him in mind when composing *La Ligue* (Taylor, pp. 161, 591, 615); and later when writing the *Histoire de Charles XII*, see J. H. Brumfitt, *Voltaire historian* (Oxford 1958), p. 11.

which the reader was not invited to question. In fact, the skill with which Daniel managed to avoid giving offence either to the Vatican or the French government elicited from Saint-Simon the caustic comment: 'C'est un plaisir de le voir courir sur ces glaces avec ses patins de jésuite'.[6] In 1710 Arouet received as a school prize Davila's irreproachably orthodox *Histoire des guerres civiles*. It is improbable that he was consulted beforehand; the choice is no doubt significant of the view of French history presented to pupils at Louis-le-Grand.

In any case, Arouet probably gave little systematic thought to history and its problems either at school or in the immediately following years. He can have had little time for historical reading during his brief but eventful diplomatic career; and even if he was able to read Abraham de (van) Wicquefort's much esteemed *L'Ambassadeur et ses fonctions*,[7] it would have added nothing to what he already knew of historiography. After his return from Holland his concern was less with history than with drama and poetry.

The evidence that we have suggests that Voltaire's first real interest in history dated from the years 1714–16[8] and was awakened by his conversations with Louis Urbain Le Febvre de Caumartin about the reigns of Louis XIV and Henry IV. As intendant des finances (1690–1715), Caumartin had lived the history of the last twenty-five years of Louis XIV's reign (M. x. 241). Like most men of his profession and class, he was deeply interested in the past of which he had an exceptional knowledge. According to Saint-Simon (iv. 5) with whom Voltaire was in agreement (M. i. 74), he 'savoit tout, en histoire, en généalogies, en anecdotes de cour, avec une mémoire qui n'oublioit rien de ce qu'il avoit vu ou lu'. His interests went back to at least the sixteenth century and, like his brother, the Abbé de Caumartin, and many of his contemporaries, he must have collected manuscripts (Taylor, p. 167). He may have shown his young friend how the study of history could provide useful political and economic lessons for the present and how to appeal to history to justify contemporary notions or claims. His enthusiasm for Henry IV, the ideal king, was such that he inspired Arouet with the

[6] Saint-Simon, *Mémoires*, ed. A. de Boislisle (Paris 1879–1931), xxiv. 4-5.

[7] In the library at Ferney was the edition issued at Cologne in 1675–1690; see *Bibliothèque de Voltaire. Catalogue des livres* (Moscou-Léningrad 1961), no. 3837; G. R. Havens and N. L. Torrey, 'Voltaire's catalogue of his library at Ferney', *Studies on Voltaire* (1959), ix. no. 3251.

[8] Cf. Brumfitt, *op. cit.*, p. 6.

idea of writing *La Ligue*. His influence can no doubt be discerned in the *Discours au roi* (Taylor, pp. 249-252), in Voltaire's views on finance and the desirable relationship between king and Parlement. The composition of his epic involved Arouet in the acquisition of the sound documentation that was then required of an epic poet; it was his desire to make his poem more easily accessible to the average French or British reader which motivated his first serious historical writings in prose, the *Histoire abrégée des événements sur lesquels est fondée la fable de la Henriade* (composed in 1722) and the *Essay upon the Civil Wars* (1727).

Recent investigation has revealed that both the latter and *La Ligue* were based on reading of surprising extent and depth. Voltaire's main source was Mézeray's three-volume *Histoire de France* (1643–51) which he valued for its picturesque elements, its 'politique' standpoint, robust independence and common-sense. These qualities were less obvious in the more elegant and more easily digested *Abrégé* which he nevertheless also consulted. To these he added 'standard' works such as Louis Maimbourg's *Histoire de la Ligue* (1684), *Histoire du calvinisme* (1682) and *Histoire du luthéranisme* (1680), Hardouin de Péréfixe's *Histoire du roi Henri IV* (1661), Gabriel Daniel's *Histoire de France* and Louis Legendre's *Nouvelle Histoire de France* (1718). All these (apart from Maimbourg's militant Gallicanism) reflected the official Catholic interpretation of sixteenth-century history and, no doubt as a corrective, Voltaire turned to Jurieu's *Histoire du calvinisme* (1683) which must have appeared to him equally partisan and intolerant (cf. M. ix. 396, xiv. 38, xix. 369). More palatable was the information in Bayle's *Dictionnaire historique et critique*, *Réponse aux questions d'un provincial* and (if Voltaire read it) *Critique générale de l'Histoire du Calvinisme de Mr. Maimbourg*.

Had he drawn only on these works Voltaire had more than enough information upon which to base the narrative of his poem. But, significantly, his curiosity and historical sense took him further, back to the sources which these 'authorities' invoked. He read the historians, memorialists and annalists of the sixteenth and seventeenth centuries, J. A. de Thou, Victor Palma Cayet, Agrippa d'Aubigné, Castelnau-Le Laboureur, Sully, Brantôme, Saulx-Tavannes and P. de l'Estoile. He investigated the polemical literature of the period, Catholic, Protestant and 'politique', for the most part in one of the learned collections or editions frequently reprinted in the seventeenth and eighteenth centuries. The memoirs by P. de l'Estoile, in editions published under the title *Journal des choses mémorables advenues durant le règne de Henri III*, were regularly accompanied by texts such as Palma Cayet's *Divorce satyrique ou les amours de la reine Marguerite*, Agrippa d'Aubigné's *Confession catholique du sieur de Sancy*, Louise de Lorraine's (?) *Histoire des amours du Grand Alcandre* and Henri Estienne's (?) *Discours merveilleux de la vie, actions et déportement de la reine Catherine de Médicis*, all illuminated by the extensive, erudite commentaries by Le Duchat and Dupuy. Similar annotations by Le Duchat were a feature of the frequent editions of the *Satyre Ménippée* to which publishers added supplementary and complementary texts such as *La Fatalité de Saint-Cloud* and the *Dialogue d'entre le Maheustre et le Manant*. Voltaire found yet other texts, though not perhaps before 1725, in Simon Goulart's *Mémoires de la Ligue*. He delved even further, consulting such relatively obscure works as Jean Boucher's *De justa Henrici Tertii abdicatione* (1589) and Thomas Artus' *Description de l'île des Hermaphrodites* (1605). He also browsed through Gilles Corrozet's *Antiquitez de Paris* (1550 etc.) and did not even scorn romanticised history. For the notes of *La Ligue* he drew on Guillaume Girard's *Histoire de la vie du duc d'Espernon* (1655) and by 1730, at the latest, he had read Valincour's *Vie de François de Lorraine, duc de Guise* (1681) and Jacques de Callières' *Courtisan prédestiné* (1668 and 1728). Finally, though it is difficult to judge to what extent, he made use of the manuscript collections of the Mesmes, Novion de Blancmesnil, Caumartin and Caumont La Force families.

Superficially, Voltaire's attitude to these sources echoes that of his historically minded contemporaries. As an epic poet, he was not obliged to enquire deeply into history, but it is clear that, despite some facile irony about the reliability of historians (Taylor, p. 271), he was convinced that the main facts of history were firmly established. In composing his poem he is content to versify the relevant passages in Mézeray's narrative and is little concerned with accuracy of detail (ibid., p. 397). Yet, as much as his contemporaries, he is drawn to the study of motive, that is to say in this context, to the study of hidden motives, psychological and political, to those elements of history that official governmental and ecclesiastical circles or conservative opinion in general preferred to ignore or gloss over. Such revelations he sought, as did others of like tastes, in printed and manuscript sources, in memoirs, in polemical writings and the commentaries attached to them. From these the truth might well emerge or, at least, some delectably discreditable or scandalous fact that would puncture the dignity of official history. Much of the information thus acquired could not, for aesthetic reasons, be included in the main historical narrative, either in prose history or in epic. Voltaire uses it with relish in his notes in which he makes effective polemical use of 'la petite histoire' (Taylor, pp. 256-259, 262-263, 269-270 etc.). The taste for the arcana of history was such that the publication of Retz's memoirs in 1717 was a major event both for the reading public in general and for Voltaire in particular.[9] Even pseudo-memoirs were welcome; and at this time Voltaire did not, it would appear, scorn them as he did later.

This is the more surprising as Voltaire's reading for *La Ligue* developed or consolidated in him a healthy grasp of the principles of historical criticism. In the notes he added to the poem in 1723 he comments scathingly on the bias of the polemical literature of the sixteenth century (Taylor, pp. 256, 279, 280) and the omission of names such as those of Maimbourg, Hardouin de Péréfixe, Daniel and Legendre is equally eloquent in the case of the later historians. He points ironically to Mézeray's occasional inaccuracies and to his credulity in the matter of the supernatural (Taylor, pp. 268, 271, 281). There seems to be little doubt but that Voltaire's reading for *La Ligue* drove home the lessons learned from Bayle who, as Dr Mason[10] and Dr Brumfitt[11] have ably demonstrated, must have been his chief mentor in this sphere. In a note (Taylor, p. 280) on the place of Henry III's death he summarises Bayle's critical examination of the evidence; in another (ibid., pp. 267-269) in which he discusses the post-mortem carried out on the body of Jeanne d'Albret, we find him applying the 'disadvantage rule' with Baylian rigour.[12]

[9] By 1722 (Best. 109), Voltaire (influenced by Bolingbroke?) may have been acquainted with Clarendon's *History of the Rebellion*, translated into French in 1704–9; but he found in the English writer no more than he had found in Retz, see F. D. White, *Voltaire's Essay on epic poetry: a study and an edition* (Albany 1915), p. 147.

[10] H. T. Mason, *Pierre Bayle and Voltaire* (Oxford 1963), pp. 128-133.

[11] *Op. cit.*, pp. 33-34.

[12] Mason, *op. cit.*, p. 130.

However, as Dr Mason (p. 129) and Dr Brumfitt (pp. 32-34) have argued, Bayle's value to Voltaire was more negative than positive. The latter never had any great opinion of the former's capacities as a historian and criticised him for his inelegant style, his diffuseness, his concern with the trifling and the scurrilous and his lack of dignity (M.xii.538-539; xiv. 38; Best. 1935 and 932). For models of synthesis Voltaire would look away from a critical dictionary, however admirable, to historical works with more unity, to theorists concerned with the aesthetic and philosophical problems of history.

In this field the amount of help he might receive from the historians he read in preparation for *La Ligue* and *La Henriade* was limited. In their theoretical pronouncements they reproduced the already familiar platitudes of humanist historiography, though Maimbourg, Daniel and Legendre followed current trends in placing added emphasis on the necessity for impartiality, accuracy, good sources and the suppression of imaginary speeches. Their Christian, providentialist interpretation of the past was no less well known to Voltaire. It was obviously as unacceptable as their patent failure to live up to their own precepts. Yet their work offered him interesting suggestions. Their main preoccupation remained political history, but there was a growing, if almost unwilling,[13] awareness of the importance of social, economic and institutional history. In his *Abrégé*[14] Mézeray inserted from time to time in his narrative a section on the condition of the Church (cf. i. 121-129; 172-180 etc.) in which he sometimes included a few rapid and haphazard comments on manners and customs, the royal household, the nobility, the nation's assemblies, military organisation (cf. i. 276-281) and the state of learning and literature (cf. iv. 398-412; vi. 393-453). No further progress can be discerned in Daniel[15] who limited himself to recording, in the course of his narrative, important changes in constitutional, ecclesiastical, judicial or ceremonial custom, listed at intervals in *Tables des usages*

[13] Cf. N. Lenglet du Fresnoy, *Méthode pour étudier l'histoire* (Paris 1713), p. 13: 'Ces matières, qui sont assez ennuyeuses, ne demandent point d'être étudiées de suite'; L. Legendre, *Nouvelle Histoire de France* (Paris 1719), vii. 203-204: 'Mais c'est assez parler des Coustumes du tems passé, ces Mœurs antiques sont si éloignées des nostres, qu'elles n'ont plus de sel pour nous; je m'arreste de peur d'ennuïer à en faire un plus grand détail . . .'

[14] Fr. Eudes de Mézeray, *Abrégé chronologique de l'histoire de France* (Amsterdam 1673, 1674).

[15] G. Daniel, *Histoire de France*, nouvelle édition (Paris 1729).

(at the end of each volume). The most impressive approach was that of Legendre who, in his seventh volume, devoted some 200 pages to a general survey of French civilisation from the beginnings (*Mœurs et coutumes dans les differens tems de la monarchie*). His review is superficial and somewhat haphazard, but its breadth and variety are astonishing. His subjects include, for instance, constitutional and administrative organisation (p. 112), the legal system (p. 145), taxation (p. 124), bondservice (p. 107) and the condition of the Jews (p. 130). There are sections on the sciences and the arts, medicine (p. 103), philosophy (p. 173), poetry (p. 179), tragedy (p. 187), comedy (p. 188), opera (p. 189), music (p. 190), painting (p. 194) and architecture (p. 199). Voltaire's references to Legendre are few in number and disparaging in tone; but it is very possible that the conception of history informing *Le Siècle de Louis XIV* owed not a little to the *Nouvelle Histoire de France*, more perhaps than Voltaire was prepared to admit.[16] Even the device of appending catalogues, lists and genealogical tables at the end of *Le Siècle* may derive in part from Legendre. In volume vi of his *Nouvelle Histoire* the latter offers a very comprehensive alphabetical list of mainly contemporary historians in which, under each name, he gives a few biographical details and a short appreciation of the author's work. In volume vii there is a genealogy of the French royal family; in volume viii lists of the great dignitaries of France.

In these early years, however, Voltaire may well have been less impressed by Legendre's example than by Rapin de Thoyras' *Histoire d'Angleterre*[17] which he began to read as soon as the first volume was issued in 1724 (Best. 183). The only specific reasons he ever gave for his long-enduring admiration for this work were Rapin de Thoyras' impartiality[18] and his knowledge of the English (Best. 2447), but these reasons must be considered in the light of Rapin de Thoyras' declared intention of writing at one and the same time the history of Prince and State which he regarded as 'un même tout, un même Corps',[19] in the light of his excursions into constitutional history (cf. i. p. iv), in the light of his considerations of 'les

[16] In 1756, in the notes to *La Henriade*, Voltaire quite unnecessarily corrects an error by Legendre. My view is that he re-read Legendre's work while composing or putting the finishing touches to *Le Siècle* (Taylor, p. 172).

[17] P. Rapin de Thoyras, *Histoire d'Angleterre* (The Hague 1724–36).

[18] Brumfitt, *op. cit.*, p. 29.

[19] P. Rapin de Thoyras, *op. cit.*, i. p. iii.

Loix, les Mœurs, les Coûtumes et la Langue des Anglo-Saxons' (i. 475) and in the light of the organic unity imposed on the work by the political thesis which emerges from his apparently impartial narrative. For Voltaire, Rapin de Thoyras' great merit must have been that he made England and her history intelligible to foreigners by unbiased analysis of psychological, social and political causes. But the *Histoire d'Angleterre* was only the brilliant illustration of a conception of history which was already in Voltaire's mind, as it was in the minds of many of his contemporaries. By 1723 it was a platitude of historiography that the annalist was a dull creature and that the purpose of history was not only to record the past, but also to make it intelligible to the reader. 'La recherche des causes est l'âme de l'histoire', comments Daniel (i. p. xxv) whose words are anticipated in Maimbourg's reference to 'les causes, & ... les motifs, en quoy consiste l'ame de l'Histoire'[20] and echoed in Legendre's pronouncements in his preface. There was a desire to find in history, not only the 'secret' motives, but also a pattern of political and psychological causality similar to that which underlay classical tragedy. This taste gave rise in the latter part of the seventeenth century to a style of history of which the most eminent representatives were Saint-Réal and Vertot. For such historians accuracy was less important than dramatic effect or the study of psychological motivation in especially significant periods of history.[21] The model was obviously Sallust; but the impulsion to admire and imitate his work stemmed, it would seem, if not from the habit of classical tragedy, at least from the mentality which produced it. Long before Voltaire, Daniel, in the preface to his *Histoire de France* (i. p. xlvi), emphasised the relationship between history and drama.

However, Voltaire was less influenced by theory than by performance. The extent and constancy of his admiration for Saint-Réal (cf. M. xiv. 131, Brumfitt, p. 30) of whose romantic inaccuracy he was well aware (Best. 6902), reveal how attractive he found this type of history (M.xiii.113; xiv.131,547; xxviii. 329; Best. 946, 4240). We do not know if he had read Saint-Réal's *Histoire de la conjuration des Espagnols contre Venise* (1674) before 1730 (M.ii. 316), but from his school-days he must have been familiar with

[20] L. Maimbourg, *Histoire du luthéranisme* (Paris 1680), p. 3.

[21] C. V. de Saint-Réal, *De l'usage de l'histoire*, in N. Lenglet du Fresnoy, *Méthode pour étudier l'histoire* (Paris 1713), p. 4.

Sallust whom he almost equally admired (M. xiv. 547). The Sallustian-Saint-Réal movement was in any case well represented in his reading for *La Ligue* in Maimbourg's *Histoire du calvinisme*, *Histoire du luthéranisme* and *Histoire de la Ligue*. Each of these works deals with an especially significant episode in European or French history. Each is written dramatically as the story of a rise and fall. Each concentrates on political and psychological motivation and on such information as is relevant to the main theme. Of this technique the *Histoire de la Ligue* is a particularly successful example. 'Je me renferme,' explains Maimbourg in the *Avertissement*, 'dans ce qu'il y a de plus essentiel à l'Histoire particulière de la Ligue, & je me suis seulement appliqué à la recherche de sa veritable origine, à découvrir ses intrigues, ses artifices, & les motifs les plus secrets qui ont fait agir les Chefs de cette conspiration.' That Voltaire leaned heavily on Maimbourg's *Histoire de la Ligue* seems more than likely from a comparison between the latter and *La Ligue*. The technique of the poet closely resembles that of the historian. There is the same sense of drama, the same dramatic presentation of the initial situation, the same limpid analysis of political and psychological factors and of personalities, the same coherent evolution of the action from the initial situation, the same elimination of all that is irrelevant to the subject.

Voltaire can have had no compunction in borrowing anything he considered of value in the work of Maimbourg. He must have been familiar with the parallel drawn by Fénelon in the *Lettre à l'Académie*[22] between the approach of the historian and that of the epic poet; and that he accepted this notion is clear both from an analysis of *La Ligue* and from his comparison between the historian and the epic poet in the *Essay upon the Epic Poetry* of 1727 (White, p. 147). By 1733 at the latest he had reached the conclusion that the approach to history should be through the epic. In his new version of the *Essai sur la poésie épique* (M. viii. 314-315) he argued that epic poetry was the first form of history and that prose history evolved out of epic. He also believed that epic poetry was a superior form of history. In Ancient Greece it had been written in verse because it must be easily remembered and sung. Its function was to transmit to posterity the religious lore of the people and the

[22] Fénelon, *Lettre sur les occupations de l'Académie française*, ed. M. E. Despois (Paris n.d.), p. 80.

memory of significant heroes or episodes in its past. Voltaire was convinced that the function of history remained unchanged, even though some four hundred years after Homer and Hesiod prose history had become a separate genre. The concern of the historian should be with significance, not with idle antiquarianism (White, p. 147). History, it is true, had lost the magic of poetry, but it should retain the aesthetic qualities, the organic unity of epic poetry. Without these, it becomes, like epic, 'une froide gazette', a mere chronicle. Unlike classical theorists, Voltaire did not consider that epic differed from history in the description of supernatural causes (*merveilleux*). Had he dared, he would have banished the supernatural from the modern epic which he would have turned into a 'poème historique' after the manner of Lucan's *Pharsalia* (Taylor, pp. 132-137). Only poetry should separate modern epic from modern history.

It was for their historical qualities, almost as much as for their poetical excellence, that *La Ligue* and *La Henriade* were admired in the eighteenth century. There was repeated praise for the vividness with which they recreated the mentality of the French sixteenth century and for the way in which they made the religious wars politically and psychologically comprehensible by bringing out the specific characteristics of the age (ibid., p. 194). This novel sense of the past Voltaire must have owed to his intelligence, but also, in part, to his examination of the problems of epic poetry during the second phase of the Quarrel of the Ancients and Moderns, to the often puerile discussions about the merits and defects of the Homeric poems. Of these, the Moderns, obsessed with the notions of progress and civility, disdainfully emphasised the rudimentary technique and the barbaric religious, ethical and social ideas which reflected the primitive state of Greek civilisation. What was not obviously inferior was irreconcilably different. Reluctantly, the idea of difference, though not the idea of inferiority, was accepted by the Ancients as the one really valid defence of Homer (ibid., pp. 90-120). The second phase of the Quarrel clarified the idea of relativity and prepared the way for a greater historical sense and a surer reconstruction of the past. In Du Bos' *Réflexions critiques sur la poésie et la peinture* (1719) Voltaire found the specific form of the theory of progress which he adopted, the theory of cyclic progress. It is possible that this literary debate was more influential than any other factor in developing Voltaire's historical sensitivity. In resurrecting the French sixteenth century he was trying to give a picture of a different and more primitive age. It was in epic poetry that he first clarified and applied many of his principles as a historian.

La Ligue and *La Henriade*, like the *Essay upon the Civil Wars*, adequately reveal the conception Voltaire had of history in these early years. The subject of his poem, the civil wars of the sixteenth century and the conquest of power by Henry of Navarre, was to Voltaire, as to Du Bos (M. xiv. 553), the most significant episode in the history of modern France. The story revealed the full dangers of religious intolerance, the true nature of the complex motives of the civil wars, the horrors of national anarchy and the historic rôle of the monarchy in France. It was of special significance to Voltaire's contemporaries, beset as they were by the problem of the succession to the throne and the English alliance, by the desire for constitutional reform, by the threat of anarchy implicit in the restlessness of parlements and nobility and in the religious quarrels of the day. The implications of sixteenth-century history are made clear in a simple, climactic action which is psychologically and politically intelligible as classical tragedy is intelligible. Nothing is more striking than the skill with which Voltaire handles his historical material, the ease and masterly clarity with which he analyses and describes the complex factors of his exposition, the logic which he imposes on the evolution of the drama. He avoids irrelevant detail, but describes fully episodes such as the massacre of Saint Bartholomew which illustrates the barbarity of sixteenth-century France or the murder of Guise which highlights the Machiavellian amoralism of the protagonists in the religious wars. His notes for *La Ligue* are in large measure devoted to the 'characteristic anecdotes' of which he will later make much use (cf. *Siècle de Louis XIV*, chap. xxv-xxviii). In these ways Voltaire makes clear the mentality, the 'esprit' and the 'mœurs' of the sixteenth century.

It would seem that the fundamental principles of Voltairian historiography were developed and formulated during the preparation for, and composition of, *La Ligue* and *La Henriade*, probably before 1723, at the latest, before 1733. As Dr Brumfitt has pointed out (p. 45), Voltaire owed a great deal to previous or contemporary theory and practice; his superiority lies in performance, based on the individual synthesis he made of the elements he borrowed. He broadened and deepened the scope of history, but, basically, the purpose of Voltairian history remains the same: the edification of the present through a rational explanation of the mentality of the past in terms of the social, political and psychological factors at work. It has sometimes been asked why Voltaire increasingly resorted to the rapid and (to us) superficial accumulation of information from secondary sources. It is possible to allege lack of time. But it would perhaps be more logical to argue that more and more Voltaire became conscious that reinterpretation of acquired knowledge was more important than detailed factual accuracy. This is the principle which he applied in his epic; to the end he remained faithful to his initial conception of history.

The composition of the Letters concerning the English Nation

Harcourt Brown

The correspondence for 1728–31 indicates that Voltaire brought from England a considerable body of material for publication. The *Histoire de Charles XII* was well advanced, the tragedy *Brutus*, begun in English prose, was planned and partly written; the *Henriade* of the 1728 quarto had to be prepared for the French public, along with a rewritten *Essai sur la poésie épique*. Lucien Foulet was convinced that Voltaire also had substantial notes to be embodied in the *Lettres philosophiques*. In spite of Lanson's doubts, A. M. Rousseau tends to concur with Foulet.[1] There are few documents which could settle the question, and we are left with the *Lettres* themselves, and their interpretation.

While other works advanced in the months after his return to France, Voltaire's correspondence, as we have it in the Besterman edition, shows no active progress with the *Lettres anglaises*, which are spoken of as a task to be taken up and finished, to be returned

[1] The present article is based on three principal texts, (1) *Letters Concerning the English Nation*, by Mr de Voltaire. London, printed for C. Davis in Pater-Noster-Row, and A. Lyon in Russel-Street, Covent Garden. MDCCXXXIII, referred to in these pages as '*Letters*'; (2) *Lettres écrites de Londres sur les Anglois et autres sujets*. Par M. D. V***. A Basle [London], MDCCXXXIV, referred to as 'Basle', and (3) *Lettres philosophiques*, édition critique . . . par Gustave Lanson, nouveau tirage . . . par André M. Rousseau, 2 vols., Paris, Didier, 1964, referred to as 'Lanson'; this text is based largely on the Jore edition (*Lettres philosophiques* par M. de V***, Amsterdam, E. Lucas, 1734—actually Rouen, C. F. Jore). The critical edition has been used for information concerning Jore's text, referred to in what follows as 'Jore'. The Harvard College copies of Basle and Jore have been used, and my thanks go to the staff in charge of the Houghton Library there. *Voltaire's Correspondence*, vols. 2 and 3, edited by Theodore Besterman (Geneva 1953) has been indispensable.

to, rather than in current development. To Formont (Best. 425) he writes that he wants to consult about how to finish his *Essai sur la poésie épique* and 'mes lettres sur les Anglois', and to Thieriot in May 1732 (Best. 472), he says in similar vein, 'Be sure I will put the last hand to them in a very short time.' Again, to Formont, in September 1732, once he has the 'travail ingrat' of replying to La Mottraye's criticism of the *Histoire de Charles XII* out of the way, he writes 'J'achèverai ces *Lettres angloises* que vous connoissez; ce sera tout au plus le travail d'un mois.'

More revealing in this context is a letter to Formont of December 1732 (Best. 524). Now 'enfin' determined to produce the *Lettres*, Voltaire has reworked entirely the section on Newton, adding a vigorous commentary on Descartes, and has revised what he had written about Locke, 'Parce qu'après tout je veux vivre en France & qu'il ne m'est pas permis d'être aussi philosophe qu'un Anglois', two statements which suggest that the passages revised had originally been written much earlier, perhaps even in England. Still more pointedly, he adds that 'Il me faut déguiser ce que je ne pourrais dire trop fortement à Londres', and that he has had to erase more than one 'endroit assez plaisant sur les Quakers et les presbytériens.'

In the summer of 1733 the book was ready, and the *Letters Concerning the English Nation* were on sale in an edition of 2000 copies.[2] The neat octavo was prefaced by about six pages of un-Voltairean prose explaining how the book had come to be written, and justifying its publication on the grounds that the English public had a 'strong desire . . . to peruse whatever is publish'd under his name.' Nobody but Thieriot can be credited with these pages; while Voltaire's letters provided general ideas of what to include, Voltaire cannot be held responsible for the utter flatness of their expression. The *Letters* 'were written in London', they 'relate particularly to the English Nation', they are written with freedom, and will be liked by 'a judicious people who abhor flattery.' They 'were not design'd for the Public'; they result from the 'Author's Complacency and Friendship for Mr Thiriot', and they do not 'observe any Method', for Voltaire 'follow'd no other Rule . . . than his particular Taste, or perhaps the Queries of his Friend.' The *Letters* appear in order of their dates; 'they were written between the latter end of

[2] Keith I. Maslen, 'Some early editions of Voltaire printed in London', *The Library* (1959), 5th series, xiv. 287-295.

1728 and about 1731.' While circumstances not related to their substance have been omitted, the public need not complain, for 'the Variety of the Subjects, the Graces of the Diction, the Solidity of the Reflexions, the delicate Turn of the Criticism, the noble Fire which enlivens all the Compositions of Mr. de Voltaire delight the Reader perpetually.' Much of this is sheer fabrication, even if the comments on style are justified.

It is clear from a letter to Thieriot of 14 July 1733 (Best. 610) that Voltaire had seen this volume before publication; several of the errata listed on the final page probably stem from his reading. Certainly the cancel A4 is a result of his comments: the Dublin edition of the same year (London: Printed, Dublin: Reprinted by and for George Faulkner) contains a sentence which contradicts the fiction that the *Letters* were written privately for Thieriot, 'to favour him with such Remarks as he might make on the Manners and Customs of the British Nation.' In the Dublin preface, on the verso of A3, we read that the Letters 'which relate to . . . Newton's philosophy will be found entertaining. Mr. de Voltaire remember'd, that he was writing to Mankind in general, and all are not Philosophers. He has infus'd . . .' The London cancel, which was delivered with the full text of the volume, omits the full sentence just quoted; it reads '. . . will be found entertaining. The Author has infus'd . . .' Recto and verso of London A4 are each reduced by one line to 23 instead of 24, and a little spacing at the end of the paragraph conceals the deletion reasonably well. This was not the only part of the Preface about which Voltaire was not happy; his irritation shows plainly in a friendly letter of July 1733 (Best. 609, see especially the 6th paragraph, p. 101), but the book was already out and the preface could not well be further shortened. 'Mon ouvrage,' to Voltaire's dismay, would have to be 'content de sa fortune.'

Thieriot's preface is almost enough to put a modern reader off the book entirely, and for some it has perhaps done just that. However, the *Letters* stood high in the English booktrade of the century,[3] and this preface must be placed in comparison with that

[3] Hywel B. Evans, 'A provisional Bibliography of English editions and translations of Voltaire', *Studies on Voltaire and the Eighteenth Century* (1959), viii. 9-121, lists ten British editions of the *Letters* in the eighteenth century. The present writer has seen three others.

prefixed to the *Lettres écrites de Londres sur les Anglois et autres sujets*, 'Basle' (actually London) 1734, from the same printer, William Bowyer. Here the letters are attributed on the title-page to 'M.D.V. . . .' and in the preface to 'une personne fort connue dans le monde.' At this time there is no attempt to justify their appearance on the grounds of content; on the contrary, several red herrings are dragged across the trail: 'Deux Anglois les traduisirent en 1732, l'une de ces Traductions fut imprimée aussitôt.' Publication of the French manuscript was begun at London, but suppressed at the author's request, as the letters had not been written for the public. Word that manuscript copies were multiplying, that publication had begun in Holland, that the English translation had been turned back into French, made it impossible to delay this edition any longer, '& nous nous flattons que si nous déplaisons malgré nous à l'auteur, nous ne déplairons pas au Public.' A sceptical modern reader may be excused for regarding this as largely prevarication, a result of Voltaire's dissatisfaction with the 1733 preface, and as an effort to suggest the illicit pleasure of reading what Voltaire did not want the public to see, while indicating clearly enough that the book contained the authentic work of its author. As the work was already dangerous to Voltaire, precautions were taken to suggest that it came to the public by way of a disavowed agent, whom nobody with any book-sense could possibly deem to be active in 'Basle'. Voltaire's letters of mid-1733 make it quite plain that we are in the presence of the prolific and devious polygraph whose unacknowledged productions are the despair of bibliographers.

II

Our chief concern is with the edition in English of 1733, a product of one of the better presses of the day, marred only by a leaf of advertisements on [A8]. Proofing in general is good, except for misprints in quotations in French. At the end of the volume, the reader of the *History of Charles XII* finds a 'Letter Concerning the Burning of Altena', a full index, and the brief and incomplete errata mentioned previously.

Reading the *Letters*, one is aware of differences in style, which appear more acute when one compares this English version with the contemporary French texts, of 'Jore' ('Amsterdam, E. Lucas') or

'Basle'. Some of the chapters read extremely well: lively, crisp narrative and witty reflections alternating with precise arguments, the equivalent of the French without being a slavish verbal translation. If one did not know that one has here a version of one of the most celebrated French books of the century, one would be hard pressed to decide which text is the original, which has been translated into the other language. One version is imaginative, picturesque, often conversational, displaying an excellent comic sense; the other is no less witty, more precise, in Voltaire's rapid and expressive French. While the two versions correspond roughly, they read as though the writer in one language had felt no serious responsibility for keeping the precise emphasis or tone of voice apparent in the other.

At other times, for instance in the chapters on Newtonian science and on Locke, the English is laboured, sometimes pedantically accurate, occasionally marred by egregious errors. One feels certain that here someone else is present, translating Voltaire's inimitable French with a dictionary before him, to make up for a lack of fluency in the language. As we shall see, the differences in style correspond with other variations, in content and the use of quotations particularly.

A tentative hypothesis, based on close reading of the *Letters* themselves, would be that part of the work, mostly that written in 1732 and 1733, was done by an only moderately competent translator, probably English-speaking, while the rest of the text, deriving largely from Voltaire's personal experiences in England, was prepared by someone close to him, capable of lively, even witty, expression, not perhaps writing English as a native, but writing it so well that these chapters justify the comments made in the eighteenth century and even much later, that these *Letters* are a worthy addition to Augustan literature, in good standing even in the age of Addison and Steele. The inept preface to the volume excludes the possibility that this version was produced by Thieriot.

This article will suggest that the only person capable of writing these lively and individual pages was Voltaire himself, and that the *Letters concerning the English Nation* are a composite production, of which at least one-half is by Voltaire, the rest being translated from his completed French text, much as we have it in the 'Basle' version. What Voltaire had originally written in English he paraphrased into French, treating his own English text as only an author is entitled to do; finding an equivalent rather than a close translation, and in many cases appearing unfaithful to his original. After the publication of his correspondence of these years there can hardly be much doubt of Voltaire's skill in English, and it is surely time to recognise that scholars can no longer write of this book as a strictly French production, written in French in France for a French public.[4] Nor can we accept without examination the persistent tradition that John Lockman was the 'translator' of the *Lettres*, which appears to stem from a statement in *Le Pour et le contre* that Prévost had seen the manuscript in Lockman's handwriting. In view of Voltaire's repeated efforts to throw off the responsibility for the Basle text, it must be considered that perhaps this attribution stems from Voltaire himself; he early learned and long remembered how useful a note in the periodicals could be in directing attention towards or away from an importunate fact. In the present case, as we have seen, manipulation of the documents was most certainly tried, and the critical reader, two centuries and more later, is challenged by that and by the incongruities of the book itself.[5]

III

The evidence of the Letters themselves, even hastily and briefly reviewed as here, is of more value than the inconsistent and fragmentary evidence of the surviving documents.

The first two Letters give us a dramatic confrontation, a moment of cultural shock, clearly sketched in a rapid interchange between

[4] As for instance, T. J. Barling, 'The literary Art of the *Lettres philosophiques*', in *Studies on Voltaire and the Eighteenth Century* (1966), xli. 7-69.

[5] It does not now seem possible to be sure who it was who suggested that Voltaire wrote some part of these *Letters* in English before putting them into French. Professor Durand Echeverría and Dr Mara Vamos noticed the variations of style in the 1741 edition, with its 25th Letter on 'Paschal's Thoughts concerning Religion'; one or two students working under direction of the former began an inquiry into the problem without reaching a definite conclusion. Almost simultaneously the present writer began a series of research seminars devoted to a detailed study of the texts in parallel. The present article has been written with the contributions of the participants in mind. Although there is reason to believe that the hypothesis set forth here appears plausible to most of these persons, responsibility for it as expressed lies with the present writer.

two speakers each well aware of his own intellectual position and its justification. Developed from Voltaire's personal experience with members of the Society of Friends, this dialogue sets the opposition around which much of the rest of the book will revolve, in a dozen areas of life and thought. It forms an excellent prologue to the other *Letters*.

The English text is lively, vigorous, idiomatic; the relationship between French and English versions is rather parallelism and equivalence than exact translation. If one reads the French after the English, one thinks of an author revising a rough draft, seeking conciseness, precision, elegance. One cannot imagine the English with all its verve as the work of a translator working far from the author's supervision.

These letters, like others later in the book, show signs of having been composed in stages, paragraphs and sentences being added at different times to bring them up to date or to meet the demands of censorship. One is not surprised that textual changes were made in the last of the Quaker letters before publishing the French version in the following year.

A simpler case is presented by the Fifth Letter, 'On the Church of England', which appears to be an English original in its first three or four pages, shifting to a late addition in French for the three final paragraphs. Such phrases as 'homme libre', rendered as 'one to whom Liberty is natural'; 'ranked among the Faithful, that is, professes himself a Member of the Church of England' equivalent with 'être du nombre des fidèles Anglicans'; or 'reason (which carries mathematical Evidence with it)' given the sense of 'raison qui est une excellente preuve', are not strikingly unsuitable translations either way, but in their English form could well be the work of Voltaire himself.

Two or three of the errata associated with this letter provide evidence in a very different direction. In the last paragraphs, referring to the greater maturity of English bishops, who are not 'call'd to dignities till very late, at a time of life when men are sensible of no other passion but avarice', the French text reads '. . . très tard, et dans un âge où les hommes n'ont d'autres passions. . . .' The phrase, 'at a time of life', seemed objectionable to the reader of proof (probably Voltaire himself, who had seen the preface) and the literal 'in an age' is advanced as a correction. Still further down page 39, we find an obscure passage: 'That sable mix'd kind of mortal (not to be defin'd) who is neither of the Clergy nor of the Laity; in a word, the thing call'd *Abbé* in France', which the errata ask us to correct to 'that mix'd being'—probably continuing with the parenthesis 'not to be defin'd'. The original wording, with the incomprehensible 'sable', suggests a degree of confusion in the French text, 'cet être indéfinissable qui n'est ni Ecclésiastique ni Séculier . . .' If one supposes a French manuscript reading 'cet être indéfini/sable qui n'est ni . . .' with a line break falling in the middle of the word, one can explain at least some of the elements of the English text, and feel sure that in this latter part of the letter one is dealing with a translation from the French made by a person not at all certain of what the author meant. The opening pages of this letter show no such uncertainties.

Letter VI, 'On the Presbyterians', appears on the whole to be an original composition in English. As Theodore Besterman and André M. Rousseau have remarked, the passage on this subject in the final paragraphs of the Leningrad Notebook (*Notebooks*, p. 43) is 'un remarquable exemple de composition en langue étrangère.' The Letter is full of words and phrases whose precise equivalent[6] is not to be found in the French text, and there are sentences which enrich our knowledge of Voltaire's thought. The last paragraph, the conclusion of his treatment of the religions of England clarifies his meaning:

> If one religion only were allow'd in England, the government would very possibly become arbitrary; if there were but two, the people wou'd cut one another's throats; but as there are such a multitude, they all live happy and in peace.

Lanson found the French version ambiguous, and his note on 'despotisme' raises a question whether it refers to the power of one religion or of a government; from the English text it seems that the latter was what Voltaire intended.

If the present hypothesis is correct, this Letter also illustrates

[6] 'Emulate the splendid luxury of Bishops'; 'this proud tho' tatter'd Reason'; 'Diogenes did not use Alexander half so impertinently as these treated Charles'; 'reduc'd him to a state of penitence and mortification'; 'and accordingly elop'd from them with as much joy as a youth does from School'. In these cases and others, the sense is in the French, but some of the spirit and energy are missing.

Voltaire's interest in improving the literary structure of his work. The third paragraph is introduced as follows:

> These gentlemen who have also some churches in *England*, introduc'd there the mode of grave and severe exhortations (p. 43).

As this repeated a reference to long Scots sermons inflicted on Charles II by his northern subjects at the Restoration, as described in the opening of the letter, the French text is modified:

> Ces Messieurs qui ont aussi quelques églises en Angleterre, ont mis les airs graves et sévères à la mode en ce pays.

The English reads like a preliminary draft in comparison with the French; no translator would render *airs* as *exhortations*, and an author's sense of appropriateness would suggest that *airs* makes a better introduction to the sentence following, which deal with Sunday blue laws, forbidding work, amusement, theatre and music on the Sabbath, allowing the masses only to 'go either to church, to the tavern, or to see their mistresses.'

There is not much concrete evidence on which to base a judgment in the case of the Seventh Letter, 'On the Socinians, or Arians, or Antitrinitarians'. The letter is brief; Lanson places it between the death of Newton in March of 1727 and that of Samuel Clarke in May of 1729; his view that Voltaire must have read Whiston's *Historical Memoirs of the Life of Samuel Clarke* before writing it, hardly seems necessary. The fifth paragraph refers to Clarke as if he were dead, the third is in the present tense; the fifth could be a late interpolation. At one point the English text agrees with 'Basle' rather than with 'Jore': 'The Emperor was going to throw the bishop out of the window': perhaps a detail too vivid for a chastened taste. Several English words are more pungent than their French counterparts: 'the most sanguine stickler for Arianism' is sharper than 'le plus ferme patron de la doctrine Arienne'; and 'he was out in his calculation and had better have been Primate of all England, than meerly an Arian parson' has a ring not audible in 'je crois que le Docteur s'est trompé dans son calcul, & qu'il valoit mieux être Primat d'Angleterre que curé Arien.' Such phrases are characteristic of Voltaire's English, reflect his view of English style as more picturesque, more lively, more vigorous than French taste allowed.

There is also the first sentence, 'There is a little Sect here', 'Il y a ici une petite Secte', which unfortunately cannot be made to prove anything, except that at some moment Voltaire intended to suggest an English origin for the letter. The use of *here* and *there*, *ici* and *là*, in the whole book is not consistent, but argument from such easily interpolated words and phrases does not always carry conviction.

The Eighth Letter, 'On the Parliament', seems on the whole to have been first written in English. In two or three respects it is independent of either French version, just as 'Basle' is independent of 'Jore'. On page 53, we read '. . . murther one another merely about syllogisms, as some Zealots among them once did.' the last seven words have no equivalent in the French. A little further down, 'The Nobles are great without insolence, tho' there are no Vassals', while the French reads 'grands sans insolence et sans Vassaux.' Again, the French text adds to the English: the Lords and Commons 'divide the legislative power under the King', while in French 'la Chambre des Pairs et celle des Communes sont les Arbitres de la Nation, le Roi est le Sur-Arbitre', which reads like an author's attempt to explain what is unfamiliar to a French public. And speaking of arbitrary power, a whole clause appears in the French, 'Mais les Anglois ne croient pas avoir acheté trop cher de bonnes loix', which has no equivalent in the English and which no translator would have felt it desirable to omit. We are not here concerned with differences between 'Jore' and 'Basle', but at least two examples show that Voltaire is here giving us three texts for three different publics. Charles I, *beheaded* in 1733, *décapité* in 'Basle', is merely *condamné* in 'Jore', while the monk who assassinated Henri III is not further described in the London editions but becomes 'ministre de la rage de tout un parti' in 'Jore'.

Peculiarities in the Ninth Letter, 'On Government', seem to show that we have here, perhaps for the first time in the book, a complete translation from a French original. Departures from the French text are easily explained as needed comments on French terms: *vilains* becomes *Villains or Peasants*; *Serfs d'un Seigneur* is rendered *Villains or Bondsmen of Lords*; *Évêques*, *Abbés*, *Prieurs* are reduced to *Bishops*, *Priors*; and finally *Haute*, *moyenne & basse justice* is not translated but explained in an eight-line footnote. Still more important indications can be pointed out. At line 30 in 'Lanson' we read *ces Lairs* or *ces Lairds*, and in the English, p. 61, *those Peers*:

a Scottish laird is not necessarily a member of the Lords, to be ranked with *margraves* and barons. And further down, at line 115, *ôtoit* is translated as *was*, apparently reading *était* in the manuscript. Voltaire would have made no such error. The preponderance of evidence is for a French original; differences between the versions here are sufficient to justify placing this letter in a category quite apart from the first eight.

The Tenth Letter, 'On Trade', brief and to the point, seems without much doubt to be a product of Voltaire's life in England, and was most probably written first in English. Three or four Gallicisms, 'Grandeur of the State', 'far-distanc'd', 'At the time when Louis XIV . . . and that his Armies', 'Monstruous', suggest rather a French hand, writing English, than an English translator working from French. On page 72, 'I need not say which is most useful to a Nation', in the French, 'je ne sçais pourtant lequel est le plus utile', suggests Voltaire seeking rather to tone down a sharp comment; this is reflected in the errata, where it is proposed that *I need not say* should become *I cannot say*. The Letter in general, in its English form, is not inconsistent with Voltaire's known powers, and there seem to be no technical reasons to reject his authorship of it.

In the Eleventh Letter, 'On Inoculation', we return to Voltaire writing French, in spite of the remark in the Édition encadrée (1775), taken up by Kehl, 'Cela fut écrit en 1727.' The final paragraphs are generally regarded as added late, in readying the book for the press. Two or three howlers enliven the English, and one hesitates to charge them to Voltaire. On page 76, 'some had this distemper very favourably three or four times, but never twice so as to prove fatal', a version not justified by the French text; and on page 80, 'twenty die of it in the most favourable season of life', translating 'vingt en meurent dans les années les plus favorables.' A literal translation produces ambiguity on page 81: 'The Duke de Villequier, father to the Duke d'Aumont, who enjoys the most vigorous Constitution and is the healthiest man in France, would not have been cut off in the Flower of his Age.' More than one idiomatic passage has been handled with skill, even though evidence to suggest Voltaire's English style is quite lacking.

On the other hand, the Letter, 'On the Lord Bacon', number Twelve, may well be another English original. There are no notable inaccuracies; an ambiguity is found, due perhaps to the lack of a comma: Bacon had approached the discovery of the weight of the air, 'but some time after Toricelli [sic] seiz'd upon this Truth.' The French offers no problem; 'La découverte de sa pesanteur, il y touchoit; cette vérité fut saisie par Toricelli'. Extracts from Bacon's *History of Henry the Seventh* in the English are literal and exact, while the French is briefer and misquotes.

The Thirteenth Letter, 'On Mr Locke', is known to have been written later than most of the others, and it is most improbable that any of it should have been composed in English. There would be no need to discuss it, were it not that it displays so clearly the incompetence of the translator. Minor infelicities may be passed over; the most egregious errors are informative: on page 96, 'believ'd that the Soul was human, and the angels and God corporeal' is offered as an equivalent for 'ont cru l'âme humaine, les Anges, et Dieu corporels.' Even worse, on page 98, is the misunderstanding of French and of Malebranche's thought; 'did not doubt of our living wholly in God' is given as a version of 'que nous vissions tout en Dieu.' The past subjunctive of *voir* and *vivre* still troubles undergraduates. Furthermore, the French text quotes Locke word for word from Pierre Coste's translation, *Essai sur l'entendement humain*, while the English sentences expressing Locke's ideas are based on Coste rather than on corresponding passages in the *Essay*.

A curious and not entirely consistent letter is the next, the Fourteenth, 'On Descartes and Sir Isaac Newton'. Lanson is willing to place it almost alone in the years 1726–29, in England, while admitting the possibility of 'morceaux écrits séparément en des temps différents.' However, several features suggest that even if two or three paragraphs may have been written originally in English, the bulk of the work was French. The word *philosophe* occurs twice in the French, each time in the special sense of the period, and not in the technical sense implied in the English context. On page 112, certain Royal Society critics of Fontenelle's *Éloge* of Newton are described as 'not the ablest Philosophers in that body', rendering 'ceux-là ne sont pas les plus philosophes.' And again, Descartes' fathering a daughter Francine is characterised as showing that he had become 'tout à fait philosophe' which is put in English 'becoming a complete Philosopher.' Admittedly the usage is special, but the strong impression cannot be avoided that Voltaire writing in English would have produced expressions somewhat less awkward than these.

In general, the French of this chapter is well written, while the English tends to stumble. The paragraph on Tides in French is better constructed than the English, the contrast between French and English thinkers is clear throughout. In a sentence on the shape of the Earth, the French is notably more precise than the English, which uses technical terms without much care. 'La terre faite comme un melon' becomes 'shap'd like a Melon or of an oblique figure.' Again, at the end, where the English refers to the 'Errors of Antiquity, and of the Sciences', we find a misreading of 'les fautes de l'antiquité & les siennes.' Essentially this letter appears to be in Voltaire's French, translated by the unnamed hand, whether written in 1727–28 or not.

As the next three Letters, XV, XVI and XVII, devoted to aspects of the thought of Isaac Newton, were written late, there can be no likelihood that Voltaire wrote them in English. The laborious and careful translation follows 'Basle' in the main, though here and there an English mathematician may have suggested emendations which reappear in Jore. Since the English text is manifestly not Voltaire's, we may leave these chapters for more fruitful areas of investigation.

With Letter Eighteen, 'On Tragedy', we pass from a realm of ideas where Voltaire's touch is inexpert and uncertain to a field he was making his own, in which he could speak with confidence. Not surprisingly one detects an individual note in the English sentences. The freedom with which the thought passes from one version to the other suggests the continuity of a single mind; no translator, particularly not he who worked on the letters immediately preceding, would venture so far from the French text.

Letters, pp. 166-167:	Lanson, lines 5-15:
Shakespear, who was consider'd as the Corneille of the first-mention'd Nation, was pretty near Cotemporary with Lopez de Vega, and he created as it were, the English Theatre. Shakespear boasted a strong	Shakespear qui passoit pour le Corneille des Anglais, fleurissoit à peu près dans le tems de Lopez de Vega; il créa le théâtre; il avoit un génie plein de force

fruitful Genius; He was natural and sublime, but had not so much as a single Spark of good Taste or knew one rule of the Drama. I will now hazard a random, but at the same time, true, Reflection, which is that the great Merit of this Dramatic Poet has been the Ruin of the English Stage. There are such noble, such dreadful Scenes in this writer's monstrous Farces, to which the name of Tragedy has been given, that they have always been exhibited with great Success.

et de fécondité, de naturel et de sublime, sans la moindre étincelle de bon goût, & sans la moindre connoissance des réglès. Je vais vous dire une chose hasardée mais vraie, c'est que le mérite de cet Auteur a perdu le théâtre anglais: il y a de si belles scènes, des morceaux si grands et si terribles répandus dans ses Farces monstrueuses, qu'on appelle Tragédies, que ces Pièces ont toujours été jouées avec un grand succès.

It is rather more plausible to suggest that the English text, with its vigour, is a preliminary draft for the more concise and muscular French than it is to claim that a translator would elaborate and dilute the French in quite this way. He would hardly break up the group of four nouns which characterise Shakespeare's genius; the 'single Spark of good Taste or knew one rule of the Drama' has a rhythm not found in the pedestrian letters on Newton through which we have just ploughed. If this English is not Voltaire's own, it was at least produced by someone who has his command of vivid phrase.

Whole paragraphs of this letter bear the same marks; not a completely idiomatic style, not as concise as Voltaire's French, but a forceful and positive manner, which grasps English words and phrases and squeezes meaning from them. The routine efforts of a translator are not evident; the sentences bear the signature of an original and lively mind:

Letters, pp. 169-170:

Nothing is easier than to exhibit in Prose all the silly Impertinences which a Poet may have thrown out, but 'tis a very difficult Task to translate his

Lanson, lines 56-64:

Il est bien aisé de raporter en prose les erreurs d'un poète, mais très difficile de traduire ses

fine Verses. All your junior academical *Sophs*, who set up for Censors of the eminent Writers, compile whole Volumes; but methinks two Pages which display some of the Beauties of great Genius's, are of infinitely more Value than all the idle Rhapsodies of those Commentators; and I will join in Opinion with all Persons of Good Taste in declaring, that greater advantage may be reap'd from a dozen Verses of Homer or Virgil, than from all the Critiques put together which have been made on those two great Poets.	beaux vers. Tous les grimauds qui s'érigent en critiques des Écrivains célèbres, compilent des volumes; j'aimerais mieux deux pages qui nous fissent connaître quelques beautés, car je maintiendrois toujours avec les gens de bon goût, qu'il y a plus à profiter dans douze vers d'Homère & de Virgile, que dans tous les critiques qu'on a faites de ces deux grands hommes.

Again it is hard to justify the English passage as a translation from the French; the sequence seems to lie in the other direction.

The letter has its word on translation as an art: 'Don't imagine that I have translated Shakespear in a servile Manner. Woe to the Writer who gives a literal Version, who by rendering every Word of his Original, by that means enervates the Sense, and extinguishes all the Fire of it. 'Tis on such an occasion one may justly affirm, that the Letter kills, but the Spirit quickens' (p. 175). The French version of the passage puts the same idea in largely different words: 'Ne croiez pas que j'aie rendu ici l'Anglois mot pour mot; malheur aux faiseurs de traductions littérales, qui en traduisant chaque parole, énervent le sens. C'est bien là qu'on peut dire que la lettre tue et que l'esprit vivifie.' Here as elsewhere, the French reads like a paraphrase, a concise summary of what the English has said, rather than as a basis from which the English text has been produced.

At the end of the letter, in the passage on Addison and *Cato*, there is a subtle but unmistakable difference in quality. These paragraphs follow the French closely, word by word, with neither interpolations or stylistic originality; the translator of the Newton chapters has been at work here.

The Nineteenth Letter, 'On Comedy', like most of the Eighteenth, could date from the English sojourn, when impressions of the stage were most vivid. While the English does not offer the striking phrases which suggest Voltaire's hand in the letter on Tragedy, several sentences have more content than is in either 'Basle' or 'Jore'. They can hardly be a translator's comments, and although Lanson attributes them to Thieriot, this seems unlikely. The last few lines of the paragraphs on Wycherley's *Country Wife* illustrate what we refer to here, as does the brief comment on the *Plain Dealer*, whose basic situation brings forth the remark, 'which by the way is not over natural', to which nothing in the French text corresponds. The letter as a whole exhibits freedom in each language, with none of the false renderings we have seen elsewhere.

Before we leave the letter, it is not inappropriate to remark that the 'vers assez connu' set apart and italicised by Lanson, 'Tout Paris les condamne et tout Paris les court', does not gain individual recognition in any of the early editions seen, in 'Jore', 'Basle', or the *Œuvres* of 1738–39 or of 1750. The phrase is treated as ordinary prose continuous with what precedes and follows. The English offers no problem: 'Plays . . . of which it might be said that the whole City of Paris exploded them, and yet all flock'd to see 'em represented on the Stage.' The line has not been traced to any poem: it is most likely a pure accident, as happens to writers in prose and verse, not excepting Voltaire. On these pages are other hemistichs ready for use: 'attirer la foule et révolter le lecteur', and again, 'les peignoit du pinceau le plus ferme et des couleurs les plus vraies', which a little adjustment would make into acceptable classic verses.

Letter XX is a trifle, 'On Such of the Nobility as Cultivate the Belles Lettres', containing half a dozen comments critical of French society, on the decay of the arts and letters among the aristocracy, on the dominance of the monarchy in matters of taste, on English democracy and the intelligence of the public, on the superior taste and wit of the professional classes. The latter half of the letter is devoted to a poem by John Lord Hervey, who called on Voltaire in Paris; these paragraphs were clearly written in France, probably in French. Phrases in the first fifty lines of the letter indicate an English original: 'Mankind in general speak well in their respective Professions' becomes 'En général, les hommes ont l'esprit de leur état.' The English is often clumsy, and does not always suggest the

French; Voltaire had found a better way of saying in French what he had already said with some obscurity in English. This opening section of the letter may have been among his first efforts in writing English.

It is consistent to say, in the light of our present criteria, that every page of Letter XXI, 'On the Earl of Rochester and Mr Waller' reveals the hand of Voltaire, competent in English, rugged in manner, but expressive and always clear. Phrase after phrase in the English is more vivid than the French. Voltaire does not always recognise a cliché, and he uses such terms for their worth, without hesitation, in ways which show the zest for idiom which a stranger enjoys once he has gained fluency in a foreign tongue. Rochester is described as the 'Idol of the Fair', in French, 'l'homme à bonnes fortunes'; 'The Graces breathe in such of Waller's works as are writ in a tender strain' passes into 'ses ouvrages galans respirent la grâce.' Such expressions are not the work of a translator; they bear the mark of a new creation, product of a freshly acquired means of expression. Here again, parallel columns would suggest the presence of a single author working over his material in two mediums, enjoying the sensations of freedom and exuberance in English, and then limiting his thought to the formal and decorous gait of elegant and precise French.

Various phrases may be cited to illustrate the originality of the English text. 'Ah, Sir! says the Ambassador, Oliver was quite another Man' hardly appears to be a translation of 'Ah! Sire, ce Cromwell étoit tout autre chose.' 'These cultivated the polite Arts with as much assiduity, as tho' they had been their whole dependance' would scarcely be produced by 'Ils ont cultivé les lettres comme s'ils en eussent attendu leur fortune.' The whole chapter should be read and compared; to this reader, both versions are Voltaire, in different garments, at ease in each.

In Letter XXII, as in XXI, there is in the English much of the quality of an informal letter, pungent, discursive, informative while not pedantic, in the tone which Voltaire tried to maintain as justification of his book as a whole. 'Mr Prior,' he writes, 'one of the most amiable English poets, whom you saw Plenipotentiary and Envoy Extraordinary at Paris in 1712. . . . I design'd to have given you some Idea of the Lord Roscommon's and the Lord Dorset's Muse. . . . Poetry is a kind of Music, in which a Man should have some Knowledge before he pretends to judge of it. . . . I only prick down, and that imperfectly, their Music; but then I cannot express the Taste of their Harmony.' The letter runs on with informal transitions, one idea leads to another, with no regard for paragraphs; Butler's *Hudibras* yields to comments on ridicule and humour, and these in turn to Swift, with a preliminary note on Rabelais, which does not lack verve. 'The former is not so gay as the latter, but then he possesses all the Delicacy, the Justness, the Choice, the good Taste, in all which particulars our giggling rural Vicar Rabelais is wanting.' In the French, Rabelais is simply 'notre Curé de Meudon'.

Letter XXIII, 'On the Regard that Ought to be Shown to Men of Letters', hardly enters into present discussion. It is dated late, from 1731 perhaps, and although it shows memories of English experiences, deriving from lost pages of the Notebooks, there is little of the English text that we can attribute to Voltaire. 'Basle' and 1733 are closer than either is to 'Jore'; one notable variant is not recorded by Lanson. The last paragraph, in a list of ways in which French legal restrictions degrade the arts, referring to actors, 'un art dans lequel nous excellons', 'Basle' reads, 'que l'on excommunie des personnes gagées par le Roy', and the English, 'that we excommunicate Persons who receive Salaries from the king.' This addition to the deficiencies of France does not appear in 'Jore', and has not been noted by Lanson.

The last letter, XXIV, 'On the Royal Society and other Academies', presents several anomalous features. Written from the point of view of France, it finds French institutions more rationally organised than their English counterparts; it makes no effort to present the fiction of a foreign visitor to England, and while the content of one or two passages is evidently late, there is no reason why these should not be interpolations in the larger part of the text. Phrases and sentences suggest that here again we are reading a draft of Voltaire's thought rather than a translation. In the French there is evidence of afterthoughts, literary rearrangements, alterations of expressions, the use of generalised summaries rather than concrete details, while the English reads like the first flow of the author's ideas. There are difficulties in this interpretation: 'Mr Prior whom we saw here invested with a public character' recalls an event in France, while on the other hand 'a Wit of this Country' refers to an

Englishman, 'un bel esprit de ce païs-là'. One could surmise that certain paragraphs were written in English before being put into French, e.g. the second to the sixth, inclusive, and the last three. They show signs of Voltaire's interests while in England, and refer to men he knew in those years, as well as to subjects debated in the circle of his acquaintance.

IV

A summary of the argument of the preceding pages would suggest that about fourteen letters (1-8, 10, 12, 18, 19, 21 and 22), were composed almost entirely in English, that three others (20, 23, 24) are of mixed origin, and that seven (9, 11, 13-17) were written in French some time after the sojourn in England. The first group deal predominantly with Voltaire's personal experiences and observations in England, the religious groups, with literature—Bacon, Swift, Butler, Pope, Waller, Rochester, and the dramatists—and with aspects of public life of his day. On the other hand, the letters composed in French are more learned, concerning themselves with philosophy, which for him included science, and other matters arising from his subsequent reading. His letters to Thieriot and others show his concern for this type of material. Thus the distinctions we have drawn from the style and presentation of the letters correspond with differences in their content. The book in its English dress was no more 'calculé pour le méridien de Paris' than had been his little *Essay on the Civil Wars of France* and the *Essay on the Epick Poetry*. It is not impossible that the French version of the latter by Desfontaines was sufficient to cause the postponement of the publication of the *Letters* in the English form until a French text was well advanced. Neither they nor their author could suffer a garbled version for French consumption.

The implications of the hypothesis outlined in these pages are by now largely apparent. If a large part of the *Letters Concerning the English Nation* was composed in England in English, then there is no difficulty in accepting L. Foulet's view that Voltaire 'rentra en France avec un Manuscrit des *Lettres philosophiques* déjà très avancé.'[7] This can be reconciled with Lanson's view that the *gros*

[7] Lucien Foulet, *Correspondance de Voltaire (1726–1729)* (Paris, Hachette, 1913), p. 308.

travail de rédaction was undertaken in 1731–32, provided one agrees that what was involved was the paraphrasing of the English material into French. As very little fresh composition was needed in much of the book, Voltaire would find the task neither lengthy nor arduous.

Moreover, the description of the book in all its English printings as 'by Mr de Voltaire' would not be completely inaccurate. Thieriot's contract with Davis and Lyon may have called for a work in English by Voltaire; this would account for the scrupulous concealing in the preface of a different hand at work in certain chapters.

Most of those who have thus far discussed the *Lettres philosophiques* have been commenting on a French book for those whose business is the study of French literature. In 1735 this was not necessarily the outlook of Voltaire. His book was written—in spite of protestations to the contrary—for a larger public, and his book circulated unchanged and under its original title long after its identity in French had been lost. As prepared by Lanson, the *Lettres* have been thoroughly denatured, as anyone who consults 'Jore' can observe; punctuation, accents, capitalisation, all are put in the mode of 1909. The tempo and tone of the book are largely lost, just as the verve and spirit of a holograph letter by Voltaire are destroyed by regularising the text.

And so the *Letters Concerning the English Nation*, a complex book, may be capable of informing us about Voltaire in ways not suspected by those who limit their attention to Lanson and his critical edition. The English text has more actuality than the author's French revision of it; the reader is closer to the impressions and events that inspired Voltaire. The sources were in the air as he wrote; the Letters, even those that treat of books, are less bookish. And finally, instead of a single conglomerate text as embodied in Lanson's edition, admirable as it may be, literature as written by Frenchmen is enriched by the complexity of three authentic versions of a fundamental book: the *Letters* of 1733, 'Basle' so-called, and 'Jore', each prepared at different times for different publics. Once more, Voltaire remains a challenge to even the most critical of editors.

Voltaire et les Sciences Naturelles

Sir Gavin de Beer

S'il est exact que Voltaire figure au tableau des causes de la Révolution française, il devient intéressant de se pencher sur les incidents dans sa vie qui le conditionnèrent à prendre ce chemin. Parmi eux on reconnaîtra un groupe, qui s'attache à quatre sujets, insolites à souhait: l'abbaye de Westminster, le plus illustre président de la Société royale de Londres, et deux artistes de théâtre.[1] Le système commence avec une de ces dernières, Adrienne Lecouvreur, dans la loge de laquelle à la Comédie-Française Voltaire eut un démêlé avec le chevalier de Rohan-Chabot qui, peu après, fit bâtonner Voltaire par ses laquais dans la rue. Une lettre de cachet, délivrée sur l'instance du chevalier, fit écrouer Voltaire à la Bastille, le 17 avril, d'où il sortit quinze jours plus tard moyennant la promesse de se rendre en Angleterre. Il se trouva à Londres lors des obsèques de Sir Isaac Newton, président de la Société royale, à l'abbaye de Westminster, le Saint-Denis de l'Angleterre, le 8 avril 1727. Peu de temps après son retour en France, Adrienne Lecouvreur mourut dans ses bras, le 15 mars 1730. Parce qu'elle avait été comédienne, le clergé de Paris lui refusa la sépulture en terre bénite, et sa dépouille fut jetée à la voirie. La même année, l'autre actrice, Anne Oldfield, mourut à son tour, et fut ensevelie à l'abbaye de Westminster le 26 octobre. C'est cette série d'événements qui est à la base du passage suivant des *Lettres philosophiques*:[2]

'M. Newton était honoré de son vivant, et l'a été après sa mort comme il devait l'être. Les principaux de la nation se sont disputé l'honneur de porter le poêle à son convoi. Entrez à Westminster,

[1] Gavin de Beer, 'Voltaire F.R.S.', *Notes & Records of the Royal Society* (1951), viii. 247.

[2] Voltaire, *Lettres philosophiques* (Amsterdam [Rouen] 1734); *Mélanges de Voltaire* (Paris, Pléiade, 1961), p. 98.

ce ne sont pas les tombeaux des rois qu'on y admire, ce sont les monuments que la reconnaissance de la nation a érigées aux plus grands hommes qui ont contribué à sa gloire; vous y voyez leurs statues comme on voyait dans Athènes celles des Sophocle et des Platon; et je suis persuadé que la seule vue de ces glorieux monuments a excité plus d'un esprit, et a formé plus d'un grand homme. On a même reproché aux Anglais d'avoir été trop loin dans les honneurs qu'ils rendent au simple mérite; on a trouvé à redire qu'ils aient enterré dans Westminster la célèbre comédienne Mlle Oldfield, à peu près avec les mêmes honneurs qu'on a rendus à M. Newton; quelques-uns ont prétendu qu'ils avaient affecté d'honorer à ce point la mémoire de cette actrice afin de nous faire sentir davantage la barbare et lâche injustice qu'ils nous reprochent d'avoir jeté à la voirie le corps de Mlle Lecouvreur. Mais je puis vous assurer que les Anglais, dans la pompe funèbre de Mlle Oldfield, enterrée dans leur Saint-Denis, n'ont rien consulté que leur goût.'

On conçoit ce que ressentit Voltaire comme haine contre la hiérarchie catholique et le despotisme arbitraire, et comme engouement pour les libertés anglaises. Du même coup, il fut porté vers les sciences naturelles, incarnées en la personne de Newton dont la supériorité sur Descartes en matière de théorie lui avait été signalée par Maupertuis, premier grand physicien français à se rallier à Newton. Mais les liens entre Newton et Voltaire étaient encore plus serrés qu'on ne se les imagine. Ce fut Voltaire qui publia en 1727, année de la mort de Newton, l'anecdote de la chute de la pomme qui déclencha toute la théorie de la gravitation.[3] Dans son livre *An Essay upon the Civil Wars of France, extracted from curious Manuscripts. And also upon the Epick Poetry of the European Nations from Homer down to Milton*,[4] Voltaire écrivit, 'Sir Isaac Newton walking in his Gardens had the first Thought of his System of Gravitation, upon seeing an Apple falling from a Tree', renseignement qui lui venait de la nièce de Newton, Catherine Barton, dont le mari John Conduitt fournit à Fontenelle les mêmes détails. Toujours dans la même année 1727, Robert Greene qui tenait ses renseignements de Martin Ffolkes, plus tard successeur de Newton comme président

[3] D. McKie & G. de Beer, 'Newton's apple', *Notes & Records of the Royal Society* (1951–52), ix. 47, 333.

[4] (London 1727), l'exemplaire de cet ouvrage conservé au British Museum porte sur la garde l'inscription autographe, 'to S^r hanslone from his most humble servant voltaire'.

de la Société royale, les confirma dans son livre.[5] Il fallut attendre l'année 1936 pour la publication des mémoires de William Stukeley,[6] qui rapporta la conversation qu'il eut avec Newton lui-même en 1726, mettant ainsi hors de doute la vérité de l'anecdote de la pomme, qui a été contestée.[7]

L'anecdote est décrite en détail par Voltaire dans ses *Letters concerning the English Nation*,[8] publiées à Londres en 1733, édition qui devança d'un an les *Lettres philosophiques* ou *Lettres écrites de Londres sur les Anglois et autres sujets*, dans lesquelles on lit:[9] 'S'étant retiré en 1666, à cause de la peste, à la campagne près de Cambridge, un jour qu'il se promenoit dans son jardin, & qu'il voyoit des fruits tomber d'un arbre, il se laissa aller à une méditation profonde sur cette Pesanteur dont tous les philosophes ont cherchez si long tems la cause en vain, & dans laquelle le vulgaire ne soupçonne pas même de mystère; il se dit à lui même, de quelque hauteur dans notre hémisphère que tombassent ces corps, leur chûte seroit certainement dans la progression découverte par Galilée: & les espaces parcourus par eux seroient comme les quarrez des tems. Ce pouvoir qui fait descendre les corps graves, est le même sans aucune diminution sensible à quelque profondeur qu'on soit dans la terre, & sur la plus haute montagne, pourquoi ce pouvoir ne s'étendroit-il pas jusqu'à la lune?' Voltaire traduit ici fidèlement la pensée de Newton dont le génie ne fut pas seulement de s'intéresser à la chute de la pomme en ligne verticale vers le centre de la terre, mais d'apercevoir que la force qui entraîne cette chute doit être la même que celle qui empêche la lune de s'échapper par force centrifuge de son orbite autour de la terre.

Voltaire reprit encore une fois l'histoire de la pomme dans ses *Éléments de la philosophie de Newton*, où il indiqua lui-même la source de ses renseignements, la nièce de Newton. Il dit:[10] 'Un jour,

[5] Robert Greene, *The Principles of the Philosophy of the Expansive and Contractive Forces, or an Inquiry into the Principles of the Modern Philosophy, that is, into the Several Chief Rational Sciences* (Cambridge 1727), p. 972.

[6] *Memoirs of Sir Isaac Newton's Life by William Stukeley*, edited by A. Hastings White (London 1936), p. 19.

[7] Sir David Brewster, *Memoirs of the Life, Writings, and Discoveries of Sir Isaac Newton* (Edinburgh & London 1855), p. 26.

[8] P. 127; l'édition anglaise devança l'édition française à cause des difficultés qu'éprouva Voltaire à publier cette dernière en France, comme il se verra ci-dessous.

[9] *Mélanges de Voltaire* (Pléiade), p. 60.

[10] M. xxii. 520; ce passage ne figure pas dans la première édition des *Elémens de la philosophie de Newton* parue en 1738, mais dans celle de 1741.

D

en l'année 1666, Newton, retiré à la campagne, et voyant tomber des fruits d'un arbre, à ce que m'a conté sa nièce (madame Conduit), se laissa aller à une méditation profonde sur la cause qui entraîne ainsi tous les corps dans une ligne qui, si elle était prolongée, passerait à peu près par le centre de la terre.'

Il n'est, peut-être, pas sans intérêt d'ajouter, que des greffons prélevés de ce fameux pommier avant sa mort, qui survint en 1820, ont été perpétués et vivent toujours, donnant des pommes à cuire, d'une variété bien connue au XVIIe siècle,[11] et qu'un morceau de bois provenant de cet arbre, qui est à coup sûr le plus célèbre du monde à l'exception de celui qui occasionna la chute, non d'une pomme mais du genre humain, est préservé dans les appartements de la Royal Astronomical Society.[12]

La publication de l'édition française de ses *Lettres philosophiques* exposa Voltaire à des poursuites judiciaires, et un mandat pour son arrestation fut lancé à Auxonne le 3 mai 1734. Il s'échappa et revint ensuite se cacher chez la marquise du Châtelet, à Cirey-sur-Blaise, où il passa quinze ans. Il y installa, avec sa maîtresse, un laboratoire de physique, qui est décrit par plusieurs visiteurs.[13] Faisant allusion à M. de Villefort, l'abbé Le Blanc écrivit au président Bouhier le 19 novembre 1736, 'on lui proposa d'aller voir Mr de Voltaire. Un escalier dérobé répondait à l'Appartement de cet Enchanteur, on le monte, on frappe à sa porte. Mais inutilement. Il était occupé à quelque opération magique et l'heure de sortir de son cabinet n'était pas venue; cependant la Règle fut enfreinte, en faveur de M. de Villefort.' A Nicolas-Claude Thieriot, Mme Denis écrivit le 10 mai 1738, 'Il se construit un appartement assez beau où il y aura une chambre noire pour des opérations de physique'; et Mme de Graffigny à François-Antoine Devaux, le 6 décembre 1738, 'dans la petite galerie . . . deux armoires; l'une de livres, l'autre de machines de physique; entre les deux, un fourneau dans le mur . . . Au delà est la chambre obscure, qui n'est pas encore finie, non plus que celle où il mettra ses machines.' Le président Hénault qui passa par Cirey y trouva 'des cabinets remplis de mécaniques et d'instruments de chimie.'

[11] D. McKie & G. de Beer, *op. cit.*, p. 53.

[12] D. McKie & G. de Beer, *op. cit.*, p. 334.

[13] Les citations qui suivent sont tirées de *Voltaire raconté par ceux qui l'ont vu* (Paris, J.-G. Prod'homme, 1929), pp. 101, 104, 108, 132.

On a la chance de savoir ce qui bouillait dans cette marmite de sorcière, et le détail des expériences scientifiques auxquelles se livraient Voltaire et son amie est donné dans le *Recueil des pièces qui ont remporté le prix de l'Académie royale des sciences, depuis leur fondation jusqu'à présent avec les pièces qui y ont concouru.*[14] Sous le déguisement d'une 'jeune Dame d'un haut rang', la marquise présenta en 1738 une 'Dissertation sur la nature et la propagation du feu'. Le chimiste Robert Boyle avait cru pouvoir expliquer l'augmentation de poids que subissent les métaux quand ils sont calcinés, en supposant que le feu consistait en particules ayant masse, et qu'elles pénétraient dans le métal calciné et ajoutaient leurs poids au sien. Ce fut l'hypothèse que la marquise décida de soumettre à l'expérience. Elle pesa des masses de fer de poids variant entre une livre et deux mille livres, d'abord chauffées et ensuite refroidies, ce qui démontre que les ressources du laboratoire, en équipement et en adresse des chercheurs, ne furent pas négligeables. Dans tous les cas, les poids restèrent invariables, d'où, comme avant elle Boerhaave, mais avec seulement huit livres de fer, Mme du Châtelet tira la conclusion que la chaleur en soi ne confère aucune augmentation de poids, et que celle-ci, dans les métaux calcinés, doit provenir de l'adhésion au métal de quelque matière dans l'atmosphère, selon l'hypothèse émise par Nicolaus Hartsoeker.

Cependant, Pieter van Musschenbrock y trouva à redire.[15] En confondant pesanteur et poids spécifique (on en était encore là), il fit observer que le fer chaud occupe un volume plus grand que quand il est froid, et, par conséquent, a un poids spécifique réduit. S'il paraissait peser le même poids quand il est chaud que quand il est froid, c'était parce que des particules de feu avaient pénétré dans le métal chaud et s'étaient ajoutées au poids de celui-ci, supposé déficitaire, pour disparaître ensuite quand le métal se fut refroidi et eut repris son poids spécifique normal. Ce fut alors qu'on vit 'Un de nos premiers poètes' soumettre un 'Essai sur la nature du feu et sur sa propagation',[16] également en 1738. Le poète, dont le nom se laisse facilement deviner, profita d'une obervation faite par Réaumur, que la fonte (alliage de fer et de carbone comme on sait

[14] (Paris 1752), iv. 104.

[15] Voir le développement historique de ce sujet dans D. McKie, 'Béraut's theory of calcination', *Annals of Science* (1936), I. voir surtout p. 278.

[16] *Recueil des pièces qui ont remporté les prix . . .* (Paris 1752), iv. 179; texte reproduit dans M. xxii, 281-325.

maintenant), à l'état chauffé, fondu et liquide, occupe un volume réduit et a un poids spécifique supérieur à celui du même métal à l'état froid. Voltaire vit le parti qu'il put en tirer pour une expérience. Il fit fondre du fer et versa dans des récipients cent livres dans l'un, trente-cinq livres dans l'autre, et vingt-cinq livres dans un troisième, opération également délicate. La calcination se fit, et quand les récipients et leurs contenus furent refroidis, les poids des métaux se trouvèrent augmentés de quatre livres dans le premier, d'une livre une once et demie dans le second, et de presqu'une livre dans le troisième. Ainsi, le métal pesait plus lourd à l'état froid, solide, et quand son poids spécifique était réduit. Impossible, dès lors, d'attribuer l'augmentation de poids à des particules de feu puisque le métal pesait moins quand il était liquide, chaud, et que son poids spécifique était augmenté.

Ces expériences réalisées par Mme du Châtelet et Voltaire, bien conçues et bien exécutées, furent de véritables apports à la science. Elles démontrèrent que la chaleur et le feu n'avaient pas de particules pesantes, et que la calcination entraîne une fixation de matières dans l'air. Il faudra attendre Lavoisier pour la preuve que ces 'matières' sont l'oxygène qui entre en combinaison chimique avec le métal, donnant un oxide dont le poids est supérieur à celui du métal original, mais il paraît que les résultats obtenus par Voltaire servirent à Laurent Bérault pour sa *Dissertation sur la cause de l'augmentation de poids, que certaines matières acquièrent dans leur calcination.*[17]

Entre temps, à Cirey, on n'avait pas négligé Newton. Voltaire publia ses *Éléments de la philosophie de Newton* en 1738, et Mme du Châtelet préparait sa traduction des *Principes* de Newton qui, cependant, ne fut publiée qu'en 1756. Pour bien saisir les difficultés avec lesquelles les hommes de sciences avaient à lutter, il faut tenir compte du fait que malgré que Newton eût publié ses *Principia mathematica* en 1687, les principes cartésiens continuaient à régner sur le continent d'Europe. Le système de Descartes[18] comportait l'extension de la matière, 'la matière subtile' qui occupait le 'vide', et les tourbillons grâce auxquels Descartes faisait tourner le monde, tourner les planètes autour du soleil, et expliquait l'action exercée à distance, qu'il ne pouvait concevoir sans enchaînement continu de

[17] D. McKie, *op. cit.*

[18] *Principia philosophiae* (Amsterdam 1644).

matière en contact reliant le corps agissant au corps subissant son action. En 1730 l'Académie des Sciences accorda un prix à Jean Bernoulli pour un ouvrage dans lequel il avait fait concorder la troisième loi de Kepler (que les carrés des temps de révolution des planètes autour du soleil varient avec les cubes de leurs distances du soleil) avec une théorie cartésienne de tourbillons, et quelques années plus tard il conclut que la force d'attraction variait selon l'inverse, non du carré, mais du cube de la distance.[19] Leibniz se refusa à abandonner l'explication cartésienne de l'action exercée à distance, et Huygens adhérait toujours au système des tourbillons, bien que Newton l'eût anéanti. Newton avait lancé la théorie générale de la gravitation universelle simplement en montrant que les corps exerçaient une attraction réciproque avec une force qui variait avec le produit des masses des corps et inversement avec le carré des distances qui les séparaient. Il se garda résolument de faire des conjectures ('hypotheses non fingo') pour expliquer la nature ou la cause de la gravitation, ou la manière selon laquelle agissait la force, même à distance. Il se borna à démontrer que les corps ont une *vis inertiae* qui résiste aux tentatives de changement de leur état, soit de repos ou de mouvement rectiligne, et qu'une force, *vis impressa*, qui a réussi à effectuer un changement dans la condition d'un corps, en lui imprimant un mouvement, se mesure par le produit de la masse de ce corps par l'accélération imprimée, celle-ci n'étant pas vitesse, mais accroissement de vitesse par unité de temps, comme Galilée l'avait constaté dans la chute des corps. On avait remarqué que dans la vitesse de mouvement d'un corps, il y avait quelque chose qui correspondait à une force, et Descartes, dans son système, était d'avis que la force d'un corps en mouvement correspondait au produit de la masse par la vitesse, formule qui en vérité donne la quantité de mouvement du corps, ou moment. Pour lui, par pur raisonnement sans aucune preuve expérimentale, la somme des mouvements dans l'univers entier était une constante; quand un corps en mouvement s'arrêtait, un autre se mettait en marche. Cependant, Leibniz insistait que la force d'un corps en mouvement, qu'il désignait force vive (*vis viva*) se mesurait par le produit de la masse non par la vitesse, mais par le carré de la vitesse. Ce fut directement à ce problème que adressa

[19] Voir le développement historique de ces théories dans Mary B. Hesse, *Forces and Fields* (London 1961), p. 157.

Voltaire dans un mémoire qu'il soumit à l'Académie des Sciences en 1741. Dans une série de propositions suivies de déductions logiques, ces 'Doutes sur la mesure des forces motrices & sur leur nature'[20] aboutissent à ce que les rapporteurs, Henri Pitot et Alexis-Claude Clairaut, désignés par l'Académie pour faire l'examen du mémoire, résument comme suit: 'Ce mémoire contient deux parties, la première est une exposition abrégée des principales raisons qui ont été données pour prouver que les forces des corps en mouvement sont comme leur quantité de mouvement, c'est-à-dire comme les masses multipliées par leurs simples vîtesses, et non pas les quarrés, ainsi que le prétendent ceux qui reçoivent les forces vives'. On en était encore au tâtonnement dans ce domaine où beaucoup restait à éclaircir et cela ressort bien de la conclusion tirée par les rapporteurs: 'Les raisons que Mr de Voltaire raporte, ne sont pas avancées comme des démonstrations, ce sont simplement des doutes qu'il propose, mais les doutes d'un homme éclairé, qui ressemblent beaucoup à une décision &c. De toutes les Questions difficiles à approfondir, que renferment les deux parties de ce mémoire, il paroît que Mr de Voltaire est très au fait de ce qui a été donné en physique, et qu'il a lui même beaucoup médité sur cette science.'

Ce fut l'ami de Voltaire, d'Alembert[21] qui, en 1743, résolut cette 'question difficile' en démontrant qu'elle reposait sur un malentendu. En raison du facteur temps, une force varie selon la vitesse d'un corps en mouvement; en raison de la distance parcourue par ce corps, la force varie selon le carré de la distance. Actuellement, pour mesurer la force, on se sert de la mesure du travail qu'elle accomplit au moyen de l'énergie cinétique qu'elle engendre, calculée selon la formule, le demi-produit de la masse par le carré de la vitesse.

Voltaire n'entra pas à l'Académie des Sciences, mais il fut admis à la Societé Royale de Londres. Ses premières relations personnelles

[20] Une analyse de ce mémoire figure dans la partie historique des *Mémoires de l'Académie royale des sciences, année 1741*, p. 149, mais l'Académie ne publia pas le texte. Il parut dans *Nouvelle Bibliothèque ou histoire littéraire des principaux écrits qui se publient* (La Haye 1741), p. 219. Il est reproduit dans M. xxiii. 165-172 (renseignements aimablement communiqués par madame Pierre Gauja et Mr S. S. B. Taylor). Un manuscrit de ce mémoire, envoyé par Voltaire à James Jurin, secrétaire de la Royal Society, a été déposé aux archives de la Royal Society par le capitaine A. K. Totton, dépositaire des papiers Jurin.

[21] *Traité de dynamique* (Paris 1743); voir à ce sujet E. Mach, *The Science of Mechanics* (Chicago 1902).

avec cette compagnie datent de 1739, date à laquelle il publia sa *Réponse à toutes les objections principales qu'on a faites en France contre la philosophie de Newton*, dont il envoya un exemplaire à Martin Ffolkes, avec une lettre du 10 octobre:[22] 'J Do my self the honour to send you this little answer j was oblig'd to write against our anti-newtonian cavillers. J am but a man blind of one eye expostulating with stark blind people who deny, there is such Thing as a Sun. J'll be very happy if this conflict with ignorant philosophers may ingratiate myself with such a true philosopher as you are.'

Dans cette supposition, Voltaire avait vu juste, et le 14 avril 1743 v.s., une candidature[23] en sa faveur fut déposée, signée par Lord Macclesfield, James Jurin, Martin Ffolkes, Shallett Turner, William Jones, James Bradley, et le duc de Richmond, Lennox & Aubigny, avec la citation suivante,

> Monsieur Arouet de Voltaire of Paris
> A Gentleman well known by Several curious and Valuable Works, being desirous of Offering himself a Candidate for Election into this Royal Society; we do accordingly propose him, and recommend him as well skill'd in Philosophical Learning, likely to be a usefull Member, and every way well qualified, and deserving of the Honour he desires.

Il fut élu le 3 novembre 1743. Sa lettre de remercîment à Ffolkes est un document[24] important pour l'histoire des sciences, et pour cette raison il est reproduit ici.

> a paris 29 n^bre n s 1743
>
> S^r
>
> one of my strongest desires was to be naturaliz'd in england; the royal Society, prompted by you vouchsafes to honour me with the best letters of naturalisation. my first masters in y^r free and learned country, were Shakespear addison dryden, pope; j made some steps afterwards in the temple of philosophy towards the altar of newton. j was even so bold as to introduce into france some of his discoveries; but j was not only a confessor to his faith; j became a martir. j could never

[22] Best. 1982.

[23] Gavin de Beer, 'Voltaire F.R.S.', *Notes & Records of the Royal Society* (1951), viii. 251.

[24] *Studies on Voltaire and the eighteenth century* (1957), iv. 252.

obtain the privilege[25] of saying in print, that light comes from the Sun and Stars, and is not waiting in the air for the Sun's impulsion, that vortices cannot be intirely reconcil'd with mathematics, that there is an evident attraction between the heavenly bodies, and such trash. but the liberty of the press was fully granted to all the witty gentlemen who teach'd us that attraction is a chimera, and vortices are demonstrated, who printed that a mobile lanch'd out from on high describes a parabola because of the resistance from the air below, that t'is false and impious to sai, light comes from the sun. even some of them printed, *col la licenza dei Superiori*, that newton ridiculously mistook, when he learn'd from experience the smaller are the pores of transparent bodies, the more pellucid they are; they alleg'd very wisely that the widest windows give the greatest admittance to light in a bed chamber. these things j have seen in our booksellers Shops, and at their Shops only.

you reward me for my Sufferings. the tittle of brother you honour me with is the dearest to me of all titles. j want now to cross the sea to return you my hearty thanks, and to show my gratitude and my veneration for the illustrious Society of wich you are the chief member.

be pleas'd Sir to be so kind as to present yr worthy bretheren with my most humble respects. j hope you will Sai to mylord duke of richemont, to mr jurin, mr turner etc how deeply j am sensible of their favours

j am with the greatest esteem, and the most Sincere respect

Sr

Yr most humble and faithfull servant, j dare not Say brother

voltaire

Comme on voit, l'abbaye de Westminster, Newton, les deux actrices, et Maupertuis, collaborèrent, à leur insu, pour faire naître chez Voltaire un intérêt passionné pour les sciences physiques. Pénétré de l'importance de l'observation objective et de la méthode expérimentale, il s'y est comporté en véritable chercheur. Cet état d'esprit, malheureusement, ne devait pas durer, et un différend

[25] Allusion au refus de privilège opposé par le chancelier d'Aguesseau à la demande de Voltaire.

s'éleva entre Voltaire et Maupertuis qui allait tout gâter. Vu l'importance des recherches que Maupertuis entreprit en Lapponie pour vérifier l'hypothèse de Newton sur l'aplatissement[26] des pôles, on se serait cru fondé de croire que les deux hommes resteraient amis, comme ils l'avaient été, et l'étaient encore le 19 janvier 1741, quand Voltaire adressa une lettre[27] à celui qu'il honora du titre de 'marquis du cercle polaire'. Ce fut même sur la recommandation de Voltaire que Frédéric le Grand appela Maupertuis à Berlin pour présider à l'Académie prussienne des sciences. Le désaccord naquit à la suite du principe de moindre action que Maupertuis énonça en 1746, mais contre lequel Samuel Koenig, autre ami de Voltaire, souleva des objections, à savoir premièrement que le principe était faux, et ensuite qu'il avait déja été énoncé par Leibniz dans une lettre adressée au professeur Hermann de Bâle, dont Koenig avait pris connaissance grâce à une copie qui avait appartenu à Samuel Henzi. Malheureusement, ce dernier avait été décapité en 1749 à Berne, inculpé de crime politique, et la lettre ne put être produite. Maupertuis réagit violemment, et sévit en faisant expulser Koenig de l'Académie prussienne comme falsificateur. A son tour, Voltaire fit explosion avec sa 'Diatribe du docteur Akakia',[28] dans laquelle, pour défendre et venger Koenig, Maupertuis est exposé aux plus outrageantes railleries et insultes, et à une moquerie implacable. Le principe de moindre action est de grande importance, et en s'attaquant à lui pour des raisons personnelles, on reconnaît en Voltaire l'apôtre de la tolérance, mais non plus l'homme de sciences.

Les sciences progressent toujours, mais la nature semble prendre plaisir à tendre des pièges et faire des niques aux chercheurs, et aux commentateurs aussi. C'est ainsi qu'un développement vient d'avoir lieu qui eût fort intrigué Voltaire. Une analyse de la forme de la terre, révélée par les trajectoires de satellites artificiels[29] (première preuve expérimentale à l'échelle cosmique des théories de Newton), a conduit à la conclusion que c'est le pôle sud qui est le plus aplati; il est plus rapproché de l'équateur de quarante mètres qu'il ne le serait si la terre avait la forme qu'on lui prêtait jusqu'ici.

[26] Voir ci-dessous.

[27] Best. 2261.

[28] *Histoire du docteur Akakia* (Berlin 1752); *Mélanges de Voltaire* (Pléiade), p. 289.

[29] D. G. King-Hele, 'The shape of the Earth', *Journ. Inst. Navigation* (1964), xvii. 1.

Le pôle nord, au contraire, est plus éloigné de l'équateur d'environ dix mètres. Nul plus que Voltaire n'aurait savouré l'ironie de la portée de la nouvelle découverte sur le travail de Maupertuis, lorsqu'il mesura l'écartement sur le terrain, des degrés de latitude au nord du cercle polaire en Lapponie, au sujet duquel Voltaire l'adjura, dans l'*Histoire du docteur Akakia*, 'qu'il ne se fasse pas seul aplatissant la terre',[30] Si Voltaire avait pu ajouter que Maupertuis avait mal aplati son pôle, l'effect aurait été retentissant.

Si l'homme de sciences en Voltaire s'est éclipsé dans son démêlé avec Maupertuis, il en est de même de ses incursions dans le domaine de la biologie; probablement à cause de l'intérêt passionné que Voltaire portait à la vie et que lui inspiraient les découvertes faites dans cette science, il n'était pas impersonnel. Comme les résultats des expériences biologiques s'y prêtaient facilement (et il y a là de quoi intéresser les transformistes), il eut vite fait d'appliquer aux hommes les connaissances acquises sur les animaux, et ne put s'empêcher de s'en servir pour garnir la moquerie ironique au moyen de laquelle il poursuivait inlassablement les objets qu'il avait en aversion, notamment l'église, contre laquelle il réussit de véritables chefs-d'œuvre de blasphème. Son 'roman', *Les Colimaçons du révérend père L'Escarbotier*,[31] en fournit un bel exemple. L'abbé Lazare Spallanzani venait, en 1768, de publier les résultats de ses expériences si remarquables sur le pouvoir de régénération de la tête chez les escargots et les limaces. Voltaire répète à son compte ces expériences, les confirme, et commence:

'Il y a quelque temps qu'on ne parlait que des jésuites, et à présent on ne s'entretient que des escargots. Chaque chose a son temps; mais il est certain que les colimaçons dureront plus que tous les ordres religieux; car il est clair que si on avait coupé la tête à tous les capucins et tous les carmes, ils ne pourraient plus recevoir de novices; au lieu qu'une limace, à qui l'on a coupé le cou, reprend une nouvelle tête au bout d'un mois.' C'est du Voltaire le plus pur, railleur, et jouant savamment, comme l'a si bien relevé René Pomeau,[32] du pouvoir évocateur et justicier des noms propres ridicules. Voltaire poursuit avec une tirade qu'il faut citer parce qu'elle décrit ses propres expériences:[33]

[30] *Mélanges de Voltaire* (Pléiade), p. 297.

[31] M. xxvii. 213-226.

[32] *Voltaire par lui-même* (Paris 1955), p. 55.

[33] M. xxvii. 214-215.

'le 27 de mai, par les neuf heures du matin, le temps étant serein, je coupai la tête entière avec ses quatre antennes à vingt limaces nues incoques, de couleur mordoré brun, et à douze escargots à coquille. . . . Au bout de quinze jours, deux de mes limaces ont montré une tête naissante; elles mangeaient déjà, et leurs quatre antennes commençaient à poindre. Les autres se portent bien; elles mangent sous le capuchon qui les couvre, sans allonger encore le cou. Il ne m'est mort que la moitié de mes escargots, tous les autres sont en vie. Ils marchent, ils grimpent à un mur, ils allongent le cou; mais il n'y a nulle apparence de tête, excepté à un seul. On lui avait coupé le cou entièrement, sa tête est revenue; mais il ne mange pas encore. *Unus est, ne desperes; sed unus est, ne confidas* [maxime à recommander aux chercheurs actuels]. . . . Dès qu'ils seront en état de manger et de faire l'amour, j'aurai l'honner d'avertir Votre Révérence.' Et alors, vient le clou: 'J'en ai souvent parlé dans mes sermons, et je n'ai jamais pu les comparer qu'à saint Denis, qui, ayant eu la tête coupée, la porta deux lieues dans ses bras en la baisant tendrement.'

Un autre exemple du génie que Voltaire savait employer pour se servir de tout bois biologique afin d'attiser son feu anticlérical est fourni par l'affaire des animalcules. John Turberville Needham, prêtre catholique anglais, avait fait des infusions de graines et de viandes qu'il versa dans des flacons en verre bouchés avec du liège ou du coton, et chauffa ensuite pour les stériliser, malgré quoi les infusions pullulèrent d'animalcules, y-compris des anguillules nématodes, que Needham démontra comme preuve de la génération spontanée.[34] Spallanzani montra ensuite que la technique employée par Needham, quoique très méritoire pour les débuts de la microbiologie au milieu du XVIIIe siècle, n'était pas suffisante pour garantir les infusions de la contagion par germes apportés dans les airs. Répétées, mais avec des flacons scellés en chauffant le verre de leurs cous, et exposés à la chaleur pendant une heure, aucune génération spontanée ne se produisit. La contre-épreuve, faite en pratiquant une ouverture dans les flacons, fut suivie de l'apparition des animalcules, et fit de Spallanzani un digne précurseur de Pasteur.

En relations avec Spallanzani, Voltaire ne tarda pas à réagir contre Needham, avec lequel il avait déja eu maille à partir, au sujet

[34] Voir Jean Rostand, *Les Origines de la biologie expérimentale et l'abbé Spallanzani* (Paris 1951), p. 26 *et seq.*

des miracles. Dans sa lettre du 26 août 1768 au marquis de Villevieille, Voltaire écrivit:[35] 'Croiriez-vous bien qu'un jésuite irlandais [Needham n'était ni jésuite ni irlandais] a fourni en dernier lieu des armes à la philosophie athéistique en prétendant que les animaux se formaient tout seuls? C'est ce jésuite Needham, déguisé en séculier, qui se croyant chimiste et observateur, s'imagine avoir produit des anguilles avec de la farine et du jus de mouton. Il poussa même l'illusion jusqu'à croire que ces anguilles en avaient produit d'autres, comme les enfants de Polichinelle et de Mme Gigogne. . . . Mon cher Marquis, il n'y a rien de bon dans l'athéisme.'

La biologie au siècle des lumières présentait cette particularité, que presque tous les progrès qui s'y marquèrent furent dans le domaine de la biologie expérimentale. La différence est frappante avec le siècle suivant, au cours duquel les sciences 'statiques' de l'anatomie comparée, la taxonomie, et la paléontologie, occupèrent les esprits, presqu'à l'exclusivité jusqu'à ce que la méthode expérimentale fleurît de nouveau, vers sa fin, avec la génétique, la physiologie, et l'embryologie. Ce fait est probablement significatif chez Voltaire, rompu à la méthode expérimentale, et pour qui ces résultats eurent sûrement plus d'attrait que les paradigmes comparatifs. On en a encore une preuve dans les expériences réalisées par Spallanzani,[36] toujours lui, sur la ressuscitation des rotifères et des tardigrades, minuscules animaux qui habitent les mares et les flaques d'eau susceptibles de se déssécher à la belle saison. Artificiellement il les dessèche, et il n'en reste alors rien que des petits corps morts endurcis; mais, humectés, ils ressuscitent, opération qu'il répète onze fois avec succès. Enthousiasmé, Voltaire lui répond,[37] le 6 juin 1776, 'Si Le Rotifero et Le Tardigrado morts, et pouris reviennent en vie, reprennent Leur mouvement, Leurs sensations, engendrent, mangent, et digèrent, on ne saura pas plus comment la nature Leur a rendu tout cela, qu'on ne saura comment La nature Le Leur avait donné; et L'un n'est pas plus incompréhensible que L'autre. J'avoue que je serais anxieux de savoir pourquoi Le grand être, L'auteur de tout, qui nous fait vivre et mourir, n'accorde La faculté de ressusciter qu'au Rotifero et au Tardigrado. . . . Il est bon aussi de savoir si ces petits animaux, qui ressuscitent plusieurs fois, ne meurent pas enfin tout de bon, et sur combien de ressurrections ils peuvent compter.'

Du temps de Voltaire, on savait déja bien à quoi s'en tenir au

[35] Best. 14229. [36] Jean Rostand, *op. cit.*, p. 95. [37] Best. 19016.

sujet des coquillages et autres fossiles, trouvés dans les couches géologiques éloignées des mers, et même sur des montagnes élevées; mais il ne put manquer l'occasion de les attribuer aux coquilles Saint-Jacques que des misérables pèlerins auraient laissé choir de leurs guenilles au cours de leurs voyages à Saint-Jacques de Compostelle ou en terre sainte. Il ne veut rien entendre de la signification des 'huîtres' sur les Alpes pour l'origine marine des couches de la terre, quoiqu'il soit prêt à admettre que les falaises de craie de Douvres et de Calais fussent autrefois continues où il y a aujourd'hui la mer qui les sépare.[38]

Le transformisme n'a pas échappé au regard de Voltaire, qui le traite avec un souverain mépris. Il aurait pu en prendre connaissance dans les œuvres de Montesquieu, Maupertuis, ou Diderot, mais ce fut contre Benoît de Maillet et son livre *Telliamed*, paru en 1748, que Voltaire se laissa aller à parler[39] 'Du système de Maillet, qui, de l'inspection des coquilles, conclut que les poissons sont les premiers pères des hommes.' Actuellement, rien de plus exact. Voltaire s'enfonce encore plus dans sa résistance au transformisme en écrivant, 'pour étayer ce système, il fallait absolument que toutes les espèces et tous les élémens se changeassent les uns en les autres. Les *Métamorphoses* d'Ovide devenaient le meilleur livre de physique qu'on ait jamais écrit.'

Comment expliquer que le même homme pût si bien conduire ses expériences sur la pesanteur des métaux calcinés, si clairement exposer les découvertes de Newton, dans un esprit strictement scientifique, et s'en prenne ensuite au principe de moindre action avec tant de fureur, attisée par des raisons personnelles, pour finir par se servir des expériences de biologie comme munitions contre l'église? La clé de l'énigme est fournie par M. Theodore Besterman dans une étude[40] où il démontre que, pour comprendre Voltaire, il faut tenir compte de sa passion pour la justice, sa croyance à la raison, son horreur de la métaphysique et des systèmes, et le facteur temps qui fait que dans toute discussion des œuvres de Voltaire, la date et les circonstances dans lesquelles elles furent écrites sont d'une importance capitale.

[38] 'Dissertation sur les changemens arrivées dans notre globe', M. xxiii. 221-230.

[39] M. xxvii. 156-157.

[40] Theodore Besterman, 'Reason and Progress', *Studies on Voltaire and the eighteenth century* (1963), xxiv. 27.

L'injustice faite à la dépouille d'Adrienne Lecouvreur s'ajoute à l'aversion contre le système le Descartes pour lancer Voltaire sur la piste de Newton, dont les découvertes lui paraissent accuser un caractère raisonnable qui va de soi. L'injustice avec laquelle, à ses yeux, Maupertuis attaque Koenig, et la monstrueuse cruauté de son projet d'étudier l'union de l'âme et du corps en procédant à la dissection du cerveau d'un criminel vivant, jettent Voltaire contre lui avec fureur, et tant pis pour le principe de moindre action, auquel, d'ailleurs, Voltaire ne tient pas. Quant aux coups décochés aux jésuites, aux moines, et aux miracles de saint Denis et de la résurrection, enveloppés dans ses commentaires sur les expériences de Spallanzani, il faut en chercher les causes dans les injustices infligées à Calas et au chevalier de la Barre.

The Encyclopédie *in Voltaire's Correspondence*

John Lough

The aim of this article is not to go over once again the ground covered by various studies of Voltaire's contribution to the *Encyclopédie*, his relations with the editors and his opinion of the work.[1] It would seem more appropriate to the occasion to try to do something rather different—to show what new light is thrown on the history of the *Encyclopédie* by both the text and the annotation of the Besterman edition of his correspondence. This is only one among several thousands of aspects of the eighteenth century which it illuminates afresh; but it happens to be the one on which I have mainly concentrated ever since its first volumes appeared in 1953. What follows is based on the notes taken as each group of volumes was published.

One tends to take for granted the enormous service rendered by the Besterman edition simply in bringing together all the letters hitherto published. However, even with letters which had already been printed, an improved text quite often means that hitherto unpublished passages have been brought to light. Several of these have some bearing on the history of the *Encyclopédie*.

No fewer than four of the letters in question (Best. 6955, 7005, 7029, 7043) were addressed to d'Argental in the period February–May 1758, at the height of the uproar caused by the article *Genève* and by d'Alembert's declared intention to have nothing further to do with the *Encyclopédie*. While the last three passages simply

[1] See R. Naves, *Voltaire et l'Encyclopédie* (Paris 1938), R. Pintard, 'Voltaire et l'*Encyclopédie*', *Annales de l'Université de Paris* (October 1952), pp. 39-56 and Marta Rezler, 'Voltaire and the *Encyclopédie:* a re-examination', *Studies on Voltaire* (1964), xxx. 147-187.

concern Voltaire's contributions to the *Encyclopédie*, the first contains a furious outburst against Diderot. The text of this letter, as it was earlier printed, broke off after Voltaire had explained that he was not worried about the articles he had sent for Vol. viii of the *Encyclopédie* as they were in d'Alembert's possession: 'Il s'agit de papiers que Diderot a entre ses mains au sujet de l'article *Geneve*, et des *Kakouacs*.' The angry tirade which followed has only now been brought to light:

> . . . il s'agit de lettres que je luy ay écrittes aux quelles il n'a pas répondu, et que j'exige qu'il me rende. Après sa lettre que j'ay reçue aujourduy 26 au bout de deux mois[2] je voudrais seulement qu'il brulât devant vous le petit billet que je luy écrivis au sujet du libelle des Kakouacs, libelle que je croiais alors fait par les jesuittes. Il a presque Désavoué Dalembert sur l'article *Geneve*. Il a abandonné son ami et son associé qui avait très grande raison, et qui n'a dit que l'exacte vérité, vérité même dont les prédicants génevois conviennent assez dans la profession de foy qu'ils viennent de Publier. Il faut d'ailleurs que Diderot soit le plus mou et le plus faible des hommes, pour continuer à travailler à l'enciclopédie sous la potence. Si luy, le chevalier de Jaucour et les autres déclarent qu'ils cesseront tout jusqu'à ce qu'on leur ait rendu la justice qu'on leur doit, et la liberté qu'ils méritent, on sera bien obligé de revenir à eux, et les coquins dont on encourage aujourdui les libelles seront obligez de se taire. Dalembert se conduit en homme libre, et Diderot en esclave. Vous pouvez mon cher ange ne luy pas reprocher sa mauvaise comédie du *Batard* et sa mauvaise foy de n'avoir pas cité le *Guldoni* dont il l'a prise presque toutte entière. Mais en vérité son procédé avec moi est inéxcusable. Je veux qu'il me rende mes lettres et je vous prie, puisque vous le connaissez, d'avoir la bonté de les retirer de ses mains. Je ne veux pas qu'il reste aucun vestige de ce que j'ay pensé sur cette sottise des Kakouacs. Aidez moy à être tranquile, car je trouve qu'il n'y a que cela de bon.

Tempers were certainly frayed in this period of crisis in the history of the *Encyclopédie*; but why should Voltaire have been so worried

[2] Best. 6946 (see Roth 89).

about the note which he had written to Diderot on the subject of Moreau's *Nouveau Mémoire pour servir à l'histoire des Cacouacs*? In his next letter to the same correspondent, written on the following day (Best. 6956), he repeats his demand that Diderot should burn in d'Argental's presence 'mon billet sur les Kakouacs dans le quel je me méprenais sur l'auteur.'

In comparison two unpublished passages in letters to Damilaville are of relatively minor interest. The first is one of the numerous occasions on which Voltaire gave vent to his impatience to see the last ten volumes of text which were finally ready for distribution at the end of 1765. On 4 March of that year (Best. 11587) he wrote: 'Voicy encor un petit mot pour Briasson. Je voudrais bien que pour réponse il m'envoiât l'enciclopédie.' The other reference (in a letter of 26 February 1766—Best. 12311) contains an unpublished passage which shows Voltaire's interest in the contents of these volumes when they at last reached Ferney. Unfortunately the copy from which these two sentences are taken has suppressed, as an editorial note points out, the vital point—the names of the articles which aroused Voltaire's curiosity, so that all we are left with is the two sentences:

> Dites moi, je vous en prie, de qui sont les articles . . .
>
> Il y en a un terrible contre les jésuites.[3]

There is more meat in some of the complete letters of Voltaire which are published here for the first time, as these include several to d'Alembert and also a number to Gabriel Cramer in the period when he was engaged in reprinting the *Encyclopédie*. One of the letters to d'Alembert (Best. 5244) throws a little more light on the early stages of Voltaire's collaboration in the *Encyclopédie*—'votre immense et belle compilation,' as he calls it. Writing from Colmar on 30 July 1754 he speaks of the 'rogatons croquez que je vous ai envoyez à l'addresse de Briasson' and adds: 'Vous ne m'avez pas accusé la réception. Cependant vous devez les avoir depuis un mois.' Another letter to d'Alembert (Best. 6126) concerns the article 'Français', despatched on 24 March 1756, and on 22 May 1757 (Best. 6568) Voltaire sent on Polier de Botens's unsigned article, 'Logomachie'. More interesting is the unpublished letter to d'Alembert of 10 April [1758] a date which is clearly established by the

[3] Unsigned, but attributed to Diderot by Naigeon.

reference to the recently published *Mémoire des libraires associés à l'Encyclopédie, sur les motifs de la suspension actuelle de cet ouvrage.* The advice which in this difficult period Voltaire sent from a safe distance to the two editors and more especially to d'Alembert tended to be somewhat contradictory. Here (Best. 7011) he is all for d'Alembert returning to his post:

> Mon cher philosophe, il est bon d'être ferme mais il ne faut pas être impitoyable. Ne résistez plus au cri du public, et au mémoire des libraires qui sont à vos genoux. Faittes vous tirer à quatre, et puis donnez grâce. Mais quand vous aurez repris les rênes, empêchez les déclamations. Quelle pitié! quels plats articles à côté des vôtres!

In this same letter we also find a reference to the possibility of Duclos replacing d'Alembert as joint-editor: 'Faudrait-il d'ailleurs que Duclos vous remplaçât, et comment vous remplacerait-il?' he asks.[4]

From another unpublished letter of Voltaire—written earlier in 1758 to the Genevan banker, Labat (Best. 6876)—we learn that at this time he had in mind to write an article 'Indes, Compagnie des,' though in the end nothing came of this. The publication of the *Dictionnaire philosophique* in 1764 led him to pen a whole series of letters denying his paternity. Among these was one (Best. 11314) to the Marquise de Jaucourt, the wife of the nephew of the Chevalier, who was an old acquaintance of Voltaire. In this unpublished letter as in a letter of the same date to Damilaville (Best. 11313), the Chevalier is enlisted among those called upon to bear witness to the truth.

> Comme m[r] le chevalier de Jaucour veut bien travailler à l'enciclopédie, et que la persécution excitée contre le dictionaire philosophique peut s'étendre jusqu'au dictionaire de l'enciclopédie, il y a quelque intérêt de connaîttre et de faire voir combien on a tort de m'imputer le petit dictionaire en question. Je proteste sur mon honneur que je n'ay aucune part à cette édition misérable.

We shall meet the Chevalier again in a moment.

The correspondence is a mine of information about both the

[4] See below, p. 57.

Panckoucke-Cramer reprint of the *Encyclopédie* and the *Supplément*. When Panckoucke abandoned his original project for a revised edition in favour of a literal reprint followed by a *Supplément*, Voltaire took up with enthusiasm the proposal that he should contribute, although he turned down with scorn the offer of a fee of 18,000 l. (Best. 14944). In an unpublished letter to Mme Denis (Best. 14956), written a week after he had promised Panckoucke a whole string of articles, he speaks of the matter thus:

> J'ai reçu les propositions de Pankouke; j'ai refusé ses offres avec colère, mais j'ai accepté le travail avec plaisir. Ce sera pour moi un grand amusement pour l'hiver, il ne m'en coûtera que la peine de dicter. Ce serait pour moi un fardeau insuportable de feuilleter et d'écrire. Cette petite occupation me consolera.

It is, however, well known that in the end Voltaire did not contribute anything to the *Supplément*; his enthusiasm for the idea resulted in the volumes of his own *Questions sur l'Encyclopédie*.

Some letters of Voltaire to Cramer brought to light for the first time make a contribution to our knowledge of the history of the publication of the Geneva edition. Not that these mostly undated missives are always absolutely clear in their meaning. For instance, Best. 15712, dated approximately October–November 1770, speaks as if Cramer and his partner De Tournes had not signed an agreement with Panckoucke on the previous 26 June to finish off the printing of the remaining volumes of text after the first three had been incarcerated in the Bastille; and are the three volumes mentioned in the second paragraph below those of Voltaire's *Questions* (as Dr. Besterman suggests in a note) or of Panckoucke's edition of the *Encyclopédie*?

> Je plains ce pauvre Pankouke à qui on lie les mains tandis que ses rivaux les ont libres. Monsieur Caro est bien heureux de ne s'être pas embarqué sur une mer si orageuse.
>
> Voicy assurément le tems de débiter ces trois volumes. J'ai bien peur que Pankouke n'ait imprimé dans ceux qui sont en prison, toutes les fautes de géographie, qui fourmillaient dans la première édition. Si ces fautes sont corrigées dans l'in 4° d'Yverdun l'in folio embastillé sera décrié sans retour. Voilà une affaire bien triste.

The competition which the Geneva reprint had to face from the *Encyclopédie d'Yverdon* is again discussed in a letter of December of the same year (Best. 15807).

> Il est très triste d'avoir été prévenus par Messieurs d'Yverdun. Il ne faut pas s'imaginer que leur entreprise soit infructueuse. Ils sont secourus par deux membres de l'académie des sciences et des belles lettres, et par un homme très savant et très laborieux. Ils ont l'avantage de corriger dans leur édition beaucoup de fautes grossières qui fourmillent dans l'Enciclopédie de Paris, et que Pankouke et De Saint ont eu l'imprudence de réimprimer. Cette faute capitale les force à donner un supplément qui renchérit le livre, et on aura l'édition d'Yverdun à une fois meilleur marché. Pour moi je sais bien que j'achêterai l'édition d'Yverdûn et non l'autre.

An editorial note points out that Voltaire did in fact acquire a set of the *Encyclopédie d'Yverdon*. On the other hand, while he was quite right to point out that de Félice's version was very substantially cheaper than the Panckoucke-Cramer reprint and the *Supplément* combined, anyone who, like himself, already owned a set of the first edition would not in any case have had any interest in buying the Geneva reprint.

Turning now to unpublished letters from Voltaire's correspondents which bear on the *Encyclopédie*, we find first a letter (Best. 5652) from that enigmatic figure, Polier de Bottens, who had succeeded his uncle as premier pasteur de Lausanne and was to contribute some strangely unorthodox articles to the *Encyclopédie*. This long screed on the subject of fornication, full of Oriental learning, was presumably an answer to a request from Voltaire whose contribution on this subject, along with that of d'Alembert, duly appeared in Vol. vii of the *Encyclopédie*.[5]

Of greater significance are a number of unpublished letters from d'Alembert. The first of these (Best. 6576) contains some pungent comments on the parsimony of the publishers of the *Encyclopédie*:

> J'ai envoyé votre lettre à Briasson. A l'égard de la proposition qu'a fait votre ami,[6] je vois bien qu'il ne connoît pas les li-

[5] In 1757, and not in 1755, as stated in the textual notes to the letter.

[6] Who was this contributor or prospective contributor?

braires. Deux exemplaires de l'Encyclopédie à donner les feront crier comme si on leur arrachoit l'âme; s'il peut en arracher un pour lui, il sera bien heureux, je lui conseille même de traiter pour cela avec eux avant de nous envoyer le reste des articles qu'il nous promet. Mandez lui de me faire parvenir la liste de ceux qu'il peut nous donner, avec les conditions aux quelles il veut travailler, & je verrai si cela leur convient; mais je ne vous réponds pas du succès.

As we have very little information about payments to authors —except for what is contained in the part of the publishers' accounts which happens to have survived—it is interesting to have d'Alembert's views on the question, bearing in mind that since it was now clear that the *Encyclopédie* was going to exceed the ten volumes originally announced, the request for two sets would seem to have been rather optimistic.

D'Alembert is also mentioned in a passage from an unpublished letter of Thieriot of 30 March 1758 (Best. 7004). This refers to a quarrel between him and Duclos who had apparently come forward as his successor as joint editor after he had given up:

C'est le Philosophe Duclos qui s'est offert de remplacer M. Dalambert pour tout ce qui n'est point Mathématique et Géométrie. C'est à l'occasion de ce remplacement qu'ils se sont querellés, mais tout est dit et convenu.

This explains Voltaire's question to d'Alembert, in his letter of 10 April (Best. 7011) quoted from above: 'Faudrait-il d'ailleurs que Duclos vous remplaçât, et comment vous remplacerait-il?' The suggestion that Duclos should take d'Alembert's place as joint editor seems to have been unknown until the publication of these two letters. Certainly there is no mention of it in Paul Meister's thesis on Duclos.[7] In any case nothing came of the proposal; indeed Duclos was apparently one of the contributors who abandoned the ship in the storms which hit the *Encyclopédie* in 1758 and 1759.

There are three unpublished letters of d'Alembert (Best. 8196, 8206, 8284) which are mainly concerned with the controversy aroused by the performance of Palissot's *Les Philosophes* at the Comédie-Française in 1760. The first of these letters, written on

[7] *Charles Duclos (1704–1772)* (Geneva 1956), pp. 63-65

26 May, shows that there was a decided rift between Voltaire and his Paris friends over what they regarded as his lack of vigour in attacking Palissot. Voltaire, anxious not to fall out with Choiseul, Palissot's patron, is upbraided for his failure to react with his customary force:

> Vous m'aviez paru, mon cher confrère, prendre le plus vif intérêt à la persécution que les Philosophes éprouvent; vous m'aviez écrit sur ce ton là, en me priant de vous envoyer ce détail très ennuyeux; vous étiez indigné il y a quinze jours, de ce que les Philosophes se laissoient *écraser*, *égorger*, *vilipender* par des *fripons* et des *fanatiques*.[8] Vous paroissiez vouloir prendre leur défense; Ils l'espéroient, le désiroient; vous m'écrivez aujourd'hui que vous vous en foutez; soyez sûr que je m'en fous encore davantage, et que je m'en fouterai encore plus par la suite.
>
> On dit que Palissot vous a envoyé sa pièce avant qu'elle fût jouée. Il vient d'imprimer une préface où il vous loue à tours de bras, sans doute pour se concilier votre approbation.... Il ajoute dans cette préface qu'il est en commerce de lettres avec vous, & qu'il s'en fait gloire. Mais, comme vous le dites fort bien *il faut rire de tout*, aussi vous ne me verrez plus que rire....

However, in his next letter (31 May) d'Alembert, having heard that as a protest Voltaire had withdrawn his *Zulime* from the Comédie-Française and that *L'Écossaise* was soon to be performed, adopted more flattering tones:

> Mon cher et illustre Philosophe, je reçois à l'instant votre lettre du 26 mai,[9] et je me hâte de vous remercier au nom de la Philosophie du parti que vous venez de prendre.... J'étois un peu fâché de votre dernière lettre,[10] j'avois cru y entrevoir un ton de plaisanterie, qui m'affligeoit pour la république, bien plus que pour moi....
>
> On dit qu'on va joüer sur le théâtre de la Comédie la pièce de l'Écossaise. Je remercie l'auteur, quelqu'il soit, de la manière dont il a parlé de l'Encyclopédie dans sa préface.[11]

[8] See Best. 8134 (25 April)

[9] Best. 8193

[10] Best. 8185 (21 May)

[11] He describes the *Encyclopédie* as 'cet ouvrage nécessaire au genre humain, dont la suspension fait gémir l'Europe'.

In the last of these unpublished letters dealing with *Les Philosophes* (1 July) d'Alembert repeats once again to Voltaire that Choiseul is behind the whole attack on the Philosophes. There is no doubt that there was dissension between Voltaire and his Paris friends over Palissot's play, and yet to the modern reader it would appear that despite his cautious behaviour in the whole matter the letters which Voltaire wrote to Palissot, who was rash enough to publish them,[12] completely unmasked the author, especially for the scandalous misquotations from the *Encyclopédie* in his preface to the play.

One last unpublished letter of d'Alembert (Best. 13623) throws some light on the disadvantages of being associated with the *Encyclopédie* for an eighteenth-century civil servant. Their friend Damilaville, the author, with Diderot, of the article 'Vingtième', had been promised the post of directeur de la vingtième for the Paris region. However, writes d'Alembert on 14 November 1767,

> un certain Sauvigni, intendant de Paris, a été le dénoncer à Mr d'Ormesson comme un athée, un Philosophe, un Encyclopédiste.

The result was that Damilaville lost this promotion.

Finally an unpublished letter written in 1767 by Count Shuvalov to Voltaire (Best. 13378) speaks both of plans for a Russian translation of the *Encyclopédie* and of the notorious Abraham Chaumeix, who after the publication of his *Préjugés légitimes contre l'Encyclopédie* had made his way to Moscow:

> Une Nouvelle qui ne vous deplaira point, C'Est qu'on traduit actuelement en Russe, un ouvrage, qui a autant honoré La France qu'il a Été Persécuté par des Français. Maitre Abraham *Chaumeix*, Enrage de nous voir devenir Enciclopédistes: mais il n'enrage point à Moscou Comme il Enrageait à Paris. Les fripons et Les sots murmurent ici dans La poussière. Je n'ai pas besoin de vous dire que C'Est *Talestris*[13] qui a désiré de procurer L'Enciclopédie à ses peuples, et qui même fait Les frais de L'Impression, mais de quoi je me Glorifierai Éternellement, C'Est d'avoir Été Le premier qui ait saisi ses vues, qui ait formé une société et arangé tout pour cette Entreprise.

[12] Best. 8214, 8257 and 8307 [13] Catherine

> Comme Enciclopédiste vous me devés quelque remerciment. Pour moi Comme Être pensant, je vous dois toujours mon homage.

Interesting as this letter is for the study of the influence of the *Encyclopédie* outside France, it seems to be the case that if what was intended was a translation of the whole work, nothing ever came of it, as only translations of selected articles ever saw the light of day in Russia.[14]

Further light is thrown on the history of the *Encyclopédie* by a number of unpublished letters written by contemporaries of Voltaire which contain references to him. These can be particularly useful because sometimes they have been dug out of remote places where the uninitiated would probably not have thought of looking for them. An example is furnished by a letter of the Chevalier de Jaucourt to Labat (Best. 6919), written in 1758 when controversy raged around the article 'Genève'. This adds one more to the meagre dozen or so letters of the Chevalier which have survived, and is especially valuable as it contains some biographical details. A letter which is interesting for Genevan reactions to the *Encyclopédie* is one from Bonnet to Haller (Best. 7448), written at the critical date of 6 March 1759. Bonnet applauds the sentiments expressed in the *réquisitoire* of Omer Joly de Fleury:

> Enfin on découvre aux yeux du Parlement, le secret de la Cabale, et l'art avec lequel elle sçait répandre son venin. Je ne puis vous dire avec quel plaisir j'ai lu d'un bout à l'autre cet Arrêt. J'y ai admiré par tout la force, la vérité, la noblesse de l'expression, et le zèle vraiement Chrêtien et Patriotique des sages Magistrats qui l'ont rendu. J'appris avant-hier que *l'Encyclopédie* a été supprimée pour toûjours, et le Privilège retiré.[15] La voilà donc supprimée par l'Authorité; elle l'auroit été bientôt par la Zizanie des Autheurs. D'Alembert avoit déclaré très expressément qu'il n'y travailleroit plus. Diderot vouloit continuer, le Chancelier lui a donné la paix malgré lui.

Such a hostile attitude to the *Encyclopédie* was not, however, universal in Geneva. It was after all in that city that the whole work

[14] See Jacques Proust, *L'Encyclopédie* (Paris 1965), pp. 198-200.

[15] The Arrêt du Conseil suppressing the *privilège* was dated 8 March.

was to be reprinted after a second edition in France itself had been made impossible.

Most interesting of all among this group of unpublished letters are those which concern the Panckoucke-Cramer reprint of the *Encyclopédie*. Two letters of Cramer to Grimm (Best. 8044 and 8172) show that as early as 1760 he was interested in printing the *Encyclopédie*. When publication of the work was held up in Paris, there was some talk of continuing the work in Holland. It is presumably to such a plan that Cramer is referring in the opening part of the first sentence below in a letter of 29 February (he goes on to suggest Geneva as a more suitable place):

> Je suis charmé que vous approuviez mon projet de n'être pas intéressé dans l'Impression de l'Encyclopédie; l'Exécution de cette entreprise ne sera pas difficile ici, & je crois que pour peu que les Libraires de Paris soyent raisonnables, nous serons bientôt d'accord. Je souhaitterois fort savoir à quel point en est le Manuscript; & si pour commencer l'Impression il est absolument nécessaire d'attendre qu'il soit antièrement achevé; je prends la liberté de vous demander cela, parceque (touttes choses d'ailleurs égales), j'aimerois beaucoup mieux aller à Paris pendant l'Été, qu'en Automne.

In May Cramer followed this up with a second letter, pressing once again his claim that Geneva would be a more suitable place than Holland in which to finish off the printing of the work:

> J'ai eu sur nôtre grand object deux ou trois conférences avec l'ami Cromelin,[16] qui par parenthèse me charge de mille choses pour vous. Il m'a détaillé sa conversation avec M. David le Libraire, & j'ai conclu que le dit David sent tout l'Inconvénient d'imprimer en Hollande; l'inégalité des papiers, la cherté de la fabrique, les droits de sortie, peut-être peu de sûreté d'ailleurs &c. Plus je réfléchis à cette affaire, & plus je crois que Genève est le lieu le plus propice de tous; j'ai six presses chez moi & des ouvriers sûrs; le papier peut se tirer du Vivarets à trente lieues d'ici & ressembler si fort à celui que l'on a employé, à Paris, qu'il sera impossible d'en faire la différence. Si le Gouvernement en France ne dit mot, l'on ne dira mot

[16] Jean Pierre Crommelin, minister for Geneva in Paris.

> ici; si le Gouvernem[t] en France veut mettre obstacle à cette impression, il l'empêchera en Hollande tout comme ici.
>
> Je compte sur vos bontés mon cher monsieur, pour vouloir dans le courant de l'Été m'informer de tems en tems de l'état des choses: Monsieur Diderot sait à quel point le Manuscript est avancé, dans quel temps il sera fini; qu'elles sont les intentions des Libraires &c. Tout cela est important: si cette affaire doit avoir lieu, il faut que le contract soit passé six mois avant qu'on commence, afin d'avoir une provision de papier telle qu'on ne soit point arrêté pendant le cours de l'Impression.

When the French government—partly to avoid losing to some foreign country the profits to be made from such a large commercial undertaking as the *Encyclopédie*—gave tacit permission for the printing to be continued secretly in Paris, Cramer's plans came to nothing. He had to wait ten years until Panckoucke's reprint was brought to a sudden stop by the incarceration of the first three volumes in the Bastille.

Cramer's association with Panckoucke—it lasted from 1770 until de Tournes and he sold back their share in the undertaking in 1775—was far from being a happy one. One of the most interesting letters, from our particular point of view, brought to light in the Besterman edition is one written by Cramer to Louis Necker de Germagny after the association had been completely dissolved (Best. 19526). In 1777 he described how seven years earlier Panckoucke had come and sought his help in his distress at the catastrophe which had befallen his new edition:

> C'étoit en 1770, au milieu de l'Été, que mon[r] Panckoucke fit un second voyage à Genêve, & qu'il arriva chés moi à la Campagne avec un abbé de ses amis: il se trouvoit disoit-il dans le plus cruel embarras; & il ne voyoit de ressource qu'auprès de moi, de qui depuis que nous nous connoissons, il éprouvoit sans cesse les meilleurs procédés: il s'agissoit de le tirer d'affaire au sujet de l'impression de l'Encyclopédie: il me conta qu'il avoit achetté tous les Cuivres, et qu'il avoit déjà fait imprimer trois vollumes tirés à deux mille examplaires, c'et [sic] à dire, six mille volumes infolio, que la police venoit de saisir par ordre de m[r] le Chancellier, que l'on avoit

> renfermés à la Bastille: Panckoucke voioit sa machine arrêtée, ces avances perduës, son crédit annéanti & sa fortune hazardée si je ne venois à son secours; il me proposa de suivre à son entreprise en m'y associant; je lui témoignai l'intérêt que m'inspiroit sa position, et l'effroy que me causoit sa proposition, il insista; m. de Tournes-Cannac mon parent & mon ami se joignit à Panckoucke, nous fimes tout ce qu'il voulut; nous achetâmes les Cuivres sur le pied de deux cent mille livres, (et nous avons sceu depuis que le prix qu'il en avoit payé n'excédoit pas la valeur de Vingt mille écus comptant); nous lui payâmes très chèrement les trois vollumes emprisonnés, dont il promettoit la libération incessamment, & que nous n'avons jamais eües; enfin je traittai Mr Panckoucke non comme un homme embarassé de qui on peut exiger quelque sacrifice, mais en vérité, (et m^r^ de Tournes vous le dira) comme un homme pour le quel on se sacrifie.

The tribulations which Cramer let himself in for are vividly described in the following passage:

> M. Panckoucke retourna à Paris; & je me mis à travailler de concert avec m. de Tournes au grand Œuvre de la réimpression Encyclopédique: nous trouvâmes l'affaire dans un état affaire pitié par la négligence, l'imprudence & l'inconséquence de m^r^ Panckoucke, entravée d'ailleurs par un impôt hors de mesure sur lentrée des livres, & sur tout par une défense expresse d'introduire ce dictionnaire dans le Royaume: Enfin, après avoir labouré pendant cinq ans, après avoir écrit plus de six mille lettres, & avoir abimé ma vue, j'eus la satisfaction de remettre la barque à flos, c'est à dire, d'avoir réparé les brêches, sauvé l'entreprise de toutte perte, achevé l'impression, & acquis la perspective d'un profit honnête.

The uneasy relations between the two men are also brought out in two unpublished letters (Best. 16075 and 17019) which Cramer wrote to Panckoucke in 1771 and 1772 when work on the new edition was still at a relatively early stage. These two letters (and others in the Manuscript Department of the Bibliothèque publique et universitaire, Geneva) are certainly written in a very acrimonious style.

Some of the initial difficulties of the whole enterprise once it had been transferred to Geneva are illustrated in a passage from a letter written from there by Louise Suzanne Gallatin to the Landgrave of Hesse-Cassel on 15 December 1770 (15800):

> A l'Égard de ce que vous me dites sur la grande anciclopédie il est vray qu'actuellement en France on n'ose pas La réimprimer, Le Clairgé se déchainant Contre tous ceux qui L'ont faite, et Cela à Caude [sic] de ce Livre *du sistème de la nature* qui est abominable a répendre. Le Clairgé a saisi cette occasion pour Examiner tout, et Critiquer tout, et Comme il a La Confiance du Souverain, on n'ose pas protéger des livres qu'il désaprouve.... Ce livre est Cause que l'on est si attentif à ce qui paroît; on devoit réimprimer l'anciclopédie, et M^r le Chancelier n'ose pas assurer qu'il puisse entrer en France, ce qui pourroit bien empêcher l'Impression.

There was also trouble with the ecclesiastical authorities in Geneva over the printing of the new edition, so much so that Panckoucke had gone behind the back of Cramer and de Tournes and tried to sell their share to the Amsterdam publisher, Marc-Michel Rey.

A further obstacle lay ahead. In July 1771 Sartines who, as well as being Lieutenant de Police, had succeeded Malesherbes as Directeur de la Librairie, wrote to the Foreign Minister, the Duc d'Aiguillon, to suggest that, while he was taking steps to prevent copies of the new edition entering France, the best course was simply to stop the work being printed in Geneva. Spurred on by this letter, d'Aiguillon wrote to Hennin, the French resident in Geneva, to order him to take the necessary steps to see that the edition was suppressed. In the meantime he received a missive from the prime mover in this whole attack on the new edition, Christophe de Beaumont, the Archbishop of Paris. If in the end nothing came of the new campaign against what the Archbishop called 'un pernicieux ouvrage', it was not for want of trying. Clearly the enemies of the work had not thrown up the sponge when the last ten volumes of text of the first edition appeared in 1765; they at least succeeded in preventing the *Encyclopédie* from ever being reprinted inside France.

The documents concerning this attempt to stop the Geneva edition are not reproduced in the Besterman edition of Voltaire's correspondence. They are however duly listed in a footnote (Best. 16292, n. 9) and invite the curious reader to make his way to the archives at the Quai d'Orsay. This example illustrates what those working in the eighteenth-century field owe to the abundant and yet suitably laconic annotation of the letters. One might like to argue with the editor about the contents of one or two of these notes; but it would be out of place in this volume and particularly in a contribution which is devoted to illustrating what one worker in this field owes to his editorial labours.

From the Inégalité *to* Candide: *notes on a desultory dialogue between Rousseau and Voltaire* (1755–1759)

R. A. Leigh

1. An unanswered letter

On 4 June 1756, Voltaire sent Thieriot three copies of a new edition of his two poems on natural law and the Lisbon earthquake for distribution to d'Alembert, Diderot and Rousseau (Best. 6203),[1] remarking, evidently in the fond belief that these three writers constituted a happy band of brothers, working harmoniously together in the common cause: 'Ils m'entendront assez. Ils verront que je n'ai pu m'exprimer autrement et ils seront édifiés de quelques notes. Ils ne dénonceront point ces sermons.' This confidence was misplaced, and the assumption on which it was founded erroneous. Spurred on, perhaps, by an urgent and indignant appeal from Geneva (but the evidence for this is unreliable),[2] Jean-Jacques sat down and drafted a weighty and considered attack on the Lisbon poem. It must have taken him the best part of a month to compose,[3] was long enough to make a fair-sized pamphlet (the earliest known printing runs to fifty-six duodecimo pages), and was obviously written with an eye to publication. Having finished this eloquent profession of faith, one or two qualms beset him. His letter, though tactful and deferential in places, was firm and outspoken, and here

[1] These references are, of course, to Theodore Besterman's monumental edition of *Voltaire's Correspondence* (Genève, Institut et Musée Voltaire, 1953–1966).

[2] See my *Correspondance complète de J.-J. Rousseau* (Genève, Institut et Musée Voltaire, 1965 s.), t. iv. no. 417 (this edition is referred to subsequently as 'Leigh').

[3] On 6 July, Thieriot informed Voltaire that Rousseau's copy of the two poems had already been handed to Duclos for delivery at the Ermitage.

and there the balance between these ingredients was apt to seem somewhat precarious. He decided to send it to Théodore Tronchin (probably through M. d'Épinay), with instructions to deliver it to Voltaire only if he thought the latter could read it without taking umbrage (Leigh 425 and 426). His remarks to Tronchin about Voltaire, which are both disparaging and patronising, strike a significantly different note from that of the letter itself, and reveal the difficulty Jean-Jacques had experienced in sugaring his massive pill.

What could have induced Rousseau to turn aside from the intimidatingly ambitious programme he had set himself to complete at the Ermitage, in order to engage in single combat a writer who was not only the outstanding literary figure of the age, but also one of its most dreaded and dangerous polemists? The point was that the Lisbon poem not only dealt with certain problems with which Jean-Jacques had been quite recently concerned, and which lay at the heart of his thinking: it had also reached him at a particularly sensitive moment in his evolution: or, if that term, applied to a man of forty-four, seems inappropriate, in that long and intermittent process of self-discovery to which the announcement of the prize competition of 1749 had given such peremptory impetus. A significant stage in that process had been reached with his return to Geneva and his readmission to the Protestant Church. The motives for this step were no doubt complex: and they certainly included one very mundane and practical one. Until his youthful conversion to Catholicism had been duly forgiven and obliterated, his claim to the title of Citizen of Geneva (a title which he had assumed even before the publication of his first *Discours*) was liable to be contested; in fact, it had been.[4] It had certainly become necessary, on the eve of the publication of an important new work, prefaced by such a loud and magniloquent flourish on the patriotic trumpet, to regularise the situation. But it would be wrong to discount the purely religious motive.[5] Whether Jean-Jacques after 1750 was ever 'really a Christian' or not, is a question which cannot be argued here: but he was certainly moving towards the active defence of a

[4] See Leigh, no. 149, note *g* (ii. 126) and A 76 (ii. 303-304).

[5] It may be noted here that, many years later, speaking of his discussions with Rousseau in Geneva in 1754, Jacob Vernes the Genevan *littérateur* and pastor, told Brissot that 'Jean-Jacques parla de la Divinité en inspiré' (Leigh, t. iii. A 132).

positive form of theism tinged with residual Christian beliefs, and above all with a certain basic Christian sensibility and colouring. Such an attitude, devoid of any systematic rancour against Christianity, and progressing steadily under its own impetus, could not fail to carry him further and further away from the *philosophes* of his circle (d'Holbach, Diderot and Grimm), with whom, in any case, his relations were becoming distinctly cooler on personal grounds.

From this point of view, the *Discours sur l'inégalité* is an interesting transitional work which already anticipates the positions of the 'Letter on Optimism'.[6] Seen as a whole, it is a solution to the classic problem of the existence of evil in a world created by an almighty and infinitely benevolent God.[7] It is Man himself who is responsible for all the ills which afflict him in modern society.[8] Admittedly, in the *Discours* itself, God is hardly mentioned at all, though he is occasionally referred to obliquely.[9] His place is taken by Nature who, exonerated from all blame, appears in the light of a benevolently conservative force, tending, indeed *intending*, to keep man perpetually in a state in which he was healthy, happy and harmless. For the deist, of course, God stands behind Nature: but since Nature was an ambiguous term acceptable to atheists and deists alike, the divergence between Rousseau's views on this point and those of the *philosophes* remained to some extent obscured.

The *Discours sur l'inégalité*, then, is already the work of a metaphysical optimist. It constitutes, in fact, a skilful set of historical and sociological variations on a traditional Christian theme: man has brought about his own misfortunes by misusing the (divine) gift of

[6] For reasons which will emerge in the course of these notes, I have preferred this title to the more usual one of *Lettre sur la Providence* (which on one occasion was used by Rousseau himself).

[7] The point is made by Émile Bréhier: 'Au total, le *Discours* [...] est une solution du problème du mal' (*Histoire de la philosophie*, Paris 1947, ii. 2, p. 473).

[8] Cp. Rousseau's own explanation of the meaning of his *Discours*: '[...] je leur criois d'une foible voix qu'ils ne pouvoient entendre: Insensés, qui vous plaignez sans cesse de la nature, aprenez que tous vos maux vous viennent de vous' (*Confessions*, *Pléiade* i. 388-389). *Pléiade* in these notes means the edition of Rousseau's *Œuvres complètes*, ed. by B. Gagnebin and Marcel Raymond (Paris 1959 ss.). In a passage immediately preceding this one, Rousseau alludes to the religious element in the inspiration of the *Discours*.

[9] Cp. *Discours sur l'inégalité*, first edition p. 161, which clarifies pp. lxviii-lxx of the *Préface*: cp. *Pléiade* iii. 186 and 126-127. See also the allusion to 'une Providence très sage' (*Inégalité*, first edition, p. 63: *Pléiade* iii. 152).

free-will. However, such are the nuances, the complexities, the ambiguities and the inner contradictions of 'providentialist' and 'optimistic' thinking in the eighteenth century, that, scarcely had the work appeared, when it was sharply criticised, in the very name of optimism, as an attack on divine Providence. In a pseudonymous open letter, signed 'Philopolis', and published in the *Mercure*,[10] the Genevan naturalist Charles Bonnet delivered a frontal attack on the *Discours*. Since, on Rousseau's own admission, society results from the development of man's faculties, society must be just as 'natural' as the state of nature. Further, since everything which happens is ordained by God ('Les faits sont-ils autre chose que l'expression de sa volonté divine?'), Jean-Jacques is revolting ('sans y penser', no doubt) against God's will. Finally, this world being only a tiny atom in a universe immeasurably vast, it is presumptuous to find fault with a detail which is merely an insignificant element in a grand design invisible to man, a design moreover which is known to be the handiwork of a perfect Being ('la planette où l'on voit ces choses, fait partie d'un Tout immense que nous ne connoissons point; mais que nous sçavons être l'ouvrage d'une SAGESSE PARFAITE'). Conclusion: everything is for the best in the best possible of worlds. This potted version of certain major themes of the *Theodicy* and the *Essay on Man* having been given, the authors themselves are then brought on to take their bow and crush Jean-Jacques under the weight of their authority: 'S'il s'agissoit de justifier la PROVIDENCE aux yeux des hommes, *Leibnitz* & *Pope* l'ont fait' etc.

Bonnet obviously occupies an extreme position. The complacent and indeed reactionary character of certain types of optimism ('cosmic toryism', Professor Willey calls it[11]) could hardly be better illustrated than in the mind and attitudes of this pillar of religious and political orthodoxy, who, a few years later, appalled by the *Profession de foi* and the *Contrat social*, was to become one of Jean-Jacques's most irreconcilable opponents and a staunch *Négatif*. But it is essential to recognise that his was precisely the sort of 'optimism' and 'providentialism' which Jean-Jacques repudiated. Indeed, though Rousseau was an 'optimist' himself, his reply to Bonnet is

[10] The letter, dated 25 August 1755, appeared in the *Mercure* for October, pp. 71-76. It is reprinted in Leigh t. iii, no. 316.

[11] B. Willey, *The Eighteenth Century Background* (London 1946), p. 43.

already, in its own way, and before *Candide* or even the Lisbon earthquake itself,[12] a satirical *reductio ad absurdum* of the kind of 'optimism' which Voltaire, four years later, was to take as his target. After a comic beginning, in which communities in an advanced state of civilisation are represented as the old age of mankind—'natural' certainly, but not to be preferred to youth, if we had the option—Jean-Jacques warms to his task. 'Nier que le mal existe est un moyen fort commode d'excuser l'auteur du mal.' The argument 'Whatever is, is right' proves too much. It can be used to justify any state of affairs, even diametrical opposites, and is particularly nonsensical when applied to the historical, evolutionary argument of the *Discours*: 'S'il y a des sociétés, c'est que le bien général veut qu'il y en ait; s'il n'y en a point, le bien général veut qu'il n'y en ait point, et si quelqu'un persuadoit aux hommes de retourner vivre dans les forêts, il seroit bon qu'ils y retournassent vivre.' Bonnet's argument means basically that 'c'est assés qu'une chose existe pour qu'il ne soit pas permis de desirer qu'elle existe autrement. Mais, monsieur, si tout est bien comme il est, tout étoit bien comme il étoit avant qu'il y eût des Gouvernemens et des Loix; il fut donc au moins superflu de les établir, et Jean Jaques alors avec vôtre sistême eut eu beau jeu contre Philopolis.' The conclusion, as far as the *Inégalité* is concerned, is that 'il est clair que l'optimisme bien entendu ne fait rien ni pour ni contre moi'. However, the argument of Philopolis also has general implications which Jean-Jacques does not neglect: and the points he makes here might well have been endorsed by Voltaire. Indeed, some of them recur, treated concretely, in *Candide* itself: 'Ce qui concourt au bien général peut être un mal particulier dont il est permis de se délivrer quand il est possible', or 'Rien n'empêche en cela que le mal particulier ne soit un mal réel pour celui qui le souffre.' Bonnet's argument should lead logically to fatalistic resignation or complete passivity: 'Pourquoi faire appeller un Médecin quand vous avez la fiévre? Que savez-vous si le bien du plus grand tout que vous ne connoissez pas n'éxige point que vous ayez le transport, et si la santé des habitans de Saturne ou de Sirius ne souffriroit point du rétablissement de la vôtre? Laissez aller le tout comme il pourra, afin que tout aille toujours bien. Si tout est le mieux qu'il peut être vous devez blâmer toute action quelconque.

[12] The reply to Bonnet was probably drafted in October 1755; see Leigh t. iii, no. 328.

[. . .] et le quiétisme le plus parfait est la seule vertu qui reste à l'homme.'[13]

The *Lettre à Philopolis* attempts, then, to refute Bonnet's particular brand of optimism whilst accepting the basic positions of optimism itself. However, this forthright statement of Rousseau's attitude remained unpublished until after his death, perhaps because he had come to realise, rather late in the day, that polemic was unprofitable and time-consuming.[14] Whatever the reason, the suppression of his reply left him in an equivocal position. The *Discours* had been denounced in one of the most widely-read journals of the day as an attack on divine Providence, and his silence[15] could be held to imply assent or even acceptance of a well-deserved rebuke. It is not without interest to note that according to Morize, Voltaire was in an analogous position about the time of the composition of *Candide*. In a book published as late as 1758, and in spite of the Lisbon poem, Voltaire is actually quoted repeatedly *in support of optimism*.[16] Just as *Candide* may have been written partly in order to make Voltaire's position clear beyond a peradventure, so Rousseau must have welcomed in his letter to Voltaire an opportunity for showing that the *Inégalité* was not an attack on Providence and that belief in

[13] In his interesting essay on the European repercussions of the Lisbon poem, Mr Besterman makes the point that Voltaire reacted against the 'fatalisme' implied in 'tout est bien': (Th. Besterman, 'Voltaire et le désastre de Lisbonne: ou la mort de l'optimisme', *Studies on Voltaire and the eighteenth century*, ii. 10 and 23-24). It will be seen that Rousseau, too, rejected the fatalism which could arise from certain types of optimism. Indeed, he was in a much better position to do so than Voltaire, for he believed firmly in free-will, whilst Voltaire had long since been converted to determinism; and many optimists were also determinists. It is true that Voltaire tried to show that determinism (rather confusingly called 'fatalisme', as was common in the eighteenth century) did not necessarily lead to apathy (*Dictionnaire philosophique*, article 'Destin'). He does so, not by a metaphysical argument, but by pointing to the facts of human nature. It is also true that *Candide* satirizes, in the person of Pangloss, the view that 'les choses ne peuvent être autrement.'

[14] Cp. Leigh t. iii, no. 340, last paragraph.

[15] It was known that Rousseau had been annoyed by Bonnet's letter and intended to reply: see Leigh t. iii, no. 330.

[16] See A. Morize, ed. *Candide* (Paris 1913), pp. xxx-xxxi. This may seem less surprising when certain pages of *Zadig* are kept in mind. Most critics would agree nowadays that the episode of the mad old Hermit (in reality the angel Jesrad in disguise) is a satire on providentialism. But it was often taken at its face value, and in the 'Letter on Optimism' itself, JJ actually quotes it against the Lisbon poem (see Leigh t. iv, no. 424, paragraph 10). Fréron's review of *Candide* also uses *Zadig* to draw attention to Voltaire's alleged inconsistency.

Providence did not involve embracing the opinions of the lunatic fringe of optimism. Between the *Lettre à Philopolis* and the 'Letter on Optimism', there is, of course, a complete change of emphasis. In the first place, instead of having to defend himself against someone professing a dangerous caricature of his own beliefs, Rousseau now found himself arguing against someone, so he believed, in the opposite camp. In the second place, the current which was to carry him from the first *Discours* to the *Profession de foi* had now gained sufficient momentum to give his thought a more decisively religious tone.[17]

In a word, the circumstances of the composition of the 'Letter on Optimism' and of *Candide* led both Rousseau and Voltaire to emphasise those aspects of their attitudes in which they differed rather than those in which they were agreed. This has obscured the fact that the area of agreement was wider than might appear at first sight.

On the 12th September 1756, Voltaire acknowledged Rousseau's 'longue Kyrielle' with a brief but quite friendly note (Best. 6306) in which he expressed, rather vaguely, his intention to reply at greater length as soon as he and his niece Mme Fontaine, both ill, had recovered; and in which he repeated, even more vaguely, a previous invitation to Rousseau to come and stay at Les Délices. Perhaps Voltaire did originally intend to reply: at all events he had Rousseau's letter copied out (probably before the end of the year) by his newly engaged secretary Wagnière.[18] But he evidently thought the better of it, and never did; and when Jean-Jacques, again through Théodore Tronchin, sounded him about publishing his letter, he declined to give his consent.[19] According to Jean-Jacques, however, he did eventually reply, though not by a letter. His reply was none other than *Candide*.

This somewhat surprising claim is first made by Jean-Jacques in 1764, in a letter to the Prince of Wurtemberg. The Prince, a great admirer of Rousseau, had just read the 'Letter', which had by then

[17] It may be noted here that during the actual composition of the letter, some amiable references to his free-thinking friends were modified or deleted: See my article 'Rousseau's letter to Voltaire on optimism', *Studies on Voltaire and the eighteenth century* (1964), xxx. 302-303.

[18] See the article referred to in the preceding note, pp. 251-252.

[19] See Rousseau's letter to Voltaire of 17 June 1760 (Dufour-Plan, *Correspondance générale de J.-J. Rousseau*, Paris 1924–34, [henceforth referred to as DP] v. 133, and Leigh t. iv, no. 447, last sentence).

been printed and reprinted several times,[20] and had written to Rousseau (31 January 1764) expressing his appreciation: 'Je viens de lire pour la première fois, et cela avec revissement, la lettre que vous avés ecritte à M. de Voltaire en response à son Poeme sur le Desastre de Lisbonne. Vous me consolés, mon cher Maitre, tandis que le Poete s'efforce de m'attrister, et je Vous avoue que la tranquilité qui regne dans ma Conscience a toujours fermé les portes de mon cœur à ce Sistème affligeant; mais ce qui m'etonne et m'afflige veritablement, c'est que cette lettre sublime n'ait point empeché Candide de naitre, ou qu'elle n'ait pas eu la force de l'etouffer dans son Indigne berceau. Mais telles sont les Erreurs de l'esprit, quand il n'est pas guidé par la Conscience, et quand l'auguste verité n'est pas le but qu'il se propose.'[21]

Rousseau did not reply until the 12 March: 'Vous étes surpris que ma lettre sur la providence n'ait pas empêché Candide de naitre? C'est elle, au contraire, qui lui a donné naissance; Candide en est la réponse. L'auteur m'en fit une de deux pages, dans laquelle il battoit la campagne, et Candide parut dix mois après. Je voulois philosopher avec lui; en réponse, il m'a persifflé.'[22] Rousseau repeats the gist of this statement in a passage of his *Confessions* (written about the beginning of 1770), worth reproducing here because it contains an interesting additional piece of information: 'Depuis lors [i.e. since September 1756] Voltaire a publié cette réponse qu'il m'avoit promise, mais qu'il ne m'a pas envoyée. Elle n'est autre que le Roman de *Candide*, dont je ne puis parler, parce que je ne l'ai pas lu.' (*Pléiade* i. 430.)

Partly because of a conspicuous inaccuracy in one of these statements,[23] partly because of the bland but damaging admission that he had not read the work on which he was passing judgment,[24] partly

[20] For the history of the publication of the letter, see the article referred to in note 17 above, pp. 258-264 and 267-268, as modified by Leigh t. iv, no. 424, *Imprimés*.

[21] Neuchâtel, Bibliothèque de la Ville, ms R 306 fol. 141-145: original in a secretary's hand, signed. First printed in G. Streckeisen-Moultou, *J.-J. Rousseau, ses amis et ses ennemis*, (Paris 1865) [henceforth SM], ii. 173-175, not quite accurately. SM's text is reprinted in DP, x. 312.

[22] Neuchâtel, Bibliothèque de la Ville, ms R 285, fol. 123 (fair copy, corrected: the original is unknown). First printed in *Œuvres* (Genève 1782 etc., 8° or 12°), xxiv. 121-123: cp. DP, x. 347.

[23] *Candide* appeared in February 1759, two and a half years (not ten months) after the date of the 'Letter on Optimism'.

[24] If Rousseau had not read *Candide*, what made him think he was satirised in the work? Hardly any of the contemporary journals condescended to notice it. Grimm gives it a good deal of space

because of the deepening egocentricity which in the end was to lead him to the firm conviction that he was the only pebble on everybody's beach, Rousseau's claim has never been investigated in detail.[25]

It must be conceded at the outset that those who dismiss his

in his *Correspondance littéraire* (1 March 1759): but apart from stressing that the *conte* is extremely amusing, making some structural criticisms and implying that it was unworthy of a mature writer, he is singularly uninformative. In any case, the *Correspondance littéraire* circulated only in manuscript to a select group of crowned heads, and Rousseau could not have seen it, having broken off all relations with Grimm on 1 November 1757. The *Journal encyclopédique* gave copious extracts (1759 ii. 3e partie, pp. 103-123) but was somewhat sparing in comment: whilst Fréron produced a long and characteristic article (*Année littéraire*, 1759, ii. 203-210). None of these notices suggested that JJ was one of Voltaire's targets. Rousseau most probably saw the review of *Candide* in the *Observateur littéraire* (1759, ii. 117-127), which categorically stated that the work was an attack on the optimism of Leibniz and Pope; and he may have deduced from this that *Candide* was an oblique reply to his letter. *Candide* is not mentioned in any of the extant letters received by Rousseau at this time: but of course many are missing, and it is quite likely that his friends and visitors discussed it. Rousseau's apparent ignorance of *Candide* is all the stranger in that he knew and appreciated Voltaire's other *contes*. The 'Letter on Optimism' itself refers to *Zadig*, whilst a little known letter of François Favre to Paul-Claude Moultou, relating a visit to Montmorency (11 December 1759), reports Rousseau as saying of Voltaire: 'Je l'estimerai comme un homme qui sait composer en vers des tragédies, et de petits bandinages en prose, rien de plus joli que *Memnon* [probably *Zadig*; this was its first title] C'est le meilleur de ses romans après *Charles XII*' (L. J. Courtois, 'Visiteurs genevois de Rousseau', *Annales de la Société Jean-Jacques Rousseau*, 1926, xvii. 152-163). On the other hand, Rousseau seems occasionally to have stated that he had not read a particular work when his intention was simply to disparage it.

[25] Mr Bottiglia, in a recent full-length study of *Candide*, does not discuss the matter at all. André Morize, in his admirable and still useful critical edition of the work, dismisses Rousseau's claim in a footnote: 'L'intervention de Jean-Jacques Rousseau a-t-elle été pour quelque chose dans la genèse de *Candide*? [...] rien ne vient à l'appui, et il ne semble pas qu'il faille donner à la *Lettre sur la Providence* une place privilégiée. Toutefois elle a dû, non pas faire réfléchir mais agacer Voltaire [...] Dans cette période de préparation, l'affaire de la lettre de Rousseau est un incident à noter,—rien de plus' (Morize, op. cit., pp. xlii-xliii, note). Professor R. Pomeau in his valuable critical edition of *Candide* (Paris 1959) discusses the matter briefly (pp. 18-19) and comes to very much the same conclusion. Professor Crocker in his edition of *Candide* (London 1958) makes some interesting points in his notes. Professor G. R. Havens remarks that 'the relation between Rousseau's *Lettre sur la Providence* and *Candide* [is] real no doubt but less fundamental than Rousseau thought', 'Voltaire, Rousseau and the Lettre sur la Providence', *PMLA* (1944), lix. 109-130. Professor Havens had already come to this conclusion in his edition of *Candide* (New York 1934), pp. xliii-xlv, where he reviews with different emphasis and from a different angle some of the points made here. I regret that I was unable to consult his edition, difficult to obtain in this country, before my paper was completed. My quotations in this paper are from Morize's edition.

assertion without further ado are in one sense right. *Candide* is the distillation of the experience of a life-time, and, although in many ways not representative of Voltaire, it is one of the most personal of all his works. It would be futile to attempt to show that it is simply an indirect answer to a long and importunate letter. In a narrower sense, too, the roots of *Candide*, regarded only as a satire on 'optimism', stretch back behind and beyond Rousseau's letter. An abortive skirmish, broken off by a tactical retreat, cannot have counted decisively in the marshalling of forces which had been proceeding for more than twenty years. Nevertheless there are some grounds for thinking that, in writing *Candide*, Voltaire had Rousseau in mind rather more than has sometimes been supposed.

2. *Candide* and the *Discours sur l'inégalité*

(a) *When did Voltaire read and annotate the* Inégalité?

There seems to have been a continual *décalage* between the publication of Rousseau's earlier works and Voltaire's reactions to them. Voltaire was in Berlin when the *Discours sur les sciences et les arts* appeared, and he missed the furore it aroused. He had not yet read it by 14 September 1751, at which date he explained to the duc d'Uzès: 'Je ne suis guère à portée, à la cour du roi de Prusse, de lire les thèmes que les écoliers composent pour les prix de l'académie de Dijon' (Best. 3982). He did eventually read it, as is shown by the opuscule originally entitled *Sur le paradoxe que les sciences ont nui aux mœurs*.[26]

Something similar seems to have happened in the case of the *Inégalité*. That Voltaire did find time to read it in the end is established by his marginal notes on the original copy sent him by Jean-Jacques.[27] But when were these notes written? Professor Havens, who has edited them with such care and skill, assumes that, with one exception, they were roughly contemporary with Voltaire's well-known letter of acknowledgment of 30 August 1755 (Best. 5792),[28] and this

[26] First printed in 1756, and ascribed by Moland and Bengesco to 1751–1753. They do not give any evidence to support this assertion, which seems to be just a guess based on the date of the polemics stirred up by the first *Discours*. It may have been composed as late as 1755. For the text, under the title 'Timon' first given to it by the Kehl editors, see M. xxiii. 483-484.

[27] These notes were first published by J.-E. Gardet in the *Bulletin du Bibliophile* (1860), pp. 1519 ss., and in a more complete and accurate form by Professor G. R. Havens in *Voltaire's Marginalia on the pages of Rousseau* (Columbus, Ohio, 1933), [referred to as *Marginalia*].

[28] See *Marginalia*, pp. 12, 16 and 25.

assumption has been accepted by the editors of the *Pléiade* Rousseau (iii. 1381–1382). Is this really likely? The letter of acknowledgment shows that Voltaire could hardly have given Rousseau's new book more than a cursory glance: it is almost entirely taken up with a minor or tangential aspect of the thesis of the *first* of the two *Discours*. True, there is, near the beginning, the famous witticism: 'On n'a jamais tant employé d'esprit a vouloir nous rendre Bêtes. Il prend envie de marcher a quatre pattes quand on lit votre ouvrage.' But this does no more than attribute to Rousseau an attitude with which he had already been credited for some time. It could easily have been inspired, for instance, by the polemic arising from the first *Discours*. Goaded by Charles Borde (a friend of Voltaire's, incidentally) Rousseau had replied,—as early as 1753: 'Il ne faut point nous faire tant de peur de la vie purement animale, ni la considérer comme le pire état où nous puissions tomber; car il vaudroit encore mieux ressembler à une brebis qu'à un mauvais ange' (*Pléiade* iii. 78).

Moreover, the tone of the marginalia, virulent, abusive and scathingly contemptuous, seems quite out of keeping with Voltaire's other references to Rousseau in 1755–1756. 'Fou que tu es', 'Qu'en sçais-tu', 'Quoi, tu ne vois pas que [. . .]', 'faux', 'ridicule', 'pitoiable', 'tarare', 'galimatias', 'singe de Diogène, comme tu te condamnes toi-même! comme tu outres tout! comme tu mets sous un faux jour', 'malheurex Jean-Jacques, dont les carnosités sont assez connues, pauvre échapé de la vérole'—such comments in the marginalia seem difficult to place or account for in 1755. It is fair to say that they convey something more than merely philosophic disagreement. The last one quoted (which, Professor Havens concedes, appears to be later than the others) recalls the tone of the *Sentiment des citoyens* (December 1764), though it need not be placed as late as that. It seems clear that the remarks as a whole belong to a period when Voltaire's attitude to Rousseau had undergone a decisive change for the worse.

When did this happen? There are two conspicuous milestones in their relations. The first is the publication of the *Lettre à d'Alembert*, which roused the anger of the author-actor-manager of Les Délices: and the second is Rousseau's gratuitously offensive letter of 17 June 1760 ('Je ne vous aime point Monsieur', etc.), which Voltaire recognised as a declaration of war, but in which he professed to discern the symptom of an illness needing to be treated with 'des bouillons rafraîchissants' (Best. 8258). Situating the marginalia after even the first of these events would take us beyond the period of the composition of *Candide*, which must have been finished between July and October 1758. There are, however, some grounds for supposing that Voltaire had turned against Rousseau before hearing about the *Lettre à d'Alembert*. His first unequivocally derogatory reference to Jean-Jacques occurs, somewhat mysteriously, in a letter to d'Alembert dated 29 August 1757 (Best. 6663): 'Si vous avez un moment de loisir, mandez-moi comment vont les organes pensants de Rousseau, et s'il a toujours mal à la glande pinéale. S'il y a une preuve contre l'immatérialité de l'âme, c'est cette maladie du cerveau; on a une fluxion sur l'âme comme sur les dents.' This letter, it is true, has come down to us only through a Kehl transcript, and in view of the way the Kehl editors are known to have treated the manuscripts at their disposal, it might be regarded with justifiable suspicion. However, even if this letter is a composite text, independent support for the date of the extract quoted is supplied by the following passage of a hitherto unpublished letter from Georges-Louis Le Sage, the Geneva mathematician and scientist, to his friend Elie-Salomon Reverdil: 'Mais voici une nouvelle bien triste: Nôtre pauvre Rousseau a l'esprit aliené. C'est à quoi les Imaginations fougueuses doivent quelquefois s'attendre.'[29]

What gave rise to these rumours that Rousseau had gone out of his mind is far from clear. Had news of his quarrel with Diderot in March–April 1757 filtered back to Geneva, perhaps through d'Alembert, who corresponded with both Voltaire and Le Sage? However that may be, and whatever the source or basis of the rumours, Jean-Jacques must have lost further ground in Voltaire's esteem with the arrival of Mme d'Épinay in Geneva early in November 1757. She saw Voltaire frequently, and her close friendship with Théodore Tronchin meant that there were now two powerful influences in Voltaire's immediate entourage which could be relied on to give him a consistently unfavourable picture of Rousseau's character and conduct. Tronchin, for instance, was probably the source of Voltaire's information about Jean-Jacques 'carnosités', whilst a certain conspicuous lack of enthusiasm in Mme d'Épinay's references to her

[29] Leigh t. iv, no. 516. The letter is undated, but must have been written c. 22 August 1757.

former protégé would be only human.[30] At all events, from February 1758 onwards, Voltaire's allusions to Jean-Jacques tend to become more and more unfavourable. For instance on the 7 March 1758 we find him writing to d'Alembert: 'Qu'est ce que c'est qu'un Citoyen de Geneve qui se dit libre et qui va se mettre au pain d'un fermier général dans un bois, comme un blérau?' (Best. 6970).

Was it about this time that Voltaire picked up the *Inégalité* again and began to annotate it? The reference to 'un Citoyen de Genève qui se dit libre' might be a pointer in that direction, whilst the reference to the 'singe de Diogène' in the marginalia could be paralleled in a letter to d'Alembert of 2 September 1758 (Best. 7133), though such expressions do not become frequent until later. All in all, the evidence is not absolutely incompatible with the conclusion that Voltaire may well have been reading the *Inégalité* in a disapproving frame of mind about the time he was actively engaged in writing *Candide* (from January 1758 onwards).[31] This tentative conclusion is supported to some extent by the text of the *conte* itself.

(b) Candide *and the themes of the* Inégalité.

With inimitable lightness of touch, Voltaire evokes in *Candide* a whole range of weighty problems which preoccupied and divided thinking men in the eighteenth century. Certainly, these problems were being discussed many years before Jean-Jacques dealt with them, but it is none the less curious to find so many of them common to both the *Inégalité* and *Candide*.

(i) *Natural Goodness*

Among these problems is the daunting enigma of human nature. Is man fundamentally good or fundamentally bad? Even before the *Inégalité*, Rousseau had proclaimed his belief in the goodness of man.[32] *Candide* discusses the question, but, as is proper in a work of art, dialectically rather than didactically. However, Voltaire's own position is indicated by the fact that belief in the goodness of nature

[30] Cp. Rousseau's complaint to Mme d'Épinay in his letter of 20 February 1758: 'J'apprends les étranges discours que tiennent à Paris vos correspondans sur mon compte, et je juge par là de ceux que vous tenez; peut être un peu plus honnêtement, à Genéve. Il y a donc bien du plaisir à nuire?'

[31] I am not asserting that this was certainly the case. The marginalia on the *Inégalité* might be later, and Voltaire may have read the *Inégalité* twice, the second time more thoroughly and in a more hostile mood. The allusion to JJ in Best. 6271 (2 August 1756) is inconclusive.

[32] *Dernière Réponse* [à Borde], *Pléiade* iii. 80.

and of human nature tends to be ascribed to that amiable repository of all absurdity, Dr Pangloss. 'Ah, que dirait Maître Pangloss', says Candide when he and Cacambo are about to be cooked and eaten by the Oreillons, 's'il voyait comme la pure nature est faite?' (Ch. XVI). A little later, it is true, when the Oreillons are persuaded to spare their victims, Candide swings to the opposite extreme: 'Mais après tout la pure nature est bonne.' This instability reflects, of course, not any indecision on Voltaire's part, but simply the comic naïveté of his hero.

Savages, however, represent only one aspect of the problem. On the more general question, we seem more than once to catch an echo of the argument of Rousseau's *Discours*: 'Il faut bien', says the good anabaptist, Jacques, 'que les hommes ayent un peu corrompu la nature, car ils ne sont point nés loups, & ils sont devenus loups. Dieu ne leur a donné ni canons de vingt-quatre, ni bayonnettes, & ils se sont fait des bayonnettes & des canons' (Ch. IV). Morize (ed. *Candide*, p. 26, n. 3) sees in this passage a refutation of Rousseau. I find this judgment puzzling, for it seems to me, on the contrary, to be perfectly consistent with Jean-Jacques's thesis, indeed to be virtually a paraphrase of it. The question is taken up again later in the tale, when Candide tentatively suggests the possibility of a historical degeneration in human nature (a major theme of Rousseau's *Discours*). The pessimist Martin dismisses the notion incisively: 'Croyez-vous [...] que les éperviers ayent toujours mangé des pigeons quand ils en ont trouvé? [...] si les éperviers ont toujours eu le même caractère, pourquoi voulez-vous que les hommes ayent changé le leur?'

It would, of course, be a mistake to identify Voltaire completely with any of the characters in his *conte*, though in his correspondence at this time he sometimes expresses views which are close to other ideas of Martin's. In this instance, Candide is allowed to object to Martin's argument, in a manner reminiscent at first sight of Zadig's famous dispute with Jesrad: 'Oh! dit Candide, il y a bien de la différance, car le libre arbitre . . .' But Voltaire no longer believed in free-will and was not in sympathy with Candide's point. It is worth noting that, in the *Inégalité*, free-will was one of the factors singled out as distinguishing man from the beasts.

Candide also seems to contain a wry comment on the personal or individual aspect of the doctrine of natural goodness: 'Je suis le meilleur homme du monde' says the hero in bewilderment at his own conduct, '& voilà trois hommes que je tue' (Ch. XV).

(ii) *Apes, Monkeys and Men*

In the *Inégalité*, Rousseau had devoted a considerable amount of space to the problem of the status of the anthropoid apes. Without committing himself too decisively on the issue, he had urged persistently that we should not conclude prematurely that the orang-outang, for instance, was not a human being: 'Toutes ces observations [...] me font douter si divers animaux semblables aux hommes, pris par les voyageurs pour des Bêtes sans beaucoup d'examen [...] ne seroient point en effet de véritables hommes Sauvages [...] On ne voit point [...] les raisons sur lesquelles les Auteurs se fondent pour refuser aux Animaux en question le nom d'hommes Sauvages [...] Nos voyageurs font sans façon des bêtes sous le nom de *Pongos*, de *Mandrilles*, d'*Orang-Outang*, de ces mêmes êtres dont sous le nom de *Satyrs*, de *Faunes*, de *Silvains*, les Anciens faisoient des Divinités. Peut-être après des recherches plus exactes trouvera-t-on que ce sont des hommes [...] ce seroit une grande simplicité de se rapporter là dessus à des voyageurs grossiers.'[33]

Candide may contain a reminiscence of these speculations in the scene in which the hero learns from Cacambo that the monkeys he has just killed were the lovers of two native women (Ch. XVI). Cacambo explains that these monkeys 'sont des quarts d'homme comme je suis un quart d'Espagnol.—Hélas! reprit Candide, je me souviens d'avoir entendu dire à Maître Pangloss qu'autrefois pareils accidents étaient arrivés & que ces mélanges avaient produit des Égipans, des Faunes, des Satires, que plusieurs grands personnages de l'antiquité en avaient vûs; mais je prenais cela pour des fables.'[34]

(iii) *Exploitation, equality and property*

Finally, there seem to be definite allusions in *Candide* to the more specifically political doctrines of the *Inégalité*. The pessimistic

[33] *Inégalité*, first edition, pp. 221-237, note 8: renumbered note X in later editions: cp. *Pléiade* iii. 208-214.

[34] Of course, the point made in the *Inégalité* and that satirised in *Candide* are really quite distinct, but no more so than is common in satire. See Morize (ed. cit., p. 94, n. 1), for an interesting passage from l'abbé Banier's *La Mythologie et les fables expliquées par l'histoire* (Paris 1740), iv. 463 ss., which may have been a common source for both Rousseau and Voltaire. Rousseau certainly knew the book: it was one of those from which he had made extracts for Mme Dupin (see *Annales de la Société J.-J. Rousseau*, 1966, xxxvi. 213.

Martin seems almost to speak on occasion with the voice of Jean-Jacques himself: 'Partout les faibles ont en exécration les puissants devant lesquels ils rampent, & les puissants les traitent comme des troupeaux dont on vend la laine et la chair' (Ch. XX).

More specifically, and more significantly, some of Rousseau's political opinions are fathered, once more, on Pangloss: 'Maître Pangloss m'a toujours dit que les hommes sont égaux', declares his pupil (Ch. XV): and, commenting on the behaviour of the friar who has robbed him and Cunégonde of all their valuables, he recalls ruefully that the theft is philosophically justifiable: 'le bon Pangloss m'avait souvent prouvé que les biens de la terre sont communs à tous les hommes, que chacun y a un droit égal' (Ch. X). We know from the Marginalia that Voltaire had been particularly outraged by Rousseau's attack on private property at the beginning of Part II of the *Inégalité*: 'Quoy, celui qui a planté, semé et enclos n'a pas droit au fruit de ses peines? Quoy, cet homme injuste [the hypothetical individual of the *Discours* who would have had the insight to defeat the first attempts to establish private ownership of land] ce voleur aurait été le bienfaiteur du genre humain! voyla la philosophie d'un gueux, qui voudrait que les riches fussent volez par les pauvres' (*Marginalia*, p. 15).

A certain number of themes, then, seem to connect *Candide* with the *Inégalité*: natural goodness, the character of savages, satirical references to radical theories on social equality and property: and, it may be added, a mock-serious vision of human happiness in ideal, but unmistakeably 'primitivistic' conditions. Is this purely fortuitous, or may we conclude, bearing in mind that Voltaire could have been dipping into the *Inégalité* at this time, that his reading of the *Discours* was a factor in the elaboration of *Candide*?

3. *Candide* and the 'Letter on Optimism'

If *Candide* toys sporadically with some of the themes of the *Inégalité*, what of its relation to the 'Letter on Optimism' itself?

The features of *Candide* which seem to have struck contemporaries most (apart from its *polissonnerie*, diversely appraised), were first of all its pessimistic view of life, and secondly its attempt to discredit the pious view that divine wisdom regulates human affairs for the best.[35] On both these points, which are already contained in the Lisbon poem, Rousseau had, in his long letter of 18 August 1756, taken up well-defined positions. On the first he disagrees sharply with Voltaire, but for a reason which is radically different from the clap-trap of the pietists and the complacent optimists. On the second point, he is really, in spite of a considerable difference in mood and tone, much closer to Voltaire's own position at this time.

(a) *The value of life: suicide: ennui and 'une vie automate'*.

If one of the leit-motifs of *Candide* is that life is full of real misfortunes, both 'moral' and 'physical', which cannot be conjured away by any metaphysical legerdemain, then Rousseau is in full agreement with Voltaire. The *Lettre à Philopolis* makes this as clear as the 'Letter on Optimism' itself. So does the *Inégalité*. Indeed, an essential function of Rousseau's belief in the immortality of the soul is to make the ills the righteous suffer in this vale of tears endurable through the firm expectation of eternal bliss in the life to come: and the converse of this proposition turns the expectation into a proof. Life is so full of tribulation and misfortune that the justice inseparable from the notion of God guarantees in itself that there will be a life to come which will make up for everything.

There may well have been many ostrich-like 'optimists' in the eighteenth century who buried their heads in post-Leibnizian or Popean sands in order to see or hear no evil: but it would be absurd to suppose that a man like Rousseau, who spent so much of his adult life in physical agony and in denouncing the evils of contemporary society, was one of them. Once the facts had been agreed, however, the question remained: what value should be placed on life? The Lisbon poem had asserted that misery was widespread, yet man's attitude to life was paradoxical and ambivalent: 'Nul ne voudrait mourir, nul ne voudrait renaître': and the point was driven home in a long explanatory note. Here again, Voltaire was touching on a subject with which Rousseau had been recently concerned. In the *Inégalité*, he had drawn attention to the high suicide rate in civilised

[35] For instance, Boswell remarks that, in *Candide*, Voltaire 'meant only by wanton profaneness to obtain a sporting victory over religion and to discredit the belief of a superintending Providence' (*Life of Johnson*, ed. G. Birkbeck-Hill, revised Powell, Oxford, i. 342).

communities:[36] and in an important footnote;[37] he had declared that it was not surprising that a recent writer (Maupertuis)[38] had concluded that the ills in a man's life outweighed the good. Maupertuis was thinking of man in his present corrupt state: but things had been different in earlier phases of human history. In the 'Letter on Optimism', Rousseau clarifies his position. Even in our present corrupt state, life is still desirable. If life were really as unbearable as was claimed, there would be mass suicides and the human race would come to an end. More to the point, he introduces a new factor into the discussion. Quite independently of the content of experience, there is 'le doux plaisir d'exister indépendant de toute autre sensation'; and that is something which those who try to cast up the balance-sheet of life always forget. Moreover, is it really true, as Voltaire had asserted, that no one would want to live his life over again on the same terms? That might well be the opinion (and even then, would it really be sincere?) of typical victims of modern civilisation: of the rich, deluded by false values, or of sophisticated intellectuals. But ordinary people, leading contented, uneventful lives, would willingly accept the offer: 'Consultez un honnête Bourgeois qui aura passé une vie obscure et tranquile, sans projets et sans ambition; un bon artisan qui vit commodément de son metier; un Paÿsan même, non de France, où l'on prétend qu'il faut les faire mourir de misére afin qu'ils vous fassent vivre, mai du païs, par éxemple, ou vous êtes, et, généralement de tout païs Libre. J'ose poser en fait qu'il n'y a peut-être pas dans le haut Valais[39] un seul montagnard mécontent de sa *vie prèsque automate*, et qui *n'acceptât* volontier, au lieu même du Paradis, *Le marché* de renaître sans cesse, pour vegeter ainsi perpetuellement' (my italics).

Is it purely fortuitous that this interconnected series of themes reappears in *Candide*? 'Nul ne voudrait mourir, nul ne voudrait renaître' is restated in a more concrete form at the close of the *Histoire de la vieille*, where Voltaire seems to take up Jean-Jacques's

[36] First edition, p. 62; cp. *Pléiade* iii. 152.

[37] First edition, note 7, p. 204; note IX in all editions after 1759: cp. *Pléiade* iii. 202.

[38] For this identification, see *Pléiade* iii. 1364, n. 2 to p. 202.

[39] For the introduction into the debate of the 'montagnards du Valais', see Leigh t. iii & iv, nos. 362, 377, 386, 403, 409, 416, 419, and 445. The correspondence between Chaignon and Gauffecourt was obligingly made available to me by M. Bernard Gagnebin who first published the documents in *Vallesia* (Sion, 1966), xxi. 179-188.

point about suicide: 'Je voulus cent fois me tuer, mais j'aimais encor la vie. Cette faiblesse ridicule est peut-être un de nos penchans les plus funestes. Car y a-t-il rien de plus sot que de vouloir porter continuellement un fardeau qu'on veut toujours jetter par terre? d'avoir son être en horreur, & de tenir à son être?

'J'ai vû dans les pays que le sort m'a fait parcourir, & dans les cabarets où j'ai servi, un nombre prodigieux de personnes qui avaient leur existence en exécration; mais je n'en ai vu que huit qui ayent mis volontairement fin à leur misère, trois Nègres, quatre Anglais, & un professeur Allemand nommè Robek.'[40]

Voltaire, then, does not concede that there is such a thing as 'le doux plaisir d'exister indépendant de toute autre sensation', and sees in human attachment to life an inexplicable enigma. What of the other half of Rousseau's argument, what of the merits of 'une vie obscure et tranquile, sans projets et sans ambition', of 'une vie presque automate', where one could 'végéter perpétuellement'? Would not such a life be intolerably tedious?

Before emerging at the conclusion of the tale, together with 'le vice' and 'le besoin', as one of the basic evils which mankind can avoid by hard work, 'l'ennui' has already acquired something of a thematic value in *Candide*. The hero and Cacambo could have 'vegetated perpetually' in Eldorado (which, incidentally, is a land of 'innocence et félicité', where their host congratulates himself on being 'fort ignorant', primitivistic phrases suggestive of Rousseau); but such a solution is shown to be incompatible with the basic urges of human nature. Again, Pococurante, who has everything, and whose life can certainly be described as uneventful, is not particularly happy either. Of course, Rousseau could have claimed that both these examples illustrated rather than refuted his thesis. However, when the ill-assorted band of adventurers settle down under Candide's leadership to subsistence farming, they find life so dull ('l'ennui était si excessif') that the Vieille actually asks 'lequel est le pire, ou d'être violé cent fois par des Pirates nègres, d'avoir une fesse coupée,

[40] In the 1761 edition of *Candide*, Voltaire changed 'huit' to 'douze', and added, after 'Anglais', 'quatre Genevois'. Morize (ed. cit., p. 71 n. 2) sees in this change 'une malice contre Jean-Jacques Rousseau'. Voltaire had noticed in *La Nouvelle Héloïse* 'un morceau admirable sur le suicide qui donne appétit de mourir' (letter of 26 January 1761, Best. 8805). But Morize does not recall that the legitimacy of suicide had been discussed at some length in the 'Letter on Optimism', and its frequency noted in the *Inégalité*.

de passer par les baguettes chez les Bulgares, d'être fouetté & pendu dans un auto-da-fé, d'être disséqué, de ramer en galère, d'éprouver enfin toutes les misères par lesquelles nous avons tous passé, ou bien de rester ici à ne rien faire?' 'C'est une grande question', replies Candide: but of course the conclusion of the tale does not leave the 'grande question' open. In fact, it brings us closer to Rousseau's 'montagnard', than we might have expected, though not, no doubt, to that secret vein of aspiration to a Nirvana-like condition which runs underground in Rousseau's work from the primitive man of the first part of the *Inégalité* to the *Rêveries du promeneur solitaire.*

Consideration of this problem leads us back again to the *Inégalité*. One of the most scandalous paradoxes of that work had been Rousseau's apparently appreciative picture of the happiness of the contented brute of Part I of the *Discours*, leading a life of complete indolence at a minimal or even non-existent level of intellectual activity. In particular, attention had been focussed on Rousseau's notorious remark to the effect that 'si elle [la Nature] nous a destinés à être sains, j'ose presque assurer que l'état de réflexion est un état contre Nature, & que l'homme qui médite est un animal dépravé.'[41] Stripped of its qualifications and torn from its context, this remark had appalled, irritated or amused nearly everyone who read the *Discours*.[42] Voltaire himself had marked the passage in his copy and had inserted a slip with the word 'dépravé' pencilled on it (*Marginalia*, p. 6), but his comments, if he made any at this time, have been lost. In the 'Letter on Optimism', Rousseau supplies an oblique gloss on his dictum, speaking of 'les gens de Lettres, de tous les orders d'hommes le plus sédentaire, le plus malsain, Le plus réfléchissant, et par conséquent le plus malheureux' (paragraph 12).

Candide itself has something to say on the subject of whether it is better to be an intellectual and wretched, or a simple person and happy. Is there not a grain of Rousseau dissolved in one of the general lessons of the tale? Metaphysical speculation, we learn, is at best futile and at worst needlessly tormenting. Martin's laconic dictum 'travaillons sans raisonner, c'est le seul moyen de rendre la vie suportable' (Ch. XXX) seems in fact a not too distant relative of Rousseau's alarming *boutade*. However, Voltaire comes closest to

[41] First edition, p. 22: cp. *Pléiade* iii. 138.

[42] Including Bonnet and Diderot, and nearly all the contemporary pamphleteers and reviewers who attacked the *Discours*.

examining Rousseau's position, not in *Candide* itself, but in a short and unduly neglected piece which he wrote soon afterwards, *l'Histoire d'un bon bramin.*[43] A life-time of study and thought has only had the effect of convincing the 'bon bramin', like Faust, of his complete ignorance, and of the futility of philosophy. Yet the problems of life and destiny continue to torment him, and his inability either to solve them or to stop thinking about them has made him profoundly unhappy. None the less, the idea of changing places with a neighbour of his, a *vieil automate* content to vegetate in ignorance and intellectual torpor, fills him with horror: 'Je me suis dit cent fois que je serais heureux si j'étais aussi sot que ma voisine, et cependant je ne voudrais pas d'un tel bonheur.' His friend the narrator agrees: 'Je vis en effect que je n'aurais pas voulu être heureux à condition d'être imbécile.' Philosophers, when consulted, come to the same conclusion, though conceding that it is illogical to prefer intelligence to happiness. No one, in fact, is prepared to '*accepter le marché* (my italics) de devenir imbécile pour devenir content'. Finally, the matter is left as one of the contradictions of human nature: 'Il y a là de quoi parler beaucoup.' This seems to be Voltaire's last word on Rousseau's favourable picture of contentment at a low level of intellectual activity, and on his defence of 'une vie automate' in the 'Letter on Optimism'.

(b) *Providence and Optimism*

This immense question has already been briefly glanced at in Section 1 of these notes, and its proliferations make it impossible to deal with it at all adequately here. Optimism in the eighteenth century is less a philosophy than a tangle of philosophical attitudes in which emphasis, tone and mood play a much greater part than a mere analysis of the arguments would indicate. It contains moreover a fundamental ambiguity: to say that this is the best of all possible worlds is not necessarily to say that it is a good one. If we go behind labels and slogans, it becomes clear that neither Voltaire nor Rousseau believed in a 'superintending' Providence which kept a close watch on human affairs, still less in one which intervened to redress the balance when things went wrong. The view of God which emerges in the 'Letter on Optimism' is that

[43] First published in 1761. A ms. copy had been sent to Mme Du Deffand in October 1759 (Best. 7806).

of a supreme being, who, though by definition infinitely good, remains aloof from the activities of man. Divine justice has nothing to do with purely natural phenomena (paragraph 24), and it is absurd to declaim against God when one has toothache or to expect him to look after our baggage (paragraph 25). God works only through general laws: '[. . .] tout tient à La Loi commune, et [. . .] il n'y a d'exceptions pour personne. Il est à croire que les événements particuliers ne sont rien ici bas aux yeux du maître de L'Univers, que sa providence est seulement Universelle, qu'il se contente de conserver les genres et les espéces, et de présider au tout sans s'inquiéter de la maniére dont chaque individu passe cette courte vie. Un Roi sage qui veut que chacun vive heureux dans ses états, a-t-il besoin de s'informer si les cabarets y sont bons? Le passant murmure une nuit quand ils sont mauvais, et rit toute sa vie d'une impatience aussi déplacée' (paragraph 25).

Is this so very different from the conception we met with in *Candide*? Except for the change of metaphor, the Derviche consulted by Candide says pretty much the same thing: 'Qu'importe [. . .] qu'il y ait du mal ou du bien? Quand sa Hautesse envoye un vaisseau en Égypte, s'embarrasse-t-elle si les souris qui sont dans le vaisseau sont à leur aise ou non?' (Ch. XXX). Does it matter very much whether we consider ourselves mice in the hold of the ship of the Universe or travellers passing a sleepless night in an uncomfortable inn?[44]

There is a similar convergence of views when Rousseau pours scorn on 'les Prêtres et les dévots' 'qui ont gâté la cause de Dieu [. . .] et pour être sûrs de Leur fait punissent et châtient Les méchants, éprouvent et récompensent les bons, indifférement avec des biens ou des maux selon l'événement [. . .] c'est une mauvaise manière de raisonner, de fonder sur le pour et Le contre les preuves de la providence, et de lui attribuer sans choix tout ce qui se ferait également sans elle.' With his usual Manichean twist and his usual concision, Martin makes very much the same point: 'Dieu a puni ce fripon, le Diable a noyé les autres' (Ch. XX).

Whether Voltaire thought he was refuting Rousseau or not, or whether Rousseau thought he was being refuted in *Candide* or not,

[44] Rousseau's views on this point could appear just as objectionable to the pious as Voltaire's: and Formey in his notes on the 'Letter' rebukes him sharply: 'Dieu ne peut conserver & diriger le tout, si sa Providence n'embrasse les moindres détails', etc. (see Leigh t. iv, no. 424, notes *yy* and *zz*).

it is clear that their views about the rôle of Providence in human affairs coincide to a great extent. Nor were they always to remain as far apart as they seem to be in 1759 on the question of optimism itself. If by optimism we mean, as Rousseau meant, hardly more than that the universe is the handiwork of an infinitely good and infinitely powerful being, then it must be said that, with one important reservation, their differences were to become narrower as time went on, just as they would have been narrower twenty years earlier. It is admittedly true that in the later writings of Voltaire the relations between God and man remain almost as chilling as they are in *Candide*, though less enigmatic; but there is some return to a more positive point of view.

Voltaire had begun his philosophical career by sharing many of the views of the metaphysical optimists: and in one sense, between 1734 and 1770, the wheel of his metaphysical opinions was to turn full circle.[45] In 1770 as in 1734, he still tries to explain phenomena in terms of two principles, God and matter; and in 1770 as in 1734, his belief in a supreme being is firmly grounded on the evidence of order, structure and design which he discerns in the universe. Nor, in spite of the ridicule of *Candide*, had he given up once and for all his belief in final causes. Final causes, in their more anthropocentric form, were the deist's substitute for Providence, especially in a rosy-tinted view of the universe which tended to see, on all sides, traces of God's benevolence towards mankind. Belief in order, structure and design, to say nothing of final causes, is completely eclipsed in the Lisbon Poem and especially in *Candide*, where simple-minded interpretations of God's activity or intentions are ridiculed, and where the stress repeatedly falls on the chaos and meaninglessness of life. However, in his later metaphysical writings, Voltaire returns to a much-modified version of his earlier beliefs. The great difference between the buoyant attitudes of 1734 and the more chastened outlook of 1770 is that Voltaire has now completely discarded the last vestigial anthropomorphic and anthropocentric elements which had unobtrusively but insistently infiltrated into his earlier opinions. This is particularly true of his conception of God (now much more of a universal force, and even less of a person than before), but it applies also in other directions. In 1770 as in 1734, the universe re-

[45] See the excellent study by I. Alexander, 'Voltaire and Metaphysics' in *Philosophy*, 1944.

mains a well-oiled mechanism: but is no longer a mechanism constructed and operated primarily for the benefit of mankind.

In reality, the issue between Voltaire and Rousseau in the *Letter* is not so much providence, or even optimism (though Rousseau uses the language of optimism, and invokes the authority of Leibniz and Pope). The real issue is the immortality of the soul, which Rousseau proclaims with fervour, and which Voltaire cannot accept. No doubt the principal reason why Voltaire declined to reply was the impossibility of joining issue publicly with Rousseau on this point.

(c) *God and Evil.*

The Lisbon poem had restated forcefully an old conundrum: if God is both infinitely powerful and infinitely good, why is there so much evil in the universe? If God is all-powerful, he is able to remove it: if he is infinitely good, he must want to do so. If he *can* remove it and *wants* to remove it, why doesn't he?

> Dieu tient en main la chaîne et n'est point enchaîné:
> Par son choix bienfaisant tout est déterminé,
> Il est libre, il est juste, il n'est point implacable,
> Pourquoi donc souffrons-nous sous un maître équitable?
> Voilà le nœud fatal qu'il fallait délier.

We have slipped back half a century, with Voltaire and Rousseau playing the rôles created half a century earlier by Bayle and Leibniz: for Rousseau answers: '[. . .] de toutes les économies possibles il [Dieu] a choisi celle qui réunissait le moins de mal et le plus de bien, ou pour dire la chose encore plus cruement, s'il le faut, s'il n'a pas mieux fait, c'est qu'il ne pouvait faire mieux. [. . .] Si L'embarras de L'origine du mal vous forçait d'altérer quelqu'une des perfections de Dieu, pourquoi justifier sa puissance aux dépends de sa bonté? S'il faut choisir entre deux erreurs, j'aime encore mieux la premiére.'

Did this hint bear fruit in Voltaire's mind? At any rate, this is precisely the solution towards which he eventually inclined. Evil can be explained by limitations on God's freedom and power: it is in this way that the enigma propounded in the Lisbon poem can be tentatively solved: 'Je demeurerai toujours un peu embarrassé sur l'origine du mal' we find Voltaire writing in 1772, 'mais je supposerai que le bon Oromase, qui a tout fait *n'a pu faire mieux*' (*Il faut prendre un parti: Discours d'un théiste*; my italics).

4. Maître Pangloss and Docteur Pansophe

It has already been noted (Section 2b) that a certain number of views expressed in the *Inégalité* are attributed in *Candide* to Pangloss. This raises the interesting question of how much of Jean-Jacques there is in Voltaire's immortal idiot. It would of course be absurd to see in Rousseau the sole or even the principal model for Candide's mentor. If we were absolutely determined to find a single protoype for him, we should probably not have to look much further than Voltaire's tediously amiable correspondent, the Duchess of Saxe-Gotha, who went on muttering the shibboleths of Leibniz and Wolff while her duchy was being devastated. In particular, it would be unfair to confuse Rousseau's brand of optimism with that of Pangloss (Bonnet's is much nearer). However, to look for fairness in a satirist would be a form of naïveté worthy of Candide himself. Rousseau certainly used the vocabulary of optimism in his 'Letter'; and a figure of fun who believes in natural equality, declaims against private property and asserts that nature and man are basically good, brings us uncomfortably close to a stereotype of Jean-Jacques as he would have looked through the artful lens of Voltaire. One cannot help wondering also whether Rousseau's 'Letter' may not have inspired Voltaire's deadly definition of optimism in *Candide*. Voltaire was slow to forget a dig. In the stately peroration to his 'Letter', Rousseau had administered a magisterial rebuke to the despondent millionaire proprietor of *Les Délices*:

> Rassasié de gloire, et désabusé des vaines grandeurs, vous vivez libre au sein de L'abondance; [. . .] Vous ne trouvez pourtant que mal sur la terre. Et moi, homme obscur, pauvre, seul, tourmenté d'un mal sans remède, je médite avec plaisir dans ma retraite, et trouve que tout est bien.

Voltaire's laconic retort is put into the mouth of Candide: '[L'optimisme] c'est la rage de soutenir que tout est bien quand on est mal' (Ch. XIX).

There are one or two other indications that from time to time Voltaire had Jean-Jacques in mind when composing the portrait of Pangloss. Except for the veneer of urbanity and *bon ton*, Voltaire had treated Rousseau's long and closely reasoned letter ('je voulois philosopher avec lui') in the same summary fashion as the Derviche treats Pangloss: '"Je me flatais, dit Pangloss, de raisonner un peu avec vous des effects & des causes, du meilleur des mondes possibles, de l'origine du mal, de la nature de l'ame, & de l'harmonie préétablie." Le Derviche à ces mots leur ferma la porte au nez' (Ch. XXX). It will be observed that (except for the Leibnizian garnishing provided by 'l'harmonie préétablie') Pangloss's agenda has an odd resemblance to the contents of Rousseau's 'Letter'.

In a more general way, Pangloss is a caricature, not simply of metaphysical optimists, but of all doctrinaires who refuse to face facts, listen to argument or learn from experience: 'Je suis toujours de mon premier sentiment' he explains, after having endured the most horrible sufferings, 'car enfin je suis Philosophe, il ne me convient pas de me dédire [...]' (Ch. XXVIII). There were literary antecedents of Pangloss, no doubt; in particular Doctor Sangrado, the demon doctor of Valladolid, who decimated a whole community thanks to his doctrine that for all illnesses 'il ne faut que saigner et faire boire de l'eau chaude [...] 'C'est une erreur de croire que le sang soit nécessaire à la conservation de la vie; on ne peut trop saigner un malade.' No doubt there is something of Dr Sangrado in Maître Pangloss, just as there is a little of Gil Blas in Candide. And in the case of both these doctrinaires, there is an additional sting (which Voltaire may well have intended for Rousseau), the implication that they did not really believe in the doctrines they professed: 'Pangloss avoüait, qu'il avait toujours horriblement souffert; mais ayant soutenu une fois que tout allait à merveille, il le soutenait toujours, & n'en croyait rien' (Ch. XXX). It will be recalled that, from the first *Discours* onwards, it had been loudly protested by Rousseau's detractors, and constantly repeated, that he could not possibly believe the paradoxes he defended, and did not in fact believe them.

The evidence is suggestive, though not, of course, conclusive. Jean-Jacques had certainly become Dr Pansophe for Voltaire by 1766: he may well have provided some of the features of Maître Pangloss in 1759.

5. The 'Letter on Optimism' a reply to *Candide*?

Rousseau firmly believed that *Candide* was a reply to his 'Letter on Optimism', but there are some grounds for suspecting that his proposition might well be inverted. The timing of the publication of the 'Letter' is curious. *Candide* appeared in February 1759: the first (unauthorised) edition of the 'Letter on Optimism' (written three years earlier) was on sale in the bookshops of Berlin by September of that year. Is this because someone felt that such an eloquent and earnest homily, discrediting Voltaire by the faults it found in his logic, justifying the ways of God to man, reasserting a rational optimism in the face of a hilarious caricature, and proclaiming a fervent belief in the immortality of the soul, would be a welcome antidote to the scandalous success of *Candide*'s 'wanton profaneness' and pessimism, and would help to reverse the 'sporting victory' it had gained over religion?

The Unity of Voltaire's L'Ingenu

Haydn T. Mason

The true nature and intention of *L'Ingénu* have constituted a problem which has exercised many critics of Voltaire. Unlike *Zadig* and *Candide*, it offers us no revealing sub-title of a thematic nature. It introduces an apparent 'homme de la nature' who, on closer investigation, turns out not to be one. It appears to criticise his own way of life, but also, through him, the way of life of French society, both provincial and courtly. The first chapters suggest another *Candide*, but the ending is tragic. Finally, as if these obstacles were not enough, Voltaire's satire concentrates not on one single aspect of French life, but ranges over theological and religious absurdities, political injustices, and even literary shortcomings.

These baffling complexities might be dismissed as inconsistencies and *L'Ingénu* as a failure, were it not that the general consensus of Voltaire criticism has always been that this is one of Voltaire's most valuable *contes*. If this is so, then the search for a central unity becomes even more important, since a significant work of art must surely possess some inner coherence to give it its vital force. But the search for that unity has proved particularly arduous, and critical analyses of *L'Ingénu*, far from abating, have increased in number in recent years. Mention must at once be made of the Brumfitt edition, which constitutes a distinguished contribution to our understanding of *L'Ingénu* by the perceptive common sense which informs it.[1] If the writer disagrees with Dr Brumfitt on the unity of *L'Ingénu* (which is, of course, not by any means the only aspect of the work that this edition treats), it is with the respectful gratitude

[1] J. H. Brumfitt and M. I. Gerard Davis, edd. Voltaire, *L'Ingénu and Histoire de Jenni* (Oxford, Blackwell, 1960). All references to *L'Ingénu* will be made to this edition.

which comes from the great help that this study has afforded him. In fact, with his usual moderation, Dr Brumfitt carefully avoids any extravagant claims about the unity of this work. '*L'Ingénu*,' he says, 'clearly does not possess the "philosophical" unity of *Candide* or *Jenni*' (xiv). 'The real central theme,' he adds, '. . . is not philosophical but political' (xvii), and he describes it as 'the abuse of arbitrary power' (xxi). But he points out that this is not the only theme, and that its claims to predominance lie in its being present 'at all the real crises of the story from the incarceration of Mlle de St-Yves in a convent to her . . . death' and always being treated with high seriousness (xvii).

At about the same time appeared a study by M. Francis Pruner.[2] Like Dr Brumfitt, M. Pruner feels that Nivat had exaggerated the influence of the La Chalotais affair upon the genesis of *L'Ingénu*;[3] and he concludes that Voltaire was thinking not only of this judicial scandal but of all the scandals against which he was campaigning in 1766. Voltaire, he decides, wanted to stress the effect of persecution upon *any* minority sect (p. 36). This seems to me an admirably sound evaluation, and it is well supported by documentary evidence, much of it derived from a careful study of Voltaire's correspondence about the time when he was apparently at work on *L'Ingénu*. It is, therefore, rather a pity that at the end the critic narrows down his general conclusion, claiming that in appearing to attack the Jesuits Voltaire is in fact attacking the Jansenists as being the most dangerous contemporary threat. If *L'Ingénu* is intended to have any polemical effect, this seems a curious proceeding, particularly when the sole Jansenist represented is clearly a sympathetic character. True, Voltaire plainly shows his disagreement with Jansenist doctrines; but the reader is going to be hard put to it to infer that he is warning above all against the political power of the *Parlements*. This deviousness contrasts strikingly with Voltaire's usual directness of attack; his target is not normally so difficult to establish.

The most recent attempt at an answer has been made by M. Roger Laufer.[4] M. Laufer makes clear that his interpretations may be

[2] 'Recherches sur la création romanesque dans *L'Ingénu* de Voltaire', *Archives des lettres modernes* (1960), xxx.

[3] J. Nivat, '*L'Ingénu* de Voltaire, les jésuites et l'affaire La Chalotais', *Revue des sciences humaines* (1952), lxvi. 97-108.

[4] *Style rococo, style des 'lumières'* (Paris, Corti, 1963).

venturesome, and indeed his approach to *L'Ingénu* has a refreshing originality about it: 'La signification de l'œuvre est plus dans son ton que dans certaines de ses affirmations' (p. 100). 'L'erreur d'optique de nombreux critiques de Voltaire est de vouloir trouver dans un conte tel que *L'Ingénu* une unité polémique et négative, alors que seul [sic] le récit romanesque et la leçon qui en découle, peuvent constituer le lieu de l'unité positive . . .' (p. 109). But the detailed findings that follow seem often to fly in the face of the facts. M. Laufer feels that Voltaire wants above all to reduce the characters to the level of marionettes and the drama to a 'petitesse ridicule' (ibid.), thereby reminding us that what counts is 'la présence du conteur' (p. 111), not the importance of the tale. He arrives at this startling conclusion by discovering, *inter alia*, that Voltaire does not mean us to take Mademoiselle de St-Yves's sorrows too seriously, for a woman who spies on the Huron while he is bathing must be exaggerating her remorse later on for what everyone assures her is a good action. This assumes that a young girl who reveals a natural curiosity must be comic if later she is involved in a virtual rape, and further that Voltaire cannot show compassion towards attitudes with which he might not wholly agree. The critic thereby reduces the breadth of Voltaire's sympathy for human nature, which is one of the main characteristics of *L'Ingénu*, and which appears in any case in Voltaire's correspondence.[5] Further, he invokes some erroneous interpretations in aid of his thesis. If St-Yves is 'enivrée de tendresse' (*L'Ingénu*, p. 45), that 'tendresse' is entirely reserved for the Huron; it is not, as M. Laufer insinuates (p. 104), St-Pouange who is responsible for its appearance. Nor is Voltaire being ironic about the Ingénu's threats of suicide, for he recognises that 'il est . . . des cas où il est permis de se tuer soi-même' and expresses nothing but horror at the penalties inflicted for suicide.[6]

By suspect arguments, therefore, M. Laufer arrives at the curious statement that *L'Ingénu* brings out 'le véritable sourire voltairien, celui de l'humain, trop humain' (p. 107), when in fact the universal irony which the critic discovers makes Voltaire sound much more

[5] Cf., e.g., Best. 12530, 14 July 1766, where Voltaire's attitude to La Barre is seen to be full of deep pity while at the same time he recognises the foolishness of the latter's conduct.

[6] *Commentaire sur le livre des délits et des peines* (1766), M. xxv. 568-569. cf. Best. 12633, 28 Aug. 1766.

like an odious God. On the contrary, Voltaire here is full (even, perhaps, too full) of sensibility. Like Gordon, 'il n'était pas de ces malheureux philosophes qui s'efforcent d'être insensibles' (p. 53); the comment, following a reflexion ascribed to Gordon but which is clearly autobiographical, may be confidently taken as Voltaire's own straightforward view. And yet, it seems to me, the Laufer 'point de départ' is the only one that will satisfactorily resolve the problem facing us. The polemical themes are too disparate; if there is a unity, it must be in the tone.

At this point it might be well to cite Voltaire's own evaluation of the *conte*: 'L'Ingénu vaut mieux que Candide, en ce qu'il est infiniment plus vraisemblable.'[7] This statement is often quoted, but usually for the wrong reasons. It is no more than a literary curiosity that Voltaire should, on one occasion, have thought *L'Ingénu* superior to *Candide*. Posterity's general failure to agree with his judgments on his own work, and his accustomed predisposition to favour what he had recently been engaged in composing,[8] nullify the significance of the judgment. But the reason given is important when one sees the key word as 'vraisemblable' (and, though it is of lesser importance, let us not forget that the sub-title of *L'Ingénu* is 'Histoire véritable'). Once we meditate upon the implications of 'vraisemblance', we quickly find ourselves heading away from the domain of the 'conte purement philosophique' and into a more strictly aesthetic field of Voltaire's work. Indeed, to find what Voltaire understands by 'vraisemblance', we can hardly do better than to look at his *Commentaires sur Corneille* (1764), echoes of which are found in *L'Ingénu*. 'Vraisemblance' for Voltaire is an essential ingredient of tragedy, and Corneille was wrong to think otherwise (M. xxxii. 347-348). It involves a close adherence to what is true 'dans la nature' (M. xxxii. 348); and it requires an element of fatality so that 'la catastrophe doit arriver nécessairement, par tout ce qui aura été annoncé dans les premiers actes' (M. xxxii. 362).

But what has all this to do with *L'Ingénu*? It would certainly be untrue to suggest that Voltaire was writing a prose tragedy. Voltaire had no sympathy with such a bastard form, which offended

[7] Best. 13360 [June/July 1767].

[8] By September 1767, Voltaire is able to write: 'Vous aurez incessamment Charlot . . . dont je fais plus de cas que de l'Ingénu' (Best. 13527).

too many rules dear to his classical æsthetic outlook.[9] Before considering the exact connexion between the 'conte' and tragedy, it is time to examine *L'Ingénu* in isolation, and to see wherein, if at all, any unity of tone may be said to reside.

This unity, it seems to me, is to be found in contrast, but not contrasts of the static kind mentioned by M. Laufer between, for example, Jansenism and Jesuitism, or sentiment and reason; rather is it of an evolutionary nature, a metamorphosis. The whole work is full of development in character; indeed, in Chapter XI, Voltaire even goes so far as to consider not only individual, but also collective metamorphoses. Whereas in *Candide* only the hero's personality evolves, here the sense of growth and change is well-nigh universal; perhaps only the 'bailli' and his son remain stock caricatures reminiscent of the puppets in *Candide*. Even the 'villain' St-Pouange 'connut le repentir' (p. 57), while the mildly maleficent abbé de St-Yves also sees the error of his ways (p. 47). These conversions would be the stuff of pure melodrama in isolation, but they must be seen in relation to the more important characters and, with them, against the general philosophical backcloth of the work. All three main characters change fundamentally. The Huron's evolution has often been pointed out, most succinctly of all by M. René Pomeau.[10] But it is significant to note that the formation of his character does not end with his awareness that he has been 'changé de brute en homme' (p. 30). Although he has learned to reflect, although his formal education is more or less complete, the total development of his sensibility still has bitter obstacles to overcome. When he leaves prison, 'l'Ingénu . . . n'était plus l'*Ingénu*' (p. 48), but he still lacks the sophistication of a man of society. He fails to guess at St-Yves's cause for grief, 'ce qu'un autre que l'Ingénu, plus accoutumé au monde et plus instruit des usages de la cour, aurait deviné facilement' (p. 46). Above all, despite Gordon's exemplary tales, he still holds to the naïve belief that virtue is enough to guarantee happiness and that happiness can be unalloyed: 'je pense qu'une âme noble, reconnaissante et sensible, peut vivre heureuse; et je compte bien jouir d'une félicité sans mélange avec

[9] Cf. Préface to *Œdipe* (M. ii. 53-58); *Discours sur la tragédie* (M. ii. 312-313).

[10] 'Roman de formation comme *Candide*, l'*Ingénu* montre la métamorphose de la "brute" en homme, sous les influences combinées du malheur, de l'amour et des belles-lettres.' 'Une esquisse inédite de "L'Ingénu" ', *Revue d'histoire littéraire de la France* (1961), lxi. 60.

la belle et généreuse St-Yves' (p. 51). It takes her death to convince him otherwise. Voltaire also preserves 'vraisemblance' in recounting the Huron's development by leaving that development incomplete. The wild impulsiveness that was so marked at the beginning remains dangerous to the end; but for the surveillance of others, he might well have killed St-Pouange and himself (p. 57). Although he has learned to some extent the art of self-mastery (pp. 49, 52), one is left with the feeling that he will always have difficulty in controlling his passionate nature.

The change in St-Yves is similarly evident. As with the Ingénu (though the latter had of course received a 'philosophic' education as well), 'l'amour et le malheur l'avaient formée' (p. 45), and the change is apparent to others (p. 48). Yet the transformation is not as inconsistent as has sometimes been suggested. St-Yves is a perfectly normal young girl throughout. At the beginning she exhibits a healthy mixture of passion and modesty: she is 'tendre, vive et sage' (p. 14). At the end she does not achieve noble pathos so much as have it thrust upon her by external circumstances which she cannot control. Indeed, Voltaire heightens the pathos by pointing out that her death is *not* that of the noble sage (p. 55), and thereby makes it the more moving. She feels, in fact, the full horror of a premature, unjustified and unwanted death; she does not 'go gentle into that good night'.

Gordon too, like the Huron, evolves: 'il était changé en homme' (p. 48). He has become wise through the experience of suffering, he has learned compassion and tolerance for such as St-Yves (p. 54). He reminds one by turns of Pangloss and Martin. Like the former, he never completely shakes off his providentialist outlook, since he can maintain to the end that 'malheur est bon à quelque chose' (p. 58); like the latter, he testifies to the generality of human sorrow (p. 51). But his main function here is not to serve as a philosophic mouthpiece. Rather he appears as a man who steadily becomes more human when acquainted with the sad complexity of human life, one who is better than his philosophy.

It is this complexity that Voltaire wishes to bring out. His presentation of character, as we have seen, testifies to this; and the hint of ambivalence is found in minor characters too, like Mademoiselle de Kerkabon, whose character is 'bon et sensible' while yet she is a 'dévote' (p. 1), who can feel jealousy of St-Yves and yet control it

(p. 5). The Jesuit Father Tout-à-tous is another case in point. Some critics have seen his advice as wholly odious,[11] yet it would appear that Voltaire's attitude to him is more complex, for a few years later he, like Tout-à-tous, explicitly approves of St Augustine's tolerant attitude towards Acindynus' wife (M. xvii. 72-73 [1770]). Clearly, this complexity is bewildering when one is accustomed to the two-dimensional caricatures of other *contes*. Yet it is in harmony with the whole tone of *L'Ingénu*. Voltaire draws our attention to one paradox after another of human existence. It is most curious how pleasure and pain are inextricably mixed, how poetry brings to the Huron 'à la fois . . . le plaisir et la douleur' (p. 32), how later, and much more intensely, St-Yves should experience a similar confusion of sorrow and joy (p. 48). It is strange how a prison can be a place of education (p. 32). Stranger yet, what is the exact relationship of body and spirit? How can emotions do physical harm? Voltaire's own musings here (p. 53) will be taken up again by 'l'homme aux quarante écus' (M. xxi. 339-340); in these poignant examples Voltaire establishes 'la confrontation de cet irrationnel et de ce désir éperdu de clarté' [12] that Camus was later to pinpoint as the heart of true absurdity in this world.

One paradox is repeatedly demonstrated. It may well be true that 'malheur n'est bon à rien' (p. 58), yet for all its gratuitous destructiveness, it is educative. In the metamorphosis that takes place in *L'Ingénu*, suffering plays a basic rôle. If the characters change, it is almost uniquely because of their acquaintance with suffering. As we have seen, the Huron's education takes place in and because of prison; St-Yves parallels this development by her own secret reading of novels while incarcerated in the convent (p. 35). Love itself aids the Huron and St-Yves in their evolution only when it has been blighted by unhappiness. It is noteworthy that the hero does not learn his final lesson until the supreme catastrophe strikes him. Voltaire insists upon the value of painful experience as a teacher, not only with individuals, but as a general rule.[13] He speaks of 'cette tristesse intéressante qui fournit des conversations attachantes et utiles' (p. 49), and points out that as Gordon recounts the evils

[11] E.g. J. Nivat, art. cit., p. 100: 'Cela vaut *Tartufe*.'

[12] A. Camus, *Le Mythe de Sisyphe* (Paris, Gallimard, 1942), p. 37.

[13] Cf. Helvétius's comment: 'Le malheur est un aiguillon puissant qui tourne les esprits du côté de la vérité,' which Voltaire annotated simply as 'vrai'. W. S. Ljublinski, *Voltaire-Studien* (Berlin, Akademie-Verlag, 1961), p. 142.

of group persecution, 'les convives écoutaient avec émotion, et s'éclairaient d'une lumière nouvelle' (p. 50). This knowledge of suffering can lead to wisdom, and with wisdom to understanding and tolerance of other human beings. Yet the hopeful aspect is more than outweighed by the darker side. For the suffering is at such great cost, and so much of it, as we see it in *L'Ingénu*, is so utterly needless and wasteful of human talent and happiness.

The characters of *L'Ingénu*, then, receive an education in sensibility, and the 'ton sensible' becomes ever more predominant as the tale progresses. But is this tone merely characteristic of the latter half, as has often been alleged? What of Jean Sareil's opinion that '*L'Ingénu*, histoire comique, tourne au sentimental sans qu'on ait jamais expliqué les raisons de ce changement que rien ne laissait prévoir'?[14] This view strikes me as oversimplified. From the start, despite the many characteristic sallies against the absurdities of the Church, the tone is more muted than in other *contes*; it lacks that cruel sharpness which is more typically Voltairean. As has been pointed out, the characters who appear, major or minor, possess a certain ambiguity that precludes open satire. Institutions may be open to attack, but these people, almost without exception, are not; at most we may be permitted an indulgent smile at their expense. Already in the early chapters certain warnings are being given of the more tragic tone to come: 'Elle sentit son triomphe; mais elle n'en sentait pas encore toute l'étendue.... Mademoiselle de St-Yves rayonnait de joie de se voir marraine ... elle accepta cet honneur sans en connaître les fatales conséquences' (p. 13). The Ingénu is already seen to have suicidal moods of depression (p. 19). Tearful scenes are not lacking (cf. pp. 20-21) which seem wholly innocent of irony. Even the hero himself sheds tears at the tales of persecution told by the Huguenots (p. 22). Ominous presages of the ending occur in these early chapters, in accordance with Voltaire's own prescription for 'vraisemblance' announced in the *Commentaires sur Corneille*.

Even so, it must be admitted that some difference of emphasis exists from that of the final chapters. Why is this? Surely the answer lies precisely in that metamorphosis which is Voltaire's constant preoccupation throughout the novel. The problem of consistency within an evolutionary context is one that has preoccupied most novelists; it is a problem of which Voltaire, albeit to a less sophisti-

[14] *Romanic Review* (1961), lii. 66.

cated degree, is aware. In discussing his tragedy *Les Scythes*, he maintains: 'rien n'est si froid que de commencer par tout avouer' (Best. 12829, 8 Dec. 1766). Predictability that yet holds the audience's interest: it is the hurdle which every writer of tragedies must face, and this is what Voltaire is facing here. Opinions may differ as to whether he has succeeded;[15] what seems certain is that Voltaire did not start out on a *conte* of the type of *Zadig* and fall into sensibility in the middle. Such a theory seems untenable when one looks at the apparent first sketch for *L'Ingénu*, which provided for the noble death of the hero at the end.[16] Such important changes as were thereafter made, most notably the transference of tragic focus to St-Yves, in no way affect the basic tragedy that Voltaire already had in mind.

Mention has again been made of 'tragedy'. It is time to return to this question. In the climactic final chapter, Voltaire invokes the aid of a patently tragic device, the appeal to pity and terror: St-Yves's words are 'tendres et terribles', the crisis arouses 'l'effroi et l'attendrissement', 'douleur et . . . pitié', while the Ingénu's state provokes 'compassion et . . . effroi'. This is but the most obvious of the ways in which the author seeks to elevate the mood to the desired level. His own views on the cathartic effect of tragedy according to the Aristotelian recipe are clearly represented in the *Commentaires sur Corneille*. He dismisses the purgative notion as meaningless, but continues: 'j'entends fort bien comment la crainte et la pitié agitent notre âme pendant deux heures, selon la nature, et comment il en résulte un plaisir très-noble et très-délicat, qui n'est bien senti que par les esprits cultivés.

Sans cette crainte et cette pitié, tout languit au théâtre. Si on ne remue pas l'âme, on l'affadit. Point de milieu entre s'attendrir et s'ennuyer' (M. xxxii. 349).

[15] To my mind, the weakest section is in the middle (Chs. X-XII), where Voltaire uses the Ingénu's education as an excuse for literary and philosophical observations. Yet the core of these is essential for the developmental theme. Could some of the material be from an earlier date? In Ch. XII, mainly on Corneille, the Huron says: 'je suis accoutumé à dire ce que je pense' (p. 33; a similar expression occurs on p. 3). Although this phrase appears, in one form or another, in correspondence during 1767 (Best. 13033, 9 Feb. 1767; Best. 13303, 25 May 1767), it occurs, more remarkably, no fewer than five times during April 1764 (Best. 10973, 10982, 10983, 11004, 11007), at a time when Voltaire had just completed his *Commentaires sur Corneille.*

[16] Pomeau, *loc. cit.*

Why this need to give such tragic expression to an 'histoire véritable'? There seem to be two reasons, one of them an historical accident to be discussed later. The first is that only in this way does Voltaire feel himself capable of giving full value here to his horror of the persecutions and intolerance of his times. There is an interesting comment in Chapter X, where the author makes manifest how pessimistic he is about the course of human events: 'En effet, l'histoire n'est que le tableau des crimes et des malheurs.... Il semble que l'histoire ne plaise que comme la tragédie, qui languit si elle n'est animée par les passions, les forfaits, et les grandes infortunes. Il faut armer Clio du poignard, comme Melpomène' (p. 29). He even proceeds in the next paragraph to sum up French history in literary terms ('si dégoûtante dans ses commencements, si sèche dans son milieu') that are curiously like his later comments on Corneille ('Je n'ai guère entendu le commencement; j'ai été révolté du milieu,' p. 33). What then more natural than that, in writing a *conte* which uncharacteristically deals with a particular historical period, Voltaire should seek to impose upon it, as in tragedy and history, 'une exposition, un nœud, un dénouement' (Best. 7090, 17 July 1758)?[17]

For Voltaire's aim, let us be quite clear, is polemical. The foregoing remarks aim to discover the underlying tone of the work, they do not deny that it is a 'pièce de combat'. While 'L'histoire nous apprend ce que sont les humains,' the narrative tells us 'ce qu'ils doivent être' (M. xix. 68). M. Pruner's comment that Voltaire wants to stress the effect of persecution upon any sect seems apposite. The themes of *L'Ingénu* do not appear to focus upon any one topic of immediate actuality, but to develop out of Voltaire's growing sense of horror at the recent persecutions, particularly of Calas, Sirven and above all of La Barre. M. Pruner shows clearly that in some respects the La Barre affair was responsible for important details of *L'Ingénu*; Voltaire's lasting and unfeigned shock at the savagery thereby revealed is too well known to be recounted once again here.[18] But Voltaire's disgust is more general, with a state of affairs

[17] Cf. 'La tragédie est le pays de l'histoire, ou du moins de tout ce qui ressemble à l'histoire par la vraisemblance des faits et par la vérité des mœurs.' *Commentaires sur Corneille*, M. xxxii. 348.

[18] It is noteworthy that Voltaire registers the same emotional reaction towards La Barre's fate as he does to St-Yves's. He ends the *Relation de la mort du chevalier de La Barre* (1766) by expressing 'l'attendrissement et l'horreur' (M. xxv. 516).

that has endured almost as long as Christianity. Writing about La Barre to Carolina of Zweibrücken, he declares: 'Je ne crois pas que depuis quinze siècles il se soit passé une seule année où l'Europe crétienne, n'ait vu de pareilles horreurs et de baucoup plus abominables, touttes produites par la superstition et par le fanatisme' (Best. 12626, 25 Aug. 1766). A little later he makes clear to the duc de Richelieu that he sees no real distinction between the Protestant victims and the others; Despinas, Calas, Sirven and La Barre all come under the general heading of 'persécutés' (Best. 12673, 15 Sept. 1766). Indeed, the seminal notion of *L'Ingénu* may well be stated in a letter written at about this time to Moultou: 'Ne pourait-on point faire quelque livre qui pût se faire lire avec quelque plaisir, par les gens mêmes qui n'aiment point à lire, et *qui portât les cœurs à la compassion*?' (Best. 12753, [Oct./Nov. 1766]: my italics). The need to move his readers by pity and horror, rather than to assault their reason, is at the heart of *L'Ingénu*.

If then the first part includes *badinage* upon curious religious customs of the Catholic Church, that only makes the subsequent tragedy more useless and terrible. What is more absurd, given the Voltairean outlook on the world, than a prohibition of marriage between a man and his godmother, the more so as the Huron was ignorant of it when committing himself? Yet from this farce all the tragedy ensues. The Huron suffers because of Catholic doctrine, because of his impulsive sympathy for Protestants, because of the political corruption at Versailles and in the provinces, which is all the worse for being capricious and wayward; the attack is generalised, upon intolerance, its causes and effects. There is an interesting parallel to the development of *L'Ingénu* in the *Avis au public sur les Calas et les Sirven* (1766), in a chapter entitled 'Causes étranges de l'intolérance' (M. xxv. 527-528). Voltaire begins: 'Je suppose qu'on raconte toutes ces choses à un Chinois, à un Indien de bon sens;' *L'Ingénu* will merely change the nationality. He continues by showing that hatred and aggression arise from subtle differences of dogma, absurd by reason of the fine distinctions that they make. But, as Voltaire goes on to point out, because of such absurdities massacres and persecution take place. Yet in fact all humanity shares the same moral code: 'les subtilités scolastiques ont fait des monstres de ceux qui, en s'attachant simplement à cette même morale, auraient été des frères.' The same path is trodden here as in *L'Ingénu*: 'il n'y a pas une seule dispute théologique qui n'ait eu des suites funestes.' Here we find the same accents of horror at the unnecessary suffering, and grief that men are so divided by institutional quarrels when they share, the St-Pouanges not excluded, a common bond of morality. Even the references to Quesnel, to whom Voltaire ascribes authorship of *L'Ingénu*, and to Le Tellier, who appears in the first sketch of the *conte*, strengthen the analogies with this chapter.

There may be one other reason for the tragic, more 'romanesque' character of this story. It lies in the curious connexion between *L'Ingénu* and *Les Scythes*. Reference to *Les Scythes* is first made in September, 1766,[19] and thereafter Voltaire reveals a very close involvement with the tragedy's success or failure. Why he should have been so sensitive to what others would feel about it is not clear; perhaps it is because he is glad to discover that his inspiration has not withered with age,[20] or because he felt he was introducing an important innovation by experimenting with a wide range of social conditions in a tragedy.[21] At any rate, from the first he is proud of his achievement: 'Des larmes! On en versera, ou on sera de pierre' (Best. 12789, 19 Nov. 1766). But the play does not find the favour he had hoped for; Cardinal de Bernis, for instance, criticises it quite severely (Best. 12938, 11 Jan. 1767). Voltaire becomes depressed, admits his limitations: 'J'ai fait humainement ce que j'ai pu. Il ne faut pas demander à un artiste plus qu'il ne peut faire' (Best. 13045, 10/11 Feb. 1767). Yet he goes on amending, apologising, hoping against hope that it will succeed. Alas! it meets with a cool reception when eventually it is performed in Paris in March. Voltaire continues the unavailing struggle, displaying a surprising vulnerability to criticism over this play: 'Ils [*Les Scythes*] avancent la fin de mes jours; ils me tuent . . . j'avais un besoin extrême du succès de cet ouvrage' (Best. 13303, 25 May 1767). And he remarks sadly a little later: 'J'ai le malheur d'aimer mieux les

[19] Best. 12701. There is an apparently earlier reference in Best. 12663, but this letter is misplaced and belongs to the period when Voltaire is amending *Les Scythes* for Lacombe, beginning on 16 March 1767 (Best. 13152). One of the corrections Voltaire demands in Best. 12663 appears in Best. 13252 (27 April 1767), which gives a reasonable indication of the former letter's date.

[20] Cf. Best. 12789, 19 Nov. 1766.

[21] Cf. Best. 12858 (19 Dec. 1766); Best. 12865 (22 Dec. 1766). F. Baldensperger stresses the aesthetic audacity of the play ('Voltaire contre la Suisse de Jean-Jacques: la tragédie des "Scythes"', *Revue des cours et conférences* (1930–31), ii. 673-689).

Scythes qu'aucune de mes tragédies' (Best. 13318, 4 June 1767). But this is the last such complaint. Quite suddenly, after months of preoccupation, he ceases to lament the tragedy. The references become much rarer and are generally quite dispassionate. The change is so clear-cut that one immediately suspects that a new work has taken hold of him and given him back the pride that had been so grievously wounded over *Les Scythes*.

Was this work *L'Ingénu*? The date would make it fit, for we know from numerous references that *L'Ingénu* was much on his mind during April and May. The suspicion grows when one looks at *Les Scythes* and even more so at some of Voltaire's comments on it. Here again a contrast is established between simple and sophisticated manners, and the blame is not entirely on one side. Obéide, the heroine, is forced to choose between two suitors, as is St-Yves, and to sacrifice herself in order to save her lover. In both, the heroine's fidelity to her lover is regarded as of supreme consequence.[22] Athamare, like the Huron, has lost his first wife (Act III, Sc. 2), he too at the end is obliged to live on after his beloved's death. When one looks at Voltaire's correspondence, the comparisons become still more closely-knit. Athamare has a 'caractère violent et emporté' (Best. 13133, 11 Mar. 1767); Voltaire writes of 'l'emportement' of the Ingénu (p. 55) and of the 'sentiments . . . violents' (p. 56) of such men as he. Athamare is 'un jeune homme beau, bien fait' (Best. 13204, 11 Apr. 1767); the Huron, on his first appearance, is described as 'un jeune homme très bien fait' (p. 2). In brief, if Athamare is 'un très jeune homme amoureux comme un fou, fier, sensible, empressé, emporté' (Best. 13250, 27 Apr. 1767), this could be an equally apt description of the Ingénu. Even Gordon's characterisation may owe something to Voltaire's difficulties in representing 'des vieillards attendrissants' in *Les Scythes* (cf. Best. 13285, 16 May 1767). It must also be remembered that during the time *L'Ingénu* is being written, Voltaire's little circle is giving several performances of the tragedy at Ferney (cf. Best. 13293 [18 May 1767]; 13300 [23 May 1767] etc). The play is very much in the forefront of his mind. One therefore wonders whether the tone

[22] During the period when Voltaire is apparently at work on *L'Ingénu* and meditating on *Les Scythes*, he refers to 'les règles ordinaires du roman, qui veulent qu'une héroïne ne fasse jamais d'infidélité à ce qu'elle aime' (Best. 13248, 27 Apr. 1767).

which *L'Ingénu* possesses, so different from that of all the other main *contes*, is not in some measure a compensatory reaction to the disappointments Voltaire suffered at the failure of *Les Scythes*.[23] If the actors at the Comédie-Française were incapable of arousing emotion by their acting, as Voltaire alleged (e.g., Best. 13230 [19 Apr. 1767]), then Voltaire had it entirely in his own power to make amends through the narrative *genre* for his failure in the dramatic. *L'Ingénu* is not a prose tragedy in Voltaire's connotation of the term, as has already been made clear; but it has all the characteristics of a work which seeks to appeal to the heart, as *Les Scythes* had tried to do, rather than to the head.

For the ultimate aim of *Les Scythes* and *L'Ingénu* is the same. *Les Scythes* is so much a work of propaganda that Professor Ronald Ridgway describes it as 'une sorte de conte voltairien'.[24] Voltaire's natural morality springs from two fundamental sources, as Professor Havens has indicated: pity and justice.[25] In *Les Scythes*, however, Voltaire eventually stresses one at the expense of the other: 'que la pitié succède à la justice' (Act v, Sc. 5), when that justice is to be as harsh as the Scythian code is. Justice must be tempered with compassion or charity; this is the theme of polemical writings of 1766 like the *Commentaire sur le livre des délits et des peines*, *Avis sur les Calas et les Sirven*, *Des conspirations contre les peuples*. The affective tone of *L'Ingénu* seeks the same end; the *conte*, or more properly *roman*, is one of Voltaire's most interesting experiments, one of his least understood but most rewarding works.

[23] It is interesting to note a somewhat similar relationship between *Candide* and *Tancrède*; but in fact the analogy is a superficial one and serves only to accentuate the deeper contrasts. Cf. A. Morize ed. *Candide* (Paris, Didier, 1957), p. 153 n.

[24] 'La Propagande philosophique dans les tragédies de Voltaire', *Studies on Voltaire and the Eighteenth Century* (1961), xv. 203.

[25] G. R. Havens, 'The Nature Doctrine of Voltaire', *PMLA* (1925), xl. 861.

Voltaire's L'Ingénu, *the Huguenots and Choiseul*

Samuel S. B. Taylor

The years which gave birth to *L'Ingénu* were those which Theodore Besterman's edition of the Voltaire *Correspondence* had reached when I joined him in Geneva to help in its completion. It was through working on the *Correspondence* that I came to know both its editor and its full significance. I offer this study to Theodore Besterman as a token of sincere regard and admiration for his achievement.

* * *

This particular *conte* by Voltaire has always presented an enigma and there have been repeated attempts[1] to plumb its meaning and to explain its apparent lack of unity in construction. The most scholarly of the critical editions, that by J. H. Brumfitt and M. I. Gerard Davis,[2] appeared before the relevant volumes of the Voltaire *Correspondence* were available and also before the discovery and publication of a first draft of this tale, found in Leningrad. A number of questions raised by earlier editors and critics may now

[1] Voltaire, *L'Ingénu, histoire véritable*, ed. W. R. Jones (Genève, &c, Textes littéraires français, 1957); J. Nivat, '*L'Ingénu* de Voltaire, les jésuites et l'affaire de La Chalotais', *Revue des sciences humaines* (1952), pp. 97-108; E. E. Rovillain, '*L'Ingénu* de Voltaire. Quelques influences', P.M.L.A. (1929), xliv. 536-545; I. O. Wade, 'The Search for a new Voltaire', *Transactions of the American philosophical society* (Philadelphia July 1958); I. O. Wade, *Studies on Voltaire with some unpublished papers of Mme du Châtelet* (Princeton University Press 1947); R. Gomard, *La Légende du bon sauvage* (Paris 1946); R. Pomeau, 'Une Esquisse inédite de *L'Ingénu*', *Revue d'histoire littéraire de la France* (1961), lxi. 58-60; Voltaire, *Romans et contes*, ed. R. Pomeau (Paris, Garnier-Flammarion, 1966); G. Chinard, *L'Amérique et le reve exotique* (Paris &c. 1934); F. Pruner, 'Recherches sur la création romanesque dans *L'Ingénu* de Voltaire', *Archives des lettres modernes* (mars–avril 1960), iii. no. 30.

[2] Voltaire, *L'Ingénu and Histoire de Jenni*, edd. J. H. Brumfitt and M. L. Gerard Davis (Oxford, Basil Blackwell, 1960); see also review by Jean Sareil in *Romanic Review* (1961), lii. 64-66.

be seen in a new light and require elucidation. We are concerned here with two of these questions, namely the reasons for the development of this tale from a first draft in typical Voltairean vein to the radically different version finally published in July or August 1767—and the establishment of Voltaire's purpose in writing it.

It was already clear that *L'Ingénu* is unique in the Voltairean *conte*, differing considerably, both from the earlier *contes* and also those which were to follow. Its historical setting is unique, it has a simpler, more dramatic structure, it portrays its characters in unusual depth and with an appeal to the sensibility and emotions of the reader reminiscent of the sentimental novel. Furthermore it shifts as the tale progresses from Voltaire's characteristic wit and irony to a bitterness and passionate anger whose impact is emotional rather than intellectual. The tone of the *conte* had hitherto been one of intellectual involvement coupled with emotional detachment. The strange feature of this *conte* is not so much that it reverses this procedure as that it begins in the usual vein and shifts in three well-defined stages towards a dramatic conclusion. No satisfactory answer to this aesthetic problem has yet been found.[3]

Some of the problems raised by the Leningrad draft are still more complex. As it was conceived, in this early state, the tale was to have been the: 'Histoire de l'Ingénu, élevé chez les sauvages, puis chez les Anglais, instruit de la religion en Basse-Bretagne, tonsuré, confessé, se battant avec son confesseur, Son voyage à Versailles chez frère Le Tellier son parent. Volontaire deux campagnes, sa force incroyable, son courage. Veut être capitaine de cavalerie, étonné du refus. Se marie, ne veut pas que le mariage soit un sacrement. Trouve très bon que sa femme soit infidèle parce qu'il l'a été. Meurt en défendant son pays. Un capitaine anglais l'assiste à la mort, avec un jésuite et un janséniste. Il les instruit en mourant.'[4]

The differences with the text that finally emerged are striking. The prototype hero, who is at no point stated to be a Huron Indian,

[3] Cp. Jean Sareil (above); '*L'Ingénu*, histoire comique, tourne au sentimental sans qu'on ait jamais expliqué les raisons de ce changement, que rien ne laissait prévoir et qui vient gâcher la seconde moitié de l'ouvrage, il faut le reconnaître'.

[4] I have followed Pomeau's modernised version in Voltaire, *Romans et contes* p. 318. Cp. R.H.L.F. (1961), lxi. 58 and I. O. Wade, 'The Search for a new Voltaire', pp. 49-50.

is a much cruder concept than his later version, nor is he subjected to the violent evolutionary changes which mark the latter. He is in the direct line of descent from Micromégas, Zadig and Candide. In so far as Mlle de Saint-Yves has a prototype, it is one in the widow of Ephesus tradition.[5] Nothing can be seen of the love between the Ingénu and Mlle de Saint-Yves and of the emotional climax that this engenders. In fact the love-drama occupies the usual subordinate position in the *conte* and is the subject of the usual profane wit. The differences between the draft and the subsequent text have been amply detailed by R. Pomeau. The most important for our purposes are those of the historical setting, the treatment of the love-theme and the army-career of the Ingénu. The theme does not emerge sufficiently strongly to warrant speculation.

Voltaire made specific changes in this first draft, as a result of which the setting was moved back from the time of Le Tellier to that of his predecessor as Louis XIV's confessor, the père La Chaise, and to the precise year of 1689, four years after the revocation of the Edict of Nantes in 1685. He retained the broad outline of the provincial satire of Breton *mœurs* of the first part of the draft, but completely changed the latter part, introducing the Bastille episode and then, in a third section, transferring the centre of interest from the Ingénu to Mlle de Saint-Yves who became the source of a pathos unique in the Voltairean *conte*. Arising out of the shift in the historical setting, Voltaire has also injected a Huguenot motif not evident in the draft.

Only the first part of the *conte* in fact bears any resemblance to the first draft, though even in this there are significant changes, as the Ingénu stops short of becoming a *sous-diacre*, let alone being tonsured. The English element is toned down and the Ingénu's army-career is compressed and brought forward into a free-booting skirmish in chapter seven.

A fresh approach to the sources suggested for *L'Ingénu* might establish which of these were drawn on for the text in its first draft and which for the subsequent changes. There are problems, however, as the 'exotic' literature of the time was immense and Voltaire

[5] The fact is noted by I. O. Wade, who first published this draft from a copy by Emmanuel Miller (Paris, BN. n.a.fr. 4822, fol. 101). In this copy there is in fact a reference (fol. 105) to a decision by St Augustine 'qu'une femme qui ne pouvait sauver la vie de son mari qu'en le faisant cocu, fit très bien de lui rendre ce service'.

assimilated elements from many different sources rather than borrowing exclusively from any single one. It would be naïve to expect him to borrow not merely incidents but also mood and approach from his sources, particularly those verging on the primitivist. Pfeil's anonymous *L'Homme sauvage* (transl. Mercier 1767), although Voltaire speaks of it in June 1767 and believed it to be by Diderot (Best. 13336), has no points of resemblance. Mandeville's *Fable of the Bees* (remark C) was favoured by Wade as the 'initial impetus' for the portrayal of the unconventional man in love,[6] but the theme was commonplace in this literature. Charles Pinot-Duclos' *Histoire de Mme de Luz* (1741) is a somewhat doubtful suggestion for the dilemma that the heroine finds herself in. There are various other suggestions including Saint-Foix, *Lettres d'un Turque à Paris* (1731), Ange Goudar, *L'Espion chinois, ou l'Envoyé secret de la cour de Pékin* (1765) of which Voltaire knew (Best. 11523, 11776, 12525), La Hontan's *Voyages* of the early part of the century, Gueudeville's *Suite du voyage de l'Amérique* (1728) and Joubert de La Rue's anonymous *Lettres d'un sauvage dépaysé à son correspondant en Amérique* (1746).

The most interesting sources suggested to date have been those by Jean Henri Maubert de Gouvest. His *L'Espion américain en Europe, ou Lettres illinoises* (Londres 1766) and earlier *Lettres iroquoises* (Irocopolis [Paris] 1752) were published anonymously and offered (respectively) both the lineage of the Ingénu himself and incidents which distinguish the draft from the final text. Among these are the religious rites satirised in the person of the Ingénu, the convent 'imprisonment', the *Lettre de cachet* affair, the Bastille, the separation of the lovers and visits by a Jansenist and others with the aim of converting the hero. The fact that Maubert de Gouvest stressed the primitivist view need not have deterred Voltaire from using promising incidents. The same author was to publish the *Traité des trois imposteurs* in 1768 (see Best, 13990 and note 3). We might speculate that the *Espion américain* offered some evidence on dating but little would emerge to pinpoint the transitions through which *L'Ingénu* passed. All that the sources so far suggested have succeeded in doing is to identify possible sources without offering firm guidance as to their dating. We must still

[6] I. O. Wade, *Studies on Voltaire etc.*, pp. 19-21. On the sources see the studies by W. R. Jones and Rovillain.

look elsewhere to find reliable evidence in tracing the genesis and growth of *L'Ingénu*.

Another possible approach is to clarify the date at which the text was finally completed, although the bibliographical complexities are as frightening as ever. It is assumed by Bengesco (no. 1470)[7] that Cramer printed the first edition. This is probably correct though by no means certain, since the first mention by Voltaire is undated and says merely: 'Nb. L'ingénu vaut mieux que Candide, en ce qu'il est infiniment plus vraisemblable. J'en ay à votre service.' (Best. 13360.) A revised date recently proposed for this letter by Theodore Besterman is [July 1767].[8] The first firmly-dated references to the *Ingénu* are d'Alembert's 'on parle d'un roman intitulé l'*Ingénu*', on 21st July (Best. 13402) and Richelieu's similar *on dit* from the provinces on 1st August (Best. 13431). There is a case to be made that the first edition was not in fact that of Cramer. Voltaire's denials were usually informatively-phrased *hocus-pocus* and his note in reply to d'Alembert that: 'je l'ai fait chercher à Genève et en Hollande' (Best. 13433) could indicate that *Utrecht* was not so far wrong as the address of the first edition. It is doubtful if Rey of Amsterdam could have been involved at this early date, but the possibility remains that the *conte* was first published in Holland or elsewhere outside Geneva, and that reports of this edition reached Paris even before printed sheets arrived at Ferney. The text of Voltaire's letter (Best. 13360) is quite consistent with Voltaire having provided Cramer with sewn, printed sheets for a reprint and not with manuscript copy for the first edition.

On the whole, however, it seems more probable that the early rumours in Paris stemmed from informed leaks from Ferney by La Harpe or Chabanon, both of whom were with Voltaire in July and may have heard extracts read aloud. Further pointers in this direction are the fact that d'Alembert still had no copy by 14 August (Best. 13469) and that Lacombe was not in a position to publish his pirated reprint before 3 September (Best. 13510), gen. note). Paris seems in fact to have had to wait upon copies that Voltaire sent from Geneva on, or shortly before, 22 August

[7] Georges Bengesco, *Voltaire: Bibliographie de ses œuvres* (Paris 1882–85), i. 455-456.

[8] Theodore Besterman now dates Best. 13441 and 13360 as [July 1767], the letters being placed in that order. I am grateful to him for his help on this question.

(Best. 13490). It was in the Genevese booksellers' hands in fact by 19 August (Best. 13486) and copies had reached Paris by the end of August.[9] It may well be that Voltaire's words to Cramer: 'Nb. L'ingénu vaut mieux que Candide' (Best. 13360) were a comment on Cramer's pre-publication blurbs, since the Genevese bookseller Chirol announced the *Ingénu* to Beccaria, before he had actually seen the book, as being 'Dans le goût de son Candide' (Best. 13428).[10] It is tempting to interpret Voltaire's postscript to Cramer (Best. 13360) as a comment on just such a printer's blurb.

If we decide in favour of Cramer as the *père putatif* of the first edition, then the text must have been complete at the latest by the second half of July 1767. Of the various references in *L'Ingénu* to events in 1767 which can be dated precisely, the latest is that to a sentence in the *Indiculus propositionum excerptum ex libro cui titulus Bélisaire*,[11] quickly dubbed the *Indiculus ridiculus*. Voltaire reproduced a sentence quoted by this work: 'La vérité luit de sa propre lumière, et on n'éclaire pas les esprits avec les flammes des bûchers' (p. 31). Voltaire must have inserted this some time after his receipt of d'Alembert's letter of 4 May (Best. 13265) which brought it to his attention. This exhausts the useful dating indications available to us in the text.

If we accept that the manuscript was not complete until late July 1767, and that this reference was inserted in May, then the text may quite probably have been complete up to the Bastille *entr'acte* in May and the period May–July spent in its completion. Other evidence in support of this hypothesis will be considered shortly. We shall assume for the time being, however, that the text *was* complete, at least so far as the Breton episodes were concerned, by this time, although allowance for the possibility of minor revisions being made is not discounted. There are references in still earlier pages of the text to the tower of Babel and to Hercules' feats of prowess with the fair sex,[12] but although these have echoes

[9] See Grimm, *Correspondance littéraire etc.*, ed. Tourneux (Paris 1879), vii. 409: 'Nous avons reçu enfin quelques exemplaires de *l'Ingénu*'. Extract under date of 1 Sept. 1767.

[10] This, if true, would suggest a [late July/early August] date for Best. 13360.

[11] [Paris 1767]. It had been printed by Marmontel's friends (see Best. 13273) not by the Sorbonne. See Voltaire, *L'Ingénu*, ed. J. H. Brumfitt, p. 31. All subsequent references are to this edition.

[12] See *L'Ingénu*, pp. 4, 14.

in letters or works of the time, they are well nigh proverbial and of little significance.

It occurs very naturally to the reader that the breaks in aesthetic continuity of the *conte* may correspond to interruptions in the composition of the work. Some corroborative evidence will be adduced later, but for the time being it will be useful to suppose as a working hypothesis that the text passed through three different states:

1. The draft.
2. A first version of the first section of the text, including the Breton chapters and perhaps some of the Bastille episode, with certain important changes in the draft 'scenario'.
3. A completed text incorporating section one in broad correspondence with the draft, and subsequent sections radically altered.

The date of the draft is not known, but we may date sections two and three provisionally in the autumn of 1766 and the spring and early summer of 1767 respectively.

For further evidence we must turn to the themes of *L'Ingénu*, in relation to Voltaire's major preoccupations in the period 1766–67. These have been repeatedly analysed over recent years. Primitivist and anti-primitivist interpretations have yielded to anti-jansenist and anti-jesuit theories. These in turn have dissolved into more serious claims that the work is directed against the use of the *lettres de cachet*, and in particular their use against the Breton *parlement* and its *procureur général*, La Chalotais. Present opinion is in substantial agreement that the *conte* refers to the succession of cases of fanaticism and miscarriage of justice which Voltaire had exposed over the years. By far the most convincing case is made by J. H. Brumfitt who notes that Voltaire enlarged his field into a protest again arbitrary authority in all forms and into a plea for political and religious liberty. Voltaire's central theme in the tale, he states, is: 'the abuse of arbitrary authority' and he develops this into 'one of his most forthright pleas for political liberty', 'tolerance and liberalism'.[13] R. Pomeau is in broad agreement with him.[14]

Earlier studies have noted that there are reminiscences of many individual victims of this persecution to be seen in the character of the Ingénu. Lt.-Gen. Lally-Tollendal, Calas, Sirven, d'Aiguillon,

[13] *L'Ingénu*, pp. xxi, xxv, xxvii.
[14] Voltaire, *Romans et contes*, ed. R. Pomeau, p. 320.

La Chalotais, La Bourdonnais, La Barre (who was of an age with the Ingénu) and even the younger Voltaire himself. We might even add to the list the young David Cavalier (*Siècle de Louis XIV*, chap. XXXVI) whom Voltaire had met in London. He had been a Huguenot guerrilla captain in the Camisard uprisings, and then later, served with the French colours. Nor has Mlle de Saint-Yves been spared this genealogical fervour. It appears that Mme Calas, the death of Mme du Châtelet and even Mme de Saint-Julien—Voltaire's 'charmant papillon de la philosophie'—who had recently interceded with Saint-Florentin on Voltaire's behalf (Best. 12847 etc.) may all be conscripted as antecedents.

There are difficulties, however, even if the sheer diversity and number of these parental links did not make their importance relatively minor. The characters of the Ingénu and of Mlle de Saint-Yves develop considerably in the course of the tale, and they quit the traditional 'puppetry' of the *conte* hero and heroine for rôles more reminiscent of the sentimental novel and theatre. The fact is important if it is remembered that much of the comic technique of the *conte* lay in its mock-*roman* techniques. The *contes* are usually, too, a shifting blend of gaiety and deep-felt emotion, but these are intellectualised emotions, refined into wit or irony, Voltaire remaining resilient even in anger. *L'Ingénu* certainly opens in the customary *conte* vein, but it seems as if, at one point, Voltaire's anger and exasperation mounted to a pitch at which he lost critical control over his material and was drawn into a rôle more nearly that of the tragedian. The story itself, with its strong, high-lighted love element, and consequent similarities with the *genre dramatique sérieux*, and also its difficulties in resorting to fantasy in a real, historical setting would tilt Voltaire's approach in the direction of involvement rather than the customary detachment of the genre.

There is little point in pursuing further the resemblances in detail between the Ingénu and his forbears. What is important is that 1766 marked a crescendo in these cases and in Voltaire's involvement with them. His relief of the Calas family had made him famous throughout Europe and the automatic recipient of pleas from all similar victims of persecution. Lally-Tollendal was executed in the summer of 1766, as was the chevalier de La Barre, a mere youngster. Sirven came to stay with Voltaire in that year pending his return to Paris to submit to the appeal procedure. The details behind the La Barre case, which was a veritable atrocity, involved a squalid succession of vices from hypocrisy, to debauchery, anti-*philosophe* bias, and jansenist zeal to purge themselves of accusations by their jesuit victims. It involved a barbarous punishment out of all proportion to the seriousness of the 'crimes' committed, and more important than any other factors—the sentence was endorsed by the parlement de Paris and subsequently by the king himself. Voltaire's anger and exasperation were immediate and uncontrollable:

'Quoi! dans Abbeville des Busiris en robe font périr dans les plus horribles supplices des enfants de seize ans! et leur sentence est confirmée malgré l'avis de dix juges intègres et humains! et la nation le souffre! A peine en parle-t-on un moment, on court ensuite à l'opéra comique; . . . Ici Calas roué, là Sirven pendu, plus loin un bâillon dans la bouche d'un lieutenant général [Lally]; quinze jours après, cinq jeunes gens condamnés aux flammes pour des folies qui méritaient Saint-Lazare.' (Best. 12545.)

Compare this with the outburst in March 1767, when the anger of Voltaire is undiminished, and when he has ceased to view these as individual cases but as symptoms of a generalised inhumanity:

'J'ai vu Fréret, le fils de Crébillon, Diderot, enlevéz et mis à la Bastille; l'abbé de Prades, traitté comme Arius par les Athanasiens; Helvétius oprimé non moins cruellement; Tercier dépouillé de son emploi; Marmontel privé de sa petite fortune; Bret son aprobateur destitué et réduit à la misère . . .' (Best. 13154.)

And again in April 1767:

'Nôtre jurisprudence a produit d'étranges scènes depuis quelques années. Elles font frémir le reste de l'Europe . . . Je voudrais que les gens qui sont si fiers et si rogues sur leurs palliers voiageassent un peu dans l'Europe, qu'ils entendissent ce que l'on dit d'eux . . . ils rougiraient, et la France ne présenterait plus aux autres nations le spectacle inconcevable de l'atrocité fanatique qui règne d'un côté et de la douceur, de la politesse, des grâces, de l'enjouement, et de la philosophie indulgente qui règnent de l'autre, et tout celà dans une même ville, dans une ville sur laquelle toute l'Europe n'a les yeux que parce que les beaux arts y ont été cultivés; . . .' (Best. 13191).

In this year 1766, in which Voltaire was to publish his *Commentaire sur le livre des délits et des peines*, a digest meant to introduce

Beccaria's enlightened ideas on penal reform and criminal justice to the French nation, Voltaire's revulsion against the 'Arlequins anthropophages' (Best. 12537) of his own nation was given further fuel. La Chalotais was imprisoned in the Bastille, the centre of national publicity, La Barre died; the *Assemblée de l'Église* met with renewed demands for repression of heresy and freethinking. Above all perhaps, a shameful difference was revealed between the state of justice in France and moves being made at that very time by Russia, Poland, Prussia and other countries to establish toleration by law and, in the case of Russia, to undertake the establishment of an entirely new code of laws. Voltaire's state of fright over the peril in which critics of the church and state were placed made him take concrete steps to leave France for Cleves, in the territory of Prussia, to found a colony of philosophers. His anger mounted in October and November 1766. His delicate, indirect contacts with Saint-Florentin for the relief of a French Protestant galley-slave, Espinas, and his family appeared doomed to failure. Russia's proclamation of toleration by law (Best. 12718) had reached him. He received documentary evidence from Moultou, his Genevese friend, of the actual scale of the Catholic atrocities against the Huguenots since the revocation of the Edict of Nantes (Best. 12753). D'Alembert's new work on the Jesuits arrived at Ferney early in November (Best. 12776) to be published in Geneva by Voltaire. To cap all, he received on the 7th of November 1766 a letter from Diderot which beyond any shadow of doubt must rank as one of the most powerful indictments of the French regime that Voltaire ever encountered, and certainly one of the most moving (Best. 12719): 'Je sçais bien qu'un honnête homme peut en vingt quatre heures perdre ici sa fortune parcequ'ils sont gueux; son honneur, parcequ'il n'y a point de loix; sa Liberté, parceque Les tyrans sont ombrageux; sa vie parcequ'ils comptent la vie d'un citoyen pour rien, et qu'ils cherchent à se tirer du mépris, par des actes de terreur. Je sçais bien qu'ils nous Imputent leurs désastres, parceque nous sommes seuls en état de remarquer Leurs sotises. Je sçais bien qu'un d'entr'eux a l'atrocité de dire qu'on n'avancera rien, tant qu'on ne brûlera que des Livres. . . . Je sçais bien qu'ils en sont venus au point que Les gens de bien et Les hommes éclairés leur sont et leur doivent être Insupportables. Je sçais bien que nous sommes enveloppés des fils Imperceptibles d'une nasse qu'on appelle Police, et que nous sommes entourés de délateurs. Je sçais bien que Je n'ai ni la naissance, ni les vertus, ni l'état, ni les talens qui recommandoient m^r^ Dela Chalotais et que, quand ils voudront me perdre, Je serai perdu . . . Si nous ne concourons pas avec vous, à écraser la bête, c'est que nous sommes sous sa griffe. . . .'[15]

There are a number of threads which are of little significance in isolation, but which taken together suggest that Voltaire may have begun composing *L'Ingénu* at this time, October–November 1766. To begin with, there suddenly appear two references, on 28 October and 5 November to the Hurons, although in a disparaging note on Rousseau's quarrels with Hume in England. In one Voltaire asked Damilaville for 'les trois lettres de ce Huron, écrites à m. du Theil' (Best. 12742): and in the other, to d'Argental in Paris he wrote: 'Vous connaîtrez Jean Jacques Rousseau; il est digne de se lier en Angleterre avec Déon et Vergy. Il est vrai qu'il n'y a point de galères en Angleterre, mais les Anglais ont des îles et possèdent le grand païs du Canada, où ces messieurs ne figureraient pas mal parmi les Hurons.' (Best. 12764.) The references in this second letter bear a close resemblance to different aspects of *L'Ingénu* and they are all the more striking in that Voltaire had earlier raised with Moultou the suggestion of making known the plight of the Huguenots otherwise than in a dry tome: '. . . Ne pourait-on point faire quelque livre qui pût se faire lire avec quelque plaisir, par les gens mêmes qui n'aiment point à lire, et qui portât les cœurs à la compassion?' (Best. 12753.)[16]

There is no certain proof that *L'Ingénu* was begun in October 1766, or thereabouts, but it is hard to resist the feeling that it was and that, even then, it incorporated substantial modifications on the Leningrad draft, which was presumably already in existence in Voltaire's notebooks. Did the version then composed incorporate the Protestant references of the final text? Did it imprint a political purpose at this point? It is not impossible, but it seems more likely

[15] See also Roth, 416 (vi. 334-337), who reads *masse* for *nasse* and who does not record Voltaire's endorsement 'de m^r^ Diderot' on the manuscript and proceeds to speculate as to whether the text derives from Diderot's fair copy and not from the letter sent.

[16] This letter is dated [October/November] by Besterman. Moultou may have produced the document read by Voltaire to correct the figures of eight 'malheureux prédicants' hanged in France since 1745 in the *Avis au public* (M. xxv. 524) of June 1766.

that it developed in a more or less conventional manner, to the end of the Breton episode, perhaps venturing into the Bastille section but then breaking off when Voltaire became otherwise engaged, with the French blockade and with his sheer unaffected panic at the appalling consequences threatened by the Le Jeune affair in December 1766 and early 1767. In one small incident[17] Voltaire faced exposure from which no influential friends could protect him and which could have forced the authorities to apply the full rigours of the law against him. The prospect of being forced to seek refuge outside France and Geneva, the economic consequences of the French blockade of the Genevese on life at Ferney, his moves over Sirven whose departure for Paris appeared imminent and his involvement both with the *natifs* of Geneva and with the production of his play *Les Scythes* by an amateur troupe at Ferney . . . all these are in themselves enough to explain the failure to complete a philosophical tale at that time . . . and we have omitted any mention of the other works he may have been writing.

It is possible to move beyond mere hypothesis, however, and to offer a closer view of the composition of *L'Ingénu* and investigate its ultimate purposes by a closer review of its themes.

L'Ingénu *and the civil rights of the French Protestants*

The connection between *L'Ingénu* and the French Protestant cause has so far escaped critics, although comment has been made on the significance of the 1689 dating and on the fact that the Ingénu is made to pass through Saumur, four years after the Edict of Nantes had been revoked in 1685. What has remained unknown is that, as the culmination of a long series of high-level contacts between Protestant leaders and the authorities, and influenced by enlightened moves on the part of a number of *parlementaires* and ministers of state, France finally made the first tentative moves to grant Protestants limited civil rights and a relief from persecution in October 1767.

There had been a succession of *initiatives* by Protestants before

[17] A contraband load of clandestine publications was seized by French officials in the luggage of a guest leaving Ferney. It contained 'beaucoup d'exemplaires de Freret, de Dumarsay, de Boulanger, de Bolingbroke, de la Metrie, des letters de Covelle sur les miracles, de dictionnaires philosophiques, des testaments du curé Mêlier; le vicaire savoyard de Rousseau et[a] et[a]'. (Best. 12876.)

1767. The respected figure of Paul Rabaut, the senior pastor of the 'desert' church, had met the marquis de Paulmy in 1752, the prince de Conti in 1755 and the duc de Fitzjames in 1762 to suggest possible terms for a settlement. These were by no means formal negotiations, authorised by the crown, but the prince de Conti was a prince of the blood and perhaps the most influential nobleman in France. The question of Protestant marriages and freedom of worship was discussed between the prince and Rabaut on 11 April 1755. The discussion with the duc de Fitzjames, who was *commandant* of Languedoc—a province with a high proportion of Protestants in the population—was clearly a move in the campaign to seek an easing of restrictions and a relief from the full rigours of the laws against the Protestants.[18]

Two major studies were made by non-Protestants in official positions of the economic and legal consequences of such relaxations, the one by Ripert de Monclar,[19] the *procureur général* of the parlement of Aix-en-Provence, and the other hitherto largely unknown, by the *conseiller d'état*, Gilbert de Voisins, working on secret orders from Louis XV, and whose report was entitled: *Mémoires sur les moyens De Donner aux Protestans un état civil en France. Composé de l'ordre du Roi Louis XV. Par feu M. Gilbert de Voisins; Conseiller d'état.* Although this latter was not published until 1787, it was probably submitted in the early months of 1767, or late 1766.[20] Whilst Ripert de Monclar's venture appears to have been a private *initiative*, Gilbert, who was one of the most distinguished state officials of his day, was instructed by the king himself to make a confidential report, based on the advice of provincial *commandants*. It was read in secret session of a sub-committee of the *Conseil du roi*, and so secret did it remain that Malesherbes himself was unable to obtain a copy when preparing his *Premier mémoire sur les protestans* in 1785–86.

The report by Gilbert stated that, despite the Revocation of

[18] On the Protestant question, see in particular: Émile Léonard, *Histoire du protestantisme*, 2e édition (Paris, P.U.F., 1963), passim; Charles Coquerel, *Histoire des églises du désert* . . . (Paris 1841); G. de Félice, *Histoire des protestants de France* (Paris 1850 and 1856); *Paul Rabaut, ses lettres à divers* (1744–94) (Paris, Fayard, 1961).

[19] Jean Pierre François de Ripert marquis de Monclar, *Mémoire théologique et politique au sujet des mariages clandestins des protestans de France* ([s.l.] 1755).

[20] On the date of Gilbert's report, see Charles Coquerel, *op. cit.*, ii. 458; British Museum copy of the report is 110g52.

1685, and the further measures of 1724, Protestantism had not been eradicated, that emigration of the population continued together with open flouting of the law, which was thereby brought into disrepute, together with the authority of the crown. There was statistical chaos, moreover, since the absence of baptismal records meant that there were no official figures for the size of the protestant population. There remained, moreover, a risk of sedition which could destroy the peace of the realm. Gilbert suggested a form of freedom which would grant a certain freedom of conscience without allowing public worship. He also recommended a compromise on marriage, which the Catholic church insisted should remain a sacrament administered by their priests. His proposals amounted to a form of 'liberté domestique et privée' with a measure of civil recognition. The civil rights question bulked far larger in the mind of the authorities than that of freedom of conscience, and such concessions as were suggested on the matter of beliefs were no doubt raised as the Protestants stubbornly refused to discuss any arrangement which did not establish their freedom to worship. The Protestants were at that time given the option of conversion to Catholicism or denial of the sacraments, including those of baptism, marriage and burial, which meant of course that marriages consecrated within their own church were officially styled 'concubinage', and the resultant children were refused the right to inherit and subject to abduction at the age of eight to be brought up as Catholics. Whilst some of these penalties were not imposed by the more tolerant local *commandants*, the persecution of those found harbouring ministers, attending worship or leading worship were very severe. They normally resulted in execution or the galleys for ministers, the galleys for male worshippers, imprisonment for womenfolk and confiscation of half one's property, the remaining half rarely being recoverable. The major obstacle to relief for the Protestants was of course the Catholic church, which still required the king, at his coronation, to swear an oath to extirpate heresy. To grant freedom for the public practice of heresy was 'unthinkable', as also the public recognition of a form of civil marriage.

The pragmatic, partial recognition of the Protestants recommended by Gilbert de Voisins was the latest in a succession of measures proposed by such enlightened persons as Élie de Beaumont[21] and Joseph Michel Antoine Servan, of the *parlement de Grenoble*.[22] Gilbert's proposals stand out, however, as the first to have achieved any success.

No news of the Gilbert de Voisins memoir is known to have leaked out to the French Protestants, and in fact their information on the subject was limited to indirect rumours of legislative moves in their favour pending in the *conseil*. We must assume, though without confirmation, that these moves followed the presentation of the Gilbert report. The lack of any information through 'official' channels is apparent from a letter of 16 May 1767, in which Rabaut wrote: 'Les nouvelles qu'on débite sont fort hasardées. On ne peut y faire aucun fonds. Mes correspondances de Paris m'en auraient appris quelque chose, s'il était vrai qu'on voulût, comme en le débite, rétablir l'édit de Nantes. Il paraît que ces nouvelles ont pour but de faire peur au pape, . . . Je ne doute pourtant pas que le gouvernement n'ait de bonnes intentions à notre égard, mais nous ignorons jusqu'où elles vont et quand il les manifestera.'[23]

There are a number of indications that the Gilbert memoir was in fact presented about 1767, though nothing definite has been discovered to corroborate this. We learn from the published version[24] that they had been written some '80' years after the revocation of the Edict of Nantes in 1685, which would place them not long after 1765, and Charles Coquerel notes that: 'des signes certains permettent de rapporter la composition de ces mémoires à l'année 1767'.[25] Whatever the exact date, it is probable that the first major legislative move in favour of the French Protestants since 1685 would have followed quite soon after the submission of Gilbert's report, which had many of the elements of the British royal commission of today.

On 30 October 1767, the *Conseil du roi* debated two motions, the one to allow Protestants freedom to practise their trade or

[21] He had published a memoir on Protestant marriages: *Question sur la légitimité du mariage des protestans françois célébré hors du royaume* ([Paris] 1764). Rabaut de Saint-Étienne opposed the undertaking of a new memoir on this subject (letter to Court de Gebelin, 25 April 1767, Paris Bibl. Soc. d'hist. du protestantisme français, Ms. 366 no. 10) on grounds that Élie de Beaumont's was excellent and could be reprinted.

[22] *Discours sur l'administration de la justice criminelle* (Genève [1766]) and *Discours . . . dans la cause d'une femme protestante* (Genève &c. 1767).

[23] Rabaut to Jean Pradel, apud *Paul Rabaut, ses lettres à divers*, *op. cit.*, ii. 69-70.

[24] (Paris 1787), p. 80.

[25] Charles Coquerel, *op. cit.*, ii. 458.

profession and the second to sanction a legal form of marriage for the use of Protestants. The first of these was passed as: 'Arrest du Conseil d'état du roi, qui règle ce qui doit être observé par tous ceux qui exercent ou voudront exercer dans toutes les Villes du Royaume, autres que celle de Paris . . . des Professions de Commerce, Arts et Métiers qui ne sont point établis en jurande . . .'

No explicit mention was made of the Protestants in the edict, to avoid offending the Catholic church, to avoid loss of face and also because the measures applied to all non-Catholics, including Jews, and not merely Protestants. The second proposal, to legitimise non-Catholic marriages, was finally defeated after being debated on four separate occasions. Some of the details of these edicts and of the reasons for the second being defeated emerge from Voltaire's letters of the time. He wrote to Damilaville in Paris on 27 November 1767: 'Vous ne me parlez point des nouveaux édits en faveur des négociants et des artisans. Il me semble qu'ils font beaucoup d'honneur au ministère. C'est en quelque façon casser la révocation de l'édit de Nantes avec tous les ménagements possibles.' (Best. 13642.) He requested a copy of the *édits* from Marin on the same day (Best. 13643) and had his first report of the outcome of the meeting by the 2 December (Best. 13654). Fuller reports were not long in reaching him, and he could state, on 18 December that: 'On a déjà donné deux arrêts du conseil en vertu desquels tous les protestans sans être nommés peuvent exercer toutes les professions et surtout celle de négociants. L'édit pour légitimer leurs mariages a été quatre fois sur la tapis au conseil privé du roi. A la fin il n'a point passé pour ne pas choquer le clergé trop ouvertement; mais on a écrit secrètement une lettre circulaire à tous les intendants du royaume: on leur recommande de traiter les protestans avec une grande indulgence. On a supprimé et saisi tous les exemplaires d'un décret de la Sorbonne aussi insolent que ridicule contre la tolérance. . . . M. de Pomaret peut compter sur la certitude de ces nouvelles . . .' (Best. 13686). There had been a number of *Arrêtés* or *Lettres patentes* on the subject of the regulations concerning entry to the trades and professions (23 June, 12 August, 23 August 1767).

Early in 1766, Voltaire's general optimism on the spread of *philosophie* had not led him to believe that toleration was a serious possibility within his lifetime (Best. 12350). Yet events in 1766 and 1767 had turned his thoughts more and more to the general subject of toleration. He was involved, through the intermediaries of Richelieu, the duc de Nivernois and Mme de Saint-Julien, not to mention Choiseul, in negotiations with Saint-Florentin on behalf of Espinas the galley-slave and Protestant. He wrote to Richelieu: 'Vous me demanderez de quoy je me mêle de solliciter toujours pour des huguenots. C'est que je vois tous les jours ces infortunez, c'est que je vois des fammilles dispersées et sans pain, c'est que cent personnes viennent crier et pleurer chez moy et qu'il est impossible de n'en être pas ému.' (Best. 12716.) The Sirven affair had also become for Voltaire a matter on which hung French national honour and prestige (Best. 12432, 13118).

Voltaire's contacts in Russia were multiplying at this time, as he came into correspondence with Vorontsov, the Golitsuins, Shuvalov and others. He was sent a copy of Catherine's *Instructions to the commissioners for composing a new code of laws* (1767) (see Best. 12550), which expressly recommended 'une sage tolérance'. The example was not lost on him: 'Puisse la France imiter bientôt la Russie et la Pologne. L'Impératrice de Russie et le Roi de Pologne me font l'honneur de m'écrire de leur main qu'ils font tous leurs éfforts pour établir la plus grande tolérance dans leurs états.' (Best. 13138.) And again: 'Je voudrais que les Sorboniqueurs qui persécutent Marmontel aprissent que l'impératrice de Russie, les rois de Dannemarck, de Pologne et de Prusse, et la moitié des princes d'Allemagne, établissent hautement la liberté de conscience dans leurs états, et que cette liberté les enrichit.' (Best. 13151.)

These letters of March 1767 and a host of similar references elsewhere reveal a sudden revival of interest by Voltaire in toleration, but in a tone not that of hope, but of bitter frustration and anger with the French, now shamed by their continental neighbours. The matter was made even worse when the Sorbonne attacked Marmontel for his defence of toleration in his book *Bélisaire*.

The example that the *Puissances du Nord* set France was given further actuality when Hennin, the French resident in Geneva and a close friend of Voltaire, began to shape a plan for the granting of privileges for Genevese immigrants into France, of whom there were an increasing number due to the political troubles in the 'tripot de Genève'. The matter had obvious relevance to Voltaire's moves to attract settlers to Ferney (Best. 12318, 12367, etc.). There began not long afterwards the first thoughts in the Versoix project, a project which was to begin as the establishment of an entrepôt for trade to the Swiss *cantons*, and which would deprive Geneva of its traditional and lucrative function. The idea germinated in January or February 1767 (Best. 13039), and matured until, towards 1770, it emerged as a proposal to create Versoix as a town in which there would be freedom of conscience and where Protestant marriages would be legally recognised (Best. 13263, 14052, 14469, etc.). The idea was even accepted by the French authorities, but fell with its patron, Choiseul.

Yet another source of shame for the French, to Voltaire, was the generous response his Sirven appeal met with on the part of the crowned heads of Europe. His *brelan de roi quatrième* as he first called his quartet of patrons (Best. 13036) expanded rapidly to include the rulers of Russia, Poland, Prussia, Hesse-Cassel, Saxe-Gotha, Hessen-Darmstadt, Baden-Durlach, Denmark and Nassau-Saarbruck (Best. appendix 202).

By the spring of 1767 the question of toleration had become immediate, practical and a cause in which he was deeply and emotionally involved. Bitterness, exasperation and anger at France's inhumane legislation were the inevitable results of this brutal contrast with the *Puissances du Nord.* Yet if this was the case in the early spring, it was not so a little later, as his despair was dissipated by news of positive legislative measures in France itself. The extent to which this may have influenced the *Ingénu* must be determined by reference to the possible influence of the *Siècle de Louis XIV* revisions which he must have begun at about the same time, in preparation for what became the expanded 1768 edition. Clearly the *Siècle* did have some influence, but if the *Ingénu* was begun in 1766, as appears at least possible, then the influence is not as clear cut as may appear. Are we to assume the Voltaire began reading for the *Siècle* revisions in 1766, or conjecture that he began the *Ingénu* only in 1767, or that having begun the *Ingénu* in 1766, he inserted the historical references *après coup*? The *Siècle* offers no help whatsoever, as Voltaire made no significant alterations to chap. XXXVI, 'Du Calvinisme au temps de Louis XIV' for this edition, though there were a number of minor additions to the preceding chapter, entitled 'Affaires ecclésiastiques'.[26]

Yet, whether the *Siècle* itself was the inspiration or not the mere fact of choosing to alter the date from a later one to 1689 must have been made with the specific intention to refer to and attack the revocation of the Edict of Nantes, made four years before. It may be that, although the affairs of Louis XIV's reign were unquestionably alive in Voltaire's mind in 1767, the references to the revocation of 1685 were prompted by an entirely different state of affairs, namely a move by the *Conseil du roi* to partially undo this revocation and restore the Protestants in some of their former rights. If so, *L'Ingénu* is a remarkably devious and inhibited move, but despite this the evidence is such as to make it not at all unlikely.

Did Voltaire actually get wind of the Gilbert de Voisins *Mémoire*? A note to the first printed version of 1787 recorded that: 'Ce [premier] Mémoire, formé dans tout le secret qu'elle avoit prescrit, a été lu dans un comité du Conseil, où il n'a pas été désapprouvé; il a aussi été communiqué secrettement par la permission du Roi à un Prélat des plus sages & des plus éclairés de la Province de Languedoc [Loménie de Brienne] . . . & à M. le prince de Beauvau . . . A l'égard de M. le Prince de Beauvau, ses vues s'accordent, presqu'en tout avec celles qui sont présentées dans le Mémoire & vont même peut-être au-delà.'[27]

The work was known to Choiseul and to the prince de Beauvau-Craon, each of whom was in regular communication with Voltaire. The prince could have given some inkling to Voltaire of what was afoot, but we have no means of knowing. It would have been a gross breach of confidence for either to have divulged the contents of the report to Voltaire. The correspondence offers no hint, as we might expect. Voltaire states that he was forced for reasons of security to avoid the subject of toleration in letters[28] and even Choiseul's mail was not free from the attentions of the *cabinet noir*.

[26] See G. Lanson, 'Notes pour servir à l'étude des chapitres 35-39 du *Siècle de Louis XIV* de Voltaire', *Mélanges offerts à M. Charles Andler* (Strasbourg, Publications de la Faculté des Lettres de l'Université de Strasbourg, 1924).

[27] Gilbert de Voisins, *Mémoires*, pp. 80-85.

[28] See Best. 12670: 'de très tristes raisons me forcent de ne pas écrire un seul mot par la poste sur la tolérance et sur la justice qu'on fait aux hommes'; and also James Marriott's reference in Best. 12766: 'Il faut que je vous avertisse qu'on fait ouvrir vos lettres au Bureau du poste en France'.

Voltaire was to be in contact with Beauvau-Craon in 1768 on a Protestant matter (Best. 12853), however. If Voltaire probably knew nothing of the Gilbert de Voisin report, then, he certainly had it on good authority that the *Conseil du roi* intended to legislate on the Protestant problem. We have it on unimpeachable authority, in the shape of an original, dated letter that he knew on or before 24 April 1767 of he intention to bring the question of the civil rights of the French Protestants before the *Conseil du roi*, and that proposals would be made relating specifically to a form of marriage valid in law. 'Voilà deux grandes nouvelles, mon cher philosophe; voilà une espèce de persécuteurs bannie de la moitié de l'Europe,[29] et une espèce de persécutés qui peut enfin espérer de jouir des droits du genre humain, que la révérend père La Chaise et Michel Le Tellier leur a [sic] ravis.

'Il faudrait piquer d'honneur Mr De Maupeou. Je réponds bien de Mr Le Duc De Choiseul et mr Le Duc De Praslin, mais dans une affaire de législation le chancelier a toujours la voix prépondérante.' The abuse to be rectified, he continued was that: 'les Welches ne permettent pas à d'autres Welches de se marier!' (Best. 13243.)

The source of Voltaire's information cannot have been official Protestant channels, as Rabaut plainly did not have the information to pass on to Voltaire.[23] It must have come through other sources, possibly Moultou himself, possibly Choiseul. Yet whether it was obtained from an official source, or merely confirmed there, Voltaire could have learnt from one or more of a number of Paris officials, Marin for example, and he appears to have had an ear very close to the ground in Paris, to be able to assure a correspondent in December that: 'M. de Pomaret peut compter sur la certitude de ces nouvelles'. (Best. 13686.)

We do not, unfortunately, possess all the correspondence that passed between Choiseul and Voltaire in 1767. Much will have arrived by courier with the military dispatches for the French troops blockading Geneva, as being more private than the mail. It is academic to speculate on the sources of Voltaire's information, but it is of more moment to know whether or not Voltaire was the source of the reports that percolated through to the French Protestants. He knew several Protestants of Geneva who were in regular contact with Rabaut (Chirol, Moultou, Manoël de Végobre)

[29] The Jesuits had just been expelled from Spain.

and Gal-Pomaret the French pastor and would-be converter of Voltaire was in correspondence with Voltaire, even Rabaut himself at times corresponding direct. At this time, however, Voltaire corresponded with the Protestants largely through intermediaries in Geneva. If there are no unmistakable traces in the extant correspondence of Voltaire having warned the Huguenots to exercise moderation and avoid irritating the authorities, there are a number of indications that he might have done so. This had been his advice in 1763, when a similar hope had been aroused after the Calas affair (Best. 10313, 10335, etc.). Although a letter to Rabaut himself on 16 May (Best. 13291) gives no clues, Voltaire noted on 29 June to Ribote-Charron that 'tout conspire à ramener la paix et la tolérance' (Best. 13356) suggesting previous correspondence on the subject. He wrote to Moultou on 20 September: 'Je commence à croire que vous serez libres' (Best. 13531) and on 22 October Gabriel de Seigneux wrote to Voltaire to complain of provocative actions by the authorities in terms that leave no real doubt about Voltaire's rôle in the matter: 'Où est donc Mon cher Monsieur la sage et humaine tolérance dont il semblait que le Ministère eût adopté le systhème? ne voulait on que leurer les Peuples d'une vaine lueur d'espérance? et se flatoit on d'arrêter par là les émigrations? En vérité, l'on n'y conçoit rien; tandis qu'on parle de paix d'un côté, on ne cesse d'affliger de l'autre. La conduite de m^r le Prince de Beauvau et celle de M^r le Duc de Richelieu ne sont pas aisées à concilier.

'Ne pouriés vous point Monsieur faire connaître à M^r le Duc de Choiseuil les inconvéniens de ces nouvelles allarmes pour *le sage but qu'il se propose*. Se pourait-il qu'on suivît en cela *ses intentions* et *la volonté du Roy*?' (Best. 13592.)

Further corroboration on Voltaire's rôle comes in the form of tributes paid to him by the Protestants after the conclusion of the affair. The relief proved to be very slight and to make no concessions either on marriage, or on freedom of conscience. Nevertheless Rabaut wrote to Moultou on 29 February 1768: 'Si la main qui nous accablait s'est relâchée, si nous jouissons de quelque tranquillité dans notre patrie, c'est à ce grand homme que nous en sommes redevables. . . . Il est heureux pour nous que cet homme célèbre soit en liaison avec des personnes en place, dont la façon de penser peut avoir la plus grande influence sur notre sort à venir.' (Best. 13860.) The same message was echoed in September, by

Gal-Pomaret (Best. 14243, general note). Both were letters intended to be shown to Voltaire, and the former is even endorsed by him. It appears amply proven that Voltaire had urged moderation on the Protestants so as not to prejudice the legislative measures, and we might also assume that he himself was involved for a considerable part of 1767 in correspondence on the subject both with the Huguenots and with Choiseul. It would not be surprising if Choiseul himself had used Voltaire to restrain the Huguenots over this vital period. Their public declarations of their grievances and intransigence over the matter of full freedom of worship had been a contributory factor in the failure of the 1763 *initiatives* in their favour. Voltaire and Choiseul faced bigotry on either side, in attempting to set matters right.

Voltaire's insistence throughout was on the civil rights to be granted and not on any religious freedom. Influential official opinion had moved towards a very limited form of toleration for economic reasons rather than humanitarian ones, and freedom of conscience was acceptable to very few indeed.[30] Voltaire was determined in this, as in most questions, not by the ideal but by what was attainable, given the state of public and government opinion. As a pragmatist, he looked forward to the limited objective of certain civil rights being extended to non-Catholics and little more. Slight though this was, it was the first official move by the authorities to better the condition of the Protestants since 1685 and its importance was out of all proportion to the actual rights they were to gain.

It remains to be seen whether these hitherto ignored links with protestant affairs in 1767 may be seen to have influenced *L'Ingénu* in any way.

The Protestants were not alone on being able to prejudice, by an indiscretion, the moves in their favour. Voltaire would know that any published contribution could mobilise and harden the opposition. His approach would have to be devious, with the problems being touched on in a general and not a specific manner. We cannot, therefore, seriously expect to find indisputable evidence in the text of *L'Ingénu*. On the other hand, as the proposed legislation was known to Voltaire by 24 April 1767, it is hardly possible

[30] 'Il paraît que le conseil cherche bien plus à favoriser le commerce et la population du royaume qu'à persécuter des idiots qui aiment la prêche et qui ne peuvent plus nuire.' (Best. 13622.)

that a work with a precise dating in 1689, and completed between May and July 1767 would not have had some connection with the moves. Voltaire had already suggested such a work, for a very similar purpose, in October or November of the previous year; and proposed a work 'qui pût se faire lire avec quelque plaisir, par les gens qui n'aiment point à lire, et qui portât les cœurs à la compassion'. (Best. 12753.) He had also suggested in 1763, for an exactly similar purpose, a witty propagandist work and not a weary tome: 'il faut être très court et un peu salé, sans quoi les ministres et mad^e de Pompadour, les Commis et les femmes de Chambre, font des papillotes du livre'. (Best. 10071.)

The idea had occurred to him in 1766, the method was one he was persuaded was effective, moreover his other works of these same months all show a concern for toleration. Whilst some of these, admittedly, do so from an angle traditional in Voltaire, and others reflect Catherine's moves in Russia, it is important to note that the link between toleration and legislation occurs in the *Lettre sur les Panégyriques* (M. xxvi. 311), and in the *Fragment des Instructions pour le prince royal de **** (M. xxvi. 443-444). The first edition of the latter also appeared in a *pot-pourri* including *De la Liberté de conscience*, since included in the *Dictionnaire philosophique* (M. xviii. 238).

References in the text are actually few, but could not, as has been said, have been explicit without prejudice to the goose which was to lay the golden egg. A Huguenot had taught the Ingénu French (p. 4), a Jesuit asks whether he is a Huguenot (p. 35), chap. VIII is devoted to table-talk with Huguenots in Saumur, and the Ingénu is later arrested as a Huguenot sympathiser and enemy of the Jesuit order. The Saumur episode is none the less very important, since it goes beyond the usual list of the economic consequences of the revocation of the Edict of Nantes and the evocation of the human misery caused, and it emphasises the view that the revocation had been a political error, the result of bad advice by the Jesuit advisers of Louis XIV, and a step which Louis XIV did not have the power to carry out (p. 22). There then comes a statement which takes on an entirely new light if we now accept that Voltaire knew of legislative moves to undo some of the damage caused by the revocation: the Ingénu leaves for Versailles, overcome by the misery of the Protestants and says: 'Je verrai le roi. Je lui ferai connaître la vérité;

il est impossible qu'on ne se rende pas à cette vérité quand on la sent' (p. 23).

The person of Louis XIV has been whitewashed, the blame being placed fairly and squarely upon his advisers the Jesuits, who in 1767 have become the whipping boys of Europe. With them cast as scapegoats, the scene is set for a graceful *volte-face* by the *Conseil du roi*.

The tribute to Choiseul (p. 52) may also take on a different hue, since the ideal minister whom everyone recognised as Choiseul[31] is basically an anti-Louvois, a man whose nature is 'incompatible avec la cruauté'. Whatever the verdict on the value or efficacy of such a contribution to the cause, it remains a fact that Voltaire's firm and constantly reiterated belief was that the privy council and persons in positions of influence were more effective converts than the public at large. The *Traité sur la tolérance* of 1763 had been conceived with an eye to its effect on ministers and members of the court. However gauche, could *L'Ingénu* have had something of the same orientation?

The unknown factor is, of course, the date at which the Saumur episode entered the text—were this to be known, together with the time at which the date-setting was introduced, many difficulties would be solved. Nevertheless, it would seem as if the legislative measures in favour of the French Protestants do form a definite influence in this *conte*. The only question remaining—and it is a vital one—is how important, or how central this influence was. Let us look, for an answer, at the political themes which merge with the religious.

L'Ingénu *and the freedom of the individual within the state*

Many specific references have been traced in the *Ingénu*, and no doubt most of these have some element of truth. We have ourselves raised yet another which we believe to have rather more importance than many others, that of the civil rights of Protestants. Yet Voltaire's *contes* raise themselves above the particular to the general statement and the same is true in the case of *L'Ingénu*. There may be reminiscences of certain individuals, of the *causes célèbres* that Voltaire himself took up, there may even be portraits that have

[31] Grimm, *Correspondance littéraire*, vii. 409: 'tout le monde y a reconnu M. le duc de Choiseul'.

been claimed to be allegorical—yet the *conte* itself transcends the individual circumstance and it sees Protestant affairs, like the many political or juridical affairs, in a much wider context. There appears to be a case for seeing *L'Ingénu*, as one of the clearest statements of Voltaire's political beliefs since the *Lettres philosophiques* of 1734.

Voltaire's position in 1734 had been the frustrating one of admiring the English constitution and yet finding it inapplicable to French conditions. The French lacked the necessary social structure, with a middle class (Voltaire's 'peuple') inarticulate, immature, and economically backward by comparison with the English bourgeoisie. Nor had it, as a class, achieved anything of a consciousness of identity. The only contenders for the rôle of constitutional check on the powers of the monarch were in fact the *parlements* and these, with their allies in the *noblesse d'épée*, could claim no powers to represent the *Tiers état*. They in fact represented a sectional interest which was economically, financially, and socially reactionary. Whatever Voltaire's preoccupation with their rôle as custodians of Justice, it by no means blinded him to the fact that their constitutional pretensions were potentially even more dangerous. In the years after 1734, Voltaire's thinking evolved considerably, principally in that it incorporated an economic, financial and historical expertise, and that it benefited from an increasing knowledge of the industrial, agricultural and social structure of the nation, weighing and assessing the various schools of thought on physiocratic, free-trade principles and bringing to bear on his opinions gifts that were unusual. These included the ability to see beyond the immediate issues of the conflict between the crown and *parlements*, a historical perspective possessed by very few in his day and a knowledge of European affairs which few could rival. He was without doubt one of the best informed observers of the French political scene of his day.

Voltaire refused to accept either the *parlements* or the crown as upholders of the ideal. He rejected outright the *parlements*' case, but he accepted that of the crown, as it then stood, only as a *pis aller*. Rousseau, whatever else may be said, was the man who defined the political ideals of the nineteenth century. In much the same way Voltaire cannot be fitted into any recognisable political system of his own day but effectively defined the political ideals of his own century, or at least those of the most enlightened proponents of the absolutist system and the 'liberalism' that inspired many opponents of absolutism. Typically succinct, Theodore Besterman has called Voltaire 'one of the pioneers of pragmatism'.[32] He would, I know, be one of the first to agree that the view of politics as the art of the possible is quite consistent with a corpus of political ideals against which events are measured. *L'Ingénu* comes closer than any other *conte* by Voltaire to a definition of Voltaire's political ideals and to his definition of the 'ideal' monarchy. It is, therefore, an important document in assessing Voltaire's exact standpoint in his later, open support of the royalist case against the *parlements*' obduracy, when Maupeou began his campaign to cut the *parlements* down to size.

What the *Ingénu* does *not* discuss is as revealing as what it does. It makes no mention whatsoever of the fundamental constitutional issue of the period, which was the clash between the crown and the reactionary elements which largely dominated the *parlements*. This is all the more surprising in that it had come to a head the year before, at the *séance de flagellation* (1766). Nor does it make any mention of the French system of justice, or of the *causes célèbres* (Calas, Sirven, La Barre, Lally-Tollendal, La Bourdonnais, etc.) except in the most general way. The fundamental fact about the imprisonment of both the Ingénu and Gordon the Jansenist[33] is that neither was imprisoned by the courts but had been denied access to these normal processes of justice. What echoes there are of the *causes célèbres* in the character of the Ingénu himself are to stimulate the imagination of the public of the day, and not to focus it precisely. It is worth remembering Gordon's words: 'le père La Chaise a obtenu du roi, son pénitent, un ordre de me ravir, sans aucune formalité de justice, le bien le plus précieux des hommes, la liberté.' (p. 27.)

[32] Theodore Besterman, 'Voltaire, absolute monarchy, and the enlightened monarch', *Studies on Voltaire* (1965), xxxii. 14.

[33] It could be noted *en passant* that Gordon's *The Independent Whig* had recently appeared in French, entitled, *L'Esprit du clergé* (Grimm, *Correspondance littéraire*, vii. 387). Voltaire knew of the work (see Best. 13536). If the prisoner named Gordon who was discovered in the Bastille by Young in 1753 had really been there for 30 years, then he would have been in prison there, during Voltaire's stay in 1726. Funck-Brentano, *Les Lettres de cachet à Paris* (Paris 1903), p. 143, notes a Jacques Gordon 'gentilhomme écossais, Entré le 18 novembre 1704, espionnage. Sorti le 27 novembre 1704'. This clashes with Young's statement. See *L'Ingénu*, pp. 120-121.

He had been imprisoned by *lettre de cachet*, as was the Ingénu. Yet even here we must beware of too narrow an interpretation, by limiting the application of the tale to this single abuse, however relevant at this precise time.[34] The use of these *lettres* had gradually become a police matter, an administrative convenience, and had ceased to be under the strict control of the *ministre de la maison du roy*. The tale is directed not against the courts, nor purely against the *lettres de cachet*, but against the dangers to personal liberty inherent in the absolutist system of the day and in its apparent contempt for the law and for the individual. The refrain runs right through the comments on the imprisonment of the Ingénu: 'Il n'y a donc pas de lois dans ce pays! On condamne les hommes sans les entendre! Il n'en est pas ainsi en Angleterre (p. 38) . . . Hélas! Monsieur, on est donc bien libéral de lettres de cachet dans vos bureaux, . . . Je respecte la liberté des hommes (p. 40) . . . le caractère des grands et des demi-grands, qui sacrifient si légèrement la liberté des hommes . . .' (p. 41).

L'Ingénu is a study in the disintegration or erosion of the ideal of Justice and Liberty under an absolutist regime. Yet it is not through tyrannical behaviour on the part of the monarch, but, paradoxically, through insufficient central control. Voltaire is attacking the corruption, venality, callousness, greed, arbitrariness, arrogance and expediency of an administrative machine which has been freed from adequate control from above, and which remains free from criticism from below. It is the tragedy of the 'absent king' unattainable, remote, uninformed and insulated from reality except through his corrupt intermediaries. It is the failure of this king to guard against improper influences and the irony of this impersonal tyranny is that it arises, not, as we have said from the one man but from the many, from an administrative, governmental machine, Kafka-esque in its invulnerability to criticism and attack. The king is charged not with viciousness, but with inertia, and the soulless machine of government is like the Paris Voltaire describes in the story (p. 34) as: 'un vaste labyrinthe, sans fil et sans issue'.

Against this corrupt machine, law is impotent, the individual

[34] Funck-Brentano, p. xli, quotes Malesherbes in 1770 as writing: 'Aujourdhui ces ordres sont prodigieusement multipliés . . . Il en résulte, Sire, qu'aucun citoyen dans votre royaume n'est assuré de ne pas voir sa liberté sacrifiée à une vengeance: car personne n'est assez grand pour être à l'abri de la haine d'un ministre, ni assez petit pour n'être pas digne de celle d'un commis des fermes.'

helpless. It is this *inefficacy* of the law that Voltaire attacks, together with the power granted to the ministers and their underlings to dispense justice outside the proper courts of justice, and by favour instead of by right. Added to this is the readiness of men in general to lend themselves, to aid and abet this evil (p. 50), and the frivolity with which the French abandon the substance of liberty for the shadow of the freedom to unburden at table and in conversation (p. 51).

The crown, which is pictured here in this inert image of Louis XV rather than in the vigorous image of Frederick II, is attacked only incidentally for its supreme irrelevance and remoteness, except in so far as it is to the crown that we look for the clock to be set back to before the revocation of the Edict of Nantes (p. 23). Yet the inference is that Voltaire looks to the prince to restore respect for the individual and for the rule of law. He wastes no time, here, on the English constitutional patterns, as they are not a practical alternative in France.

Considerably less attention is paid to the sovereign, however, than to the ideal minister, and it is here that the major ray of hope emerges in a depressing political picture. Choiseul is set up as the archetype of the enlightened minister. His eulogy (pp. 51-52) is far from being naïve adulation, however. It occurs at the height of a discussion of the principle of freedom and stands as a symbol of Voltaire's hope for an uncorrupt, reforming administration, the precise opposite to that of Louvois in more than one respect. The opposition is pointed in the reference to Choiseul's freedom from 'la cruauté' (p. 52).

Voltaire was writing, at about this time, his prescription for the ideal monarch in the *Fragment des Instructions pour le prince royal de* ***, and here, as in *L'Ingénu*, the insistence is on the need for the rule of law, and for a law simple, unified and fair, which will respect the rights of the individual (M. xxvi. 444).

For Voltaire, who had no illusions on *parlement* or king, the only hope for France lay in the emergence and strengthening of enlightened elements in the councils which advised the king. It is not naïve optimism, but the pragmatism of the social pessimist. All the abuses raised are those within the absolutist regime, and yet Voltaire does not fly, as did nearly all the Paris *philosophes*, to the *thèse nobiliaire* as a panacea. Instead he stated the conditions which were the prerequisite of an enlightened absolutist system: government in accordance with the law, respect for the freedom of the individual within the law, and a gradual reform of the body of law itself.

Many of the conclusions offered in this essay have necessarily been tentative and the evidence adduced has at times been circumstantial. Yet the whole builds into a case which is rather more than a mere hypothesis and which has the advantage of offering some explanation for the halting construction of the tale and for the gradual abandonment by Voltaire of the plan laid down in his original draft. It seems highly probable that the first part of the tale was composed in the closing months of 1766, following very broadly the existing draft and the usual *conte* style and tradition. On composition being resumed in the spring of 1767, Voltaire's intentions were substantially modified, and his earlier, more specific causes of anger had become assimilated into a mounting indignation against the corrupt regime of which they were in fact symptomatic. However, in this picture of a generalised contempt for justice and for the rights of the subject a symbol of hope appeared in the figure of the enlightened minister, the means of the restoration of respect for the sanctity of the individual and for liberty within the law. Emerging from this is a profound conviction of the ultimate value and dignity of the cultured, formed individual, the prototype of the Liberal. There can be little doubt that a distinct Protestant theme underlies the tale, or became absorbed into it, in the course of composition. Yet it has been absorbed into its true place in a general commentary on the individual in an absolutist state.

The aesthetic transformation within the tale appears, therefore, to be a result of interruptions in its composition and of substantial changes in Voltaire's intentions as he wrote it. It is the product of both a deep social and political pessimism, and yet, paradoxically, of a note of new hope arising from the prospect of the first enlightened moves in favour of the Protestants since 1685.

This transformation is multiple. From scything wit, fantasy and irony—the habitual mask of feeling for the *conteur*—Voltaire has slipped over the brink into commitment and the rôle of dramatist he knew so well. From the *conte*'s usual parody of the *roman*, the tale moves to an emotional intensity which Voltaire claimed to be deeper and more sincere than the 'romans nouveaux' (p. 39). From being mere puppets the characters become persons of stature and maturity, poise and dignity. The only satisfactory explanation of this is that sheer involvement and depth of feeling on the part of Voltaire broke the mastery of mood which had always been the hallmark of the *conte*, a detachment all the harder to preserve, given the immediacy of the issues at the time of writing and the limitations imposed by a historical subject.[35]

[35] I have been greatly indebted for the courteous and kind help received from M. le pasteur Henri Bosc, curator of the *Bibliothèque de la Société de l'histoire du protestantisme français*, where I was granted free access to manuscript material. The work was considerably helped by a grant awarded from the Sir Ernest Cassel Educational Trust fund in 1965, for which I wish to express my appreciation.

Voltaire et le peuple

Roland Mortier

L'attitude de Voltaire devant les masses populaires n'a jamais fait, à notre connaissance, l'objet d'une étude spécifique. La plupart des critiques ont évité ce sujet avec une étrange réserve ou ne l'ont abordé qu'avec réticence, en couvrant Voltaire d'excuses et de justifications. Les autres, comme Faguet, ont cru pouvoir tirer de deux ou trois citations adroitement rapprochées la preuve de ses contradictions et de l'inconsistance de sa pensée politique.[1] Le silence ou la gêne des uns, le triomphe bruyant des autres s'expliquent sans peine. Assurément, Voltaire n'avait rien d'un démocrate, au sens moderne du mot,[2] mais de combien de penseurs du XVIIIe siècle pourrait-on dire le contraire? Rousseau lui-même n'hésite pas à écrire: 'A prendre le terme dans la rigueur de l'acception, il n'a jamais existé de véritable démocratie et il n'en existera jamais. . . . S'il y avait un peuple de dieux, il se gouvernerait démocratiquement. Un gouvernement si parfait ne convient pas à des hommes.' Du moins Rousseau est-il républicain et partisan de la souveraineté populaire, mais l'écrasante majorité des écrivains politiques, de Montesquieu aux physiocrates, s'accorde à exclure les masses

[1] E. Faguet, *La Politique comparée de Montesquieu, Rousseau et Voltaire* (Paris 1902), pp. 78, n. 1, 80 ('il ne s'est jamais assez surveillé pour ne point tomber dans les contradictions') et 83 ('Voltaire n'est rien moins que systématique dans ses idées politiques et peut être accusé même de les avoir eues quelque peu flottantes'). Ce jugement se fonde sur la comparaison de trois lettres: à Damilaville, Best. 12358 (1er avril 1766); à Linguet, Best. 13143 (15 mars 1767); et à La Chalotais, Best. 10238 (28 février 1763); il ne touche pas réellement au fond du problème.

[2] De là à qualifier l'ancienne victime du chevalier de Rohan d''aristocrate . . . par désir de fonder (l'autorité souveraine) sur l'ignorance populaire . . . par passion de maintenir une énorme distance entre le peuple et les hautes classes' (Faguet, p. 78) il y a une marge que seules la distorsion des textes et une hostilité de principe permettent d'ignorer.

populaires de la gestion publique et à réserver celle-ci aux seuls propriétaires. Mably n'a que mépris pour le peuple, 'cette lie de l'humanité . . . destinée à servir de lest au vaisseau de la société' et d'Holbach, si radical à d'autres égards, est persuadé que 'c'est la propriété qui fait le citoyen' (*Encyclopédie*, art. 'Représentants'; 'Éthocratie', ii. 16). Dès lors, pourquoi glisser pudiquement sur certaines phrases de Voltaire, pourquoi aussi vouloir en tirer des conclusions abusives et faciles?

La pensée voltairienne constitue un ensemble cohérent et solide, à condition de la voir dans son ensemble et dans sa vraie perspective. En ignorer certains aspects fondamentaux serait la preuve d'une déférence mal inspirée. En isoler quelques formules brillantes et amères serait plus tendancieux encore, et nous laisserait sur l'image d'un Voltaire grimaçant et caricatural.[3] Reste donc à ouvrir le dossier et à retourner aux textes, mais à tous les textes ou du moins à un choix très largement représentatif. On évitera ainsi de tomber dans les simplifications outrancières d'un Faguet, tout en rompant le pieux silence d'un Barni (*Histoire des idées morales et politiques en France au XVIIIe siècle*, Paris 1865), trop soucieux de ne pas ternir l'image d'un Voltaire humaniste libéral pour faire un sort à cette question gênante. Récemment encore, un exégète voltairien s'inquiétait en constatant que certaines déclarations de Voltaire pourraient le rendre suspect 'aux yeux des critiques marxistes qui y verront la marque d'un historien de classe, de la classe bourgeoise'[4] et il s'empressait de conclure sur ce point en affirmant: 'il ne faut donc pas exagérer le mépris de Voltaire pour le peuple.'[5]

L'examen attentif des nombreux textes répartis sur un demi-siècle nous prouve que le problème est loin d'être simple et qu'il s'accommode mal d'une réponse en noir ou blanc. Surtout, il n'est pas fondamentalement politique en dernière analyse. L'attitude de Voltaire envers le peuple s'inspire de considérations sociales, philosophiques, éducatives, mais avant tout économiques et religieuses

[3] Nous aimerions reprendre à notre compte deux remarques excellentes de R. Pomeau: 'la pensée de Voltaire n'est . . . pas aussi courte que le donnerait à croire un groupement de textes partiel et partial' et 'il serait . . . injuste de s'en tenir aux textes où l'humeur voltairienne rétrécit comiquement le débat' (*La Religion de Voltaire*, pp. 393-394).

[4] Voir e.a. l'étude de J. Varloot sur 'Voltaire et le matérialisme' dans *Europe* (mai-juin 1959), pp. 73-74.

[5] Ch. Rihs, *Voltaire. Recherches sur les origines du matérialisme historique* (Genéve, Droz, 1962), p. 138 n. 310 et p. 140.

dont on ne saurait faire fi sans la trahir. C'est ce que trop de commentateurs ont oublié, tout comme on a négligé de vérifier quel sens Voltaire accordait au mot 'peuple' et quelles distinctions il y établissait.

Il n'y a pas lieu de s'attarder beaucoup aux textes où le concept de *peuple* se confond avec celui de masse flottante et versatile, la *turba* dont parle Sénèque, et qui ne s'identifie pas nécessairement avec la *plebs*. Ce point de vue remonte aux stoïciens, et plus haut sans doute; il imprègne la pensée des 'libertins' du XVIIe siècle qui se veulent, selon le P. Garasse, des 'esprits transcendans' (Naudé compare la 'populace' au caméléon ou à 'la sentine et cloaque dans laquelle coulent toutes les ordures de la maison'). Il est typique d'un groupe minoritaire, mais éclairé, qui se tient pour 'déniaisé' et n'a que mépris pour les erreurs du vulgaire. En ce sens, c'est aussi l'attitude de Diderot.[6]

Dans *Brutus*, Messala traite avec dédain 'l'erreur des peuples imbéciles' et réclame un chef 'dont le nom seul impose à ce peuple volage' (I, 4; M. iii. 336), Ce reproche d'inconstance reparaît dans une variante au texte de *Mariamne* (III, 3; M. ii. 221), où Varus déclare à Hérode:

> Vous connaissez le peuple: on le change en un jour;
> Il prodigue aisément sa haine et son amour.
> Si la rigueur l'aigrit, la clémence l'attire.

vers qui se retrouvent presque mot-à-mot dans *La Mort de César* (I, 4; M. iii. 330):

> Je sais quel est le peuple: on le change en un jour;
> Il prodigue aisément sa haine et son amour.
> Si ma grandeur l'aigrit, ma clémence l'attire.

Dans la même pièce, Brutus dit à Cassius (II, 4; M. iii. 338):

> Ce peuple mou, volage, et facile à fléchir
> Ne sait s'il doit encor l'aimer ou le haïr.

Une note du *Traité sur la tolérance* (Chap. VIII, M. xxv. 46) reprend la même idée:

[6] Cf. notre article sur 'Diderot et la notion de "peuple" ', dans *Europe* (janvier–février 1963), pp. 78-88.

> Tacite, qui connaît si bien le naturel des princes, devait connaître aussi celui du peuple, toujours vain, toujours outré dans ses opinions violentes et passagères, incapable de rien voir, et capable de tout dire, de tout croire, et de tout oublier.

Ailleurs, la critique porte plutôt sur l'ignorance et la superstition des foules. Hermogide, parlant à Ériphyle dans la pièce du même nom (M. ii. 477), déclare:

> Pour qui ne les craint point, il n'est point de prodiges;
> Ils sont l'appât grossier des peuples ignorants . . .
> Pensez en roi, Madame, et laissez au vulgaire
> Des superstitions le joug imaginaire.

Mais ce sont là des lieux communs qui ne permettent aucune conclusion sur la pensée profonde de Voltaire.[7] Son inquiétude devant le peuple vient d'ailleurs, et tout d'abord de sa longue réflexion sur l'histoire des hommes, passée et présente.

L'abondante documentation que Voltaire a recueillie, en vue de *La Henriade*, puis de ses ouvrages historiques, l'a amené à la conclusion désolante que les masses populaires sont la proie facile de la superstition et du fanatisme, mais aussi qu'elles sont capables des atrocités les plus révoltantes et des crimes les plus inhumains. La 'populace', comme l'appelle Voltaire, va d'instinct aux formes les plus basses du sentiment religieux et sympathise spontanément avec la partie la plus rétrograde du clergé.[8] Voltaire ne cessera de rappeler aux rois que ces masses fanatisées et aveugles sont le pire danger pour l'État, pour l'autorité royale et pour le progrès de la pensée. L'inquiétude, encore diffuse dans *La Henriade*, éclate dans l'*Essai sur les mœurs* où elle se nuance parfois d'une sorte d'horreur.

[7] Ces textes n'ont pas été suffisamment exploités dans la seule étude consacrée à la question, 'The People in eighteenth-century tragedy from *Œdipe* to *Guillaume Tell*', par J. Van Eerde (*Studies on Voltaire and the eighteenth century*, xxvii. 1703–13).

[8] Cf. *Le Pauvre Diable*, 'le peuple est l'âne, et le moine est le singe' (M. x. 102); lettres à d'Alembert (4 juin 1769, Best. 14699): 'un capucin prêchant à Saint-Roch a plus de crédit sur le peuple que tous les gens de bon sens n'en auront jamais'; à d'Argental (20 avril 1769, Best. 14626): 'un cordelier véhément . . .', à Condorcet (27 janvier 1776, Best. 18750): 'Il y a une autre canaille à laquelle on sacrifie tout; et cette canaille est le peuple . . . c'est pour elle qu'on va à la Messe . . . qu'on rend le pain béni . . . qu'on a condamné le chevalier de La Barre.'

Songeant aux excès de la Ligue, il fait dire au bon roi Henri (M. viii. 67):

> Vous connaissez le peuple, et savez ce qu'il ose
> Quand, du ciel outragé pensant venger la cause,
> Les yeux ceints du bandeau de la religion,
> Il a rompu le frein de la soumission (Chap. II).

Ailleurs, il avertit les rois du danger de subversion qui les menace en leur rappelant les théories politiques des Ligueurs (M. viii. 163-variante de l'éd. de 1723):

> Partout on entendait cette fatale voix,
> Que le peuple en tout temps est souverain des rois.
> Ces maximes alors, en malheurs si fécondes,
> Jetaient dans les esprits des racines profondes (Chap. IX).

Dans *Le Siècle de Louis XIV* (Chap. XXXVII, 'Du jansénisme', M. xv. 62), il ironise sur les prétendus miracles du diacre Pâris, puis se ravise et en tire la leçon à l'usage de ses contemporains. De telles absurdités restent possibles. 'La religion peut encore aiguiser les poignards. Il y a toujours, dans la nation, un peuple qui n'a nul commerce avec les honnêtes gens, qui n'est pas du siècle, et sur qui l'atrocité du fanatisme conserve son empire comme certaines maladies qui n'attaquent que la plus vile populace'. N'avait-il pas écrit plus haut que 'la populace est presque partout la même'? (Chap. X, M. xiv. 257-258).

Mais c'est dans l'*Essai sur les mœurs* que les accents de dégoût et d'horreur se multiplient, soutenus par un foisonnement d'exemples. L'histoire, pour Voltaire, n'est qu'une longue succession d'erreurs, de préjugés, de cruautés et de crimes. Les masses, laissées à elles-mêmes, retournent aussitôt aux instincts les plus barbares: il n'en veut pour preuve que les violences infligées aux frères de Witt, ou les scènes de cannibalisme qui firent suite à l'assassinat de Concini:

> La populace, toujours extrême, toujours barbare, quand on lui lâche la bride, va déterrer le corps de Concini, inhumé à Saint-Germain-l'Auxerrois, le traîne dans les rues, lui arrache le cœur; et il se trouva des hommes assez brutaux pour le griller publiquement sur des charbons, et pour le manger.
>
> (Chap. CLXXV, M. xii. 576)

Ce même peuple n'a cessé de freiner le progrès et de faire obstacle aux rois les plus éclairés. Voltaire rappelle le triste sort de l'empereur Henri IV, humilié par Grégoire VII, et il s'exclame, s'adressant directement aux rois de son temps:

'Arrêtez-vous un moment près du cadavre exhumé de ce célèbre empereur Henri IV, plus malheureux que notre Henri IV, roi de France. Cherchez d'où viennent tant d'humiliations et d'infortunes d'un côté, tant d'audace de l'autre, tant de choses horribles réputées sacrées, tant de princes immolés à la religion: vous en verrez l'unique origine dans la populace; c'est elle qui donne le mouvement à la superstition. C'est pour les forgerons et les bûcherons de l'Allemagne que l'empereur avait paru pieds nus devant l'évêque de Rome; c'est le commun peuple, esclave de la superstition, qui veut que ses maîtres en soient les esclaves. Dès que vous avez souffert que vos sujets soient aveuglés par le fanatisme, ils vous forcent à paraître fanatique comme eux; et si vous secouez le joug qu'ils portent et qu'ils aiment, ils se soulèvent. Vous avez cru que plus les chaînes de la religion, qui doivent être douces, seraient pesantes et dures, plus vos peuples seraient soumis; vous vous êtes trompé: ils se servent de ces chaînes pour vous gêner sur le trône, ou pour vous en faire descendre' (Chap. XLVI, M. xi. 398).

Voilà pour les enseignements du passé. Mais ne peut-on mieux augurer du présent, et le peuple est-il définitivement voué à cette condition proche de la brute? La réponse de Voltaire à cette question n'est pas invariable, mais on finit par découvrir, au-delà des mouvements d'humeur et des réactions liées aux circonstances, un fond de doctrine dont il ne s'est guère écarté et qui s'accorde d'ailleurs logiquement avec l'ensemble de sa pensée.

Une des grandes questions qui se sont posées au siècle des lumières, depuis Fontenelle jusqu'à Condorcet, a été de savoir s'il convenait de diffuser ces lumières de façon extensive et d'en faire bénéficier le peuple. Voltaire estime que le problème a été mal posé, et qu'il importe de distinguer ce qu'il faut entendre par 'peuple' et par 'lumières', tout en s'accordant sur le processus même de cette diffusion.

Le peuple, pour Voltaire, n'est nullement un tout homogène. Il se compose d'une masse de travailleurs misérables et peu qualifiés, et d'une élite d'artisans spécialisés et cultivés. Voltaire n'attend rien des uns et beaucoup des autres. Il estime nécessaire le maintien d'une main-d'œuvre inculte, non scolarisée et il redoute visiblement que la généralisation d'une éducation populaire n'aboutisse à dépeupler les campagnes et à vider les ateliers:[9] argument économique émanant d'un gros propriétaire qui d'ailleurs ne s'en cache pas. Qu'on en juge par la lettre à Damilaville du 1er avril 1766 (Best. 12358):

> Je crois que nous ne nous entendons pas sur l'article du peuple que vous croyez digne d'être instruit. J'entends par peuple la populace qui n'a que ses bras pour vivre.[10] Je doute que cet ordre de citoyens ait jamais le temps ou la capacité de s'instruire, ils mourraient de faim avant de devenir philosophes, il me paraît essentiel qu'il y ait des gueux ignorants.[11] Si vous fesiez valoir comme moi une terre, et si vous aviez des charrues vous seriez bien de mon avis, ce n'est pas le manœuvre qu'il faut instruire, c'est le bon bourgeois, c'est l'habitant des villes, cette entreprise est assez forte et assez grande . . . Je suis de l'avis de ceux qui veulent faire de bons laboureurs des enfants trouvés, au lieu d'en faire des théologiens; du reste il faudrait un livre pour approfondir cette question.

Il ne s'agit point là d'une boutade ou d'un paradoxe. Voltaire

[9] On retrouve ici l'incidence d'un problème qui a vivement préoccupé le XVIIIe siècle, la hantise de la dépopulation. Diderot y voyait la conséquence de l'attrait des villes et de la transformation des paysans en soldats et en laquais, c'est-à-dire en sujets improductifs. La question a été fort bien étudiée au congrès de Genève (1963) sur *Le siècle des lumières*, particulièrement dans les contributions de Sir Julian Huxley, 'A Factor overlooked by the philosophes: the population explosion' et de Mme Agnes Raymond, 'Le problème de la population chez les Encyclopédistes' (*Studies on Voltaire and the eighteenth century*, xxv. 861-883 et xxvi. 1379-1388).

[10] L'article 'Peuple' de l'*Encyclopédie*, rédigé par Jaucourt d'après une dissertation de l'abbé Coyer, constate également qu''autrefois le peuple étoit l'état général de la nation, simplement opposé à celui des grands et des nobles', mais que l'évolution du mot depuis une vingtaine d'années a limité fortement son acception: 'il ne reste donc dans la masse du peuple que les ouvriers et les laboureurs.' Cependant Jaucourt et Coyer, à la différence de Voltaire, éprouvent la plus vive sympathie pour le sort des masses laborieuses.

[11] On voit mal comment concilier cette formule, et celles qui suivront, avec l'affirmation de M. Antoine Adam: 'Voltaire ne dit pas que le peuple doit être tenu à l'écart du progrès des Lumières' ('Voltaire et les lumières', dans *Europe*, mai–juin 1959, p. 16). Ce n'est pas rendre justice à Voltaire que d'ignorer certains aspects de sa pensée parce qu'ils s'harmonisent difficilement avec nos idéologies contemporaines.

est très sérieux et il ne variera pas sur cet article, comme le prouve une lettre à Linguet du 15 mars 1767 (Best. 13143):

> distinguons dans ce que vous appelez peuple, les professions qui exigent une éducation honnête et celles qui ne demandent que le travail des bras et une fatigue de tous les jours. Cette dernière classe est la plus nombreuse. Celle-là pour tout délassement et pour tout plaisir, n'ira jamais qu'à la grand'messe et au cabaret, parce qu'on y chante et qu'elle y chante elle-même. Mais pour les artisans plus relevés, qui sont forcés par leurs professions mêmes, à réfléchir beaucoup, à perfectionner leur goût, à étendre leurs lumières; ceux-là commencent à lire dans toute l'Europe.

Dans une lettre à d'Alembert (du 2 septembre 1768, Best. 14239), il est plus net encore et plus caustique:

> Il [=Damilaville] doit être content, et vous aussi, du mépris où l'inf... est tombée chez tous les honnêtes gens de l'Europe. C'était tout ce qu'on voulait et tout ce qui était nécessaire. On n'a jamais prétendu éclairer les cordonniers et les servantes; c'était le partage des apôtres.

Quand éclate à Lyon une émeute populaire qui se termine par une fusillade, Voltaire écrit à Tabareau (le 3 février 1769, Best. 14499):

> A l'égard du peuple il sera toujours sot et barbare, témoin ce qui est arrivé à la canaille de Lyon. Ce sont des boeufs, auxquels il faut un joug, un aiguillon et du foin.

Il confie à Damilaville, le 12 octobre 1764 (Best. 11299), que 'la vérité n'est pas faitte pour tout le monde. Le gros du genre humain en est indigne';[12] le 19 mars 1766, même son de cloche dans une lettre au même correspondant: 'il est à propos que le peuple soit guidé, et non pas qu'il soit instruit. Il n'est pas digne de l'être' (Best. 12338) ainsi que le 28 avril 1766 (Best. 12398): la majorité des gens 'ne méritent pas qu'on les éclaire . . . Il est certain . . . que la raison fait de grands progrès, mais ce n'est jamais que chez un petit nombre de sages.'

[12] Il rejoint ainsi l'attitude de celui qu'il appelle 'le lâche Fontenelle'. Nous comptons aborder dans une autre étude le problème de cette opposition.

Lorsqu'il lit, en 1763, dans l'*Essai d'éducation nationale* de La Chalotais: 'Le bien de la société demande que les connaissances du peuple ne s'étendent pas plus loin que ses occupations. Les frères de la Doctrine chrétienne, qu'on appelle "ignorantins", sont survenus pour achever de tout perdre: ils apprennent à lire et à écrire à des gens qui n'eussent dû apprendre qu'à dessiner et à manier le rabot et la lime, mais qui ne le veulent plus faire', Voltaire ne peut s'empêcher d'applaudir à ces vues qui rejoignent les siennes et il s'empresse d'écrire à l'auteur (le 29 février 1763, Best. 10238): 'Je vous remercie de proscrire l'étude chez les laboureurs. Moi qui cultive la terre, je vous présente requête pour avoir des manœuvres, et non des clercs tonsurés.'[13]

Pour autant que le paysan n'abandonne pas sa charrue, Voltaire est prêt à glorifier son état: 'Celui qui défriche un champ rend plus de service au genre humain, que tous les barbouilleurs de papier de l'Europe' (aux d'Argental, le 11 mars 1763, Best. 10270).

Ces textes sont clairs et explicites. Ils émanent d'un philosophe qui méprise les erreurs de la 'populace', d'un bourgeois qui redoute ses soulèvements et d'un propriétaire soucieux de se réserver une main-d'œuvre abondante et peu coûteuse.

Faudrait-il dès lors rejeter Voltaire parmi les théoriciens soucieux de maintenir le peuple dans ses ténèbres afin de sauvegarder leurs privilèges économiques et sociaux? En dépit des apparences et de la dureté de certaines formules, rien ne serait plus faux.

Sans doute Voltaire est-il persuadé qu'il serait dangereux d'ouvrir des écoles dans tous les villages et de vouloir répandre le savoir humain dans toutes les classes, mais ce n'est ni par opportunisme ni par mépris pour l'espèce humaine, L'explication profonde se trouve dans sa philosophie de l'histoire et dans sa conception du progrès. Celui-ci est lent, peu spectaculaire et toujours précaire. Accélérer le mouvement de l'histoire, brusquer les faits, c'est leur faire violence et risquer de tout gâter par un zèle mal inspiré.

Les lumières doivent donc se diffuser, et se diffuseront un jour, mais par étapes successives. Le peuple finira par en bénéficier insensiblement, non par une initiation brutale qui le jetterait dans l'oisiveté et dans la subversion, mais par une sorte de lente osmose.

[13] Cf. *Dictionnaire philosophique*, article 'Propriété' (M.xx.293): 'on a besoin d'hommes qui n'aient que leurs bras et de la bonne volonté.'

On lit dans *Le Siècle de Louis XIV* (Chap. XXXVI, 'Du calvinisme au temps de Louis XIV', M. xv. 38):

> Il faut d'abord qu'elle [la raison] soit établie dans les principales têtes; elle descend aux autres de proche en proche, et gouverne enfin le peuple même qui ne la connaît pas, mais qui, voyant que ses supérieurs sont modérés, apprend aussi à l'être. C'est un des grands ouvrages du temps, et ce temps n'était pas encore venu.

Cette théorie de l'éducation progressive par l'exemple, et non par l'instruction, lui tient visiblement à cœur. Dans la lettre, déjà citée, écrite à Damilaville le 13 avril 1766 (Best. 12376), il la développe in-extenso:

> Il est bien certain que les pélerinages, les prétendus miracles, les cérémonies superstitieuses ne feront jamais un honnête homme: l'exemple seul en fait; et c'est la seule manière d'instruire l'ignorance des villageois. Ce sont donc les principaux citoyens qu'il faut d'abord éclairer. Il est certain, par exemple, que si à Naples les seigneurs donnaient à dieu la préférence qu'ils donnent à st Janvier, le peuple au bout de quelques années se soucierait fort peu de la liquéfaction dont il est aujourd'hui si avide. Mais si quelqu'un s'avisait à présent de vouloir instruire ce peuple napolitain, il se ferait lapider. Il faut que la lumière descende par degrés. Celle du bas peuple sera toujours fort confuse; ceux qui sont occupés à gagner leur vie ne peuvent l'être d'éclairer leur esprit: il leur suffit de l'exemple de leurs supérieurs.[14]

Il faut entrer dans les articulations profondes de la pensée voltairienne pour comprendre comment il concilie, sans l'ombre d'un paradoxe, la nécessité d'éclairer les masses avec le refus de les instruire. Cette association peut nous paraître spécieuse; elle ne l'était nullement pour lui.

Voltaire s'est toujours dressé avec indignation contre ceux qui voulaient maintenir le peuple dans un état d'abrutissement. Une

[14] La même idée est développée dans le *Dictionnaire philosophique*, art. 'Superstition' (M. xx. 456): 'l'exemple de ces magistrats n'éclairera pas la canaille . . . leurs mœurs adoucies adouciront celles de la plus vile et de la plus féroce populace.'

chose est de croire le peuple, dans sa majorité, rebelle à la raison,[15] une autre de vouloir perpétuer et exploiter sciemment cet état. Dans un petit pamphlet intitulé *Jusqu'à quel point on doit tromper le peuple* (M. xxiv. 71) il écrit:

> C'est une très grande question, mais peu agitée, de savoir jusqu'à quel degré le peuple, c'est-à-dire neuf parts du genre humain sur dix,[16] doit être traité comme des singes.

L'article 'Fraude' du *Dictionnaire philosophique* (M. xix. 205-208) pose la question de savoir *S'il faut user de fraudes pieuses avec le peuple* et Voltaire, par la bouche du sage Ouang, s'élève contre cette scandaleuse théorie:

> Nos lettrés—dit Ouang—sont de la même pâte que nos tailleurs, nos tisserands et nos laboureurs . . . et il y a bien moins de crimes parmi les lettrés que parmi le peuple. Pourquoi ne pas daigner instruire nos ouvriers comme nous instruisons nos lettrés?[17]

Nous sommes arrivés ici à un point crucial du problème et nous pouvons nous demander si Voltaire ne se contredit pas ou si son attitude n'a pas évolué. La suite du texte nous éclaire bientôt. L'instruction à laquelle songe Voltaire n'est ni littéraire, ni philosophique, ni historique, ni théologique surtout; elle ne se confond en rien avec l'enseignement que Diderot, Talleyrand et Condorcet voudront voir dispenser à tous les citoyens. Diffuser la culture et le savoir à des millions d'hommes lui paraîtrait absurde et périlleux; autre chose est de répandre 'une religion sans superstition', la croyance à 'un Dieu qui punit et qui récompense', puisqu'aussi bien le rôle du philosophe est d''annoncer un Dieu'.

La lettre à Damilaville (1er avril 1766, Best. 12358) ne disait pas autre chose:

> Confucius a dit qu'il connaissait des gens incapables de sciences, mais aucun incapable de vertu; aussi doit on prêcher

[15] 'Le peuple ne raisonnera jamais: on ne raisonne que dans l'oisiveté. Le peuple est entre l'homme et le bête' (*Voltaire's Notebooks*, éd. Besterman, ii. 381).

[16] Ce calcul de proportions a fait l'objet d'échanges de correspondance entre Voltaire et Frédéric II, cf. Best. 12310 et 12338.

[17] Voir le première *Épître aux fidèles* (Best. app.149, t. lii. 266). Voltaire souhaiterait qu'à l'exemple des Anglais on puisse 'éclairer à la fois le chancelier et le cordonnier.'

> la vertu au plus bas peuple; mais il ne doit pas perdre son temps à examiner qui avait raison de Nestorius ou de Cirille, d'Eusèbe ou d'Athanase, de Jansénius ou de Molina, de Zwingle ou d'Œcolampade,[18] et plût à dieu qu'il n'y eût jamais eu de bon bourgeois infatué de ces disputes, nous n'aurions jamais eu de guerres de religion, nous n'aurions jamais eu de st Barthélemy, toutes les querelles de cette espèce ont commencé par des gens oisifs et qui étaient à leur aise; quand la populace se mêle de raisonner, tout est perdu.

L'instruction à donner aux masses se précise, et se limite du même coup, à une sorte d'évangélisation déiste. Dans sa lutte contre l'Église romaine. Voltaire sait qu'il ne triomphera que lorsque son église personnelle aura trouvé des adeptes. Comme l'a très bien dit René Pomeau, 'la propagande voltairienne . . . ne fait pas table rase, elle dresse temple contre temple' (*op. cit.* p. 376).

Voltaire n'a pas assez confiance dans les 'lumières' du peuple pour vouloir l'initier à la philosophie des 'frères', ou à ce qu'il appelle 'les mystères de Mitra' (Best. 14040), mais il espère réussir à le gagner à une forme de religion plus humaine, plus tolérante, plus douce. On s'est demandé souvent s'il était sincère, et certains de ses propos ont contribué à entretenir le doute:

> La croyance des peines et des récompenses après la mort est un frein dont le peuple a besoin. (*Lettres à S.A. Mgr. le Prince de . . ., du curé Meslier*, M. xxvi. 511-512).

Qu'un dieu soit indispensable pour contenir la 'canaille', Voltaire en est intimement persuadé[19] et c'est ce qui l'éloigne du curé Meslier:

'Pourquoi adresser ce testament à des hommes agrestes qui ne savaient pas lire? Et, s'ils avaient pu lire, pourquoi leur ôter un joug

[18] Voltaire, on le voit, s'insurge surtout contre le fait que l'Église, ayant le monopole de l'enseignement, ne recrute des élèves dans le peuple que pour en faire des prêtres ou des moines; cf. supra la lettre à La Chalotais (28 février 1763, Best. 10238): 'des manœuvres, et non des clercs tonsurés'. Bien des remarques surprenantes de Voltaire s'expliquent par le contexte de l'époque et par sa haine de l'Église toute-puissante.

[19] Cf. *Dict. philosophique*, art. 'Athéisme' (M. xvii. 463): 'Il est très vrai que par tout pays la populace a besoin du plus grand frein.' De même, Voltaire note en marge de *Le Vrai Sens du système de la nature* (Londres 1774), p. 134, ligne 13: 'la populace est une bête féroce qu'il faut enchaîner par la crainte de la potence et de l'enfer' (cf. W. S. Ljublinski, *Voltaire-Studien*, Berlin 1961, pp. 121 et 142).

salutaire, une crainte nécessaire qui seule peut prévenir les crimes secrets?'[20]

Ce même sentiment le dressera plus tard contre d'Holbach et sa 'synagogue' avec une violence qui n'est pas inspirée seulement par l'intérêt ou par l'opportunisme, mais aussi par une sincère conviction. Car enfin, s'il est vrai qu'il faut un dieu à la 'populace', Voltaire croit aussi qu'il en faut un aux philosophes; seulement, ce n'est pas tout à fait le même. Inutile de revenir là-dessus après le beau livre de René Pomeau.

Il arrive, on l'a vu, que Voltaire se laisse aller au découragement devant tant de sottise, tant d'aveuglement, tant de férocité. Le peuple ne serait-il donc que cette 'populace', cette 'canaille' toujours capable du pire, toujours sollicitée par le fanatisme?

> —Distingue toujours les honnêtes gens, qui pensent, de la populace, qui n'est point faite pour penser. (*Questions sur l'Encyclopédie*, art. 'Blé', section VI, M. xviii. 16.)
> —Ce monde-ci (il faut que j'en convienne) est un composé de fripons, de fanatiques et d'imbéciles, parmi lesquels il y a un petit troupeau séparé qu'on appelle *la bonne compagnie*; ce petit troupeau étant riche, bien élevé, instruit, poli, est comme la fleur du genre humain; c'est pour lui que les plaisirs honnêtes sont faits. (*Conversation de M. l'Intendant des Menus en exercice avec M. l'abbé Grizel*, M. xxiv. 247.)
> —Par quelle fatalité est il plus aisé de rassembler des laboureurs et des vignerons que des gens qui pensent? (à d'Alembert, 23 juillet 1769, Best. 14787.)
> —Nous aurons bientôt de nouveaux cieux et une nouvelle terre; j'entends pour les honnêtes gens: car pour la canaille le plus sot ciel et la plus sotte terre est ce qu'il lui faut! (à d'Alembert, 13 janvier 1769, Best. 14464.)

[20] D'Alembert pose la même question à Frédéric II, mais en des termes très différents (29 janvier 1770). Sa morale repose sur 'la liaison du véritable intérêt avec l'accomplissement de nos devoirs', mais elle se heurte à un insurmontable obstacle, 'c'est de savoir si ceux qui n'ont rien, qui donnent tout à la société et à qui la société refuse tout, qui peuvent à peine nourrir de leur travail une famille nombreuse, ou même qui n'ont pas de quoi la nourrir; si ces hommes, dis-je, peuvent avoir d'autre principe de morale que la loi, et comment on pourrait leur persuader que leur véritable intérêt est d'être vertueux, dans le cas où ils pourraient ne l'être pas. Si j'avais trouvé à cette question une réponse satisfaisante, il y a long-temps que j'aurais donné mon catéchisme de morale' (éd. Belin, 1822, v. 289).

—La canaille créa la superstition; les honnêtes gens la détruisent. (*Le Dîner du comte de Boulainvilliers*, 3e entretien, *Pensées détachées de M. l'abbé de Saint-Pierre*, M. xxvi. 560.)

Pourtant ces accès de dépression et de pessimisme ne sont pas le dernier mot de Voltaire, tout comme la vie ne se résume pas pour lui à un dilemme entre les ratiocinations de Pangloss et le fatalisme du derviche. Il y a une issue, mais elle est lointaine et son accès est ardu. Voltaire se refuse à désespérer de l'homme et à abandonner la majorité du genre humain au sort de la brute.

L'attentat de Damiens lui inspire, dans le *Précis du siècle de Louis XV*, ces considérations nuancées:

> L'esprit des Poltrot et des Jacques Clément, qu'on avait cru anéanti, subsiste donc encore chez les âmes féroces et ignorantes! La raison pénètre en vain chez les principaux citoyens: le peuple est toujours porté au fanatisme; et peut-être n'y a-t-il d'autre remède à cette contagion que d'éclairer enfin le peuple même; mais on l'entretient quelquefois dans des superstitions, et on voit ensuite avec étonnement ce que ces superstitions produisent (M. xv. 394).

On retrouve la même lueur d'espoir, la même nuance dans un *Dialogue entre un philosophe et un controleur général des finances* (M. xxiii. 502) où l'ignorance des masses est expliquée par leur condition économique et par la politique délibérée des grands:

> La populace reste toujours dans la profonde ignorance où la nécessité de gagner sa vie la condamne, et où l'on a cru longtemps que le bien de l'État devait la tenir.

Peut-être faut-il chercher le dernier mot de Voltaire dans le *Sermon des cinquante* (M. xxiv. 453). Le troisième et dernier point développe l'idée qui lui est chère: que le moment est venu de dissocier christianisme et religion, qu'il faut prêcher aux hommes la religion naturelle,

> On nous dit qu'il faut des mystères au peuple, qu'il faut le tromper. Eh! mes frères, peut-on faire cet outrage au genre humain?

Bien des superstitions ont déjà disparu, parmi les plus choquantes. Pourquoi donc désespérer?

> Il faut avoir le courage de faire encore quelques pas: le peuple n'est pas si imbécile qu'on le pense; il recevra sans peine un culte sage et simple d'un Dieu unique, tel qu'on dit qu' Abraham et Noé le professaient, tel que tous les sages de l'Antiquité l'ont professé, tel qu'il est reçu à la Chine par tous les lettrés . . . lorsque la raison, libre de ses fers, apprendra au peuple qu'il n'y a qu'un Dieu . . . certes alors, mes frères, les hommes seront plus gens de bien, en étant moins superstitieux (M. xxiv. 453).[21]

En définitive, on peut dire que Voltaire n'a jamais cru qu'il fallait instruire la masse des travailleurs manuels,[22] mais qu'il fallait l'éclairer moralement par l'exemple et lui proposer une forme de religion plus pure et plus rationelle. L'histoire et l'expérience lui ont appris à se défier du peuple dont l'action a souvent contrarié le progrès des 'lumières'. De toute manière, celui-ci restera lent, et ses résultats fragiles: Voltaire préfère placer ses espoirs dans des réformes venues d'en haut, inspirées par les 'philosophes' aux souverains éclairés, soutenues par le 'petit troupeau' des 'honnêtes gens' et dont le peuple finira par bénéficier à la longue, par une sorte de réfraction discrète et efficace.

Sur ce plan, tout comme sur d'autres, il se sépare à la fois de Diderot, du baron d'Holbach et de Jean-Jacques. Certains lui en sauront gré, comme le Nietzsche du brillant parallèle Voltaire-Rousseau dans *Der Wille zur Macht*. D'autres le blâmeront de ce qu'ils jugent une faiblesse: Robespierre, bien sûr, mais aussi Germaine de Staël, peu suspecte de jacobinisme pourtant et qui écrira dans *De la littérature* (éd. Van Tieghem, p. 278): '[Voltaire] aimoit les grands seigneurs, il aimoit les rois; il vouloit éclairer la société plutôt que la changer'. Jugement sommaire, fondé sur une simplification excessive, mais qui illustre l'ancienneté d'un malentendu que cet article a tenté de lever ou, du moins, d'éclairer quelque peu.

[21] Cf. Fréret, dans le 3e Entretien du *Dîner du comte de Boulainvilliers*, 'L'adoration pure de l'Être Suprême commence à être aujourd'hui la religion de tous les honnêtes gens; et bientôt elle descendra dans une partie saine du peuple même.'

[22] Il est curieux de constater que Rousseau partage cet avis, mais pour une raison diamétralement opposée; cf. *Émile*, Livre I (éd. 1826, t. viii. 41-42): 'Le pauvre n'a pas besoin d'éducation; celle de son état est forcée; et il n'en sauroit avoir d'autre.' On comparera ces positions intransigeantes et théoriques aux solutions raisonnables et concrètes proposées par Diderot dans le *Plan d'une université pour le gouvernement de Russie* et dans l'*Essai sur les études en Russie* (AT., iii. 415, 417, 429, 520).

The financial history of the Kehl Voltaire

Giles Barber

Horace Walpole greeted the slightly premature news of Voltaire's death by writing to his friend William Mason 'I heard last night that Voltaire is dead; now one may buy his works safely, as he cannot write them over and over again' and there was evidently an element of truth in this remark.[1] The underlying exasperation of the letter writer is moreover echoed by Quérard who heads his section on the Kehl edition 'Troisième âge. Nous sortons enfin de ce labyrinthe inextricable d'éditions publiées depuis 1756, et composées de pièces, de morceaux imprimés successivement, et formant des collections indigestes dont il est difficile, pour ne pas dire impossible, de coordonner les parties'.[2] These remarks indicate well how welcome a definitive edition of Voltaire's works would seem to have been at the time of his death. Numerous articles and reference works have mentioned and discussed the edition, produced under Beaumarchais' general management at Kehl and designed to meet that need and it is not intended here to consider the important bibliographical, typographical or textual problems which it raises, but rather to attempt to see what happened commercially to this apparently promising publication, described by Brunet as the undertaking 'la plus vaste et la plus dispendieuse peut-être qu'on ait jamais faite en librairie dans un si court espace de temps'.[3]

[1] *Horace Walpole's correspondence with William Mason*, ed. W. S. Lewis [and others], i. 343 (17 Jan. 1778).

[2] J. M. Quérard, *La France littéraire*, x. 374.

[3] J. C. Brunet, *Manuel du libraire* 5e éd. (1864), v. col. 1354. For other work, on the Kehl Voltaire besides those quoted in the footnotes of this article see P. H. Muir, 'The Kehl edition of Voltaire', *The Library*, 5th ser., iii. 85-100; J. G. Dreyfus, 'The Baskerville punches 1750–1950', *The Library*, 5th ser., v. 26-48; G. Peignot, *Recherches sur les ouvrages*

In 1775 Voltaire's printers for the last twenty years, the Cramer brothers of Geneva, had attempted to provide a more nearly definitive edition of his works than had hitherto been available through the purchase of their sixty-five volume edition in octavo which had been in progress since 1757. This new edition, which because of the decorative frame to each page, is called the 'edition encadrée', was, however, clearly incomplete and could not be considered the worthy and definitive edition both the public and the trade wanted. This wish to do due honour to Voltaire is indeed one of the most striking features of most of the early transactions concerning the Kehl edition.

The prime mover of a definitive edition was the publisher Charles-Joseph Panckoucke, whose vision and enterprise were perhaps unparalleled in the late eighteenth-century book-trade, and who, as an old friend, had visited Voltaire at Ferney in September 1777 together with his sister, Madame Suard, and his compatriot J. J. M. Decroix, an enthusiastic Voltairian, in order to persuade him to co-operate on this project. Voltaire agreed and at once began emending and correcting an interleaved copy of the 'edition encadrée' but his death on 30 May 1778 came before much progress had been made. Panckoucke, who had already amassed a certain number of Voltaire manuscripts, lost no time. In early August he completed his purchase of the d'Argental correspondence and in September he collected from Madame Denis the corrected volumes together with 'le reste des manuscrits'. On 29 November he secured Condorcet's services as general editor. Unfortunately, however, his numerous financial commitments were leading Panckoucke into bankruptcy and, after seeking aid from Catherine II, whose apparently affirmative but tardy answer he could not afford to await, he finally agreed to sell his material to Beaumarchais, who was prepared to undertake the publication of the complete works.[4] The sale contract was signed on 29 February 1779.

de Voltaire (Paris 1817); P. Bonnefon, 'Une correspondance inédite de Grimm avec Wagnière', *Revue d'histoire littéraire de la France* (1896), iii. 481-535; L. de Loménie, *Beaumarchais et son temps* (Paris 1880); A. Bettelheim, *Beaumarchais* (Frankfurt 1886), pp. 422-452; G. Bengesco, *Voltaire. Bibliographie de ses œuvres* (Paris 1882–90).

[4] See George B. Watts, 'Catherine II, Charles-Joseph Panckoucke, and the Kehl edition of Voltaire's *Œuvres*', *Modern Language Quarterly* (1957), xviii. 59-62. See also G. B. Watts, 'Panckoucke, Beaumarchais, and Voltaire's first complete edition', *Tennessee studies in Literature* (1959), iv. 91-97.

Beaumarchais' motives, and indeed even the manner in which he was drawn into an undertaking which was to occupy and burden his life for a number of years, are far from clear but it may well be that a feeling that he alone was capable of organising this worthy monument to the memory of the leading literary figure of the century was the mainspring of his decision. The difficulties inherent in publishing the complete works of so outspoken an author as Voltaire led Beaumarchais to set up the Société littéraire et typographique of which he was in fact the only shareholder and director. Most of the accounts and letter books of the society on which this article is based thus eventually became part of the Beaumarchais estate and are now to be found at the Bibliothèque historique de la ville de Paris.[5] Important complementary papers are also to be found in the Institut et Musée Voltaire in Geneva.

But for Beaumarchais, fired with enthusiasm, the responsibility of providing a full text was not enough. The edition must also be worthily printed and therefore Baskerville's typographical material, reputed the finest of the century, was purchased from his widow and special processes for making paper and ink were investigated. The vigour and optimism behind the undertaking were evidently those of Beaumarchais and are reflected in all the early activities of the Society. The English prospectus sets the tone:

> Silent admiration and fruitless regrets restore not to society the good and the great, nor to the Republic of letters, men of genius and learning, who are no more. As publick benefactors they have a claim to more evident, more lasting proofs of publick veneration. And it is no less a measure of prudence than a duty of gratitude to admit the claim in its fullest extent.

[5] F. Bournon, *Catalogue des manuscrits de la bibliothèque de la ville de Paris* (Paris 1893), no. 268. These manuscripts came from the library of F. de Marescot. They consist of:

(1) Registre de la correspondance littéraire et typographique sur la nouvelle édition des œuvres de Voltaire (1779–90);
(2) Copies de lettres d'affaires de Beaumarchais (1780–88);
(3) Copies de lettres (1788–1802);
(4) Compte d'achat des caractères typographiques;
(5) Livre de caisse (1784–89);
(6) Journal de la vente de l'édition de Voltaire (1785–90);
(7–9) Papers relating to Beaumarchais' estate. References are given in this article as BHVP 268/1 etc.

It is naturally a pleasure to acknowledge my indebtedness to Dr Th. Besterman who originally drew my attention to the Geneva manuscripts.

> The honors we pay the dead give animation to the minds of the living: they awaken genius and call it into action.
>
> It is in perusing the works of men of learning, in forming our taste and improving our minds, by the lessons they may have left us, that we best shew our respect for their memory: it is the tribute that insures their immortality. Authors (that is the few who deserve that name) die not. The hand of Death, which consigns the rest of mankind to oblivion, only draws a veil before authors. Though become invisible, they remain with us, they daily converse with us: they accompany us in retirement, to entertain and instruct us: they meet us in publick, to form the life and pleasure of society.
>
> These reflections, enforced by the death of Voltaire, together with the great abuse of the works of that much admired author, and the impositions practised on the Public, under the sanction of his name, have induced some gentlemen of affluent fortunes and distinguished rank in Paris, philanthropists and encouragers of learning, to form themselves into a society, and lay foundation for a permanent typographical establishment in order to enrich the world with correct and complete *posthumous* editions of the authors who merit most from society.

But this early optimism extended to the material benefits to be gained from the publication as well, and by June 1779 matters appeared to be sufficiently advanced for Cantini, the treasurer of the Society, to write to Farquharson, who was negotiating the purchase of the Baskerville type, giving details of the edition and pointing out how much he could make by acting as the English agent. 'Nous ouvrons la souscription de 12,000 exemplaires en 60 vol. 8° moyen, c'est à dire entre la grandeur proposée par M. Pankouke un papier dit carré de france, et celle du Grand-raisin de france qui est aussi large et moins long que le Royal de Londres. Nous adoptons le format pour que les marges soient plus belles et les alinéa interlignes d'un léger espace', and he goes on to explain the trade terms and lottery. 'Chaque volume à 5 livres en feuilles: pour les 60 volumes 300*ll.*; 424,000*ll.* en 1,500 lots sur 12,000 billets ce qui fait un lot par huit billets, le dixième des lots gagnés par les souscripteurs gagnans, à ceux de nos correspondans qui auront procuré leur souscription. Le 1/10 du prix de l'exemplaire, c'est à dire 30*ll.* sur chacun, abbandonnés à nos correspondans qui placeront douze exemplaires.

'Exemple du bénéfice d'un correspondant sur 12 exemplaires:

12 exemplaires à 30		360 : 0 : 0
1 lot ½	424,000 en 1500 lots donnent 282*ll.* 2s pour le dixieme pour 1 lot et demi est	42 : 7 : 6
		402 : 7 : 6

M.M. les voyageurs jouiront de la même remise sur tout ce qu'ils placeront directement, et ils auront en outre le 1/10 du dixième accordé à chaque correspondant des villes comprises dans leur district.

'Le votre, Monsieur, est l'Angleterre, je suppose qu'il s'y place 2,400 exemplaires, que vous en placiés directement 480 il vous reviendra 40 foix 402*ll.* 7s. 6d. cy 16,095*ll.*

'Reste 1920 exemplaires, faisant 160 dousaines à 402*ll.* 7s. ou 64380*ll.* dont le 1/10 est pour vous cy 6,438

22,533'

Even allowing for advertisement and travel expenses, he continues, the profit should be over 16,000*ll.*—and this to one agent! Moreover the Society is prepared to pay him 500*ll.* a quarter during his negotiations for the type and later to employ him regularly at this salary.[6]

Farquharson's reply was evidently highly cautious and by August 1779, when Beaumarchais was reading the proofs of the prospectus, there was evidently still much uncertainty about the terms to be allowed. It was moreover being suggested that an official duodecimo piracy should be produced but this was rejected as liable to reduce the number of subscribers for the full octavo edition. The possibility of a quarto edition for bibliophiles was also examined but it was felt that it was better to try to fill the octavo subscription list first. Meanwhile it was to be announced that only six thousand copies were to be printed, although this number would be raised if the number of subscriptions warranted it. The prospectus eventually appeared in January 1781 and announced three editions totalling five thousand copies. Four thousand of these were in the octavo edition at fifteen guineas, six hundred in medium quarto at twenty-five guineas and four hundred in royal quarto

[6] BHVP 268/1 ff. 4-5.

at forty guineas, the prices, according to the English prospectus, being for the work in sheets and without carriage or customs charges which would probably be about twelve per cent.[7] The same prospectus indicates that subscriptions could be made at various bankers, in London at Sir Robert Herries and Co., in Edinburgh at Sir William Forbes, J. Hunter and Co., and in Dublin at Messrs. Black and Murray. Similarly in London at Elmsley's, the bookseller, Woodmason, the stationer's, or with Farquharson himself as agent to the Society, at John Henderson's, Mitre-Court, Milk-Street, Cheapside.

But the professional bookselling world was evidently already organising itself to meet this powerful, if chaotic, amateur invasion. Beaumarchais and his incompetent architect assistant, J. F. Le Tellier, were having difficulty in completing their equipment and in establishing themselves just outside France at the fort of Kehl in the territory of the Margrave of Baden. Moreover Panckoucke himself was far from giving them every assistance and encouragement. On 27 February 1780 Beaumarchais wrote to Le Tellier '[Panckoucke] arrive de Lyon. On s'y apprète à accaparer tous les libraires de l'Europe aussitôt que notre prospectus paraitra, pour une contrefaçon in 8° à bon marché, qui sera promise pour trois mois après notre livraison générale. Certes nous n'avons ni droit ni moyen de nous y opposer; car il y a grande apparence que cela se fera hors le Royaume—Mais qui nous empechera, ai-je-dit, de la faire nous même?—Personne; mais tout le monde sera accaparé, tous les marchés seront faits, avant que vous y songiez. Il n'y aura plus moyen de réparer ce tort: parce que, votre édition lachée, la contrefaction est au premier occupant, et tout étant arretté d'avance, on vous cueillera le fruit qui vous appartient—Que faudrait-il faire? Un sousfermage pour la contrafaction qui se donnerait à 3–10^{s} au public et 50^{s} aux libraires; le nombre de 4000 ne pouvant satisfaire à tout, on ne vous saura nul mauvais gré d'avoir permis une edition plus commune que la votre—Cela se peut; mais nous ne pouvons y songer que notre souscription ne soit remplie—Mais pendant ce tems là vous allés être devancé par un accaparement

[7] New York Public Library *KF 1782. I am indebted to Professor Harcourt Brown for this reference as well for information concerning his interesting collection of printed documents relating to the Kehl edition. A similar collection is to be found in the Bibliothèque Nationale MS. n.a. 22188.

général, dès que votre prospectus va paraitre—Mais un pareil marché connu, casserait le col à notre édition in 8vo de Baskerville—Cela peut y nuire un peu, mais le bénéfice de l'autre dédommagera et par de là. Vous pouvez faire tel marché qui vous assure un très grand bénéfice sans aucune avance. Mais si vous en manquez la moment, d'autres sont prêts à le faire. Réfléchissez-y, la nouvelle société se chargera aussi des supplements. Vous n'aurez d'autre soin à donner qu'à votre belle édition.... Telle a été notre conversation.'[8]

By June 1781 when Le Tellier was beginning to print off the four thousand copies the situation was no better. A worried Beaumarchais expressed alarm at printing so many for, as he protests to Le Tellier, there are only thirteen hundred real subscribers on the list. The figure appears to be higher he adds, but the

> 200 billets réservés sur les premiers numeros, pour la Russie et la Prusse, 100 reconnaissances prises et payées par Mde De Necker, autant par Mr De Montran ne doivent pas etre regardées comme solvables si une speculation quelconque ne peut s'etablir en leur faveur sur cet objet. D'autre part les prospectus des contrefacons paraissent. Nous en avons un de Palisot qui meriterait bien des coups de baton: mais comme il n'est pas permis d'en donner, nous nous réservons seulement la vengeance de lui faire perdre tout le bénéfit de son déplacement: Il est à Berne. Le tems est venu où nous devons traiter pour l'édition commune, et il nous parait que cette société de Berne est autant et plus en état que personne de remplir nos vues, par sa richesse et ses grandes relations: mais ma 1ere condition serait qu'elle renvoyat *Le Palisot*, et c'est de quoi nous nous occupons. Les gens de Neuchatel sont liés d'affaire avec eux: ils pourraient se partager la besogne, voila ce à quoi nous travaillons.[9]

[8] Institut et musée Voltaire Dossier 'Affaires de Kehl', 27 février 1780. Panckoucke's proposal raises some interesting questions. He appears to suggest that terms should be agreed with the potential pirates for an authorised, but unrecognised, edition, a piracy in all but fact. Was this an original suggestion or does it reflect a certain eighteenth-century practice? The answer to Beaumarchais' particular problem was to give up the quarto edition and put out an official duodecimo one.

[9] Institut et musée Voltaire Dossier 'Affaires de Kehl', 1 juin 1781.

During the next two years the problems of the piracy faded into the background as Le Tellier's inefficiency brought the production at Kehl to a standstill. Beaumarchais continued to protest his support, 'ma confiance en vous a été la baze de tout ce que j'ai fait', to decry Panckoucke 'que je ne consulte point, parce que le grand tripotage ôté, tout le reste est vague dans son esprit' and to push the date of publication further and further forward. Panckoucke had moreover refused to hand over all the manuscripts, claiming he had not been fully paid according to the agreement of 25 February 1779. The original sum was 300,000 livres of which 200,000 were to be paid from the profits of the edition. Panckoucke's refusal clearly impeded the progress of the edition and Beaumarchais sought arbitration for, as he said 'L'Europe attend'.[10] The manuscripts appear to have been forthcoming and a second agreement on 26 November 1786 reduced the price to 160,000 livres, of which 100,000 had already been paid and the remainder of which Beaumarchais paid by issuing that day four undertakings of 15,000 livres each, payable in December 1789, 1790, 1791 and 1792. Panckoucke later boasted of the cost of that evening's dinner.[11]

At Kehl matters were going from bad to worse under Le Tellier's direction and, in Beaumarchais' phrase 'l'Europe librairienne' was full of rumours of the collapse of the Society. The production of the *Mariage de Figaro* (26 April 1784) led the assistant editor Decroix to write on 12 May 'Je voudrais qu'il [le Patron] eut autant de success à Kehl qu'au faubourg St. Germain'. A number of volumes of the first instalment were nevertheless ready and in late May the collective and individual title pages were to be printed off. Moreover the combined Berne and Neuchâtel piracy had been abandoned, probably against some compensation, and it was hoped that this would increase the number of subscribers. Matters were rapidly coming to a head and by the end of August it was generally known that Claude Vincent Cantini, Beaumarchais' accountant, had disappeared. The debt was rumoured to be about 800,000 livres but at least by 1800 it was, according to papers dealing with Beaumarchais' estate, then no more than the agreed figure of 164,000 livres. Nevertheless this incident also led to the departure

[10] BHVP 268/1 8 mars 1787 and Institut et musée Voltaire Dossier 'Affaires de Kehl', 17 mars 1783. See also *Œuvres complètes de Beaumarchais*, ed. É. Fournier (Paris 1876), pp. xlii-xlvi.

[11] G. B. Watts *op. cit.*, p. 62.

of Jean François Le Tellier as chief administrator at Kehl and thus, on the eve of the delivery of the first volumes of the complete works, closed the first part of the history of the Kehl Voltaire. Beaumarchais had spent enormous sums in the past six years and so far received virtually no return. The next six years, the last of his life, were to bring, if no unqualified honour and success from this project, at least some return on his expended capital and energy.

First of all the team was overhauled and de la Hogue, formerly French commissioner in the Spanish part of Haiti, was appointed to Le Tellier's place. The editorial work seems to have continued to lie with Condorcet, assisted by Nicolas Ruault, Beaumarchais' bookseller, and Jacques Joseph Marie Decroix, who read proofs in Lille and came up to Paris for three or four months a year to lend a hand generally. Gudin de la Brenellerie seems to have overseen much of Beaumarchais' general finances and, in one of his explanatory and encouraging letters to de la Hogue, Beaumarchais writes 'M. Ruault, c'est moi. M. Gudin, c'est moi: comme vous même etes moi'.

The first volumes appear to have been delivered to subscribers either at the end of 1784 or in the first weeks of 1785. There were thirty for the octavo edition and thirty-seven for the duodecimo, containing in general, the theatrical, poetical and philosophical works. It is difficult to ascertain from the extant account books how many sets were subscribed and the subscription book, which evidently existed, appears not to have survived. Subscription numbers referred to in the account books fall into the following blocks 36-71, 442-552, 690-1032, 1205-1280, 1392-1430, 1525-1747, 1865-2044, 2182-2431. Among the gaps come presumably the two hundred reserved for Russia and Prussia, the hundred for Madame Necker, the hundred for M. de Montran and another hundred subscribed by Decroix. There would seem to be little evidence for thinking that the total number of subscriptions was over two thousand five hundred. The subscriptions traced are nearly all under the names of booksellers of whom the frères La Bottière of Bordeaux probably head the list with about one hundred and fourteen. At least seventy-five sets, of one format or another, were subscribed in England. Ten per cent of the subscribed sets, in fact all those ending with the figure four (a number chosen by adopting the final figure of one of the royal lotteries), reached their subscribers free as a result of Beaumarchais' publicity lottery.[12]

In fact no official publicity had been possible in French periodicals or newspapers since the work was not officially allowed in the country and the same difficulty complicated distribution. Until Maurepas' death in 1781 Beaumarchais counted on his support and even after that he evidently profited from tacit protection. In March 1782 after difficulties at Kehl Le Tellier had suggested moving to France, whereupon Beaumarchais wrote 'Le defaut de Kehl est peut être d'être trop près de la longuer des bras: la griffe peut croitre jusqu'à vous y atteindre. Comment supposés-vous aussi que je puisse engager un ministre, quoique plein de bonne volonte, de se compromettre en se rendant le protecteur public de l'édition de Voltaire? Ils peuvent abattre les coups—si on en porte: mais, lorsqu'on est obligé de sortir de France pour faire la presse, vous voulés qu'ils protègent ouvertement ailleurs ce qu'ils n'osent tolérer chez eux! Vous me croyez donc un charme pour les empecher de raisonner! Chacun courant à telle chose; mais personne ne veut être cite pour y avoir aidé. Voila quels sont les ministres; et dans leur position je sens que je ferais de meme.'

After the first delivery the opposition mounted. The work was condemned by the Archbishop of Paris in his message for Lent 1785 and the Arrêt du Conseil d'État du Roi of 3 June 1785 ordered the suppression of the edition. Nevertheless deliveries do not seem to have been much impeded and distribution continued from Paris. A later note to de la Hogue upbraids him for having put 'des livres étrangers' in some consignments as Beaumarchais has apparently assured 'les puissances inquiètes' that there would be none. Later the Paris bookseller Jean-Nicolas Barba recalled in his *Souvenirs* (Paris 1846, pp. 119 et seq.) that he had smuggled copies of the Kehl Voltaire in through the Saint-Martin control in the company of one of Volland's assistants and the son of the younger Didot.

In fact once the subscribers' copies had been issued sales started on a regular basis from Beaumarchais' Paris house and on 21 April 1785 Nicolas Ruault entered into a formal agreement with Beaumarchais to be responsible for selling the productions of the Société littéraire. He agreed to keep a ledger, to hand over the takings, and

[12] For details of the lottery see Bengesco *op. cit.*, pp. 115-116.

to keep to the prices fixed. Beaumarchais provided the premises and allowed him two thousand livres a year plus a free twentieth copy on duodecimo and octavo works and a free thirteenth on quarto ones.[13] The agreement was confirmed in October 1787 and continued until June 1790 when Ruault was said by Beaumarchais to have taken 'un parti plus avantageux que celui de diriger ma librairie'. One of Ruault's ledgers is evidently that which survives among Beaumarchais' papers and from this and the latter's personal accounts we get a glimpse of how retail sales went during the years immediately following publication.[14]

The ledger is a day book in which orders and despatches were entered chronologically. Each client also had a reference number which presumably led to his page in the Grand livre or account ledger. The daybook shows that through 1785 Ruault was very busy selling not so much sets of Voltaire, although a certain number were sold, but rather other works which had either been produced at Kehl or were held for Beaumarchais. According to one note this stock consisted of 96 copies of Beaumarchais' own *Mémoires*, two parts in quarto, 100 *Barbier de Séville*, 50 *Eugénie*, 25 *Mânes de Louis XV* 12°, 7997 copies of the ordinary paper octavo first edition of the *Mariage de Figaro*, 1506 of a better paper edition with engravings and 192 of the English paper Kehl edition with engravings (being a load of two hundred minus the eight withheld as usual by the Chambre syndicale), 115 *Géorgiques* Latin and French 8°, 87 Virgils, 69 La Bruyère and 43 *Œuvres complètes de J.-J. Rousseau* 19 volumes 12°. With the exception of the *Mariage* most of these works were sold during 1785. The *Mariage* sold some 1,400 copies but the remaining stock seems unaccounted for. Ruault rendered regularly numbered accounts to Beaumarchais which cover the period January 1785 to August 1787. By far the highest return is for February 1785 and this presumably covers the first issue of the Voltaire. The returns tail off through 1785 and 1786 and are again high in May, June and July 1787 at the time of the third issue (8° edition volumes 46-51, 12° edition volumes 59-67). The figures are strangely low at the date of the second issue, January 1786 (volumes 31-45 and 38-58). The annual totals are: 1785 85,516 livres: 1786 4,706; 1787 61,242 (total 151,464).

[13] Institut et musée Voltaire Dossier 'Affaires de Kehl'.

[14] BHVP 268/6 Journal and 5 Livre de caisse.

These rather disappointingly low sales appear to have been made to about a hundred booksellers in Paris and the provinces. The chief amongst these were the Bordeaux booksellers with the La Bottière in the lead, although Blaizot, 'libraire du Roi à Versailles', and Robiquet l'aîné at Rennes also bought heavily. Foreign booksellers presumably received stock direct from Kehl to the agents in their own countries and few are even mentioned. Robert Hay at St Petersburg is an early exception and others include the Frères Faure at Parma, Reycends of Turin, Cramp, Bulkeley & Co. of St Petersburg, Antony Gerna of Dublin, and an account for 'Chevalier fils, directeur des paquebots à New York'. In 1788 the ledger records the despatch of thirty-seven copies of the complete Voltaire (at that date still without the correspondence only issued in 1789) to Theodore-Charles Mozard, the printer, journalist and poet of Port au Prince, Haiti, for 9,169 livres. The books were bound, some at least in 'veau ecail, dorés sur tranche par Biseaux' and a letter to Mozard indicates that 'Nous avons recommandé la reliure propre au climat que vous habitez; on a inseré dans les ingredians qui le compose, de l'arsenic et de la colloquinte, pour préserver les livres des insectes qui les rongent sans cette précaution'.

In July 1786 Beaumarchais discussed with De la Hogue how he should deal with the booksellers. 'Je vous ai promis quelques observations sur la manière de vendre aux libraires & je vais les mettre sous vos yeux et les soumettre à votre bonne judicaire. L'usage ou la routine de toute librairie de l'Europe n'est point de faire la remise ou le rabais au marchand en forme de tant pour cent en bas des factures; cette remise se fait par exemplaire meme du livre lequel a deux prix; le prix m^d^ [marchand] et le prix particulier ou public. Je ne crois pas qu'on doive d'écarter de cet antique usage. Ainsi l'on pourait fixer, comme il fait, le prix de chaque Voltaire in -12 et in -8° dans une circulaire consacrée aux libraires. La remise en argent serait de 20 pour cent et le 11e ou le 13e gratis lorsqu'on en prendra 10 ou 12 exemplaires en une seule emplette. La remise de 30 pour cent suit comme sur 50 exemplaires ne me paroit pas juste parceque celui qui se charge de 50 exemplaires fait une avance considerable de ses fonds, parcequ'il est probable qu'il est pour en revendre une partie à des colporteurs de province auxquels il faut accorder un petit bénéfice; et voila pourquoi les fortes maisons de librairie nous demanderont toujours un rabais considerable; il faut qu'ils partagent le bénéfice avec leurs petits correspondans; s'il en vaut pas la peine d'être partagé, ils ne feront pas de demande ou seulement de très petites. Il faut des credits assez longs à leurs pratiques, et tout ne se vend pas au particulier. Il faut decider si vous donnerez le 11e ou le 13e gratis. Le 13e avec 20% en argent equivaut à 27½, le 11e à 29¼%, si je ne me trompe. Ainsi il conviendrait d'adopter ce dernier. M. Le Tellier l'a d'ailleurs annoncé jadis dans une circulaire qu'il fit imprimer et que l'on a repandu dans la librairie tant nationale qu'étrangère.

in -12°	à 24s. le vol. prix md	80	prix particulier 96*ll.*
	à 30	96	120
	à 40	130	160
	à 50	160	200
	à 4.10	300	360
in -8°	à 40s	96	120
	à 3*ll.*	150	180
	à 4*ll.*	200	240
	à 6*ll.*	300	360
	à 7*ll.*	420	510

Le papier velin n'est point assez cher à 7.10 pour le particulier en comparaison avec originale à 6*ll.* il est vrai qu'il y a eu un mille à vendre et c'est un grand nombre, mais on sera toujours le maitre, s'il languit trop longtemps dans les magazins, d'augmenter le rabais aux libraires seulement. Il n'en faut pas faire aux particuliers sous quelque pretexte que ce soit. Le prix de l'exemplaire ne doit jamais être relacher à leur égard. Si on avait cette faiblesse elle serait bientôt connue des marchands et leur confiance serait perdue. Si vous trouvez ces principes raisonnables et justes faites imprimer un circulaire dans lequel vous annoncerez ces prix doubles, au marchands seulement avec le 11e *gratis* et 6 mois de credit, en [illegible] sur Paris si vous pouvez l'obtenir, ce qui sera assez difficile, generalement parlant. D'après ces arrangems vous pouvez repondre au Genevois. Soyez persuadé que vous avez la préférence sur les *tourneisen* et consorts; il n'a qu'une édition à offrir, et vous en avez dix en caracteres de Baskerville à des prix faciles d'acquisition. Si ces Genevois demandent 8 ou 10 mois de credit il ne faudrait pas leur refuser ce prolongement de terme, en supposant toutes fois que l'emplette soit considérable. Les livres ne s'écouleront, par gros nombre, qu'autant que l'on donne de facilités aux acquereurs solides et qui font un grand commerce.'[15]

The rival edition mentioned is that produced at Basle by J. J. Tourneisen, 'avec les caractères de G. Haas', and also available with the imprint of the Gotha bookseller Charles-Guillaume Ettinger (Bengesco 2143), which was an octavo reprint of the Kehl edition with an extra volume of letters.[16] Nor was this rival edition the only difficulty facing the Société littéraire in 1786. There was again trouble from the Margrave over the activities of the Kehl press and Decroix several times suggested that the correspondence, the next and last major section of the edition and due to go to the press in the course of the next year, should be printed somewhere else abroad. On the French side too there was trouble and, the Garde des Sceaux having written to Kehl, Beaumarchais wrote to protest to de Calonne on 25 September saying 'J'ai la preuve en main que c'est d'accord avec les ministres du Roi, qui j'ai commencé cette grande et ruineuse entreprise que me tient plus de 2 millions dehors, avec le risque affreux de les perdre. Il s'agissait alors de l'honneur de la nation et de l'émulation de plusieurs arts qui nous étaient dans la dépendance de l'étranger. Aujourd'hui c'est une persecution qui n'a pas d'exemple, quoi qu'on m'ait bien promis qu'il n'y en aurait jamais.'[17]

Beaumarchais' long letter on trade terms betrays another worry, that of attracting large wholesale contracts. In 1787 the third and last instalment of Voltaire's works was published and thus whole sets could now be sold. The correspondence, containing about four thousand seven hundred letters, of which only a few hundred had previously been published, was to all intents and purposes a new work and thus fully able to find its own market.[18] It would, as Beaumarchais commented to de La Hogue on 4 May 1787, complete the octavo editions of Voltaire's works published at Geneva, Lausanne and Lyon as well as the Kehl one and could therefore expect a good sale. To over-print as many as six thousand

[15] BHVP 268/2.

[16] Tourneisen also produced another edition in 1790 and 1791. See Th. Besterman, 'Quelques éditions anciennes de Voltaire inconnues à Bengesco', *Genava* (Genève 1954), p. 201.

[17] Institut et musée Voltaire Dossier 'Affaires de Kehl', incomplete letter.

[18] See Th. Besterman, 'The Beaumarchais transcripts of Voltaire's correspondence', *Times Literary Supplement* (23 April 1949), p. 272. Reprinted with emendations in Best., app. 7 (vol. i. pp. 359-362).

three hundred in octavo seemed reasonable but for the duodecimo, where besides Kehl there was only the old Liège edition, he recommended only a thousand to fifteen hundred.[19]

The first large wholesale contract was signed on 20 September 1786 and by this the Paris booksellers Belin, Volland and Maradan bought 1602 copies (of which collection of volumes is not clear) for the agreed price of twenty-four thousand livres plus a packing charge of five hundred and forty. In May 1787 negotiations were in hand with a Le Roy of Caen and on the eighth the Paris office of the Société littéraire, probably in the person of Nicolas Ruault, wrote to De la Hogue: 'J'ai repassé l'état ou apercu du prix de fabrique du 8º à 2 et à 3*ll.* suivant lequel le volume revient, l'un dans l'autre, *rendu à Paris*, à 26s. Il faut y ajouter la part que chaque édition doit supporter de l'acquisition des manuscrits. . . . Aussi donc ce n'est pas taxé trop haut chaque volume de 26s., à 5s. de manuscrit, ce qui le porte à 31s. Or 126,000 volumes [presumably 1,800 sets] à 5s. font 31,500 à ajouter avec 163,000 prix de fabrique suivant votre apercu, ci 194,830. C. à.d. 200,000 pour faire un compte rond, et pour établir le projet de vente à M. Le Roy, auquel je travaille. Ce libraire offre 50s. du volume l'un dans l'autre. On croit au premier coup d'œil qu'il y a un bénéfice honnête et considerable; cependant je crains qu'en vendant ainsi toutes les éditions on ne puisse atteindre la somme totale des debourses faites et à faire: la sottise et la folie de Jean François Le Tellier d'éxécrable memoire doivent rencherir beaucoup tous ces ouvrages.'[20] The figures given to Le Roy himself the same day do not exactly tally with this calculation. 'Je n'ai encore reçu du directeur de l'imprimerie de Kehl que le nombre juste des exemplaires in 8º à 40s. et à 3*ll.* Chacun de ces papiers n'a été tiré qu'à 1050, ce qui fait au juste 2,100 exemplaires. Il y a environ 400 souscriptions du 1ᵉ et 150 de celui à 3*ll.* C'est donc 5 à 600 exemplaires retenus et par consequence 1500 à vendre. . . . Les in -12 ont été tirés à un nombre plus haut que les in -8º. L'in -12 à 30s. à 3000 exemplaires; celui à 40s. à 1,000, celui à 24s. à 1,250, à 2 10 à 500'. Orders, he notes, can be sent for any of these.

However a few days later the total costing of the Kehl edition was completed and on the twenty-sixth the results were broken to de La Hogue. 'Deux millions, 231,438*ll.* 14s. 7d.—Voila, mon cher

[19] BHVP 268/2. [20] BHVP 268/2.

ami, la somme déboursée par M. de Beaumarchais depuis l'origine de la Société littéraire en 1779 jusqu'au 20 de ce mois, compris les traites à echeoir, dont avis à été donné jusqu'au dit jour 20 mai courant. Vous me dites dans votre lettre du 14, que pour finir ce cher Voltaire, il en coutera à peu près 40 milliers. Ajoutez cette somme à celle ci-dessus et vous avez environ 100 mille louis de depenses ci ... 2,400,000*ll.* pour tout ce qui a été imprimé et que l'on achevera d'imprimer dans l'imprimerie de la Société littéraire. Il convient de deduire de ce capital la valeur des types de Baskerville 100,000*ll.*, celle des papeteries d'Arches, d'Archettes et Plombières environ 50,000*ll.*, la vente du J. J. Rousseau et autres petits objets environ 30,000*ll.*, ci 180,000*ll.* Il en restera deux million 220 milles livres pour les Voltaire en 12° et en 8°, compris 5 ou 600 mille francs de gaspiller du J. F. Le Tellier, ce qui les rencherit d'autant. Simulez maintenant une vente de toutes ces éditions, et voyez à quel prix on peut la passer en gros, au plan bas. Je ne pense pas, qu'aux prix où elles reviennent, on puisse jamais les vendre en gros. Les libraires savent trop bien calculer ce qu'un livre coute de fabrique; ils n'en offriront que le prix comptant fort peu de choses audessus de ce qu'elles coutent à la Société dans l'état actual. La détestable administration de Le Tellier, qui augment d'un quart toutes les éditions, empechera toujours de la ceder en gros; ce quart était le bénéfice qu'on pouvait espérer en les vendant de cette manière.' The negotiations with Le Roy have fallen through because of a misunderstanding about the price as he was only offering 30s. for the 3*ll.* and 20s. for the 2*ll.* edition, or only 25s. per volume—half the price previously understood!

This sobering experience was renewed in October 1787 when some 850 copies of the 67 existing volumes of the duodecimo edition were sold to Maradan at 24s. a volume. It was clearly necessary to sell as much as possible from the shop at a discount. More negotiations were tried early in 1788 with Bernuset of Lyon but the discount sales picked up during this year and a number of entries cover sales of fifty to eighty copies of the works. Indeed with the completion of the correspondence in sight Beaumarchais, who had earlier written 'Cette funeste imprimerie empoisonne mon existence de toutes les manières possibles', could now hopefully say 'l'affaire de la fourniture des œuvres de Voltaire touche à sa fin'.

The last batch of texts of the correspondence with d'Alembert, which seems to have been the last item to be printed, was sent to Kehl on 1 August 1788 and though there is no mention of the volumes of correspondence in the ledger until January 1789 it would seem likely that the majority was in print by November 1788. The first sign that the total Kehl edition was complete and beginning to reach the wholesale market was probably a printed circular letter issued by Maradan, together with Desenne and Volland, on 30 October 1788 in which, outlining the interest of the correspondence, he advertised his ability to provide both that and the works proper.[21] In March 1789 moreover the consortium made heavy purchases under the ledger heading 'marché du Voltaire à 40s. en 70 volumes'. An entry also shows that a considerable number of sets of the correspondence had been delivered to the booksellers' joint warehouse, rue St-Étienne-des-Grecs, since November 1788. These deliveries included over 2,500 copies of some volumes and over 6,000 of the d'Alembert correspondence which is always mentioned as volumes 17 and 18.[22] This wholesale transaction was finally settled in May 1790 when Volland is shown as having a thousand and fifty-six copies of the correspondence unsold.

No business was transacted at all during mid July 1789. Beaumarchais' private accounts, beyond recording the 'pension de Mlle Eugenie au couvent', her clavichord and geography lessons and the usual 2200 livres a month allowed Madame de Beaumarchais for housekeeping, show only an exceptional payment for the poor of the parish (8,000 livres) on 21 July, 336 to Pierre François Harnon, the sculptor, for a bust of Voltaire on 10 August and on 19 August a small payment for 'Drapeaux et un simulacre de la Bastille'. In the shop small sales were heavy in August and September and large orders emanating from St Petersburg and London were at last attended to. The former, to the Frères Hay, was for some fifty copies at a cost of 9,393 livres; the latter, to Peter Elmsley, was for 118 copies of the octavo edition and eighty-one of the duodecimo, nearly all 'satiné', for some 71,342 livres.

These sales were probably the final major ones handled by Ruault, who left Beaumarchais' service in January 1790, and are almost the last in the ledger. It is perhaps worth noting, however, that in May 1790 six hundred sets of engravings, 107 copper plates and 107

[21] Institut et musée Voltaire shelfmark Rf. c. 64.

[22] See also Roux Devillas catalogue 64 (1966), item 648.

original drawings by Moreau le jeune were sold to Saugrain for 19,000 livres. Saugrain had apparently also sold over a hundred copies of the octavo edition. The following year saw the winding up of most of the sales machinery. Beaumarchais, pressed, amongst other things, by his debts to Panckoucke which now began to fall due, still sold some books direct from his house. Sets of the Voltaire are said to have been virtually all the crowd found in the house, Boulevard St-Antoine, when they invaded it in August 1792.[23] Otherwise sets were available from Bossange's depository, rue des Noyers.[24] But already in March 1791 Clavelin had sold off sets at the Hôtel Bullion. The Société littéraire still had a correspondent at Strasbourg, who was evidently responsible for Kehl despatches, but eventually the majority of this stock was, by 1796, deposited with E. J. Faesch at Basle. It seems likely that this stock was then remaindered by Faesch and Decker.[25] Among other final auction sales one for 1570 copies in octavo and duodecimo by J. M. Hausset on 5 November 1804 is worth noting.[26]

It would unfortunately seem impossible to work out any accurate balance sheet for the Kehl edition. Clearly amateur organisation, Le Tellier's maladministration, professional rivalry, the political situation and a host of minor problems made the production of this edition hazardous from the beginning. Threats of piracy, and later piracy itself, complicated the marketing of an edition probably far too large for the existing market. In 1787, when sales were beginning to get under way, the edition had, as we have seen, cost Beaumarchais about two and a quarter million livres. In 1791 presenting a copy to the nation he claimed a deficit of over a million livres. The inventories made after Beaumarchais' death in 1799 show, under heading or 'cotte' 20 which contains most of the booksellers' debts, a sum owing to him of 97,757 livres. This is divided into 44,482 due from Bons débiteurs; 37,420 from the Douteux and 11,855 from the Mauvais. The highest figure by far is that owed by Peter Elmsley of London,

[23] For details of the copy Beaumarchais presented to the nation in July 1791 see E. Dacier, 'Le *Voltaire de Kehl* de la Bibliothèque Nationale', *Trésors des bibliothèques de France*, v. 208-213.

[24] See the *Moniteur* (12 Sept. 1791). Also letter from Beaumarchais to Bossange, 27 Vendémiaire an VII in *Bulletin du bouquiniste* (1862), pp. 35-36.

[25] See Institut et musée Voltaire Correspondance relative au magazin de Voltaire à Bâle. (Letters of 1796.)

[26] The prospectus for this sale was kindly brought to my attention by Professor Harcourt Brown who possesses a copy.

some 29,000 livres. The correspondence relating to the pursuit of this debt is in the Institut Voltaire and shows the complexity of this type of problem, for the matter was still being negotiated a year or two after the battle of Waterloo. However, from all these figures it would seem tempting to suggest that in all probability a high proportion of the capital costs of the Kehl edition may well have been recovered. Certainly there was no profit and the loss to Beaumarchais on the capital involved was evidently colossal. This was his own conclusion too, for shortly before the final printing was complete, he wrote 'L'Europe sera satisfaite et moi j'aurai perdu au moins 600 mille livres sans les interets de 3 millions depuis 5 ans—Quelle vie je mene! Bondieu! Heureusement je vieillis et fais peu de cas de ce qui m'echappe'. Later, however, when the great edition of the great man was complete he looked back at the difficulties past and wrote with justified pride 'J'ai eu l'audacieux courage de tenir parole à l'Europe'.

Sagesse et Morale dans Jacques le Fataliste

Jean Fabre

'Le tic d'Horace est de faire des vers, le tic de Trébatius et de Burigny, de parler d'antiquité; le mien, de moraliser.'[1] Tout au long de l'œuvre de Diderot, la plus secrète comme la plus répandue, la préoccupation morale paraît à la fois si tenace et si paradoxale qu'elle n'a pu manquer d'arrêter les critiques et de susciter en leur esprit les motivations les plus diverses. Déjà Pierre Hermand, lorsqu'il s'efforçait d'ordonner dans une très consciencieuse et mémorable étude 'les idées morales de Diderot', n'avait pu réussir à lier convenablement sa gerbe ou son faisceau.[2] Fallait-il accuser la cruauté du destin qui avait empêché ce jeune érudit, mort au combat en 1916, de donner une forme mieux élaborée à son enquête? Mais la contre-épreuve était fournie, à la même époque, par René Hubert qui, s'efforçant en bon 'philosophe' de mettre de la logique, là où le 'littéraire' Hermand se bornait à relever des contradictions, n'aboutissait pas à un résultat plus convaincant.[3] Aucune morale cohérente ne semblait pouvoir être déduite d'un chaos d'aspirations véhémentes mais confuses, ni d'affirmations catégoriques mais apparemment contradictoires. De cette double enquête, il ne restait guère qu'un répertoire ou un arsenal de textes, offert à tous ceux qui continuaient à prétendre qu'à l'image des girouettes de Langres, 'le Philosophe' s'était contenté d'osciller, au gré de son humeur, dans le champ des idées morales.

Depuis lors, en effet, on ne peut dire que les réflexions et

[1] AT. vi. 315 (Satire I, Sur les caractères . . .).

[2] *Les Idées morales de Diderot* (Paris, Presses Universitaires de France, 1923).

[3] 'La morale de Diderot', *Revue du 18e siècle* (1914 et 1916), ii. 329-340, iii. 29-42.

recherches sur la morale de Diderot aient marqué des progrès décisifs. Elles ont permis cependant de mieux dégager et motiver la contradiction, sinon l'antinomie, sur laquelle Diderot lui-même était venu buter, mais sans perdre l'espoir de la résoudre ou de la dépasser. Comment aurait-il pu sacrifier l'une ou l'autre des deux assurances ou convictions qui coexistaient et parfois se heurtaient au fond de lui-même, l'une de raison, l'autre de sentiment? D'une part un matérialisme et un déterminisme sur lesquels, depuis au moins la *Lettre sur les aveugles* il ne reviendra plus, puisqu'il les considère comme expérimentalement démontrés: en leur rigoureuse et nécessaire conséquence, ils autorisent et même ils impliquent une médecine, une pédagogie, une politique, un ordre social et moral, qui permettront de régler le comportement des hommes et même de modifier leurs habitudes au mieux du devenir de l'espèce. Mais c'est alors qu'apparaît inévitablement l'autre évidence: tout cela ne sera jamais une morale, c'est-à-dire non pas un code sur lequel chacun réglera sa conduite, mais une déontologie, un idéal qui garantira son aspiration au bonheur, mais aussi à la justice, ou simplement motivera l'impulsion qui le porte à sortir de lui-même, à s'indigner, à aimer, à se dévouer, à sacrifier même sa vie. Soumis, il doit le savoir, aux lois d'un universel déterminisme, l'homme sait aussi que la vie lui offre mille occasions de se déterminer et que cette détermination, où il trouve au moins une illusion de liberté, car il se sent responsable au moins dans les suites qu'elle entraîne, risque de l'engager pour jamais.

Telle est la double évidence qui, à mesure que Diderot avance en expérience et en âge, s'impose toujours davantage à lui. Au lendemain de son *Interprétation de la nature*, qui marque dans l'expression de son matérialisme un tournant décisif, il se plaisait à en durcir les termes et à en outrer les conséquences, ou l'inconséquence qui s'y attache. D'un côté la fameuse lettre à *Landois*;[4] de l'autre presque simultanément, ce théâtre qui sert à un moralisme intempérant d'exutoire plus que de tribune, en donnant à l'homme qui vient d'établir 'que le mot liberté est un mot vide de sens' et qu'en conséquence 'il n'y a ni vice ni vertu', l'occasion de pousser jusqu'à la

[4] Il est indispensable de la lire à sa place: dans la *Correspondance littéraire* de Grimm du 1 juillet 1756. Cette lettre a fait l'objet de nombreuses interprétations qui n'ont pas toujours tenu compte des commentaires qui la précèdent et la suivent. Il serait grand temps de donner de cet ensemble (v. *Correspondance littéraire*, ed. Tourneux, iii. pp. 244-256), une édition critique.

frénésie l'exaltation de ce qu'il continue d'appeler 'le mérite et la vertu', comme au temps où il s'exerçait en marge de Shaftesbury.

Quelque dix ans plus tard, rien apparemment n'est changé: 'J'enrage,' prétend Diderot, 'd'être empêtré d'une diable de philosophie que mon esprit ne peut s'empêcher d'approuver et mon cœur de démentir.'[5] Mais cette fois, la constatation prend l'allure d'un badinage, ce qui donnerait à penser que l'antinomie est moins poignante ou l'illogisme moins flagrant que naguère. Peu importe que le matérialiste Naigeon 'fasse dépendre du passage d'une comète' l'amour qui se réveille ou s'éveille au cœur d'un galant philosophe. Ce qui compte, c'est que cet amour soit sincère et que, contre toute raison, il veuille rimer avec toujours. 'Peu s'en faut que je ne me fasse chrétien pour me promettre de vous aimer dans ce monde tant que j'y serai; et de vous retrouver, pour vous aimer encore dans l'autre. C'est une pensée si douce que je ne suis point étonné que les bonnes âmes y tiennent.' Mais ces 'bonnes âmes' en seront pour leurs frais de prosélytisme. Monsieur le Philosophe ne s'enrôlera pas dans leur troupe. Il vient d'écrire l'*Entretien avec d'Alembert* et il répète, avec le matérialiste Bordeu, qu'on est 'irrésistiblement entraîné par le torrent général', par le mouvant déterminisme d'un monde en perpétuelle mutation. Mais il sait aussi que 'l'athéisme est tout voisin d'une espèce de superstition presqu'aussi puérile que l'autre' et que s'il 'est impossible de lui résister, il est dur de s'abandonner aveuglément au torrent universel.' Ce qui compte après tout dans cet 'ordre', c'est qu'il n'exclue pas les 'efforts' et que ces efforts aient une chance d'être 'victorieux'. A défaut de liberté, le déterminisme autorise la sincérité de l'amour, comme l'exigence d'une morale. L'heure est venue sans doute, non plus d'exalter celle-ci dans le vide, mais de la fonder.

Écrire un traité de morale: c'était pour Diderot un très ancien projet, mais qui avait pris la forme d'un vœu, voire d'un rêve, et

[5] Cette phrase célèbre, ainsi que les propos qui suivent, figurent comme on sait dans un fragment de lettre conservée par une copie Naigeon. On a beaucoup épilogué sur la destinataire de cette lettre: Mme de Meaux selon M. Jean Pommier, Sophie Volland, selon l'opinion commune, étayée par M. Herbert Dieckmann de solides raisons (cf. Roth, ix. 154-155 et notes). Mais la date, qui importe davantage, ne peut faire de doute, car la lettre et celles qui l'entourent, se réfèrent au passage de la comète, visible dans l'horizon de Paris, à partir du 20 septembre 1769. Diderot a travaillé tout le mois d'août au *Reve de d'Alembert*, dont il annonce l'achèvement à Sophie Volland dans sa lettre du 11 septembre (ibid. p. 140).

il en renvoyait la réalisation au terme de sa carrière. 'Vous voyez,' écrivait-il, vers 1758, à un pasteur de Genève 'combien la louange du bien est séduisante. Quoique je n'aie pas tardé à rentrer en moi-même et à reconnaître combien le sujet était au-dessus de mes forces, je n'y ai pas tout à fait renoncé, mais j'attendrai. C'est par ce morceau que je voudrais prendre congé des lettres. Si jamais je l'exécute, il serait précédé d'un discours dont l'objet ne vous paraîtra ni moins important ni moins difficile: ce serait de convaincre les hommes que, tout bien considéré, ils n'ont rien trouvé de mieux en ce monde que de pratiquer la vertu.[6] J'y ai déjà pensé, mais je n'ai encore rien trouvé qui me satisfasse. Je tremble lorsqu'il me vient à l'esprit que, si la vertu ne sortait pas triomphante du parallèle, il en résulterait presqu'une apologie du vice.'[7] On comprend le 'tremblement' du philosophe: sur le plan du raisonnement pur, en fonction de cette 'diable de philosophie' dont la lettre à Landois tirait si cruellement la conséquence, sa démonstration risque de tourner court, ou plutôt de ruiner ce qu'elle aurait voulu démontrer. Épris de logique, le philosophe a quelque peine à admettre que la morale ne se déduit pas, mais qu'elle s'expérimente; qu'elle ne peut se prouver qu'en s'éprouvant. Son argumentation réduite à quia, le seul parti qui lui est provisoirement offert est celui du contradicteur de Zénon: prouver le mouvement en marchant. A cet impossible traité 'toujours imaginaire, toujours futur', se substitue la forme d'expérimentation que représente la création littéraire, reflet, substitut ou symbole de l'expérience vécue.

Telle est la conclusion qu'Herbert Dieckmann tirait naguère d'un débat qui opposait entre eux les commentateurs de Diderot et les

[6] Cf. *Le Neveu de Rameau*: 'Lui—Mais à votre compte, il faudrait donc être d'honnêtes gens—Moi—Pour être heureux? Assurément' et la note 158 de mon édition (Librairie Droz, pp. 43 et 186), qui renvoie à Pierre Hermand, selon lequel l'accord de la vertu et du bonheur est 'la clef de voûte' de la doctrine morale de Diderot, et à l'une des déclarations les plus explicites de Diderot (*Le Temple du Bonheur*, AT. vi. 439): 'J'étais bien jeune,' déclare le Philosophe, 'lorsqu'il me vint en tête que la morale entière consistait à prouver aux hommes qu'après tout, pour être heureux, on n'avait rien de mieux à faire en ce monde que d'être vertueux; tout de suite, je me mis à méditer cette question et je la médite encore.'

[7] Ce texte, tiré d'une lettre de Diderot à 'M.N.^{xx} de Genève', était cité par Pierre Hermand dans son Introduction p. xii, d'après Assézat et la version tronquée de cette lettre qui figurait dans les pseudo-*Mémoires* de Mme d'Épinay. L'édition Georges Roth se réfère à l'original autographe de la lettre pour en désigner le destinataire: le pasteur Jacob Vernes et en fixe la date probable: 9 janvier 1759. (v. Roth, no. 106, ii. 106-109).

révélait aussi ardents que lui-même à le suivre en sa préoccupation morale. 'Le traité le préoccupe, mais il ne *peut* pas le rédiger. Mais ce que Diderot a fait, c'est de la morale communiquée dans des contes, des romans, des essais etc.'[8] La proposition vaudrait au premier chef pour *le Neveu de Rameau* qui, en sa première rédaction, a vraisemblablement ouvert la voie à cette forme d'expérience morale, ou plutôt, l'a rendue à la fois nécessaire et possible; Monsieur le Philosophe tient bon contre l'immoraliste Rameau, dont l'assaut lui a rendu le fier service de faire place nette et de dissocier l'exigence morale de l'inconsistant moralisme où il n'avait que trop tendance à se complaire. Sur le chemin où il s'est désormais engagé, *Jacques le Fataliste* va marquer une étape probablement décisive.

'Diderot n'a pas encore commencé son traité *De vita bona et beata*, mais il a fait un conte charmant, intitulé *Jacques le Fataliste*' écrit à Bodmer Meister père, premier témoin d'un chef-d'œuvre, le 12 septembre 1771. En fait Diderot n'est pas encore prêt à concurrencer Sénèque, ni même à se mesurer avec ce stoïcien quelque peu compromis et compromettant, pour lequel au temps où il faisait ses premières armes de Philosophe, il ne professait que mépris mais qui, à mesure qu'il vieillit et jusqu'à son dernier *Essai*, va lui servir de pierre de touche et de garant. Mais c'est le roman qui va prendre la place du traité ou lui frayer le chemin. Ce qu'est ce roman (ou anti-roman) en son intention, sa genèse, ses sources, ses structures, sa signification, ce n'est pas le lieu de le rappeler ou de l'établir.[9] Il suffira de dire quelles conditions et quelles ressources il offre à l'expérience morale.

Conçu, esquissé et même écrit en sa première forme, au cours des mois qui ont suivi le retour du fameux voyage à Bourbonne et à Langres en l'été de 1770, *Jacques le Fataliste* prolonge sur le plan de l'imaginaire les premières vacances que sa vie laborieuse ait offertes sans doute à Diderot. Dans un pays familier et présent comme un terroir, mais qui ne se laisse situer nulle part, sur des

[8] On se reportera aux *Cahiers de l'Association Internationale des Etudes Françaises* (juin 1961), no. 13, p. 397 et à l'ensemble de la discussion qui a suivi les divers exposés sur Diderot dont on trouve là, à défaut d'une sténographie complète, un raccourci à l'emporte-pièce.

[9] Sur ces questions je me permets de renvoyer à mon étude 'Allégorie et symbolisme dans *Jacques le Fataliste*', *Europäische Aufklärung, Herbert Dieckmann zum 60. Geburtstag* (Munich 1967), pp. 69-75, ainsi qu'à ma communication destinée au second colloque international sur le Siècle des Lumières, à paraître dans les *Studies on Voltaire*.

routes et chemins où aucune borne n'indique d'où ils partent et où ils conduisent, en quelques journées d'un été hors du calendrier, deux êtres ni de réel ni de rêve, ni de vérité ni de roman, ne sont pas les héros d'une histoire, mais ils vivent ou revivent leurs histoires, leur passé redevenant un présent, et avec elles les cent histoires, aventures ou spectacles dont ils ont été ou deviennent les témoins, selon les caprices du hasard ou plutôt du romancier démiurge qui dispose de ce hasard. Tout naît apparemment de sa fantaisie et d'abord ces deux êtres qu'on prend tantôt pour des symboles, tantôt pour des projections de lui-même, tantôt pour des fantoches dont ce Vaucanson du roman règle et remonte le mécanisme. Mais voici qu'ils se détachent de lui ou lui d'eux; ils mangent, boivent, dorment, regardent, écoutent, s'égayent, s'indignent, compatissent, agissent, se mêlent de tout et inlassablement bavardent, raisonnent et disputent, si bien que le spectateur dérouté ne peut savoir s'ils sont de chair ou de raison. En Jacques et son maître, couple indissociable: antagoniste et complémentaire, le philosophe reconnaîtra une caricature de raison pure et une exaltation de raison pratique; le psychologue, une relation maître-valet, directe ou inversée; l'historien, un noble et un 'jacques'; l'amateur de romans, une variation sur le couple picaresque fondamental, Don Quichotte et Sancho, mais ramené à l'état de schéma ou d'épure, allégé de toute obligation ou destination, sans attache de métier, de famille ni de cœur, libéré du projet mais non du souvenir, merveilleusement disponible à l'événement. A tous, le romancier donnera tour à tour raison, un romancier qui ne cesse de faire intrusion dans son roman: ingénieur, régisseur, confident, voyeur, bonimenteur, poète; inlassable interlocuteur de ses personnages, de ses lecteurs et de lui-même, se moquant de son métier et de la philosophie autant que de la littérature, s'amusant de tout et de tous et visiblement en vacances. Tel est en gros *Jacques le Fataliste*: roman du 'fatum', mais dans un climat d'allégresse et de liberté.

Plus encore que dans la structure, cette liberté éclate dans les idées et les propos. 'J'abandonne mon esprit à tout son libertinage,' disait le Philosophe rêvant sur le banc d'Argenson et suivant de l'œil le manège des courtisanes dans l'allée de Foy. 'Je le laisse maître de suivre la première idée sage ou folle qui se présente (. . .) Mes pensees ce sont mes catins.'[10] *Jacques le Fataliste* s'inscrit tout

[10] *Neveu de Rameau*, édition citée, p. 3 et note 4.

entier à la suite. Foin de l'honnêteté et même du sens commun! 'Il n'y a peut-être pas sous le ciel une autre tête qui contienne autant de paradoxes que la tienne,' dit le Maître à Jacques. Mais Jacques-Diderot de répondre: 'Et quel mal y aurait il à cela? Un paradoxe n'est pas toujours une fausseté,'[11] et le Maître en convient. La pudeur n'est pas mieux traitée: tant pis pour ceux qui seraient tentés d'en faire une vertu! 'La fable n'est pas trop morale; mais elle est gaie,' seront-ils obligés de conclure comme le Maître, après le gaillard apologue de la gaîne et du coutelet.[12] Leur délicatesse acceptera-t-elle la verdeur avec laquelle Jacques conte ses amours et celles d'autrui? Pour en prévenir ou en accentuer l'effet, l'auteur se lance à corps perdu dans son roman afin d'y plaider le droit à l'indécence et même à l'obscénité, littéraire et morale. Pourquoi tant de véhémence? Et pourquoi tant de pusillanimité puisqu'il termine en se retranchant derrière la morale et Montaigne: 'La licence de son style m'est presqu'un garant de la pureté de ses mœurs . . . Lasciva est nobis pagina, vita proba.'[13]

Qu'on nomme les choses par leur nom, qu'on parle et écrive naturellement d'activités, de besoins ou de désirs naturels à l'homme, que la franchise du langage dévoile l'hypocrisie de certains interdits, n'est pas en soi une revendication si nouvelle; quand on connaît Diderot, l'on ne s'étonnera pas de le voir renouer, contre un siècle de libertinage frelaté, non seulement avec Montaigne, mais avec Rabelais. On admirera seulement qu'il y mette tant de chaleur et qu'il pose la question en termes de morale. Car enfin sa philosophie devrait le libérer de toute préoccupation de ce genre, moraliste ou immoraliste. De cette philosophie Jacques, qui lui ressemble alors comme un frère, se fait placidement l'écho et, s'il le faut, le Philosophe vient à la rescousse, comme pour attester qu'il s'en tient toujours, sur les principes, à ce qu'en exposait la lettre à Landois. 'Jacques ne connaissait ni le nom de vice, ni le nom de vertu; il prétendait qu'on était heureusement ou malheureusement né. Quand il entendait prononcer les noms de récompenses ou de châtiments, il haussait les épaules. Selon lui, la récompense était l'encouragement des bons; le châtiment l'effroi des méchants. Qu'est-ce autre chose, disait-il, s'il n'y a point de liberté et que notre destinée soit écrite là-haut? Il croyait qu'un homme s'acheminait aussi nécessairement

[11] *Jacques le Fataliste*, AT. vi. 30.

[12] *Ibid.*, p. 119.

[13] *Ibid.*, p. 221-223, cf. *Neveu de Rameau*, édit. cit. p. 71 et note 239.

à la gloire ou à l'ignominie qu'une boule qui aurait la conscience d'elle-même suit la pente d'une montagne; et que, si l'enchaînement des causes et effets qui forment la vie d'un homme depuis le premier instant de sa naissance jusqu'à son dernier soupir était connu, nous resterions convaincus qu'il n'a fait que ce qu'il était nécessaire de faire. Je l'ai plusieurs fois contredit, mais sans avantage et sans fruit.'[14]

Vraiment? D'aucuns regretteront que le Philosophe se fasse pour une fois si discret et seront tentés de porter à sa place la contradiction. Car s'il est impossible de convaincre et encore davantage de convertir un fataliste 'très têtu', qui fait si volontiers parade de son fatalisme qu'on pensera nécessairement à ce qu'évoque le mot parade en ses sens les plus concrets: un bouclier et un tréteau, il ne doit pas être trop malaisé de battre en brèche le 'fatalisme', aussi vulnérable que tout autre système dans un tournoi d'idées. L'argumentation changera seulement de caractère selon que ce fatalisme se réfère à la prédestination des théologiens, se drape dans Spinoza ou se fonde sur 'l'enchaînement des causes et des effets', tel qu'un déterminisme matérialiste et mécaniste a le devoir ou la prétention de l'établir.[15] Puisqu'il s'agit alors d'une philosophie qui se veut 'expérimentale', l'expérience devrait tout trancher. Hélas! l'expérience est faite ou plutôt se fait *in vivo*, et lorsqu'il s'agit non de l'homme en soi mais d'un homme, de tout homme vivant, on aura beau répéter qu'il est déterminé, l'impossibilité de dénombrer tous les facteurs de cette détermination en rendra le calcul illusoire, même *ex eventu*, et beaucoup plus illusoire encore la prétention de donner à ce calcul un caractère prévisionnel. En admettant que ce qui constitue pour un homme, d'un mot cher à Diderot, son 'individualité naturelle' puisse être quelque jour défini à sa naissance par une formule biologique, une sorte de fiche signalétique établie par la science la plus rigoureuse, qui témoignerait de son moi originel et serait comme l'équivalent matérialiste de sa 'monade', ce moi étant appelé non à être mais à exister, la 'modification' intervient alors, dont aucun Helvétius ne pourra jamais régler le détail. 'Puis-je n'être pas moi,' objecte Jacques. 'Et n'étant que moi, puis-je être autrement

[14] *Ibid.*, p. 180.

[15] Parmi les considérations et études innombrables suscitées par ce problème, je me contente de signaler une des premières et des plus caractéristiques, parce qu'elle se réfère directement à *Jacques le Fataliste*: 'Diderot and the Abbé Dulaurens', by Otis E. Fellows and Alice G. Green, in *Diderot Studies* (Syracuse University Press, 1949), i. 64-93.

que moi? Puis-je être moi et un autre?'[16] Sans doute, mais le même Jacques proclamera aussi bien que ce moi lui échappe, puisqu'il ne lui apparaîtra jamais qu'en son devenir. De ce devenir l'homme ne sera-t-il pas, en quelque mesure, l'artisan? Être conscient et agissant, déterminé sans doute, mais se déterminant, capable de prendre conscience de ses actes, sinon d'agir d'après sa conscience, son comportement ne sera jamais réductible à celui de quelque animal-machine. Le 'fatalisme', quel qu'il soit, qu'il lui plaira alors d'invoquer, ne lui servira jamais que d'assurance contre les caprices de ce qu'il appellera 'fortune' ou 'hasard' et, davantage encore, contre le vertige de cette indétermination pratique, à laquelle il serait tenté de redonner le nom de liberté.

Ainsi pourrait argumenter le Philosophe, s'il en était encore à son apprentissage philosophique, au temps de *la Promenade du sceptique*, dans le pays des doctrines et des systèmes. Mais l'heure n'est plus de raisonner, mais de vivre ou, comme il aime à dire, de 'cheminer'. En sa trame même, *Jacques le Fataliste* figurera la vivante allégorie de ce cheminement. Le fatalisme va être mis à l'épreuve non de quelque argumentation, mais de l'expérience ou plutôt de cette multitude d'observations et d'expériences prises sur le vif, auxquelles l'invention de Jacques et de son maître va servir de réceptacle et de banc d'essai. Il ne s'agit pas de glorifier une philosophie, ni moins encore de réfuter une doctrine par l'absurde, d'écrire un 'Jacques ou le fatalisme', dans l'esprit de *Candide ou l'optimisme*. Car, après tout, le fatalisme n'est pas plus absurde, théoriquement, que tout autre système, et, pratiquement, il a même beaucoup de chances de l'être un peu moins. Mais il est piquant de voir comment raisonne et agit celui qui se proclame fataliste, lorsqu'il est mis en présence de tout ce que la vie ou la fertile imagination d'un romancier lui ménage de rencontres et de hasards.

Que la réponse ne se laisse pas déduire de l'idée, la personne de Jacques, mieux que toute anecdote ou tout propos, en portera d'abord et constamment témoignage. Il suffit de se reporter à la suite d'un portrait commencé comme un évangile selon Spinoza. 'D'après ce système on pourrait s'imaginer que Jacques ne se réjouissait, ne s'affligeait de rien; cela n'était pourtant pas vrai. Il se conduisait à peu près comme vous et moi. Il remerciait son bienfaiteur pour qu'il lui fît encore du bien. Il se mettait en colère contre l'homme

[16] *Jacques le Fataliste*, AT. vi. 15.

injuste; et quand on lui objectait qu'il ressemblait plus au chien qui mord la pierre qui l'a frappé: "Nenni," disait-il, "la pierre mordue par la chien ne se corrige pas; l'homme injuste est modifié par le bâton." Souvent il était inconséquent comme vous et moi, et sujet à oublier les principes, excepté dans quelques circonstances où sa philosophie le dominait évidemment; c'était alors qu'il disait: "Il fallait que cela fût, car cela était écrit là-haut." Il tâchait à prévenir le mal; il était prudent avec le plus grand mépris pour la prudence. Lorsque l'accident était arrivé, il revenait à son refrain: et il était consolé. Du reste bonhomme, franc, honnête, brave, attaché, fidèle, très têtu, encore plus bavard . . .'[17]

Le tout constitue un assez fier démenti à ce qu'on pourrait attendre de la doctrine: cynisme ou veulerie. Quant au détail, il permet de définir une sagesse et même de formuler une morale, par référence au moins implicite à un ensemble de 'valeurs'. Le plus étonnant n'est pas que cette morale existe, ni même qu'elle ne diffère guère de la morale des bonnes gens, de 'vous et moi', au gré de la générosité de Diderot ou de son optimisme. Plus merveilleux encore paraîtront 'l'inconséquence' primordiale, qui fait de Jacques le fataliste un être moral par excellence et le permanent illogisme avec lequel il s'abandonne au même 'tic' que Diderot, cet autre 'bavard'. Pour tous deux, et d'ailleurs pour tous les personnages qui surgissent dans le roman, moraliser est un passe-temps de prédilection et une amorce irrésistible, 'tant le naturel a de force'.

> Il se moque de tout, certain âge accompli
> Le vase est imbibé, l'étoffe a pris son pli . . .
> Qu'on lui ferme la porte au nez,
> Il reviendra par les fenêtres.[18]

Et voilà la morale installée le plus naturellement du monde au cœur d'un roman où elle semblait n'avoir que faire.

Son irruption ne saurait aller sans fracas. De même que *Jacques le Fataliste* est un anti-roman, la morale qui s'y affiche le plus ouvertement est une anti-morale, en dérision de toutes les morales d'obligation, de tradition ou de convention. Peut-il en être autrement dans un monde où l'on nous rappelle sans cesse que 'tout est néces-

[17] *Ibid.*, pp. 180-181.

[18] La Fontaine, Fables, II, 18: *La Chatte métamorphosée en femme.*

saire'? Or 'ce qui est nécessaire n'est en soi ni bon ni mauvais, ni beau ni laid . . .'[19] Pas de vice, pas de vertu en soi; ce que l'on décore de ce nom ne saurait être que relatif, et souvent plus déconcertant qu'édifiant. Au gré du milieu et au moment, 'chaque vertu et chaque vice se montre et passe de mode'.[20] Méfions-nous de ceux qui font étalage de leurs principes: 'Je ne sais,' dit Jacques, 'ce que c'est que des principes, sinon des règles que l'on prescrit aux autres pour soi': en vertu de quoi, il ne serait pas loin de penser que la plupart des prédicateurs ont chance d'être des imposteurs ou des escrocs. Méfions-nous des bons sentiments: c'est sur eux que l'on construit la morale la plus niaise et la plus ruineuse. Une analyse qui se veut clairvoyante les décape impitoyablement et les réduit à leur principe: l'amour-propre, le besoin de dominer. C'est ainsi que s'explique, selon Jacques, l'attachement des femmes ou des petites gens pour les animaux: 'l'animal se trouvant dans la société immédiatement au-dessous de la classe des citoyens commandés par toutes les autres classes, ils[prennent] un animal pour commander aussi à quelqu' un'.[21] Toute la vie se passe en faux-semblants, fausses interprétations ou, comme dit Jacques, en *quiproquo*: 'Il y a les quiproquo d'amour, les quiproquo d'amitié, les quiproquo de politique, de finance, d'église, de magistrature, de commerce, de femmes, de maris . . .'[22] Au-delà de cette permanente hypocrisie, se découvre le seul sentiment dont on ne puisse douter: l'égoïsme: 'Mon maître, mon maître, vous n'y avez pas bien regardé: croyez que nous ne plaignons jamais que nous . . .'[23] A certains moments, Jacques semble tout près de parler comme celui que Diderot appelle 'le tigre à deux pieds', l'homme au 'cœur velu', ce Fougeret de Monbron qui fait dire à son *Cosmopolite*: 'Je suis parfaitement convaincu que la droiture et l'humanité ne sont en tous lieux que des termes de convention, qui n'ont, au fond, rien de réel et de vrai, que chacun ne vit que pour soi; et que le plus honnête homme n'est, à proprement parler, qu'un habile comédien.'[24] Qu'en résulte-t-il? La raison du plus fort? La loi de la jungle? Un immoralisme radical va-t-il être érigé en système?

Pas le moins du monde. Tout système étant nécessairement faux, la logique de celui-là ne vaut pas mieux qu'une autre. C'est que

[19] Article 'Laideur', AT. xv. 410.

[20] Cf. *Neveu de Rameau*, édit. cit. note 124.

[21] *Ibid.*, p. 177-178

[22] *Ibid.*, p. 60

[23] *Ibid.*, p. 25.

[24] *Neveu de Rameau*, édit. cit. note 124.

l'homme n'est pas simple et qu'aucun ne se laisse mettre en formule. Est-il bon? Est-il méchant? La question favorite de Diderot, n'ayant pas de sens en soi, n'est susceptible d'aucune réponse. Cet être imprévisible qu'est l'homme va s'empresser de démentir par sa conduite, qui seule réellement importe, le jugement que l'on serait tenté de porter sur lui. Le moraliste, qui ne s'en persuade pas d'emblée, s'expose à de cinglants démentis et à de cruelles bévues. 'Je n'aime pas,' dit Jacques, 'à parler des vivants, parce qu'on est de temps en temps exposé à rougir du bien et du mal qu'on a dit; du bien qu'ils gâtent, du mal qu'ils réparent . . .'[25] *Jacques le Fataliste* roman du paradoxe, s'ouvre largement à ces paradoxes de conduite: anecdotes, histoires et rencontres ne s'y accumulent que pour en présenter le plus large éventail, le plus déconcertant recueil. Prenez un homme comme Gousse, qui fait alterner dans sa conduite les actes les plus vils et les plus généreux. 'D'après cette action héroïque, vous croyez à Gousse un grand fonds de morale? Eh! bien, détrompez-vous, il n'en avait pas plus qu'il n'y en a dans la tête d'un brochet . . . Il n'est pas plus malhonnête quand il me vole, qu'honnête quand il se dépouille pour un ami; c'est un original sans principes.'[26]

Grâces soient rendues aux originaux de cette espèce! Comme celle du *Neveu de Rameau* naguère, leur manifestation ne peut être que salutaire: ils confirment le Philosophe dans son aversion pour toute morale conventionelle et dans son espoir de trouver un autre fondement à son besoin de moraliser que la 'modification' dont ne rêve que trop, en ce siècle, un matérialiste qui se veut éclairé. Une telle entreprise s'est toujours révélée tyrannique: Sparte façonnait ses enfants à tolérer le mensonge et le vol, à condamner la pusillanimité ou le métissage, au nom de la patrie et pour la sauvegarde de la cité. Au nom de quoi la philosophie militante, lorsque les rois seront philosophes ou les philosophes seront rois, va-t-elle préparer des hommes à servir le bien de l'espèce? La 'modification', certes, est efficace et un autre 'original sans principes', le bourru bienfaisant, le brutal au cœur tendre qu'est le mari de la bonne hôtesse, n'en disconvient pas. 'Nature,' dit-il, 'm'a fait l'homme le plus dur et le plus tendre; je ne sais ni accorder ni refuser.'[27] Ne pourrait-il en être autrement? Sans doute, et l'éducation aurait pu en faire le héros

[25] *Jacques le Fataliste*, VI, p. 59.
[26] *Ibid.*, p. 70-71. [27] *Ibid.*, p. 105.

de quelque drame honnête ou d'un conte moral à la Marmontel. A tout prendre, ne vaut-il pas mieux qu'il soit resté ce qu'il est? L'esthétique s'accorde en Diderot avec la morale pour lui faire souhaiter de ne pas trop émonder les arbres, de respecter en l'homme son individualité naturelle et de ne pas tarir cette source d'émerveillement et d'instruction que lui offre le spectacle des originaux.

Il en résulte un ensemble de précautions ou de règles, négatives peut-être, mais dont le respect constitue, à défaut de morale, un préalable à toute morale. La première est un 'tu ne jugeras point', que Diderot semble reprendre de l'Évangile, mais avec une chaleur singulière. Chaque fois que Jacques intervient dans la dispute, c'est toujours pour s'y conformer. Ce n'est pas lui qui condamnera les 'monstres', qu'ils s'appellent le P. Hudson ou Mme de La Pommeraye. Leur fils? Ce serait peut-être un scélérat fieffé, peut-être un parfait honnête homme . . . Mais à eux-mêmes qui aura le courage de jeter la pierre? Ceux que la voix populaire désigne si volontiers comme des scélérats ne sont pas à condamner, mais à comprendre. Diderot intervient directement pour cette mise en garde: 'Ah! lecteur, vous êtes bien léger dans vos éloges et bien sévère dans vos blâmes . . .' On ne forcerait pas sa pensée en lui attribuant telle maxime que le marquis de Sade mettra plus tard dans la bouche de son sage Zamé. 'Tout est à prendre dans le cœur de l'homme, quand on veut se mêler de le conduire.'[28] Ce n'est, après tout, qu'une variante pragmatique de l'*Homo sum* de Térence et de son corollaire: 'et nihil humani a me alienum puto'. *Jacques le Fataliste* s'inscrit tout entier à la suite de ce vieil adage. Il suffit à dicter cette première vertu de compréhension et d'indulgence envers ses semblables qui découle pour tout homme d'une nécessité bien entendue.

Le même devoir d'acceptation vaut aussi et d'abord pour lui-même. Nier la nécessité est insensé; s'insurger contre elle, futile; s'y plier de mauvaise grâce ôterait tout plasir à la vie. Ici encore, la plus vieille sagesse s'accorde avec la plus neuve: non pas se résigner, mais consentir. 'Jacques mène son maître': invité à faire de cette évidence un accord, le maître objecte: 'Et que fait notre consentement à une loi nécessaire? Jacques:—Beaucoup. Croyez-vous qu'il soit inutile de savoir une bonne fois nettement, clairement, à quoi

[28] *Aline et Valcour, Œuvres complètes du marquis de Sade* (Paris, au Cercle du Livre Précieux, 1962), iv. 328.

nous en tenir? . . . Le maître: Mais où diable as-tu appris tout cela? Jacques:—Dans le grand livre . . .' Il aurait pu aussi bien le trouver, sous forme de recommandation, dans Sénèque. Mais lire dans 'le grand livre' de la nature et du monde élargit les horizons et les idées. On ne saurait mieux faire l'apprentissage de deux vertus opposées, mais complémentaires. Au 'nihil admirari' que Jacques met si naturellement en pratique, la vertu de prudence vient apporter non certes un correctif, mais un condiment, dont le capitaine de Jacques lui faisait apprécier la saveur, car il prétendait 'que la prudence ne nous assurait point un bon succès, mais qu'elle nous consolait et nous excusait d'un mauvais'.[29] Comprise de la sorte et définie avec cet humour, la prudence contribue à la tranquillité de l'âme et est indispensable à la bonne humeur. Voilà la recommandation essentielle, celle qui engage Jacques et son maître à s'enrôler allégrement parmi ceux qu'ils appellent 'les sectateurs de la gourde'.[30] Ils s'y retrouveront en robuste et joyeuse compagnie, fidèles à l'esprit de ceux qui, leur vie durant, ont illustré ces vertus fondamentales: indulgence, gaieté, curiosité, car si l'homme s'interroge en vain pour savoir d'où il vient et où il va, il serait aussi ingrat que sot de ne pas faire de sa chance de vivre un émerveillement perpétuel. Sous l'apparence capricieuse du hasard, la nécessité se charge de lui donner l'attrait de l'imprévu et le charme de l'absurde. S'il était donné aux hommes de régler en raison leur propre vie et, à plus forte raison, celle de leurs semblables, nul doute qu'ils n'en fissent un trajet monotone et fastidieux. Par bonheur, 'nous croyons conduire le destin, mais c'est toujours lui qui nous mène; et le destin pour Jacques était tout ce qui le touchait ou l'approchait, son cheval, son maître, un moine, un chien, une femme, un mulet, une corneille'.[31] Autant de contraintes peut-être, ou de soucis, mais aussi d'occasions, peut-être de signes. Au voyageur de garder les yeux ouverts et disponible au moins quelque partie de son cœur. Voilà pour l'essentiel de quoi est faite la sagesse de Jacques, non pas en dépit, mais en vertu de son fatalisme. Il en résulte un art de vivre, le plus traditionnel du monde, mais qu'il appartient à tout homme d'actualiser et de rajeunir.

Mais de cette sagesse peut-on tirer une morale? Donner sens à la vie? Instruire et faire des hommes? La réponse n'est pas une

[29] *Jacques le Fataliste*, AT. vi. 20. [30] *Ibid.*, p. 234. [31] *Ibid.*, p. 37.

thèse ni un credo, mais un homme: Jacques, tel que Diderot, substitut et ordonnateur du destin, a voulu le faire et l'a fait. Non pas fils de personne, mais enraciné dans un terroir, héritier d'une lignée, formé par l'éducation villageoise qui, au lieu de brimer sa nature lui a permis de s'épanouir. En lui se retrouvent des 'fibres', se conjuguent et s'harmonisent des héritages qu'on aurait pu croire discordants: celui de son grand-père Jason, le brocanteur puritain, celui de son parrain Bigre, le gaillard tonnelier. Pratiquement, il en est résulté un homme qui, aux yeux des professeurs de morale, n'est pas plus mauvais qu'un autre, peut-être un peu meilleur et, en tout cas, plus facile à vivre.

'J'ai beau,' dit-il, 'revenir sur le passé, je ne vois rien à démêler avec la justice des hommes, je n'ai ni tué ni volé ni violé . . .'[32] En quoi il ressemble sans doute, comme disait Diderot, à 'vous et moi'. Mais certains traits le distinguent davantage. Il a l'attendrissement facile, particularité assez étonnante chez un 'fataliste'. Quand il évoque le souvenir de son aîné mort à Lisbonne, lors du tremblement de terre, et que son maître lui représente que 'cela était écrit là-haut—Il est vrai, Monsieur, répond-il, je me le suis dit cent fois; et avec tout cela, je ne puis m'empêcher de pleurer.'[33] De quel obscur atavisme, de quelle faiblesse naturelle ou acquise, ces larmes si peu raisonnables peuvent-elles témoigner? Et quelle motivation plus obscure attribuer à cette maîtrise de soi qui, en d'autres circonstances entraine un refus de pleurer? Le Maître s'en indigne: 'Jacques, vous êtes un barbare, vous avez un cœur de bronze.—Non, Monsieur, j'ai de la sensibilité: mais je la réserve pour une meilleure occasion. Les dissipateurs de cette richessse en ont tant prodigué, lorsqu'il fallait en être économe, qu'ils ne s'en trouvent plus quand il faudrait en être prodigue.'[34] De quel nom appeler la nécessité, qui permet à un homme de régler ainsi sa compassion, ou de lui donner l'illusion qu'il la contrôle, d'en fixer ainsi la valeur?

Brusquement, cette sensibilité devint active et, sans qu'il sache pourquoi, pousse Jacques à des actions que, selon le cas, son Maître s'empressera d'appeler courage, héroïsme, bienfaisance, vertu. Contre quoi Jacques s'indigne; aucun mérite particulier ne s'y attache; elles n'ont aucune motivation morale et, quant à lui, il y verrait plutôt inconséquence ou sottise. Quand il se dépouille par exemple des 'deux gros écus', son seul bien, pour les donner à la

[32] *Ibid.*, p. 63 [33] *Ibid.*, p. 46. [34] *Ibid.*, p. 206.

bonne femme qui vient de casser sa cruche d'huile. C'est le contraire d'un acte libre, si l'on entend par là une action volontaire et délibérée; non pas 'une bonne action', mais une sorte d'impulsion élémentaire, viscérale à laquelle on ne peut se dérober. Réflexion faite, Jacques s'empresserait de la désavouer, 'gâtant,' dit-il, 'par mon regret, l'œuvre que j'avais faite.'[35] Qu'importe, puisqu'elle est faite et qu'en ses conséquences elle devient un acte moral? Car la bienfaisance est contagieuse, comme l'atteste l'histoire de M. Le Pelletier, ce chrétien qui, à la différence de tant d'autres, se conforme si spontanément à l'Évangile. D'aucuns s'en étonnent ou scandalisent. 'L'Évangile,' dit le Maître, 'est dans mon cœur et dans mon fourreau, et je n'en connais pas d'autre . . .' Celui de Jacques est 'écrit là-haut', sur le grand rouleau: 'chacun apprécie l'injure et le bienfait à sa manière', et le jugement diffère selon les hommes et même en chacun d'eux, à l'infini.[36]

Rien de cela n'est raisonnable; rien de cela n'a de sens. Mais tout prend un sens; nos actes ne nous suivent pas, ils nous précèdent. Sur quel chemin, nul ne le sait. Mais tout se passe comme si la nature s'orientait en nous et nous orientait avec elle vers quelque inconcevable fin. Jacques en paraît, malgré lui, si intimement persuadé, qu'un autre que lui serait tenté d'appeler Providence le Destin qu'il invoque. 'Dieu fait bien ce qu'il fait,' disait un autre Jacques, le Garo de La Fontaine. Le hasard serait-il le ministre de quelque providence en devenir? En discuter serait le plus vain des exercices. Tandis que son maître fait des phrases, comme on en trouve dans les livres, sur la vie à venir, Jacques garde obstinément les pieds sur terre. 'Je n'y crois ni décrois, dit-il; je n'y pense pas. Je jouis de mon mieux de celle qui nous a été accordée en avancement d'hoirie.' Mais il faut croire que dans cette vie même et dans l'émerveillement de vivre se trouve quelque chose de sacré. Suprême inconséquence, il arrive à Jacques de prier et à Diderot de transcrire sa prière: 'Toi qui as fait le grand rouleau, quel que tu sois et dont le doigt a tracé toute l'écriture qui est là-haut, tu as su de tous les temps ce qu'il me fallait; que ta volonté soit faire. Amen.—Le maître—Est-ce que tu ne ferais pas mieux de te taire?—Peut-être que oui, peut-être que non. Je prie à tout hasard.[37]

Le mot est trop accidentel, trop inattendu, pour qu'on en tire une conclusion. En *Jacques le Fataliste*, Diderot n'a pas voulu

[35] *Ibid.*, p. 85. [36] *Ibid.*, p. 62. [37] *Ibid.*, p. 167-168.

élever un autel au 'Dieu inconnu', ni s'en remettre pour le désigner à quelque nouveau saint Paul. Mais cette brusque élévation est bien dans la logique ou, si l'on veut, l'illogisme fondamental de *Jacques le Fataliste*, et elle en accentue le caractère déconcertant. Pas si déconcertant cependant que l'on ne puisse reconnaître dans cet étrange roman le départ de la grande quête qui, de Diderot à Camus, a lancé sur les chemins de Jacques tant de pèlerins qui, sans avoir l'illusion de donner un sens à la vie, ont été persuadés qu'il fallait penser et vivre comme si la vie avait un sens. A chacun d'eux Diderot a donné mieux qu'un exemple: un antidote. A l'angoisse et à la nausée de tant d'autres, s'opposent sa verdeur, son allégresse, sa confiance, le refus du tragique, l'absence de prétention. Libre à chacun d'interpréter *Jacques le Fataliste* à sa fantaisie, de lui donner un autre sens. Diderot ne s'y oppose pas; il l'a même voulu ainsi. Cette liberté aussi est dans l'esprit du roman; elle fait corps avec lui. Mais elle ne s'exerce pas dans le vide et ne saurait se réduire au simple divertissement. Qui lira ce chef-d'œuvre dans l'esprit que Rabelais souhaitait pour le sien s'apercevra que la réflexion morale, sans aucune trace de lourdeur ni de pédantisme, lui donne sa portée véritable et sa très piquante dignité.

The concept of mœurs *in Diderot's social and political thought*

Arthur M. Wilson

Mœurs is a word that often flowed from the pens of the *philosophes*. Old though the term already was in the French language, some of the most exciting and most original books of the eighteenth century bore in their titles the promise that the study of *mœurs* would be their central focus—Voltaire's *Essai sur les mœurs*, Duclos' *Considérations sur les mœurs de ce siècle*, Toussaint's *Les Mœurs*. The subtitle of *L'Esprit des lois* is *du rapport que les lois doivent avoir avec ... les mœurs*. And Rousseau, in his famous prize essay, was responding to the question 'si le rétablissement des sciences et des arts a contribué à épurer les mœurs.' The *philosophes* very generally accepted the dictum of Duclos that 'les mœurs, plus que les lois, font et caractérisent une nation.'[1]

Two reasons, each of them very characteristic of the Age of Enlightenment, are prominent in explaining this eighteenth-century interest in *mœurs*. In the first place, anti-clericals such as Toussaint were eager to argue that the morals inculcated by natural religion are just as good, better in fact, and certainly more universal, than those taught by any single cult, Christianity included.[2] In the second place, for the historiographers and social scientists of the Enlightenment (and there were both among the *philosophes*), the study of *mœurs* helped to get at the heart of the understanding of history,

[1] Charles Pinot Duclos, *Œuvres complètes*, 10 vols. (Paris 1806), vi. 59.

[2] Toussaint wrote in his *Avertissement*: 'la Religion n'y entre qu'en tant qu'elle concourt à donner des mœurs; or, comme la Religion naturelle suffit pour cet effet, je ne vais pas plus avant. Je veux qu'un Mahométan puisse me lire aussi-bien qu'un Chrétien: j'écris pour les quatre parties du monde.' Regarding Toussaint, see T. J. Barling, 'Toussaint's *Les Mœurs*,' *French Studies* (1958), xii. 14-20.

the explanation both of continuity and of change. Under the influence of Montesquieu one studied *mœurs* as an aspect of historical relativism, affected by climate and geography. Under the influence of Voltaire one studied *mœurs* as an example of the importance of cultural history as well as in a context of historical relativism. Moreover, *mœurs* were being discovered to be of an almost infinite variety. The abundant literature of exploration and travel served to draw attention to this variety, thus raising the question of what, if anything, could be predicated of all men, a topic that the eighteenth century found irresistible. 'The discrimination of the historically unique from the humanly universal is an unavoidable obligation of those who pretend to discover the dynamics of . . . change,' writes a twentieth-century social scientist, and the *philosophes*, we can now see, had an instinct for that discrimination.[3] The nascent sciences of ethnology and anthropology were illuminated by this realization that *mœurs* are basic in a society and that they vary greatly, while moralists and reformers dilated upon the evidence that *mœurs* are dangerously subject to deterioration and corruption.

Diderot, too, used the word *mœurs* very frequently, so that, by leafing through his works, it is easy to find several hundred instances. The word *mœurs* has a multitude of meanings, as everyone knows, by this fact making it a plague to persons whose mother tongue is not French. Diderot often used the word, as does everybody else, to refer to an individual's standards of conduct. Thus he spoke, in references to individuals, of their having *bonnes mœurs*, or *mauvaises mœurs*, or *mœurs corrompues*, the word *mœurs* constituting a sort of measuring stick for evaluating standards or norms of socially acceptable behaviour, accompanied by an overtone of what is socially acceptable with regard to sexual behaviour. Diderot prided himself upon his own possession of *mœurs* in this private and individual sense. For example, in an autobiographical passage in 'De la poésie dramatique', he described a person named Aristes in a way that must be confessed to be fondly narcissistic. Among all the other praise heaped upon Aristes, Diderot remarked that he was 'sévère dans ses *mœurs*.'[4] Again, when trying to advise the somewhat way-

[3] K. H. Silvert, *Expectant Peoples: Nationalism and Development* (New York [1963]), p. 4.

[4] Denis Diderot, *Œuvres complètes*, ed. Jules Assézat and Maurice Tourneux; 20 vols. (Paris 1875–1877), vii. 390, henceforth cited as AT.

ward young actress, Mlle Jodin, Diderot sounded a great deal like Polonius. 'Tâchez donc d'avoir des mœurs.'[5] 'Les mœurs de mon père ont toujours été bonnes,' wrote Mme de Vandeul. 'Il n'a de sa vie aimé les femmes de spectacles ni les filles publiques.'[6]

All of the *philosophes*, Diderot first among them, liked to think of themselves as possessing *mœurs* in the happy sense of the term. All of them save perhaps La Mettrie, who apparently did not care. Thus they tried to counteract the imputation that men critical of the established religion must be depraved. 'Il est bien plat de juger sans cesse les mœurs par les principes spéculatifs,' wrote Diderot in a letter published anonymously in the *Mercure de France* in June 1771.[7] Palissot's play, *Les Philosophes*, enraged the men who were his target because the whole point of the piece was to suggest that the *mœurs* of the *philosophes* were vicious and corrupt. 'Le philosophe qui manque de religion,' Diderot once wrote, 'ne peut avoir trop de mœurs.'[8] His biographers can probably be made to admit that Diderot was more than averagely aware of his 'image'. It is evident that he used the concept of *mœurs*, in the private and personal sense of the word, as a tactic of self-justification and self-praise. 'Il faut défendre ses opinions par ses mœurs; et moins les opinions sont populaires, plus il importe que les mœurs soient irrépréhensibles.'[9]

Diderot continued to use the word *mœurs* in self-vindication up to the end of his career. Proof of this can be seen in the frequency with which he mentioned *mœurs* in his *Essai sur les règnes de Claude et de Néron*, the second edition of which has for its subtitle *et sur les mœurs et les écrits de Sénèque*. It has often been observed that in this *Essai* Diderot identified with Seneca.[10] This constituted a rather remarkable turnabout, for in the *Essai sur le mérite et la vertu* Diderot had been very critical of Seneca.[11] What came to fascinate Diderot, once he had succumbed to the blandishments of Holbach and Naigeon and had begun to write an introduction to La Grange's

[5] Denis Diderot, *Correspondance*, ed. Georges Roth (Paris 1955–), vi. 240.

[6] AT. i. lxi.

[7] Roth, xi. 51.

[8] Roth, v. 105 (Aug. 21, 1765).

[9] Roth, viii. 100 (Aug. 28, 1768).

[10] Fritz Schalk, *Diderots Essai über Claudius und Nero* (Köln & Opladen [1956]), pp. 20, 26; J. Robert Loy, '*L'Essai sur les règnes de Claude et de Néron*,' *Cahiers de l'Association Internationale des Études Françaises* [henceforth cited as *CAIEF*], no. 13 (juin 1961), 248; Douglas A. Bonneville, *Diderot's* Vie de Sénèque: *A Swan Song Revised* (Gainesville, Fla., 1966), p. 40.

[11] AT. i. 118 n.; see Diderot's later comments upon this passage (AT. iii. 176-178).

translation of Seneca's works, was whether Stoic virtue could really survive a close association with despotic power. Seneca, once he had accepted a position as Nero's tutor, found that he could not disengage and was forced step by step into the most horrendous of moral compromises. Did he thereby lose his virtue, or did he not? We know that Diderot asserted that he did not, though with a stridency and an inflated rhetoric that makes the *Essai sur les règnes de Claude et de Néron* his least pleasing work. But there is an excellent reason for this identification—and, indeed, for this stridency. Diderot, too, had accepted favours from a despot and found, too late, that he could not disengage. Catherine the Great was Diderot's Nero.[12] And there were many of Diderot's countrymen who thought that he had compromised or even forfeited that virtue, those *mœurs*, of which he was so proud. So, when Diderot praised the *mœurs* of Seneca, as he so often did, he was also praising his own.[13]

All this is of course of interest biographically. But more significant than that, especially to the student of the history of ideas during the Enlightenment, is an examination of how Diderot used the concept of *mœurs* as a point of focus in the unfolding of his social and political philosophy. His earliest works show that he then used the word very sparingly. But when he began to meditate, as he did in the *Entretiens sur le Fils naturel* (1757) and in *De la poésie dramatique* (1758), upon the rôle that the theatre could be made to play in the life of a nation, the references to *mœurs* became frequent.[14] 'Le théâtre,' Diderot continued to say, in 1772, 'peut être une école capable de former les mœurs par sa nature.'[15] This growing interest in the part played by *mœurs* in the life of a nation broadened and deepened as Diderot became increasingly familiar with art. The *Salons* show him musing upon the relation of art to *mœurs*, show him praising Greuze—'prédicateur des bonnes mœurs'—, accusing Boucher of being a corrupter of *mœurs*, and castigating Baudoin for having bad taste because he had bad *mœurs*.[16] In the *Salons* Diderot

[12] Jean Fabre, in *CAIEF*, no. 13 (juin 1961), p. 396.

[13] AT. iii. 14, 25, 29, 38, 71, 144 n., 159, 269.

[14] A.T., vii. 108, 130, 313, 369-373, 394.

[15] Roth, xii. 15 (Jan. 6, 1772).

[16] Greuze (Denis Diderot, *Salons*, edd. Jean Seznec and Jean Adhémar, 4 vols. [Oxford 1957-]), i. 143; ii. 140, 155; AT. x. 501 [*Essai sur la peinture*]). Boucher (Diderot, *Salons*, ii. 76; AT. x. 501). Baudoin (Diderot, *Salons*, ii. 140; iii. 198, 201; AT. xii. 92-93 [*Pensées détachées sur la peinture*]).

studied Le Prince's pictures of Russia for their depiction of Russian *mœurs*, and speculated upon the *mœurs* of the Ancients and the *mœurs* of Christianity as he gazed upon the *grandes machines*, the large so-called historical paintings, that hung in the positions of greatest honour at the Louvre during the biennial exhibitions.[17] Art forms, Diderot believed, do not create *mœurs*—it is the other way round. *Mœurs* are more fundamental and deep-seated than art forms, but they are revealed by the arts. 'Les beaux-arts ne font pas les bonnes mœurs; ils n'en sont que le vernis.'[18] Diderot trained himself to observe instances of art forms that are affected by *mœurs*: 'Mais admirez ici l'influence des mœurs. Il semble qu'elle devienne la base de tout. Vous allez à Constantinople et là ... il semble que plus un édifice, une maison ressemble à une prison, plus elle soit belle.'[19]

The deep-seatedness of *mœurs* in the life of a nation confers upon them, in Diderot's estimation, a tenacity that makes them very hard to change. Why, he asked, did Chinese *mœurs* remain constant in spite of the successive conquests of China? It was because, though only a handful of men were needed to conquer China, it would have required millions to change her.[20] In Diderot's estimation, *mœurs* have an authority over a people that is not easily deflected and, when once corrupted, not easily repaired. For a *philosophe* who desired, on the one hand, to improve social behaviour or, on the other, to prevent or delay its corruption, an understanding of the nature of *mœurs* offered an opportunity to explore the potentialities (and also the limitations) of social engineering.

The process, the dynamics by which a change in *mœurs* may be either stimulated or retarded, became in Diderot's later life one of the centres of preoccupation of his social philosophy. This can be seen by turning especially to his *Supplément au Voyage de Bougainville*, his *Mémoires pour Catherine II*, his *Observations sur le Nakaz*, and

[17] Le Prince (Diderot, *Salons*, ii. 172, 173, 174, 177). *Mœurs* in art (Diderot, *Salons*, i. 214-215).

[18] AT. iii. 469. Cf. Diderot, *Observations sur le Nakaz* (Denis Diderot, *Œuvres politiques*, ed. Paul Vernière, Classiques Garnier, p. 446): 'Ce ne sont pas les beaux-arts qui ont corrompu les mœurs.'

[19] Roth, iv. 130 (Sept. 2, 1762). Diderot had alluded to this aspect of Turkish architecture once before (Denis Diderot, *Lettre sur les sourds et muets*, ed. Paul H. Meyer, *Diderot Studies* (Geneva 1965), vii. 98). On Diderot's doctrine of the arts and *les mœurs*, see Henry Vyverberg, *Historical Pessimism in the French Enlightenment* (Cambridge, Mass., 1958), pp. 190-194.

[20] AT. ii. 327-328; cf. Diderot's 'Fragments échappés du portefeuille d'un philosophe' (AT. vi. 447).

his *Essai sur les règnes de Claude et de Néron*. In all of these his references to *mœurs* are numerous. As early as 1760 Diderot had remarked that 'la politique et les mœurs se tiennent par la main,' and his experience in later life, during which he became ever more interested in politics, confirmed rather than altered this conviction.[21] What he was attempting to analyse were the principles of morals and legislation. This subject, later to be the title of Jeremy Bentham's most famous book, fits very aptly the earlier and equally utilitarian concern of Diderot, namely the relationship of *les mœurs et les lois*.

It is interesting to note that Machiavelli, too, was greatly interested in this question of the relationship of legislation and morals. Thus he writes in the *Discorsi sopra la prima deca di Tito Livio*: 'Perchè, cosi come gli buoni costumi [*mœurs*], per mantenersi, hanno bisogno delle leggi; cosi le leggi, per osservarsi, hanno bisogno de' buoni costumi [*mœurs*]'.[22] A systematic examination and comparison of Diderot's and Machiavelli's works would undoubtedly reveal some very interesting parallels. Certainly both men were anxiously concerned with what it is that brings about the decay and corruption of a people's *mœurs*.

Diderot operated from the definition of *mœurs* that appeared in the *Encyclopédie* and which he may have written himself.[23] *Mœurs* are 'actions libres des hommes, naturelles ou acquises, bonnes ou mauvaises, susceptibles de règle & de direction.' The phrase 'naturelles ou acquises' is standard to definitions of *mœurs* found in French dictionaries: it appeared in *Le Dictionnaire de l'Académie Françoise*, edition of 1694—and in the edition of 1935; it appeared in the 1702

[21] Roth, iii. 130 (Oct. 12, 1760). On Diderot's increasing interest in political theory, see Arthur M. Wilson, 'The Scope and Development of Diderot's Political Thought', *Studies on Voltaire* (1963), xxvii. 1871–1900.

[22] Machiavelli, *Discorsi*, Book I, cap. xviii. For the equivalence of the Italian word *costumi* and the French word *mœurs*, see *Nouveau Dictionnaire françois-italien*, 2 vols. (Geneva 1677), ii. 464, s.v. 'Costumi'; Francesco de Alberti di Villanuova, *Nuovo dizionario italiano-francese* (Nizza 1788), p. 240, s.v. 'Costume'; Ottavia Cesana, *Lingua viva francese in relazione coll'italiano* (Milano-Roma-Napoli 1912), p. 103, s.v. 'Costume'; Giorgio Alessandroni, *Dizionarietto delle difficoltà per ben tradurre dall' italiano in francese* (Ferrara [1921]), p. 78, s.v. 'Costume'. Cf. the Amelot de la Houssaye translation of Machiavelli's *Le Prince*, cap. iii.

[23] *Encyclopédie*, x. 611b. Jacques Proust, *Diderot et l'*Encyclopédie (Paris 1962), p. 536, rejects Diderot's authorship of the article 'Mœurs'; *per contra*, John Lough, 'The Problem of the unsigned articles in the *Encyclopédie*', *Studies on Voltaire and the Eighteenth Century* (1965), xxxii. 369, thinks the article 'may reasonably be attributed to Diderot despite the absence of Naigeon's guarantee.'

edition of Furetière, and in the 1771 edition of the *Dictionnaire de Trévoux*; and it appears in the current edition of the *Petit Larousse*. However, the phrase 'susceptibles de règle & de direction' is peculiar to Diderot, a part of his definition that does not appear in other dictionaries and encyclopaedias, and smacks of that social determinism characteristic of him and reminiscent of his *Lettre à Landois* (1756).

The phrase 'susceptibles de règle & de direction' is fully compatible with Diderot's philosophy of the nature of man. Man is by nature neither all good nor all bad. What *can* be predicated of man is that he is modifiable and he is educable. 'L'homme, libre ou non, est un être qu'on modifie.'[24] Man is by his nature neither vicious nor virtuous—he is *bienfaisant* or *malfaisant*.[25] *Mœurs* signified to Diderot, to use a Freudian term, the internalization of controls. It follows, then, that in dealing with human nature the norms of socially acceptable behaviour, that is to say *les mœurs*, should be aimed towards *bienfaisance* instead of *malfaisance*. Even Rousseau, though he declared man a being naturally disposed to goodness, insists with impressive gravity upon the importance of *mœurs* in a society, and declares that the shaping of *mœurs* is the most important thing that the Legislator does.[26] How much more important even than this were *mœurs* in Diderot's system of social ethics, for his system was oriented much more deterministically than Rousseau's.

If man, then, is 'susceptible de règle & de direction,' where does this model and guidance come from? In Diderot's opinion, it comes from laws, but only slowly. He was enough of a sociologist to know that habits of behaviour are only very gradually responsive to legislation. 'Il n'en faut pas douter, les lois, avec le temps, changent les mœurs d'un peuple. Mais la loi a son effect dès qu'elle est publiée, et les mœurs qui consistent dans un certain tour de tête commun à tous les membres d'une société n'en restent pas moins d'abord dans

[24] *Encyclopédie*, x. 601-602, s.v. 'Modification, Modifier, Modificatif, Modifiable'. Naigeon listed this article as being by Diderot (Lough, art. cit., p. 355). Lester G. Crocker, *An Age of Crisis: Man and World in Eighteenth Century French Thought* (Baltimore [1959]), p. 278, points out how the doctrine in this article is similar to that in the *Lettre à Landois*. Cf. Pierre Hermand, *Les Idées morales de Diderot* (Paris 1923), pp. 86-87.

[25] *Encyclopédie*, ix. 945, s.v. 'Malfaisant'; attributed to Diderot by Naigeon (Lough, art. cit., p. 355).

[26] Rousseau, *Du contrat social*, livre II, cap. xii.

toute leur force: ce n'est qu'à la longue qu'une action conforme aux mœurs et proscrite par la loi devient moins commune à force d'avoir fait éprouver les inconvénients de ce contraste.'[27]

This conviction led Diderot to speak of *mœurs* almost invariably in terms of *habitudes*, of customary patterns of action that are not easy to change by legislation. The social approval given to duelling in spite of severe laws against it was a case in point.[28] Were he alive today he would no doubt observe that the United States' difficulties with the enforcement of its civil rights legislation is a striking instance of the impediments to bringing *mœurs* into conformity with laws. Similarly, it is equally difficult for laws to retard that corruption of *mœurs* which Diderot so frequently mentioned, always with abhorrence and dread.[29]

Nevertheless, Diderot believed that to bring *mœurs* into conformity with legislation while trying to prevent their decay and corruption was one of the chief purposes and most important functions of government. Eager improver and utilitarian that he was, he looked to enlightened legislation to modify and ameliorate standards of socially acceptable behaviour. In his *Mémoires pour Catherine II* he often pointed out her opportunities in this respect.[30] And in the *Observations sur le Nakaz* he wrote that 'Je crois que les mœurs sont des conséquences des lois,' and again, 'L'amélioration des mœurs tient à la bonne législation.'[31]

In the *Supplément au Voyage de Bougainville*, Diderot gives another and quite complex definition of *mœurs*. Replying to the question 'Qu'entendez-vous donc par les mœurs,' he wrote, 'J'entends une soumission générale et une conduite conséquente à des lois bonnes ou mauvaises. Si les lois sont bonnes, les mœurs sont bonnes; si les lois sont mauvaises, les mœurs sont mauvaises; si les lois, bonnes ou mauvaises, ne sont point observées, la pire condition

[27] AT. vi. 390 (1769).

[28] AT. vi. 390-392.

[29] AT. i. 12; iii. 180 n., 218, 269-270, 275, 317, 324; vii. 130; xi. 92; xviii. 61; Diderot, *Œuvres politiques*, p. 446.

[30] Denis Diderot, *Mémoires pour Catherine II*, ed. Paul Vernière (Paris [1966]), pp. 66, 143, 180.

[31] Diderot, *Œuvres politiques*, p. 372; cf. ibid., p. 349: 'Les mœurs sont partout des conséquences de la législation et du gouvernement.' Roth, viii. 117 (Sept. 6, 1768). 'Il n'y a de mœurs générales constantes que celles qui ont la législation pour base' (Diderot, *Œuvres politiques*, p. 376). In *Sur l'inconséquence du jugement public de nos actions particulières*, Diderot speaks of '. . . nos législations absurdes, sources de mœurs aussi absurdes qu'elles . . .' (AT. v. 357).

d'une société, il n'y a point de mœurs.'[32] This is uniting morals and legislation with a vengeance. It is to be noticed that in this passage Diderot emphasises that legislation, though a necessary cause, is not in itself a sufficient cause in establishing *mœurs*. Laws can be nullified by non-observance. Here Diderot is talking of mass behaviour—'C'est par la majeure partie d'une nation qu'on juge de ses mœurs.'[33] Nor is this a fanciful or unrealistic way of visualising the dynamics of social conduct and socially acceptable ethical forms. The ill-starred American experiment with Prohibition illustrated exactly what Diderot was talking about. Many were the observers who agreed with his diagnosis of just such a situation: non-observance of the law, even a bad law, is the worst condition that a society can find itself in.[34] What resulted in the United States was precisely the corruption of *mœurs* that Diderot would have predicted.

Diderot was an activist in politics. He believed that melioration was feasible. He believed that reforms could be accomplished. As an activist he plainly felt that governments had both the opportunity and the moral obligation to take the initiative in social improvement, in preserving *bonnes mœurs* and in forestalling *mœurs corrompues*. Thus Diderot did believe in Progress. But he was no mere Utopian, save by snatches, as when he brooded over the *mœurs* of the Tahitians or imagined an ideal society on the island of Lampedusa.[35] He was a social thinker who balanced his hopes of what could be accomplished through laws and administration by a realistic recognition that there can be a disheartening gap between a law conducive to good *mœurs* and the general observance of that law. He was also quite aware of the possibility of stagnation or retrogression. With his apprehension that the corruption of *mœurs* might overset the balance, Diderot could scarcely be said to be a naïf believer in the inexorable inevitability of Progress.

[32] Denis Diderot, *Œuvres philosophiques*, ed. Paul Vernière, Classiques Garnier, p. 504. Diderot repeats this almost *verbatim* in the *Observations sur le Nakaz* (Diderot, *Œuvres politiques*, p. 372).

[33] AT. iii. 18 n. [a note added in the 1782 edition of the *Essai sur les règnes de Claude et de Néron*].

[34] 'Pour la masse générale des sujets, la vertu est l'habitude de conformer ses actions à la loi, bonne ou mauvaise' (Diderot, *Œuvres politiques*, p. 321).

[35] For an analysis of the Utopian elements in Diderot's thought, see Hans Hinterhäuser, *Utopie und Wirklichkeit bei Diderot: Studien zum 'Supplément au Voyage de Bougainville'* (Heidelberg [1957]), passim and esp. pp. 24, 127-129; see also Herbert Dieckmann's comments in his edition of Diderot, *Supplément au Voyage de Bougainville* (Geneva 1955), pp. xlviii-lxiv, xciv.

Because of his conviction that progress is not automatic and inevitable, Diderot expected leadership from government and was made restive when it did not develop. His quite harsh criticisms of the policy of Catherine II, amply deserved, prove how great was his disappointment.[36] In his satirical *Principes de politique des souverains* (1774), aimed at Frederick the Great, he had the unnamed sovereign say, 'Je me soucie encore moins des mœurs, mais bien de la discipline militaire.'[37] Recent historical writing has demolished the older view that the *philosophes*, Diderot among them, favoured benevolent despotism.[38] When Diderot spoke of the rôle of legislation, therefore, it was from the position of one who believed in constitutionalism, and who, when frustrated, spoke approvingly (though privately) of the need for revolution. His dissatisfaction with the governments of Europe was eloquently expressed in 1778 in his *Essai sur la vie de Sénèque le philosophe*: 'Après des siècles d'une oppression générale, puisse la révolution qui vient de s'opérer au delà des mers, en offrant à tous les habitants de l'Europe un asile contre le fanatisme et la tyrannie, instruire ceux qui gouvernent les hommes sur le légitime usage de leur autorité.' May 'these brave Americans' be able to forestall the corruption of *mœurs*, he continued: 'Qu'ils songent que ce n'est ni par l'or, ni même par la multitude des bras, qu'un État se soutient, mais par les *mœurs*.'[39] This solicitude about the Americans' preserving their *mœurs* is like Jefferson's concern lest his countrymen, by leaving the land and crowding into cities, lose their vigour.[40] It

[36] Furio Diaz, *Filosofia e politica nel settecento francese* (Torino 1962), pp. 562-563; Diderot, *Œuvres politiques*, pp. 343-344, 355-357. Cf. Wilson, art. cit., pp. 1889–1891, 1895–1896. Catherine II was greatly offended by Diderot's comments when she came across them in his manuscripts in 1785. 'Cette pièce,' she wrote to Grimm on Nov. 22, 1785, 'est un vrai babil. . . .' (Maurice Tourneux, *Diderot et Catherine II*, Paris 1899, p. 519.)

[37] Diderot, *Œuvres politiques*, p. 180.

[38] Peter Gay, *The Party of Humanity: Essays in the French Enlightenment* (New York 1964), pp. 274-277; Wilson, art. cit., pp. 1890-1891; Alfred Cobban, *In Search of Humanity: The Role of the Enlightenment in Modern History* (London [1960]), pp. 166-167; Diderot, *Œuvres politiques*, pp. xxvi-xxxiv; Robert Derathé, 'Les Philosophes et le despotisme', in *Utopie et institutions*, ed. Pierre Francastel (Paris 1963), pp. 57, 66; Franco Venturi, 'Oriental Despotism', *Journal of the History of Ideas* (1963), xxiv. 136. Cf. Diderot's vigorous and unambiguous observation in AT. ii. 381-382.

[39] Diderot, *Œuvres politiques*, pp. 491, 492.

[40] Thomas Jefferson, *Notes on the State of Virginia*, Query XIX: 'Corruption of morals in the mass of cultivators is a phenomenon of which no age nor nation has furnished an example . . . generally speaking, the proportion which the aggregate of the other classes of citizens bears in any State to that of its

is an interesting instance of the close parallels between Jefferson's and Diderot's social and political thought.

In the article 'Toucher' in the *Encyclopédie* Diderot had written that 'il est dangereux de toucher aux choses de la religion, des mœurs & du gouvernement.'[41] But touch upon them he did, and ever more daringly. In the last thing he ever published, the *Essai sur les règnes de Claude et de Néron*, he raised the question of whether or not it should be allowable for a philosopher to express himself freely on religion, politics, and *mœurs*. 'Il me semble enfin que, si, jusqu'à ce jour, l'on eût gardé le silence sur les mœurs, nous en serions encore à savoir ce que c'est que la vertu, ce que c'est que le vice. Interdire toutes ces discussions, les seules qui soient dignes d'occuper un bon esprit, c'est éterniser le règne de l'ignorance et de la barbarie.'[42]

To the end Diderot was concerned with the importance of *mœurs* in the well-being or pathology of a nation. If sometimes he was gloomy or bitter, he wrote disconsolately of 'la dépravation de nos mœurs,' or of what he called 'notre décrépitude.'[43] Thus he would complain of how luxury was corrupting *mœurs*.[44] And in such moments of discouragement, thinking of Seneca, he would argue that the only seemly rôle for a *philosophe* was one of withdrawal. 'Lorsque le philosophe se désespère de faire le bien, il se renferme, et s'éloigne des affaires publiques; . . . il s'exhorte à la vertu, et apprend à se raidir contre le torrent de mauvaises mœurs qui entraîne autour de lui la masse générale de la nation.'[45] At other times, when he was more in a fighting mood, he looked forward to the possible reinvigoration of a nation's *mœurs* in spite of the tyrannical or inept policies of governments. His solution—startlingly drastic—reveals to us the revolutionary Diderot, the Diderot of the final edition of Raynal, the Diderot who first and last attributed a preponderant rôle to *mœurs*:

husbandmen, is the proportion of its unsound to its healthy parts, and is a good enough barometer whereby to measure its degree of corruption. . . . It is the manners and spirit of the people which preserve a republic in vigor.'

[41] *Encyclopédie*, xvi. 446b, s.v. 'Toucher'; for attribution to Diderot, see Lough, art. cit., p. 383.

[42] AT. iii. 249.

[43] AT. ii. 94-95, 432; vi. 349; xvii. 469.

[44] 'Satire contre le luxe, à la manière de Perse' (Diderot, *Salons*, iii. 121-126). cf. 'Du luxe' in *Mémoires pour Catherine II* (Diderot, *Œuvres politiques*, pp. 284-300, esp. 286-287).

[45] AT. iii. 29.

On demandait un jour comment on rendait les mœurs à un peuple corrompu. Je répondis: *Comme Médée rendit la jeunesse à son père, en le dépeçant et le faisant bouillir.*[46]

[46] AT. ii. 276 (*Réfutation d'Helvétius* [1774]). Cf. Diderot to John Wilkes, Nov. 14, 1771 (Roth, xi. 223); the same idea is expressed in the third edition (1780) of Raynal's *Histoire des deux Indes*, probably one of the many passages contributed to this edition by Diderot (Denis Diderot, *Textes politiques*, ed. Yves Benot (Paris [1960]), p. 52 n.).

Mme du Châtelet and Leibnizianism: the genesis of the Institutions de physique

William H. Barber

The goings-on at Cirey-sur-Blaise have attracted the interest of gossips since the 1730s, but only during our present generation has it become widely recognised, thanks chiefly to the researches of Professor I. O. Wade, that the intellectual activities in that rather out-of-the-way château were of real significance for an understanding of Voltaire. That for a decade both Mme du Châtelet and her lover devoted much time there to scientific and philosophical study is commonplace knowledge, derived both from the publications which it produced and from their correspondence. Two areas of relative obscurity remain, however. First, the nature of the intellectual relationship between them is not easy to determine. The hostile opinions of contemporaries such as Mme du Deffand and König, who had their own reasons for sneering at Mme du Châtelet's intellectual preoccupations, may be discounted, but it is plain from her letters that she saw herself as no more than a humble (if intelligent) disciple of creative scientists and mathematicians such as Maupertuis and Bernoulli, and made no real claim to originality. Remarkable woman though she was, can she have exercised the guidance over Voltaire's activities in these fields which has sometimes been suggested?[1] How far, rather, did they not each go their own intellectual way; benefiting, obviously, from the mutual stimulus of discussion, but pursuing rather different reading, coming to their own conclusions, and composing works, under the same roof, of which the other had often little or no real knowledge

[1] E.g. by I. O. Wade, *Voltaire and Mme du Châtelet* (Princeton 1941), pp. 193-196.

until they were completed?[2] Secondly, the history of the evolution of Mme du Châtelet's scientific and philosophical opinions, and especially of her attitudes to Leibnizian and Newtonian thought, has not been easy to establish firmly, important though it is for an understanding of her relationship to Voltaire. Some new evidence has been made available, however, in Dr. Besterman's editions of Voltaire's correspondence and of the letters of Mme du Châtelet, and what follows is an attempt to throw a little further light on these problems with the help of that evidence and of further consideration of the manuscripts of Mme du Châtelet in the Bibliothèque Nationale.

Little information is available concerning Mme du Châtelet's education. Voltaire, describing the beginning of their liaison from a distance of a quarter of a century, tells us that her father had given her a thorough knowledge of Latin and its literature, but that 'son goût dominant était pour les mathématiques et pour la métaphysique'.[3] How seriously these tastes had been nourished up till 1733 is not easy to determine, but it seems likely that her encounter with Voltaire brought a strong new intellectual stimulus into her life.

Voltaire was aware within a few months of the beginning of their relationship that Mme du Châtelet's intellectual capacities were far above those of the average members of the fashionable society she frequented. His earliest description of her, in a letter to Cideville of 14 August 1733,[4] makes the point quite plainly:

Voicy ce que c'est qu'Emilie:
Elle est belle et sait être amie,
Elle a l'imagination
Toujours juste et toujours fleurie.
Sa vive et sublime raison
Quelquefois a trop de saillie:
Elle a chassé de sa maison
Certain enfant tendre et fripon,

[2] It was certainly possible for Mme du Châtelet to submit an entry for the essay competition on the nature of fire held by the Académie des Sciences in 1738 without Voltaire's knowledge: see Mme du Châtelet to Maupertuis, 21 June [1738]. *Lettres de la marquise du Châtelet*, ed. Besterman (Geneva 1958), no. 129. (Subsequent references to this edition will use the abbreviation C. followed by the number of the letter.)

[3] *Mémoires pour servir à la vie de M. de Voltaire, écrits par lui-même*, M. i. 7.

[4] Best. 624.

Mais retient la coqueterie;
Elle a je vous jure un génie
Digne d'Horace et de Neuton
Et n'en passe pas moins sa vie
Avec le monde qui l'ennuye,
Et des banquiers de Pharaon.

In a document of 1735, she herself comments on her situation, and alludes to her retirement to Cirey and perhaps also to her first contacts with Voltaire and his circle, in rather similar terms:

'Je suis persuadée que bien des femmes ou ignorent leurs talents, par le vice de leur education, ou les enfoüissent par preiugé, et faute de courage dans l'esprit. Ce que i'ay eprouvé en moy, me confirme dans cette opinion. Le hazard me fit connoitre de gens de lettres qui prirent de l'amitié pour moy, et ie vis avec un etonnement extreme, qu'ils en faisoient quelque cas. Je commençai a croire alors que i'etois une creature pensante. Mais ie ne fis que l'entrevoir, et le monde, la dissipation, pour lesquels seuls ie me croyois née, emportant tout mon tems et toute mon ame, ie ne l'ay crû bien serieusement, que dans un age ou il est encor tems de devenir raisonable, mais ou il ne l'est plus d'acquerir des talents.

'Cette reflection ne m'a point decouragée. Je me suis encor trouvée bien heureuse d'avoir renoncé au milieu de ma course aux choses frivoles, qui occupent la plus part des femmes toute leur vie, voulant donc employer ce qui m'en reste a cultiver mon ame.'[5]

Along with his literary distinction, his wit and his many personal qualities, Voltaire's capacity to open up new fields of interest for her—to give her, even, new insights into her own capabilities—may well have formed an important element in her first attraction to him. It was certainly as a direct result of her new association with Voltaire that she began to apply herself seriously to mathematical and scientific studies.

Voltaire's contact with Maupertuis had begun when on 30 October 1732 he had written to the author of the *Discours sur les différentes figures des astres*, then just published, to ask him his advice on points concerning the exposition of the Newtonian theory of gravitation which was destined to appear in the *Lettres philoso-*

[5] 'Préface du traducteur, 1735' to Mme du Châtelet's translation of Mandeville's *Fable of the Bees*; Ms at Leningrad reproduced in I. O. Wade, *op. cit.*, Appx. III, p. 232; and again in *id.*, *Studies on Voltaire* (Princeton 1947), pp. 136-137.

phiques.[6] The earliest extant letters of Madame du Châtelet show that by January 1734 she was already on familiar terms with Maupertuis and working hard at algebra under his tuition.[7] Maupertuis's protégé Clairaut, then in the first flush of his youthful mathematical fame, was also among her acquaintance by this period.[8] The early stages of her mathematical education, of the process of intellectual self-discovery to which she was to allude in 1735, were thus entrusted, thanks to Voltaire, to the guidance of one of the most distinguished mathematical scientists in contemporary Europe: and moreover, to the pioneer exponent of Newtonian views in France. At this point, both she and Voltaire were indeed very much his pupils: Voltaire where an understanding of Newton was concerned,[9] Mme du Châtelet more generally. The document of 1735 from which we have already quoted indicates that she soon came to a realisation that her scientific abilities (however remarkable for a woman, in the eyes of her contemporaries) would never go beyond the point of a capacity to understand and perhaps expound the work of others; that her bent might consequently lie in exposition and translation:

'Sentant que la nature m'avoit refusé le genie createur qui fait trouver des verités nouvelles, ie me suis rendüe justice, et ie me suis bornée a rendre avec clarté, celles que les autres ont decouvertes et que la diversité des langues rendent inutilles pour la pluspart des lecteurs.'[5]

She was, indeed, to make two brief ventures into the field of independent scientific enquiry, with her *Dissertation sur la nature et la propagation du feu*, entered for the essay competition on the subject held by the Académie des Sciences in 1738, and her public controversy with Mairan over the Leibnizian doctrine of 'forces vives',[10] but her major efforts certainly went into the less ambitious task of disseminating among French readers the intellectual achieve-

[6] Best. 515.

[7] C.2, 5, 8, 9, 10: all assigned by Dr. Besterman to January 1734.

[8] C.11, probably April 1734. See P. Brunet, *La Vie et l'œuvre de Clairaut* (Paris 1952), chap. II.

[9] Cf. the deferential tone, on such matters, of Voltaire's letters to Maupertuis: Best. 515, 516, 517, 519, 520, of the autumn of 1732.

[10] M. D. de Mairan, *Lettre à Madame *** sur la question des forces vives, ou Réponse aux objections . . . dans ses Institutions de physique* (Paris 1741). Mme du Châtelet, *Réponse de Madame *** à la lettre que M. de Mairan, Secrétaire perpétuel de l'Académie Royale des Sciences, lui a écrite le 18 février sur la question des forces vives* (Brussels 1741).

ments of others, and especially of Englishmen. In addition to her *Institutions de physique* and her translation of Newton's *Principia*, she left in manuscript a chapter on Newton's optics and the partial translation of Mandeville's *Fable of the Bees* from whose preface we have quoted.[11]

Mme du Châtelet's discipleship to Maupertuis and, through him, her allegiance to the cause of Newton in the struggle with Cartesianism, is very clear from her correspondence during the early years at Cirey. Her earliest known allusion to Newton, in a letter to Maupertuis of 23 October 1734,[12] is a contemptuous reference to a clerical author of a forthcoming anti-Newtonian treatise: 'Il ne sait pas cet homme-là que vous le foudroyerez'. In the autumn of 1735, Algarotti made an extended stay at Cirey and was welcomed as a fellow enthusiast in the crusade: 'Il a mis les sublimes découvertes de Mr Newton sur la lumière en dialogues qui peuvent (au moins) faire le pendant de ceux de Fontenelle'.[13] She even, it seems, set herself to learn Italian in order to read these dialogues (published in 1737 as *Il neutonianismo per le dame*) and may have toyed with the project of translating them.[14] 1736 seems to have marked the peak of purely Newtonian enthusiasm at Cirey: on 1 December, Mme du Châtelet announced to Maupertuis that Voltaire had completed 'une introduction à la philosophie de Neuton' (the *Éléments*, published after various vicissitudes in 1738), that Maupertuis had in fact succeeded in his ambition to 'faire un philosophe du premier de nos poètes'.[15] In the same letter, she insists upon the modesty of her own talents in this field—'Pour moi vous savez à peu près la dose dont je suis capable en fait de physique et de mathématique', but it would appear, from a remark addressed to Thieriot three weeks later, that she had at least a superficial acquaintance with the *Principia Mathematica*[16] by this time. Her curiosity about Newton, indeed, even seems to have led her to read his *Chronology of Ancient Kingdoms amended* in English:[17] in so far as this may in-

[11] Her unpublished Biblical commentary, the *Examen de la Genèse*, seems to be work of a similar type in a different field: see Wade, *Voltaire and Mme du Châtelet*.

[12] C.24.

[13] C.52: to an unidentified correspondent, 3 Jan. 1736.

[14] C.63: to Algarotti, 20 [April 1736] It is tempting to see in this perhaps not very serious proposal a hint that the idea of Newtonian translation was already taking shape in her mind.

[15] C.73.

[16] C.78: to Thieriot, 21 Dec. [1736]—a comment on the Latin verses by Halley which preface Newton's work.

[17] C.92: to Thieriot, 16 Jan. [1737].

dicate an interest in Newton's religious views, the fact perhaps has some significance.

This Newtonian year of 1736, however, was also the year in which the philosophy of Leibniz began to intrude upon the scene at Cirey. As we have suggested elsewhere,[18] Voltaire's concern with Leibniz before this date probably went scarcely beyond an acquaintance with Fontenelle's *Éloge* of him, and an interest in the areas of controversy between Leibniz and Newton as they emerge in the Leibniz–Clarke correspondence and the other relevant documents included in Desmaizeaux's *Recueil* of 1720.[19] This latter interest Voltaire's personal contacts with both Clarke and Desmaizeaux in London can hardly have failed to stimulate. There is nothing to indicate whether or not Mme du Châtelet was introduced to this topic by Voltaire during their first years at Cirey: references to Leibniz in her correspondence begin only in February 1738.[20] However, from August 1736 until late in 1738 Frederick of Prussia in his correspondence with Voltaire pressed upon the latter the claims of Wolff's Leibnizian ideas in the field of metaphysics and took up a position on the subject of free will which Voltaire assumed to Leibnizian;[21] he sent Voltaire translations of philosophical works by Wolff,[22] in part by the hand of his close friend baron Dietrich von Keyserlingk, who paid a brief visit to Cirey in July 1737.[23] Mme du Châtelet can scarcely have failed to acquire some awareness of Leibnizian ideas from this, but there is no evidence that they attracted her at this date.[24] Her first active concern with Leibniz sprang rather from her mathematical studies.

[18] *Leibniz in France* (Oxford 1955), pp. 175, 178.

[19] Pierre Desmaizeaux, *Recueil de diverses pièces sur la philosophie* (Amsterdam 1720), 2 vols.

[20] C.120: to Maupertuis [*ca.* 10 Feb. 1738.]

[21] *Leibniz in France*, pp. 178-182, 200-203.

[22] J. Deschamps, *Logique, ou réflexions sur les forces de l'entendement humain et sur leur légitime usage, dans la connaissance de la vérité* (Berlin 1736): a translation of C. F. von Wolff, *Vernünfftige Gedanken von den Kräfften des menschlichen Verstandes und ihrem richtigen Gebrauche* (1712); a manuscript French translation by Ulrich von Suhm of Wolff's *Vernünfftige Gedancken von Gott, der Welt und der Seele des Menschen, auch allen Dingen überhaupt* (1720). Frederick to Voltaire, 4 Nov. 1736 (Best. 1139); [*ca.* 5 Jan. 1737] (Best. 1192); 8 May 1737 (Best. 1763); 16 Aug. 1737 (Best. 1302).

[23] Voltaire to Frederick [*ca.* 30 July 1737] (Best. 1297).

[24] In a fragment of a letter to an unknown correspondent dated 15 November 1737 (Best. 1327) Voltaire describes Mme du Châtelet as 'une âme éclairée par tout ce que les Lokes, les Clarkes, les Leibnits, les Volf ont de bon . . .

The problem of kinetic energy, which had furnished Leibniz with the spearhead of his attack on Cartesian mechanics at the end of the previous century, remained a subject of debate until the publication of d'Alembert's *Traité de dynamique* in 1743. At Cirey, Voltaire was apparently the first to be concerned with it. He read, and was convinced by, Mairan's anti-Leibnizian *Dissertation sur l'estimation et la mesure des forces motrices du corps* during August 1736,[25] after having originally been lent a copy by the author himself in Paris the previous June or earlier.[26] When Mme du Châtelet read it is not exactly ascertainable, but that it made a considerable impression upon her is clear from the fact that in her *Institutions de physique*, published four years later, she discusses parts of it in detail (at that date of course critically, from a Leibnizian standpoint), and even specifically mentions having studied it with her young son.[27] It seems at least possible, then, that Voltaire, here as in other matters, may have been the agent through which her interest in the subject was aroused, and that it was in consequence of this that she read the treatise which won her over to the Leibnizian view, Johann Bernoulli's *Discours sur les lois de la communication du mouvement* (Paris 1727). She wrote to Maupertuis on 2 February 1738[28] to enquire, deferentially, whether he favoured Mairan or Bernoulli, and in response, apparently, to a letter (which has not survived) from him upholding Bernoulli she committed herself in a second letter later in the month to support for Leibniz.[29] Her change of view, when it came, must have been relatively swift, as it was to be later on the much wider issue of Leibnizian metaphysics.

une femme qui sait l'optique de Neuton aussi bien que les S'Gravesandes et les Muchenbrocks'. This would apparently imply a critical, eclectic attitude; and the tone of the remark is in any case rhetorical.

[25] Voltaire to Henri Pitot, 31 Aug. 1736; to Berger [*ca.* 1 Sept.] 1736 (Best. 1092, 1093). Mairan's essay had been published in 1730 in the *Mémoires de l'Académie des Sciences* for 1728. A later version was published independently in 1741.

[26] Voltaire to Mairan, 9 Nov. 1736 (Best. 1146).

[27] *Institutions de physique*, pp. 429-433. Mairan replied to these criticisms in his *Lettre à Madame *** sur la question des forces vives, ou réponse aux objections ... dans ses Institutions de physique* (Paris 1741), and elicited a rejoinder from her: *Réponse de Madame *** à la lettre que M. de Mairan ... lui a écrite le 18 février 1741 sur la question des forces vives* (Brussels 1741). Mme du Châtelet also mentions having just re-read Mairan's *Dissertation* in a letter to Maupertuis of 1 Sept. 1738, C.139.

[28] C.118.

[29] C.120: [*ca.* 10 Feb. 1738].

She had completed only a few weeks earlier[30] her entry for the essay competition on the nature of fire organised by the Académie des Sciences. This had included an incidental reference to Mairan's *Dissertation sur les forces motrices* which implied approval, and when she learned later[31] that her essay (together with Voltaire's) was to be published with the prizewinning essays, she went to considerable trouble to have her text amended.[32] To this the Académie would not consent, but when the volume finally appeared it contained an *errata* list in which figures a correction making perfectly clear Mme du Châtelet's new Leibnizian allegiance in the matter of 'forces vives'.[33]

In discussing the problem of kinetic energy in her letters to Maupertuis, it is clear that she is more disposed than he is to widen the matter out from a purely technical point of mathematical physics to a question with philosophical implications. With Voltaire's concurrent controversy with Frederick over free will no doubt in her thoughts, she hesitates as to whether the Leibnizian theory may not have unacceptably deterministic implications,[34] and, reproaching Maupertuis with his lack of concern with metaphysics—'Vous ne voulez point éclairer ses profondeurs, vous avez cependant bien tort'—she sketches a hypothesis concerning the nature of God's intentions in the matter of the laws of motion which would reconcile the findings of the physicists concerning the conservation of energy or movement with the morally necessary existence of free will in human beings.[35] It is clear, nevertheless, that

[30] Voltaire had begun experimental work with a view to entering for this competition as early as June 1737 (Best. 1279, 1280), and may have completed his essay by mid-December, when the steady bombardment of requests for scientific apparatus and materials aimed at the long-suffering Abbé Moussinot in Paris seems to cease abruptly. Mme du Châtelet, once again following Voltaire's lead, conceived the idea of competing herself only a month before the closing date, when his work was almost finished (C.129: to Maupertuis, 21 June, [1738]), and worked alone in secret and at night, presumably submitting her entry just before the new year. Cf. Mme de Graffigny, *Vie privée de Voltaire . . .* (Paris 1820), p. 141.

[31] C.132: to Maupertuis, 7 July [1738].

[32] C.148, 149, 151, 152: to Maupertuis, 24 Oct., *ca.* 5 Nov., 19 Nov., *ca.* 1 Dec. 1738.

[33] *Pièces qui ont remporté le prix de l'Académie Royale des Sciences en M. DCC XXXVIII, selon la fondation faite par feu M. Rouillé de Meslay, ancien Conseiller au Parlement* (Paris 1739). Mme du Châtelet's entry, pp. 85-168: footnote on p. 105 corrected in *errata* list, pp. 218-219.

[34] C.122: 30 April [1738].

[35] C.124, 9 May [1738]: 'J'ai envie de faire un moment le conciliateur comme

this metaphysical bent, however significant for later events, did not induce her at this stage to accept any other aspect of Leibnizian thought.[36] Throughout 1738 she remains preoccupied with Newtonian ideas, and especially with the obstacles Voltaire's *Éléments de la philosophie de Newton* is encountering in France. She even attributes Leonhard Euler's victory over Voltaire and herself in the Academy's essay competition to French Cartesian prejudice against Newtonian principles, referring to Euler as 'un leibnisien et par conséquent un cartesien'.[37] She seems, indeed, to assume in general that Leibnizians and Cartesians form a common front of opposition to Newton (primarily perhaps because of their rejection, on philosophical grounds, of the vacuum and of the force of attraction).

This would explain the impatient scorn of her and Voltaire's reactions to Wolff, that 'grand bavard en métaphysique',[38] her regret that Frederick has been so misguidedly brought up in the Leibnizian way of thinking.[39] At a rather deeper level, it may also to some extent account for her apparently sudden 'conversion' to Leibnizian metaphysics a few months later. Her admiration for Newton and his achievements was real and lasting, but it is apparent even from her discussions with Maupertuis over 'forces vives' that analyses of natural phenomena which were merely scientific in the modern sense (as Newton's were) did not satisfy her intellectually: she wished to

Mr de Mairan, et de dire, que Dieu peut avoir établi des lois de mouvement pour le choc des corps inanimés par lesquelles, ils conservent, ou communiquent, ou consomment dans des effets, la force qu'on leur imprime, mais que cela n'empêche point qu'il ne réside dans les êtres animés un pouvoir soi mouvant, qui est un don du créateur comme l'intelligence, la vie etc. Car si je suis libre, il faut absolument que je puisse commencer le mouvement, et si ma liberté était prouvée il faudrait bien convenir que ma volonté produit de la force quoique le *quomodo* me soit caché. La création, qu'il faut bien admettre quand on admet un Dieu n'est-elle pas dans ce cas-là, et n'y a-t-il pas mille choses qu'il nous sera toujours également impossible de nier, et de comprendre?'

[36] C.120: to Maupertuis, [*ca.* 10 Feb. 1738]. 'Le docteur Clarke dont Mr de Mairan a rapporté toutes les raisons dans son mémoire traite Mr de Leibnits avec autant de mépris sur la force des corps, que sur le plein, et les monades, mais il [a] grand tort à mon gré, car un homme peut être dans l'erreur sur plusieurs chefs, et avoir raison dans le reste. Mr de Leibnitz à la vérité n'avait guère raison que sur les forces vives, mais enfin il les a découvertes . . .'

[37] C.127: to Maupertuis, 22 May [1738]; cf. also Best. 1461, Voltaire to Thieriot, 21 [June 1738].

[38] C.146: to Maupertuis, 29 Sept. 1738.

[39] C.129: to Maupertuis, 21 June [1738].

relate theories in physics to a metaphysical framework which would also accommodate deism and a belief, for example, in the freedom of the will. Cartesianism might have served her had its physics not fallen into discredit precisely at the hands of Newton: but where Voltaire retained a Lockean cautiousness in these matters, she was less critical and more easily attracted by speculative theorising. As long as Wolff and Leibniz appeared to her as denigrators of Newton, like the Cartesians, she had little inducement to find their metaphysical doctrines acceptable. Contact in the early months of the following year with the Wolffian enthusiast Samuel König seems however to have brought her to the conviction that Wolffian metaphysics was in itself a satisfying account of the ultimate nature of things, and one which (contrary, it would seem, to her initial assumptions in 1737–38) did not necessarily impede acceptance of Newton's physics, provided Newtonian theories were taken as concerning themselves solely with *phenomena*. This is the attitude which seems to inspire that (in some ways) odd hybrid of Wolffian and Newtonian doctrine, the *Institutions de physique*, in the form in which it appeared in print in 1740.

While it may thus prove ultimately in a sense to be true that Mme du Châtelet was concerned with 'merging Leibnitzianism and Newtonianism', in Professor Wade's phrase,[40] there is no real evidence that this process began before König's arrival at Cirey in March 1739. Beyond the translations of Wolff which Frederick had sent to Cirey, and the original article by Leibniz on the subject of 'forces vives' which Mme du Châtelet mentions looking up,[41] the only other works by either philosopher of which she reveals any knowledge are Leibniz's correspondence with Clarke,[42] and Wolff's major Latin treatise on mathematics and physics, the *Elementa Matheseos Universae*.[43] Professor Wade has also

[40] I. O. Wade, *Voltaire and Candide* (Princeton 1959), p. 46.

[41] C.122: to Maupertuis, 30 April [1738]. Leibniz, 'Brevis Demonstratis erroris . . . Cartesii . . .', *Acta Eruditorum*, Mar. 1686; 'De Primae Philosophiae emendatione', *ibid.*, Mar. 1694; or 'Specimen Dynamicum', *ibid.*, April 1695.

[42] See above, p. 205.

[43] She wrote to Maupertuis, 3 Sept. [1738] (C.141) 'En lisant quelque chose de Volf l'autre jour je trouvai ces mots, que je veux vous mander car peut-être ne les connaissez-vous pas: *Vir a lumine singulari praeditus cel. de Maupertuis demonstravit vi motus vertiginis astrorum fieri posse, ut inducant figuram disceam, ac inde rationem reddit, cur nunc appareant, nunc iterum dispareant.*' The passage occurs (though with the readings *vir acumine singulari* and *ut induant figuram*) in the *Elementa*, 2nd edition (Halle

suggested[44] that the invitation to König was the result of an existing concern with the philosophical works of Leibniz and Wolff, rather than the occasion for its development, at Cirey. There seems to be no evidence in her or Voltaire's correspondence, however, to support the supposition that they had any prior knowledge of König's philosophical opinions before his arrival. The occasion for König's employment at Cirey seems rather to have been, simply, that Mme du Châtelet's enthusiasm for mathematical studies had been re-kindled, after a period spent primarily on problems in physics, by a brief visit paid to Cirey by Maupertuis in January 1739.

He had gone on to Basle to stay with the Bernoulli family, and she wrote to him there soon after his arrival: 'Vous m'avez donné un désir extrême de m'appliquer à la géométrie et au calcul. Si vous pouvez déterminer Bernoüilli à apporter la lumière dans mes ténèbres j'espère qu'il sera content de la docilité, de l'application, et de la reconnaissance de son écolière.'[45] The upshot of this, and the outcome of a long campaign by Mme du Châtelet to persuade Maupertuis himself to stay and help her, was that he came back from Basle in mid-March bringing both the younger J. Bernoulli and König with him to Cirey.[46] Bernoulli stayed for only ten days, but König, whom Maupertuis had known as a fellow-pupil in the Bernoulli household during his stay in Basle in 1734, remained with Mme du Châtelet until late in the year. He accompanied her from Cirey to Brussels in mid-May, and it seems that it was about this time that he initiated her into Wolffian metaphysics.[47] In September, however, in Paris, König gave her great offence by his indiscretions

1735), iii. 754-755 (*Elementa Astronomiae*, chap. IX, §1126). It is no doubt to this 3-volume 2nd edition of the work that she refers in C.146, to Maupertuis 29 Sept. 1738, and it may also be the 'mathématiques universelles' she mentions as owning in her letter to Prault of 16 [?Feb. 1739], C.186.

[44] *Op. cit.*, p. 37.

[45] C.175: 20 [Jan.] 1739. Maupertuis had been at Cirey 12–16 January: Mme de Grafigny, *op. cit.*, pp. 198, 202.

[46] O. Spiess, 'Voltaire und Basel', *Basler Zeitschrift für Geschichte und Altertumskunde* (1948), xlvii. 112; this article is based upon the Bernoulli correspondence in the Basle University Library.

[47] C.241: to J. Bernoulli, Brussels 30 June 1740. 'Enfin en vivant avec Mr de Koenig je parlais souvent de métaphysique avec lui, dans le voyage surtout en venant ici [i.e. that of May 1739] elle faisait le sujet de nos entretiens. Il me parla de celle de Leibnits et me fit naître l'envie de la connaître. J'avais apporté avec moi la métaphysique de Volf traduite en français que le p. royal de Prusse, à présent roi, m'avait fait traduire et m'avait envoyée manuscrite. Je la lus donc avec attention, et j'y trouvai de très belles idées, très neuves et que l'on ne connaissait point du tout en France.'

concerning the *Institutions de physique*,[48] and they finally parted in December 1739.[49] Dr Besterman's publication for the first time of Mme du Châtelet's letters to Bernoulli makes it possible to establish these facts more reliably and more precisely than in the past: they cannot, however, be fully elucidated outside the context of the history of the composition and publication of the *Institutions de physique* itself, and it is to this that we must now turn.

Mme du Châtelet addresses the *avant-propos* of her book to her son, and also says elsewhere that her original motive in writing a general work on physics was to provide him with an introduction to the subject. Too much importance clearly cannot be attached to this, but it might suggest that the idea was unlikely to have occurred to her before the boy's ninth birthday, in November 1736, by which time Voltaire was on the point of completing his *Éléments de la philosophie de Newton*. A more important factor was her realisation that in fact no up-to-date introductory textbook on physics was available in French,[50] and that the gap would not be filled by Voltaire's work whose scope was more limited. In her letter to Bernoulli of 30 June 1740 (C. 241), in which she is concerned to refute König's assertions of late 1739 that the book was virtually dictated by him, she claims that the complete manuscript was taken to Paris by her friend and neighbour Mme de Champbonin in 1738, before she had ever met König. It is clear from her and Voltaire's correspondence that Mme de Champbonin was in Paris in June 1738, and back at Cirey by early October,[51] so that Mme du Châtelet's work was plainly complete by mid-1738. It was submitted, anonymously, for official scrutiny to the physicist Henri Pitot, and his *Approbation*, printed in the book, is dated 18 September 1738.

It thus appears that, as with her *Dissertation sur la nature . . . du feu*—whose composition must have interrupted her work on the

[48] He both disclosed her authorship of the work and claimed the credit for its good qualities for himself, so she alleges: C.241, *cit. supra*.

[49] C.228, 229: to Bernoulli, 18 Dec., 28 Dec. 1739.

[50] *Inst. phys.*, p. 4. (All references are to the first edition, Paris, Prault, 1740. The London edition of 1741, Vaillant, has the same pagination.) Cf. also C.241, where Mme du Châtelet indicates that Mme de Champbonin drew her attention to this point and encouraged her to publish anonymously.

[51] Voltaire to Thieriot, 21 [June 1738], Best. 1461; Mme du Châtelet to d'Argental [*ca.* 5 Oct. 1738], C.147, Best. 1552 (both dates are well established).

Institutions de physique—she was essentially following a lead already given by Voltaire in writing a general book on physics, even if her intentions were to cover a wider field. And in making preparations for it to be published, she trod very closely in his footsteps, for Pitot was in contact with Voltaire and had been consulted by him concerning the *Éléments* in 1737;[52] and her publisher, with whom she dealt anonymously through Mme de Champbonin,[53] was Prault, who brought out the Paris ('London') edition of Voltaire's *Éléments* in the summer of 1738, and had been in touch with him since 1733.[54] She seems, too, to have written her book in complete secrecy. In her letter to Bernoulli (C. 241) she describes how in the summer of 1739 she finally brought herself to confide in König in order to obtain his expert advice, once she had decided to include some discussion of Leibnizian metaphysics:

> 'Je balançai longtemps si je me confierais à lui, enfin me croyant sûre de sa probité et de son attachement, je lui confiai mon secret. J'y trouvai l'avantage de lire mon ouvrage à un habile homme et d'être sûre par conséquent qu'il n'y aurait point de fautes, ce dont je doutais fort, n'ayant consulté personne.'

And in the same letter she says that in the first instance she was persuaded by Mme de Champbonin to publish partly because 'étant assurée de l'incognito parce que je ne me confiais qu'à elle, je jouirais du plaisir de me voir juger, sans courir aucun risque si le jugement n'était pas favorable'. The parallel here with her diffidence concerning her entry for the Académie's essay competition is plain, and altogether in keeping with her general lack of confidence in her scientific abilities. The implication seems clear that her work on the *Institutions* was concealed even from Voltaire, as was that on the prize essay. It is likely, however, that he may have been let into the secret after Pitot's official approval had been obtained (and the authoress's self-doubts quieted). In a letter to Lefranc de Pompignan of 30 October 1738 (Best. 1570) he deplores the backwardness of France in scientific matters, and the necessity of depending upon foreign authors in this field, remarking, in terms directly reminiscent of Mme du Châtelet's own comments, that 'Nous n'avons pas encore de bons élémens de physique' and announcing 'On va imprimer

[52] Best. 1268, 1281. [53] Best. 1572. [54] Best. 587.

enfin des Institutions physiques dont M. Pitot est l'examinateur et dont il dit beaucoup de bien'—though without, of course, naming the author.[55]

Matters moved slowly after Pitot's *Approbation* was obtained in September 1738. The *Privilège* was not taken out until 21 April 1740, and the book seems to have been published in November, though an advance copy was sent to Frederick in early September.[56] An explanation for this delay is offered in an *Avertissement du libraire* in the book itself:

> 'le premier Tome[57] des *Institutions de Physique* étoit prêt à être imprimé dès le 18 septembre 1738 comme il paroît par l'Approbation, et l'Impression en fut même commencée dans ce temps-là; mais l'Auteur ayant voulu y faire quelques changemens, me la fit suspendre; ces changemens avoient pour objet la Métaphysique de M. de Leibnits, dont on trouvera une Exposition abrégée au commencement de ce Volume.'

This would imply that the only reason for postponing publication was Mme du Châtelet's decision to include an exposé of Leibnizian metaphysics in her book: and since on the traditional view she can have decided this only after her conversations with König in May 1739, seven or eight months later, there is an apparent discrepancy which might seem to call the whole interpretation into question.[58] In fact, however, the situation was a good deal more complicated.

It is clear from a letter from Mme de Champbonin to Prault of 1st November 1738 (Best. 1572) that the immediate cause of the

[55] It is not wholly impossible that when he wrote to Pompignan Voltaire genuinely knew nothing of the authorship of the *Institutions*. Mme du Châtelet had contributed an anonymous 'Lettre sur les Elemens de la Philosophie de Neuton' to the *Journal des Sçavans* for September 1738 (pp. 534-541), praising Voltaire's work, and ending, in what is really a quiet puff for her own forthcoming book, with a plea in very similar terms to those used by Voltaire to Pompignan for a French 'Traité de Physique complet'. Voltaire would certainly have read this article shortly before writing to Pompignan: did he know who was its author?

[56] C.252, 249.

[57] No more were ever published. It seems possible however that Caussy was right in his assumption that the manuscript at Leningrad entitled *L'Essay sur l'optique: chapitre 4 De la formation des couleurs* by Mme du Châtelet was intended for the *Institutions de physique*, but for a further volume. See Wade, *Studies on Voltaire* (Princeton 1947), p. 119 and, for the text of the MS., pp. 188-208.

[58] Wade, *Voltaire and Candide*, p. 36.

delay was that Mme du Châtelet was having a fair copy made from the original, which is described as 'extrêmement brouillé'. And Mme du Châtelet herself later explains that the book 's'imprima très lentement parce que mon libraire qui ne me connaissait point . . . me quittait pour tous les romans qui se présentaient', so that when she went to Paris in September 1739 it was merely 'plus qu'à moitié imprimé'. It was only at this stage, she says, that she introduced the Leibnizian material of the early chapters, preparing the new text at speed and with König's help:

'J'engageai le libraire à recommencer les feuilles où je voulais mettre ma nouvelle métaphysique, et à faire quelques cartons, et je me mis à travailler. Il fallait pour bien faire lire plusieurs chapitres des ouvrages de Volf, comme ontologie, cosmologie &a, outre sa métaphysique que j'avais lue et que j'avais avec moi. Je n'avais point le temps de chercher dans les gros in-quarto les idées qu'il me fallait. Je priai Mr de Koenig de me faire des extraits des chapitres qui m'étaient nécessaires, ce qu'il eut la bonté de faire, et sur quoi je travaillai en partie.'[59]

Since Mme du Châtelet left Paris for Cirey in early November, returning at the beginning of December and leaving again for Brussels by the middle of the month, it seems likely that the bulk of this work was done in September and October.[60] These new early chapters were available in proof by April 1740, since she sent Frederick a copy of them, as 'mon essai de métaphysique . . . imprimé' on the 25th.[61] Her hopes, however, that the complete volume would be ready for sending to him 'vers la Pentecôte' (25 May that year) were not to be fulfilled, as we have seen.

Mme du Châtelet's explanations, however, occur in a letter to Bernoulli in which she is defending herself against König, and might therefore be felt to be in some degree suspect. In fact, corroboration of her account in certain respects is available from two quarters. In the first place, her statements about her Wolffian sources can be

[59] C.241 (30 June 1740).

[60] Best. 2000, C.227, 228.

[61] C.237. It would thus appear that the *Privilège* (21 April 1740) was not obtained until this new material was in print. One wonders whether it may not in fact have been necessary to obtain Pitot's approval for the revised text, and whether the description 'cet ouvrage dans lequel on a exposé les principes de la Philosophie de M. Leibnits & ceux de M. Newton' may in fact be an amendment of the original wording of the *Approbation*, although the original date of 18 Sept. 1738 has been retained in the version printed in the book. Solid evidence, however, is lacking.

substantially confirmed. She specifies her debts to Wolff's *Ontologia* in a footnote to her *avant-propos* (p. 13), and these are quite unmistakable, as I have shown elsewhere.[62] It would also be possible to demonstrate in detail that her second chapter, 'De l'existence de Dieu' closely follows Chapter 6, 'Von Gott', of Wolff's *Vernünftige Gedanken von Gott, der Welt und der Seele des Menschen, auch allen Dingen überhaupt*, the 'métaphysique' sent to Voltaire in French translation by Frederick and which she mentions as having with her. In both Wolff's and her own chapter, the same arguments, by and large, are presented in the same order.

Further confirmation is also provided by the substantial collection of manuscript material for the *Institutions de physique* to be found in the Bibliothèque Nationale.[63] These papers may be divided into three groups. The first consists of drafts in Mme du Châtelet's hand for the *avant-propos*, the first ten chapters[64] and the beginning (§§211-229) of Chapter XI of the *Institutions* as published (ff. 1-190). The second group is made up of material related to the same chapter: a set of page proofs numbered 137-164, comprising a 'Chap. X. Des Loix du Mouvement en général, & du Mouvement simple' preceded by the final page of a previous chapter (not identifiable in the published work), with autograph corrections to provide the text of the rest (§§229-270) of Chapter XI, 'Du Mouvement, & du Repos en général, & du Mouvement simple', as published (ff. 194-207); and a copyist's draft of an earlier state of the material, amended and expanded by Mme du Châtelet to give the text reproduced in the page proofs (ff. 208-218). Lastly, the third group comprises drafts of the remaining chapters, XII-XXI, of the *Institutions* as published. These are for the most part in the copyist's hand, with autograph corrections to give the published text,[65] apart from minor variants which presumably result from further revision at the proof stage. The draft of Chapter XVI, 'De l'Attraction

[62] *Leibniz in France*, pp. 138-139.

[63] Paris, BN, fonds fr. 12265: a volume of 371 ff.

[64] The numbering of the chapters throughout the MS. shows signs of several rearrangements and does not always correspond to that finally adopted in the published work (see Wade, *Voltaire and Candide*, pp. 42-43). To avoid confusion, in what follows only the published chapter numbers and titles will be used.

[65] A second copyist seems to have been employed for chap. XIX, 'Du Mouvement des Projectiles'; and Professor Wade believes that the additions (ff. 263-267) to the copyist's draft of chap. XV, 'Des Découvertes de M. Newton sur la Pesanteur' are in Voltaire's hand (*op. cit.*, p. 43).

Newtonienne' is, however, in Mme du Châtelet's hand (ff. 275-285). This gives substantially the text as printed, except that it omits the final paragraph (obviously an afterthought) discussing Bouguer's report of deviant gravitational phenomena in Peru. For Chapter XXI 'De la Force des Corps' there is also an autograph re-drafting (ff. 326-334) of substantial passages which are scored through in the early part of the copyist's draft (ff. 338-353), together with an autograph draft (ff. 354-361) of the last part of the chapter (beginning at §585) followed by a fair copy of this made by the copyist and further amended (and shortened) by the author to give approximately the printed text (ff. 362-363, 367-370).[66]

The presence of a 48-page set of printed proofs at the centre of this volume of manuscripts immediately strikes one as odd, especially since they form a kind of buffer-state between the autograph material which precedes them and the copyist's work which predominantly follows. A consideration of this state of affairs may lead us, however, to important new evidence concerning the genesis of the *Institutions de physique*. These printed pages are exactly similar in layout and typeface to those of the first edition: that they are proofs is demonstrated by the fact that p. 138, the first page of 'Chap. X', has a blank space at the top, above the chapter heading, of exactly the size of that occupied by a vignette at the head of the corresponding Chapter XI on p. 215 of the 1740 edition. The disparity between the proof and the published version is, however, considerable: substantially the same chapter is numbered 'X' and occupies pp. 138-164 in the proof, but becomes Chapter XI on pp. 215-242 in the book itself.[67] This also implies a marked disparity between proof and final text in the earlier part of the book: ten chapters filling 214 pages apparently began as nine chapters needing only 137 pages. In the light of the evidence already discussed concerning the re-shaping of the early part of the book after printing had begun, it seems an inescapable conclusion that these are proof-sheets of the original version, printed by Prault from the fair copy promised him by Mme de Champbonin in her letter of 1 November 1738 (Best. 1572).

[66] ff. 364-366 are occupied by a misplaced passage from an earlier chapter.

[67] The apparent identity in length of the two versions conceals a further disparity: the content of the proof form of the chapter, occupying 27 pp., is condensed into pp. 222-242 of the published text, while pp. 215-222 are occupied with new material, derived from the preceding ff. 184-190 of the MS. volume.

If this is accepted, the question then arises as to why these particular proof sheets, and these alone, should have been preserved in this way. The answer here would seem to take us to the heart of the matter. There is a fair amount of manuscript correction to these proofs, but not such a quantity as to make the operation inconvenient for either author or printer. This, however, is a chapter primarily concerned with mechanics, a field in which Mme du Châtelet's conversion to Leibnizian metaphysics would have only minor relevance, if that conversion was indeed the occasion of her revision: to revise upon existing proof, with the addition only of a new introductory section of a general nature,[68] would be the simplest procedure to follow. Earlier chapters, however, were to be replaced by the new exposé of Leibnizian metaphysics which now fills Chapters I–VIII; and ground covered in Chapter IX, 'De la divisibilité & subtilité de la Matière', and Chapter X, 'De la Figure, et de la Porosité des Corps', which is part-metaphysical, part-scientific, may well have been treated more fully, as well as from a different philosophical standpoint, in the first version. It is highly likely, in consequence, that the proof-sheets would be useless for revision here; and for these ten chapters we have in fact a complete set of new autograph drafts. It is perhaps significant also that the fate of the original copyist's draft of these early chapters seems to parallel that of the proofs. It has vanished, together with the (useless) proofs for Chapters I-IX of the 1739 printing; but that for Chapter X has survived with the proofs, and follows them at

[68] This section, discussing and defining notions of relative and absolute motion and rest (§§211-229) was probably necessitated by changes in earlier chapters: the final paragraph of the previous chapter in the proof text (chap. 'IX') seems to be the end of a discussion of the absolute or metaphysical nature of movement, somewhat Newtonian perhaps in tone, to which nothing in the final printed version corresponds:

> §194. 'Nous sçavons bien à peu près ce que le mouvement n'est pas; nous sçavons qu'il n'est ni un Etre Physique, ni une substance particuliere de son genre, &c. Mais lorsqu'il s'agit de connoître ce qu'il est, il faut que nous avouyons notre ignorance; ainsi les disputes sur la nature du mouvement, ne pouvoient rien apprendre aux hommes, & nous devons nous contenter d'examiner ses loix & ses effets, puisque cette connoissance suffit à nos besoins, & qu'il ne nous est pas donné de connoître sa nature' (fol. 194*r*: 'p. 137').

The new introductory section, however, contains two references to 'la raison suffisante' (§§227, 228). It would appear to be an attempt at compromise between Leibnizian relativism and the Newtonian concept of absolute space and time; the examples used (§§217, 218) seem derived from Newton's *Principia*, Definitions, schol. iv (transl. Mme du Châtelet, i. 9-10).

ff. 208-218 in the present MS. volume. These pages, in a copyist's hand with copious corrections and additions by Mme de Châtelet, no doubt formed part of the 'original . . . extrêmement brouillé', to which Mme de Champbonin refers in her letter, of which a fresh fair copy was sent to Prault; they may have been preserved, when the corresponding draft of earlier chapters was discarded, because in the case of this chapter alone the authoress decided merely upon a further revision of her text in proof, and reference to her own previous draft would be useful in such circumstances.[69]

If this interpretation is valid as far as the early autograph chapters and the proofs corrected to give Chapter XI are concerned, the rest of the manuscript is relatively easy to account for. There is no reason whatever to think that Mme du Châtelet's new metaphysical persuasion would involve her in any need for revising the remaining chapters where their context is predominantly scientific: if proofs of these chapters had been available, they could have been amended to suit the new conception of the book with as little or less trouble than those of the original Chapter X. Their absence consequently suggests that they never existed—that Prault had not set up more than ten chapters (pp. 1-164) in type by the date in the summer of 1739 when Mme du Châtelet decided to rewrite the early part. A fair copy of the later chapters may even never have been prepared for him: what we have for these chapters is a first copyist's draft, with autograph corrections (in most chapters relatively few) to give a text very close to that published in 1740. The one exception here is significant. Chapter XVI, 'De l'Attraction Newtonienne' is, like the opening chapters, not copyist's work but an autograph draft: and the reason here is the same—this chapter involves philosophical issues, and the latter part, in particular, contains criticism of the Newtonian hypothesis of universal attraction on the grounds that it is incompatible with the Leibnizian principle of sufficient reason. Secondly, the set of autograph and copyist's drafts for parts of Chapter XXI, described above, shows the same procedure—very clearly indeed for the opening part of the chapter, since the rejected first version here survives scored through (ff. 338-343) in the copyist's draft, and is replaced by the autograph material at ff. 326-334, which reshapes the original discussion of Leibniz's 'forces

[69] Eighteenth-century French printers do not appear to have been in the habit of returning MS. copy with the proofs.

vives' (already favourable, since Mme du Châtelet had accepted this theory since early 1738, as we have seen) to fit it into the fully Leibnizian philosophical context of the whole work in its revised form.

One last feature of this manuscript deserves mention here. It is clear that this whole collection of material for the revised version of the book was intended to be re-copied for submission to the printer: no doubt its survival among Mme du Châtelet's papers means that such a fair copy was actually made, and sent to Prault. There would thus be scope for two further revisions of detail, on the fair copy itself and on the proofs, and the minor discrepancies that are discoverable between manuscript and printed text can no doubt be accounted for in this way. There is also evidence of a more direct sort. At the head of the autograph draft of Chapter III (fol. 76*r*) is Mme du Châtelet's instruction 'laissés deux marges'—a practice generally followed in the copyist's work here preserved. On the second page of the proof version of Chapter XI (fol. 195*r*) is a further note: 'ne copiés point les chifres dans tout l'imprimé ni ce qui est renfermé entre quatre lignes',[70] and on a later proof page (fol. 201*v*) 'il faut laisser icy un feuillet entier de papier blanc et reprendre a ces mots, au bas de la page, *un corps perds &c.*'

The manuscript of the *Institutions de physique* thus seems to offer indications which strongly support the view that the early part of the work was completely rewritten after Mme du Châtelet had been won over to Leibnizian metaphysics by König in May 1738. But if the early chapters as published are plainly Leibnizian, can anything be known concerning what it was that they replaced? How complete a transformation was effected? In view of the fact that nothing of the text of the original first nine chapters has survived, except the last few lines of Chapter IX on p. 137 of the proofs for Chapter X, the answers to such questions might seem to be beyond our grasp: to a great extent they are, but a few grains of information can nevertheless be gleaned.

[70] These boxed-in marginalia, particularly frequent in the autograph sections of the manuscript, make it clear that Mme du Châtelet submitted her work at this stage to someone for comment. She often herself queries the clarity or correctness of what she has written ('cela est-il bien?' One such query is prefaced by the initial V. (f. 140*r*)), and her reader often criticises in peremptory tones—'expliquer', 'exemple', 'que veut dire . . .'. The handwriting here often seems to differ little from Mme du Châtelet's, but one may surmise that the reader was Voltaire. That König was of course also consulted is confirmed by three marginal mentions of his name: ff. 48*r*, 202*r*, 203*r*.

The proofs discussed above, and the copyists' drafts of later chapters (initially intended, of course, for the original version of the book) contain in all eleven references to certain of the 194 numbered paragraphs in the 'lost' early chapters; and from the context of these references a few hints can be obtained. The work seems to have begun with a statement of Newtonian principles of scientific enquiry: §10 contained 'la 3e loy donnée par Mr Neuton pour se conduire dans la recherche de la nature' (fol. 267*r*), and the context indicates that this concerned the uniformity of nature. Specifically scientific matters seem to have been reached quite quickly, however: references to §29 (fol. 196*v*), §44 (fol. 197*r*) and §58 (fol. 196*v*) all relate to the general laws of motion. §94 (fol. 197*v*) was apparently concerned with the applicability of the mathematical notion of infinity to the speed of moving bodies. Soon after this paragraph, however, a new chapter must have begun: §98 (fol. 368*r*), §119 (fol. 247*v*) and §124 (*ibid.*) all relate to the general properties of matter—hardness and porosity. Finally, questions of dynamics were under discussion in §133 (fol. 338*r*), §141 (fol. 194*v*) and §144 (fol. 200*v*). It thus seems probable that the brief introductory generalities of the original version were more concerned with scientific method than with any form of metaphysical doctrine; and that some of the fundamental laws of physics may have been discussed at greater length than in the final version. The work, in fact, probably began as a scientific textbook in a much narrower sense than subsequently. In view of Mme du Châtelet's enduring interest in the philosophical implications of scientific theory, she may have felt some dissatisfaction with this state of affairs from the start, and her Leibnizian illumination would then merely provide a further stimulus, with the necessary philosophical material, to give her *exposé* the metaphysical foundation which in her view was an essential prerequisite for scientific thinking.

The shape of the *Institutions de physique* is proof enough that, however uneasy the marriage between Leibnizian metaphysics and Newtonian science may seem to us today, it imposed no discomfort on Mme du Châtelet. The tenor of her later preoccupations, her long labours, terminating only on her death-bed, on her translation of the *Principia Mathematica* and its commentary, may indeed suggest that Newton remained the more fertile source of inspiration of the two. But in spite of Voltaire's assertions, and no doubt his wish to believe, that her concern with Leibnizian metaphysics was no more than a transient infatuation,[71] there is some evidence that she continued in her new-found faith. The 1744 edition of her *Dissertation sur la nature . . . du feu* contains a revised final paragraph for Chapter IV in which, for the first time, she attempts to enlist the support of Leibnizian metaphysics in the solution of the problem under consideration.[72] And in 1746 she expresses regret to Bernoulli that her work on Newton leaves her no time to submit an entry in defence of the theory of monads for the essay competition on the subject announced by the Berlin Academy for 1747.[73] We have no grounds for supposing that the remaining three years of her life produced any substantial change in her attitude.

Mme du Châtelet's scientific and philosophical ideas appear, on re-examination, to be essentially derivative. Her happiest rôle here is perhaps that of disciple—of Voltaire, of Maupertuis, of König—in spite of her in other respects somewhat masterful personality. Yet in view of the obstacles society placed in the path of intellectual women of high birth, and of her dissatisfaction with her own intellectual powers, this is scarcely surprising. Remarkable in its historical context as her achievement is, we should perhaps accept her own verdict that it was by means of translation and exposition rather than original work that she was best equipped to help the cause of enlightenment. It seems unlikely, then, that in this sphere she can have exerted any real influence on Voltaire's thought, beyond perhaps the sharing of an infectious enthusiasm for scientific and mathematical studies. Her acceptance of Leibnizian metaphysics

[71] 'Après avoir rendu les imaginations de Leibnitz intelligibles, son esprit . . . comprit que cette métaphysique si hardie, mais si peu fondée, ne méritait pas ses recherches . . . Ainsi, après avoir eu le courage d'embellir Leibnitz, elle eut celui de l'abandonner.' *Éloge historique de Madame la Marquise du Châtelet* (1752), M. xxiii. 516. Cf. also *Mémoires*, M. i. 8.

[72] Her concluding discussion was on the question of whether fire could be considered a form of matter: for her original suggestion that this problem could be solved experimentally by establishing whether or not fire possessed the essential characteristics of matter, weight and impenetrability, she now substitutes a paragraph implying that it may be a phenomenon resulting from a combination of monadic entities of a different kind from that underlying the phenomena of matter; and a footnote explains 'On sent aisément qu'on suppose ici les principes de la Philosophie Leibnitienne'. *Dissertation sur la nature et la propagation du feu* (Paris, Prault, 1744), pp. 17-18. Cf. 1739 edn., *cit. supra*, pp. 96-97.

[73] C.357, 358: to Bernoulli, 6 Sept., 20 Nov. 1746. Cf. also C.364, to J. Bernoulli, 23 July 1747, in which she expresses her dissatisfaction at the news that 'Le prix a été donné à Berlin à un destructeur de monades'.

may seem disconcerting in its suddenness, and was less easy to accommodate to her Newtonian views in physics than perhaps she realised.[74] Within the context of eighteenth-century rationalism it is a revealing example, however, of the difficulty, even for emancipated minds, of establishing any clear frontier between scientific knowledge and philosophical speculation; of studying the behaviour of the material world without also seeking some key to ultimate truth. Voltaire's perhaps deeper understanding of Newton, and certainly his exasperation with Wolffian pedantries, made him at the time appear to take the sounder attitude in his gentle mockery of her new-found dogmas: but he himself, as his later career shows, was never able to escape from the fact that rationalist deism entailed *some* form of metaphysical basis for science. One of Mme du Châtelet's important contributions is perhaps to have made it clear, by the indiscretion of her conversion to Leibnizianism, how strongly rooted in the past deism of this sort remained.

[74] Christian Wolff, who was a fervent proselytiser, was in correspondence with Mme du Châtelet from January 1740 onwards, partly it seems in the hope of also converting Voltaire. Though delighted with the *Institutions de physique*, he seems to have had little confidence in the firmness of her faith, and to have assumed that there was a constant danger of her being won back to Newtonianism by Voltaire. Wolff wrote to Manteuffel in January 1742, with reference to the then forthcoming Amsterdam edition of the *Institutions*: 'Man wird sehen, wann die holländische Edition herauskommen wird, wo sie vieles ändern wollte. Wenn sie dem Voltaire mit seiner Newtonianischen Philosophie Gehör gibt, wird die Änderung keine Besserung sein' (See H. Droysen, 'Die Marquise du Châtelet, Voltaire und der Philosoph Christian Wolff', *Zeitschrift für französische Sprache und Literatur* (15 Jan. 1910), xxxv. 226-238). For the Wolffians at least, no accommodation with Newton was possible.

The Encyclopédie *and Freemasonry*

Robert Shackleton

Towards the end of the eighteenth century a number of writers, *émigrés* prominent among them, expressed the view that the French Revolution had been brought about by freemasonry, or by an alliance of the freemasons and the *philosophes*. An Eudist priest, Jacques-François Le Franc, published in 1791 a work with the suggestive title *Le Voile levé pour les curieux* in which, after a detailed consideration of the anti-religious aims of the freemasons, he advanced the conclusion 'La Franc-Maçonnerie veut renverser le trône, comme elle a renversé l'autel'; and in the following year he pursued the same theme in his *Conjuration contre la religion catholique et les souverains*. An exiled officer called La Tocnaye declared in *Les Causes de la Révolution de France* (Edinburgh 1795) that the masons had a primary responsibility for the Revolution, and asserted: 'trois objets principaux sont consignés à l'exécration et à la vengeance des maçons . . .: le Pape . . ., le Roi de France . . ., et le Grand-Maître de Malte.'

An Italian prelate, Mgr Giovanni Marchetti of Empoli, surveying in his *Che importa ai preti?* (Cristianopoli [=Rome] 1797) the diversity of contemporary sects and parties, concludes: 'il general risultato che dobbiamo raccoglierne con evidenza, si è, che lo scopo o nelle Logge, o ne' Circoli, o de' Massoni, o degl'Illuminati, Egiziani, ecc., sempre era quello generale e comune a tutti, *di abbattere la Religione col Trono*.' Marchetti documents his case with reference to d'Alembert, Diderot, Voltaire, Frederick the Great, and especially—if surprisingly—Mercier, whose *L'An 2440* he sees as a particularly dangerous work.

These claims about freemasonry may seem no more than normal if they are judged in the light of French attitudes of the nineteenth and twentieth centuries. In their own day they were new; for although Clement XII in his Bull *In eminenti apostolatus specula* of 1738 had placed an interdict on the order, his condemnation had not been universally accepted in France, to the point that as late as the 1770s there existed lodges consisting solely of ecclesiastics, and even of monks.

In 1797 a professor in the University of Edinburgh, John Robison, published a work lengthily entitled *Proofs of a Conspiracy against all the Religions and Governments of Europe, carried on in the secret meetings of Free Masons, Illuminati, and Reading Societies.* The author, who in his youth had himself been initiated into the order, stresses the difference between French and Scottish freemasonry; he sees an affinity between French freemasonry and the ideas expressed by Boulanger in his *Recherches sur l'origine du despotisme oriental*; he attaches importance to the masonic affiliations of Robinet, whom he sees as a highly significant figure, and Condorcet. How much happier and wiser than these are the English:

> O fortunatos nimium, sua si bona norint
> Anglicolas!

In a postscript to the second edition, which appeared later in 1797, he speaks of a recently published work by the Abbé Barruel. This is the *Mémoires pour servir à l'histoire du jacobinisme*, first appearing in 1797–98 and frequently reprinted.[1] The eighteenth century was marked, he says at the outset of the work, by three bitter enemies of Christianity: Voltaire, d'Alembert, and Frederick the Great. To these he adds, by way of afterthought, Diderot, describing him as *l'enfant perdu* of the anti-Christian movement. These conspirators—for they and relatively minor figures were in his view united in a conspiracy—used a variety of means to overthrow the Church. Their first means was the *Encyclopédie*. Their aim was 'de faire de l'*Encyclopédie* un immense dépôt de toutes les erreurs, de tous les sophismes, de toutes les calomnies qui, depuis les premières écoles de l'impiété jusqu'à cette énorme compilation, pouvaient avoir été inventés contre la religion'. In the second of his five volumes Barruel turns to freemasonry and produces a violent denunciation which is based on a much fuller historical knowledge

[1] On Barruel see B. N. Schilling, *Conservative England and the Case against Voltaire* (New York 1950), pp. 248-277.

than that displayed by previous opponents of the order. He then explains the union which was effected between the *philosophes* and the freemasons: 'Les Sophistes de l'impiété et de la rébellion ne furent pas longtemps à s'apercevoir combien les Francs-Maçons fraternisaient avec toute leur philosophie. Ils voulurent savoir ce que c'étaient que des mystères dont les profonds adeptes se trouvaient leurs plus zélés disciples. Bientôt les philosophes français se firent tous maçons.'[2]

From this assertion of Barruel sprang the opinion, on which modern scholarship has been divided, that the *Encyclopédie* was a masonic enterprise.

Lanson, in an article of 1912, wrote: 'Il est curieux de noter, et l'on n'a assez marqué dans nos histoires de la littérature et de la philosophie au XVIIIe siècle, que l'*Encyclopédie* est une entreprise maçonnique, ou du moins que l'idée en naquit chez les Francs-Maçons'.[3]

L.-P. May, writing in 1939, took the argument further.[4] Franco Venturi, in his valuable *Le origini dell'Enciclopedia*,[5] Jean Gigot, in a useful article entitled *Promenade encyclopédique*,[6] Jean Pommier, in a review of Gigot,[7] lean with varying degrees of reservation to the view that there was a significant connection between the *Encyclopédie* and the order. Mornet meanwhile, in *Les Origines intellectuelles de la Révolution française*,[8] though claiming that Diderot was a freemason, was sceptical about the relationship between freemasonry, and the *Encyclopédie*, as Joseph Le Gras, in his *Diderot et l'Encyclopédie*,[9] had been before him. A serious and sustained examination of the problem appeared in 1954 in an article 'L'*Encyclopédie* fut-elle une entreprise maçonnique?' by G.-H. Luquet.[10] Using abundant evidence and arguing with vigour, Luquet concludes negatively; but the editor of the journal in which the article appeared, Jean Pommier, avowed himself still not wholly persuaded.

The specific pieces of evidence on which the case for the masonic

[2] ii. 438.

[3] 'Questions diverses sur l'histoire de l'esprit philosophique en France avant 1750', *Revue d'histoire littéraire de la France* (1912), pp. 313-314.

[4] 'Note sur les origines maçonniques de l'Encyclopédie', *Revue de synthèse* (1939), pp. 181-185.

[5] (Rome &c. 1946); second edition (Turin 1963).

[6] *Les Cahiers Haut-Marnais* (1951, 1er trimestre), pp. 52-71.

[7] *Revue d'histoire littéraire de la France* (1951), pp. 377-379.

[8] (Paris 1938), pp. 375-387.

[9] (Paris 1928), pp. 28-31.

[10] *Revue d'histoire littéraire de la France* (1954), pp. 23-31.

character of the *Encyclopédie* has been based are three in number: the speech of Ramsay, the masonic membership of the printer Le Breton, and the frontispiece of Cochin. It is not my intention now to re-examine these pieces of evidence, which have been much discussed in recent years. It can be said that they are not decisive. Ramsay's speech shows an affinity between freemasonry and both dictionary-making and the study of manual arts and crafts; there is no evidence to show that André François Le Breton was a freemason;[11] the frontispiece, if its masonic character is to be accepted, is some twenty years subsequent to the publication of the first volume of the *Encyclopédie* and can throw no light on its original inspiration. This paper embodies an investigation of the extent to which freemasonry was to be found among the contributors to the *Encyclopédie*, based on the masonic archives which are now in the *domaine public*.

It was first necessary to establish a list of the contributors to the *Encyclopédie*, no simple and straightforward task. The published lists are as follows:

Encyclopédie méthodique, *Beaux-Arts* (Paris and Liège, 1788), i. p[ii], 153 names.

L'Encyclopédie et les encyclopédistes, (Paris, Bibliothèque nationale, 1932), 179 names.

L.-P. May, in *Revue de synthèse* (1939), pp. 186-190: 218 names.

Kuwabara Takeo, Turumi Syunsuke, Higuti Kiniti, in *Zinbvn* (Kyoto), no. 1 (1957), pp. 1-22: 171 names.

J. Proust, *Diderot et l'Encyclopédie* (Paris 1962), pp. 511-539: 160 names.[12]

F. A. Kafker, in *French Historical Studies* (1963), pp. 106-122: 218 names.[13]

In this diversity it was necessary to establish a new list. This was done by including all names mentioned as contributors in the *Discours préliminaire*; all names mentioned in lists of abbreviations;

[11] In the valuable and decisive work by P. Chevallier, *Les Ducs sous l'acacia* (Paris 1964), confirmation is given to the earlier researches of Luquet and it is proved that the Le Breton who had been cited as a freemason was not the publisher of the *Encyclopédie*.

[12] M. Proust expressly disavowed any claim to completeness for his list, and did not include contributors to the *Supplément* or the artists who produced the plates.

[13] Mr Kafker's list includes contributors to the *Supplément* but does not include artists.

all names mentioned in the *avertissements* to vols. i-vii and to the *Supplément*; all names of contributors mentioned in the account book of the *libraires associés*; the signatures appended to all signed articles; the signatures of the engravers and designers of the plates, and the names mentioned in the prefatory material to the volumes of plates. In addition an appreciable number of names were supplied by secondary sources and by scholarly writing on the *Encyclopédie*. These were included only when confirmation could be obtained. The total number of names thus arrived at, excluding some not yet confirmed, was 272. The artists who produced the plates were included because their contribution to the work was as closely linked to the aim of the *Encyclopédie* as that of the authors of very many of the articles; in any case a large number of the artists also produced written contributions.[14]

On 13 August 1940 a law of the Vichy Government dissolved all secret or partially secret societies; and as a result the archives of the *Grand Orient de France* and the *Grande Loge de France* were sequestrated. These archives, up to the year 1850, are now to be found in the Cabinet des Manuscrits at the Bibliothèque nationale. A significant complement to them is provided by the Joly de Fleury Collection, some volumes of which relate to freemasonry. The *Grand Orient* Collection, which is much more important than the other elements, makes possible a close study of the personal identity of eighteenth-century freemasons. The *Grand Orient* was established in 1773 and provoked a great resurgence of masonic activity in France. A large number of new lodges was founded, and lodges already existing sought recognition from the *Grand Orient*. In requests for recognition the antiquity of the lodge making the request is insisted on. As a result the papers of the *Grand Orient* disclose much though by no means complete information about the state of freemasonry in France before the year 1773, though naturally the records are much fuller after that year. The documents forwarded to the *Grand Orient* by each lodge in correspondence with it are of two kinds, the *planches*, which are *procès-verbaux* of the meetings of the lodge, and the *tableaux*, which are lists of members and which, in the majority of cases, give details sufficient for

[14] A complete inventory of articles in the *Encyclopédie*, including the names of the authors, is at present being prepared for publication by Professors R. N. Schwab and W. E. Rex of the University of California (Davis).

the identification of members: full name, address, date of birth, date of becoming a mason, and profession. The necessary exercise was to ascertain how many of the contributors to the *Encyclopédie* are listed in the *tableaux* of the different lodges.

Such an exercise is far from simple. The volume of documentation is immense, and that part of it which is chronologically relevant can be identified only by examining the whole. It soon became clear that the task of making a complete check, though intellectually fairly straightforward, would require not months but years, even though the inevitable formalities of the library were reduced to the minimum.[15] Accordingly, some other method than a complete *dépouillement* was needed.

Here it was possible to take advantage of the happy discovery that M. Alain Le Bihan, working on the rôle of freemasonry in the Revolution, had made a complete *dépouillement* of the papers of all the Parisian lodges, and was willing to check against his list of their members the new list of Encyclopædists. His kindness and detailed knowledge of the field made possible a far more decisive result than could otherwise have been achieved.

There remained for personal scrutiny the papers of the non-Parisian lodges. These were the provincial, military, colonial and foreign lodges, of which the provincial lodges were both the most important and the most voluminous. These were handled in two ways. In the first place the geographical spread of the lodges was compared with the geographical spread, both by birth and by residence at the time of activity, of the Encyclopædists. In the second place a complete *dépouillement* was made of masonic records relating to the areas where the Encyclopædists were most numerous.

For the geographical spread of lodges throughout France, the card-index to the archives of the *Grand Orient* provided the basic information. This was supplemented by the extremely useful *état des loges existant en France en 1771* which is appended to G. Bord, *La Franc-Maçonnerie en France des origines à 1815* (Paris 1908), and by the *Collection Chapelle* of the archives of the *Grande Loge de France*, which, like those of the *Grand Orient*, are in the Bibliothèque

[15] It is a pleasure to record my indebtedness to the kindness and patience of M. R. Lecotté of the Bibliothèque nationale, who is in charge of the masonic collection, and whose expert knowledge is made readily available to scholars working in this field.

nationale. The list was finally checked and completed by reference to the excellent article, 'La Franc-maçonnerie en France jusqu'en 1755' by Mlle F. Weil.[16] The result of this investigation is shown on the accompanying map I. It can be seen that there is a concentration in the vicinity of the seaports, Dunkirk, Rouen, Le Havre, Brest, Bordeaux, Sète, Marseilles, Toulon, and that an abundance of early lodges can be observed in the south, in the present departments of Hérault, Tarn, Aude, Tarn-et-Garonne, Gers, Haute-Garonne, Gard, Vaucluse and Bouches-du-Rhône. If the map were extended beyond 1759 a very rapid extension would be seen, penetrating into most parts of France, but with a particularly high density of lodges in the north, in the area of La Rochelle and Bordeaux, within a region of eighty miles radius from Toulouse, on the Mediterranean coast, and in the vicinity of Lyons.

With this distribution may be compared the birthplace of the Encyclopædists. Leaving on one side 43 who were born outside France, and 67 whose place of birth is at least for the present unascertainable, the origin of the remainder (162 out of 272) is as follows:

Paris	43	Languedoc	19
Béarn	1	Limousin	2
Berry	2	Lyonnais	9
Burgundy	17	Maine	4
Britanny	7	Normandy	7
Champagne and		Orléanais	3
Brie	10	Picardy	3
Dauphiné	4	Poitou	1
Franche-Comté	3	Provence	5
Guyenne and		Metz, Toul,	
Gascony	5	Verdun	5
Île-de-France	8	Lorraine	4

There are both correspondences and discrepancies between this distribution and that of the masonic lodges. Paris is strong in both lists, as is Languedoc; but Champagne and Burgundy, where Encyclopædists are numerous, are barely touched by freemasonry. After 1770 a number of lodges were founded in Burgundy, but before that date there were very few; while in Champagne there

[16] *Studies on Voltaire and the Eighteenth Century* (1963), xxvii. 1787-1815.

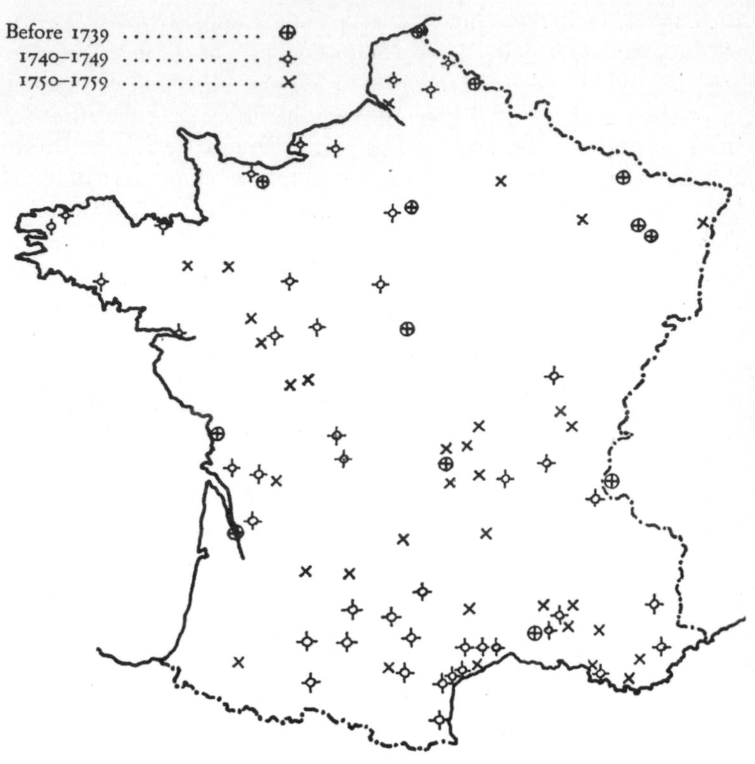

MAP I: Masonic Lodges established.

were but few lodges even at the end of the century. There is, to say the least, no firm pattern of correspondence between Encyclopædists and freemasons. Indeed, if instead of freemasons one considers the spread either of Protestants or of Jansenists in the eighteenth century, the degree of correspondence is scarcely less.[17]

The place of birth is not necessarily the decisive geographical fact. Map II shows the place of residence at the moment of writing, when it is not Paris, for those of the Encyclopædists for whom it can be identified. The *Supplément* is excluded from consideration at this point. Here some coincidence is shown in the area of Lyons, and more still in the region of Montpellier; but the overall pattern

[17] For Protestantism, see S. Mours, *Les Églises réformées en France* (Paris &c. 1958), p. 160, and for Jansenism, E. Préclin, *Les Jansénistes du XVIII*ᵉ *siècle et la constitution civile du clergé* (Paris 1929), facing p. 124.

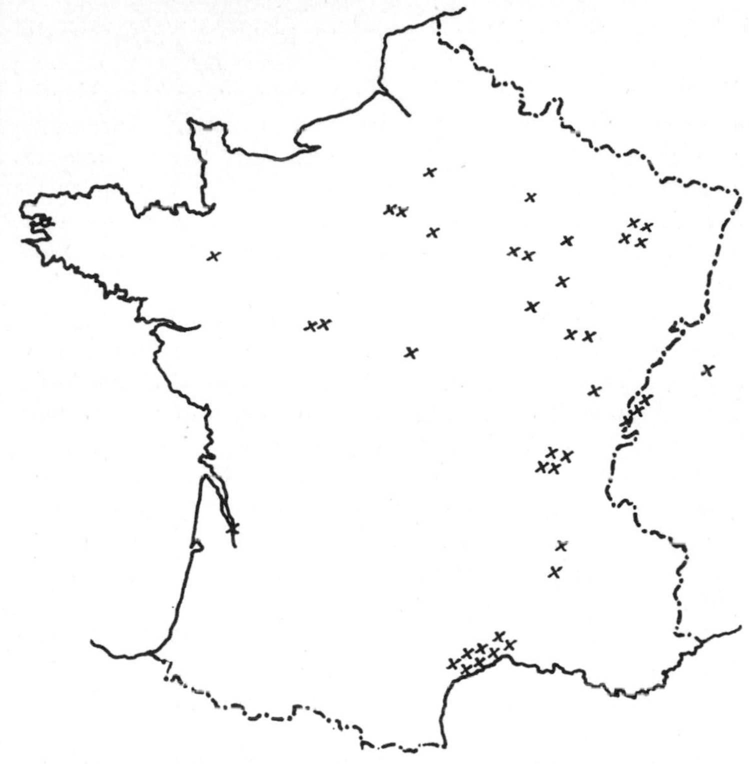

MAP II: Residence of Encyclopædists at moment of writing (excluding *Supplément* and those resident in Paris).

shows no clear relationship between the two. A complete *dépouillement* of the masonic archives for Lyons and Montpellier seemed thus to be indicated, and it was effected for the whole of the eighteenth century, the total number of *tableaux* examined being 50 for Montpellier and 64 for Lyons.

Eight Encyclopædists were born at Lyons or elsewhere in the Lyonnais: these are Bourgelat, Briasson, Buisson, Falconet, Milly, Gautier de Montdorge, Morellet and Willermoz. Five of these, at the time of publication of the *Encyclopédie*, had moved away from the region. These were Camille Falconet, the celebrated doctor and bibliophile, whose aid was acknowledged in the *Discours préliminaire*, but who did not write any articles for the work; Briasson the printer, who was one of the *libraires associés* and a fully fledged

Parisian by adoption; Morellet, who contributed to volumes vi and vii, whose rôle as a minor *philosophe* was not insignificant, but who is best known now as the author of the celebrated memoirs; Gautier de Montdorge, who had some responsibility for the articles on engraving in volume vii, and the Comte de Milly, whose rôle was limited to having furnished (perhaps unwittingly) information for the article 'Porcelaine de Saxe' which appeared in the fourth volume of the *Supplément*. To the three names remaining, Bourgelat (whose contribution to the *Encyclopédie* was in fact a significant one), Buisson (who is mentioned in the *Discours préliminaire* as having sent in memoirs on subjects connected with textiles but who did not actually write any articles), and Willermoz, should be added the name of Antoine-François Brisson who became inspector of manufactures in the *généralité* of Lyons, and who wrote two articles, 'Suisses' and 'Tuileries', which appeared in volumes xv and xvi. These are the names one should look for especially, in the *tableaux* of the masonic lodges of Lyons.

In the whole of the eighteenth century there are known 27 lodges at Lyons. The oldest were *La Sagesse* (1743), *La Bienveillance* (1752), *L'Amitié* (1744), *Saint-Jean de Jérusalem* (1756), *Grande-Loge écossaise* (1750), *La Parfaite Amitié* (1756), *Amis choisis* (1744). All the *tableaux* surviving of all the lodges of the eighteenth century were examined, a search being made not only for the names of the Encyclopædists mentioned as being domiciled in Lyons, but those of all the 272 who figured on the list. One only of all these appeared in the *tableaux*: Pierre-Jacques Willermoz. His brother Jean-Baptiste was a very prominent freemason.[18] He himself was admitted a mason on 11 November 1759, according to the *tableau* of a later lodge called *Deux Loges réunies*. Here there is an undoubted link between the *Encyclopédie* and freemasonry. Its limited nature, however, is shown by the fact that Willermoz wrote only one article for the *Encyclopédie*: the article 'Phosphore' which appeared in volume xii.

No fewer than 18 Encyclopædists were born in Languedoc, such diverse figures as Dortous de Mairan (whose claim to be a contributor is dubious, since it is mainly based on posthumous utilisation of his papers in the *Supplément*) and the Abbé de Prades being

[18] See Alice Joly, *Un Mystique lyonnais et les secrets de la franc-maçonnerie* (Mâcon 1938).

among them; but no fewer than eight were resident at or very near Montpellier while contributing. Jean Bouillet, a doctor of Montpellier, and his son Jean-Henri-Nicolas both made modest contributions on medical subjects. A manuscript memoir on the father written by his son attributes to him the articles 'Facultés: Sensitive, Appétitive, Vitale',[19] and the articles 'Faculté appétitive' and 'Faculté vitale' are in fact signed by him. According to the *avertissement* to volume iii the son collaborated in the father's articles. The article 'Consultation', signed by the son, is withdrawn from him by the errata to volume v. Father and son probably lived in Béziers rather than Montpellier. Guillaume d'Abbes, who was an official of the Chambre des Comptes of Languedoc, wrote the article 'Figure (Physiologie)' in volume vi. Gabriel-François Venel was one of the regular team of contributors, writing articles for each volume from the second to the first of the *Supplément*. He had a vigorous character, being described by his tutor Rouelle (himself an Encyclopædist) as *Le Démon du Midi*. His colleague at Montpellier, Charles Le Roy (brother of Jean-Baptiste who was already a contributor, and son of Julien the watch-maker) contributed an article to volume vi; the astronomer Ratte, a well-known personality at Montpellier, wrote a number of articles for volume vii and one for volume xi; Ménuret de Chambaud was a prolific contributor throughout the period of clandestinity, appearing extensively in each volume from viii to xvii. Jean-Guillaume La Fosse wrote many articles for the *Supplément*. It is thus clear that a connection with Montpellier, established at an early date by Venel, was extended after 1755, possibly through Venel, possibly though the influence of Jean-Baptiste Le Roy on his brother. Certainly there was at Montpellier, based on the University, the nearest approach to a team of Encyclopædists to be found anywhere outside Paris.

Here, if a relationship between freemasonry and the *Encyclopédie* is to be discovered, it might most readily be found, the more so as Montpellier was, as has been seen, an important centre of the order. Some records survive of twenty lodges in the eighteenth century, and all these were examined for the names of the 272 Encyclopædists. One of the lodges, *Les Cœurs réunis*, had a particular and explicit connection with the University. But neither there nor in the *tableaux* of all the other lodges does one find the name of an Encyclopædist.

[19] *Archives du département de l'Hérault* D. 201, fol. 11.

The list of *Les Cœurs réunis* includes the name of one Louis-Pierre Montet, who is doubtless related to Jacques Montet who wrote one article in each of volumes xv, xvi and xvii. The lodge entitled *L'Ancienne et réunion des élus* lists as having been present at its inauguration Scipion Allut and Allut *fils aîné*, both doubtless related (the first, according to the *Nouvelle Biographie générale*, being cousin) to Antoine Allut, who furnished descriptions of glass-working for the fourth volume of plates of the *Encyclopédie*. The lodge has in 1781 a member called Barthès who, since he is described as a judge, cannot be the same as the Encyclopædist Paul-Joseph Barthès who was a physician, though he was probably related. Jean La Fosse, member in 1779 of the lodge *Amis fidèles*, described as *maître menuisier*, may be a relative of Jean-Guillaume mentioned above, but he is not the same. From this it would seem that the Montpellier Encyclopædists came from *milieux* sympathetic to freemasonry but were not themselves masons.

The overall survey now becomes most important. In effecting it, the assistance of M. Le Bihan was invaluable. In addition, a scrutiny was made of 220 *tableaux* of provincial lodges of the *Grand Orient* obedience, selected from the areas where a connection was most likely to be found, and including 22 military lodges, 50 *tableaux* of lodges affiliated to the *Ancienne Grande Loge de France* (Collection Chapelle), and 24 *tableaux* found in the papers of Baron Toussaint. In addition a large number of secondary works were examined; they are too numerous to list, but they include most notably and fruitfully the works of Amiable[20] and of Bord above-mentioned, as well as works of local relevance. From all these sources there results a list of 17 Encyclopædists who were freemasons. Of these, eight contributed to the main body of the work:

Cochin (Charles-Nicolas)
Marnésia (Charles-Adrien-Louis, marquis de Lezay-)
Montesquieu (Charles-Louis de Secondat, baron de)
Paris de Meyzieu (Jean-Baptiste)
Péronnet (Jean-Rodolphe)
Tressan (Louis-Élisabeth de La Vergne, comte de)
Voltaire (François-Marie Arouet)
Willermoz (Pierre-Jacques)

[20] L. Amiable, *Une Loge maçonnique d'avant 1789. La R. L. Les Neuf Sœurs* (Paris 1897).

The first of these was responsible for the frontispiece of the *Encyclopédie*, drew up the plan for the section *Dessin* of the third volume of plates, and himself drew three plates. The first volume of the Collection Chapelle of the archives of the *Ancienne Grande Loge de France* mention the admission as a freemason, on 23 November 1765, of (*inter alios*) Charles Cochin. His identification with the artist is hypothetical, but the close proximity of this date to that of Cochin's drawing the frontispiece for the *Encyclopédie* is at least suggestive, and it would not be unreasonable, pending a proof to the contrary, to list Cochin as a freemason.

Marnésia was a member of the lodge *Les Neuf Sœurs* (the major 'philosophical' lodge) in 1782–83, that is, seventeen years after the publication of his single article 'Voleur' in volume xvii. Montesquieu had been admitted as a freemason in London in 1730; in 1737 he was forbidden by Cardinal Fleury to remain a member of the order, and there is no evidence of any subsequent connection.[21] Voltaire was admitted to the lodge *Les Neuf Sœurs* very shortly before his death and some thirty years after contributing to the *Encyclopédie*. Péronnet is recorded as being *vénérable d'honneur* at the lodge *Uranie* in 1787–88, at least twenty-five years after his single article for the *Encyclopédie*.

This leaves, apart from the dubiously identified Cochin, three Encyclopædists who were freemasons at the moment of contributing. Paris de Meyzieu was admitted to the lodge of the Duc de Villeroy on 4 June 1737;[22] the Comte de Tressan was admitted to the lodge *Devoir du fendeur* (a military lodge) in *c.* 1747;[23] Willermoz has already been seen to be a member of a Lyons lodge. To see these pieces of information in proportion it should be added that Paris de Meyzieu wrote a single article for the *Encyclopédie*, 'École Royale Militaire', that Tressan wrote only four in all, on military topics, and the Willermoz wrote the one article already mentioned, 'Phosphore'. No major contributor to the main body of the *Encyclopédie* was then a freemason at the time of contributing, four contributors only were freemasons when contributing, and their rôle was a modest one in any case.

[21] See R. Shackleton, *Montesquieu, a critical biography* (Oxford 1961), pp. 138-141 and 172-174.

[22] Ms Joly de Fleury 184, fol. 144*v* (information from M. R. Maudet).

[23] A. Bouton, *Les Francs-maçons manceaux et la Révolution française* (1741–1815) (Le Mans 1958), p. 64.

The following nine contributors to the *Supplément* were freemasons:

Andry (Charles-Louis-François)
Béguillet (Edme)
Cadet de Gassicourt (Louis-Claude)
Chabrol (Matthieu-Charles)
Lalande (Joseph-Jérôme Le Français de)
Milly (Nicolas-Christophe de Thy, comte de)
Monneron (Charles-Claude-Ange)
Pommereul (François-René-Jean)
Turpin (François-Henri)

Of these Andry was a member of the order twelve years after contributing, at the Lodge *Les Frères initiés*, 1788–92, and Béguillet six years later (at *Les Amis de la vertu*, 1782–83, and *La Réunion des étrangers*, 1785). Andry was a minor, and Béguillet a major contributor to the *Supplément*. Milly, already mentioned as the author of a single article, became a mason at *Les Neuf Sœurs* two years later. Turpin, who wrote many historical articles for the *Supplément*, appears to have joined *Les Neuf Sœurs* probably slightly later, though the identification is not completely secure. Of the remaining five, four were simultaneously freemasons and Encyclopædists: Chabrol, who belonged to the military lodge *Union parfaite du Corps du génie* at Mézières in 1774, and who wrote on surgery, Monneron, who wrote a single article 'Échecs' and who belonged to the lodge of Annonay; Pommereul, loosely connected to the *Encyclopédie* through the use made of his manuscript history of Corsica, was a founder member in 1777 of *L'Amiable Concorde* at Fougères; and Lalande. This celebrated astronomer was a very prolific contributor to the *Supplément*, for which he wrote the article 'Francs-maçons', an important contribution to the history of the order. He was himself a prominent mason, belonging to the lodge *Les Neuf Sœurs* and being an officer of the *Grand Orient*. Cadet de Gassicourt was a freemason and an officer of the *Grand Orient*, but no information is available about the dates of his membership. He wrote two articles for the *Supplément*.

There is no doubt that the connection between the *Supplément* and freemasonry is much closer than that between the main body of the *Encyclopédie* and the order. If Barruel is right in describing

Robinet and Condorcet as freemasons the connection is closer still, especially in view of the fact that at Bouillon, where Robinet edited the *Supplément*, there appears to have existed an autonomous *orient*.[24] This is in no way surprising. Freemasonry was very much more widespread in the 1770s when the *Supplément* was being prepared than it had been twenty years before. It is true also that far more records have survived from the seventies, when the *Grand Orient* had been formed, than from the earlier years, and that it is much more possible that a masonic affiliation could go unrecorded in the fifties than in the seventies. And it should be repeated that the conclusions do not rest on a complete examination of all the surviving records.

Those conclusions, nevertheless, may be worth accepting, provisionally, for what they are. Of the affinity in spirit between speculative masonry, basing itself firmly on operative masonry, and the outlook of Diderot and his contributors, believing in the dignity and the intellectual importance of manual arts and crafts, there can be no doubt; nor is there doubt of the similarity between Diderot's aim and that of compiling a universal dictionary which was proclaimed by Ramsay in his famous speech. From this common base there were two developments, freemasonry and the *Encyclopédie*, which were separate and independent, or which at least touched each other only insignificantly and fortuitously. In the 1770s, however, when freemasonry had gained considerably in extension, it came into much closer contact with the *Supplément* to the *Encyclopédie* than it ever had done with the main work. The contributions of masons now became far more numerous, and there was a genuine and significant connection. Meanwhile, however, the originality and vigour and audacity which had marked Diderot's compilation had faded away. The *Supplément* is, with the exception of a very few articles, a pale, dull, anodyne work, very far from conspiratorial in character.

So far then from the *Encyclopédie* being a masonic conspiracy, it became significantly masonic only at a stage when not even the most timorous critic could possibly describe it as conspiratorial.[25]

[24] P. Duchaine, *La Franc-maçonnerie belge au XVIIIe siècle* (Bruxelles 1911), p. 116, and Bord, *op. cit.*, pp. 236-240.

[25] In addition to my gratitude to MM. Lecotté and Le Bihan, I am glad to express my thanks to MM. R. Maudet and R. Chevallier and to Mlle F. Weil for ideas, suggestions and information.

La surprise et le masque dans le théâtre de Marivaux

René Pomeau

Il est, dans l'œuvre d'un écrivain, des textes justement dédaignés qui méritent pourtant l'attention du critique: ouvrages mineurs, esquisses abandonnées, productions mal venues mais où se laissent entrevoir les secrets du créateur. Un peu au hasard énumérons le *Don Garcie de Navarre* de Molière, le *Pygmalion* de Rousseau, la première *Éducation sentimentale* de Flaubert. Et chez Marivaux *L'École des mères.*

Le titre de cette pièce en un acte annonce le dessein de rivaliser avec Molière. Parvenu à la pleine maîtrise de son art (*L'École des mères* se situe, en 1732, entre le *Jeu* et les *Fausses Confidences*), Marivaux a voulu reprendre le sujet de *L'École des femmes*[1]: il manifeste clairement son propos dans le dialogue même par une référence explicite à Agnès. Ce faisant, il corrige Molière, non sans pertinence. Comme Agnès son Angélique fut maintenue dans une complète ignorance; sans un instinct naturel d'intelligence, elle eût été réduite à une quasi stupidité. Mais ici le responsable n'est pas un Arnolphe, barbon amoureux. C'est la mère de la jeune fille, mère oppressive qui, plus ou moins consciemment, s'efforce d'écarter une rivale: après avoir tenté d'étouffer la personnalité de sa fille, elle veut marier celle-ci à un vieillard. De nouveau se manifeste en cette comédie un Marivaux curieusement ennemi des mères, de ces Madame Argante multipliées dans une œuvre où pourtant les personnages franchement antipathiques sont rares. De plus, tout en

[1] Mme Desvignes a démontré qu'il a beaucoup emprunté également à une pièce de Dancourt, *La Parisienne* ('Dancourt, Marivaux, et l'Éducation des filles', *R.H.L.F.*, 1963).

apaisant on ne sait quelle rancune, il s'assure sur Molière l'avantage de la vraisemblance. Il paraît plus naturel assurément qu'une jeune fille soit élevée par sa mère, et Marivaux fait l'économie des péripéties romanesques d'une Agnès retrouvant juste à point les parents qu'elle avait perdus à l'âge de quatre ans.

Marivaux n'aimait pas Molière: aversion qui sur le plan de la création devait être salutaire. Au XVIIIe siècle, comme on sait, la tyrannie des classiques fait obstacle au renouvellement des formes littéraires. Après les périodes brillantes, refuser les chefs-d'œuvre de la veille devient la condition de la libération. A Molière Marivaux a signifié une fin de non-recevoir, que ne surent opposer à ce maître ni Dancourt, ni Regnard, ni Dufresny, non plus que Voltaire ne put rompre avec Corneille et Racine. Selon le jeu de mots de Beaumarchais, il fut, lui, cet auteur 'oseur', injuste pour ses prédécesseurs mais créateur. Il a eu l'audace de se créer un empire comique dans un monde, sinon ignoré, du moins peu exploré par Molière, celui de l'amour. Il a développé une comédie de l'amour, et il l'a fait en mettant en œuvre avec prédilection deux 'figures' (au sens où l'on parle de 'figures de ballet'): la surprise, le masque. A cet égard son *École des mères* paraît significative: à la fois pour ce que nous y apprenons sur l'usage du masque au XVIIIe siècle, et par l'absence paradoxale que nous y constatons de l'autre figure, celle de la surprise.

De tous les sujets de Molière, *L'École des femmes* est le plus proche de Marivaux: l'action y prend son départ dans une 'surprise de l'amour'; entre le regard d'Agnès sur son balcon et celui d'Horace, passant dans la rue, une étincelle s'allume, entretenue par les saluts réitérés, puis par les sourires. A partir de cet instant, les deux jeunes gens naissent à la vie, et Agnès, qu'Arnolphe avait voulu rendre sotte autant qu'il se peut, sera 'polie par l'amour'. Situation typiquement 'marivaudienne', que pour cette raison sans doute Marivaux a retranchée de son *École des mères*: il ne nous dit rien de la rencontre de son Angélique avec un Éraste, équivalent à l'Horace d'Agnès. Lui qui avait un si vif amour-propre de l'originalité a-t-il voulu éviter d'attirer l'attention sur le fait que la surprise, l'une des figures maîtresses de son théâtre, avait déjà été employée par Molière?

C'est au théâtre sans doute que tout est dit. Mais il reste possible, heureusement, de donner un sens nouveau à des scènes mille fois traitées. S'il n'a pas inventé le jeu de la surprise, Marivaux pouvait à bon droit se targuer de l'avoir développé avec un esprit très original.

Il en avait peut-être pressenti les ressources dans ses œuvres de jeunesse, puisque Georges Poulet a rencontré une 'surprise' dans son roman les *Effets de la sympathie*.[2] Néanmoins il ne débute vraiment que sept ans plus tard, quand pleinement conscient de sa découverte, il fait de la surprise la péripétie décisive d'*Arlequin poli par l'amour*. Ce beau brunet enlevé par la fée végétait sottement dans la demeure enchantée; l'esprit et le cœur vides, il poursuit machinalement une balle de volant. S'étant baissé pour la ramasser, soudain près de lui il voit Silvia: 'Il demeure étonné et courbé; petit à petit et par secousses, il se redresse le corps; quand il s'est entièrement redressé, il la regarde'. Il n'en faut pas plus: le choc électrique de ce regard a réalisé instantanément le prodige que n'avait pu opérer la baguette de la fée: de brute qu'il était, Arlequin est devenu homme.

A vrai dire, dans cette courte pièce en un acte, nous ne comptons pas moins de trois surprises. Outre celle-ci, il est fait mention de deux autres, incomplètes en ce sens qu'elles ne sont pas réciproques. Avant le lever du rideau, la fée est tombée amoureuse d'Arlequin par surprise: elle l'a vu dans un bois, assoupi, beau comme l'Amour endormi. C'est un émoi purement physique, puisqu'elle ne sait rien de ce splendide garçon et n'a pu apprécier son esprit, ni son caractère. Mais elle n'en a cure; il suffit que ses yeux aient *surpris* son cœur: elle fait enlever le brunet avant même qu'il ne se réveille. Une troisième surprise est destinée à créer une situation symétrique à celle qui existe entre Arlequin et la fée: Silvia est aimée d'un berger qu'elle n'aime point. Comment cela s'est-il fait? Il l'a vue: 'voilà tout'. Ce jeu de la surprise demeure pourtant dans *Arlequin* bien rudimentaire. Du premier regard, son amour et celui de Silvia ont atteint une intensité telle qu'aucun progrès n'est plus possible. Le développement de l'action n'intéressera pas les sentiments, définitivement fixés au zénith de l'amour: il ne s'agira plus que de montrer comment l'amoureux, croissant rapidement en esprit et en politesse, pourra vaincre les obstacles dressés par la fée jalouse.

Dans les pièces suivantes, Marivaux nuancera cette même situation. A la surprise 'coup de foudre', créant en un éclair un amour parfait, il préfère un choc presque imperceptible, si léger que les

[2] G. Poulet, *La Distance intérieure* (Paris, Plon, 1952), p. 11.

futurs amants d'abord n'en ont pas conscience. Ainsi il faudra du temps à la comtesse et à Lélio dans la première *Surprise*, à la marquise et au chevalier dans la *Seconde*, pour sentir que leur cœur est pris; il en faudra pour qu'ils donnent son vrai nom à cet émoi, et y consentent. Dans les *Serments indiscrets* qui sont une troisième surprise de l'amour, il faudra cinq actes, et cette fois ce sera trop long. *La Dispute* enfin nous ramène à la pureté en quelque sorte métaphysique d'*Arlequin poli par l'amour*: nous sommes comme à la création du monde; tels Adam et Eve s'éveillant dans le premier jardin, Azor et Églé ignorant même ce qu'est un homme, ce qu'est une femme, sont saisis par la plus fondamentale des surprises.

Le recours habituel à cette figure oriente le théâtre de Marivaux vers l'analyse. La comédie du 'plaisant détour' qui est la sienne détaille avec une agréable précision les progrès du sentiment. A partir d'un initial 'étonnement' (ce mot, équivalent du mot plus usité de *surprise*, se lit dans le *Petit Maître corrigé*), le dialogue donne au spectateur le plaisir de suivre dans sa croissance un amour qui se fait grand sans le savoir; et cela institue entre Marivaux et son public un jeu qui prend fin au moment précis où cet amour accepte de se reconnaître.

Marivaux est incomparable pour conduire ces analyses dialoguées. Mais il faut bien voir qu'à l'origine, il pose un fait qui n'est susceptible d'aucune analyse: la surprise, donnée immédiate, gratuite. Cette psychologie de l'amour est celle du *Je ne sais quoi* dont il fait la théorie dans la deuxième feuille de son *Cabinet du philosophe*. Il y distingue deux allégories: la Beauté et le *Je ne sais quoi*. Aimer la Beauté, voilà qui est bien normal, naturel, ennuyeux en un mot. La surprise, c'est-à-dire la vie, c'est d'aimer le *Je ne sais quoi*. Mais qu'est-ce que ce *Je ne sais quoi*? Sa définition, bien entendu, est d'être indéfinissable: un 'charme répandu sur un visage et qui rend une personne aimable sans qu'on puisse dire à quoi il tient'. C'est la perception instantanée de ce charme qui crée la surprise.

On sent bien que l'amour véritable procède du *Je ne sais quoi*. Il va donc échapper à toute prise. Un des thèmes de Marivaux est l'échec des stratégies tendant à susciter l'amour. Voyez combien la fée prend de peine pour séduire Arlequin. Elle a de la beauté, plus sans doute que sa rivale Silvia. Elle s'habille avec plus d'élégance. Et elle est fée. Pourvue de tant d'avantages, elle espère provoquer chez Arlequin, comme elle dit, 'la surprise la plus amoureuse'. Elle épie le moment où ce corps balourd sera, selon son expression, 'retouché par l'amour', où cette âme obtuse, par la vertu du même amour, pourra 'se sentir elle-même'. Espoir vain. Sur la fée guettant son réveil Arlequin jette un regard, mais 'le regard le plus imbécile', et il se rendort. A son second réveil, comme elle lui demande s'il est 'surpris' de la voir, il répond que oui, mais qu'il a faim. Pour la personne de la fée, toute aguichante qu'elle soit, il ne sent pas le moindre désir. La méthode de séduction par le chant et la danse ne réussit pas mieux, pour la simple raison qu'il n'existe pas de méthode pour séduire.

Du moins Marivaux en est-il persuadé. A deux reprises il a tourné en dérision les stratégies amoureuses: dans *La Fausse Suivante*, puis dans *Le Triomphe de l'amour*, une femme sensible se laisse enflammer par une cour assidue; mais il se trouve que dans les deux cas le séducteur n'est autre qu'une femme déguisée en homme. Tant Marivaux est assuré que les tentatives préméditées de conquête ne peuvent susciter qu'un sentiment factice. L'amour vrai jaillit, lui, spontanément comme un effet sans cause. Tout au plus est-il préparé par une attente vague, ignorante de son objet. C'est l'attente de Silvia, nerveuse au lever du rideau dans le premier acte du *Jeu*: mais elle ne prévoyait pas que dans la place préparée par l'attente viendrait se loger le galant Bourguignon, ou du moins l'homme prétendu tel.

Que fréquemment l'amour naisse ainsi à l'instant même de la rencontre, qui le niera? Mais on ne peut non plus contester que des naissances de l'amour fort différentes de celle-ci appartiennent aussi bien à l'expérience concrète. Non moins véritable que les surprises marivaudiennes est l'amour sans surprise de Swann. Le personnage de Proust d'abord n'éprouve pas la moindre attirance vers la demi-mondaine Odette de Crécy qu'il connaît depuis assez longtemps; les avances même de celle-ci n'ont pu l'émouvoir. L'amour s'éveille en lui seulement lorsque cette femme assez vulgaire lui apparaît mise en valeur dans le cadre mondain du salon Verdurin, et surtout magnifiée par les analogies avec la musique et la peinture. Swann, amateur d'art, s'éprend d'elle en même temps que de la petite phrase musicale de Vinteuil, associée désormais à la présence d'Odette; il se met à l'aimer beaucoup du jour où il reconnaît dans son profil celui de la Séphora de Botticelli, qu'il avait admirée dans la Chapelle

Sixtine. Ainsi l'amour de Swann naît progressivement, selon la même loi du devenir qui enchaînera ses tribulations et sa lente agonie.

C'est dire que cet amour, naissant dans la durée, convient parfaitement au roman proustien, lequel dispose librement du temps. En revanche, la surprise est une forme essentiellement dramatique de l'éveil amoureux. Dans le théâtre de Racine, elle produit le choc initial de la passion: 'Je le vis, je l'aimai'. Dans le roman même, c'est à la surprise qu'a recours le narrateur pour se donner un commencement absolu. Ainsi la rencontre de Frédéric Moreau et de Mme Arnoux sur le bateau de Nogent: 'ce fut comme une apparition'. Par son caractère inexplicablement abrupt, la surprise laisse pressentir un décret du Destin: si Marivaux en avait eu le goût, il eût pu développer les virtualités tragiques d'un tel amour, indiquées dans sa comédie héroïque du *Prince travesti.*

Il préférait, conformément à l'optimisme de son époque, orienter l'action née de la surprise, non vers la catastrophe, mais vers l'avenir heureux d'un mariage d'amour. Comme l'a souligné Georges Poulet,[3] cette surprise fait passer les cœurs sans transition d'une sorte de néant à une existence pleine. Elle donne une âme à Arlequin qui végétait dans l'hébétude; elle communique la vie aux personnages expérimentaux de la *Dispute*. Sur un mode moins allégorique, ce même choc arrache à la torpeur sentimentale les protagonistes des deux *Surprises*, de même qu'il suscite la jubilation de Silvia, quand celle-ci, au dernier acte du *Jeu*, consent au bonheur de la surprise: 'c'est un mariage unique, c'est une aventure dont le seul récit est attendrissant, c'est le coup de hasard le plus singulier, le plus heureux, le plus . . .' Comme le dit un autre personnage de Marivaux (Lélio, dans la première *Surprise*, I, 2), le cœur est 'un vrai paralytique'; il ressemble aux 'eaux dormantes qui attendent qu'on les remue pour se remuer'; il faut que 'l'aiguillon de l'amour' l'éveille. Alors sa vérité se déploie. Car Marivaux, qui intitula l'une de ses premières comédies *L'Amour et la verité*, a réussi à rajeunir un très vieil adage. Dans son théâtre l'âme vraie est celle qui aime, rejetant le masque de l'indifférence ennuyée.

Cette dernière métaphore indique que la figure de la surprise apparaît solidaire de l'autre figure, celle du masque.

[3] *La Distance intérieure*, p. 2, où est cité le texte de la *Première Surprise.*

Il est connu que le théâtre se plaît à ériger sur sa scène un second théâtre: le drame de *Hamlet*, *L'Illusion comique* de Corneille produisent à l'intérieur de leur spectacle un autre spectacle; comme Molière dans *L'Impromptu de Versailles* donne la comédie de la répétition d'une de ses comédies. Sous une forme plus élémentaire, le déguisement d'un personnage en un autre est un artifice banal que Marivaux n'a pas inventé: on peut compter chez Molière jusqu'à sept scènes de l'amoureux travesti. Et dans *Le Jeu de l'amour et du hasard*, l'idée qui vient à Silvia et à Dorante de se déguiser n'a pas exigé de leur part un puissant effort d'imagination. Mais, de même que celui de la surprise, Marivaux a su arracher à la banalité ce lieu commun théâtral du déguisement, et ce, pour deux raisons: l'une tenant à sa psychologie propre, l'autre aux habitudes sociales de son temps.

Au XVIIIe siècle le masque était entré dans les mœurs à un degré qui nous surprend aujourd'hui. L'usage venait, semble-t-il, d'Italie, et particulièrement de Venise. Dans cette terre classique du carnaval, on allait en masque six mois de l'année. Le 'masque noble', ou 'masque national' des Vénitiens, la 'baoute', comportait tout un costume: non seulement le loup de toile blanche qui couvrait le visage, mais encore une sorte de capuchon de soie noire garni de dentelle, tombant jusqu'à la taille. Un manteau, noir aussi, le *tabarro*, enveloppait le tout, et l'on portait sur la tête un tricorne. Un tel masque assurait un rigoureux anonymat. Il permet de se soustraire aux règles, restées très strictes, des convenances, morales ou sociales; il donne le moyen aux sénateurs de cette république tyrannique, d'échapper à l'espionnage policier des Dix, et de se mêler aux divertissements populaires, ou de fréquenter des lieux de plaisir. Aux femmes, il procure une liberté d'allure dont elles ne jouiraient pas à visage découvert.

De Venise la pratique du masque s'était répandue dans toute l'Europe. Ainsi à Pétersbourg, selon Casanova, dans les bals du Palais d'hiver où se pressaient cinq mille personnes, Catherine II incognito sous le masque se promenait dans la foule, pour écouter ce qui se disait de son gouvernement. En France, il semble que dès le XVIIe siècle le masque était considéré comme une sorte de tenue de cérémonie. Un personnage de Molière, dans *Le Mariage forcé*, acceptant une invitation aux noces de Sganarelle, ajoute qu'il s'y rendra en masque 'afin de les mieux honorer'.

Pour le XVIIIe siècle, le théâtre de Marivaux fournit plusieurs témoignages. L'un d'entre eux se rencontre dans cette *École des mères* dont nous parlions. Pour les fiançailles d'Angélique, il est prévu qu'après le souper on se déguisera. Ce qui permet à Damis, vieillard fiancé à la jeune fille, d'écouter sous le travesti la conversation de celle-ci avec celui qu'elle aime. Damis a endossé un masque complet à la vénitienne, de telle sorte que la mère d'Angélique le prendra pour une jeune fille. Cette péripétie amène le dénouement: levant le masque, Damis déclare sagement qu'il renonce à épouser Angélique malgré elle. Autre masque, dans la *Méprise*: deux jeunes filles habitant un village proche de Lyon ont l'habitude de prendre l'air chaque jour sur la promenade publique, le visage couvert d'un masque. Elles entendent ainsi préserver leur teint contre les rayons du soleil. Dans les *Sincères* enfin, un fade complimenteur prétend avoir reconnu une dame malgré son masque: c'est qu'elle avait enlevé son gant, découvrant une main unique au monde. Cette scène prenait place à Paris au cours de l'un de ces bals masqués qui, à partir de la Saint-Martin, avaient lieu à l'Opéra de onze heures du soir au lever du jour. On y portait le domino sur le haut du visage, mais aussi le masque entier, comme on le voit dans un tableau de Coypel représentant Mme de Mouchy en robe de bal, le masque à la main.

S'inspirant d'une pratique sociale aussi vivante, le jeu du masque dans le théâtre de Marivaux échappe à la convention. Développé avec une délicate finesse, il prend un intérêt psychologique qu'il n'avait pas dans la comédie de Molière.

Tout d'abord le personnage déguisé rayonne de cette joie d'être un autre. On a parlé de saturnale à propos de l'*Ile des esclaves*. Effectivement les valets devenus maîtres savourent un vif plaisir à jouer ce rôle qu'ils connaissent si bien, mais dont ils pouvaient se croire séparés à tout jamais par la barrière de la domesticité. C'est ainsi que Cléanthis, la fille suivante de *L'Ile des esclaves*, imite avec une verve étourdissante les manières de sa maîtresse. Elle charge. Dans la caricature qu'elle dessine, une intention de satire s'insinue; mais elle cède aussi au plaisir de 'jouer à la maîtresse', comme le font les enfants. De même l'Arlequin du *Jeu de l'amour* s'en donne à cœur joie dans son habit de Dorante. Il se hâte, car il sait que l'intermède sera bref. Faisant une entrée fracassante, il accumule les butorderies non par pure maladresse, car s'il est balourd il n'est pas sot; il pourrait tenir son emploi avec plus de vraisemblance, s'il voulait s'en donner la peine. Puis ce sont des galanteries en style extravagant, des manières de tranche-montagne avec ses maîtres réduits au rôle de domestique. Arlequin-Dorante s'exclame 'Ah! les sottes gens que nos gens', et quand il connaît l'identité véritable de la prétendue Silvia, il a l'audace de poursuivre un jeu autorisé par son travesti: à celle qu'il sait devoir être demain sa maîtresse, il ne craint pas de dire: 'Bonjour, Lisette: je vous recommande Bourguignon; c'est un garçon qui a quelque mérite'.

Le jeu d'être un autre sous le masque devient tout à fait pur quand il s'agit de personnages qui par leur rang social n'en peuvent tirer aucune revanche. Ainsi l'héritière déguisée en chevalier dans *La Fausse Suivante* ou, dans *Le Triomphe de l'amour*, la reine de Sparte travestie en Phocion. Toutes deux se donnent le régal d'un masque double. Car femmes, elles se font passer pour hommes; et quand elles doivent avouer leur sexe véritable, elles prolongent le jeu en s'attribuant une fausse identité féminine. Elles se donnent le plaisir d'être plusieurs 'autres', successivement ou à la fois. C'est Phocion qui pratique cette substitution des masques avec la virtuosité la plus vertigineuse. Plus forte que Don Juan courtisant simultanément deux femmes, cette créature de Marivaux fait dans le même temps la cour à une femme sous une identité masculine, et à deux hommes sous une identité féminine, fausse celle-là aussi. On la voit passer d'un rôle à l'autre avec un sans-gêne qui frise l'invraisemblance. De sa part ce jeu paraît presque entièrement gratuit: nous entendons bien qu'elle a pris ces masques multiples pour parvenir jusqu'au jeune homme qu'elle aime; mais certainement, étant la reine, elle pouvait aboutir à ses fins à moindres frais.

Marivaux discerne aussi dans le déguisement d'autres motivations, plus profondes qu'une activité purement ludique. L'expérience des mascarades révèle cette évidence: la vérité des êtres s'exprime sous le masque. Une fois supprimé le vêtement social par la substitution d'un autre qui ne compte pas, toutes les inhibitions qu'imposait le rang à tenir sont levées. Silvia n'eût pas écouté les douceurs de ce garçon qui lui plaît, si son tablier de soubrette ne l'avait pas dégagée de ses responsabilités. Dorante de son côté aurait eu scrupule à débiter des galanteries à une Lisette, sans la livrée de Bourguignon qu'il va quitter bientôt: aventure sans avenir, sans danger par conséquent, croit-il d'abord.

Marivaux connaissait assez le théâtre pour savoir que les rôles que choisit un acteur expriment sa personnalité vraie. Dans un dialogue d'une de ses pièces les plus oubliées (*La Réunion des amours*, sc. 5), il a logé cette réplique qui va loin: 'ceux que vous travestissez prennent le masque que vous leur donnez pour leur visage'.

La figure masculine de Phocion est-ce un masque, ou un visage? La jeune fille se sent très à l'aise dans son costume d'homme. Elle en prend avec aisance toutes les allures. Elle calcule froidement ses entreprises de séduction; elle attaque avec un esprit de décision tout viril. C'est une reine, qui a de naissance l'instinct de commander. Sans doute, mais l'autorité royale ne lui suffit pas: elle lui ajoute les droits d'initiative que lui confère le costume masculin. On ne peut écarter tout à fait le soupçon que Marivaux a assuré l'originalité de ce personnage au dépens de sa vraisemblance. Mais si l'on cherche à cet androgyne une justification psychologique, on émettra l'hypothèse qu'en cette jeune fille un refus de la féminité inspire une jalousie du rôle masculin qui s'exprime dans le déguisement en homme. La vérité de ce personnage, s'il en a une, s'exprime dans son masque.

Ce sérieux du déguisement, Marivaux est allé jusqu'à le prendre pour sujet d'une de ses dernières comédies: la pièce en un acte, *Les Acteurs de bonne foi*, si curieusement proche de Pirandello ou d'Anouilh. A l'occasion d'une fête, les domestiques d'une maison ont décidé de donner une comédie composée par l'un d'entre eux, nommé Merlin. Or chacun joue le personnage qu'il est réellement et, chose plus grave, l'action fictive n'est autre que ce qui est en train de leur advenir, à savoir une inconstance double, et réciproque. Merlin, fiancé de Lisette, abandonne celle-ci pour Colette, jeune paysanne coquette, qui de son côté, n'aimant pas son fiancé le lourdaud Blaise, trahit celui-ci pour le beau Merlin. Les deux infidèles ont trouvé le moyen de la comédie pour se confesser leur sentiment, sous les yeux même des deux délaissés. Mais ceux-ci ne sont pas dupes. Ils sentent très bien que Merlin et Colette sont en train de vivre l'amour qu'ils jouent. 'Ils font semblant de faire semblant', s'écrie le pauvre Blaise, moins insignifiant qu'on pourrait le croire: devant la comédie qu'il voit jouer, le malheureux garçon éprouve une gêne, un malaise intolérable. A chaque instant il interrompt les acteurs, prenant pour vérité les paroles de leurs rôles, et certes il ne se trompe pas. Finalement par la faute de ce balourd clairvoyant Merlin devra renoncer à faire jouer une comédie où les masques sont des visages.

On peut apercevoir dans ces *Acteurs de bonne foi* une illustration anticipée du *Paradoxe* de Diderot *sur le comédien*. Mais on pensera plutôt que s'y révèle un désarroi de Marivaux en présence du masque.

Si l'on voulait tenter une 'psychanalyse de Marivaux', on scruterait l'étrange fable qu'il conte dans son *Cabinet du philosophe* sous le titre *Le Voyageur dans le Nouveau Monde*. Un jeune chevalier apprend un jour, par une lettre interceptée, que la femme qu'il aime le trompe. Il provoque en duel son rival, le blesse, doit s'enfuir à l'étranger. Il y rencontre un mentor d'une cinquantaine d'années qui lui propose de le conduire dans le pays où les hommes et les femmes sont vrais. Après un voyage en mer il débarque donc dans ce nouveau monde: or il le trouve tout semblable à la France qu'il a quittée; il reconnaît Paris, et dans ce Paris, sa rue, et dans cette rue sa maison. Il entre dans cette maison et y trouve ses domestiques. Nous attendons, nous, que dans ce nouveau monde, double de l'ancien, le voyageur rencontre son propre double. Mais Marivaux n'est pas en train de raconter un cauchemar, pas même un rêve. Ce nouveau monde, c'est l'ancien, et c'est réellement à Paris que le mentor a conduit le voyageur. La seule différence c'est que désormais celui-ci sait distinguer la vérité sous l'apparence. 'Dans chaque homme,' écrit Marivaux, 'il y en a deux . . ., l'un qui se montre, l'autre qui se cache.' Auparavant le jeune homme était dupe, maintenant il sait lever les masques, et sous son regard ce monde est devenu le monde vrai. Ainsi il surprend les dévergondages de sa gouvernante, à l'office: il perce à jour l'hypocrisie d'un parent qui tente de lui dérober sa part d'héritage; devenu riche, il lit dans les intentions d'un père qui lui offre sa fille en mariage. Bref, comme lui dit son mentor: 'vous avez appris à connaître ces hommes, et à percer le masque dont ils se couvrent, vous les verrez toujours de même; et vous serez le reste de votre vie dans ce monde vrai, dont je vous parlais comme d'un monde étranger au nôtre'. Ce mouvement du monde faux vers un monde vrai, qui est le même une fois le masque ôté, est essentiel à Marivaux. C'est celui qu'il éprouva, à l'âge de dix-sept ans, selon l'anecdote qu'il conte dans la première feuille de son *Spectateur français*. Il s'était épris d'une jeune fille, belle, mais qui semblait ignorer qu'elle l'était. Il l'aimait pour cette simplicité. Or un jour, il la surprend devant son miroir s'appliquant à prendre des mines naturelles, repassant tous ses airs naïfs. Du coup, il fut dégrisé: 'Mademoiselle,' lui dit-il, 'je viens de voir les machines de l'Opéra; il me divertira toujours, mais il me touchera moins'.

Marivaux ajoute qu'à partir de cette aventure il a passé sa vie 'à examiner les hommes et à s'amuser de ses réflexions'. Il ne ressemble nullement au Baudelaire des *Petits Poèmes en prose*, reprochant au 'mauvais vitrier' de n'avoir pas 'des verres roses, rouges, bleus, des vitres de paradis [...] qui fassent voir la vie en beau'. Bien loin de chercher l'illusion, Marivaux en ressent un malaise, et le besoin de le dissiper. Ce trouble devant le masque, il est un sujet où traditionnellement il affleure: celui des *Ménechmes*; le jumeau ou le sosie joue, par rapport à l'autre, la fonction d'un masque, en se substituant à lui. Mais c'est un masque vivant, autonome, par là particulièrement inquiétant.

Nous ne sommes pas surpris que Marivaux ait choisi pour donnée l'existence d'un être en partie double, dans une de ces œuvres dédaignées[4] mais significatives, dont nous parlions plus haut. Les deux jeunes filles de la *Méprise* qui se promènent en masque sur le mail du village sont, sinon jumelles, du moins très ressemblantes: même taille, même visage, même robe, et même masque. Le jeune Ergaste en est tombé amoureux, ignorant qu'elles sont deux: il rencontre tantôt l'une, tantôt l'autre, croyant qu'il parle toujours à la même. Il en résulte un imbroglio que le désarroi d'Ergaste empêche d'être tout à fait plaisant.

Déjà *Le Jeu de l'amour et du hasard* avait exprimé ce même trouble d'un personnage amoureux en face d'un objet énigmatique. C'est ce qu'éprouve Silvia devant cet incompréhensible Bourguignon, qui a de l'esprit, des manières, de la délicatesse dans le langage et dans le cœur autant qu'un homme de qualité, et qui avec tout cela n'est qu'un laquais. Réciproquement celui-ci n'est rien moins qu'à l'aise devant Silvia, cette soubrette qui a l'air d'une princesse. C'est aussi le tourment d'Angélique dans *L'Épreuve*: elle se croyait aimée par Lucidor, et voici que ce jeune homme passe froidement au rôle de seigneur de village occupé à trouver des partis avantageux pour les filles à marier. Est-ce un masque qu'il prend pour dissimuler son amour, ou bien cet amour n'a-t-il existé que dans

[4] Cette petite pièce en un acte a pourtant été reprise, avec un certain succès, à la Comédie-Française en 1959.

l'imagination d'Angélique? L'infortunée reste au supplice jusqu'à ce que Lucidor consente à s'expliquer. Toute comédie de Marivaux est ainsi plus ou moins une épreuve, laquelle prend fin quand le masque est levé.

Il est possible maintenant de concevoir comment les deux figures dont nous parlons s'associent au cours de l'action. Il arrive que l'étonnement devant le masque se confonde avec la surprise de l'amour, c'est le cas dans le *Jeu*, à la première rencontre de Silvia et de Dorante. 'Cette fille m'étonne', dit l'un. Et Silvia: 'voilà un garçon qui me surprend'.

Ensuite, dans le délai qui sépare la surprise du dénouement espéré, un masque se forme, qui n'a rien de matériel, un masque, si l'on ose dire, intérieur. Ce n'est plus un visage, ce sont des sentiments qu'il s'agit de cacher, et à soi-même autant qu'aux autres. En général toute la réalité de ce faux-semblant consiste dans le nom qu'on lui donne; le jeu verbal étant primordial, dans le théâtre de Marivaux, comme l'a montré Frédéric Deloffre. C'est, par exemple, le pacte d'amitié dans la *Seconde Surprise de l'amour*: une amitié exclusive entre la marquise et le chevalier, qui donne droit à la jalousie, qui ne diffère de l'amour que par le nom même d'amitié. Dans *Le Jeu*, Silvia, honteuse d'aimer un laquais, déguise son sentiment en 'esprit de justice': si elle défend avec tant de chaleur Bourguignon, ce n'est pas qu'elle l'aime, non certes: c'est qu'elle veut être juste avec lui. Dans *Les Sincères*, la marquise se joue à elle-même la comédie de la sincérité. De même le 'Petit-maître corrigé', jeune homme au fond timide, n'osant pas s'abandonner à son amour pour Hortense, dissimule celui-ci sous les affectations de l'homme à bonnes fortunes. Ce qui compose un étrange personnage à deux tons, sensible et ricanant.

Car ce masque intérieur est une gêne pour le cœur qui le porte. Il a d'abord procuré une certaine aise par l'expression qu'il permet au sentiment refoulé. Mais expression incomplète, dont on souffre. Enfin libéré du mensonge le personnage s'épanouit, telle Silvia soupirant après l'aveu de Dorante: 'Ah! je vois clair dans mon cœur', et: 'j'avais grand besoin que ce fut là Dorante'. Ce sont les grands moments que guettent dans chacune de ses pièces les amateurs de Marivaux. C'est le moment délicieux où l'Araminte des *Fausses Confidences* répond à un autre Dorante doutant qu'elle puisse l'aimer: 'Et voilà pourtant ce qui m'arrive'.

Nous avons tendance à détacher de leur époque les écrivains qui lui survivent, particulièrement les écrivains de théâtre. Au bout de quelque temps, une pièce ne peut plus être jouée comme elle l'était à sa création. A plus forte raison, après plus de deux siècles. Marivaux n'échappe pas à cette mise à jour, qui fait de lui notre Marivaux. Nous ne devons pourtant pas oublier à quel point il fut homme de son temps.

De son temps, par ce qui se mêle à son comique de cet attendrissement si insupportable dans les comédies larmoyantes et les drames bourgeois. De son temps surtout par l'esprit de vérité qui anime son théâtre. Il demeure sans doute indifférent à l'idéologie de son époque. On a pu parler d'une philosophie de Molière et même les critiques qui ne veulent reconnaître aux idées énoncées dans les pièces de celui-ci qu'une valeur d'accessoires, ne peuvent pas nier qu'elles y soient présentes. Aucun débat en revanche n'est possible sur une philosophie, inexistante dans le théâtre de Marivaux. En comparaison de ses contemporains, Montesquieu, Voltaire, et même l'abbé Prévost, il est un écrivain qui ne pense pas.

Pourtant, il s'affirme bien, lui aussi, 'philosophe', en ce que l'erreur et l'imposture lui sont insupportables. Le mouvement de son théâtre épouse celui de la vérité qui libère. C'est à cette fin qu'il fait jouer les deux figures majeures: la surprise qui révèle les êtres, le masque qui laisse apparaître la vérité par transparence, puis, ôté, en fait valoir la belle nudité. D'autres ont douté que l'acte de démasquer convienne vraiment à la gaîté de la comédie. Baudelaire dans les *Fleurs du mal* montrera un masque au sourire voluptueux couvrant un visage convulsé. Une inquiétude parfois crispe les masques de Marivaux, mais quand se découvrent les visages, la 'surprise' qu'il nous communique est celle du bonheur. Sans parti pris 'philosophique', ce créateur a réalisé le dessein, vainement tenté par d'autres en son siècle: celui d'un théâtre des 'lumières'.

Un Abbé philosophe à la Bastille (1751–53): G.-A. de Méhégan et son Zoroastre

John S. Spink

Les années qui suivirent la signature du traité d'Aix-la-Chapelle en 1748 furent marquées par une grande effervescence intellectuelle à Paris. C'est l'époque où le marquis d'Argenson prévoyait de grands changements dans l'État et l'Église.[1] Cette agitation a laissé de nombreuses traces dans les dossiers de la police. Le cas du *Zoroastre* de l'abbé de Méhégan est éclairé par quantité de documents conservés à la Bibliothèque nationale et à la Bibliothèque de l'Arsenal.

Zoroastre, histoire traduite du chaldéen, est peut-être le premier roman philosophique qu'on ait décrit comme tel au moment de sa parution: Grimm emploie ce terme en en rendant compte le 17 mai 1751:

'Un nouveau roman occupe maintenant les esprits. Il est intitulé *Zoroastre.* Ce philosophe, né et élevé au milieu des erreurs de son siècle, en sent l'absurdité et entreprend de longs voyages pour acquérir des lumières. La superstition qu'il trouve partout le dégoûte des hommes, et il se retire dans une profonde solitude où, à force de réflexions, il découvre l'existence et l'unité de Dieu, la spiritualité

[1] D'Argenson écrivait en 1753: 'On ne sauroit attribuer la perte de la religion en France à la philosophie anglaise qui n'a gagné à Paris qu'une centaine de philosophes, mais à la haine des prêtres qui va au dernier excès. A peine osent-ils se montrer dans les rues sans être hués. Tous les esprits se tournent au mécontentement et à la désobéissance et tout chemine à une grande révolution dans la religion ainsi que dans le gouvernement.' Cf. Aubertin, *L'Esprit public au 18e siècle* (1873), pp. 281-282.

et l'immortalité de l'âme, la vérité et la nécessité du bien et du mal moral, et par conséquent les peines et les récompenses à venir. Dès qu'il s'est bien affermi dans des principes raisonnables, il entreprend d'en persuader ses semblables. Il trouve une nation qui a précisément les mêmes opinions que nous, chrétiens, et il entreprend de les combattre. Il vient à bout de désabuser les gens qu'il instruit, et de les persuader. Le voilà législateur, et roi bientôt après. Le petit roman philosophique dont je vous parle est écrit avec assez de force et de chaleur, mais d'un style souvent poétique et presque toujours boursouflé. L'auteur, dont on ignore le nom, mais qu'on assure être ecclésiastique, n'a pas beaucoup d'idées, mais il en a d'assez agréables. Le succès de l'ouvrage est dû aux raisonnements et aux plaisanteries qui s'y trouvent contre la religion chrétienne.'[2]

Funeste renommée! Un ouvrage qui occupait les esprits ne pouvait manquer d'attirer l'attention de la police. Comme on va voir, c'est celui même qui vendait le livre qui par sa maladresse allait mettre les limiers sur la piste.

Dans le registre tenu par le lieutenant de robe courte Joseph d'Hémery, où figurent, classées selon l'ordre alphabétique, ses notes sur les gens de lettres et assimilés, on peut lire ce qui suit au sujet d'un compagnon imprimeur nommé Dufour:

'Le 15 mai 1751 il a vendu un livre intitulé Zoroastre Libelle contre la Religion que le Prieur a imprimé. Cet ouvrage est du S. Abbé Mégan.

'Quelques jours après que ce jeune homme a mis ce livre en vente, il a vû qu'il faisoit du bruit, il est venu a ce sujet me voir et me dire qu'on lui avoit adressé plusieurs exemplaires avec une lettre dont la copie est cy jointe, et qu'il ne connoissoit pas la personne ni l'auteur; je l'ay engagé a faire l'impossible pour les decouvrir, ce qu'il n'a point fait, bien au contraire quelque tems après il a vendu la critique, ou plutôt l'apologie de cet ouvrage, ce qui a fait que le Magistrat a décidé qu'il seroit arrête. En conséquence le 7 juin 1751 nous avons été en perquisition chez lui, et il a été

[2] *Correspondance littéraire*, éd. Tourneux, ii. 60-61. Cette référence est fournie par Belin, *Le Mouvement philosophique* (Paris 1913), p. 39. Belin, qui consacre une courte notice à Méhégan, a utilisé les documents contenus dans la collection Anisson-Duperron, vol. 49 (B.N. Français 22. 109, f. 49) et dans le volume consacré aux affaires de la librairie (Paris, BN, naf. 1214, fol. 17) et les documents fournis par Ravaisson (*Archives de la Bastille*, Paris, 1866, xii. 362), mais non le dossier Méhégan à la Bibliothèque de l'Arsenal (11758).

ensuite conduit au fort l'Eveque, ou il a persisté a ne vouloir rien dire. Le 8 juin 1751 il a tout avoué.'[3]

Voici le texte de la lettre que Dufour prétendait avoir reçue d'un inconnu:

'Un de vos amis, Monsieur, qui s'interesse pour vous, et qu'il n'est besoin de nommer ici, m'a engagé de m'adresser à vous pour me faire distribuer un ouvrage que j'ay fait imprimer et dont je suis l'auteur; Jose me flatter sans prévention, sur le rapport de gens d'esprit qu'il est bien écrit et qu'il pourra prendre, il est d'un stile comparable à celui des mœurs[4] a l'auteur duquel il est dédié. Le porteur vous en remettra une douzaine; si vous jugés apropos de vous en charger, faite le moi sçavoir; il passera chés vous de tems à autre, et vous en laissera autant que vous en ferés demander. Vous etes je le sçais plus que personne en état de m'en faire distribuer a des colporteurs. afin que vous puissiés etre recompensé des peines que vous prendrés, je vous les passerai à onze livres la douzaine pour les donner aux Colporteurs a vingt sols et selon que vous m'en procurerés le débit je vous accorderay le vingt cinquiéme. vous venderés seul, si vous le voulés, mon édition qui n'est pas considerable, Et pour vous faire un plus grand avantage, vous ne payerés une douzaine qu'en recevant une autre, je suis très veritablement, Monsieur, en attendant le plaisir de me faire connoitre a vous, et de vous remercier de vive voix

Votre tres humble serviteur
DL.h[5]

Ce 29 avril 1751'

Écroué au Fort l'Évêque, Dufour fut interrogé le mardi 8 juin 1751 par Rochebrune, commissaire enquêteur et examinateur au Châtelet. Voici l'essentiel de procès verbal de l'interrogatoire.

'Premierement Interrogé de Ses noms Surnom age pays Qualité et demeure

'A dit aprés serment de repondre verité se nommer Pierre Dufour

[3] Paris, BN, naf. 10781, fol. 163.

[4] C'est-à-dire Toussaint, l'auteur des *Mœurs*.

[5] Paris, BN, ms. fr. 22109, fol. 51. Ce texte porte la note suivante *alia manu*: '1er May 1751 Copie de la pretendue Lettre qui a été ecrite a Dufour au sujet du livre Intitulé Zoroastre qu'il a vendu'. Cette note ne saurait être du 1er mai 1751, puisque d'Hémery affirme que Dufour a mis l'ouvrage en vente le 15 mai. Grimm en parle le 17 mai comme d'une nouveauté.

agé de vingt deux ans natif de paris et apprentif imprimeur demeurant a paris ruë de la Tisseranderie avec ledit Pierre Dufour son perre paroisse Saint Jean en Gréve. Interrogé quel est l'auteur d'un Imprimé Intitulé Zoroastre.

'A dit qu'ayant presté serment de dire Verité il ne nous doit rien cacher pour satisfaire a sa Conscience et que c'est l'abbé Mégan qui demeure en chambres garnies chez un perruquier au dessus de la porte cochere du sieur Mercier imprimeur ruë Saint Jacques.

'Interrogé quel a été l'imprimeur de cet ouvrage et combien il y a Eu d'éxemplaires.

'a dit qu'il s'est adressé au S. Pecquet Libraire demeurant ruë de la huchette et qu'il y en a eu sept cent cinquante d'imprimés dont il ne lui reste que douze Exemplaires qui sont dans une boëte quarrée appartenante au Repondant et qui est dans l'imprimerie dud. Sieur Prieur Imprimeur; ajoute que dans la même boëtte il y a six a sept Critiques de Zoroastre Et une brochure intitulée la touriere des Carmelites qui lui a été prestée il y a trois ans par le sieur chateau vieux alors clerc de Notaire.

'Interrogé quel est l'auteur et l'imprimeur de la Critique de Zoroastre.

'a dit que ledit Sieur abbé Megan l'a composé et que le repondant s'est adressé pareillement aud. Sieur Pecquet qui en a tiré quatre cens exemplaires ou environ de parfaite [*sic*] parce que le surplus montant a six cens s'est trouvé imparfait à cause d'une transposition.

'Interrogé combien il a donné d'argent aud. Abbé Megan.

'A dit qu'il peut lui avoir donné cent francs ou environ en differentes fois et en Excluant les exemplaires qu'il lui a donnés Montant a Soixante ou Environ Ajoute que ledit sieur Megan n'a point Composé Zoroastre et la Critique dans la vuë d'aucun interest ayant Engagé le repondant d'en tirer le meilleur parti qu'il pourrois [*sic*]. Ce qui est cause que le repondant les a vendus sur le pied de dix huit a vingt sols.

'S'il n'est pas vrais que le repondant ayant été trouver le sieur d'Hemery lieutenant de Robe Courte au sujet dudit livre de Zoroastre il lui à montré une lettre par laquelle il est mention que cet ouvrage à esté envoyé au repondant par une personne inconnüe et Nous l'avons interpellé de nous declarer s'il n'a pas fait ecrire ladite lettre pour donner le change audit sieur d'hemery.

'A dit qu'il convient d'avoir fait écrire ladite lettre par un jeune homme qu'il connoist sans scavoir sa demeure et que l'ayant rencontré dans la ruë de la Tisseranderie il le mena chez le pere du repondant ou il l'Ecrivit ajoute que ledit jeune homme se nomme Robert et est clerc de notaire.'

Dufour donne à Rochebrune la clef de la boîte où se trouvent les exemplaires de *Zoroastre* et l'interrogatoire se termine comme suit:

'Ajoute que les vers qui se sont trouvés chez lui lui ont été donné il y a plus de deux ans et demie, Lorsqu'il étois clerc du sieur Quentin notaire ruë Saint Antoine et qu'il ne se souvient point par qui lui ont été donné les vers, sur la paix n'en reconnoissant point l'Ecriture.'[6]

Le lendemain, d'Hémery fit au lieutenant général de police Berryer le rapport que voici:

'J'ai l'honneur de vous rendre compte que la declaration que le Nommé Dufour a faite au Commissaire de Rochebrune que le Nommé Pecquet avoit imprimé Zoroastre et la Critique de ce Livre et qu'il en avoit laissé plusieurs exemplaires dans une petite Cassette chez le Sr Le Prieur ou il travailloit, nous nous sommes transportés M. Le Commre Et moy chez led. Pecquet pour y faire perquisition, mais comme il ne s'y est rien trouvé nous l'avons accompagné en votre hotel ou il est convenu de tout. Ensuite Nous avons été chez Le Sr. Le Prieur qui nous a dit que la mere de Dufour etoit venu hier chercher la Cassette en question et qu'il la luy avoit remise Nous avons été tout de suite chez cette femme en la presence de laquelle nous avons fait l'ouverture de lad. Cassette dans laquelle il s'y est trouvé sept exemplaires de Zoroastre et deux de la critique qui ont été saisis ainsy qu'il est constaté par le procès verbal que led. S Commissaire a dressé à ce sujet.

'N[ot]a on n'a pas encore arrêté l'abbé Megan parce que la mere de Dufour l'a été avertir.'[7]

L'abbé Guillaume-Alexandre Méhégan ou de Méhégan était déjà connu d'Hémery, puisque celui-ci notait le 1er février 1751, dans son registre, qu'il était 'petit, blond, bossu et d'une assez jolie figure'. C'est, observait-il, 'un jeune abbé de condition qui a beaucoup d'esprit, 1000 livres de pension sur l'Evêché de S.-Claude, 200 livres sur le trésor royal. Il a un frère qui fait joliment des vers, qui est

[6] Paris, BN, ms. fr. 22109, fol. 49-50. [7] Paris, BN, naf. 1214, fol. 17-18.

major au régiment de la couronne. Il est clerc tonsuré du diocèse d'Alais, et il auroit pu être évêque.'[8]

L'abbé participe activement à la vie intellectuelle. Il est lié avec La Beaumelle, qui a à peu près le même âge que lui et a fait ses études au collège des jésuites d'Alais (Alès), dans ce même diocèse dont l'abbé est ressortissant. Les deux jeunes gens projettent, en 1750, de faire publier à Amsterdam une gazette des lettres et La Beaumelle, nommé professeur de français à Copenhague et désireux de faire une leçon inaugurale, s'adresse à son ami qui lui en fournit une qui est un véritable programme de littérature comparée rédigé sous l'égide de l'*Esprit des lois*. La Beaumelle était l'auteur d'un petit ouvrage, publié à Amsterdam sous le couvert de l'anonyme, qui prend la forme d'un conte oriental, mais qui est en réalité un discours en faveur de la liberté de conscience et contre la révocation de l'édit de Nantes.[9] En 1751 il a déjà rejoint son nouveau poste, mais il va bientôt faire circuler à Paris quelques exemplaires de ses *Pensées* où un lecteur attentif pourra découvrir un radicalisme politique qui n'était pas moins prononcé pour être présenté d'un point de vue protestant.

Chose plus grave, le nom de l'abbé venait de figurer dans une épigramme connue de la police, à côté de celui de Boindin, libre-penseur notoire. D'Hémery fit un rapport au sujet de cette

[8] Paris, BN, naf. 10781, art. Méhégan.

[9] Sur le projet de publier une gazette des lettres, voir Nicolas, M., *Notice sur la vie et les écrits de Laurent Angliviel de la Beaumelle* (Paris 1852), p. 7. La Beaumelle accepta d'abord une place de gouverneur du fils du baron de Gram, à Copenhague où il arriva le 15 avril 1747. Lorsqu'il fut nommé à la chaire de langue et de littérature françaises, il fit un voyage à Paris et y séjourna du mois de mars au mois de décembre 1750. La Beaumelle laissa publier sous son nom par l'imprimerie royale du Danemark, une belle édition du discours, mais ne protesta pas lorsque Méhégan en réclama la paternité quatre ans plus tard.

L'ouvrage de la Beaumelle qui prend la forme d'un conte oriental s'appelle *L'Asiatique tolérant, traité à l'usage de Zeokinizul* (Louis XV), *roi des Kofirans* (François), *surnommé le chéri, ouvrage traduit de l'arabe du voyageur Bekrinoll* [Crébillon] *par M. de ***, Paris, chez Durand, rue St. Jacques à St Landry et au Griffon* [Amsterdam, M.-M. Rey ?] l'an xxiv du traducteur [1748], in 8⁰, xxviii + 145 p. La préface est signée des initiales L.B.L.D.A. (Laurent Beaumelle la de Angliviel, c'est-à-dire Laurent Angliviel de la Beaumelle). On attribue à Crébillon fils l'ouvrage intitulé *Les Amours de Zeokinizul* auquel l'*Asiatique tolérant* est une manière de suite, mais certaines pages très téméraires au début des *Amours de Zeokinizul*, semblent sortir de la même boutique que l'*Asiatique tolérant*, étant écrites d'un point de vue protestant et libéral. De plus, il est peu probable que Crébillon fils eût signé de l'anagramme transparente de 'Krinebol' un ouvrage aussi dangereux pour son auteur. Je pencherais à en chercher l'auteur parmi les amis de La Beaumelle.

épigramme, au mois de février 1751.[10] On en trouve le texte dans son journal:

> Boindin regent du Caffe de Procope
> vient de quitter ses éleves cheris:
> je vois du coup l'athéisme au syncope;
> rassurez vous mécreans de Paris,
> Petit Abbé Predicateur en bosse[11]
> peut de la secte assurer les progrés
> par sa doctrine il a manqué la crosse
> sa preuve est faite, il a droit aux sifflets.[12]

Pour d'Hémery, le nom de Méhégan symbolise le déisme, comme celui de Boindin symbolise l'athéisme. Quand paraît la brochure intitulée *Zoroastre*, il note dans son journal, en date du 6 mai 1751: 'je crois par le déisme qui y règne qu'elle est du sieur abbé de Megan'.[13]

D'Hémery note encore, le 18 février 1751,[14] que Méhégan travaille à une tragédie intitulée *Julien*, L'on pense à l'empereur Julien, si admiré des Philosophes, mais Méhégan l'appellera, dans la suite, au cours d'un interrogatoire, le *comte Julien*, ajoutant qu'il l'a proposée aux comédiens et l'a retirée ensuite 'pour ne pas déplaire à sa famille'.[15] Le comte Julien doit être celui qui, gouverneur d'Andalousie, se révolta contre le roi Roderic qui avait fait violence à sa fille. Méhégan avait composé encore un roman intitulé *Mémoires du sieur de Terville*,[16] mais ne l'avait pas publié. Ce roman paraîtra en 1756, sous le titre d'*Histoire de la Marquise de Terville*.[17] Il se distingue par son mépris de la convention romanesque et par certaines remarques qui montrent que l'auteur était Philosophe.

[10] Ravaisson, *op. cit.*, xii. 357-358.

[11] *En marge*: 'l'abbé de Mégan'. Méhégan était bossu (cf. les remarques de d'Hémery, ci-dessus).

[12] Paris, BN, ms. fr. 22156, fol. 39. Au sujet du déménagement de Boindin, d'Hémery notait, en date du 18 février 1751: 'Le Sr Boindin qui frequente depuis longtems le Caffé de Procope ou il attiroit beaucoup de monde par les conversations curieuses qu'il y tenoit vient de le quitter pour aller Caffé de Maillard parce qu'il a trouvé dans ce quartier une vieille dame qui lui donne la table' (*ibid.*, fol. 34*r*). Cette dame habitait la rue Brunbourg; elle ne le laissait manquer de rien, pourtant il la quitta en octobre 1751, pour aller loger dans la rue de la Comédie, où, dit d'Hémery, 'il veut absolument mourir' (*ibid.*, 21 oct., 1751, fol. 133). Il mourut en effet peu après.

[13] *Ibid.*, fol. 63*r*-63*v*.

[14] Le 18 février 1751, *ibid.*, fol. 34*r*.

[15] Paris, Archives de la Bastille, 11758, fol. 29*v* (numéroté également 35*v*).

[16] *Ibid.*

[17] 'Londres', in-8° (Paris, Bibliothèque de l'Arsenal, 8° B.L. 21687).

Madame de Terville ne trouve pas le bonheur dans l'amour; son mariage clandestin échoue, ruiné par les forces sociales qui s'y opposent et les époux finissent par se séparer. La préface déclare que le roman peut être aussi 'utile' que la tragédie. Dans le texte on trouve des passages qui servent à préciser très nettement l'attitude politique de l'auteur. Terville est royaliste, mais 'citoyen'. 'N'oubliez jamais,' dit-il à son fils, 'que vous êtes Citoyen. Respectez votre Prince, honorez-le en homme éclairé: il est dépositaire de ces Loix qui font votre sureté' (p. 45). Un certain comte de Mérolles est présenté comme étant un de 'ces Nobles paresseux qui se persuadent que le mérite de leur pere les dispense d'en avoir: d'ailleurs dur, avare, attaché à son or. En un mot, il joignoit toute la vanité d'un noble campagnard au ridicule orgueil d'un Financier opulent' (pp. 41-42). Si la seconde de ces deux dernières phrases se ressent de la comédie de mœurs du début du siècle, la première laisse prévoir celle de l'époque de Figaro. Une troisième citation montrera que l'auteur avait une conception du rapport entre l'individu et la communauté qui est celle de la plupart des Philosophes: 'Ainsi le pere vertueux cherchoit à faire voir que notre intérêt étoit nécessairement lié avec celui des autres, et que la vertu n'étoit que l'art de se rendre heureux en faisant la félicité de la société où l'on vivoit' (p. 46).

L'on voit que l'abbé Méhégan méritait bien le titre de Philosophe. Voici comment il fut amené, selon lui, à composer son *Zoroastre*:

'j'étois un jour a diner a l'hotel nôtre dame. La conversation tomba sur Zoroastre. on le maltraitoit beaucoup. j'en fis l'apologie. J'assurai qu'il n'avoit jamais suivi que le religion naturelle, La seule lumiere capable de nous guider quand on est privé du flambeau de la revelation. on me flata: on m'invita a mettre par écrit ce que j'avois dit. Que ne peut point l'illusion de l'amour propre! de retour chez moi je travaillai. L'imagination m'offrit de nouveaux traits. Je m'y laissai aller et en vingt quatre heures l'ouvrage fut tel que vous le voyez. un nouveau vertige de vanité m'engagea a le montrer. il ne fut que trop applaudi. On en porta a mon insçu une copie chez l'imprimeur. quelques jours après on m'en montra une épreuve et je consentis alors a le faire paroitre. Comme on cherchoit a grossir le volume, j'y ajoutai la piêce du bonheur qui m'etoit chere, parce qu'elle contenoit une foible ébauche de ma respectueuse admiration pour mon souverain. Ainsi parut cette brochure avec tant d'indifference de ma part que j'ignore encore le nom de l'imprimeur et que je n'en ai donné aucun exemplaire aux librairies et aux colporteurs.'[18]

Ne reprochons pas à l'auteur de cette lettre ses réticences. Il était entre les mains de l'ennemi lorsqu'il la composa. Reconnaissons certes, qu'elles jettent le doute sur tout ce qu'il dit au sujet de la genèse de son ouvrage, mais rappelons d'autre part le rôle que jouaient les propos de table dans la vie intellectuelle de l'époque. Quant aux mobiles qui ont pu l'inciter à prendre la plume, reconnaissons, comme lui, que la vanité d'auteur n'y a pas été étrangère. Méhégan était un jeune auteur à l'affût du succès; celui de son premier ouvrage dépassa sans doute ce que sa prudence devait espérer, mais on voit que son amour-propre y trouve une récompense. Ce qu'il ne pouvait dire, et que nous devons dire pour lui, c'est que le désir d'être utile et de témoigner de la vérité y eut aussi sa part. Rappelons que Dufour insiste sur le désintéressement de l'auteur, devant un enquêteur qui, tout en serrant de très près la vérité matérielle, excluait d'office tout idéalisme et posait l'intérêt le plus sordide comme seul mobile plausible.

Méhégan fournira plus tard des précisions au sujet de ses relations avec Dufour:

'Interrogé s'il n'a pas composé et fait imprimer differens ouvrages.

'A répondu qu'il est auteur de Zoroastre petite brochure, qu'il l'avoit donné a mettre au net au nommé Berard écrivain qui travailloit pour le repondant, que ce Berard l'a donné au nommé Dufour Compagnon Imprimeur de Prieur du moins le Sr Dufour le lui a dit ainsi, et qu'il ne sçait pas qui l'a fait imprimer; que ledit Dufour lui apporta une épreuve dudit ouvrage qui avoit été imprimé à son insu, mais convient qu'alors lui Repondant donna son consentement pour qu'il fût imprimé, et rendu public, qu'il y fit même alors differentes corrections et augmentations que ledit Dufour lui a donné environ 60ˡˡ a compte sur les exemplaires qu'il avoit vendus, et qu'il lui a donné en outre 60 exemplaires qu'il a vendus ou donnés pour son compte. Ne sçait ce qu'est devenu le surplus de l'édition qu'il a laissé audit Dufour et qui en a fait ce qu'il a voulu.'[19]

[18] Méhégan à Berryer, 14 août 1751 (Paris, Archives de la Bastille, 11758, fol. 25, numéroté également 30). Le texte de cette lettre a été publié par Ravaisson (*op. cit.*, xii. 362).

[19] Interrogatoire de l'abbé devant Berryer, lieutenant général de police, le mercredi 1er septembre 1751, à 9 heures du matin dans la salle de conseil du château (Paris, Archives de la Bastille, 11758, fol. 29 (35)).

Il ajoutera un an plus tard la déclaration que voici:

'dans le marché que je fis avec le nommé *du four* pour la coupable bagatelle qui m'a jetté ici, nous étions convenus d'en partager tous les hazards. je n'en ai que trop essuyé les peines. j'en ai peu eu des avantages. on m'a assuré qu'il avoit tiré plus de douze cens exemplaires. il m'en a confessé huit cens cinquante de son aveu, en quatre jours il avoit retiré ses frais, en en vendant deux cens, a vingt sols piece. il en restoit donc six cens cinquante à partager. il m'en a donné ou en argent ou en papier, cent cinquante. Ainsi ce seroit encore pres des deux cens dont il me seroit comptable, où en papier, qu'il faudroit brûler, où en argent qu'il devroit me donner.'[20]

L'abbé n'avait plus rien à cacher au moment où il fit cette déclaration et il songeait plutôt à sa situation financière qu'à des aveux supplémentaires, mais ce qu'il dit laisse voir que son accord avec Dufour avait été tout à fait explicite. En mettant ensemble les témoignages des deux hommes on peut reconstituer les événements comme suit.

Méhégan donne son manuscrit à copier à un écrivain public nommé Bérard, qui le passe à un compagnon imprimeur nommé Dufour, qui s'entend avec un libraire nommé Pecquet, demeurant rue de la Huchette qui l'imprime ou la fait imprimer chez Le Prieur. Dufour apporte l'épreuve à Méhégan qui, pour grossir le volume, ajoute certaines pièces, y compris le poème intitulé *Le Bonheur*, et compose la *Critique*. Pecquet tire 750 ou 850 exemplaires de *Zoroastre* et 400 de la *Critique*. Dufour donne 60 exemplaires de *Zoroastre* à Méhégan. Il lui donne aussi 60 ou 100 livres en argent comptant. L'ouvrage se vend 18 ou 20 sols l'exemplaire. Dufour en vend 200 en quatre jours, probablement du 15 au 19 mai. Puis il va voir d'Hémery et cherche à parer le coup dont il se sent menacé à cause du succès même de l'entreprise. Il ne reste plus que 7 exemplaires de *Zoroastre* et 2 de la *Critique* au moment de l'arrestation de Dufour, le 7 juin. Dès le 10 juin, Méhégan, averti par la mère de Dufour, a quitté son logement de la rue Saint-Jacques.

Il ne resta pas longtemps en liberté. Bientôt Duval, secrétaire du lieutenant de police, à l'hôtel s'Aligre, notait sa nouvelle adresse:

'chez la dame Le Roux qui loue des chambres garnies rue de Vaugirard Hôtel S. Louis, je crois.'[21]

[20] Déclaration faite le 9 juin 1752 (*ibid.*, fol. 38-39 (54-55)).

[21] *Ibid.*, fol. 4 (5).

Le 10 août d'Argenson contresignait une lettre de cachet. Le lendemain soir, de Rochebrune et d'Hémery se présentaient devant la maison à porte cochère où Françoise Bonnemain, veuve d'Antoine Le Roux, louait des chambres garnies, pour arrêter l'abbé qui occupait depuis un mois une chambre du deuxième étage, sur le derrière, et saisir 'les manuscrits contraires à la religion à l'Etat et aux bonnes mœurs' qui s'y trouveraient. L'abbé était dans son lit. On fouilla les tiroirs de la table et de la commode, mais aucun document ayant rapport au sujet de la perquisition ne fut découvert.[22] On emporta la robe de chambre du prévenu et dans la poche de ce vêtement furent trouvées, le lendemain, quelques feuilles de papier sur lesquelles le jeune homme avait fait le récit d'une promenade à pied de Paris en Bourgogne. On pense à J.-J. Rousseau en lisant ce petit exercice de débutant, daté de 'la nativité 1749'. On y voit une certaine recherche du pittoresque et d'une certaine atmosphère de liberté et d'insouciance que créent des allusions aux sétiers de vin qu'on a bus et à une bourse mal garnie. Le manuscrit resta dans les dossiers de la police.[23]

[22] Procès verbal signé de Rochebrune (*ibid.*, fol. 8-11).

[23] *Ibid.*, fol. 16-24. Voici un extrait de ce texte inédit. (Je mets entre parenthèses ce qui est barré dans le texte.)

'Je passai une nuit fort agité. je ne dormis point et souffris beaucoup. la fatigue de la veille m'avoit accablé. je me levai sur les sept heures je demandai le Compte. on me taxa a 15 sols ce fut un coup de foudre. je compris n'en avoir que dixsept. je donnai ce qu'on me demandoit. je sortis en cachette cachant mon trouble [mais] j'évitai le grand chemin je cotoyois la riviere et là je reflechis tout entier a mon sort. je n'avois point mangé. il ne me restoit qu'une moitié de cervelas (mais il faloit du pain du vin) et deux sols pour faire huit lieues a pied dans la plus grande chaleur. Le plus court eut été [d'aller demander] d'attendre jusqu'au diner et d'aller [demander a diner] chez quelque curé. mais ma vanité ne pouvoit s'accommoder de ce parti. j'ai toujours trouvé honteux de demander les choses les plus legeres a un homme qui n'est pas mon ami. d'ailleurs cet homme pourroit etre insolent et que d'humiliations a souffrir dans ce cas. enfin je pouvois etre reconnu, ou demasqué par la suite par quelqu'un [qui m'auroit] je pris donc une autre résolution. elle fut d'aller acheter dans quelque vilage pour deux sols de pain, d'y boire un verre d'eau et de manger sous quelque arbre mon [demi] cervelat. ensuite pour appaiser ma soif [d'aller] de cotoyer les vignes et d'en prendre de tems en tems quelques grappes [muries] avec ces idées je repris la joye. Mais comme j'avançois sur le bord de l'yonne, j'aperçus une cariolle, [c'est a dire] une charette couverte d'une toile cirée rouge tirée par quatre vigoureux chevaux, c'est dans ces voitures que vont tous les grands du pays. On y est tres cahoté et l'on va fort vite. [j'aperçus] je vis en même tems cinq ou six honêtes gens qui y montoient, et le cocher qui croyoit que je venois [aussi m'y] remplir la voiture m'attendit. toute ma crainte etoit d'etre vû distinctement par des gens de sens qui me feroi[en]t ensuite rougir de ma misere. je r[ebroussai] chemin alors, je feignis de

A onze heures et demie la porte du château fort s'ouvrait devant l'abbé, escorté par d'Hémery. Celui-ci fit par devant Rochebrune un procès verbal que le prisonnier refusa de signer.

Le lieutenant de police Berryer le laissa attendre plus de quinze jours avant de l'interroger, sans même le laisser se procurer des livres pour se distraire. Quand il eut finalement cette permission, l'abbé demanda l'*Histoire de France* de Mézeray, l'*Abrégé chrono-*

me promener sur la riviere et m[ême] de gagner du coté de Montereau. ils le crurent et partirent. je les laissai s'eloigner un peu et je repris ma route. on voiage pendant une demi lieue le long de la riviere. ensuite on monte, mais assez doucement. j'arrivai a 9 heures a Cannes un petit bourg très joli dont la situation est admirable. derriere, c'est une campagne belle et fertile. de l'autre coté, une pente insensible conduit jusqu'a la riviere [au dela vous voyez quantité] et vous decouvrez [une vaste] la plaine ou [serpente l'yonne] que [je] decrirai bientot. [apres] sur les neuf heures j'arrivai à un bourg qu'on nomme Villeneuve la guiare. il me le fallut traverser et là je trouvai trente Carioleurs [?] qui redoubloient ma honte par leur rires. j'abaissai mon chapeau sur mes yeux, et je passai vite, ensuite je m'éloignai du grand chemin. au sortir de villeneuve on entre dans une plaine immense [et qui est le chef d'œuvre] qui vous conduit jusqu'a Sens eloigné d'environ six lieues. d'abord vous rencontrez [a droite de vertes] des prairies entrecoupées de noyers et de peupliers qui forment des promenades, des ombrages charmans. ensuite en avançant tout droit, vous découvrez [la riviere] à droite la riviere d'yonne qui serpente au milieu, au dela de la riviere, vous voyez sur ses bords, quantité de petites villes de tours, de ports [?] au dela [des] vous apercevez dans le lointain des plaines coupées de taillis et semées de vilages et tout cela terminé par des montagnes cultivées et chargées de differens fruits, à votre gauche vous avez une infinité de petites colines qui se succédent les unes aux autres toutes couvertes de vignes (chargées de raisins) de noyers et (de chanvre) (un vilage) de vergers charmans et de vilages au bas de quart de lieue en quart de lieue. Vous continuez ainsi jusqu'à Pont, ou la riviere partage la plaine et se jette sur la droite, [Pont est] on compte trois lieues de villeneuve la, mais j'en fis bien cinq. le chemin est uni [comme] au niveau. je ne fis que monter et descendre. c'est que je gagnai par les colines [pour] et j'allai de montagne en montagne pour deux vuës. la premiere etoit d'eviter le monde qui alloit a Sens la 2ᵉ d'attraper en passant des grappes de raisin qui pourroient me soutenir. en effet j'en mangeai tant que je ne sentis ni faim ni soif. mais je me fatiguois beaucoup a descendre et a monter continuellement. joint a cela le vent qui me secouoit, et le soleil qui me rotissoit. j'arrivai sur les mydi au pont. je passai par les derrieres de cette bicoque qui n'a de mérite que par sa situation. on passe l'yonne par un fort beau pont [j'entrai ensuite a la derniere auberge pour m'y refraichir] j'allois entrer dans une maison de paysan pour [demander] acheter du pain. en fouillant dans ma poche je sentis plusieurs piéces. je les comptai. je trouvai que j'avois cinq sols et demi. un fanatique eut crié miracle. c'est que deux pieces de six liards s'étoient cachées dans le replis de ma poche. c'etoit un prodige dans les circonstances ou je me trouvois. j'entrai fierement dans l'auberge. J'y bus un demi setier de vin fort joli, j'y mangeai mon cervelas et du pain le tout pour quatre sols. Ce fut là tout mon diner. Je le fis durer le plus longtems que je pus pour me délasser et sur les deux heures je rentrai dans ma belle plaine. j'avançai a grands pas et apres avoir fait une lieue je me reposai sous des arbres ou je *logique* du président Hénault, l'*Histoire universelle* de Bossuet, un mappemonde, une carte de l'Europe et une carte de la France.[24]

L'interrogatoire eut lieu le 1er septembre. Nous en avons déjà cité cette partie qui concerne le livre incriminé. Citons maintenant la partie qui intéresse le prévenu:

'Après serment fait par répondant de repondre vérité Interrogé de ses noms, surnom, âge, qualité, pays, demeure, profession et Religion.

'A dit se nommer Guillaume Alexandre de Méhégan, natif de la petite ville de Salle [La Salle] dans les Cevennes agé de vingt six ans et demy.[25] clerc tonsuré du diocèse d'Alais [Alès], Ecuyer—demeurant rue de Vaugirard de la Rel. Catholique apost. et romaine.

'Interrogé en quel tems est venu à Paris et a quelle occasion.

'A repondu qu'il est venu a Paris en 1741 pour faire ses etudes et solliciter des Graces auprès de M. le Card de Fleury.

'Interrogé en quel tems la dame de Méhégan sa mere y est venue demeurer.

'a repondu qu'elle est venue a Paris en 1741 pour veiller a l'education du repondant qui a demeuré avec elle jusqu'en l'année 1743 qu'il est entré au seminaire de S. Nicolas du Chardonnel ou il a demeuré jusqu'en 1746. qu'il est revenu chez sa mere qui demeuroit alors rue Platriere a l'hotel du Saint Esprit, et qu'il a resté avec elle jusqu'en l'année 1748 qu'elle est allée demeurer à Sens.

chantai, je déclamai, je mangeai quelques noyes que j'avois ramassées dans le chemin. je restai la jusqu'a quatre heures ensuite je me mis en marche et me promenai le long de la riviere. il fesoit chaud, l'eau etoit claire, je lavai mes pieds ensuite je me deshabillai et me jettai a l'eau. je n'osois pourtant avancer de peur de manquer la terre. j'y restai quelque tems [ensuite je me rabi] je me rehabillai et je continuai ma route. j'aperçus assez pres de moy un gros clocher et quelques autres. Je crus que c'etoit Sens. Comme j'etois fort aise de n'entrer que tard, je m'assis sur le bord de la riviere en attendant que le soleil se couchat et [deux] une heure apres je rencontrai un paysan qui me dit que j'avois pris le bon chemin.'

On reconnaît sans peine les lieux que nomme l'auteur, Montereau, Cannes, Villeneuve-la-Guyard, Pont-sur-Yonne, mais l'on s'étonne de le voir affirmer que la rivière se trouve à sa droite, à la sortie de Villeneuve; elle se trouve à gauche pour quelqu'un qui traverse cet endroit en direction de Sens.

[24] Lettre de Méhégan à Berryer du 2 septembre 1751 (*ibid.*, fol. 31); lettre de Chevalier, gouverneur du château, à Berryer, 10 septembre 1751 (Ravaisson, *op. cit.*, xii. 366). Cf. Paris, Archives de la Bastille, 12518, fol. 128 (ce dossier contient la correspondance de Rochebrune au sujet des vêtements et autres objets qu'on permet au prisonnier de recevoir).

[25] Il est donc né en 1725, et non en 1721, comme l'affirment la *Bibliographie universelle* et l'avertissement de son *Tableau d'histoire* (édition posthume de 1778).

'Interrogé s'il a des freres et des sœurs a repondu qu'il a un frere ainé qui a servi longtems dans le Regt de la Couronne et qui est actuellement major dans les Grenadiers de France. qu'il a une sœur aînée qui demeure avec la dame falliere que son pere est mort il y a 18 ou 19 ans, qu'il étoit Irlandais qui avoit passé en France avec le Roy Jacques et commandoit dans les Cevennes lorsqu'il est mort.'[26]

Ensuite Berryer l'interrogea au sujet de ses ouvrages. Nous avons reproduit ci-dessus la réponse du prévenu en ce qui concerne *Zoroastre*. En dernier lieu il fut question de ses autres ouvrages:

'Interrogé s'il n'a point composé d'autres ouvrages soit en vers soit en prose:

'a repondu qu'il a composé un roman moral intitulé Memoires du Sr de Terville, qu'il a remis entre les mains de Merigot libraire qui le devoit porter a la Censure, qu'en outre il a composé une Tragedie intitulée Le Comte Julien qu'il avoit remis a Dubreuil Comedien pour la presenter aux Comediens, et des mains duquel il l'a retirée pour ne pas déplaire a sa famille.'[27]

Combien de temps Berryer voulait-il le garder en prison? Un an, semble-t-il, car son secrétaire Duval écrivit le 13 juin 1752 dans la minute d'une lettre: 'la faute qui l'a fait mettre a la Bastille est a peu pres expiée; il y a un terme à tout'.[28] S'il y était encore au mois de mars 1753, après 29 mois d'incarcération, il faut attribuer cette rigueur, dont Berryer lui-même semble avoir conscience,[29] aux efforts infatigables de la mère de l'abbé, appuyée par l'archevêque de Sens et l'ancien évêque de Mirepoix.[30] Berryer était plein d'égards pour le jeune abbé à cause de sa naissance et le considérait évidem-

[26] Le père de l'abbé, Jacques de Méhégan, chevalier, baronnet d'Angleterre et Chevalier de l'ordre royal et militaire de Saint-Louis, avait épousé Elizabeth Russell, de la même maison que les ducs de Bedford. Son fils aîné, Jacques-Antoine-Thadée, était chevalier et pensionnaire de l'ordre royal et militaire de Saint-Louis et colonel du régiment de grenadiers royaux de son nom. La sœur de l'abbé se nommait Catherine-Elizabeth. (Aubert de la Chenaye-Desbois et Badier, *Dictionnaire de la noblesse*, 1868, xiii. col. 583.)

[27] Paris, Archives de la Bastille, 11758, fol. 29 (36).

[28] *Ibid.*, fol. 40 (56).

[29] 'Le prisonnier ne cesse aussi de demander sa liberté promettant de ne plus travailler a aucun ouvrage qui puisse déplaire au Gouvernement ni qui soit contraire a la Religion. . . . Je crois que 29 mois de prison à la Bastille pourront le corriger et qu'on peut le rendre libre.' (Note de Berryer, *ibid.*, fol. 68 (84).)

[30] Languet, archevêque de Sens, écrivit à Berryer, le 31 août 1751, pour appuyer la demande de la mère. Sa lettre se trouve dans Ravaisson, *op. cit.*, xii 365. 'Cette dame', écrivait-il, 'quoique très noble et vertueuse a le malheur d'avoir un fils aussi dérangé, ce dont elle n'est pas plus contente que le public édifié.' L' intérêt que Languet portait à la ques-

ment comme récupérable, mais la mère accusait son fils de s'être endetté et affirmait que, s'il restait en prison, ses pensions s'accumuleraient et lui permettraient finalement de faire face à ses créanciers. Il est vrai que l'abbé avait pour 1825 livres de dettes et ne disposait, semble-t-il, que de 1250 livres. Il affirmait lui-même en avoir 1832 et proposait d'en donner 1200 à ses créanciers et réserver 500 pour lui. Mais la mère faisait remarquer que l'abbé possédait 582 livres de moins qu'il ne croyait.[31] On peut s'étonner qu'une mère voulût laisser dans une de ces cellules malsaines 'de dix pas de circonférence' nommées 'calottes'[32] un fils dont la santé n'avait jamais été bonne, à cause de 582 francs, et en effet elle avait d'autres raisons; ses lettres montrent qu'elle désirait ardemment l'avoir en son pouvoir et l'empêcher de rien faire 'qui déplût à nos maîtres'.[33] Sa première lettre, adressée à d'Argenson et datée de Sens, du 9 septembre 1751, donne le ton. En voici les premières phrases:

'Cet une mere qui se jette a vos pieds pour implorer l'authorité de Vostre Grandeur, afin de pouvoir metre un fils derangé en lieu de sureté, et quelle ne soit plus exposée a craindre les dangers quentraine un libertinage effrené, que ny les prieres, ny les Menace reiterees depuis plusieurs annees nont pu arreter.

tion tient sans doute dans ces trois derniers mots, qui terminent la lettre. Le 4 septembre, l'ancien evêque de Mirepoix envoya son secrétaire chez Berryer pour lui demander de garder l'abbé en prison 'jusqu'à ce que la famille ait pris un parti à son égard'. (Paris, Archives de la Bastille, 11758, fol. 33 (39).)

[31] *Ibid.*, fol. 49 (54). (État des affaires du Sieur Méhégan—liste de ses dettes, été 1752.) Il avait des dettes à billet (perruquier, tailleur, chirurgien, blanchisseuse, cordonnier, etc.) au total de 1252 livres et des dettes sans billet au total de 571 livres. Sa pension sur l'Evêché de Saint-Claude pouvait lui rapporter 1500 livres (mais le mère affirme qu'on en retient un sixième, soit 250 livres). Sa pension du roi de 500 livres pouvait lui en rapporter 332, toutes réductions faites (mais, disait encore la mère, elle ne devait être payée qu'au mois de février 1753). Il croyait donc disposer de 1832 livres, mais ne disposait en réalité que de 1250 livres.

[32] Méhégan à d'Argenson du 13 décembre 1752 (*ibid.*, fol. 69*v*). Méhégan était au quatrième étage 'du coin' depuis le 18 août 1751 (il avait d'abord été 'au troisième étage du coin'; cf. British Museum, Egerton 1667, Livre des entrées au château de la Bastille, fol. 87); il devait donc être dans une des 'calottes'. 'Les calottes étaient les chambres de l'étage supérieur. En été la chaleur y était extrême, et, en hiver, le froid, malgré les poêles. C'étaient des chambres octogones dont le plafond, comme le nom l'indique, était en forme de calotte. Assez élevées dans la partie centrale, elles allaient se réduisant vers les bords. On ne pouvait se tenir debout qu'au milieu de la pièce.' (F. Funck-Brentano, *Les Secret de la Bastille*, 1932, pp. 68-69.)

[33] Mme de Méhégan à d'Argenson (Paris, Archives de la Bastille, 11758, fol. 34 (41)).

'Cet abbé de M . . . depuis longtems, il fesoit profession de precher dans les Cafés, et dans les lieux qu'il frequentoit, lindependance et lirreligion,—il a eté dans plusieurs colege, et Seminaires, ou en luy reconoissant des talens pour reussir dans les etudes, il a toujours mecontenté ses superieurs, par son derangement de conduite cherchant la compagnie des plus mauuais sujets, au sortir de ces maisons il alloit en chambre garnie se reduisant toujours a la misere la plus affreuse par ses debauches et par ses deptes, et n'ayant de gout que pour lindependance.'

Et vers la fin:

'une annee de cloture pouront le ramener au devoir, par les reflections, car ce que le tems seul, joint aux personnes judicieuse qu'il frequentera, qui peuvent operer sur un esprit aussy gaté aussy foug[u]eux aussi independant

'J'ai parlé a M larcheuuesque de Sens, de la conduite de mon fils, et de son caractere, il la savoit deja, ce prelat est convenu avec moy, que lunique moyen denpecher un plus grand derangement et de preuenir le deshonneur qu'il pouroit faire a la famille, etoit de le faire metre dans quelque endroit honorable, ou obligé de demeurer par lauthorité du Roy, il eut le tems de faire des reflections salutaires sur sa conduite passée.'[34]

Cette lettre a été apostillée comme suit par la main de Duval, secrétaire de Berryer: 'le laisser un peu séjourner à la Bastille'. D'autres lettres suivent. La dame apprend en passant à son correspondant qu'elle 'doit plus de 1000 livres un procès qui a achevé de [l']abimer' et demande que l'argent des pensions de son fils soient payé par son entremise, 'sans quoi il se moquerait' d'elle.[35] Le caractère hautain et autoritaire de la dame se révèle dans chacun de ses propos. De son côté, l'abbé déclare que sa mère ne l'a jamais aimé et laisse entendre qu'il pourrait facilement se justifier, 'mais il vaut mieux n'être pas justifié, que de l'être en se plaignant de l'auteur de ses jours'.[36] Les dernières lettres de la mère montrent qu'au moment de la libération de son fils elle finit par comprendre que ceux qui avaient feint de s'intéresser au sort de l'abbé étaient en réalité ses ennemis: 'Je crains', écrit-elle, le 9 janvier 1753, dans une lettre à Berryer, 'que ceux même qui paroisse[nt] sinteresser a nous,

[34] *Ibid.* Le texte de cette lettre a été publié par Ravaisson, *op. cit.*, t. xii.

[35] Paris, Archives de la Bastille, 11758, fol. 46*v* (62*v*).

[36] *Ibid.*, fol. 56 (70).

soposeroi[en]t qu'il fut libre' et, dans une autre lettre écrite quelques jours plus tard: 'il a des ennemis qui doivent implorer Monsieur le Compte [d'Argenson] et se servir du nom de sa famille sous le pretexte qu'il se feroit remettre a la Bastille et vous implorer pour l'exiler dans les provinces'.[37] A ce moment-là, son fils était auprès d'elle et se montrait disposé à lui être serviable; elle déployait une énergie considérable pour lui obtenir des protections: il ne se mariera qu'en 1763.[38]

Le volume qui avait motivé l'arrestation de l'abbé était un petit in-12 d'une centaine de pages, portant, sur la page de titre, les mots: *Zoroastre, histoire traduite du chaldéen, Nec vanos timuit strepitus Acherontis avari, A. Berlin, à l'enseigne du Roi Philosophe, M.DCC. LI.* Il contenait, après une épître adressée à T[oussaint] A[uteur] D[es] M[œurs], une préface, un poème adressé à l'abbé et une *Lettre à un gentilhomme de province ou réfutation d'un libelle intitulé Zoroastre, histoire traduite du chaldéen.* Comme nous avons vu plus haut, cette dernière pièce est de Méhégan lui-même, selon le garçon imprimeur Dufour; le récit de ses relations avec ce dernier permet même de croire que toutes les pièces du volume sont de la plume de l'abbé. Le livre est devenu très rare. La Bibliothèque de l'Arsenal en possède deux exemplaires, dont l'un (8° B 18532) vient d'Hémery lui-même.

La préface renferme une défense de Zoroastre et des Guèbres contre Pierre Bayle. Les Guèbres ne croient qu'un Dieu; suivre la nature est leur règle unique; ils pensent que pour pratiquer les vertus ils n'ont besoin que de ce cri du cœur qui nous avertit d'être justes et humains.

Cette préface contient encore une déclaration au sujet d'un manuscrit qui aurait été pieusement conservé par les Guèbres et qu'un voyageur aurait rapporté de l'Orient, subterfuge transparent dont ni le magistrat ni le prévenu ne firent mention pendant l'enquête.

Le conte débute par une description de la vie des premiers hommes qui semble anticiper sur celle de Rousseau, et des observations sur les sentiments naturels des hommes qui font penser au

[37] *Ibid.*, fol. 66*v* (82*v*).

[38] Il épousa en 1763 Thérèse-Charlotte Boitel (Aubert de la Chenaye-Desbois et Badier, *loc. cit.*). Mme de Méhégan collaborera, comme son mari, à la rédaction du *Journal encyclopédique.* (Notice en tête du *Tableau d'histoire* de Méhégan, ed. de 1778.)

Traité de métaphysique de Voltaire, inédit à cette date. Toutefois, la prédilection du jeune auteur débutant pour les effets de style, et notamment l'emploi excessif des épithètes, trahit l'influence persistante de la classe de rhétorique et indique peut-être en même temps la source première de ses idées, à savoir les *Métamorphoses* d'Ovide. Les premiers hommes adoraient par sentiment l'auteur de la nature. Un second sentiment les attachait à leurs semblables et un sentiment plus doux encore à leurs compagnes. 'La terre ouvroit son sein à leurs mains laborieuses et les tendres voluptés étoient le prix de leurs fatigues passées, jusqu'à ce qu'un sommeil paisible les préparât à de nouvelles.' Mais à l'âge d'or succède un âge de fer et de sang:

'Bientôt la terre but le sang de ses enfans. Les Conquérans parurent avec les paricides. La gloire, le prix de la vertu, fut le partage des crimes heureux. La prêtre avare vendit sa voix à l'injuste puissance, et pour comble de maux la basse superstition mit les mensonges sanguinaires à la place des vérités bienfaisantes. L'Univers gémissoit sous le triomphe de l'erreur. Les mœurs et le culte raisonnable se perdoient dans les absurdes préjugés; quelques hommes éclairés appercevoient le nuage, mais leurs mains impuissantes faisoient de vains efforts pour écarter le bandeau, ou leur voix timide n'osoit indiquer les foibles lueurs qui se présentoient à eux.'[39]

Alors un sage parut et osa dire vérité. Suit une vie imaginaire de Zoroastre et un récit tout aussi imaginaire de ses voyages en Asie et en Europe et de ses méditations solitaires sur Dieu, sur le lien qui rattache l'individu à la société, sur la bienfaisance, sur la vie à venir où l'ordre sera rétabli, après le désordre de l'existence terrestre. Zoroastre arrive en Bactriane au moment où l'on va sacrifier sur l'autel un être humain, une belle jeune fille. Il se précipite, la libère, est acclamé par le peuple, dénoncé par les prêtres, sauvé par le roi qui, éclairé par Zoroastre, proclame la religion d'un Dieu bienfaisant et aimant. Le roi fait bâtir des écoles, encourage le commerce et l'industrie, ferme les couvents. Quand le roi meurt, Zoroastre lui succède, triomphe des Scythes, mais devient le prisonnier des Assyriens et de leur reine Sémiramis. On l'envoie chez des bergers féroces; il les éclaire et les civilise: ce sont les Guèbres qui, heureux grâce à lui, ont conservé pieusement sa mémoire jusqu'à nos jours et suivent encore ses lois.

[39] pp. 4-5.

On voit que les procédés caractéristiques du conte philosophique — un récit qui prend la forme d'un voyage, un personnage principal dont la fonction est d'éclairer les hommes ou qui cherche à s'éclairer lui-même—tels que les pratiquaient Cyrano et Foigny au siècle précédent, Montesquieu et Voltaire dans celui de l'auteur, sont employés dans ce conte. Méhégan eût-il su exploiter cette veine, si ses malheurs ne l'en eussent détourné? Qui sait? Il avait du courage et était certainement très intelligent. Avait-il l'esprit suffisamment trempé pour être capable d'humour? On peut en douter. Un *Zoroastre* n'est pas encore un *Zadig*. Mais ne pouvait-on pas espérer de lui des *Bélisaire*, des *Incas*? Quoi qu'il en soit, les 29 mois qu'il passa dans une cellule étroite brisèrent sa volonté de faire de la critique sociale. Il n'avait plus, en sortant, que l'ambition d'être nommé à un poste au bureau des affaires étrangères.[40] Cette ambition ne se réalisa pas, échec qu'on peut compter pour une chance, car dans la suite la très réelle originalité de son esprit put se révéler dans une série d'ouvrages consacrés à l'histoire de la civilisation. Disciple encore de Voltaire dans ce domaine, il le fut en même temps de Montesquieu et l'on peut voir en lui un précurseur de Mme de Staël critique et théoricienne des lettres.

Dans le même volume que *Zoroastre* figure un poème, qui doit être de Méhégan, où le poète se félicite de ne pas avoir prononcé de vœux irrévocables. Comme le sujet de ce poème est peu banal, comme les vers en sont faciles, et que ce texte est à peu près introuvable, citons-le en entier.

> C'en est fait, j'ai brisé ma chaîne.
> Un Dieu puissant m'a conservé:
> Un Dieu protecteur m'a sauvé:
> Une obéissance inhumaine,
> Alloit m'enchaîner à l'Autel.
> Victime d'une loi suprême,
> J'allois subir l'arrêt cruel
> Qui me ravissoit à moi-même.
> Déja des Prêtres odieux
> Préparoient les liens horribles,

[40] Lettre de Méhégan à d'Argenson, 13 décembre 1752 (Paris, Archives de la Bastille, 11758, fol. 53 (69): lettre de Mme de Méhégan à d'Argenson, mars, 1753 (*ibid.*, fol. 90 (107*r*)).

Déja le ministre des Dieux
Me dictoit les sermens terribles
Qui devoient captiver mes vœux.
L'injuste Démon de l'envie
A soufflé sa noire fureur,
Par la main de la calomnie
J'ai vu briser ces nœuds d'horreur.

Doux mouvemens de la nature
Renaissez célestes désirs.
Brillans amours, tendres soupirs,
Etouffez la vile imposture
Qui fait un crime des plaisirs.
Ne craignez plus un vain murmure,
Doux enfans de ma liberté,
Revenez troupe aimable et pure
Ramenez la felicité.

Suspendons ces chaînes brisées
Aux myrthes heureux de Paphos.
Déchirons ces sombres livrées
Monumens de mes noirs travaux.
Accourez, rendez-moi ma lyre;
Resonnez sublimes accens;
Amis partagez mon délire.
Joignez votre voix à mes chants.
Portez les fleurs, donnez l'encens,
Venez dans ce lieu solitaire,
Je veux sous ces berceaux charmans
Honorer le Dieu tutélaire
Qui me rend vos embrassemens.
Que le Dieu des repas brillans
Préside à ce riant mystere.
Que les ris, les folâtres jeux
En réglent la cérémonie.
Qu'un Faisan immolé par eux
Soit la victime qui expie.
Que les flots d'un Beaune fumeux
Arrosent cet autel joyeux

Où ma liberté sacrifie.
Qu'au lieu de cantiques Thalie
Inspire les vives chansons.
Qu'Apollon laisse à la Folie
Le soin d'en diriger les sons.
Que l'aimable et tendre Sylvie
Que les Graces suivent toujours,
Sur leurs pas mene les Amours.
C'est la galante hiérarchie
Où je consacre mes beaux jours.

Abbé je le sçais. L'opulence
Ne sourit pas à ces projets.
Les honneurs, la dévote aisance
Pouvoient flatter mon espérance.
Mais ce phantôme vue de près
Que présente-t-il? mille peines,
Des faux plaisirs, des vrais malheurs:
Des routes sans cesse incertaines
Qu'affligent les pâles terreurs,
Où marche en tremblant la bassesse,
Rampant sous un fat protecteur
Dont elle encense la foiblesse:
L'envie armant la main traitresse
De l'ami volage ou méchant[:]
Ou d'un sot crédule, imprudent[:]
Des refus moins durs que les graces
Qu'on vous accorde avec hauteur:
Et la contrainte et les disgraces.
Laissons un éclat imposteur
A l'illusion du vulgaire.
Dans une pompeuse misere
Laissons le chercher le bonheur,
Je l'ai dans mon indépendance,
Dans mes amis, dans ta constance,
Ma lyre, l'étude et mon cœur.

Poète, Méhégan prise son indépendance, comme ses prédecesseurs, les poètes 'libertins' du XVIIe siècle. De plus, le poème sur le bonheur qui suit le texte de son *Zoroastre* montre en lui un de ces esprits qui, au dix-huitième siècle, comme déjà à la fin du dix-septième, unissent au déisme philosophique la doctrine morale d'Épicure. C'est la forme que prend la libre-pensée 'gassendiste'. Chaulieu, Parrain, Claville, Diderot jusqu'à l'âge de quarante ans, Voltaire pendant toute sa carrière ont été 'gassendistes' dans ce sens. Dans *Le Bonheur*, après avoir écarté successivement la Fortune, l'Ambition, la Gloire et la Volupté, mot auquel il attache le sens de 'luxure', le poète se déclare partisan de la nature: nous pouvons être heureux—les bêtes ne le sont-elles pas?—en suivant les douces lois que la nature nous prescrit:

> Regarde autour de toi, consulte la nature.
> Tout retrace ses dons, tout t'offre le bonheur.
> Il est dans les plaisirs: on l'a dans la puissance:
> Il suit le solitaire au milieu de ses bois:
> Il ne dédaigne point l'innocente indigence:
> Il luit sous la chaumiere; il brille chez les Rois,
> La Prudence partout s'asservit à ses loix.
> Connois-toi, suis ton cœur, sa route est toujours sûre.
> Le sentiment y veille, il guidera tes vœux.
> Sa voix ne fut jamais sujette à l'imposture.
> Son instinct, ses remords sont un sûr conducteur.
> Il mène à la Sagesse: elle mène au Bonheur.

Méhégan sortit de la Bastille le 13 mars 1753.[41] Il avait beaucoup souffert de la solitude et s'en était plaint dans une lettre à d'Argenson:

> On se représente aisément ce que souffre un malheureux continuellement enfermé dans un trou affreux, privé de tout commerce, uniquement livré à lui-même, ne connoissant jamais rien du présent, n'envisageant l'avenir qu'a travers ses craintes.[42]

Cette solitude il l'avait remplie de lectures d'histoire et de ce qu'il appelle 'géographie raisonnée, c'est-à-dire cette géographie qui indique non seulement la situation respective des lieux, mais encore les mœurs des peuples, les loix des sociétés, et les interêts

[41] *Ibid.*, fol. 74 (90), cf. 12493, fol. 75.
[42] Lettre de Méhégan à d'Argenson, 13 déc. 1752 (*ibid.*, fol. 53 (69)).

réciproques de leurs chefs'.[43] Il avait composé dans sa cellule diverses dissertations, parmi lesquelles notons un *Essai sur les progrès des arts*, une *Description de l'Europe*, des *Considérations sur le progrès du mahométisme*, des *Réflexions sur l'Espion turc* [de Marana], et des *Observations sur l'auteur Rousset d'Hollande*, c'est-à-dire Rousset de Missy, historiographe de Guillaume d'Orange.[44] C'est à des travaux de ce genre, toujours fortement influencés par Voltaire et par Montesquieu, qu'il consacrera sa carrière d'homme de lettres professionnel, carrière qui ne se terminera qu'à sa mort, survenue à Paris le 23 janvier 1766. Cette carrière mériterait d'être étudiée pour elle-même, mais comme notre auteur, devenu le chevalier de Méhégan en sortant de la Bastille, n'est plus, à partir de sa libération, un abbé philosophe, nous devons réserver à une autre occasion l'étude de ses travaux de philosophe historien.

[43] *Ibid.*

[44] Lettre de Méhégan à Berryer du 15 mars 1753 (pour demander qu'on lui rende ses manuscrits); reçu signé par Méhégan, le 8 juin 1753 (*ibid.*, fol. 76, 80 (92, 96)).

Jean-Jacques Rousseau and the Problem of 'Original' Language

Ronald Grimsley

Rousseau's attitude towards language is ambiguous. Since language, like all other human values, has been corrupted by the degeneration of modern life, it is used for the concealment and distortion of truth rather than for its revelation and communication. Society is dominated by a polite jargon that bears no relationship to genuine human feelings, whilst the reflection of modern thinkers has merely produced the sterile subtlety and sophistication of *une philosophie parlière*. Moreover, even in the most favourable conditions, language, according to Rousseau, cannot express the deepest human emotions, absolute 'felicity' being ultimately indescribable; the enjoyment of a 'full, perfect and sufficient happiness' is marked by a silence that is far more expressive than the most eloquent words. On the other hand, Rousseau recognises that few human beings are able to achieve the ecstatic contemplation of *la matinée à l'anglaise* described in *La Nouvelle Héloïse* or the silent reverie he himself enjoyed on the Ile de Saint-Pierre. With all its limitations and imperfections language still remains the indispensable instrument of human communication, whether of thought or emotion, and, consequently, the modern thinker's main problem is not to replace language by something else, but to rediscover its essential purpose and function. In other words, as soon as he seeks to understand the 'nature of man', he has to devote some attention to the problem of language and ask himself what are its 'original' features and how they can be restored to a world corrupted by artificial social values.

Contemporary philosophers tended to approach this problem in two ways. Some, like Locke and Condillac, were inclined to relate the question of language to the development of ideas. This genetic method was used to a very limited extent by Rousseau in *Émile* when he tried to describe the development of language in the child. His main emphasis, however, was not placed on the nature of language as such but upon its relationship to the progressive development of the child's other capacities. A second and more ambitious approach to the subject involved the use of the 'historical' method, which treated the emergence of language as a significant moment in man's development from primitive to social existence. Various attempts were made to discover or reconstruct the characteristics of 'primitive' language by tracing back existing languages to their older forms. It is especially in the *Discours sur l'origine de l'inégalité* that Rousseau discussed this problem of the origin of language, only to conclude that it was insoluble. While admitting the stimulating effect of Condillac's work upon his own reflections, he considered that this philosopher had really assumed the very point which was in question—the interdependence of language and society. So difficult did the question of the origin of language appear to Rousseau that he was half inclined to accept the Biblical explanation of language as a gift from God!

If the problem of the ultimate origin of language appeared to present insuperable difficulties, Rousseau in another less well-known but perhaps intrinsically more interesting discussion tackles it in a rather different way. The *Essai sur l'origine des langues*, part of which may have been contemporary with the *Discours sur l'origine de l'inégalité*,[1] does not examine the origin of 'language' itself but of 'languages'. This enables him to adopt a more specifically historical approach; if the birth of the earliest languages is

[1] The exact date of composition is not known. In view of Rousseau's statement that the essay was first intended to form part of the *Discours sur l'origine de l'inégalité*, Lanson's assertion (*Annales Jean-Jacques Rousseau*, viii. 5) that the main part of the *Essai* was already in existence by 1750 seems untenable. It may have been written about 1754 and revised and completed in 1761–63 when Rousseau thought of publishing it as a separate work. (Cf. *Confessions*, Bk. XI, *Pléiade*, i. 560.) The exact date of composition does not affect the argument of the present study. The *Essai sur l'origine des langues* is an extremely rich text which can be analysed from various points of view—linguistic, aesthetic, anthropological, etc. I am here concerned with only one significant aspect of a complex work. A discussion of its bearing on the views of modern linguists, especially Otto Jespersen, is to be found in the article by E. Claparède, 'Rousseau et l'origine des langues', in *Annales Jean-Jacques Rousseau*, xxiv. 95-119. P. M. Masson has also examined the chronological question in the *Annales*, ix. 45-49.

irremediably lost in the remoteness of the past, it is none the less possible to compare existing languages with those of which records are still available. It must be admitted that Rousseau does not pay much heed to historical accuracy—in any case, his own linguistic knowledge was extremely limited and he was forced to rely for the most part on secondary authorities—but he accepts the principle that the nearer we get to the source of older languages, the more clearly shall we be able to perceive what they were like before their corruption by the advent of society with all its concomitant evils. The *Essai*, therefore, assumes the existence of language as such, vaguely attributing it to 'une faculté propre à l'homme' which makes him use his organs for the purpose of communication.

According to Rousseau, a study of the oldest known languages would suggest that their primary function was not the communication of thoughts and ideas but the expression of feelings and passions. 'Le premier cri de l'homme est le cri de la nature.' In this respect Rousseau was following the trend of contemporary thinkers and friends like Condillac and Diderot who were also stressing the affective, non-rational nature of primitive language. At the same time—and the point is of cardinal importance for Rousseau's subsequent argument—he refuses to define its 'expressive' function too narrowly, insisting that even the expressive language of primitive man already contained a rudimentary, if merely implicit, element of communication; he believes it to have been used by a 'kind of instinct', in moments of stress or danger, to invoke the help of other people. Rousseau seems to be suggesting that any use of language, however subjective at first sight, has always involved some reference to an object. When, however, we are considering the language of very early communities, it is misleading to speak of the separate functions of 'communication' and 'expression', for primitive man had no genuinely reflective awareness of the meaning of his activities; he identified himself spontaneously with the immediate feeling of his existence. Any 'language' he might use would simply be an extension of this undivided consciousness.

If early man thus attained an effortless expression of his whole being, it was largely because he was concerned with the satisfaction of very simple and, for the most part, physical or instinctive needs. Since these needs involved the activity of his whole being, his 'speech' would at first take the form of bodily gestures, although these might sometimes be reinforced by inarticulate cries. Gesture-language had an immediate appeal, as is proved by its effective use at a more advanced stage of human development.[2] 'Ainsi l'on parle mieux aux yeux qu'aux oreilles. . . . Le langage le plus énergique est celui où le signe a tout dit avant qu'on parle' (Ch. I). Visual signs have the great advantage of making a direct impact upon the imagination. As soon as primitive man rose above the demands of elementary appetites and began to experience deeper emotional needs, his use of language became correspondingly more complex. The chief limitation of gesture-language is that it cannot 'move the heart and inflame the passions'. It is sounds, not gestures, which express human feelings, the 'successive impression of speech' exerting a more powerful emotional influence than the presence of the object itself. The use of sounds, therefore, was a significant stage in man's development because it revealed the existence of feelings which could not be conveyed by mere gestures. 'Il est donc à croire que les besoins dictèrent les premiers gestes, et que les passions arrachèrent les premières voix' (Ch. II). The expression of joy and sorrow involved far more than the desire to appease hunger and thirst. Moreover, the need for emotional satisfaction brought men together in a way that physical appetite never did. 'Toutes les passions rapprochent les hommes, que la nécessité de chercher à vivre force à se fuir' (Ch. II). Whereas nature alone provided them with the means of satisfying their physical desires, feelings like love, hatred, pity and anger needed the presence of other human beings to give them meaning; the 'accents, cries, laments' elicited by these emotions drew men to one another and so led to the development of rudimentary social relationships, of which the family was probably the first form. Having become organised into social communities, men then began to develop their reason; but it was the affective rather than the intellectual rôle of early lan-

[2] In the very first chapter of the *Essai* Rousseau gives some vivid examples of ancient leaders who conveyed important messages by means of gesture-language. He had already been preceded by Condillac who, in turn, had drawn upon Bishop William Warburton's *The Divine Legation of Moses*, part of which had already been translated into French in 1744 under the title of *Essai sur les hiéroglyphes*. In later years Rousseau came to attach particular personal significance to the use of 'signs' as an extremely effective, if somewhat esoteric, form of 'immediate' language. Jean Starobinski (*Jean-Jacques Rousseau: la transparence et l'obstacle*, Paris 1958, pp. 172 ff.), has devoted some very illuminating pages to a discussion of this point.

guages which determined their first characteristics. 'Les premières langues sont chantantes et passionnées avant d'être simples et méthodiques' (Ch. II).

Because of their emotional function, early languages were used to express the 'almost inevitable impressions communicated by passion'. Since passion 'fascinates the eyes' and causes men to see the world through an 'illusory image', its language will consist of 'images, feelings and figures'. Original language is, therefore, 'figurative' or representational; only when men acquire a clearer and more balanced view of their situation does it become consciously 'metaphorical'. Rousseau gives the example of a lonely savage frightened by the sight of a stranger whom his imagination at once transforms into a 'giant'; when experience has taught him that this 'giant' is not very different from himself, he uses the term 'man' to describe them both, the word 'giant' being henceforth confined to the 'false object' which first alarmed him. The essential point for Rousseau is that the primary characteristics of primitive language do not depend upon 'articulations' which are the result of 'convention', but upon the 'natural' effect of 'voices, sounds, accents and number' capable of expressing man's immediate reaction to his situation. Euphony, harmony and the beauty of sounds are the principal features of the oldest languages. From this point of view, Rousseau looks sympathetically upon Plato's suggestion in the *Cratylus* that there is a mysterious link between an object and its name.

The invention of writing as a means of 'fixing' language was a late development which seriously altered its 'original' character; accuracy and clarity gradually replaced intensity and expressiveness as the primary requirements of language which, with the growth of rationality and abstraction, lost its vital energy. It does not fall within the scope of the present paper to analyse Rousseau's account of the subsequent evolution of language under the influence of physical and climatic conditions; he uses these factors to explain the increasing diversity of languages and the difference, for example, between the sonorous, eloquent, lively character of the languages of the South and the harsher, shriller and more heavily articulated languages of the North. What is more relevant to our purpose is the conclusion which Rousseau draws from the affective quality of 'original' language. As in the *Discours sur l'origine de l'inégalité*, he recalls the idyllic happiness of the early communities based upon the family rather than the nation. It was soon clear, he says, that the first *fêtes* of these primitive societies could not be limited to mere gestures, for man began to experience emotions of joy and affection which impelled him to some kind of vocal utterance. 'Les pieds bondissaient de joie, le geste empressé ne suffisait plus, la voix l'accompagnait d'accents passionnés; le plaisir et le désir, confondus ensemble, se faisaient sentir à la fois: là fut le vrai berceau des peuples; et du pur cristal des fontaines sortirent les premiers feux de l'amour' (Ch. IX).

A particularly fascinating aspect of this stage of human existence was not only the uninhibited enjoyment of the immediate present, which eliminated the problem of time since 'nothing marked the passing of the hours', but also the simultaneous enjoyment of various feelings which conferred a spontaneous unity on the experience. Early languages, therefore, expressed the affective unity of the beings who used them and could be described in the broadest sense as 'poetic', which meant that they contained the essence of what modern man now knows as 'poetry, music and discourse'. Primitive peoples were ignorant of such distinctions, because, all being inspired by the same emotional needs, they were wont to pass effortlessly from one form of expression to another. 'Les vers, les chants, les paroles ont une origine commune.' Rousseau refers with approval to Strabo's statement that in the ancient world 'speaking and singing were the same thing'.

This brings us to the heart of Rousseau's essay by reminding us of its full title: *Essai sur l'origine des langues où il est parlé de la mélodie et de l'imitation musicale.* Since poetry and music have the same origin inasmuch as they add 'rhythm and sounds' to 'feelings and images', they both express emotions through the 'melodious inflexions' of the voice. This explains Rousseau's tireless insistence on the idea that the essence of music is to be found in melody, not harmony; whereas he considers the latter to consist of a merely intellectual manipulation of physical sounds, melody lies closer to the origin of music because it expresses vital human feelings. The same principle is applicable to other arts. Just as music involves far more than physical sounds, so does painting consist of more than the mere arrangement of colours, the exact significance of which is determined by their relationship to 'design' and the 'imitation of feelings'. In each case the artist infuses something of his own inner being into the physical material. 'Il faut que les objets parlent pour se faire entendre; il faut toujours, dans toute imitation, qu'une espèce de discours supplée à la voix de la nature.' The physical components of any art, therefore, have a representational function; but if Rousseau insists, like most of his contemporaries, upon the notion of imitation as the basis of art, he is careful to point out that what the artist imitates is not the object itself, but the emotions or 'movements which its presence evokes in the heart of the beholder'. The purely sensuous impressions are simply 'occasional causes' for the production of 'intellectual and moral impressions'. Colours and sounds are 'representations and signs' of something other than themselves, namely, the human emotions with which they are associated; as mere 'objects of sense' they are without meaning and cannot 'speak'. Rousseau concludes, therefore, that any musician who believes his art to be based on the production of physical reactions in the listener is completely mistaken about its real purpose. The more closely he concentrates on the physical aspect, the further does he draw away from the true source of his art. The ultimate effect will almost certainly be a loss of creative energy and inspiration.

Rousseau extends the same argument to language itself. In the same way as the artificial invention of the 'harmonic interval' serves to obliterate the 'passionate accent', the intellectual organisation of words and concepts obscures the original function of language as the expression and imitation of feelings. In Rousseau's view it is not accidental that vocal inflexions should play such a large part in poetry, eloquence and music. Although language—like music and poetry—originally 'imitated' or expressed the emotions elicited by the objects to which it referred, the 'progress of reasoning' and the 'perfecting of grammar' have unfortunately destroyed the 'lively, passionate tone' which inspired the 'singing' quality of the older languages. Indeed, the very separation of eloquence, poetry and music into distinct 'arts' is a sure indication of their decline, for they are today incapable of giving full and effective expression to human emotions. Instead of being the common characteristic of several arts, melody is no longer recognised as the essence of even one, having been nearly ousted—in France at least—from music itself by the prevailing love of harmony. Modern civilisation has lost its true aesthetic sense and forgotten that men were poets before they were philosophers or geometers.

The general deterioration of human values has had serious effects upon the development of language. The exaggerated role of 'reflection' has led to a diminution and enfeeblement of emotions which in turn have caused language to lose its force and energy. When contrasting ancient with modern languages, Rousseau always stresses the superior 'energy' of the former. Moreover, this loss of energy has also led to the disappearance of unity and simplicity. Whereas language, as a mode of communication should bring men together, its restriction to an unnatural analytical function has merely served to isolate them from one another by the creation of endless subtleties and distinctions. Primitive man, it is true, was also a solitary creature, but only because the self-sufficiency of his instinctive, almost animal-like, existence made language unnecessary; living in harmony with his physical environment, he could satisfy his simple needs without recourse to other men. Modern man, on the other hand, remains imprisoned in a private, artificial world because his language is a mere jargon or 'affected language' which reflects the superficial banalities of 'opinion' and 'appearance' and so bears no relationship to his essential character as a human being.

To understand the original function of language man has first of all to rediscover the meaning of his own nature and to reaffirm the unity, simplicity and vitality of his being. As Rousseau so often points out, human nature was intended to be a unity and in spite of all its obvious limitations, this unity was, as we have seen, a genuine characteristic of primitive existence. No doubt man cannot return to this early stage of his history, nor is it desirable for him to do so, for this would involve a renunciation of all his possibilities as a moral being; but primitive man was at least content to be himself and readily accepted the intrinsic quality of his own nature. The unity and robustness of his existence stand in striking contrast to the incoherence and weakness of a modern world which, as Rousseau insists in his first *Discours*, has lost both its physical strength and its 'vigour of soul'.

At the very end of his *Essai sur l'origine des langues* Rousseau emphasises once again the essential difference between the language of the Ancients and that of modern man—between 'les langues sonores, prosodiques, harmonieuses' of the ancient world and 'le bourdonnement des divans' so frequently heard today! Characteristic examples of the physical inadequacy of modern discourse are the modern preacher who vainly exhausts himself in his efforts to reach his congregation and the academician whose speech can barely be heard at the end of the room. How inferior they are to those ancient orators who spoke for a whole day in the open air without suffering any incommodity! If, affirms Rousseau, a Frenchman of today tried to address his fellow-citizens on the Place Vendôme, nobody would hear a word of what he was saying! On the other hand, the generals of old harangued their troops without difficulty, whilst Herodotus 'lisait son histoire aux peuples de la Grèce assemblés en plein air, et tout retentissait d'applaudissements'. Unlike modern speakers who imprison themselves and their audience in some confined space, which merely serves to bring out the weakness of their utterance, ancient orators were inspired by the invigorating presence of a physical nature that appeared to lend strength to their discourse. If they felt themselves to be in harmony with their physical environment, they were also sustained by the knowledge that they were addressing either the whole nation or a large audience of sympathetic citizens. The speaker and his hearers did not constitute separate units, but formed part of the same human entity. The direct contact with nature and the effortless enjoyment of common feelings helped them to realise that their language, like all true language, was that of freedom. 'Toute langue avec laquelle on ne peut se faire entendre au peuple assemblé est une langue servile' (Ch. XX).

If such conditions were ideally suited to the needs of genuine communication, the peculiar effectiveness of ancient language was not due mainly to the physical strength of those who used it, but to the special quality of the sound itself. Both orator and audience being inspired by the same emotions (the discourse, for example, often dealt with some patriotic or religious theme), language became permeated by a sonorous, 'singing' quality which, as we have seen, Rousseau deemed to be the distinguishing characteristic of ancient languages. In short, language was an integral part of human nature; the words, the subject and the feelings of both speaker and audience were imbued with the same unity and intensity.

If modern man cannot restore language to its 'original' (as opposed to its merely 'historical') rôle by returning to the past, he ought at least to recapture the spirit of the ancient world. The *Lettre à d'Alembert* contains a number of interesting reflections on this point. To the artificial, prison-like atmosphere of the modern theatre with its audience silently absorbed in a private world that cuts them off from the rest of society, Rousseau opposes the example of Greek tragedy, 'ces grands et superbes spectacles, donnés sous le ciel, à la face de toute une nation'. Once again he stresses the contact with nature and the link with the community. 'Tragedy' was not something apart from the rest of the nation's life, but an experience through which the Greeks could 'échauffer leurs cœurs de sentiments d'honneur et de gloire'. That is why it always had a musical resonance; as Rousseau points out in his *Observations sur l'Alceste de Gluck*, Greek tragedies were 'true operas' because the 'harmonious and musical' quality of the Greek language already possessed a 'melodious accent' and required only the addition of rhythm to make declamation musical too. Moreover, when speech itself contains this musical element, it becomes much easier for a good actor to communicate feelings to the 'soul of a sensitive spectator'. As both speech and music originate in human emotion, the 'accents of melody' and the 'cadence of rhythm' will 'imitate the inflexions which passion gives to the human voice' and so 'penetrate the heart and move it by feelings'. Since the power of language and music depends ultimately on 'the energy of the feelings and the vivacity of the scenes' they describe, they can, in favourable circumstances, reinforce each other, so that the great artist will make 'language sing and music speak'.

Language and music become very effective partners on public occasions which allow a community to abandon itself freely to the enjoyment of truly patriotic feelings. In the *Lettre à d'Alembert* Rousseau dreams of the day when his fellow Genevans will be able to participate in national celebrations inspired by feelings which are both patriotic and human. Unlike the 'dark cavern' of the modern theatre, with its 'timid, motionless' audience lost in 'silence and inaction', 'happy peoples' rejoice in the spontaneous expression of their natural emotions. 'C'est en plein air, c'est sous le ciel qu'il faut vous rassembler et vous livrer au doux sentiment de votre bonheur.' Of the Genevans' pleasures he says: 'Qu'ils soient libres et généreux comme vous, que le ciel éclaire vos innocents spectacles'. The similarity between the setting and spirit of the ancient Greek tragedy and those of these ideal Genevan *fêtes* is unmistakable. In each case we are transported to a land of 'peace, freedom, equity and innocence', where every citizen shares fully in the 'simplicity' and 'secret charm' of genuine patriotism.

A still more striking, though equally idealised, example of Rousseau's desire to regenerate language by bringing it closer to music is to be found in the description of the grape-harvest in *La Nouvelle Héloïse* (Part V, Letter VII).[3] Here again we are in the presence of a collective activity—'on se rassemble pour aller à la vigne'—and the whole community of Clarens takes part in an experience that combines work and play, the 'useful' and the 'pleasant'. Amid 'the simplicity of pastoral and country life' and 'all the charms of the golden age' everything contributes to 'l'aimable et touchant tableau de l'allégresse générale qui semble étendu sur la face de la terre'. The spirit of joyful abundance inspires the happy workers to singing, story-telling and (later in the day) dancing. Their songs are based on 'simple, naïve, often sad and yet pleasing words'. On all sides can be heard the 'concert' of voices singing in unison. (Even in a letter such as this Saint-Preux-Rousseau cannot forbear to castigate the contemporary love of harmony as a sure sign of 'depraved taste', nothing being more contrary to the 'impulse of nature'!) At Clarens too song, speech and laughter mingle with other sounds such as the hooping of casks and vats, the continual tramping of the harvesters bringing the grapes to the wine-press, and the 'hoarse sound of the rustic instruments inciting them to work'. All these different sounds seem to be but part of a single scene in which freedom and equality combine to form a joyous *air de fête*. 'La douce égalité qui règne ici rétablit l'ordre de la nature.'[4] The simplicity, freedom, peace, innocence and equality of this busy community suggest that man has at last discovered his real nature and with it a 'language' capable of giving outward expression to all the feelings of his innermost soul.

Even though idyllic scenes such as these describe a possibility rather than an achievement of modern man, Rousseau clearly believes that the rediscovery of authentic language is inseparable from the rediscovery of human nature itself. The narrow social conventions in which man has allowed himself to become imprisoned

[3] There is detailed commentary of this episode by Bernard Guyon in *Pléiade*, ii. 1707 ff. as well as by Jean Starobinski in a valuable section of his *Jean-Jacques Rousseau: la transparence et l'obstacle*, pp. 114 ff.

[4] As Jean Starobinski points out (*op. cit.*, pp. 120 ff.) this 'equality' is in many ways deceptive, the system of Clarens being strictly paternalistic.

must give way to a more spontaneous and sincere form of human utterance. Although he uses a number of contemporary ideas about the affective origin of language, Rousseau gives them a personal emphasis which brings his view of language into accord with his fundamental philosophical principles. He believes that through the use of a regenerated language man will at last be able to show himself as the being who *is* what he appears and proclaims himself to be.

L'exemplaire des Œuvres de Vauvenargues annoté par Voltaire, ou l'imposture de l'édition Gilbert enfin dévoilée

André-M. Rousseau

A une date incertaine, mais antérieure à 1819, année de sa mort, Fauris de Saint-Vincent, fils de l'ami et correspondant de Vauvenargues, déposa à la bibliothèque municipale d'Aix un exemplaire de l'édition de 1746 des œuvres du moraliste, portant, de la main de son père: 'Les notes qui sont à la marge de cet exemplaire sont de la main de M. le marquis de Vauvenargues, auteur de cet ouvrage, et c'est sur cet exemplaire qu'a été faite l'édition publiée en 1747'. Deux affirmations, deux erreurs.

Un lecteur attentif de l'édition de Suard (1806) pouvait déjà rectifier la première, puisque celui-ci, on ne l'a jamais fait remarquer, donne l'une de ces notes, correctement attribuée à Voltaire.[1] Mais ce n'est qu'en 1856 que D. L. Gilbert, préparant sa grande édition, examina le volume en compagnie du Conservateur et de J. Mouan, sous-bibliothécaire. A en croire son *Avertissement* (pp. vi-vii), il fut le premier à 'affirmer que ces notes étaient de Voltaire et ne pouvaient être que de lui', convainquit le Conservateur et fit publier ses conclusions par Mouan dans une petite brochure[2] malheureusement fort rare, car elle seule contient à peu près tout ce qui a été dit de précis et de raisonnable sur la question.

[1] Suard tirait sa documentation, grâce à l'entremise de Voltaire, du marquis de Villevieille, fils de l'ami de Vauvenargues. Villevieille a pu transmettre le souvenir d'une annotation isolée, sans que Suard soupçonnât l'existence du reste.

[2] *Quelques mots sur un exemplaire de la 1ère édition des Œuvres de Vauvenargues avec notes manuscrites aux marges* (Aix 1856).

Dans la longue, vive et futile querelle qui s'ensuivit, peu nous chaut de savoir auquel des trois hommes revient l'honneur de cette capitale trouvaille. Plutôt que d'en faire l'historique dans une longue étude au titre trompeur,[3] G. Saintville, à qui nous devons cependant les meilleures recherches sur la biographie de notre auteur, eût mieux fait d'établir le texte même des dites annotations, et point n'était besoin pour cela d'une édition en *fac-simile*, qu'il aurait, dit-on, projetée avant sa mort prématurée. Auréolé de gloire, cet exemplaire n'a cessé, depuis un siècle et plus, d'être pieusement feuilleté, sinon examiné, par d'innombrables zélateurs de Vauvenargues (plus que de Voltaire, il est vrai), dont l'émotion, apparemment, a obnubilé le sens critique. Tel fut le cas, entre autres, d'Émile Henriot qui, en 1925,[4] commente avec esprit quelques annotations choisies parmi les plus classiques, ce qu'il aurait très bien pu faire chez lui avec la seule édition Gilbert.

Tous les biographes, de Lanson à Mlle May Wallas, et de Gaillard de Champris à Cavallucci, répètent plus ou moins les dires de Gilbert. Je suppose que Lanson, dont l'œil d'aigle n'eut guère de défaillance, ne tint jamais l'exemplaire entre ses mains;[5] sinon, comment n'eût-il pas remarqué ce que soupçonna vaguement May Wallas, dont l'objectivité, pour une fois, l'emporta sur le lyrisme, à savoir que l'édition Gilbert n'offre qu'une invraisemblable caricature de l'original? Tout le monde avant nous pouvait formuler les remarques qui vont suivre. Sans prétendre expliquer cette mystérieuse cécité collective, assurons-nous donc du fait, comme dans la fable de la dent d'or, avant de faire des systèmes.

Gilbert laisse au lecteur non prévenu l'impression que le texte de 1747 suit de près celui de 1746, simplement agrémenté ici et là de commentaires marginaux du seul Voltaire.[6] Rien n'est plus loin

[3] *Le Vauvenargues annoté de la bibliothèque Méjanes* (Paris 1933).

[4] *Vauvenargues annoté par Voltaire*, publié dans le feuilleton litteraire du *Temps*, recueilli dans *Courrier littéraire, XVIIIe s.*, nlle éd. augm., (Paris 1961), i. 295-298.

[5] Dans son *Marquis de Vauvenargues*, il se contente d'une brève allusion (pp. 98-99). Notons au passage (p. 115) une curieuse bévue de ce grand savant qui date la seconde édition de l'année suivant la mort de l'auteur, alors qu'elle n'est postérieure que de quelques semaines.

[6] Nous laissons de côté les *marginalia* mises par Voltaire sur un exemplaire de le seconde édition, publiées par Suard et correctement reproduites par Gilbert, ce qui n'a pas empêché certains éditeurs récents, M. Mohrt par exemple (Paris 1957), de mêler étourdiment les deux séries. Plus libres et de portée plus générale, ces notes, interrompues à la p. 101, n'ont évidemment jamais été connues de Vauvenargues.

de la réalité. L'exemplaire d'Aix fourmille des corrections les plus variées: traits de plume en tous sens et signes divers; notes au crayon, à l'encre, et de plusieurs encres et écritures; ratures, additions, repentirs, parfois superposés, rien n'y manque. Dira-t-on que Gilbert a tiré le meilleur et le plus clair d'un obscur grimoire? Point du tout, car il suffit d'un peu d'attention pour le déchiffrer. Mais il est temps d'instruire en règle ce procès.

'J'ay crayoné un des meilleurs livres . . .', écrivit Voltaire.[7] Il faut le prendre au pied de la lettre. Si Gilbert a pris la peine de transcrire l'une des remarques écrites au crayon, fort célèbre d'ailleurs, mais sans souffler mot de la graphie,[8] que n'a-t-il fait de même pour les pages 19, 23, 24 et 25, notes minimes certes, mais très positives? Le groupement des références nous donne à penser que Voltaire rouvrit d'abord par hasard le volume à la page 19, commença à l'annoter au crayon à main levée, puis, devant l'ampleur de la tâche, s'y adonna méthodiquement à son bureau.

Passons sur de menues négligences.[9] Les lectures franchement fautives sont rares: *bien* au lieu de *bon* (A 14, G 19), mais l'une d'elles mérite le pilori des interprétations grotesques. En bas de la page 268, qui se termine par la maxime: 'Les grands philosophes sont les génies de la raison', figurent incontestablement les deux lettres *Y A*. Les rares remarques placées en cet endroit de la page sont toutes de Vauvenargues, et rien n'indique que ces lettres, au demeurant peu claires, se rapportent à cette maxime. Tout autre commentateur se serait tû, mais non Gilbert, qui s'écrie: 'Ici Voltaire emploie ironiquement l'affirmation allemande *ia*, comme pour signifier que la proposition de Vauvenargues va de soi, et n'a pas besoin d'être énoncée' (G 476)!

Parfois, sans aucun motif, il supprime quelques mots: *un peu* devant *plus de détail* (A 79, G 43); *ni l'incivilité*, après le remarque de la p. 135 (G 69). Mais, le plus souvent, il enjolive: *très beau* devient *tout cela est très beau* (A 11, G 14); *on ne peut mieux*, *on ne peut mieux dire* (A 11, G 14), ce qui ne donne pas tout à fait le même sens. Ici il ajoute: *il lui manque*, devant: *l'art de faire des vers* (A 21, G 35); là, *idée*, devant un sec *frivole* (A 90, G 49). Brusque, le *non*

[7] Best. 3072.

[8] 'Comment a-t-on pu voir si bien étant si jeune?' (A 24, G 16). Dans toute cette étude, A et G désignent les pages de l'exemplaire d'Aix et du tome i de l'édition Gilbert, respectivement.

[9] Note sans appel dans le texte (A 14, G 20); remarque de Voltaire sans indication d'édition (G 24).

de A 249 s'étire en: *universelle, non, prématurée, non* (G 269); neutre, *cela n'est point frivole* se colore en: *il n'y a pas là de jeux frivoles* (A 235, G 245). Innocente manie, dira-t-on. Voire, car Gilbert affadit, alanguit et orne abusivement une réalité souvent brève et vigoureuse.

Ne parlons pas d'un énergique *et aussi pour s'envoyer faire f*, que sa pudibonderie traduit en *envoyer promener* (G 491), mais avec un commentaire qui suggère assez clairement l'original.[10] Nombre de remarques, pourtant anodines, au lieu d'être simplement reproduites dans leur éloquence dépouillée, sont diluées dans un long discours inutile (A 66, G 37), où parfois elles se noient tout à fait (A 90, G 49, où il ne reste plus un mot du libellé authentique). Encore heureux lorsque l'éditeur ne fond pas sournoisement deux annotations en une seule (A 82, G 44). Un exemple suffira. Là où Vauvenargues écrit (A 18): '[Un esprit étendu] les [=les rameaux des choses] réunit à leur source et dans un centre commun; il les met sous un même point de vue', Voltaire, frappé de ce galimatias, souligne *source*, *commun* et *sous*, et ajoute: *même définition que pour la profondeur*, tandis qu'il faut à Gilbert deux lignes et demie pour dire exactement la même chose (G 13-14).

Ces diverses fioritures ne sont rien à côté des omissions. Quelquefois, la raison se devine aisément: quand la remarque porte sur un passage retranché qui ne figure plus dans la seconde édition, elle disparaît avec le passage lui-même et c'est parfois bien dommage (A 248). Le plus souvent, ces innombrables silences restent inexplicables. Admettons qu'un éditeur du milieu du siècle dernier n'ait pas vu l'intérêt de très nombreux signes: traits verticaux, horizontaux, obliques, ondulés, en marge ou dans le corps de la page; mots soulignés, croix (très nombreuses) en guise d'astérisques; chiffres inversant l'ordre de mots ou de phrases, etc., signes muets en apparence, éloquents pour qui veut bien les interpréter. Mais comment Gilbert a-t-il pu négliger tant de remarques, qui vont des plus brèves[11] aux plus considérables, par la longueur et par le sens: *manque de liaison et de clarté* (A 62, G 35); *terme qui conviendrait*

[10] Vauvenargues avait écrit: 'Il ne tient qu'à nous d'admirer la religieuse franchise de nos pères, qui nous ont appris à nous égorger pour un démenti'. Voilà une admiration que Voltaire, qui souligne aussi *religieuse*, ne risquait certes pas d'éprouver! D'où le ton de sa remarque.

[11] *Fort bien* (A 10); *louche* (A 81); *recherche faible* (A 84); *trop commun* (A 85); *faites-les donc* (2 fois, A 88).

mieux à l'orgueil (A 63, G 36); *vous n'en avez pas parlé* (A 64, G 36); *est-ce un ridicule? pourquoi vous efforcez-vous de l'approfondir?* (A 77, G 42); celle-ci enfin, riche de nuances, sur la présence occulte de Pascal entre Voltaire et Vauvenargues, dans un court chapitre sur le 'divertissement' (A 66, G 37): 'L'âme d'un pêcheur . . . se détache en quelque sorte de son corps pour suivre un poisson sous les eaux', à quoi Voltaire rétorque: '*En quoi cela est-il humiliant?*'.

Ces quelques exemples sont loin d'épuiser la liste des omissions. C'est par dizaines que Gilbert écarte des annotations fort lisiblement écrites. Quelques chiffres donneront la mesure des pertes: A 98: 4 remarques; Gilbert: néant —A 81: 4 remarques; Gilbert: 3 absentes, 1 fautive —A 90: 4 remarques; Gilbert: 2 absentes, 1 travestie, 1 seule correcte —A 181-5: 6 remarques; Gilbert: une seule; et ainsi de suite. En comptant les signes muets, nous pouvons dire que Gilbert ne restitue pas 50% de l'original, et ceci sans que le lecteur puisse le soupçonner.

A cette étrange désinvolture, nous ne voyons qu'une seule cause: fier de sa découverte, Gilbert estima qu'un relevé approximatif des annotations les plus frappantes suffirait à sa gloire. Ou bien il s'est contenté d'une séance de quelques heures pour en transcrire lui-même le texte, ou a confié cette tâche à quelque scribe, qui s'en est acquitté à la diable. On aimerait voir ici la vengeance de Mouan qui avait tiré pour lui les marrons du feu.

Non content de ces retranchements, Gilbert en prend à l'aise avec son texte. Nous voulons bien lui pardonner d'avoir attribué à Voltaire une correction faite par Vauvenargues (A 77),[12] tant la décision dépasse le coup d'œil superficiel qui fut le sien. Mais quelle singulière outrecuidance d'effectuer, sans prévenir, une correction demandée par Voltaire et refusée par Vauvenargues (A 14, G 11),[13] ou, pire encore, de prendre à son compte ce qui n'appartient qu'à Voltaire et Vauvenargues.[14] Et que dire de certaines notes où

[12] Voltaire avait souligné le mot *importants* et mis une note en marge, mais c'est Vauvenargues qui a biffé le mot.

[13] Le premier paragraphe du chapitre *Du bon sens*, contient 3 fois l'expression *le bon sens*, la dernière fois au sens de *direction*, évidemment une négligence, que Voltaire corrige par *de leur vray côté*. C'est bien la leçon de Gilbert, mais non celle de l'édition de 1747 qu'il prétend suivre.

[14] A 195, G 472, n. 5—Tout en la jugeant *belle*, Voltaire avait cru reconnaître la répétition d'une maxime figurant dans un autre endroit, sans préciser la page. Vauvenargues la retrouve et donne la référence en marge, mais maintient la répétition. Faussement modeste, Gilbert s'attribue le mérite d'avoir décelé la redite et supprime l'un des deux passages.

Gilbert prend Voltaire à parti et lui dit son fait avec suffisance? (G 50).

En un mot, sous couleur d'édition critique, Gilbert, sans la moindre méthode,[15] n'a fait que rétablir de temps en temps dans ses notes des paragraphes de 1746 supprimés en 1747, sans apporter le moindre secours à qui veut suivre de près le travail de l'écrivain. Une simple comparaison des deux éditions révèle au contraire plusieurs centaines de variantes. Or, si les progrès d'un jeune auteur méritent toujours notre intérêt, il est ici multiplié par la qualité de l'annotateur. Ce qui nous touche et nous passionne, c'est de saisir sur le vif le dialogue du maître et du disciple, le détail, voyant ou discret, de leur accord ou de leur mésentente, les esthétiques et les philosophies en présence, les patients efforts de deux écrivains également, quoique diversement exigeants, qu'apprécieront ceux qui savent le prix, la peine et le poids d'un seul mot. Voilà tout ce que Gilbert efface avec la brutalité satisfaite d'un demi-archéologue capable de saccager un site par sa précipitation, son aveuglement ou sa vanité.

L'exemplaire d'Aix, Dieu merci! reste intact, et nous pouvons encore le feuilleter à loisir. La place manque ici pour exposer en détail les précautions techniques dont il faut s'entourer:[16] distinction entre les encres, celle de Voltaire plus décolorée et virant au bistre, celle de Vauvenargues noire et forte; entre les écritures, coulée pour Voltaire, bâtarde pour le moraliste, sans négliger les déformations dues au manque de place et à la hâte; emplacement des annotations dans les marges ou entre les lignes; dessin des divers traits. A titre d'exemple, voici l'énonce de quelques problèmes d'attribution, allant du plus simple au plus litigieux.

'Il y a une distraction assez semblable au sommeil', écrit Vauve-

[15] Ainsi (G 38), Gilbert signale la suppression d'un paragraphe de 1746 'd'après de conseil de Voltaire', mais ne le donne pas, alors qu'il le fait p. 1 et 2. 'Nous ne croyons pas qu'il y ait lieu de le rétablir contre l'intention de l'auteur', ajoute-t-il comme excuse, tout en étouffant aisément ses scrupules ailleurs.

En G 242, Vauvenargues ayant mis dans la 2ème édition une phrase sur Corneille qui ne figure pas dans la 1ère, Gilbert écrit: 'C'est un correctif que Vauvenargues accorda sans doute à Voltaire', hypothèse absolument arbitraire, alors que des dizaines d'additions et de corrections n'éveillent chez lui aucun écho.

En revanche, pp. 239-253, soudain pris d'un beau zèle, il donne en note presque toutes les variantes.

[16] On souffre en pensant que seul Gilbert a pu consulter les manuscrits de Vauvenargues, détruits ensuite sous la Commune.

nargues (A 41, G 26). Voltaire met une croix devant 'sommeil' et, en marge, *rêves du.* Vauvenargues corrige en 'assez semblable aux rêves du sommeil'.

Exemple de navette à élucider (A 248, G 253 n. 2): Vauvenargues écrit: 'Racine [a] la dignité et l'éloquence'. Voltaire biffe les deux mots et, en marge, *le sentiment.* Vauvenargues garde la suggestion mais rajoute *et l'éloquence.* Finalement, tout le paragraphe sera supprimé.

En A 73, G 40, en face de 'les jeunes gens sont aussi très sensibles, très constants et neufs à aimer', Voltaire a simplement tiré un petit trait vertical. Il s'agit d'une correction de style, mais aussi d'un je ne sais quoi entre un homme de 53 ans et un de 32. Le texte définitif est: 'Les jeunes gens sont aussi très sensibles et très confiants.'[17]

Enfin, on se heurte parfois à des obscurités, telles le *plus pu* mystérieux de A 85 ou le *qui est peu, est pourtant* de A 46.

Tout ce travail n'est que le préambule de la véritable étude, celle de l'aide apportée par Voltaire à Vauvenargues pour polir son ouvrage. Nous nous bornerons ici à quelques exemples. *Aucun d'entre eux*—nous y avons mis de la coquetterie—ne figure dans l'édition Gilbert, ce qui ne veut pas dire qu'un exposé complet et approfondi doive négliger ce que Gilbert a publié. Il faudrait aussi examiner les variantes qui n'ont pas été suscitées par Voltaire, mais ceci dépasse notre propos.

Loin de se limiter à un commentaire marginal et très théorique, les annotations de Voltaire sont minutieuses, précises, pédagogiques même, et portent sur le métier plus encore que sur l'art d'écrire. Le style de Vauvenargues en effet frappe les moins avertis par son manque de grâce et de souplesse. Laborieux souvent, guindé même, parfois bizarrement rocailleux, il déroute par des constructions forcées, l'usage insolite des prépositions. Vagues et abstraits, trop de termes créent l'équivoque ou l'obscurité. L'auteur tout le premier, savait ce qu'il devait faire: 'Je me suis attaché autant que j'ai pu', avoue-t-il dans le *Discours préliminaire* de la deuxième édition (G 3), 'à corriger les fautes de langage qu'on m'a fait remarquer dans la première; j'ai retouché le style en beaucoup d'endroits'. Chez ce type de moraliste-philosophe fort peu attentif au monde extérieur concret, la pensée emprunte son existence aux mots qui en sont à la fois l'essence et la traduction sensible. Sachant, par la conversation, que Vauvenargues avait réellement quelque

[17] Gilbert (40 n.) déclare que Voltaire a rayé *neufs à aimer*, ce qui est faux.

chose à dire, Voltaire souffrait avec lui de le voir chercher un véhicule adéquat.

Dans sa sollicitude, il ne craint donc pas de s'abaisser à reprendre jusqu'à des fautes d'impression (A 179), de ponctuation et d'orthographe (corrigeant *foiblesse* en *faiblesse*, l'une de ses manies). Bon nombre de remarques portent sur l'enchaînement des pensées: ordre des paragraphes, redites, contradictions (parfois à plusieurs dizaines de pages de distance). Ainsi: *vous n'en avez pas parlé* (A 64); *peu lié* (A 65); *répété dans le chapitre du bien et du mal* (A 132); *liaison outrée* (A 192). Ces propos furent peu efficaces. Quiconque a tant soit peu écrit, sait combien il est malaisé de déplacer fût-ce une simple phrase, même si le genre adopté par Vauvenargues se prêtait bien au décousu. Lorsque celui-ci reconnaît le bien-fondé de l'observation, il se borne le plus souvent à la suppression pure et simple de tout le passage.

Si Voltaire réagit parfois en simple grammairien,[18] ses conseils sur la propriété des termes, nombreux et précis, touchent au cœur du style. Il ne se contente pas d'interroger ou de censurer, il offre des synonymes, un, deux, trois même. Vauvenargues n'aura plus qu'à choisir. 'La paresse [naît] de notre impuissance', lit-on en A 85. *Du manque de passion, d'aiguillon*, propose Voltaire.[19] Ici (A 110), il biffe *vertueux* et suggère *grands ou bien criminels, ou?*; là (213), au lieu de *nuire*, il offre *noircir*, *médire*, *calomnier*, ou bien, pour remplacer *qualités*, donne à choisir entre *différences*, *détails* et *objets* (A 13).[20] Dans l'ensemble, s'il relève mainte gaucherie (comme en A 31), il dénonce surtout l'obscurité, vice capital chez un moraliste,[21]

[18] 'Quel [Voltaire: *que*] sens que l'on considère' (A 11)—'Modérations sur [Voltaire- *dans*] les plaisirs' (A 116)—'Qui les flatte et [Voltaire: *on attend un que*] malheureusement' (A 128)—'On peut se consoler d'être dans leurs faiblesses (A 173); Voltaire a rayé *dans leurs* et noté: *barbarisme recherché*. La 2ème édition porte *d'éprouver*.

[19] Sans l'écouter, Vauvenargues accentue la bizarrerie: 'La paresse naît d' impuissance'. Par une sorte de remords et de compensation, deux lignes plus bas ('la tristesse [naît] de notre misère'), il raie *misère* qu'il remplace par *impuissance*. Finalement, il gardera *misère*.

[20] *Différences* est tracé d'un trait noir et épais avec une plume que l'on vient de charger d'encre. Les deux autres mots, au contraire, quoique placés en dessous, trahissent la fin de l'encre. Ce sont donc eux qui furent écrits les premiers, mais Voltaire, tenant à faire les choses à fond, a repris de l'encre pour ajouter le troisième.

[21] *Louche* revient souvent. Ex.: 'Il était juste d'assurer à la vieillesse ce qu'elle prêtait à l'enfance'. Volta re-souligne *assurer* et *prêtait*, le tout étant qualifié d'*obscur et recherché*. La 2ème édition a: '. . . les secours qu'elle avait prêtés à l'enfance' (A 68, G 38).

ou encore, guidé par l'âge et l'expérience, insère un prudent *souvent* (A 19) ou un sage *quelquefois* (A 76), nuances qui ne coûtent rien.

Si l'étude détaillée de ces annotations paraît aride, combien plus aride encore dut être la tâche de les écrire. Nous pouvons croire Voltaire lorsqu'il déclare avoir 'relu [l'ouvrage] avec un extrême recueillement' (Best. 3072). Cette re-lecture dut en effet exiger entre dix et vingt heures d'examen au microscope. Combien d'écrivains peuvent se vanter d'en avoir distrait autant des journées de Voltaire pour un but analogue? Par comparaison, les commentaires plus personnels portant sur le fond, révélateurs de toute une pensée à nos yeux, n'aidaient pas Vauvenargues à progresser dans son métier. Loin d'être toujours amènes,[22] ces réflexions se teintent parfois d'ironie.[23] En voici un exemple amusant: 'Que je vous estime, mon enfant, de mépriser les petites finesses . . .', écrit Vauvenargues (A 185, G 122), s'adressant à Hippolyte de Seytres (ils ont respectivement 25 et 16 ans!). *Cela est bon à un patriarche*, s'écrie Voltaire. Sensible au ridicule, l'auteur lui substitue *mon très cher ami.*

Souvent, la remarque va plus loin et amorce une discussion en règle; ainsi: *Voyez la préface des abeilles*, *Shaftesbury*, *Pope* (A 92, G 50), et, plus loin, *la fable des abeilles*, une seconde fois (A 98, G 53).

Au total, comment Vauvenargues a-t-il accepté ces conseils? Son attitude varie beaucoup. Tantôt il se soumet sans barguigner, docilité qui va d'une minime modification[24] à l'addition d'une phrase entière.[25] Tantôt il se corrige à demi, mais alors peut aussi bien aller dans le sens de Voltaire qu'en faire simplement à sa tête.[26]

[22] 'Il y aurait là-dessus des réflexions à faire' (A 88)—*Faites-les donc*, et, dans la même page 'J'ignore l'art d'embellir'—*Réflexion n'est pas ornement*. Deux pages plus loin: *Nulle analogie*.

[23] 'La vertu ne satisfait pas', écrit Vauvenargues. *Il est vrai*, commente Voltaire en mettant une croix après *vertu*.

[24] '[Il y a une autre éloquence] . . . dans les sentiments plus encore que dans l'expression' (A 90, G 19) devient: *jointe à celle de l'expression.*

[25] *La joie est un sentiment plus pénétrant* de A 47, G 29, appartient entièrement à Voltaire.

[26] '[La modération] est une espèce de, satiété, une richesse de tempérament, enfin une disposition à toutes les vertus civiles'. Voltaire souligne *richesse* et *tempérament*, et note: *mauvaise expression et fausse idée.* La phrase deviendra: 'la modération est l'état d'une âme qui se possède . . .' (A 116, G 61).

'. . . qui peut se sauver des misères qui suivent la médiocrité' (A 140). Voltaire souligne *misère* et propose *humiliations*; ce qui devient: 'qui peut se sauver des faiblesses que la médiocrité traîne avec soi' (G 71).

Ce sont ces demi-ententes qui sont les plus révélatrices.

Enfin, plus d'une fois, refusant tout net, il maintient son texte, par amour-propre semble-t-il, quand il ne s'entête pas dans l'incorrection, l'obscurité ou la maladresse.[27]

Les *Réflexions et maximes* forment un cas à part. Des 575 numéros de l'édition de 1746, Vauvenargues en a retranché 245, soit 43%. Sur les 247 annotations de Voltaire dans cette section, 121 ont porté au but et provoqué le retrait d'autant de maximes, soit 22% du total primitif. Gilbert—chose curieuse—étant à peu près irréprochable dans cette partie de son édition, tout lecteur pourra apprécier lui-même le rôle de Voltaire.

Nous pouvons maintenant poser les principes d'une édition véritablement critique. Par une typographie appropriée, elle devrait faire apparaître les diverses étapes qui séparent les deux éditions. Nous pouvons aussi répondre à la seconde question de notre préambule. Contrairement à ce que répètent tous les biographes après Gilbert, le texte de 1747 n'est absolument pas ce que donnerait l'exemplaire d'Aix imprimé en tenant compte de toutes les marques qu'il porte. Il faut supposer que Vauvenargues ne s'en servait que comme exemplaire de travail, mais préparait par ailleurs un exemplaire définitif destiné à l'imprimeur.

Les preuves ne manquent pas. Tantôt le texte d'Aix, quoique dûment corrigé par Voltaire et souvent revu derrière lui par l'auteur, n'est pas celui de la seconde édition (cf. A 51, G 57; A 114; A 148), tantôt le texte change d'une édition à l'autre bien que l'exemplaire d'Aix ne porte aucun signe, ni de Voltaire, ni de Vauvenargues (G 7 par exemple).

Ce dernier cas, extrêmement fréquent, permet de résoudre un point litigieux. Gilbert et ses successeurs affirment tous que ces corrections sont le fait des abbés Trublet et Séguy, qui surveillèrent l'impression posthume. Passe encore pour les passages signalés à leur attention par quelque marque, mais pourquoi auraient-ils altéré tant de phrases que rien ne distinguait du reste? En réalité, Vauvenargues étant mort le 28 mai, et l'approbation étant du 10 juin,[28] la seconde édition ayant été composée chez le même Briasson d'après un exemplaire de la première,[29] mais avec une mise en page

[27] 'Le jugement va plus loin que le sens, mais ses principes sont plus variables' (A 14, G 11). Voltaire propose *plus déliés ou plus profonds*, mais en vain.

[28] Le privilège de la première, daté du 27 janvier 1746, était encore valable.

[29] Ce que prouve l'analyse des coquilles.

différente par suite du nombre des corrections, il ne fait pour nous aucun doute qu'il suffit de croire Suard sur parole[30] et d'admettre qu'avant sa mort Vauvenargues avait déjà confié à Briasson l'exemplaire dont nous venons de parler. Quant à celui d'Aix, trouvé par ses amis parmi ses maigres hardes, il fut pieusement conservé par Fauris de Saint-Vincent qui n'eut jamais la curiosité de le comparer au texte de 1747.

Toute main étrangère à celle de l'auteur étant ainsi écartée, nous sommes plus à l'aise pour juger de Voltaire lecteur de Vauvenargues et de Vauvenargues lecteur de Voltaire, écoutant le maître, faisant la sourde oreille ou ne prêtant qu'une oreille distraite ou critique. Mais les pages ci-dessus ne sont encore qu'une introduction à une étude complète de leur collaboration. Il faudrait élargir la perspective, y faire entrer non seulement la controverse sur Corneille et sur Racine, mais pratiquement toutes les œuvres, car nous savons, depuis leur premier commerce épistolaire en 1743, que Vauvenargues avait envoyé à Voltaire la plupart de ses textes en manuscrit et en avait reçu conseils et corrections.[31] Loin d'être un cas exceptionnel, l'exemplaire d'Aix demeure comme le seul et précieux vestige d'un travail mené en commun, d'un échange continu, inlassable, exigeant et fructueux. Pendant un trop bref moment, ce livre nous permet de saisir sur le vif le dialogue curieux, parfois divertissant et toujours instructif, de deux écrivains également épris de perfection.

[30] 'La seconde [édition] revue et corrigée par lui était fort avancée lorsqu'il mourut', *Œuvres*, t. I, p. i.

[31] Cf. en particulier Best. 2845, 2852, 2876, 3076. Dans cette dernière lettre, il s'agit entre autres des *Portraits* dont la publication posthume sera faite directement sur le manuscrit corrigé par Voltaire, aujourd'hui malheureusement perdu.

Broggia e Vico

Franco Venturi

Una sola persona seppe osservare con libertà di giudizio e con indipendenza di carattere la realtà napoletana dei primi dieci anni di Carlo Borbone a Napoli (1734–1744), trovando in se stesso abbastanza coraggio per proclamare apertamente le proprie idee e per esporre pubblicamente le proprie conclusioni, e questi fu Carlantonio Broggia. 'Aromatarius', e cioè droghiere all'ingrosso, egli aveva una esperienza commerciale diretta ed una personale conoscenza di tutti gli innumerevoli ostacoli che le tradizioni, le leggi, le vecchie abitudini burocratiche frapponevano allo svolgersi del mestier suo. Autodidatta, egli aveva saputo profittare d'un giovanile soggiorno a Venezia, circa tra il 1718 ed il 1720, in un mondo economico che lasciò profonde tracce in tutta la sua mentalità. Tornato a Napoli aveva trovato nella meditazione solitaria e nell'ambiente di Bartolomeo Intieri e di Alessandro Rinuccini i mezzi con cui sviluppare le sue idee politiche ed economiche. Avidamente aveva assorbito, nella Napoli degli anni 20 e 30, tutto quanto gli era riuscito di imparare dai maestri della vecchia generazione, da Paolo Mattia Doria e, soprattutto dall' 'acutissimo nostro Vico'.[1] Carlantonio Broggia era così vissuto, nel cuore della sua Napoli, isolato e pur aperto alla

[1] Carlantonio Broggia, *Trattato de' tributi, delle monete e del governo politico della sanità* (Napoli, Pietro Palombo, 1743), p. 486. Curioso che questo rapporto tra Broggia e Vico non sia stato abbastanza notato. Probabilmente la responsabilità di questa lacuna risale a Pietro Custodi che, nella sua collana di *Scrittori classici italiani di economia politica* pensò bene di riprodurre il *Trattato* di Broggia tagliandone via la terza ed ultima parte, riguardante la sanità, la dove appunto si trova la menzione di Vico. Ma la mentalità ed il vocabolario di Broggia rivelano, a parte ogni esplicita citazione, una forte impronta vichiana, i suoi assiomi egli li chiama *dignità*, la *sapienza riposta* è una delle sue formule preferite, non mancano le fantasiose etimologie e, come vedremo, una delle sue idee chiave, quella dell'eccesso di civilità, deriva da Vico.

cultura e alla vita del suo tempo, figura originale e uomo di carattere, 'di mezzana statura, di corpo esile . . . , il dorso curvo, la fronte crespa, il naso aquilino, il sopraciglio grave e la barba folta.' Si era via via interessato ai problemi economici come a quelli medici, leggendo largamente e disordinatamente libri d'ogni genere, sempre più preso ed oppresso dal suo mestiere di commerciante e da una grossa, sempre crescente famiglia, desideroso ogni giorno più di consacrarsi ai grandi problemi, di vivere per il bene comune e sempre più scontento di non poterlo fare.[2] Nel 1742 aveva presentato al duca di Montealegre una memoria, o come diceva, un trattato, intitolato *Il ristoro della Spagna causato dalla libertà concessa alle nazioni amiche del commercio d'America.*[3] Era una puntuale risposta alle molte voci che si andavano diffondendo in quegli anni sulla possibilità, per il regno di Napoli, di profittare del monopolio spagnolo nelle Indie Occidentali. Broggia rispondeva con un programma di liberalizzazione integrale, additando in quel monopolio precisamente una delle cause essenziali della decadenza spagnola. 'La sicurezza di esser all'intutto propri beni sì vasti ha resi pigri e gonfi di se stessi i spagnuoli. . . .'[4] Questi avevano creduto di poter dominare gli olandesi, i portoghesi, i catalani come avevano assoggettato, o, come egli diceva, 'signoreggiato' gl'indigeni del l'America e così avevan finito col perdere il loro impero. 'Fu la negata libertà all'americano commercio ciò che causò tutt'il male e fece perdere alla Spagna quello spirito di economica industria che possedeva per avanti.'[5]

[2] I dati essenziali su di lui stanno in Michelangelo Schipa, 'Il Muratori e la coltura napoletana del suo tempo', in *Archivio storico per le province napoletane* (anno XXVI [1901], fasc. iv. pp. 614 sgg; Luigi dal Pane 'Una memoria sulla Pantelleria di Carlo Antonio Broggia', *Archivio storico italiano* (anno CXVI [1958]), disp. iii. pp. 381 sgg; id, 'Di un' opera sconosciuta di Carlo Antonio Broggia e del suo carteggio con L. A. Muratori', estratto del *Giornale degli economisti e annali di economia* (novembre dicembre 1958). Larga bibliografia in Oscar Nuccio, 'Broggia Carlo Antonio', appendice al IV e V volume, parte antica, della raccolta di Pietro Custodi, *Scrittori classici italiani di economia politica* (Roma, Bizzarri, 1965).

[3] E' perduta, ma un ampio riassunto ce ne forniva lo stesso Broggia nella sua *Memoria ad oggetto di varie politiche ed economiche ragioni e temi di utili raccordi che in causa del monetaggio di Napoli s'espongono e propongono . . .* (Napoli 1754). pp. cv sgg.

[4] *Ibid.*, p. cvi.

[5] *Ibid.*, p. cxi. Inutile notare come queste discussioni siano l'eco, a Napoli, della guerra tra Spagna ed Inghilterra. Il distacco dal mondo spagnolo del nuovo Regno avviene in un momento di gravi ed importanti esperienze per la penisola iberica. E, come si vede anche da questo esempio, Napoli è attivamente coinvolta nell'atmosfera spagnola di quegli anni.

L'anno dopo, nel 1743, era pubblicato il *Trattato*. I problemi della decadenza europea erano ormai sostituiti da quelli, ben più vicini e brucianti, della debolezza, della fragilità, della pericolosità della situazione napoletana. Il *Trattato* rispondeva appassionatamente, con apparente disordine e in realtà con forte coerenza interna alle domande che sempre più insistentemente si levavano sul l'orizzonte del nuovo Regno nell'anno che trascorse tra l'incursione, l'umiliazione inglese e il gran gioco d'azzardo della campagna di Velletri. La corruzione era profonda nel Napoletano e derivava, affermava Broggia, da un sempre più accentuato distacco tra la 'buona pratica', tra il 'vivere semplice, economico, ed operante', tra 'lo spirito dell'industria'[6] e il falso raziocinare la legge concepita come pura forma, la politica intesa come mera astuzia. Napoli insomma viveva sotto il segno di quella che Vico aveva chiamato la 'barbarie della riflessione'[7] e che Broggia definisce come 'eccedente coltura'.[8] Da questo giudizio sul proprio tempo Broggia sembrava qua e là trarre una moralistica ripulsa, un accorato ritorno al passato, un'angosciosa ricerca di certezza religiosa, una condanna d'ogni pensiero e ricerca moderna, empirica, epicurea, razionalistica. Ma là pure, in questo suo appassionato giudizio, egli trovava il punto di partenza d'una energica volontà di riforma. L'eredità di Doria e di Vico poteva condurre alla contemplazione platonica, al provvidenzialismo. Ma, per Broggia, fu stimolo a ritrovare una 'politica fondata nell'economica.'[9]

La situazione era grave. Avrebbe il Napoletano continuato ad esser preda di successivi conquistatori, mutando padrone senza cambiar davvero di condizioni? Quella breve luce di autonomia che si era accesa nel 1734 sarebbe stata di nuovo spenta ed il Napoletano sarebbe tornato provincia? Per Vico, nella conclusione della *Scienza nuova* la conquista era apparsa una giusta e naturale punizione della corruzione e delle 'malnate sottigliezze degl'ingegni maliziosi', della 'barbarie della riflessione', peggiore perfino della primitiva 'barbarie del senso'. Vico si appagava pensando che la storia, la provvidenza stabilivano il dominio delle 'nazioni migliori' su quelle peggiori,

Cfr. J. Vicens Vives, *Historia economica de España* (Barcelona, Teide, 1959), pp. 518 sgg.

[6] *Prefazione*, p. v.

[7] *Ibid.*, p. 486. Broggia si riferisce alla *Scienza nuova, Conclusione dell'opera sopra un'eterna repubblica naturale, in ciascuna sua spezie ottima, dalla divina provvidenza ordinata*. Cfr. ed. Fausto Nicolini (Bari, Laterza, 1928), ii. 163-267.

[8] *Ibid.*, *Prefazione*, p. v.

[9] *Ibid.*, p. iv.

che tutto era nell' 'ordine naturale' e che perciò 'chi non può governarsi da sé si lasci governare da altri che l'possa'. Era evidente che al mondo prevalevano 'sempre quelli che sono per natura migliori'.[10] Ma Broggia non poteve rassegnarsi a questa visione dell'eterno corso delle umane cose. Il problema per lui era quello di che cosa bisognava fare perché la conquista diventasse più difficile, impossibile. 'Si tratta di sollevar la patria, di sostenere il proprio principe, di rilevar il nome e la gloria della propria nazione.'[11] Se otto o diecimila uomini possono conquistar un paese, se 'un pugno di soldati si rende padrone di un milione di uomini',[12] è perché i ricchi ed i potenti non pagano le tasse, perché i contadini sono oppressi, perché la miseria è terribile, perché manca l'iniziativa economica, perché non viene appoggiato il commercio, perché l'intera vita economica del paese deve essere rinnovata.

'Uno de' motivi più efficaci ed essenziali donde uno stato porta seco il brutto titolo di conquista ed è esposto al ludibrio de' conquistatori dipende dalle varie arti delle quali, col soccorso de' sofisti, si servono i ricchi... per esimersi da que' soccorsi e da quelle contribuzioni ordinarie e straordinarie per le quali per ogni legge e specialmente ne' straordinari ed urgenti bisogni sono strettamente tenuti.'[13] Tutto il *Trattato dei tributi* parte da questa constatazione. Di là nascono le sue critiche al sistema del catasto, di là le sue proposte di non tassare direttamente i beni mobili, i capitali e i redditi provenienti dall'industria e dal commercio per far pagare invece i beni immobili, le proprietà terriere. Non esclude, è vero, dazi e gabelle, ma avverte che non bisogna mai aggravarli in tempo di guerra.[14] Tutta la sua riforma fiscale è indirizzata a favorire l' 'industria', a tentare di sviluppare l'attività economica facendo ricadere il peso dei gravami sul lusso, sulla ricchezza improduttiva e sulla rendita.[15]

Broggia è particolarmente sensibile alle implicazioni sociali d'una simile politica. Si proclama apertamente 'difensore della povertà industriosa e faticatrice'.[16] Si tratta, innanzi tutto, dei contadini. Egli sa che la loro condizione sta peggiorando con l'accrescersi

[10] *Scienza nuova*, p. 162.

[11] *Trattato*, p. 21.

[12] *Ibid.*

[13] *Ibid.*

[14] *Ibid.*, p. 43.

[15] Cfr. Carlantonio Broggia, *Memorie ad oggetto di varie politiche ed economiche ragioni*, p. lix: 'Il mio trattatello de' tributi molto si affatica e quasi tempesta per far vedere che le tasse sulle industrie e sì sui danari impiegati a negozi son tribbuti dannosi ed i peggio concepiti'.

[16] *Trattato*, p. 68.

delle affittanze e con la diminuzione dei salari bracciantili. La loro condizione sta diventando peggiore di quella degli schiavi. Essi conducono 'una vita più meschina' e patiscono 'la più spietata miseria'.[17] Il contadino . . . il pane di grano non ha possibilità di mangiarlo che quando sta infermo e si trova coll'anima a i denti.'[18]

Eppure sui contadini gravano le tasse personali, che debbono essere soppresse, su di loro ricade ogni aumento delle gabelle ed, in genere, il peso maggiore del sistema fiscale e sociale esistente. Proprio in questo sta una delle principali debolezze del Napoletano. 'A ché dobbiamo fra l'altre cose essenziali attribuire le perdite lacrimevoli che in guerra soffrono gli stati se non al non potere che per poco contare sulla gente contadinesca?'[19] La miseria, lo spopolamento delle campagne costringono gli stati come il Napoletano 'a servirsi della gente vile, infesta e di poco cuore delle città, che poco resiste alle fatiche e tosto si ammala o pure bisogna ricorrere a mercenari dai quali viepiù di rado puote sperarsi frutto e serviggio convenevole.'[20] Debolezza militare dunque che affonda le sue radici nella situazione sociale di tutto il paese. 'Dee il principe più temere e guardarsi dalle maledizzioni de' poveri e specialmente pe 'l motivo de' mal situati tributi che dall'armi de' nemici.'[21] Ben lo sanno questi ultimi che sono animati alla conquista 'riflettendo al cattivo governo, alla debolezza de' popoli, all'invito de' medesimi.'[22] Il pericolo più grave sta sempre in una politica che intende 'tener avvilita ed oppressa la gente povera, affaticata e industriosa anco per mezzo de' tributi mal situati', in una politica 'conferente all'interesse privato de' ricchi' e 'altrettanto nocevole, pestifera e letale al vero interesse del principe.'[23] Inutile cercar di mascherare questa politica di oppressione per i contadini con delle concessioni alla plebe delle grandi città. Quest' ultima è generalmente meglio trattata perchè maggiormente la si teme. I contadini sono dispersi e apparentemente meno pericolosi. 'Per essere una sì fatta gente di sua natura e per se stessa le più umile, le più quieta, le più sofferente' se ne fa 'il più spietato abbuso.'[24]

[17] *Ibid.*, p. 79.

[18] *Ibid.*, p. 80.

[19] *Ibid.*, p. 80.

[20] *Ibid.*, cfr. p. 89: 'E sempre sarà vana quella fiducia del legislatore che fonda ogni sua tutela sul solo esercito e nella gente forastiera, conciosiachè dato, come è pur troppo facile a darsi che l' esercito soccomba, il tutto è perduto.'

[21] *Ibid.*, p. 86; cfr. p. 93

[22] *Ibid.*, p. 89.

[23] *Ibid.*, pp. 89-90.

[24] *Ibid.*, p. 87.

Ma fin dove la misera situazione dei contadini derivava da una errata politica economica, o non piuttosto dalla situazione feudale della società napoletana? Broggia si poneva chiaramente il problema, anche se non lo esaminava a fondo. Come Bartolomeo Intieri qualche anno prima[25] egli sapeva che la situazione del Napoletano non permetteva di pensare ad una vera risoluzione della questione feudale. Diceva chiaramente perciò in proposito la sua opinione, senza trarne tuttavia conclusioni politiche. Certo, affermava, bisognerebbe pur studiare 'le cagioni per le quali certi stati, pieni sin alla gola e come soffocati di feudi sono ordinariamente i più esposti alle invasioni de' nemici e sono i meno atti per far sosta a i mali sì interni che esterni, sì di pace che di guerra'. Era questo un gravissimo difetto del Napoletano, e ormai inveterato. I feudi avevano una forte e deleteria incidenza sulla situazione fiscale. 'D'ordinario accade che in simili stati il maggior pondo de' tributi, per quanto un qualche buon legislatore si affatichi per avventura nel suo tempo d'instituir altrimenti, abbia in fine sempre a ridursi sulle spalle de' poveri.'[26] Ma sembrava difficile, forse impossibile ogni tentativo di rimediarvi. I feudi apparivano a Broggia come una gravosa, penosa realtà. Ma come riuscire anche soltanto ad intaccarla?

Se i contadini costituivano per Broggia il greve e grigio fondo, carico di miseria e di sofferenza, di tutta la società napoletana, la sua attenzione immediata si rivolge tuttavia alle classi che stavano, per così dire, in primo piano, agli uomini delle manifatture e dei commerci. Le sue proposte si fanno, quando parla di loro, più dettagliate e precise. La sua profonda simpatia per i contadini lascia allora il posto ad un più articolato programma pratico. La 'coltivazion del commercio', come egli diceva, è al centro di tutto il suo pensiero. Qui la lotta contro il lusso si fa più ravvicinata e trova la sua applicazione in una serie di precise e dettagliate proposte. Broggia è un mercantilista, ma non crede possibile un intervento dello stato per creare compagnie internazionali di commercio, manifatture privilegiate ecc. Son cose queste da lasciare ai paesi ricchi e industriosi, come ad esempio la Francia. Per il Napoletano non si potrà stabilire dei rigidi sistemi protezionistici o, peggio ancora, proibizionistici per impedire la concorrenza delle merci straniere e per evitare che

[25] Cp. Franco Venturi, 'Gli anni 30 del Settecento', in *Miscellanea Walter Maturi* (Torino, Giappichelli, 1966), pp. 129-130.

[26] *Trattato*, pp. 27-28.

il denaro delle classi ricche vada tutto speso in merci di lusso che provengono dall'estero. Le dogane saranno uno strumento importante per cercar di ottenere un risveglio delle attività economiche locali, ma quel che più conterà sarà, nel paese stesso, di invitare, spingere ad investimenti proficui, combattendo la mentalità stessa del lusso, risvegliando 'lo spirito di economia', facilitando le esportazioni, permettendo così la formazione di un capitale nuovo di origine mercantile, favorendo in ogni modo i mercanti del posto, così come ogni iniziativa che permetta di migliorare la bilancia commerciale. Al limite di questo programma sta la visione, lontana, di quel che si potrebbe ottenere dal paese con una politica economica che colpisca i ricchi proprietari terrieri, nobili ed ecclesiastici, che liberi da ogni intralcio i commercianti e gli imprenditori, concentrando su di loro gli investimenti e le facilitazioni fiscali. Ma non è che un limite, un ideale punto d'arrivo. Broggia sa benissimo che deve cercar d'agire in un mondo in cui privilegi e concentrazioni di ricchezze impediscono piani tanto vasti ed arditi. Vuole piuttosto una qualche riduzione dei consumi quando le merci che li alimentano provengono dall'estero. Soltanto così, più che attraverso le dogane, si otterrà una limitazione delle importazioni. L'allargarsi dei consumi di lusso gli pareva un male per combattere il quale egli ricorreva all'immagine di una società più arcaica e più austera. Quale era stato il risultato del fatto che, in cinquant'anni, il prezzo dello zucchero fosse diminuito della metà? Che la gente vi si era abituata, ed ora ne consumava tre o quattro volte di più che non facesse cinquant'anni prima, con gran danno della bilancia commerciale del paese.[27] E quale il risultato, in tutta Italia, dello stabilirsi di sempre nuovi porti franchi, attraverso i quali erano penetrati sempre più numerosi i prodotti stranieri? I prezzi delle merci erano indubbiamente diminuiti, si erano anzi, come egl idiceva, 'prostituiti'.[28] Ma ne aveva approfittato soltanto una ristretta cerchia di nuovi ricchi, di mercanti in grado di accumulare rapide fortune, ma incapaci poi di rinvestirle fruttuosamente. In terre generalmente andavano a finire i denari così speculati sui traffici di lusso. Il lusso si era sempre più diffuso, mentre l'iniziativa economica era in ultima analisi diminuita.[29] I

[27] *Ibid.*, p. 106.

[28] *Ibid.*, p. 109.

[29] *Ibid.*, p. 110. Gli studi recenti di A. Caracciolo hanno dimostrato quando l'analisi di Broggia corrispondesse alla verità, almeno per quanto riguarda il porto franco di Ancona. Alberto Caracciolo, *Le port franc d'Ancône. Croissance et impasse d'un milieu marchand au XVIII*[e] *siècle* (Paris, S.E.V.P.E.N., 1965).

porti franchi erano stati 'l'ultimo colpo' della decadenza italiana.[30] Lo stato avrebbe dovuto invece appoggiare i commercianti locali, proteggendoli contro simili speculazioni internazionali, così come avrebbe dovuto in ogni modo favorire il commercio di esportazione, fonte di vera ricchezza e che era invece in tutti i modi intralciato dalle 'tratte' (le licenze per il commercio estero), dagli innumerevoli controlli, dalla onnipresente concorrenza del contrabbando nonchè dagli ebrei.[31] La situazione economica degli ultimi anni avrebbe ovviamente dovuto spingere il governo in questo senso. I prezzi delle derrate d'esportazione erano aumentati, il commercio estero si era sviluppato. Erano sintomi positivi. 'Allorchè le derrate sono a vil prezzo questo è uno de' contrasegni che uno stato è oppresso dalla debolezza e dalla miseria.'[32] Di quali merci si trattasse, Broggia ce lo indica chiaramente. 'Nell'anno 1740 il regno di Napoli divenne creditore quasi tutt'in un colpo e fuori dell'usato per le gran summe di frumento e per gran partite d'oli ed altre derrate estratte e da estrarsi fuor di stato.'[33] Di questa situazione bisognava approffittare. Un commercio dunque non di speculazione, non quello che era solito svilupparsi in occasione di carestie. Un commercio basato sui prezzi alti delle merci d'esportazione, derrate agricole e materie prime. Contemporaneamente era necessaria una trasformazione del costume e della mentalità e un sistema di prezzi che regolasse e mantenesse ad un basso livello l'importazione delle merci di lusso, destinate alle classi ricche e privilegiate. In mezzo, tra esportazione e importazione, una classe di commercianti nazionali in grado di profittare dell'una e dell'altra, senza monopoli, senza privilegi, in virtù della sua stessa capacità ed iniziativa economica.

Come si vede, un programma che aveva un aspetto conservatore (niente avventure economiche internazionali, ostilità per i grandi mercati, lotta contro il lusso e l'allargamento dei consumi) ed un aspetto riformatore (simpatia profonda per le classi povere, larga iniziativa economica della classe commerciante). I due aspetti erano

[30] *Ibid.*, p. 109.

[31] All' inizio del 1746 Broggia scrisse a Muratori una lettera, oggi perduta, sulla definitiva cacciata degli ebrei dal Regno di Napoli, dopo il tentativo, presto naufragato, di riammetterli nell' Italia meridionale (1740-46). I suoi apprezzamenti si indovinano, anche troppo chiaramenti dalla risposta dello studioso modenese. L. A. Muratori, *Epistolario*, edito e curato da Matteo Campori (Modena, Società tipografica modenese, 1907), xi. 4930.

[32] *Ibid.*, p. 159.

[33] *Ibid.*, p. 361.

strettamente saldati insieme nella sua battaglia contro il lusso, inteso insieme come una corruzione morale, una decadenza, una 'barbarie della riflessione', per dirla vichianamente, e come un investimento sbagliato, una attività economica negativa.[34] Broggia odiava il lusso e sapeva insieme, come Paolo Mattia Doria, che esso *non* sviluppava le manifatture in una situazione simile a quella del Napoletano.[35] L'elemento morale e quello economico erano ambedue alla radice del suo programma di riforme.

Intendeva imporlo al più presto all'attenzione del governo, sospinto come era dalla ripulsione che provava per il mondo in cui viveva e convinto d'altra parte della pericolosità e precarietà della situazione che lo attorniava. Ancora pochi mesi prima che la corte di Carlo di Borbone desse inizio alla campagna di Velletri, Broggia presentava al duca di Montealegre una memoria sulla riforma da operarsi nella dogana di Napoli in cui gli elementi essenziali del suo pensiero erano ribaditi. Lo scopo di ogni politica economica era quello di aiutare quei cittadini che costituivano 'la parte migliore dello stato, come quella che travaglia e fatica'.[36] Per far questo era necessario facilitare le esportazioni, abolendo le imposte che gravavano su di esse, costruendo strade ecc. 'In vece di chè—concludeva —la credenza e la cura di contribuire al detto gran bene col sostenere e promuovere il lusso de' propri sudditi, oltrechè una tal via è molto circoscritta e limitata, ella è sommamente letale e dannosa al proprio stato ed al proprio commercio ed è piena di demerito presso Dio, non essendo nè cosa prudenziale nè cosa giusta che per dar da vivere ad una parte de' cittadini abbiano le migliori parti a rovinarsi e impoverire di beni non meno fisici che morali, ed abbia la società, per causa del lusso, ad esser altamente travagliata da un diluvio di mali ed errori per ogni verso i più dannosi e crudeli.'[37]

La campagna di Velletri, l'esperienza del 1744, impedirono una

[34] Cfr. pure Carlantonio Broggia, *Memorie ad oggetto di varie politiche ed economiche ragioni*, p. xcvi.

[35] *Ibid.*, p. xcix. 'Si crede in oltre che il proprio lusso promuova nello stato le manifatture. Ma questo egli è un altro grosso errore. Un tal bene non si conseguirà mai se coloro i quali più degli altri dovebbero attendere a spendere per far fiorire le arti e il commercio, come sarebbono i ricchi e i nobili, son quegli che d' ordinario il medesimo lusso rende pigri, vani, spregiatori dell' industria, bisognosi e incapaci di attendervi. E que' popolani che vi attendono, arricchiti che si sono, urtuno al medesimo scoglio e abandonano l'industria, e così le arti e il commercio trovansi sempre più in mano di gente povera, e che comincia ad arricchire.'

[36] *Ibid.*, p. cxxiii.

[37] *Ibid.*, p. cxxiii.

effettiva applicazione di queste idee di Broggia—che rimase così un isolato, un solitario. Alla radice stessa del suo pensiero stava la spiegazione di questo fallimento. Egli condivideva con i suoi contemporanei quegli elementi di stanchezza, di distacco dalla politica delle grandi potenze, di ripiegamento che prevalsero—attraverso l'esperienza della guerra—con il ministero del marchese Fogliani. Broggia era stato la punta più avanzata, la mente più ardita e conseguente della breve e complessa spinta riformatrice del primo decennio di Carlo di Borbone. Ne era stato il frutto più maturo. Ma l'analisi del suo pensiero ci ha rivelato anche tutti gli elementi conservatori, rivolti verso il passato che esso portava con sé. L'esempio di Venezia, neutrale e prudente, sembrava dominare sempre più l'orizzonte politico di Broggia e dei suoi contemporanei—dopo gli anni di grandi programmi, di accese speranze e di grandi delusioni.[38]

[38] Per la sua visione di Venezia, cfr. *Trattato*, pp. 107, 122, 129, 261, 444, 475, ecc. e *Memorie ad oggetto di varie politiche ad economiche ragioni*, p. xvi ecc.

Le conte philosophique

Yvon Belaval

L'apogée du conte philosophique se situe avec tant d'éclat au XVIIIe siècle, qu'on en vient à se demander s'il ne se définit point par l'esprit des Lumières. Pratiquement, il disparaît ensuite. Remonte-t-on le cours du temps—de *Télémaque* à Cyrano, B. Gracian, Rabelais, *Till Eulenspiegel*, Marguerite de Navarre, Boccace, Noël du Fail, Bonaventure des Periers, les Devis, Propos, Fabliaux, le *Satyricon*, *l'Ane d'or*, pour citer à vue de mémoire—peut-être n'est-ce pas sans projeter sur ces récits, par illusion rétrospective, un type d'intention qu'ils n'avaient pas encore. N'importe! On s'en tiendra à la question: qu'est-ce que le conte philosophique au XVIIIe siècle? En quoi est-il philosophique? En quoi la philosophie a-t-elle affaire avec un conte? Serait-elle, elle aussi, à sa manière, un conte?

On n'essaiera pas d'enfermer le conte dans une formule, car 'ce n'est pas un genre littéraire distinct, comme la tragédie, l'épopée, la comédie, l'ode ou, même, la satire'.[1] Il varie de forme et de ton selon le milieu où l'on conte. Si le conte philosophique atteint son apogée au XVIIIe siècle, il faut par conséquent que le milieu lui ait alors imprimé une force particulière. Cette force a son origine dans la conversation telle qu'elle s'exerçait dans les salons et les cafés. Ce qui la caractérise dans sa forme, c'est que l'art de la conversation appartient désormais à des gens de lettres qui accèdent à l'indépendance; quant au fond, c'est l'esprit de contestation politique et religieuse qui envahit alors toutes les classes sociales et toutes les sectes. Cette contestation ne s'exprime pas sans danger. La liberté a des degrés: elle peut être plus grande dans un café, malgré les mouchards, que dans certains salons; dans une lettre, que dans un écrit publié, même sous pseudonyme. Pour combattre, elle exploitera

[1] H. Dieckmann, *Contes de Diderot* (London 1963), p. 10.

les événements présents, les anecdotes, les on-dit; elle couvrira ses attaques en procédant par allusions, antiphrases, faux-noms, anagrammes, jeux de mots, paraboles, etc. La conversation sera donc brillante et polémique. Brillante, elle doit plaire à l'imagination. Polémique, elle doit user de prudence. Voilà déjà deux traits que l'on retrouve dans les contes dont on peut dire comme des fables qu'il se peut très bien 'que, les hommes aimant naturellement les images et les contes, les gens d'esprit se soient amusés à leur en faire sans aucune autre vue', mais aussi, des hommes libres ayant peu besoin de déguiser la vérité, que l'on 'ne peut guère parler à un tyran qu'en paraboles, encore ce détour même est-il dangereux'.[2] La genèse du conte se conformerait donc assez facilement à un modèle théorique. On part de la conversation à bâtons rompus, avec ses traits et ses clins d'œil. On s'élève à quelque *narration continuée* par un des interlocuteurs: il lui faut jouer sa partie, tenir l'attention en haleine, conserver l'unité dans la variété des anecdotes et des dialogues. Que l'on suppose maintenant cette narration jouée par un homme de lettres—un Fontenelle, un Voltaire, un Diderot, un Galiani[3]—de même que la nature imite l'art, de même cette narration de salon imitera un récit littéraire. Sans doute, ce n'est pas assez: tout fin diseur, s'il ne récite pas, n'est pas capable d'écrire. Mais un Fontenelle, un Voltaire, etc., est capable, lui, d'opérer la transposition du parlé à l'écrit, de l'improvisé dans la chaleur d'une conversation à l'improvisé travaillé la plume à la main: désormais, l'imitation littéraire qui avait—ou pouvait avoir—inspiré la narration de salon devient, à son tour, imitée dans une narration écrite qui donne l'illusion de la parole spontanée.[4] Dans cette imitation d'imitation transparaissent les procédés de dramatisation et de dissimulation déjà sensibles dans le dialogue des gens d'esprit. Il n'est pas toujours possible, aujourd'hui, de saisir les allusions du conte, et même une fiche d'érudit n'en restitue pas le contexte qui en faisait une réalité vivante. Dans la mesure où il imitait une narration de

[2] Voltaire, *Dictionnaire philosophique*, au mot: 'Fable'.

[3] Sur Voltaire raconteur d'histoires, voir le témoignage du baron de Gleichen, cité par William F. Bottiglia, *Voltaire's Candide* (Genève 1964), pp. 57-58; sur Diderot, témoignage de Marmontel, *Mémoires* (Paris 1891), ii. 243 sq.; sur Galiani, témoignage de Diderot dans la Correspondance (éd. Roth).

[4] Est-il besoin de rappeler les paroles de Diderot? 'Lorsqu'on fait un conte, c'est à quelqu'un qui l'écoute: et pour peu que le conte dure, il est rare que le conteur ne soit pas interrompu quelquefois par son auditeur. Voilà pourquoi j'ai introduit dans le récit qu'on va lire . . .' AT. v. 311.

salon, datée et située, le conte philosophique a perdu pour nous une partie de son contenu objectif et de son sens philosophique. A oublier ce côté salonnard, journalistique, compère de Revue, on s'expose à ne pas comprendre les plaisanteries les plus simples—par exemple, pourquoi Frederic II s'appelle Luc et pourquoi il devient le roi des Bulgares[5]—à soumettre la structure du conte à une logique qui n'est pas la sienne, et à fausser les intentions.

En tout cas, le conte est appelé philosophique. L'adjectif est caractéristique du siècle. Et le siècle se caractérise, depuis Locke, Newton, et sous l'influence de Bayle—soit dit pour simplifier—par son hostilité aux systèmes métaphysiques. On ne croit plus la raison humaine capable d'atteindre aux trois objets fondamentaux de l'ontologie traditionnelle: l'âme, le monde, Dieu. Ni la substance ni la cause n'étant accessibles, on s'en tiendra aux accidents et aux effets, d'un mot: aux phénomènes. Attentif à l'expérience, on renoncera aux belles déductions du dogmatique. En apprenant à bien douter, on découvrira combien l'intolérance est insoutenable en théorie et insupportable en pratique. A railler les systèmes—l'optimisme de Leibniz, le fatalisme imputé à Spinoza—on luttera pour une meilleure harmonie entre les hommes. On exposera au lecteur l'*expérience formatrice* des personnages. L'argument sera remplacé par l'exemple. Le conte philosophique est un petit *Bildungsroman.* D'où certains thèmes qui, cette fois, ne doivent rien à des motivations mondaines, mais se rattachent à des considérations 'philosophiques'. D'abord, le thème du couple maître-disciple: Don Quichote était un enfant devant le bon-sens solide de Sancho; *El Criticon* —peut-être a-t-il servi à *Candide*—mettait en scène un voyageur naïf avec son tuteur réaliste; Télémaque suit Mentor; Candide a pour instructeur Pangloss ou Martin; Jacques n'est jamais sans son maître ou, plutôt, le maître ne va jamais sans Jacques. Ensuite, le voyage. Il a une fonction éducatrice. Sorti de la sujétion des précepteurs et, explique Descartes, 'me résolvant de ne chercher plus d'autre science, que celle qui se pourrait trouver en moi-même, ou bien dans le grand livre du monde, j'employai le reste de ma jeunesse à voyager, à voir des cours et des armées, à fréquenter des gens de

[5] On lit avec étonnement dans Paolo Alatri: *Voltaire, Diderot e il 'partito filosofico'* (Messina-Firenze 1965), p. 59, n. 1: '*Luc* era il soprannome che Voltaire dava a Federico II: e cio perché a Ferney aveva una scimmia che portava quel nome' (cf. S. Bettinelli, *Opere* (Venezia), xxi. 27-28). —Pour 'Bulgare', voir à ce mot le *Dictionnaire philosophique*.

diverses humeurs et conditions, à recueillir diverses expériences, à m'éprouver moi-même dans les rencontres que la fortune me proposait, et partout à faire telle réflexion sur les choses qui se présentaient, que j'en pusse tirer quelque profit. Car il me semblait que je pourrais rencontrer plus de vérité, dans les raisonnements que chacun fait touchant les affaires qui lui importent, et dont l'événement le doit punir bientôt après, s'il a mal jugé, que dans ceux que fait un homme de lettres dans son cabinet, touchant des spéculations qui ne produisent aucun effet, et qui ne lui sont d'autre conséquence, sinon que peut-être il en tirera d'autant plus de vanité qu'elles seront plus éloignées du sens commun, à cause qu'il aura dû employer d'autant plus d'esprit et d'artifice à tâcher de les rendre vraisemblables'.[6] La citation énonce le programme du XVIIIe siècle et définit au mieux une des intentions de ses romans—du picaresque au purement pédagogique comme l'*Émile* au Livre cinquième—et de ses contes. On ouvrira donc le livre du monde, on y accompagnera Candide sur trois continents, ou Jacques et son maître à travers une province de France. Enfin, la *naïveté* (ou l'*ignorance*) que corrige l'expérience. On civilise un homme naturel, on réveille un rêveur. Don Quichote, le voyageur naif de Gracian, Télémaque avaient précédé les persans de Montesquieu, Gil Blas, Candide, l'Ingénu, le maître de Jacques, etc.—et l'on observera combien leur naïveté schématisée, pour pédagogues, diffère de la naïveté plus médicale, métaphysicienne, héritière de la voyance du génie romantique—que l'on aura avec *l'Idiot* de Dostoïevski ou, plus modestement, avec *Goha le simple*, d'Adès et Josipovici. En antithèse, non la raison du philosophe, mais le bon sens, nourri d'expérience, de Sancho, du tuteur, de Mentor, de Martin, de Jacques, etc.

Si le conte est philosophique, il doit enseigner une vérité, non plus par déduction suivie de concepts, comme en philosophie, non plus comme le dialogue, qui, s'il peut avoir la verve d'un conte, n'argumente pas, en principe, sur la variété des aventures, non plus comme la fable—encore que la dernière phrase de *Candide* ou de *Jacques le fataliste* formule une moralité—dont l'allégorie est plus scolaire et la fausseté 'souvent sensible, comme lorsque l'on fait parler des animaux ou des arbres'.[7] Mais il doit enseigner à la manière d'un roman ou, plutôt, d'un 'petit roman'.[8]

[6] *Discours de la méthode*, AT. vi. 9-10.

[7] D'Alembert, dans ses *Synonymes* aux mots 'Conte, fable, roman'.

[8] C'est l'expression, par exemple, de la

Comment concilier entre elles la vérité philosophique et la vérité d'un récit d'imagination, même s'il en conte de belles? La vérité philosophique est—ou devrait être—logique: abstraite, universelle, déductible. La vérité du récit est la semblance au vrai, la vraisemblance: concrète, individuelle, imprévisible. D'un côté, une déductibilité intemporelle; de l'autre, une suite d'événements, et déduit-on l'Histoire? Encore le roman 'réaliste'—le XVIIIe siècle l'appelait historique—fera-t-il de *l'exemple* un *intermédiaire* entre la généralité des maximes morales et l'individualité de l'expérience: ainsi professait un Huet ou un Aubert de la Chesnaye des Bois,[9] et cette profession demeure la doctrine—ou le prétexte—d'un Prévost, d'un Diderot, d'un Rousseau, d'un Laclos[10]. Toutefois, tandis que le roman offre l'exemple d'*une destinée*, c'est-à-dire, en imitation, l'exemple d'une vérité historique, le conte, même quand il prend pour thème *la* destinée—sous-titre de *Zadig*—en fait un thème philosophique où la liberté d'invention éloigne encore plus de l'Histoire. Qui ne voit la contradiction? La vérité profonde du 'petit roman' n'est pas romanesque, mais philosophique—ses personnages ne proposent pas des exemples, mais des illustrations d'idées, des idées illustrées—, et le philosophique doit avoir la vie imaginative d'un conte. A certains—André Le Breton, David F. Strauss—la contradiction paraît insoluble: le conte philosophique est un genre faux.[11] Leur tort, réplique justement William F. Bottiglia,[12] est d'en vouloir juger d'après les critères du roman réaliste. Qu'en est-il?

Si, avec la psychanalyse, on entend par dramatisation la mise de l'idée ou, plutôt, du désir, en images, on peut chercher comment une philosophie se dramatise dans le conte. Ce n'est plus par la disparition de la pensée vigile: au contraire, cette pensée se veut plus que jamais alerte et en alerte. Souvent, elle doit tromper la censure; aussi use-t-elle de fables, mais consciemment, par calculs, et non, à la façon du rêve, par symbolisation involontaire. Et puis

Correspondance littéraire du 1 mars 1759: 'M. de Voltaire vient de nous égayer par un petit roman intitulé *Candide ou l'optimisme . . .*'.

[9] D. Huet, *Traité de l'origine des romans* (1ère éd. 1760), p. 216. Aubert de La Chesnaye des Bois, *Lettres amusantes et critiques sur le roman . . .* (1743), p. 20.

[10] Prévost pour présenter *Manon*; Diderot, dans l'*Éloge de Richardson*; Rousseau, dans la seconde Préface de *La Nouvelle Héloïse*; Laclos, dans l'article 'Sur le roman', *Mercure de France* (17 avril 1784).

[11] André Le Breton, *Le Roman français au XVIIIe siècle* (1898), pp. 216-220. David F. Strauss, *Voltaire*, trad. (Paris 1876), pp. 169-174.

[12] *Op. cit.*, p. 57.

elle veut faire un conte, amuser, inventer des imaginations riantes. Pour échapper à la censure ou pour plaire, elle recourt à la dramatisation philosophique. D'où vient l'image? De deux sources. D'abord, l'auteur a observé, il a vécu: il a rencontré des hommes, entendu des mots de caractère, épié le manège d'un chien, suivi les échos d'un tremblement de terre; toutes sortes de circonstances lui ont fourni l'occasion de réflexions 'philosophiques', si bien que, reprenant ces réflexions, il en a, pourrait-on dire, les illustrations toutes prêtes. D'autre part, l'auteur a médité, il a lu: il peut puiser dans ses lectures—ainsi, démarquer des passages de *Tristram Shandy*—et, souvent, déduire sans peine d'un thème philosophique—la relativité de toutes choses, par exemple—les figures qui le concrétisent: Gulliver, Micromégas, la nouvelle Mélusine. En principe, les images issues de la première source sont les plus 'réalistes', elles appartiennent à l'ordre du souvenir. Les images issues de la seconde source sont plus libres, plus disparates. Que l'image donne à penser, que la pensée s'image, l'idée entre en action et l'on peut commencer un conte. Le titre en indique le thème. Tout y paraît improvisé sur canevas, comme une *Commedia dell'Arte*. C'est le canevas d'une leçon de scepticisme ou, ce qui revient au même, de sagesse et de tolérance. La syntaxe du récit reste simple, elle a pour règle la rencontre qui multiplie les points de vue: l'auteur rencontre bien ou mal selon l'imprévisible de sa verve. Le vocabulaire, ce sont les images. Il va du réalisme à l'abstraction allégorique, renvoie à la vie quotidienne ou parle par l'énigme des symboles. Dès lors, a-t-on à exposer la relativité de nos croyances? On fera voyager le lecteur pour le déconcerter par la diversité des mœurs, soit réelles, soit utopiques, on le dépaysera dans un monde à une autre échelle. A son vocabulaire on juge le conteur. Inépuisable en réalismes avec *Jacques*, Diderot manque d'imagination orientale avec *Les bijoux indiscrets*; élégant dans ses turqueries, Voltaire aurait reculé devant le bric-à-brac d'emblèmes maçonniques de *La flûte enchantée* et n'aurait pas été capable de l'élever à l'onirisme d'un *Conte* de Goethe.[13] Que l'on compare *Gulliver*, *Micromégas*, *La Nouvelle Mélusine*: combien une même pensée permet de dramatisations diverses! Cependant, Diderot, lorsqu'il décalque la réalité au plus près, intitule significativement son récit: *Ceci n'est pas un conte*. Dans le

[13] Généralement traduit en français sous le titre: *Le Serpent vert*. On se rappelle que *Die neue Melusina* est, aussi, de Goethe.

pays du conte, le temps ne dure pas, l'espace est imaginaire. Il en résulte que les personnages se changent vite en pantins, en marionnettes. Paul Vernières l'a dit de *Jacques*,[14] Naves, Hazard, etc. l'ont dit des protagonistes de *Candide*;[15] on incrimine la rapidité des événements qui les entraînent sans leur laisser le loisir de vivre d'une façon très individuelle; on découpe leurs gesticulations de fantoches 'portant cependant quelques unes des marques profondes de l'humaine condition' (Hazard). Quoi! les événements sont incroyables, et l'on s'y attache? les personnages sont des fantoches, mais vivants?

Vivants, oui. Ce réalisme de l'imaginaire ne doit pas étonner, puisque, déjà, la perception choisit, ne retient que ce qui intéresse, guide, signifie. A plus forte raison, toute description artistique ne se forme que sur des sens: l'acteur représente la marche, il ne marche pas; la pomme peinte représente la pomme; le repas est un accessoire de théâtre, non un besoin physiologique; le Nouvel Orléans, à la fin de *Manon*, n'a pas à respecter l'information géographique, il signifie, l'exil, un lieu sauvage, la tyrannie du gouverneur, l'espoir déçu d'un nouveau monde, comme l'Eldorado, en *Candide*, est le symbole de l'Eldorado. En bref, le réel n'est jamais donné, mais choisi, et il n'y a pas plus de vraisemblance absolue que de vrai absolu. La vraisemblance de l'*Astrée* n'est pas celle du *Roman comique*; celle de *Marianne* n'est pas celle de *Madame Bovary*; *l'Assommoir* n'est pas plus vrai que *La Princesse de Clèves*. Il suffit que l'auteur séduise à son jeu. On appelle 'réalisme' un genre seulement du réalisme de l'imaginaire: la maison du père Goriot est déjà le portrait du père Goriot dans un certain style; le château de Thunder-ten-tronckh, c'est le portrait d'une baronnie dans un autre style. Si l'on garde pour modèle un certain réalisme, alors, faudra-t-il dire, les marionnettes sont plus vraies que vraisemblables: elles n'expriment que l'essentiel, comme le masque tragique ou comique; un enfant peut les reconnaître; il rit ou il pleure avec elles, Leur pureté géométrique les cerne en un sens univoque. Il semble qu'ici comme ailleurs l'univocité de sens exige un traitement opératoire; la seule façon d'animer ces marionnettes est de les combiner dans une action perpétuelle, multiple, à suspens, alors qu'inversement, dans le roman psychologique, où les personnages sont multivoques, l'action importe moins que l'analyse et peut, même, être supprimée. De plus,

[14] Paul Vernière: *Diderot et l'invention littéraire, à propos de Jacques le Fataliste* (R.H.L.F., avril–juin, 1954).

[15] Bottiglia, *op. cit.*, p. 70.

dire que la marionnette est univoque—qu'elle est, d'un bloc, le fataliste, l'ingénu, le candide, etc.—équivaut à la définir par un seul attribut: elle est donc à la fois un personnage singulier et un universel vide, une substance qui n'est rien de plus que ce qu'elle apparaît, qui ne peut pas être la source interne de ses prédicats et ne peut recevoir ses accidents que du dehors, qui demeure même en dehors de ce qui lui arrive, le temps ne la modifiant guère, une intériorité figée dans une extériorité tumultueuse. Le conte est une expérimentation mentale où l'on montre comment réagit une qualité pure dans différents milieux. Cette qualité pure, abstraite, obtenue par analyse, est, en général, la candeur, l'ingénuité, l'innocence, où l'on reconnaît aussitôt la *tabula rasa*, le *white paper* de l'empirisme. Le personnage principal est ainsi l'homme naturel. C'est donc un homme théorique dont peut user le pédagogue, soit pour exposer la conflit de la nature et de la culture, soit pour dénoncer la folie de s'obstiner au théorique dans la pratique—l'irréalité du système contre la réalité de l'expérience—soit pour combiner ensemble les deux enseignements. Comme l'imagination, chez Kant, doit servir d'intermédiaire entre la sensibilité et l'entendement ou la raison, il convient que le personnage du conte philosophique tienne à la fois du concret et de l'abstrait, offre le symbole aisément perceptible non pas tant d'une idée théorique que d'une idée pratique; ou, plutôt, puisqu'il doit être un personnage, disons que ce symbole est un idéogramme. Le conte philosophique est un conte idéogrammatique.

Ce discours idéogrammatique ne saurait avoir les mêmes articulations que le discours logique du philosophe. Ils n'ont pas la même grammaire, le même dictionnaire. Le conteur utilise une espèce de langage d'action, le gestuel; le philosophe, un langage de convention—parfois des pires conventions! A propos de l'art des pantomimes, Voltaire a souligné la différence, car cet art 'ne peut plaire que lorsqu'on représente une action marquée, un événement théâtral qui se dessine aisément dans l'imagination du spectateur. On peut représenter Orosmane tuant Zaïre . . . Mais comment des pantomimes peindront-ils la dissertation de Maxime et de Cinna sur les gouvernements monarchiques et populaires?'[16] Diderot est allé plus loin dans la *Lettre sur les sourds et muets*. Et l'on pourrait citer toute le littérature du XVIIIe siècle sur le langage. On se contentera ici d'observer qu'un discours idéogrammatique ne se prête pas à un

[16] *Dictionnaire philosophique*, au mot: 'Chant, Musique'.

développement philosophique. Ce que gagne la vie se perd pour l'abstraction. Nos marionnettes vivantes ressemblent à des personnages, mais les schématisent; elles sont jetées dans une suite de rencontres qui ressemble à de l'Histoire, mais cette Histoire ne se déroule pas dans un temps historique; elles dialoguent mais c'est sans réfléchir, en récitant la leçon qu'on leur souffle, sans procéder à l'analyse réflechie du philosophe. Au résultat, la philosophie enseignée se ramène à des remarques de bon sens sur un thème philosophique; elle réflète le schématisme des personnages; elle ne dépasse pas la moralité d'une fable.

Est-ce à dire que le conte philosophique soit un genre faux? Non pas! Nous y prenons trop de plaisir—et, il est important de le noter, un plaisir qui se renouvelle à chaque lecture—pour qu'il ne satisfasse pas à une vérité fondamentale. Mais, de même que l'on s'égare à réduire le réalisme à un type de réalisme—celui que Balzac et Flaubert porteront à sa perfection—de même s'égarerait-on à vouloir enchaîner la philosophie tout entière aux chaînes de raisons d'un Spinoza ou d'un Hegel. La philosophie du conte fût-elle puérile, il n'en serait pas, du coup, condamné *comme genre littéraire.* Or, elle n'est puérile que si l'on en fausse l'intention: elle ne se veut pas théorique, mais polémique. C'est une *idée* qu'elle défend, ce n'est pas un système qu'elle échafaude. Et cette idée, qu'elle défend, —qu'est-ce qu l'homme naturel? qu'est-ce que l'homme?—est bien digne d'un philosophe.

Il se pourrait, d'ailleurs, que la philosophie fût un conte, et non pas seulement au sens où le XVIIIe siècle était toujours prêt à le dire ironiquement pour ne voir en tout système dogmatique qu'une fable. Au reste, ce ne serait pas la priver de valeur que de lui accorder sans ironie, le sérieux d'une fable, d'en faire une mythologie de la raison, propre à nous désigner, comme le mythe chez Platon, des vérités inaccessibles à la science. Les réflexions, aujourd'hui, de bien des philosophes sur la poésie fondatrice et révélatrice de l'être ne vont-elles pas parfois en ce sens? Pour parler en psychologue, on peut se demander si l'emploi d'un vocabulaire technique là où il ne saurait définir univoquement un objet ou une manœuvre, ne dissimule pas une technique de l'imagination.[17] Que de fois le philo-

[17] C'est ce que j'ai essayé de montrer dans mon Essai: *Les philosophes et leur langage* (Paris 1952). translated by Norbert Guterman: *Philosophers and their Language* (Ohio University Press 1967).

sophe ne semble-t-il pas personnaliser des notions abstraites, quand, les utilisant comme sujets grammaticaux, il en fait des agents de verbes, si bien que l'attention observe, la volonté décide, la liberté choisit, etc.? Est-il certain que ces notions ne soient pas alors des marionnettes, plus abstraites que celles du conte? Est-il certain que leurs aventures logiques ou dialectiques—plus éloignées encore de l'Histoire que les aventures du conte—ne passionnent pas celui qui peut les suivre à la manière d'un roman? Ne faut-il pas prendre à la lettre l'expression de Schelling: Odyssée de la conscience?

Quoi qu'il en soit, le conte, tel qu'il s'est développé au XVIIIe siècle, devait à coup sûr disparaître avec un certain art de la conversation, un certain public limité, une certaine forme de censure, etc. Qu'en reste-t-il? Il renaît, il subsiste avec de nouveaux moyens d'expression: les dessins animés, les 'comics', dont la philosophie simpliste relève moins de la polémique et davantage de la propagande; avec, surtout, les science-fictions, que peuvent lire les ignorants de la science et qui, dans le pays imaginaire des merveilles scientifiques, soulèvent des questions dont on découvrira demain, peut-être, qu'elles sont des questions de vie ou de mort.

Scotland and the French Enlightenment

J. H. Brumfitt

The dawn of the eighteenth century witnessed the extinction of the political independence of Scotland. Yet it also saw the beginning of that country's greatest period of intellectual and literary achievement. During the next hundred years or so, men like Hume, Robertson, Adam Smith, 'Ossian', Burns and Scott—to mention only the greatest—were to give Scotland an influence on the development of European culture out of all proportion to the smallness of her population. Moreover, though the union with England undoubtedly contributed to this florescence by furthering the economic well-being of the country, by strengthening Scots' contacts with a then more developed culture and by providing a wider reading public for the new Scottish writers, yet in both the literary and philosophical spheres, Scotland was to maintain an independent life of its own. Indeed, the second half of the eighteenth century, when the Scottish renaissance was bearing fruit, was for England a period of relative decline. This contrast was noted as far afield as Italy by the perspicacious Carlo Denina of Turin. Not surprisingly, his *Discorso sopra le vicende della letteratura* which stressed the importance of the Scottish achievement was to be published by the Glasgow printer Foulis and in September, 1764, passages from it were given pride of place in *The Scots Magazine*.

If Scottish intellectual life was to maintain some degree of independence, so too, though in a rather different way, was Scottish political life. This, of course, was markedly true of the first half of the century where the outstanding events of the political scene were the two Jacobite risings. At this time a relatively tumultuous Scotland confronted a quiescent England. In the second half of the century, however, the rôles tended to be reversed. Whilst England witnessed the growth of political radicalism associated particularly with the Wilkite movement, Scotland remained superficially passive. The agitation for a Scottish militia aroused some enthusiasm, but its appeal was a limited one. The demands for borough and parliamentary reform only really developed towards the end of the century. In part this estrangement of the Scots from developments in England was due to the xenophobic anti-Scottish prejudices of Wilkes himself who could discern no sense in the struggle of 'Goth against Goth' and who regarded all Scots as the tools of Lord Bute. In part, no doubt, it resulted from unpleasant memories of 1745 and from the determination to avoid at all costs yet another outburst of civil strife. Yet this situation was to change rapidly with the advent of the French Revolution when Scotland suddenly became the scene of a wave of democratic political agitation which outstripped, in speed at any rate, that of the radical societies south of the Border; so much so that in 1793 Edinburgh was chosen as the meeting place of the ill-fated British Convention of reformist societies and forty-five Scottish societies sent delegates. If the Scottish Jacobins, as they were called, were soon crushed in what was little short of a reign of terror, the speed and intensity of their growth suggest that, beneath the apparently calm surface of Scottish life in the previous decades, things had been happening which were parallel, though by no means identical, with developments in England.

The primary causes of these independent developments lie, no doubt, in the nature of Scottish society. Yet it is at least possible that they may also owe something to the continued influence—literary, philosophical and political—of Scotland's old ally, France. In these circumstances it is of interest to examine both the debt of the Scottish Enlightenment to French thought and the general dissemination of the ideas of the French Enlightenment in Scotland. Though the first of these tasks has been partly accomplished by biographers of men like Hume and Smith, there are still many aspects of the problem which remain to be investigated. This paper, however, is not concerned with them, but has the more restricted aim of investigating some of the media by which French Enlightenment thought penetrated Scotland.

The most obvious, but at the same time the most striking way in which the Scots learnt of the French Enlightenment was by direct contact. The traffic was one-way, for the *philosophes*, even when they visited England, did not penetrate to Scotland. But for centuries the Scots themselves had turned to Europe—to France and Holland in particular—for their intellectual contacts and professional training, and if these bonds began to be loosened in the eighteenth century in favour of closer links with England, they were still very strong. The links with the Dutch universities were particularly close, especially for the study of medicine and law. Two distinguished but typical cases may serve to illustrate this. The Edinburgh physician, Archibald Pitcairne—an outspoken freethinker and Jacobite—had taught at Leyden and had had the great Boerhaave and Mead among his pupils,[1] and the legal reformer Duncan Forbes of Culloden had also, like many leading Scots jurists, studied in Holland.[2] The Scots, moreover, were financially and commercially active in Europe. The career of John Law or that of the Hope family of bankers in Holland are two examples in the former category; that of John Black, wine-merchant in Bordeaux, friend of Montesquieu and father of the chemist Joseph Black may serve to illustrate the commercial links between France and Scotland[3]—though this particular link was to be somewhat slackened by the English insistence that the Scots should drink Port (from England's oldest ally) rather than their traditional claret.

Such ties, of course, do not necessarily imply direct contact with the French Enlightenment, though at times they could lead to this as in the case of the correspondence (now lost) between Black and Montesquieu. But the intellectual predominance of France in Europe meant that any visitor with philosophical or literary pretensions, whatever the ostensible purpose of his visit, was almost bound to make contact with the thought of the *philosophes*. Here we may cite as typical the experience of Boswell in Holland. Boswell came to Utrecht to study law, but he devoted his spare time to reading Voltaire and writing French free compositions, longed for the day when he could visit Paris and had little but contempt for the small-town life of the Dutch provincial city. How he

[1] H. G. Graham, *Scottish men of letters in the eighteenth century* (1901), p. 8.

[2] C. R. Fay, *Adam Smith and the Scotland of his day* (1956), p. 15.

[3] R. Shackleton, *Montesquieu* (1961), p. 209.

envied his friend and compatriot George Dempster his sojourn in the French capital![4]

If the union with England was tending to diminish these traditional contacts, two other important factors had the effect of increasing them. The first of these was the exile, voluntary or otherwise, of the Scottish Jacobites. Many were to play a significant rôle in European life and thought—Rousseau's protector 'Milord Maréchal', for example, or, perhaps most significant of all, the chevalier Ramsay, whose influence on the growth of French freemasonry and whose rôle in sponsoring the idea of the *Encyclopédie* were of paramount importance. Nor did the exiles cease to have influence in their own country. Ramsay, for example, encouraged the Foulis brothers, who visited him during their European travels, to open their Glasgow bookshop and publishing house.[5]

Another important factor was the extent to which Scots, and more particularly Scots academics, travelled abroad as tutors to the sons of the aristocracy, for they were far more venturesome than their colleagues in the English universities.[6] It was in this way, for example, that Adam Smith visited France, and Scots tutors were much sought after by both Scots and English nobles embarking on the grand tour. How numerous the former were, and how keen they were to establish contact with the French Enlightenment may be judged from the number of them who took the trouble to visit its patriarch at Ferney. Approximately a third of 'Voltaire's British Visitors' listed in the study of that name by Sir Gavin de Beer came from remote and relatively underpopulated Scotland.[7]

Many of the leading figures of the Scottish Enlightenment were among the European travellers, including Adam Ferguson and, of course, David Hume who received an almost triumphal reception in Paris. But those who did not travel, or who travelled but rarely, had to rely on other sources of information. The most obvious of these was the press; obvious, but not extensive, for in the eighteenth century Scotland boasted only one journal with pretensions to seriousness—or at any rate only one to survive for any length of time. The *Scots Magazine*, moreover, was often parochial in outlook

[4] *Boswell in Holland, 1763–1764*, ed. F. A. Pottle (1952), pp. 12-13, 38-39 and *passim*.

[5] G. D. Henderson, *Chevalier Ramsay* (1952), p. 199.

[6] Fay, *op. cit.*, p. 18.

[7] *Studies on Voltaire and the eighteenth century* (1957), iv. 7 ff.

and when it did look further afield it was often content to borrow articles from the *Gentleman's Magazine* or book reviews from other English sources such as the *Monthly Review*. It hardly seems to prepare the way for the achievements of the *Edinburgh Review* early in the following century. Nevertheless, it did contain a considerable amount of information about the French *philosophes*—a fact which is all the more striking because it contrasts with the journal's general colourlessness.

Foreign literatures other than French find little or no place in its pages, but French literature is well represented, above all in the person of its most distinguished practitioner, Voltaire. Translations from his works are numerous. In 1750–51 one finds extracts from his *History of the Crusades* and a brief summary of *Zadig*. In 1752, passages from the *Siècle de Louis XIV*. In 1755 an account of *L'Orphelin de la Chine*, in 1757 his description of the 1745 rebellion, in 1758 an 'Ode to the King of Prussia' and a long extract from *The Travels of Scarmentado*; in 1764, part of the final prayer of the *Treatise on Tolerance*; in 1773, a descriptive passage dealing with Oliver and Richard Cromwell. In addition, there are numerous letters, genuine and spurious, by Voltaire, three portraits of the man, numerous anecdotes about him and, of course, notices of many and reviews of some of his books. The reader of the *Magazine* could not fail to be acquainted with much of his work. Yet his direct acquaintance would be restricted, on the whole, to the relatively non-controversial side of this work—to the histories, the plays and the *contes*. Voltaire is praised as a champion of religious tolerance, but such an attitude was not regarded as unorthodox in Protestant Scotland. However, one finds no extracts from his philosophical or deistic works and such reviews of these as there are are predominantly hostile. *Candide*, for example, receives unsympathetic treatment (May 1759), the reviewer being mainly concerned to point out that Voltaire has failed to understand the doctrine of optimism. The reviewer of the *Dictionnaire philosophique* (December 1764) after a brief tribute to Voltaire's literary genius, passes to a condemnation of him for 'the prostitution of those abilities on trifling and obscene subjects, for his prejudices against revealed religion and for his affecting on every occasion to ridicule the sacred writings especially those of the Old Testament'. In April 1766, an article entitled 'Misrepresentations of Voltaire confuted', which deals with passages in *La Philosophie de l'histoire*, adopts a similar tone, the author pointing out the need for such criticism 'as there appears a strong bias, expecially among the younger sort, to rely upon him as a sure guide in history, on account of his spritely and agreeable manner of writing, while his principles are irreligious, and favourable to the gratification of criminal passions.' In January 1767, there is a brief notice of *Le Philosophe ignorant* couched in similar terms and in August of the same year, a review of Larcher's *Supplément à la philosophie de l'histoire* is made the occasion for an even longer diatribe against the pernicious influence of the Sage of Ferney. Thus, although Voltaire's unorthodox views are never given a fair hearing in the pages of *The Scots Magazine*, they are certainly brought to the reader's notice. One suspects moreover, that the ponderous denunciations of their immorality, coupled with the indications of their popularity with the young might well have increased rather than diminished the number of their readers.

No other *philosophe* receives such thorough treatment, and only Rousseau comes anywhere near to doing so. A translation of the *Discours sur les sciences et les arts* is no more than listed (April 1752), though two years later, in its next reference to Jean-Jacques (anent the *Lettre sur la musique française*), the *Magazine* is already referring to him as 'The famous M. J. Rousseau of Geneva'. In January 1761 there appears a review of *La Nouvelle Héloïse* and from then onwards a number of his letters appear as well as a remarkably inexact account of his life (January 1766), a description of his disputes with Geneva (1765 and 1766) and, of course, a full account of his celebrated quarrel with Hume (December 1766). From these extracts and comments the reader could hardly piece together a coherent view of Rousseau's thought, though it may be noted that their tone often indicates that the author expects him to be acquainted with Rousseau from other sources.

Apart from these two main figures, however, the French Enlightenment receives little notice. Surprisingly, in view of the extent of his influence on the Scottish Enlightenment, Montesquieu is hardly mentioned save that translations and editions of his works are listed among new books. Diderot, Condillac, the *Encyclopédie* are passed over in silence. Maupertuis is more fortunate, for in 1759 there are long extracts from a 'Letter to the King of Prussia from M. de Maupertuis on the progress of the sciences'. D'Holbach's *Système de la nature*, *Système social* and *Le Bon sens* all receive brief hostile notices (February 1771, January 1773, August 1773) though Raynal's *Histoire philosophique* is reviewed in most favourable terms (August 1772). But *The Scots Magazine* can hardly be said to give its readers any hint of the existence, let alone of the doctrines of the 'philosophical movement'. They were, it is true, made aware of political opposition to the regime, but only of opposition from the Parlements whose struggles against royal authority are described in some detail and with some sympathy. In June 1771, for example, there appears a description of the state of Paris which ends prophetically in the following terms: 'The King is deaf to all this distress which he has occasioned, indulging himself with the company of Mme Barré, going a hunting, etc.; but it is the opinion of every thinking man there, that a speedy revolution cannot fail to take place, as it is daily expected to hear of the King's assassination.'

Though, as the links with England grew, more English periodicals found their way north of the Border, *The Scots Magazine* continued to maintain its almost unique position. There was, however, one significant, though short-lived attempt to establish a rival. In 1755–1756 there appeared two numbers of *The Edinburgh Review*—a journal which was to some extent a propaganda vehicle for the moderate party within the Scottish Church and had the support of many of the leading figures of the Scottish Enlightenment, Robertson and Blair among them. The contributors included Adam Smith whose review of continental literature shows that the journal, had it survived, would have had a refreshingly cosmopolitan as well as an enlightened outlook. Smith discusses the *Encyclopédie* at some length, emphasising its debt to English thought, summarises the new scientific work of Buffon and others, lavishes the highest praise on Voltaire and analyses Rousseau's *Discours sur l'inégalité*. The breadth of his view contrasts markedly with the absence of any similar perspective in *The Scots Magazine*.[8]

The *Edinburgh Review* did not escape the attacks of the Church traditionalists, though it had certainly attempted to do so. In par-

[8] *The Scots Magazine* itself printed part of the article (March 1756). See also John Rae, *Life of Adam Smith* (1895), pp. 123-124 and W. L. Mathieson, *The Awakening of Scotland* (1910), p. 202.

ticular, the project appears to have been kept secret from Hume despite the latter's close links with many of the contributors.[9] The participation, perhaps even the overt support of a noted atheist might have prejudiced the journal's chances. This caution on the part of the leading figures of the Scottish Enlightenment and the intolerance characteristic of the defenders of tradition manifest themselves in other ways too: in, for example, Adam Smith's reluctance to arrange for the publication of Hume's *Essay on Suicide*, in the troubles Smith brought upon himself by his defence of Hume after the latter's death, in the reprimand which Hume himself received when, as Librarian of the Advocates' Library, he introduced to its shelves such immoral works as the *contes* of La Fontaine.[10] It follows that the contents of public libraries cannot be taken as an indication of the reading habits of the public. Private libraries, however, can provide some useful information, one of the best examples here being that of Adam Smith. Smith's library clearly demonstrates the importance of French influences on one leading figure in the Scottish Enlightenment, for nearly half the books are in French and they include works of d'Alembert, Bayle, Boulanger, Condillac, Diderot, Helvétius, Holbach, Mably, Montesquieu, Raynal and, of course, the complete works of Voltaire and Rousseau, as well as more specialised writings on economics and volumes of the remonstrances etc. of the Parlements.[11]

However, if we seek to find which books were most widely read, our surest method is to discover which ones Scottish publishers found it profitable to translate and publish. An examination of these suggests a considerably greater measure of Scottish interest in the work of the *philosophes* than is indicated by the pages of *The Scots Magazine*.

Edinburgh was the main centre of the Scottish book trade and though increasingly the Edinburgh publishers forged links with their London counterparts, they still retained a large measure of independence. Their activities in the past had often been restricted to the publication of works of religious edification and controversy, but after 1745, when Scotland was recovering rapidly from the effects of the Rebellion, their attitude quickly broadened. The

[9] E. C. Mossner, *The Life of David Hume* (1954), p. 338.

[10] *Ibid.*, p. 253.

[11] James Bonar, *A Catalogue of the library of Adam Smith* (1932).

juxtaposition of the old world with the new, together with an interesting example of the convergence of the two, may be observed in the titles of three books published in Edinburgh in 1755 and advertised in *The Scots Magazine: The Deist stretched upon a death-bed; or, A lively portraiture of a dying infidel; Mahomet the impostor, A tragedy. By M. de Voltaire*, and *Earthquakes explained and practically improved.*

However, from 1750 onwards, Edinburgh publishers, particularly Donaldson, Kincaid, Hamilton and Balfour, produced a steady stream of editions and translations of the works of the major French *philosophes*. In the cases of Montesquieu, Voltaire and Rousseau, these have been listed in a useful bibliographical study by A. K. Howard.[12] Montesquieu's *Esprit des lois* was published in 1750 by Hamilton and Balfour who also, in the same year, published a translation of the two chapters dealing with the English constitution. An English translation of the complete work appeared in Aberdeen in 1750 and five further editions were published in Edinburgh later in the century. The *Lettres persanes* and the *Considérations* also appeared in Edinburgh, the first in translation, the second both in translation and in the original French. Voltaire, as one might expect, was even more frequently published and translated. The *Histoire de Charles XII*, *Mahomet*, *Le Siècle de Louis XIV*, *The History of the war of 1741*, The *Essay on customs* (under various titles like its French original), *Candidus* (three editions), *The History of the misfortunes of John Calas*, *An Essay on crimes and punishments* (three editions), all these, together with lesser writings and letters, were published in Edinburgh during the second half of the century. As for Rousseau, he is represented by a ten-volume translation of the complete works (1773–74) as well as by translations of *The Cunning Man* [*Le Devin du village*] (1786), *Julia or the new Eloisa* (1794) and *Emilius* (1763, 1768 and 1773).

One might expect that Edinburgh, the capital city and traditional cultural centre of Scotland would respond in this way to the growing interest in the French Enlightenment. The case of Glasgow, however, furnishes more striking evidence. At the beginning of the eighteenth century, Glasgow was a small town of about twelve thousand inhabitants with little culture and a reputation for Calvin-

[12] Alison K. Howard, 'Montesquieu, Voltaire and Rousseau in eighteenth century Scotland', *The Bibliotheck* (1950), vol. ii.

istic austerity. It did not boast a bookshop until 1741 when the Foulis brothers returned from their continental tour to set up their printing and bookselling business. But from mid-century onwards, Glasgow expanded rapidly, its population rising by 1790 to sixty-two thousand.[13] Its culture blossomed simultaneously, and to this the book trade was no exception. The Foulis brothers themselves produced many excellent editions, particularly of the Classics and of English literature. Though on the whole they were Jacobite and latitudinarian in sympathies and more in tune with the Christian humanism of Fénelon or Ramsay than with the ideals of the French Enlightenment, they did publish a translation of Voltaire's *Charles XII*, d'Alembert's *La Destruction des Jésuites*, and, most surprisingly, Voltaire's *Pucelle d'Orléans*.[14]

However, a far more interesting case is that of the other important Glasgow printer and publisher, Robert Urie. Comparatively little is known about the man save that he was a printer and bookseller from about 1740 until his death in 1771. On the whole, his editions have no particular appeal to the bibliophile, being relatively cheap and sometimes rather carelessly printed. But the catalogue of his publications compiled by H. A. M'Lean[15] reveals strikingly the growing interest in the French Enlightenment. Urie started in a modest way in 1740 by printing four theological works by Andrew Gray and James Durham's *On Scandal.* In the forties he began to branch out from theology into literature with editions of Tacitus and Terence and *The Spectator*. In 1746 he published his first French work—the ever-popular *Télémaque*. In 1749, though theology is still predominant, there also appears a translation of Fontenelle's *Pluralité des mondes.*

In the fifties, Urie's output begins to increase (37 volumes in 1750) and so too do his publications in and translations from French (three volumes of Fénelon and two of Vertot in that year). In 1751 his first Voltaire translation, *The Temple of Taste*, appears, as do also Montesquieu's *Reflections* and *Persian Letters*. The next few years see further Voltaire editions (*Letters* and *The Age of Louis*

[13] H. G. Graham, *The Social life of Scotland in the eighteenth century* (1899), i. 136-137.

[14] Richard Duncan, *Notices and documents illustrative of the literary history of Glasgow* (1831), pp. 75 ff.

[15] Hugh A. M'Lean, 'Robert Urie, Printer in Glasgow', *Records of the Glasgow Bibliographical Society* (1913–14), iii. 89 ff. I am grateful to Professor I. D. McFarlane for drawing my attention to this article.

XIV) as well as a turning from Scottish theology towards the works of the English Enlightenment (Pope, Swift, Locke, Addison). But it is in the sixties that the output of French Enlightenment works becomes most striking. Sixteen volumes of Voltaire are published during this period, including the *Elements of Newtonian philosophy*, *The Philosophy of history*, the *Philosophic dictionary*, *The Ignorant philosopher*, *L'Ingénu* and the *Letters concerning the English people.* Some of the translations, like those of *La Philosophie de l'histoire*, *L'Ingénu*, *L'Homme aux 40 écus*, *La Princesse de Babylone* and *Le Philosophe ignorant* are published within a year of the original French edition. And though Urie specialises in Voltaire, he also publishes, for example, d'Alembert's *Miscellanies*, Formey's *Philosophy and Philosophers* and Rousseau's *Thoughts.*

From all these contacts, articles and publications it becomes apparent that a knowledge of the thought of the French Enlightenment was fairly widespread in the Scotland of the second half of the eighteenth century. How far and in what ways it influenced the Scottish Enlightenment is a complex question beyond the scope of this enquiry. It may, however, have had an influence of Scottish social and political life at the end of the century considerably greater than is immediately obvious.

The political and social ferment which characterised Scotland during the early years of the French Revolution was a remarkably wide phenomenon as has been demonstrated by H. W. Meikle in his study of *Scotland and the French Revolution.*[16] However, it lasted only a short time and was followed by a long period of repression. Many of the early radical enthusiasts like Thomas Somerville reacted sharply against the excesses of the Revolution and understandably sought to draw a veil over their earlier attitude and the reasons for it.[17] Even Burns, who probably remained a Jacobin at heart, found it expedient, after the outbreak of war, to write patriotic British ballads. It is only from his correspondence that we learn, for example, that the song which has become the Scottish national anthem was inspired as much by the struggle of the French revolutionaries as by those of Robert Bruce.[18] The nineteenth-century liberals, in their desire to establish the respectability of their ideas,

[16] Henry W. Meikle, *Scotland and the French Revolution* (1912).

[17] Thomas Somerville, *My own life and times* (1861), p. 264.

[18] See Meikle, *op. cit.*, pp. 121-122.

were often tempted to assert, as did Henry Cockburn in his description of the repression at the turn of the century, that there had never been any such thing as Scottish Jacobinism.[19] For these reasons there is probably a certain reluctance to admit to, let alone to describe, the influence of the more radical forms of French thought. Not that we would wish to suggest that these were in any sense decisive—it was Tom Paine's *Rights of Man* which above all stirred the minds of the reformers. But that they may have played their part in preparing the way for this awakening is suggested by the fact that one of them at least—and significantly the most 'respectable', Montesquieu—is often cited by the reformers.[20]

Other, more radical, thinkers were known too. A final example of the influence of one of these comes not from the great cities, but from remote and conservative Saint Andrews.[21] Thomas Chalmers was a student there in the nineties and was, as were a number of his contemporaries, strongly influenced by the teaching of James Brown who, although a 'marked man' continued to expound liberal ideas. In the sphere of politics it was the influence of Godwin that was paramount in this milieu. But what nearly ended Chalmers's distinguished ecclesiastical career before it had fairly begun was his reading, whilst still a divinity student, of Mirabaud's [*sic*] *System of Nature*. This produced a more shattering effect on him than it had on the young Goethe, though happily (if surprisingly) he was later reconverted by the arguments of the Aberdeen theologian, James Beattie.[22] Yet this evidence of the impact of radical 'philosophic' ideas in the very citadel of the established order is one further indication of how far they had been able to penetrate.

[19] Henry Cockburn, *Memorials of his time* (1856), p. 81.

[20] See, for example, Meikle, *op. cit.*, p. 17, re Macgrugar and *Letters of George Dempster to Sir Adam Fergusson*, ed. James Fergusson (1934), p. 347. But many other thinkers of the Scottish Enlightenment acknowledge a debt to Montesquieu.

[21] The University's Chancellor was Henry Dundas and the town was one of the first to introduce 'loyalty oaths' for suspected Jacobins (See Meikle, *op. cit.*, p. 116).

[22] William Hanna, *Memoirs of Thomas Chalmers* (1865), i. 8 and 29. D'Holbach's work was originally, and in the English translation, attributed to Mirabaud.

Molière à la fin du Siècle des Lumières

Otis Fellows

> Il est un petit nombre d'écrivains qui ont un privilège: ils ont peint l'homme, l'humanité même, et comme elle ils deviennent un sujet inépuisable, éternel, d'observations et d'études. Tels sont et seront toujours Molière, La Fontaine, Montaigne.
>
> (Sainte-Beuve, *Nouveaux Lundis*, mars 24, 1862)

En essayant de lier le nom de Molière à la fin du siècle des lumières et surtout à la Révolution française on risque de provoquer immédiatement l'une des répliques les plus célèbres de son théâtre: 'Que diable allait-il faire dans cette galère?'—le 'il' se rapportant, bien entendu, à Molière et non au jeune Léandre des *Fourberies de Scapin.*

Il est pourtant incontestable que Molière se trouva étroitement mêlé à la tourmente révolutionnaire et que sa présence continua à se faire vivement sentir pendant toute cette période.

Les divers aspects de la fortune de Molière pendant la Révolution ont été maintes fois étudiés, mais nul essai n'a été tenté, autant que je sache, de présenter une synthèse générale de la question. C'est justement ce que je voudrais faire ici dans les limites étroites dont nous disposons.

Le premier de ces aspects qui a fait l'objet de patientes études au dix-neuvième siècle est celui du sort réservé aux dépouilles mortelles du grand auteur comique. Au premier abord, le sujet peut certes paraître macabre; mais il ne manque pas de jeter une lumière inattendue sur la vénération parfois équivoque qu'on eut alors pour Molière et les à-côtés singuliers de l'idéalisme révolutionnaire.[1] Rappelons-en les grandes lignes.

[1] Le sort probable des restes de Molière, surtout pendant la Révolution et les années qui l'ont suivie, a souvent piqué la curiosité des savants français,

Depuis de longues années Jean-Baptiste Poquelin, dit Molière, et le grand fabuliste, Jean de La Fontaine reposaient dans le petit cimetière Saint-Joseph à Paris. Les philosophes n'ignoraient pas l'endroit et Denis Diderot avait écrit ces mots aussi touchants qu'éloquents: 'Ce lieu sera toujours sacré pour les poètes et pour les gens de goût' (AT., vi. 333). 'Toujours', voilà bien un grand mot et Diderot n'aurait pu se tromper davantage. Un quart de siècle s'était à peine écoulé que Molière et La Fontaine étaient arrachés à leur éternel repos. Voici comment se passèrent les choses.

C'était en 1792, la Révolution commençait à battre son plein. Cette année fut marquée par un nombre d'incidents qui n'étaient que les signes avant-coureurs de la fureur populaire: la prise des Tuileries par le peuple, la destitution de Louis XVI, les 'Massacres de septembre', et l'élection de Robespierre à la Convention.

Le règne de la Terreur n'a pas encore commencé, mais les esprits en fermentation conçoivent bien des idées, bien des projets dont les plus singuliers, les plus fantaisistes, concernent directement Molière enterré depuis plus d'un siècle. Paris est alors divisé en sections dont la plupart portent des noms du passé, des noms militants ou évocateurs des vertus civiques de la Rome antique.

Or une de ces Sections armées avait son siège dans la chapelle Saint-Joseph qui était entourée de cette partie du cimetière où l'on croyait que Molière ainsi que La Fontaine reposaient. Pour faire honneur aux deux grands écrivains classiques et en même temps

qui ne se sont d'ailleurs jamais trouvés entièrement d'accord sur ce sujet si longtemps enveloppé de mystère. Voici une bibliographie sommaire des ouvrages suscités par la question:

Jean François Cailhava d'Estendoux, *Études sur Molière, ou Observations sur la vie, les mœurs, les ouvrages de cet auteur et sur la manière de jouer ses pièces* (Paris an X–1802); Alexandre Lenoir, *Musée des monuments français, ou Description historique et chronologique des statues* (Paris 1821), viii; Ulrich Richard Desaix, *La Relique de Molière du cabinet du baron Vivant Denon* (Paris 1880); Louis Moland, 'Histoire des restes de Molière de 1792 à 1799', *Revue de la Révolution* (1883), ii. 405-425.

Voir aussi *L'Intermédiaire des chercheurs et des curieux* (1864), i. 86 (M.T.: 'Les Tombes de Molière et de La Fontaine'); p. 109 (V.D.: 'Les Tombes de M. et de L.F. au P.L.'); p. 246 (Fr. L.: 'Tombes de M. et de L.F.'); (1875), viii. 452 (Saint-Frusquin: 'La Mâchoire de M.'); p. 538 (O.D.: 'La Mâchoire de M.'); (1959) nouvelle série, ix. 104 (un néophyte: 'Tombe commune de M. et de L.F.'); pp. 638-639 (Le Raboliot des Lettres: même titre); p. 1033 (Pierre Vernois: même titre).

Il y a, du reste, dans *Le Temps* du 17 novembre 1885 l'essai de Jules Loiseleur intitulé 'Les nouvelles controverses sur Molière à propos de récentes publications, VIII, Si les restes de Molière ont eu le sort de ceux de Voltaire'.

honorer ce coin de Paris, La Section abandonna son nom d'alors pour s'appeler 'Section de Molière et de La Fontaine'.

A peine la Section eut-elle reçu son nouveau nom que les citoyens, qui en faisaient partie, décidèrent d'ériger des monuments dignes de ces illustres morts. Or pour donner à ces monuments un éclat et une grandeur exemplaires, il fut décidé de chercher et de trouver les restes mortels—ou 'restes sacrés' pour employer la formule contemporaine—de ces deux géants de la littérature française.

L'exhumation de Molière eut lieu le 6 juillet 1792, et celle de La Fontaine le 21 novembre de la même année. Les restes, selon les documents du jour, furent mis dans deux coffres fermés à clef, et aussitôt transférés dans des caisses de sapin 'de deux pieds de long sur un pied et demi de large et un demi pied de haut'. La chapelle Saint-Joseph ayant été démolie pour faire place à un corps de garde les sectionnaires mirent les deux caisses dans le grenier du corps de garde.

L'Assemblée avait proclamé la patrie en danger à cause de l'avance des armées alliées; la chute de la royauté étant devenue un fait accompli, l'exécution de Louis XVI n'allait pas tarder. Tant d' événements importants firent bien vite oublier le prestige si récemment acquis par la présence matérielle et spirituelle de deux personnalités littéraires du 17e siècle. Avant la fin de l'année, la Section des poètes n'était qu'un souvenir fugitif; son nouveau nom était la Section Brutus. *Sic transit gloria mundi*![2]

Aussi, soucieux d'art et de littérature, ces quelques sectionnaires voulaient trouver le moyen de rendre hommage, à leur manière, à ce que, à leurs yeux, représentaient 'les restes augustes' de deux Français de grande renommée, aux activités pacifiques et apolitiques.

De ces fidèles il y en a surtout un qu'il serait impossible d'accuser de négligence ou d'indifférence vis-à-vis des augustes débris. C'était l'écrivain et l'auteur dramatique Jean François Cailhava d'Estendoux. Son dévouement sans bornes au souvenir du grand poète comique, son zèle féroce pour tout ce qui le concernait élèvent Cailhava au premier rang de ceux qui l'aimaient non pas sagement, peut-être, mais à la folie. Quand, en 1779, d'Alembert

[2] Nous lisons, par exemple, dans le *Journal de la Montagne*: 'Une députation de Molière-et-Lafontaine communique un arrêté qui change le nom de cette section en celui de section *Brutus*. Pour célébrer l'adoption de ce nom auguste, elle fera prononcer solennellement demain à 5 heures de relevée, l'oraison funèbre des patriotes Marat et Lepelletier.' (16 septembre 1793), no. 106, p. 744.

présenta le buste de Molière aux quarante immortels, c'est Cailhava qui composa le *Discours prononcé par Molière le jour de sa réception posthume à l'Académie.* C'est lui aussi qui nous raconte l'émotion qu'il ressentit au moment de la prétendue exhumation des squelettes de Molière et de La Fontaine. Ce fut, semble-t-il, une émotion égale à celle que Hamlet, prince du Danemark dut éprouver devant le tombeau d'Ophélie. Mais laissons la parole à Cailhava lui-même:

> J'ai pressé sur mon sein les têtes de ces deux hommes de génie; je les ai baisées religieusement: celle du fabuliste inimitable m'a fait verser des larmes d'attendrissement; je me suis prosterné devant celle du premier des comiques, et j'ai sollicité, j'ai obtenu la permission de la ceindre d'un papier sur lequel est écrit ce vers: 'C'est un homme qui . . . Ah! . . . un homme . . . un homme enfin.' (*Tartuffe*, acte I. scène vi.[3])

Or les dépouilles de Molière avaient été enfermées dans leur caisse quatre mois et demi avant l'exhumation de La Fontaine. Pour que Cailhava pût avoir les crânes des deux poètes dans ses mains, il est évident que la caisse de Molière dut être rouverte au moment de l'exhumation de La Fontaine. On a nettement l'impression, du reste, en lisant des documents que Louis Moland et d'autres savants ont mis au jour, que chacune des deux caisses a été ouverte à plusieurs reprises. Poussés soit par la curiosité, soit par une vénération quelque peu déplacée, certains enthousiastes, soyons-en sûrs, n'ont pas toujours montré la plus grande discrétion à l'égard des ossements devenus reliques sacrées. Avec tout ce remue-ménage d'ossements il n'est pas surprenant que certains des os de Molière se soient retrouvés dans la caisse de La Fontaine, et un ou deux des os de La Fontaine dans celle de Molière. Beaucoup plus grave est le fait que dans cette série d'ouvertures et de fermetures des deux caisses quelques-uns des restes se soient doucement évaporés.

Le baron Dominique Vivant Denon, Directeur des musées impériaux et royaux pendant de longues années, fut toute sa vie un grand épicurien et un grand collectionneur. C'est lui, apparemment, qui justifia si bien l'axiome d'Erik Satie: ' Si vous voulez vivre longtemps, vivez vieux'. Vivant Denon mourut à Paris parmi ses collections en 1825. D'après Anatole France il avait rempli d'une

[3] C'est ainsi que Cailhava conclut—la Révolution enfin terminée—son livre très lu à l'époque: *Études sur Molière*, p. 355.

quantité de reliques profanes un reliquaire, vidé pendant la Révolution de ses reliques de saints: cendres d'Héloïse, cheveux d'Inès de Castro, moustache de Henri IV, dent de Voltaire, sang de Napoléon. Dans le coffret, parmi ce bric-à-brac macabre, il y eut aussi des fragments d'os de Molière et de La Fontaine. C'est ce que nous explique une brochure publiée en 1880, et intitulée *La Relique de Molière du cabinet du baron Vivant Denon.* Collectionneur enthousiaste d'œuvres d'art et de souvenirs, le baron, même aux heures les plus sombres de la Révolution, eut amplement l'occasion de recueillir une variété de reliques dont aucune n'était, semble-t-il, plus facilement accessible que celles de nos deux poètes.

Pendant de longues années au dix-neuvième siècle l'on pouvait voir sous un globe au musée de Cluny un fragment de mâchoire, selon toute probabilité celle de Molière. Si c'était bien son maxillaire inférieur, comme le disait longtemps un certificat apposé sur le socle qui supportait le fragment, comment se fait-il que cette partie de sa mâchoire ait fini par avoir le sort peu enviable d'être transformée en simple curiosité de foire? Les origines de l'histoire remontent à la Révolution. C'est une des plus singulières de cette période, qui n'en manquait pas.

Sous la Convention nationale, l'assemblée révolutionnaire qui succéda à l'Assemblée législative le 21 septembre 1792 pour gouverner la France pendant trois années mémorables, eut une idée géniale. Ce n'était rien moins que de recueillir les os des Français illustres du passé pour les convertir en verre phosphate par une opération chimique. Dans quel dessein? Pour en faire des coupes mortuaires ou—terme plus patriotique—des coupes républicaines; ou bien, et l'expression quelque peu ambigue est encore plus élégante: des coupes 'consacrées à la reconnaissance publique'.

En ce qui concerne le pauvre Molière, les comptes rendus que nous possédons se ressemblent tous. Aucun, pourtant, n'est aussi lapidaire que celui publié par un personnage bien informé dans le périodique intitulé l'*Intérmediaire des chercheurs et des curieux* pour l'année 1864. Nous lisons:

> '. . . à l'époque de la Convention, sur un ordre du Comité de salut publique, le chimiste Darcet fut mis en possession d'une partie des ossements de Molière et de quelques autres morts illustres, . . . à l'effet d'en tirer du phosphate de chaux qui

devait être employé à la fabrication d'une belle coupe en porcelaine de Sèvres où l'on aurait bu patriotiquement à la 'République.' J'ignore si ce vase a été fabriqué . . .'[4]

Quelques temps après, il paraît que l'ordre en cause fut révoqué. Il en résulta que les corps des 'morts illustres' furent rendus aux cimetières et ceux de Molière et de La Fontaine à leurs caisses dans la mansarde mentionnée plus haut. Tout laisse croire, pourtant, que Darcet ne fut pas le seul chimiste choisi par l'État pour ce travail de vitrification. Il y a, par exemple, la lettre-requête adressée au ministre de l'Intérieur par Beaumarchais. Dans cette lettre de protestation, le dramaturge déplorait le fait qu'en visitant les collections du Jardin des Plantes, il y avait rencontré au coin d'un laboratoire de chimie, dans la poussière des fourneaux et des matériaux servant à des distillations, le corps exhumé de Turenne portant—ajouta-t-on après—toutes ses médailles.[5]

On a souvent dit que la période révolutionnaire, marquée par un bouleversement politique et social en général et par les excès de la Terreur en particulier, ne fut pas prête à suivre l'exemple de Philinte:

[4] V. D., 'Les Tombes de Molière et de La Fontaine au Père-Lachaise', p. 109.

[5] Voir *Œuvres complètes de Beaumarchais*, éd. Édouard Fournier (Paris 1876), p. 690, 'Lettre LII'. Il serait à-propos, peut-être, de citer au moins une partie de cette lettre à François de Neufchâteau, homme d'état français et ministre de l'intérieur du Directoire:

'1 [*sic*] brumaire an VII
(11 novembre, 1798).

Ministre Citoyen,
Les soins constants que vous mettez pour embellir le jardin national, conservatoire des plantes exotiques, des arbres et des animaux qui arrivent de tous les points du globe, nous prouvent que vos sages vues s'étendent à tout ce qui peut être utile au public, ou sembler digne de sa curiosité. Mais j'avoue qu'au plaisir de voir ces collections se mêle en moi un sentiment pénible, toutes les fois que j'y trouve, au coin d'un laboratoire de chimie, dans la poussière des fourneaux, des matras, et des matériaux servant à des distillations, le corps exhumé de *Turenne*, sans que je puisse m'expliquer les motifs d'un pareil dédain pour les restes d'un chef d'armée que le roi le plus fier de son rang jugea digne de partager la sépulture de sa maison.

'Que peut donc avoir de commun le squelette du *grand Turenne*, avec les animaux vivants que cette enceinte nous conserve?

'Qu'aurait dit Montecuculli, de voir son vainqueur figurer au milieu d'une ménagerie? . . .

'Je vous prie donc, ministre ami de l'ordre, dont la haute magistrature est de surveiller les objets de décence publique, de prendre en considération cette remarque sur Turenne, qu'un bon citoyen vous soumet.

'Je pourrais bien signer mon nom, ou même en donner l'anagramme, si cette singularité ajoutait quelque chose au mérite d'un aperçu: *qu'importe qui je sois*, si je dis la vérité? C'est de cela seul qu'il s'agit.'

'Je prends tout doucement les hommes comme ils sont.'
(*Le Misanthrope*, I, i)

La formule est dans *le Misanthrope*; et *le Misanthrope* est bien la pièce de Molière qui fut, sinon la plus en vogue, du moins celle qui fit le plus de bruit pendant la Révolution. Une des raisons en fut *la Lettre à d'Alembert sur les spectacles* de Jean-Jacques Rousseau, publiée en 1758. L'attaque de Rousseau est d'une importance historique particulière en ce qu'elle montre les changements qui ont eu lieu dans la société et dans l'opinion publique depuis l'époque de Molière. Elle eut un profond retentissement dans la seconde moitié du siècle, et surtout durant les années révolutionnaires.

Comme les deux *Discours* qui la précédèrent, *la Lettre* fut dans une grande mesure une déclaration de guerre contre le caractère artificiel de la société de l'époque.[6] Ce caractère artificiel est reflété en partie dans l'esprit des salons du jour et en partie dans le théâtre contemporain. *Le Misanthrope* est justement un chef-d'œuvre comique qui a pour cadre les salons de Paris sous l'ancien régime. Le seul personnage de la pièce qui soit sincère aux yeux de Jean-Jacques est, bien entendu, Alceste. Du reste, Alceste a le très grand mérite d'avoir justement les mêmes défauts qu'on reproche à Rousseau: tous deux se piquent de leur franchise et de leur honnêteté; tous deux ont peu de patience pour la dissimulation ou l'hypocrisie; tous deux se trouvent aussi vertueux qu'on peut l'être dans une société non seulement artificielle, mais même dépravée. A cause de ces traits, tous deux tombent dans le ridicule.[7] Tout comme Alceste, Rousseau refuse d'accepter la société contemporaine. Il est donc prêt à s'identifier complètement avec celui qui dit au moment où la pièce touche à sa fin:

> Trahi de toutes parts, accablé d'injustices,
> Je vais sortir d'un gouffre où triomphent les vices,

[6] Voir l'édition critique du *Discours sur les sciences et les arts* par George R. Havens (Modern Language Association of America—Monograph Series, no. XV—New York et Londres, 1946). Dans son introduction et son commentaire se trouve une analyse très utile de l'état d'esprit de Rousseau à partir de 1749.

[7] Sans se nommer, Jean-Jacques se désigne en termes assez transparents pour le lecteur de son temps: 'Vous ne sauriez me nier deux choses: l'une qu'Alceste dans cette pièce est un homme droit, sincère, estimable, un véritable homme de bien; l'autre que l'Auteur lui donne un personnage ridicule. C'en est assés, ce me semble, pour rendre Molière inexcusable' (Rousseau, *Lettre à Mr. D'Alembert sur les spectacles*, ed. M. Fuchs, Lille, Genève, 1948, p. 48).

Et chercher sur la terre un endroit écarté
Où d'être homme d'honneur on ait la liberté.
(*Le Misanthrope*, V, iv)

Non seulement Rousseau défend le caractère et les actions d'Alceste, mais il part aussi en guerre contre l'honnête homme par excellence de la pièce, Philinte. Il lui reproche et sa modération et sa fausseté. Bref, il trouve que Philinte, ce sage de la pièce, n'est qu'un homme du haut monde dont les maximes ressemblent à celles des fripons. Pire encore, toujours selon Jean-Jacques, Philinte rappelle ces grands seigneurs qui ne se soucient point du peuple affamé et misérable.

Et voilà Rousseau le porte-parole le plus éloquent de 1789 avant la lettre.[8] En attaquant le théâtre, et, plus précisément, *le Misanthrope* de Molière, il obéit à la logique de son système, système qui est à la fois hostile aux raffinements de la société sous l'ancien régime et à son indifférence à la sincérité et à la vertu. Les répercussions en furent, comme on le sait, longues et retentissantes.[9]

Surtout en ce qui concerne les deux personnages principaux de la pièce on était prêt depuis longtemps à accepter une interprétation qui allait être celle donnée par Jean-Jacques. L'acteur Baron, formé par Molière lui-même et mort en 1729, avait refusé de jouer un Alceste ridicule; il tenait à accentuer les qualités supérieures de ce caractère où les exagérations semblaient être légitimes et justes.[10] Du reste, les acteurs qui suivirent peu après Baron furent en général fidèles à son interprétation d'Alceste, homme de cour digne et noble.[11] D'ailleurs La Bruyère avait déjà proposé un Alceste sympathique.[12] Et, dans sa réplique à Rousseau, d'Alembert démontra

[8] A cet égard les remarques d'un des plus grands disciples de Rousseau au vingtième siècle semblent parfaitement à-propos. La *Lettre* selon Romain Rolland est 'un torrent d'éloquence passionnée qui enflamma l'opinion'. Et il ajoute: 'Elle est déjà, par endroits, un discours de la Révolution'. (*Les Pages immortelles de J.-J. Rousseau choisies et expliquées par Romain Rolland*, Paris 1938, p. 24.)

[9] Voir, parmi tant d'autres, l'étude importante de Margaret M. Moffat, *La Controverse sur la moralité du théatre après La Lettre à d'Alembert de J.-J. Rousseau* (Paris 1930).

[10] Cf. Maurice Descotes, *Les Grands rôles du théâtre de Molière* (Paris 1960), p. 9.

[11] Sujet traité en détail par Edward Daniel Sullivan, *The Interpretation of Molière's Alceste from 1666 to the present* (unpublished doctoral dissertation, Harvard University, 1941), pp. 122-123.

[12] '... le misanthrope peut avoir l'âme austère et farouche; mais extérieurement il est civil et *cérémonieux*: il ne s'échappe pas, il ne s'apprivoise pas avec les

qu'il n'était pas loin de partager les vues de son adversaire quand il dit du personnage d'Alceste: 'Il n'y a personne qui ne l'estime, qui ne soit même porté à l'aimer et à le plaindre'.[13] D'autres, suivant l'exemple de Rousseau et de d'Alembert voulaient voir en Alceste, même avant la Révolution, un parangon de vertu. Tantôt se rangeant tout à fait du côté de Rousseau, on s'accordait avec lui pour dire que l'on ne devrait pas présenter le Misanthrope comme un personnage risible. Tantôt—c'est le cas d'Élie Fréron par exemple[14]—on refusait catégoriquement d'admettre avec Jean-Jacques que Molière eût fait de son mieux pour rendre Alceste ridicule.[15]

La vérité est que Rousseau n'était pas si éloigné de Molière qu'il le prétendait. Dans son portrait d'Alceste et ailleurs, Molière avait donné un sens nouveau à la notion de liberté en faisant de l'homme l'auteur de ses propres actions morales et de sa propre vertu. Et c'est précisément la position de Jean-Jacques, homme des lumières, dans ses diverses œuvres et tout particulièrement dans le *Vicaire savoyard* et le *Contrat social.* Molière aussi bien que Rousseau reconnaissait la souveraineté d'un impératif moral qui n'était pas dicté par le ciel mais que l'homme s'imposait à lui-même.

Autre fait capital: à mesure que le siècle progresse et que le caractère d'Alceste est regardé de plus en plus favorablement, celui de Philinte baisse dans l'estime du public. Ici encore d'Alembert semble accepter le jugement de Rousseau, et il reproche à Philinte d'être 'un caractère mal décidé, plein de sagesse dans ses maximes et de fausseté dans sa conduite'.[16] Mais c'est en 1790 que les nouvelles interprétations du rôle d'Alceste et de Philinte allaient être exploitées avec grand succès. Depuis quelque temps les affiches de la Comédie-Française avaient fait sensation en annonçant une nouvelle pièce, *le Philinte de Molière ou La Suite du Misanthrope.* Tout le monde se demandait qui avait bien pu avoir l'effronterie de

hommes; au contraire, il les traite honnêtement et sérieusement.' La Bruyère, *Les Caractères*, 'De l'homme' (Paris, Piazza, 1928), ii. 189-190.

[13] D'Alembert, *Mélanges de littérature d'histoire et de philosophie*, 'Lettre à M. Rousseau' (Amsterdam, Nouvelle édition, 1764), ii. 422.

[14] *Année littéraire* (1758), vi. 306.

[15] Cet intérêt renouvelé pour Alceste augmenta encore davantage l'énorme prestige dont jouissait Molière. En 1769, il entra, d'une manière posthume, à l'Académie Française et nombreux furent les écrivains qui concoururent pour son éloge. En 1773, on célébra le centenaire de sa mort, la fameuse édition Le Bret parut et les Comédiens français décidèrent de jouer sans aucune rémunération jusqu'à ce qu'une somme suffisante pour faire élever une statue soit amassée.

[16] D'Alembert, *op. cit.*, p. 423.

s'ériger en continuateur du grand poète comique. La pièce eut sa première le 22 février, six mois après la prise de la Bastille. C'était une période d'enthousiasme et d'idéalisme qui avait vu l'écroulement de l'ancien régime et qui témoignait du plus grand espoir pour l'avenir. C'est dans cette atmosphère que la pièce de Fabre d'Eglantine s'attira une importance que ses qualités littéraires ne justifiaient pas. Pour le spectateur de 1790 c'était un manifeste de propagande politique émouvant; pour nous, deux siècles plus tard ce n'est plus qu'un document politique et social, une manière de curiosité.

Fabre d'Eglantine, comédien, homme politique et opportuniste, avait su bien accorder sa réfutation du *Misanthrope* avec le climat du début de la Révolution. Molière, quoique toujours vénéré, avait momentanément perdu de sa popularité, et un critique de l'époque pouvait s'écrier: 'Qui est-ce qui donne aujourd'hui quarante-huit sous pour voir du Molière?'[17] En effet, la Révolution négligeait les aspects littéraires du théâtre.[18] Fabre, pourtant, avait tout de suite attiré l'attention des spectateurs parisiens en profitant en même temps de la gloire établie de Molière[19] et de la popularité de Rousseau.[20] Fidèle à l'esprit de son âge, il se déclarait publiquement

[17] Voir A. V. Arnault, *Œuvres* (Paris, Bossage, 1826), ii. 421.

[18] Cf. Jacques Hérissay, *Le Monde des théâtres pendant le révolution 1789–1800* (Paris 1922), p. 69.

[19] L'admiration que Fabre témoignait pour l'auteur du *Tartuffe* et du *Misanthrope* était sans doute sincère et, déjà avant la Révolution, il avait chanté les louanges du 'sublime Molière' dans un poème intitulé *A un poète comique*, *Œuvres mêlées et posthumes de Ph. Naz. Fabre d'Eglantine* (La Veuve Fabre d'Eglantine, Paris, Vendémiaire, an XI), ii. 4. En publiant la pièce, il ajouta un Prologue où il proclamait: 'A côté de Molière, enfin, je me hasarde' (p. 56); on dirait même, en lisant les vers qui suivent, que le poète révolutionnaire s'abrite à l'ombre du grand homme:

'Mais voyez-vous encor cet essain [*sic*] ténébreux
D'aveugles partisans . . .
Qui, pour mieux me haïr, feignant d'aimer Molière,
Fanatiques menteurs de cet homme immortel,
M'immolent à leur haine au pied de son autel?'

(*Le Philinte de Molière*, Paris, Prault, 1791, p. 58.) Il se pose aussi en interprète infaillible de Molière dans une assez longue critique défavorable de la première représentation d'une suite au *Misanthrope*, écrite par Charles-Albert Demoustier, intitulée *Alceste à la campagne* (voir l'article de Fabre dans *Les Révolutions de Paris* du 4 au 11 décembre, 1790, lxxiv. 479-482). Cette critique, cependant, est, comme *le Philinte de Molière*, une réfutation de la pièce de Molière.

[20] C'est toujours dans le Prologue que nous lisons:

'Mon cher, c'est à ce livre, à son intention,
Que je dois mon ouvrage et sa conception,
Je le dis hautement. Si le méchant m'assiège,
Qu'il sache que Rousseau lui-même me protège.'

(Paris, Prault, 1791), p. 58.

disciple de Jean-Jacques et avouait même avoir pris l'inspiration originale de son Philinte dans *la Lettre sur les spectacles*. Au fond, il ne faisait que suivre l'avis de Diderot qui avait écrit dès 1757: 'Telle est encore la vicissitude des ridicules et des vices que je crois qu'on pourrait faire un *Misanthrope* tous les cinquante ans' (AT., vii. 151). Pour Fabre, Alceste représente un citoyen de 1790, homme sensible et bon, et dévoué aux idées nouvelles.[21] Philinte est peint, par contre, comme un aristocrate borné et égoïste et tout à fait satisfait des conditions politiques et sociales de l'ancien régime. Alceste symbolisait tout ce qui est juste, Philinte, d'autre part, tout ce qu'il y a de pervers dans la société: deux portraits que le spectateur contemporain pouvait reconnaître sans la moindre difficulté.

Bien entendu, sans Molière et sans Rousseau il n'y aurait pas eu de *Philinte de Molière*. Mais il y avait d'autres facteurs qui contribuèrent à la genèse de la pièce. Le portrait que Fabre donne de lui-même ressemble assez à celui de l'Alceste auquel Rousseau s'identifiait une trentaine d'années auparavant.[22] Et puis, par jalousie et animosité personnelle, il voulait attaquer, coûte que coûte, un dramaturge très en vogue à l'époque: Collin d'Harleville. Non seulement Fabre attaquait celui-ci dans le Prologue malicieux de sa propre pièce, mais aussi dans la pièce même; car il tenait à faire croire au spectateur que son personnage principal, Philinte, égoiste et réactionnaire, ressemblait à Collin comme un frère. On peut invoquer comme autre origine de la pièce, le fait que Fabre, membre du club politique de Danton, *les Cordeliers*, voulait faire d'Alceste un déclamateur politique. De tout ceci, il résulte que, pour les spectateurs de l'époque, l'Alceste de Molière prend une signification nouvelle. Dès lors, les acteurs jouant ce rôle aspirent à se faire applaudir en mettant en relief les passages où Alceste s'en prend aux institutions et à la société de l'ancien régime. Quant à Fabre, il n'est peut-être pas sans intérêt de rappeler qu'avant d'être guillotiné il s'est tourné vers un de ses juges en lui adressant les paroles sui-

[21] Cf. le portrait de l'Alceste de Fabre fait par Wilhelm Fischmann, que le savant allemand conclut en disant: 'Alceste ist wohl noch ein Misanthrop, aber er ist menschlicher, sensibler, wohltätiger. Sein Menschenhass und seine Menschenverachtung entspringen dem Mitgefühl für diejenigen, die unter den Boshaften schuldlos zu leiden haben (Greifswald, Julius Abel, 1930), p. 108.

[22] 'Je suis âpre, franc, . . . ennemi implacable et éternel de la flatterie, haut, fier, quoique timide . . .' (Cité par A. Aulard, 'Figures oubliées de la Révolution', *La Nouvelle Revue*, Paris 1885, xxxv. 65).

vantes: 'Fouquier, tu peux faire tomber me tête, mais non pas mon Philinte'.[23] Et il avait raison, car sa pièce lui survécut—ne fût-ce que jusqu'à la fin du siècle.

N'oublions pas non plus que le succès d'une pièce à l'époque révolutionnaire, comme dans tous les temps d'ailleurs, dépendait souvent en grande partie du prestige des acteurs. Ceci était tellement vrai alors que des critiques dénoncèrent l'engouement des spectateurs pour certains acteurs et les accusèrent d'accorder une importance plus grande aux diverses interprétations qu'aux chefs-d'œuvre même. Toujours est-il que pendant presque toute cette période le grand acteur Molé jouait, paraît-il, si bien l'Alceste de Molière et celui de Fabre qu'on serait justifié de croire que le monde courait plutôt applaudir son art que celui des deux auteurs.

Mais Molé jouait dans *le Misanthrope* un Alceste tout à fait différent de celui que nous connaissons. Cet acteur renommé travaillait avec Dorat-Cubières, poète médiocre, et révolutionnaire ardent, pour réviser, changer, même 'mutiler', dit-on, le répertoire classique, surtout les pièces de Corneille, de Racine, de Voltaire et de Molière. Une de leurs tâches fut d'éliminer toutes les expressions à resonnance aristocratique, depuis 'valet de chambre' jusqu'aux mots 'cour', 'vicomte', et 'roi'. Car, pour les citoyens de la Révolution, il n'existait plus de valets de chambre ni de rois.[24]

Le livre de Molé intitulé *Le Misanthrope de Molière avec des variantes du Citoyen Molé*, Paris an II de la Révolution, est assez bien connu même aujourd'hui. Au dix-neuvième siècle cette adaptation de la comédie par l'acteur fut l'objet d'une attaque célèbre de Jules Janin. Dans de tels changements Janin vit des 'crimes littéraires de la Terreur', commis par 'une main impie'. Il se trompait; il y avait plusieurs mains! On n'a que l'embarras du choix parmi

[23] Voir Georges de Froidecourt, 'Fabre d'Eglantine, plaideur', *La Révolution Française* (1938 nouvelle série), xiii. 84.

[24] Bien qu'il ait jugé nécessaire de corriger Molière, Cubières ne perdit pourtant jamais l'occasion de l'appeler le plus grand des Français. Dans la *Correspondance dramatique* (Paris 1810), où il défend la pièce de Mercier, *la Maison de Molière*, et sa propre pièce, *la Mort de Molière*, il écrit: 'Molière est notre dieu en littérature' (p. 30). Et dans son *Épître à Molière* (Paris, s.d.) nous trouvons les vers suivants:

La Grèce eut des Myrons; la France des Coustous.
Tous ces Mortels sont grands, nous les admirons tous;
Ils marchent tous de front dans leur noble carrière,
Mais quel Mortel jamais fut l'égal de Molière? (p. 80)

les passages éloquents et passionnés du fameux chapitre XIII de sa *Littérature dramatique*, passages pleins d'indignation vertueuse; quel est celui qui l'emporterait sur tous les autres? Celui-ci peut-être ferait notre affaire:

> 'Eh! que voulez-vous que comprenne au Molière du XVIIe siècle, la nation de 93, abrutie par l' alcool et par les discours des clubs, haletante dans les rues pour voir passer les morts qui la saluent, dévergondée, hideuse, sanglante, détachée violemment de son double passé royal et chrétien? Molière en 93, déchiré en lambeaux dans la coulisse et luttant avec peine contre les mélodrames et les tragédies du *Salut public*. O la triste immolation!'

Comme *le Misanthrope*, *le Tartuffe* subit également des indignités. Les critiques auraient pu s'écrier avec Janin: 'O la triste immolation!' en entendant les acteurs dire:

'Ils sont passés ces jours d'injustice et de fraude, . . . etc'

au lieu de:

'Nous vivons sous un prince ennemi de la fraude, . . . etc'

Les argus du dix-neuvième siècle remarquèrent, du reste, que le dénouement du *Tartuffe* avait été à tel point remanié que 'La République, au lieu du prince, exerce sa justice contre l'hypocrite démasqué'.[25] Ces critiques se trouvaient cependant dans une position plus avantageuse que ceux qui vivaient à l'ombre du Tribunal Révolutionnaire. Les hommes de lettres sous Louis-Philippe, par exemple, regardaient souvent d'un œil méfiant cette époque où la modération ne fut pas une vertu. On jugeait donc avec grande sévérité les variantes apportées par le citoyen Molé et d'autres. Changer un groupe de mots, quelques phrases dans l'œuvre dramatique de Molière et de ses confrères fut, pourtant, peu de chose à côté des 16,594 condamnations à mort prononcées dans le pays en dix-sept mois.[26] Du reste, ceux qui remaniaient les pièces de Molière ne faisaient que suivre les ordres du jour. Dans le décret de la Convention Nationale du 2 août 1793 relatif à la représentation

[25] Voir A. Liéby, 'L'ancienne répertoire des théâtres de Paris à travers la réaction thermidorienne', *Révolutions françaises* (1905); cf. Victor Hallays-Dabot, *Histoire de la censure théâtrale en France*, Chap. VI, 'La Censure pendant la Révolution' (Paris 1862), pp. 143-206.

[26] Provenant des recherches et des travaux de Donald Greer, ce nombre est généralement accepté par les historiens.

des pièces de théâtre on peut lire ce qui suit: 'Tout théâtre sur lequel seroient représentées des pièces tendant à dépraver l'esprit public, et à réveiller la honteuse superstition de la royauté, sera fermé, et les directeurs arrêtés et punis selon la rigueur des loix.'[27]

Mais Molière lui-même fut dépeint pendant la Révolution comme un grand homme du passé en révolte contre l'ancien régime. Forcé de louer Louis XIV, disait-on, il faisait ses prologues mauvais, et détestables à plaisir.[28] Il employait les platitudes, les lieux communs les plus vulgaires avec une intention marquée, comme pour avertir la postérité du dégoût et de l'horreur qu'il avait pour un travail que lui imposaient les circonstances, son état, et la soif de répandre ses talents et sa philosophie.[29] Mais c'était une manière de justifier Molière qu'on trouve couramment exprimée pendant la Révolution.

Ainsi nous pouvons déjà voir que certaines conclusions du regretté Albert Thibaudet ne sont pas tout à fait acceptables. Il remarquait, il y a une trentaine d'années: 'Rousseau et la Révolution l'avaient même traité, avec tous les écrivains de son temps, comme un suppôt de la tyrannie qui ridiculisait les Jacobins en la personne d'Alceste' (*Revue de Paris*, 1930, p. 367). Mais la réfutation de ce point de vue ne doit pas être limitée uniquement au *Misanthrope*. *Le Journal des spectacles* notait que *le Bourgeois gentilhomme* était, par exemple, plus révolutionnaire qu'on ne le pense.[30] Camille Desmoulins disait dans le *Vieux Cordelier*: 'Molière dans *le Misanthrope* a peint en traits sublimes le caractère du républicain et du

[27] Et pour corollaire C.-G. Étienne et A. Martainville nous disent dans la Préface à leur *Histoire du théâtre français* (Paris an X–1802), 'Le trône et l'autel, journellement présentés sur le théâtre comme des objets d'horreur et de mépris, accoutumèrent le peuple à se jouer de ce qu'il avait long-tems vénéré' (I, iii). On dirait que la scène parisienne ne faisait que suivre les ordres du *Journal de la Montagne* où l'on lit pour le 11 septembre, 1793: 'Plus de rois sur notre théâtre, s'ils n'y paraissent cruels, sanguinaires, barbares, ou faux hypocrites; en un mot, tels qu'ils sont. Plus de nobles, sinon avec les traits qui, depuis tant de siècles, ont caractérisé cette caste. Plus de prêtres, sinon démasqués.'

[28] Aux yeux de Dorat-Cubières le grand crime du roi-soleil fut d'une netteté frappante:

'Les beaux-arts autrefois n'étaient-ils pas esclaves
Des tyrans odieux? . . . .
Louis, de Despréaux deshonora les pages
Et de Molière même il souilla les ouvrages'

(*Les Progrès des arts dans la République*, Paris, an V, p. 2.)

[29] *Révolutions de Paris* (an II, déc. 1790), no. 74, pp. 457-458.

[30] 9 frimaire l'an IIe (29 nov. 1793); pour confirmation de cette position, voir L. de La Pijardière, 'Le Maître d'armes et le maître à danser pendant la Révolution', *Le Moliériste* (avril 1888), x. 2026.

royaliste; Alceste est un jacobin; Philinte un feuillant achevé.'[31] D'ailleurs, le *Journal de la Montagne* s'écriait en pleine Terreur: 'Molière a démasqué, d'une manière heureuse, les fourberies des prêtres; son Tartuffe est volé à notre révolution.'[32]

'Plus de prêtres sur nos scènes, sinon démasqués' devint un cri de ralliement pendant la Révolution.[33] Voilà une explication de la grande popularité du *Tartuffe*, des adaptations du *Tartuffe*, et des suites du *Tartuffe* pendant toute cette période. Un écrivain se plaint à la Préfecture de Police à Paris: 'On donne le Tartufe partout . . . pourquoi ne donnerait-on pas ma pièce?'[34] Les attaques contre l'Église et le clergé finirent par devenir si acerbes sur la scène parisienne que le public commença à déplorer une telle violence prolongée contre un ennemi déjà terrassé.

Mais la Révolution, surtout au moment de la Terreur, n'eut aucune intention de fuir les extrêmes, quand même il se fût agi de Molière. Le ministre de l'Intérieur, par exemple, reçut une lettre en septembre 1793 caractérisant un aspect outré du jour: 'Que les marquis cèdent la place aux patriotes, brûlons, s'il le faut, les chefs-d'œuvre de Molière. . . . Les arts y perdront quelque chose, mais à coup sûr, les mœurs y gagneront.'[35] Et, en effet, on supprima *les*

[31] *Œuvres* (Paris 1874), ii. 254.

[32] 4 sept. 1793.

[33] Déjà en 1790 on lit dans *Révolutions de Paris*: 'Le Tartufe [*sic*] a montré et mis à la portée du peuple le [*sic*] *jésuites* et le *jésuitisme*; pas à pas ces hypocrites impérieux, qui s'insinuoient dans les familles, se sont trouvés soumis à la comparaison que faisoient d'eux les pères, les mères, les fils et les filles, avec l'*hypocrite* de Molière; petit à petit les yeux se sont ouverts, la méfiance s'est étendue, la conviction en a résulté; et quand les jésuites attaqués, ont crié au secours, ils n'ont trouvé que des ennemis. Telle est, nous l'osons dire, l'influence puissante des représentations.' (No. 74, p. 456.)

[34] Les deux pièces dérivant du *Tartuffe* qui ont fait le plus de bruit à l'époque sont *Le Tartuffe révolutionnaire ou la suite de l'Imposteur* et *Papelard ou le Tartuffe philosophe et politique*. Il y avait aussi *Hypocrite en révolution, par P. J. Bourlin* [pseud. Dumaniant]. Par contre, parmi d'autres, l'*Autre Tartuffe, ou la mère coupable*, par Beaumarchais, n'eut qu'un succès modeste. On pourrait mentionner aussi: *Les Victimes cloîtrés*, *A Bas les calottes*, *ou les Déprêtrisés*, *L'Esprit des prêtres*, *Le Prélat d'autrefois*, *La Journée du Vatican*, *ou le mariage du pape*, *Le Prêtre réfractaire ou le nouveau Tartuffe* et *La Papesse Jeanne*.

[35] Cité par Alexandre Tuetey, *Répertoire général des sources manuscrites de l'histoire pendant la Révolution Française* (Paris 1916), ix. 382-383. Dans le même esprit, Aristide Valcour écrivait dans le *Journal de la Montagne*: 'Il seroit à souhaiter que nous fussions assez sages pour nous priver, pendant au moins dix ans de la représentation de nos chefs-d'œuvres [*sic*] dramatiques' (66:423, 6 août, 1793). De tels sentiments font l'objet mal caché de *la Décade*: 'C'est une mesure nécessaire à laquelle tout bon patriote doit souscrire. Mais du moins les

Fourberies de Scapin et *George Dandin* pour des raisons de moralité. A Angers on trouva même *le Médecin malgré lui* une 'pièce absolument immorale'.[36] A Caen, un poète se lamentait:

'Hélas! Qu'êtes-vous devenus
Divin Molière! O Regnard! O Destouches!'[37]

On voit ainsi que les réactions aux pièces de Molière furent nombreuses et variées pendant la décade entre 1789 et 1799, mais que le théâtre de Molière lui-même, sans compter les adaptations et les imitations, eut un succès fort impressionnant. Il est difficile d'arriver au nombre exact de représentations à Paris pendant ces années à cause de la multiplicité des théâtres. Fondant mes chiffres sur Joannidès, qui dans ses tables de représentation ne comprend que les pièces jouées à la Comédie-Française, sur la table préparée par

Molière, les Corneille, les Racine ne seront jamais exclus d'aucune bibliothèque. L'homme de lettres ira encore s'instruire en silence avec ces grands maîtres; et jamais il ne sera défendu de rire avec *Scapin*, de politiquer avec *Cinna*, de pleurer avec *Andromaque*' (1:140, 30 floréal, an II—19 mai, 1794).

[36] Voir C. Post, 'Molière immoral', *Le Moliériste* (1880), ii. 94.

[37] L'histoire du théâtre dans les villes de Province pendant la Révolution a fait l'objet de nombreuses études. On retrouve presque toujours les mêmes attitudes: le rire et la comédie ne sont guère à la mode dans une époque d'idéalisme et de violence. Molière lui-même est souvent respecté comme par le passé, mais il arrive qu'un citoyen, animé d'un zèle patriotique et révolutionnaire trop enthousiaste, condamne son œuvre au nom de la pureté.

Sans vouloir donner une bibliographie complète du sujet, nous signalons les travaux suivants: A. A[ulard], 'La Police des théâtres en l'an IV', *Révolution française* (1928), lxxxi. 245-246; Jean-Julien Barbé, 'Le Théâtre à Metz pendant la Révolution (1790–an II)', *Annales historiques de la Révolution française* (1927), iv. 359-388; Ch. Boell, 'Les spectacles républicains à Autun pendant la Révolution', *Mémoires de la Société Éduenne* (1908); Adolphe de Cardevacque, *Le Théâtre à Arras avant et après la Révolution* (Arras 1884); E. G. de Clérambault, *Le Théâtre à Tours à l'époque de la Révolution* (Tours 1916); Henri Clouzot, *Le Théatre à Fontenay-le-Comte pendant la Révolution, le Consulat et l'Empire jusqu'en 1806* (Fontenay-le-Comte 1899); Victor Combarnous, *Notes et souvenirs: l'histoire du grand théâtre de Marseille (31 octobre 1787–13 novembre 1919)* (Marseille 1927); Paul Courteault, *La Révolution et les théâtres à Bordeaux* (Paris 1926); Lucien Decombre, *Recherches d'histoire locale, notes et souvenirs. Le Théâtre à Rennes* (Rennes 1899); Robert Deschamps La Rivière, 'Le Théâtre au Mans pendant la Révolution', *Revue historique et archéologique du Maine* (1901), xvix. 78-100, 191-218, and l. 71-104; Étienne Destranges, *Le Théâtre à Nantes, depuis ses origines jusqu'à nos jours (1430–1893)* (Paris 1902); J. Durandeau, 'Le Théâtre à Dijon pendant la Révolution', *Revue bleue* (1888), xlii. 748-750; Louis Duval, *Le Théâtre à Alençon au XVIIIe siècle* (Paris 1912); Paul d'Estrée, *Le Théâtre sous la Terreur (1793–94)* (Paris 1913); A. Fray-Fournier, *Le Théâtre à Limoges avant, pendant et après la Révolution* (Limoges 1900); Gaston-Martin, 'Le Théâtre et la politique à Toulouse en l'an

M. Listener pour la série *les Grands Écrivains de la France*,[38] et mes recherches personnelles pour lesquelles j'ai dépouillé des périodiques révolutionnaires jour par jour, je suis arrivé aux chiffres suivants, chiffres qui sont assurément en deçà de la réalité.

Pendant cette dizaine d'années dix-huit pièces de Molière furent jouées plus de 500 fois. *Tartuffe* l'emportait sur toutes les autres avec 84 représentations; il était suivi de près par *l'École des maris*, *le Médecin malgré lui* et *l'Avare*. Quant au *Misanthrope*, généralement considéré son chef-d'œuvre à l'époque, il n'eut que 34 représentations, peut-être parce que cette comédie partageait la scène et les talents de l'acteur Molé avec *le Philinte de Molière*.

Nous venons de parcourir la décade 1789–99, une des époques les plus mouvementées dans l'histoire de la France moderne. Elle provoqua comme on ne le sait que trop bien de profonds bouleversements dont les répercutions continuent à se faire sentir. Nous avons essayé d'examiner la fortune de Molière pendant ces années. Nous avons vu que la présence du grand poète comique se fit constamment sentir d'une façon ou d'autre. D'une manière générale, on peut remarquer un désir prolongé et déterminé de l'honorer et

V', *Révolution Française* (1927), lxxx. 193-211; E. Gautier-Lachapelle, 'Les Théâtres pendant la Révolution (d'après une étude inédite de M. Thomas Latour)', *L'Investigateur de l'Institut historique* (1856), pp. 65-76; Gaston Lavalley, *La Censure théâtrale à Caen en l'an VII* (Caen 1908); Paul de Longuemare, *Le Théâtre à Caen, 1628–1830* (Paris 1895); P. Moulin, 'Le Théâtre à Marseille pendant la Révolution', *Congrès des Sociétés Savantes de Province* (1906); Théodore Muret, *L'Histoire par le théâtre 1789–1851, Première série, La Révolution, le Consulat, l'Empire* (Paris 1865); J. Noury, *Le Théâtre-Français de Rouen* (Rouen s.d.); René Paquet, *Le Théâtre à Metz* (Metz 1908); Jules Pellison, 'Le Théâtre à Saintes pendant la Révolution', *Bulletin de la Société archéologique, historique et artistique* (1910–11), ix. 58-60; Edmond Poupe, *Le Théâtre à Toulon (1791–1792)*, Extrait du *Bulletin historique et philosophique* (1905) (Paris, Imprimerie nationale, 1906); Ulysse Rouchon, *Le Théâtre au Puy à la fin du XVIIIe siècle* (Paris 1909); Henry Rousset, *Le Théâtre à Grenoble, histoire et physionomie, 1500–1890* (Grenoble 1891); Gilbert Stenger, 'Les Théâtres pendant le Consulat: les spectacles de l'an VIII', *Revue d'Art dramatique* (1903), pp. 263-270; Aurélien Vivié, *Les Théâtres de Bordeaux pendant la Terreur (1793–1794): Fragments d'histoire d'après des documents inédits* (Bordeaux 1868).

[38] *Œuvres de Molière*, nouv. édition, éd. Eugène Despois (Paris 1873), i. 550. La table de Listener est fondée sur les représentations données sur les cinq principaux théâtres autres que le Théâtre de la Nation pendant les années de la Révolution où les registres de la Comédie n'offrent aucune indication; ces théâtres sont: Théâtre de la République; Théâtre de l'Égalité; Théâtre Feydeau; Théâtre Louvois; Théâtre de l'Odéon—mais il y a au moins une demi-douzaine d'autres théâtres à Paris à cette époque.

de le révérer. Une des premières manifestations de ce respect fut, ainsi que nous l'avons noté, l'extraordinaire engoûment qui se manifesta pour ses dépouilles mortelles. La majorité de ses pièces furent représentées durant cette période et connurent la plus grande popularité. L'homme Molière devint un héros qui, quoique sujet d'un monarque—et la royauté était alors synonyme de la tyrannie—sut néanmoins faire front à la tyrannie de l'Église et de l'État. On aima à retrouver dans ses pièces l'esprit même de la Révolution. Selon les exigences du jour, cependant, elles durent subir certains remaniements plus ou moins importants, comme d'ailleurs les pièces de Corneille, de Racine et de Voltaire. Selon des critiques du siècle suivant, elles furent même gravement mutilées. Le fait que suites, adaptations, imitations, 'singeries' de ses pièces se multiplièrent alors est un témoignage de plus de sa popularité.[39] Ce n'est que durant la Terreur, quand la violence et l'intolérance atteignirent leur paroxysme, que quelques-unes de ses pièces furent bannies du théâtre au nom de la moralité et de la vertu.

D'une manière générale donc, la grandeur et le renom de Molière survécurent à la période révolutionnaire, qui donna même à son œuvre des dimensions nouvelles. Celles-ci allaient être exploitées dans la première moitié du siècle suivant par l'école romantique. Tartuffe deviendra un monstre sinistre, Don Juan, un grand humanitaire, Arnolphe, un homme aussi malheureux que le Werther de Goethe; et quant à Alceste, il pourra dire avec le Rousseau des *Confessions*, 'Je suis autre'.[40]

L'anecdote bien connue que nous raconte Paul Stapfer dans son *Molière et Shakespeare* nous convaincra facilement que Molière survécut à la Révolution française et fut bien reconnu comme un génie universel: 'En l'année 1800, un célèbre acteur anglais, Kemble, vint à Paris. Ses confrères de la Comédie-Française lui offrirent un banquet. A table on causa d'abord des poètes tragiques des deux nations; la supériorité de Shakespeare sur Racine et sur Corneille était vivement soutenue par l'Anglais contre ses hôtes, qui, par

[39] Rappelons entre autres: *Alceste à la campagne*, *Le Misanthrope corrigé*, *La Suite des précieuses*, *Le Dépit amoureux* (*en deux actes*), sans compter plusieurs de ses comédies mises en musique; et comme nous l'avons déjà vu, un nombre considérable de pièces inspirées du *Tartuffe*. On trouve aussi de fréquentes allusions à Molière lui-même dans des pièces à la mode telles que: *La Maison de Molière*, *Le Souper de Molière*, *Les Deux Figaro*, *Molière à la nouvelle salle*, ainsi de suite.

[40] Cf. O. Fellows, *French Opinion of Molière* (*1800–1850*), (Providence 1937).

politesse ou par conviction, commençaient à céder le terrain, quand tout à coup le comédien Michaut s'écria: "D'accord, d'accord, Monsieur; mais que diriez-vous de Molière?" Kemble répondit tranquillement: "Molière? c'est une autre question. Molière n'est pas un Français."—"Bah! un Anglais, peut-être?"—"Non, Molière est un homme." . . . Devant lui s'évanouissent les petites différences de temps et de lieux; aucun peuple, aucun siècle ne peut le revendiquer comme sien; il est à tous les âges et à toutes les nations.'[41]

Si cette anecdote n'était pas véridique, elle mériterait de l'être. Pendant une dizaine d'années la Révolution avait donné une nouvelle valeur à Molière comme elle l'avait fait pour Corneille, Racine, Montesquieu, Buffon, et tant d'autres grands écrivains de l'ancien régime. Malgré la violence parfois faite à Molière, à l'homme et à son œuvre, au nom du nouvel ordre, ordre marqué par l'emportement et l'idéalisme, le grand poète comique en est sorti l'égal de Voltaire et de Rousseau—c'est-à-dire non seulement un des plus grands hommes de lettres de la France, mais aussi comme une arme politique des plus redoutables contre les forces réactionnaires du passé.

Tout cela est d'autant plus étonnant que Molière émergeait, avec éclat, d'une époque où l'art théâtral, comme la littérature pure, comptait pour relativement peu de chose. C'était une période où le bourgeois, le marchand et l'artisan jouèrent pour la première fois un rôle capital dans les affaires publiques. Ce sont ces hommes-là, autrefois si peu importants et sur la scène politique et comme spectateurs au théâtre, qui couraient au spectacle et y faisaient prévaloir leur propre goût. A cette époque ce sont les pièces faisant appel aux émotions plutôt qu'aux ressources de l'esprit qui étaient le plus à la mode. Comme l'a fait remarquer un critique qui avait vécu ces années de bouleversement des vieilles valeurs traditionnelles,[42] 'la tragédie s'est soutenue dans une médiocrité honorable,

[41] Paul Stapfer, *Shakespeare et Molière* (Paris 1887), pp. 23-24.

[42] Alexandre Ricord, *Quelques Réflexions sur l'art théâtral* (Paris 1811). Il y avait pourtant ceux qui étaient capables de voir le côté amusant de la question. Ainsi, le 5 janvier 1793, on voit à Paris pour la première fois *la Chaste Suzanne*, petite pièce en deux actes agrémentée de couplets dans laquelle l'Écriture sainte et le Vaudeville se mêlent. Dans le dénouement on se moque du théâtre de l'époque tout en faisant l'éloge de Molière. Voici le refrain de Suzanne:

'De noirs effets pour du tragique,
Du calembour pour du comique,
Du bel esprit pour du plaisant,
Voilà le théâtre à présent.
Mais réunir, comme Molière,
Dans une intrigue régulière,
Et la morale et l'enjoûment,
Oh! c'est de l'ancien testament.'

et la comédie est dans le plus grand dépérissement' (p. 19). C'était un moment où les dramaturges de talent, tenant à faire plaisir au nouveau public, s'adonnèrent d'abord au drame, puis à un genre qui faisait beaucoup souffrir la bonne comédie—le mélodrame avec ses coups de théâtre sensationnels, ses cris d'horreur, et son amour du sang répandu sur la scène. En dépit de tout cela, Molière, auteur de pièces comiques où dominaient le naturel et la finesse ainsi que le bon sens, fit partie avec Voltaire et Rousseau, de la trinité des trois hommes de lettres les plus vénérés en France au temps où la Révolution touchait à son terme.

Swiss in Great Britain in the Eighteenth Century

Béat de Fischer

In a book intended to commemorate the merits of a great English connoisseur of the work of Voltaire, a Swiss friend and admirer might be tempted to take as the starting point of his contribution the great philosopher, the 'Suitzerman V.'[1] and his visit to England of 1726–28. No doubt Monsieur de Voltaire came across few Genevans or Swiss whilst over here; but what sort of Helvetic society might he and his contemporaries have found if they had felt inclined to look for it?

Thus it is the Genevan[2] and Swiss society in eighteenth-century England which will provide the subject of this essay. The temptation to write it was all the stronger because that period was also the golden age of the Swiss colony in the British Isles.

INTRODUCTION

In the eighteenth century many Genevans and Swiss played a particularly notable part in an astonishing number of sectors of English life. True, there already existed before this time close, strong and even vital links between England and some of our republics, our cities and our eminent men. Until then, however, relations had been almost exclusively confined to questions of religion—aspects of the organisation of the churches—and the political and military

[1] This was the way in which Voltaire signed a letter to George Keate from Monrion, near Lausanne, on 17 February 1757 (British Museum. Add. MSS., 30991, Fol. 4, Best. 6466).

[2] Geneva was not to enter the Confederation (with Vaud, Valais and Neuchâtel) before 1814.

solidarity to be established among the Protestant powers; and the main factor was the Engish interest in the homes of the new faith, especially Zürich and Geneva.

This changed during the course of the eighteenth century. Protestant England and her Protestant sovereigns, of course, continued to constitute a strong attraction for Geneva and the Protestant cantons, and a large number of their citizens came here, and were welcomed, for religious reasons. But the dialogue broadened considerably from this century onwards, and was to be long sustained with great intensity on both sides.

Several circumstances brought this change about. First of all, the 'Back to Nature' movement, inspired primarily by the publication of 'The Seasons' (1730) by the Scot James Thomson (1700–48), turned English attention to the Helvetic people and their mountains, whose beauty was to be revealed in Albert de Haller's *The Alps* (1729) and Rousseau's *Nouvelle Héloïse* (1761). This enthusiasm soon manifested itself in numerous poetic works. In 'Liberty' (1731) Thomson himself celebrated the virtues of the simple cowherds of our valleys. Then, in his letters of 1739, Thomas Gray described the blissfulness of the City of Geneva and the beauty of her lake. In his 'Helvetiad' (1756) George Keate sang of our fights for freedom; he then wrote a history of the City of Calvin (1761), which he dedicated to the 'Genevan' Voltaire, and in which he held up that community as an ideal for republics; finally, in *The Alps* (1763), he described the attractions of our mountains. Oliver Goldsmith dedicated his book *The Traveller* (1764) to us, as did William Wordsworth his *Descriptive Sketches* (1793).

This was also the period when numerous Englishmen began to travel more widely in Switzerland and to settle there. The 'Grand Tour' almost inevitably brought to our country the sons of wealthy families, and William Coxe speaks kindly of it in his *Travels in Switzerland* (1779). Edward Gibbon (1737–94), following the example of many others of his countrymen, resided in Lausanne for a total of sixteen years between 1753 and 1793, and even contemplated marrying the handsome Suzanne Curchod, the future Madame Necker, mother of Madame de Staël.[3] Philip Stanhope and his sons

[3] *The Letters of Edward Gibbon* (London 1956), vol. ii: Letters of Edward Gibbon to Suzanne Curchod 1758–63.

lived in Geneva. Many British lovers of Swiss nature had Swiss scenes engraved by famous artists like Hentzi and others. In England itself works by Lavater, and Gessner's *Idylls*, were being read in English translations.

But this English interest in Switzerland provoked, in its turn, an intense interest in England among many Swiss. In Geneva the publication in 1726 of the *Lettres sur les Anglais et les Français*, by Béat de Muralt, created a sensation in a society which was growing tired of French influence and tutelage. And Geneva did not cease, during the whole of the century, from taking an interest in things English, a fascination which was to reach its climax in the founding by the Pictet brothers in 1796 of the 'Bibliothèque britannique'. That journal so courageously defended England's liberal ideas on the Continent that Talleyrand was prompted to say to Pictet de Rochemont: 'Your review has behind it such a weight of public opinion that its suppression would amount to a coup d'état'. And Sismondi added: 'Geneva is a town which speaks and writes French, but thinks and reads English'.

In Zürich J. J. Bodmer discovered England on reading *The Spectator*, and disseminated her ideas through the periodical which he himself founded with some friends—*Die Discourse der Mahlern* (1721–23). He subsequently translated Milton's *Paradise Lost* into German. Bodmer's enthusiasm soon spread to wider circles, and it was under his influence that Wieland translated 22 of Shakespeare's plays, which were then published in Zürich by Orelli, Gessner & Co. Thanks to Bodmer, Shakespeare was even to be read by a humble Toggenburg peasant, Uli Braecker, who wrote the astonishing *Etwas über Shakespeare*.

Numerous other Swiss, such as Albert de Haller, Gaudenz de Salis-Seewis, Bridel, Madame de Montolieu, Samuel Constant, Johannes von Müller[4] and Vincenz Bernhard von Tscharner,[5] found inspiration in English models, in the field of either literature, politics, philosophy or agriculture. For a short while Switzerland became the channel through which English ideas flowed to the Continent, and from her sprang a new flowering of German letters.

It goes without saying that such anglophile feelings increased

[4] Edgar Bonjour, *Johannes von Müllers Verhältnis zu England* (Basel 1957).

[5] Conrad Bäschlin, *Die Blütezeit der ökonomischen Gesellschaft in Bern 1759–1766* (Laupen 1913).

Swiss visits to England and had a very favourable influence on the welcome accorded to the Swiss and Genevans by English society. Truth to tell, Monsieur de Voltaire mocked this enthusiasm: 'Genève' he said 'imite l'Angleterre comme la grenouille imite le bœuf. Elle est le Gille de l'Angleterre.'

A second and powerful factor which helped the Swiss to blossom out in England in the eighteenth century was the interest that Protestant England, her sovereigns and the Whigs on the one hand, and the Reformed Cantons and Geneva on the other hand, took in each other.[6]

The accession of William of Orange to the English Throne was warmly welcomed by Geneva and the Protestant Cantons. His policy towards them remained that of his successors throughout the century: its aim was to check French influence in Switzerland, to rally to the Allied cause at least the Protestant Cantons, and to obtain soldiers from them. English and Swiss interests were not always fully in harmony, for each side acted upon very different motives. But on the whole the Swiss neutrality served singularly well the policy for European balance pursued by England. Apart from that, England saw in Switzerland—placed in the centre of the Continent and where so many foreign interests overlapped—a first-rate observation post. All this worked very much in favour of England's friendly policy towards Switzerland and Geneva, and it also motivated the despatch to our land of successive diplomatic missions.

But there also were very special reasons for the kindly dispositions towards Switzerland of the different sovereigns. William III came from a country long linked by a close friendship with Reformed Switzerland, and, already in the Netherlands, he himself had had in his service numerous officers from our country. It is natural that in England, too, he should have maintained his friendly feelings for them and continued to rely on their loyalty. In its turn the Hanoverian dynasty liked to surround itself with Protestant Swiss, Genevans and Neuchâtelois. Of German origin, slow to learn the English tongue and get used to the English way of life, these sovereigns and their equally Germanic wives were quite glad to welcome Swiss people who spoke or at least understood their own

[6] Markus Meier, *Die diplomatischen Beziehungen Englands mit der Schweiz im 18. Jahrhundert* (Basel 1952).

language, adhered to the same faith, belonged to the same culture or were familiar with it, and willingly served a court which was not always popular and sometimes struggled with financial difficulties. Moreover, after the founding in 1735 of Göttingen University, where many Swiss taught and studied, new links were forged between the royal family and Swiss circles. Was not A. de Haller a professor at that illustrious centre of learning? Did not King George III refuse to allow Haller to accept a Bernese diplomatic mission in London in order to keep him in Göttingen?[7] And was it not typical that Ph. A. Stapfer, for instance, should spend a period there before completing his studies in England?

All this helps to explain the favourable welcome extended to some of the Swiss in England, a welcome which was all the more cordial because the Confederation kept no diplomatic agents in London, and it was precisely these Swiss who ensured regular contacts between their country and the English Court and Government. Our diplomatists and officers in the service of the Crown played a substantial part in Anglo-Swiss relations, notably where the Prussian succession to the Throne of Neuchâtel and the enrolment of Swiss troops were concerned.

Thirdly, it is worth remembering that, from the beginning of the eighteenth century, London, separated from our country by a long and difficult journey, was sheltering Swiss groups and institutions which had grown strong enough to give real help to newly arrived compatriots, guide them, and introduce them to those personalities and circles which could play a useful part in their future evolution.[8]

Indeed even before the eighteenth century there existed in London and in other parts of Great Britain a considerable nucleus of Genevans and Vaudois.[9] The Genevans gathered in the 'Compagnie des Genevois', while the Vaudois, numbering 700 to 800, were not yet organised. In 1703, however, the Vaudois approached other compatriots and together they constituted the United Society of Swiss in London. In 1718 that organisation again amalgamated with another and then, after absorbing also the Ancient Company

[7] Emil Boesch, *Albrecht von Hallers Lebenslauf* (Bern 1877).

[8] Ernest Boos, *Die Schweizerkolonie in England nach Berufsgruppen* (Bern 1966).

[9] There must have existed a small colony of Genevans in Ireland too. The father of General Dufour met it there when he emigrated (Marcel Du Pasquier, *La Suisse Romande, terre d'accueil et d'échanges*, Lausanne 1965, p. 85).

of Genevans, became in 1720 the powerful and solid Mutual Aid Society of the Swiss in London, which is still flourishing.

The Genevan and Swiss community of those days seems to have been quite comfortably off, since it is known that some of its members (with such names as Pages, Marcet, Favrot, Buisson, Saladin, Lullin, Perdriau, Favre, etc.) decided in 1703 to invest jointly in government bonds the substantial sum of £300,000, 'which would return an annual income of £20,000'.

Between 1722 and 1725 a Glarus man, Stehelin, and a Vaudois, Hollard, were the pastors of a bilingual 'Church of the Switzers', which depended on the Bishop of London and for which King George I had given the land near Charing Cross. (This particular piece of land was not used, however.) A second religious community was set up in 1762, in the form of a French-speaking 'Église suisse de Londres',[10] whose first pastors were Antoine Bugnon (1762–1771), A. J. Roustan (1764–91), an admirer of Jean-Jacques Rousseau and himself a writer, and A. Sterky (1792–1839), French Reader to the future Queen Charlotte.

At that time there also existed a French Hospital (a different one from that founded in 1867) which was open to the Swiss and to which wealthy Genevans such as Anne Colladon and Pierre Gaussen made important donations. Ten members of the Duval family, of Geneva, were successively directors of this institution.

These institutions soon lay at the heart of Swiss life in London. But one should not forget, either, the houses of diplomats, high civil servants and officers, the scholars' chambers and the artists' studios where Swiss who had already attained important positions gave their juniors, in a splendid spirit of mutual aid, the benefit of their professional guidance and social support.

One might also recall here the presence of numerous and remarkable Huguenots from France, who had found refuge in London after the revocation of the Edict of Nantes and who readily regarded the Genevans and the Protestant Swiss as members of their own great family. Such was, for instance, the case with Sir Samuel Romilly, M.P.; Samuel Bosanquet, a Governor of the Bank of England; and John Francis Rigaud, a painter and Member of the Royal Academy. They were all very close to Geneva by virtue of their marriages, their visits to that city, their studies or their business life.

[10] Albert Roehrich, Claude Reverdin, *L'Église suisse de Londres* (London s.d.).

But the decisive factor in the extraordinary efflorescence of the Swiss in England in the eighteenth century was certainly that that period was intellectually one of the most brilliant both in the Old Confederation and in Geneva, and that our country, too small to utilise the talents of all its children, had to let a surprising number of distinguished citizens go abroad—men eminent not only in literature, the sciences and the arts, but also in such fields as the army, the administration and banking. But one must also remember here the part played by Huguenot families who, having sought refuge in Geneva or in Switzerland for religious reasons, saw, after staying for various lengths of time, some of their members leaving again for different countries, where they were welcomed as Swiss.

Here, then, are sufficient factors to explain the remarkable influx of Swiss into Great Britain in the eighteenth century, and the part they were able to play there, thanks to the active sympathy and goodwill with which they met.

I

The series of literary, scientific and philosophical journeys which Genevans and Swiss undertook to the British Isles in the eighteenth century began in 1701 with the little-known one made by the Genevan Georges-Louis Le Sage (1676–1759), the teacher of a considerable number of young Englishmen. As a result, he wrote his *Remarks about England*. But it was the *Lettres sur les Anglais et les Français*, the fruit of an earlier pilgrimage to England (1694–1695) by the Bernese officer of a Swiss regiment in Paris, Béat de Muralt (1665–1749), which unleashed the Anglomania of the Swiss when the book appeared in Geneva in 1725. (It is not certain whether Voltaire did read the 'Letters' on the occasion of his visit to England; he never mentioned them in his correspondence; the 1753 edition of the book was, however, found in his library.) In his turn, Albert de Haller (1708–77), who much enjoyed the works of Milton and Pope, came to London and to Oxford at a very early age. Later on he was to dedicate to George III his book *Arthur, King of England*, in which he declares himself in favour of a constitutional state modelled on England; he was hoping to get some reward for his efforts, but his book did not evoke quite the desired response.

Charles-Victor de Bonstetten (1745–1832), of Berne, was in England in 1769–70, at the age of 24, and met many celebrities there. He visited London, Oxford, Bath and Berkshire. He had the privilege of being introduced to Thomas Gray at Pembroke College and immediately a deep friendship united the great poet of nature with the young son of the Alps.[11] Johann Gaspar Scheuchzer,[12] son of Johann Jakob, came to England in 1720, at the age of 18, worked as librarian to Sir Hans Sloane and helped him to compile the catalogue of his collection of books, which was to become the Library of the British Museum. He was also a Fellow of the Royal Society.

Benjamin Constant (1767–1830) attended Edinburgh University from July 1783 to April 1785, and it was there that he entered upon 'the happiest year' of his life. There, too, he learnt, so his biographer says,[13] always to take work seriously. The town which he described later at the beginning of *Adolphe* undoubtedly has some features of Edinburgh.

Étienne Dumont (1759–1829), of Geneva, stayed in England from 1786 to 1789 and again from 1791 to 1814.[14] Former tutor to Lord Shelburn's children, and his librarian, he became an intimate friend of Jeremy Bentham, whose great treatises on punishments and rewards, on political economy and on judicial evidence he published; but for him, these unique works might never really have become known.

Jean-Jacques Rousseau[15] (1712–78), tired of the persecutions he suffered in France, Geneva and the Canton of Berne as a result of his writings, sought asylum in England and hoped to find peace in this oasis of freedom in Europe. At the prompting of Milord Maréchal, George Keith, and in the company of the Scottish philosopher David Hume, who wanted to 'show the lion' in London, he landed in Dover in January 1766. From the moment he arrived in the capital, everyone from commoner to King was interested in him. His *Le Devin du village* was staged at Covent

[11] Marie-L. Herking, *Charles-Victor de Bonstetten* (Lausanne 1921).

[12] Gavin de Beer, 'Johann Gaspar Scheuchzer', *Notes and Records of the Royal Society of London* (1949), ix. 56.

[13] Gustave Rudler, *La Jeunesse de Benjamin Constant 1767–1794* (Paris 1909).

[14] Jean Martin, *Étienne Dumont* (Neuchâtel 1942).

[15] Louis John Courtois, *Le Séjour de Rousseau en Angleterre* (Lausanne 1911). Gavin de Beer, 'Quelques considérations sur le séjour de Rousseau en Angleterre', *Genava*, n.s. (Genève 1955), iii. 1. Henri Roddier, *J.-J. Rousseau en Angleterre au XVIIIe siècle* (Paris 1950). Jacques Voisine, *J.-J. Rousseau en Angleterre à l'époque romantique* (Paris 1956).

Garden. The painter Allan Ramsay[16] and the sculptor Gosset immortalised his features. The King himself secretly offered him a pension. But the malicious *Lettre du roi de Prusse*, which also circulated in London, upset him and gave him the idea that his enemies were poisoning public opinion. After toying with the idea of going to 'Wild Wales', of which he had been told that it resembled Switzerland, he accepted the hospitality of Richard Davenport in his house (since pulled down) at Wootton, in Staffordshire. However, he soon fell out with Hume—it was the famous 'quarrel'—and, after a stay in England of only 16 months, he returned to the Continent in April 1767. Nevertheless, his influence continued to be felt strongly on this side of the Channel: Priestley and Godwin supported his ideas; Goldsmith, Byron and Shelley were to be influenced by his cult of feeling.

Madame de Staël[17] came to England in 1793, not as a refugee but to rejoin her lover, the Count of Narbonne, for whom she had rented Juniper Hall, in Surrey. But she was soon thought to be something of a Jacobin, and when the Anglo-French war broke out she returned to Switzerland. She had arrived at Juniper Hall at the same time as the news of Louis XVI's death, which made still sadder the exile of the friends whom she met again there: Talleyrand, Montmorency and Jaucourt. But she spent there with Narbonne 'quatre mois de bonheur échappés au naufrage de la vie', and is supposed to have written at that time the second chapter of *De l'influence des passions sur le bonheur des individus et des nations*, entitled 'Est-ce là du bonheur?' She also met Fanny Burney, with whom she felt herself in sympathy and whom she later called 'la première femme d'Angleterre'.

It is worth while adding here that Mademoiselle Necker had already visited England with her parents[18] at the age of 10, in 1776.[19] She was then much impressed by the acting of Garrick at Drury Lane; she later considered him and Talma to be 'les premiers

[16] A copy of Ramsay's portrait of Rousseau was ordered from the artist by Madame Necker who educated her daughter according to the the ideas of the philosopher. It now adorns the Château de Coppet.

[17] J. Christopher Herold, *Mistress to an Age* (London 1959), pp. 116-123.

[18] The reader may be interested to know that the Neckers adopted the coat of arms of a Necker who lived according to genealogists in Ireland in the days of William the Conqueror.

[19] Comtesse Jean de Pange, *Le Mystérieux Voyage de Necker en Angleterre* (1776) (Paris 1948).

génies du théâtre'. When she was 17, her mother, who was very eager for a Protestant marriage, planned to wed her, the wealthiest Protestant heiress in Europe, to the young but already famous William Pitt, whom she met at Fontainebleau. Nothing came of this, however, since Germaine could not resign herself to living permanently in England away from her father. Mr Pitt, she said 'a le nez trop long et je n'aime pas les brumes de Londres'.

If most of these travellers came to England as visitors, curious to get to know the country in general, others—the greatest number of them apparently from Zürich and Geneva—were anxious to pursue special studies at Oxford or Cambridge or to fulfil some scientific or religious mission. Thus one could meet at those famous universities such scholars as Pastor Ami Lullin (1748–1816); the jurist Jean-Jacques Burlamaqui (1694–1748), who, inspired by Locke, Cumberland and Pope, published his *Principes du droit naturel et du droit public*, of which no fewer than eleven English translations appeared between 1748 and 1817 and which became the textbook of the Cambridge professors; the theologian Jean Alphonse Turrettini (1671–1737), who, with William Wake, Archbishop of Canterbury, tried to reconcile all the Protestant churches; the mathematician Nicolas Fatio (1664–1753), a friend of Newton and a Fellow of the Royal Society at 23; Firmin Abauzit (1679–1767), Pastor Benedict Pictet (1625–1724), Doctor Théodore Tronchin (1709–81); and Louis de Lolme (1741–1806), of Geneva, the author, in particular, of an essay on the British constitution which, translated into English and running into many editions, was in its turn for a long time a standard textbook for teachers and students.

The presence in London of Swiss scientists manifested itself more especially when certain great English societies for the advancement of the sciences and the arts came into being. For instance, the Royal Society of Arts, created in 1754, had as one of its founders the agronomist Jean Rodolphe Vautravers (1723–1815), of Romairon (Vaud), and counted among its early members many other Swiss. The same can be said of the Royal College of Surgeons. And it goes without saying that The Royal Society, from its foundation in the seventeenth century, had Swiss scholars among its Fellows such as Nicolas Fatio; Abraham Trembley of Geneva, pedagogue, writer and tutor to the Duke of Portland; Albert de Haller; and Johann-Jakob Scheuchzer, of Zürich (1672–1733), the author of the *Itinera Alpina*. Let me add in passing that Joseph de Planta (1744–1827), the future Chief Librarian of the British Museum, was one of its Secretaries (1776–1804). Furthermore, the close personal relationships between Swiss and British scientists are reflected in the friendship that united Newton, Johann-Jakob Scheuchzer, Hans Sloane, Nicolas Fatio and Firmin Abauzit.

The Genevese influence upon the Methodist movement also deserves a reference here. Jean Guillaume de la Fléchère, of Nyon (1729–85), called Fletcher in England and Vicar of Madeley (Shropshire), was for twenty years Wesley's most faithful collaborator and adviser. Moreover, he was the principal of the first Methodist seminary, founded by Lady Huntingdon in Trevecka, and the lawgiver of his church. Wesley himself, in two big volumes, erected a lasting monument to him. In his turn Vincent Perronet (1693–1785), son of a citizen of Château-d'Oex naturalised in England, a famous preacher, worked closely with Wesley and Fletcher. He was called the 'Archbishop of the Methodists'.

At the time of the political troubles in Geneva at the end of the century and while Geneva was under French occupation, many of her citizens sought shelter in England. This was the case, for instance, with Sismondi; with François d'Ivernois, who took British nationality, was knighted and became a friend of Pitt; with Charles-Ami Lullin, who became friendly with William Wickham; with Mallet Du Pan, the founder of the *Mercure britannique* in 1798, who, having exhausted all his energy and resources, took refuge in London, where he died, the ancestor of a brilliant line of English civil servants and diplomats.

The century closes on inflammatory speeches at Westminster, in which famous parliamentarians like Pitt, Grenville, Fox, George Canning and others stigmatised France for having destroyed, when invading Switzerland, the very cradle of liberty. Samuel Taylor Coleridge, W. L. Bowles, J. Montgomery and William Wordsworth deplored this tragedy in bitter verses.

II

Perhaps more brilliant still, but in any case wider in scope than the part played by Swiss writers, philosophers and scientists, was that of Swiss artists in eighteenth-century England.

Their tradition had already been established by Hans Holbein, of Basle, when he became painter to Sir Thomas More and later to King Henry VIII, and by the famous Genevan miniaturists James Petitot and Jacques Bordier, whose many works still adorn castles, stately homes and museums in this country.

But it was in fact in the eighteenth century, when the Royal Academy of Arts was founded in 1768, that there first came to light the astonishing number of Swiss painters established in London and that their profound influence on contemporary art was recognised. Three of the Founders, five of the Members first elected, and no fewer than three of the first Keepers of that illustrious institution were Swiss.

Behind the back of Sir Joshua Reynolds, whom he disliked, King George III discussed intensively with the chaser, enameller and medallist George Michael Moser, of Schaffhausen (1704–83), the constitution of the new Academy, the nomination of Members and the commissioning of certain paintings. The reason was that Moser had been drawing-master to the sovereign when the latter was Prince of Wales, an honour he owed, apart from his personal merits and his friendly manner, to the fact that he had been the Principal and Treasurer of the celebrated painting academy founded by Hogarth in 1735 at St Martin's Lane, the cradle of the future Royal Academy. The latter having come into existence, Moser quite naturally became its first Keeper. Sir Joshua Reynolds himself (1723–92) wrote his obituary: 'Of him [Moser],' he pointed out, 'it can truly be said in every sense that he was the father of the present race of artists.'[20]

After his death in 1783 he was succeeded by another Swiss, Agostino Carlini (d. 1790), of Geneva, a well-known sculptor and painter. Somerset House is indebted to him for two allegorical statues representing English rivers. But his best-known work is without doubt Dr Ward's portrait.

The fourth Keeper of the Academy was yet another Swiss: Heinrich Füssli (1741–1825), of Zürich, or Henry Fuseli as he was called in England. As a painter, art teacher (Blake, Flaxman and Thomas Lawrence were among his students), writer, philosopher and man of the world, he played a primary rôle in the artistic, philosophical and literary life of London. He illustrated Shakespeare

[20] James Northcote, R.A., *The Life of Sir Joshua Reynolds* (London 1819).

and Milton, and his historical drawings helped people to understand better the symbolism of his friend William Blake. Although his paintings in the heroic vein were not to everyone's taste, he was much appreciated as a teacher, and his *Lectures on Painting* were much in demand. Nothing shows more clearly the esteem in which this original and powerful personality was universally held than the fact that he was buried in St Paul's Cathedral, where he rests, not far from Sir Anthony van Dyke and Sir Christopher Wren, immediately next to Sir Joshua Reynolds.

Of Basle extraction, but passing as the son of a Pole because his father had been at King Stanislaus Poniatowski's court, Philip de Loutherbourg (1740–1812) was among the first to be elected a Member of the Royal Academy. Originally engaged by David Garrick as 'Superintendent of scenery and machinery' at the Drury Lane Theatre, he became, with the encouragement of Sir Joshua Reynolds and Thomas Gainsborough, an excellent painter of landscapes and historical battle-pieces. At the end of his life he met Casanova and, curiously enough, turned faith-healer with thousands of patients under his care.

One of his pupils was Sir Francis Bourgeois (1756–1811), of Giez,[21] who in his turn was among the first Members of the Academy. He is remembered today less as a painter of animals, battle scenes and landscapes, or as painter to George III, than as the donor of the paintings in the imposing Gallery of Masters at Dulwich College. One of his friends, Noël Desenfans, had bought for King Stanislaus a number of classical works intended to form the nucleus of a Polish national collection. But upon the partition of that unfortunate country, the whole collection came into the hands of Bourgeois, who donated it, with substantial funds for its upkeep, to the institution of which it is still the pride. The monumental mausoleum of this generous benefactor still stands in the lovely building designed by Sir John Soane to house the collection.

Another Swiss well known to his contemporaries and also an early Member of the Academy was Johann Waeber (d. 1793), of Berne, John Webber in English, painter, a pupil of Aberli, and official artist of Captain Cook's Third Voyage to the Pacific Ocean (Tahiti) in 1776. He it was who drew the famous scene depicting the great explorer's death. The British Admiralty afterwards pub-

[21] D. Agassiz, *Sir François Bourgeois* (Lausanne 1937).

lished a large album of his drawings. Captain Cook wrote in his journal that he had engaged Webber to travel with him in order to supplement the inevitable deficiencies of written descriptions . . . and to make the results of his efforts interesting and instructive to the seaman, the scholar and the general reader.

One of the only two women elected among the first Members of the Royal Academy was Swiss: Mary Moser (Mrs Lloyd) (1744–1819), daughter of George Michael Moser and herself a celebrated flower painter and art adviser to Queen Charlotte.

J. F. Rigaud, an excellent artist and a favourite portrait painter with English society, and also an early Member of the Academy, was thought to be Genevan, but was in fact of French extraction, although related to the family bearing the same name in Geneva.

In 1802 H. Singleton painted the famous picture showing the Members of the Royal Academy that year, grouped around their President, Benjamin West, and each one of them a celebrity. No Swiss can contemplate without emotion the faces of so many illustrious compatriots who belonged at that time to such an exalted assembly.

But it was not only in this great institution that one met Helvetic artists. Outside its compass others were also able to make a name for themselves in this country. The foremost of these was, of course, Jean-Étienne Liotard (1702–98), of Geneva, who came to London for the first time about 1756 and then from 1772 to 1774, and whom some English connoisseurs have placed as high as the great Joshua Reynolds himself. At another level, one could also see at work his pupil, L. A. Arlaud (1751–1829), and the miniaturist J. H. Hurter (1734–99), of Schaffhausen; the painter David Morier (1705?–70), of Château-d'Oex, who was protected by William, Duke of Cumberland, and who excelled in painting animals, especially horses, and executed battle-pieces and equestrian portraits (George II, George III, the Duke of Cumberland)—he made no fortune as an artist but became the ancestor of a splendid family of British diplomats; the landscape painter and poet Samuel Hieronimus Grimm (1733–94), of Burgdorf; the famous topographical draughtsman Jakob Schneebeli (d. 1792), of Zürich; Salomon Gessner, son of the poet of *Idylls*; James Anthony Dassier (1715–59), of Geneva, engraver at the Royal Mint; and F. H. Müntz, another engraver, who enjoyed Walpole's patronage.

To these painters and engravers must be added members of other liberal professions, such as the architect Charles-Paul Dangeau de La Belye (1704–81), born in Vevey of Huguenot parents, the builder of the first Westminster Bridge and the author of plans for a new Palace of St James; Andreas Schalch (1692–1776), of Schaffhausen, who cast the Woolwich bells; Burkhart Tschudi (1718–1773), of Schwanden, a famous harpsichord maker, some of whose instruments, remarkable as much for musical quality as for superb cabinet-making, can still be seen at Chatsworth, Chirk Castle, etc.

A special place belongs to J.-J. Heidegger (1666–1749),[22] of Zürich, known both for his breath-taking ugliness, delineated by Hogarth's pencil, and for the valuable and effective help he gave Handel, both as devoted friend and admirer and as librettist and skilful director of the King's Theatre, where they collaborated most amicably.

III

Numerous also were the Swiss, Genevans and Neuchâtelois who, in the eighteenth century, discharged special functions at Court, whether at Whitehall, St Theobald and St James's, or at Hampton Court and Kew. They were almost always French-speaking, and often pastors or pastors' sons, whose appeal lay mainly in the fact that they were both Protestants and heirs to the French civilisation.

William III had as his preceptor Samuel Chappuzeau. When he became King of England in 1688, he took with him his bodyguard of 50 Bernese who, as tradition says, entered London to the strains of the 'Bernermarsch'.[23] As his physician, he took over from his predecessor Sir Theodore Colladon (d. 1707), of Geneva, the chief medical officer at Chelsea Hospital, whose last descendant, Anne Colladon, left a considerable part of her fortune to the French Hospital, to which Swiss were also admitted. Sir Theodore's successor was Étienne Rougeat, another Genevan. On scientific matters, King William liked to refer to Nicolas Fatio, Newton's friend. It was he who tried, though without success, to persuade Firmin Abauzit to leave Geneva for Cambridge.

Queen Anne had in her Palace Guard three Swiss captains:

[22] Th. Vetter, *Johann Jakob Heidegger ein Mitarbeiter Handels* (Zürich 1902).

[23] Richard Feller, *Geschichte Berns* (Bern 1955), iii. 97.

Pachoud, Bonnard and Delachaux; she had no doubt inherited them from her brother-in-law.

From the time the Protestant Hanoverians arrived in England, the Swiss and Genevan colony, with its large Reformed majority, had excellent relations with them. In 1745, when the second Jacobite rebellion broke out, it offered to levy in support of George II a 500-strong battalion which could be mobilised within 24 hours. This volunteer corps, organised by Sir Luke Schaub, however, never saw action, but the sovereign reviewed it and handed to it on that occasion a flag which is still in existence, and which is similar to those of the Swiss regiments in France.[24] The inscription on the cross of the Colour seems to have been: 'Ubi libertas ibi bene'.

George II, who had a marked aversion to all he called 'bainting, blays and boetry', was nevertheless fond of masquerades. It was the peculiar 'Swiss Count', the J.-J. Heidegger, of Zürich,[25] already mentioned, who became his rather licentious Master of the Revels. The severe Andreas de Planta, on the other hand, was appointed Italian Reader to Queen Caroline. F.-O. Petitpierre and Joshua Amez-Droz (d. 1793) were teachers of French and tutors to the future King George III, and he had George Michael Moser as his drawing-master. Gaspar Wettstein acted as chaplain, English teacher and librarian to the Prince of Wales, who even sent him to Gotha on a delicate mission to his future fiancée.

But it was George III who assembled the greatest number of Swiss around himself, the Queen and the Royal Princes. He employed successively as French Reader the Reverend Charles de la Guiffardière, of Geneva, nicknamed 'Mr Turbulent'; Antoine Jacques Roustan; Bugnon and Sterky; while the physicist Jean-André de Luc, a Fellow of the Royal Society, held the same appointment to the Queen. His influence was quite important as he gathered round him a group of well-known Genevese emigrants. Joseph de Planta was the King's adviser on books and libraries, and Colonel

[24] Felix Staehelin, *Der jüngere Stuartprätendent und sein Aufenthalt in Basel 1754-1756* (Basel 1949). The Young Pretender lived in Basle, accompanied by Mrs Walkinshaw, as Chevalier William Thompson and said he was a doctor. When in Rome, Charles-Victor de Bonstetten was very much impressed by his young wife, the Countess of Albany, the 'Reine des Cœurs'. (Herking, *op. cit.*, pp. 109-111). It is of interest to note that some Catholic Swiss fought in the ranks of the Jacobites.

[25] E. S. Turner, *The Court of St James* (London 1960), p. 206.

Polier ensured the liaison between him and the Court at Hanover. De Salgas educated the Princes William and Edward, and Lieutenant-General Jacques de Budé (1737–1818), of Geneva, gave them military instruction. The King commissioned Paul Mallet to write a History of the House of Brunswick, to which the Queen belonged. Mademoiselle de Montmollin, Mesdemoiselles P. and B. de Planta, and Mademoiselle Mula were governesses to the Princesses, and also dealt with the Queen's correspondence. The English teacher, Mademoiselle Bab de Planta, was, in particular, a companion in grief of the famous Fanny Burney[26] under the formidable Miss Schwellenberg, Lady-in-Waiting to Queen Charlotte.

It was not only the King who surrounded himself with Swiss. The nobility shared his habits and we see the Dukes of Portland and Newcastle, the families of Lords Dysart, Mountstuart, Limerick, Bentinck, Chesterfield, Walpole, Lansdowne, Waldgrave, Cecil and many others entrusting the education of their sons to Swiss tutors and sending them together on the 'Grand Tour', on which several of our towns and cities constituted traditional stops. The Duke of Chandos even had his own Swiss Guard.

IV

The most surprising form of the Swiss presence in England in the eighteenth century was perhaps that constituted by our bankers.[27]

Since before the Reformation, but mostly after the revocation of the Edict of Nantes (1685), bankers from Geneva—which was the cradle of one of the forms of modern capitalism—and Huguenot refugees in that town had been emigrating to London, where they soon established trading counters, while jealously maintaining close ties with their families and the parent enterprises in their hometown, which had become too small for them. This emigration continued during the whole of the eighteenth century, so that, by the end of it, an impressive number of Genevan and Helvetic merchant bankers were to be found in London. Among them might be mentioned Pierre Chauvet, Louis Guiguer (one of whose relatives

[26] *The Diary of Fanny Burney* (London 1966), pp. 130-135, 137-143, etc.

[27] Swiss Bank Corporation, *Swiss Merchant Bankers in London* (London 1954). Herbert Lüthy, *La Banque protestante en France* (Paris 1961).

owned Prangins Castle where Voltaire lived in 1754 before he bought Les Délices), Charles-Henri Rigaud, Jacques Achard; and above all Pierre Isaac Thēlusson and Anthony Francis Haldimand, who played such a prominent part in the English business world.

Always in close contact with compatriot bankers and co-religionists in Amsterdam, Lyons and Paris, these businessmen constituted what one would call today a Huguenot Internationale. They mostly dealt in the money market. But they also acted occasionally as intermediaries between London's flourishing financial market and certain Swiss cantons, primarily Berne and Zürich, which sometimes borrowed from and sometimes lent capital to the British Government and financiers. Several Swiss agents were on the spot to help them. Berne, for instance, had recourse to representatives such as Captain Hans Jakob Otth (= Ott) and to such firms as Muller & Co., while at the same time also keeping a special financial commissioner in the kingdom. Towards the end of the century, Berne had deposited in London some £440,000, and Zürich about £50,500, which sums they were thus able to save from Napoleon's grasp and which they withdrew intact when the wars were over, the accrued interest for the years 1798 to 1814 being used to pay off the so-called 'Helvetian public debt'. Less would have sufficed to create a firm tradition of financial collaboration and mutual trust between the two countries.

The Genevan and Swiss bankers were, at certain times, almost the only financial links between the continent and isolationist England, which was almost continuously at war with some adversary there. This fact enabled them, when the Revolution of 1789 was impending, to render services to the French aristocrats who, foreseeing trouble, were eager to transfer their fortunes to England. It was in this context that Pierre Isaac Thélusson, whose family's office in Paris had had Monsieur Necker[28] as a partner, played a particularly active rôle. His enigmatic will became a test case well-known to British lawyers.[29]

Extremely well informed, cultivating valuable international and local relationships and controlling very large assets, the Genevan

[28] When Paris was suffering from famine in 1789, Necker offered his whole fortune in England as a guarantee of payment for English wheat to be imported by France (Édouard Chapuisat, *Necker*, Paris 1938, p. 181).

[29] John J. Moss, *A Study in the private use of eighteenth century legal formalism. Historical evidence for an understanding of Peter Thellusson's Will* (London 1958).

and Swiss bankers in London[30] were naturally more and more in demand for their services. A number of them became British, married well in the Kingdom, were raised to the peerage or were elected Members of Parliament. Their brilliant position made it possible for several of them to accede to the highest offices in the City, some becoming directors and even governors of the Bank of England. Thus it was that Peter Gaussen, of Geneva (1723–88), held this high appointment between 1777 and 1779, that is to say, during the American War of Independence. Peter Isaac Thélusson and William Haldimand, the son of Anthony Francis, were among the directors at the turn of the century.

It is also interesting to mention here the bankers who were directors of the very important East India Company: Peter Gaussen, already referred to, and Pierre Henri Cazenove, of Geneva, the founder of the Cazenove firm in London, which is still flourishing.

V

The enrolment in England of Genevan and Swiss soldiers during the eighteenth century is explained by a twofold factor: on the one hand, the hostile attitude of Louis XIV towards the Protestants, whom he drove out of France by means of the Revocation of the Edict of Nantes, had shocked the Protestant cantons and had encouraged them to be more liberal in their policy of considering recruitment also for nations other than France. Louis XIV had, moreover, upset the Swiss by constructing the fortress of Huningen just outside Basle, by occupying Strasbourg in spite of its federal links with the Swiss, by reducing the pay of the Swiss regiments in France and by limiting the commercial privileges of Swiss tradesmen in France. On the other hand, the Protestant Genevans, Vaudois and Neuchâtelois, who did not benefit from the 'capitulations' signed by the Thirteen Cantons, at that time liked to offer their sword to Protestant powers.

So it happened that in 1692 William III was able to conclude in Zürich a treaty of 'Offensive and Defensive Union', the parties being, on the one side, the Protestant cantons and the town of St

[30] These bankers were mainly Boissier & Sellon, Cazenove, Ami Gampert, A. Haldimand, Barthelemy Huber, Mark Liotard & Aubertin, Nicolas Marcet, Marcet & Cie, Samuel Müller, Peter Thélusson, Naville & Aubert, Ami Rilliet, Tourton & Guiguer, etc., etc.

Gall, and on the other side His Britannic Majesty 'for the services of Holland'. Thanks to this arrangement, it was possible for Lord Galloway and Jean de Sacconay, of Bursinel, to sign in 1695 a 'capitulation' for the levy of a Swiss regiment 1,600 strong. This excellent corps, comprising mainly Vaudois and four companies of the former Oberkan Regiment, rendered important services to the Duke of Marlborough when fighting against the armies of Louis XIV in the sieges of Kaiserswerth, Venloo, Ruremonde, Liège, Huy and Limbourg (1702–3), actions which were celebrated in Berne as if they were Switzerland's own achievements.

But already in the years 1689 to 1692, during the Irish campaign, the British sovereign had employed several Swiss officers, whose valour he had no doubt had occasion to recognise in Holland (they were de la Bastide, Bonnard, de Bonstetten, Desjean, d'Erlach, de Morsier, de Montmollin, de Saussure, de Steiger and Vischer).

However, it was principally in the American Colonies and in India that our regiments and our individual officers and soldiers fought in large numbers for the British crown, although some of them served at home also. Peter Elias, of Berne, for instance, introduced physical training into the Royal Navy and the British Army. With Sir Luke Schaub as intermediary, four companies of 140 men each and an artillery company of 71 men had been recruited in 1751 for the East India Company.[31] Once in India, they were incorporated into Major Lawrence's and Captain Clive's small army and lined up against the French, who were then thrown out of the country. In these companies, two officers distinguished themselves particularly: Daniel Frischmann, who became Commandant of the Comorin Province and Governor of Madras, and Colonel Louis Henri Polier, to whom the Calcutta command was entrusted. According to Sir John Fortescue and Malleson, Clive's real teachers were the two Swiss captains, Paradis of Fribourg and de Gingins of Vaud. Another unit, Count Charles-Daniel de Meuron's (1738–1806) Swiss Regiment, entered His Britannic Majesty's service in Ceylon in 1795, the Netherlands having been occupied by France and its allegiance to the Stadthouder brought to an end. In 1799 it joined General J. Harris's army and achieved wonders in the historic

[31] J. E. Kilchenmann, *Schweizer Söldner im Dienste der engl.-ostindischen Kompagnie in der Mitte des 18. Jahrhunderts* (Gümligen 1911). Arnold Lätt, *Der Anteil der Schweizer an der Eroberung Indiens* (Zürich 1934).

capture of Seringa Patham, the capital of Tippoo Sahib, when the Swiss grenadiers and light infantry formed the vanguard. At the end of the campaign Major-General Pierre-Frédéric de Meuron, the brother of the proprietor of the regiment, became Governor of Ceylon.

In America there were Swiss in the Royal American Regiment,[32] formed at the request of the British Parliament in 1754 by Henri Bouquet (1719–66), of Rolle, and Frédéric Haldimand (1718–91), of Yverdon. This corps, which, apart from the two Swiss battalions, was composed of four battalions of Scots and Dutch, had the task of repelling the French of Canada and of ensuring communications between the various forts along the whole territory under English control. Placed under the orders of the British Commander-in-Chief, this regiment was used in the defence of Canada in 1758–59; in the struggle against the Red Indians in 1763–64, when Henri Bouquet covered himself with a glory that still shines today; and in the American War of Independence (1775–83). Bouquet carried British rule beyond the Alleghany Mountains and into the Ohio Valley. Frédéric Haldimand organised the defence of Canada, which he succeeded in preserving for the British crown through his skilful handling of the situation. The three Prévost brothers, of Geneva, Augustin (1723–86), Jacques (1725–76) and Marc (1736–81), distinguished themselves during these campaigns. Augustin in particular helped defend Georgia and Florida against the American rebels.

But many of these officers also made names as administrators: Henri Bouquet became Governor of the Southern Colonies; Major-General Augustin Prévost Governor of Georgia; Sir Frederic Haldimand Governor of Montreal, then of Florida, and finally, from 1778 till 1804, Governor-General of Canada. Sir George Prévost (1767–1816) was Governor of Nova Scotia, then Governor-General of Canada (1812–14) also. These last two owed their high office, apart from personal merit, to the twofold fact that they were at once French-speaking and Protestant, which made them acceptable to both the English and the Canadians. 'A French-speaking Protestant', the latter would say, 'is a Swiss.'

Sir Frederic Haldimand's[33] record of service is impressive: he

[32] Arnold Lätt, *Schweizer Offiziere als Indianerkrieger und Instruktoren der englischen leichten Infanterie* (Zürich 1933).

[33] Arnold Latt, *Zwei Schweizer General-Gouverneure in Kanada* (Zürich 1926).

reconciled the Catholic French Canadians to British rule; he established law and order in a country devastated by 20 years of war; he introduced the constitutional government of 1784, built the first canal in the country, created its first public library and organised the colony's defence system so that his successor, Sir George Prévost, was able to hold it in 1812 against the United States in spite of their twelve-fold superiority in numbers. Several historians (Kingston, J. Winsor, Sir C. P. Lucas, MacIlwraith, for instance) have called him one of the 'makers of Canada'. Unfortunately, the last years of his mandate were marred by the attacks of a journalist called Pierre du Calvet, who accused him of being a tyrant. These accusations were fully refuted, but nevertheless they did obscure his glory for a short time.

It may be of interest to note here that almost all the Secretaries of the first Governors-General of Canada were Swiss, mainly Vaudois: Conrad Gugy, J. Bruyère, H. Cramahé, F. Mourrier, F. Mazères, F. L. Genevay.[34]

In this chapter the colonial achievements of two very enterprising gentlemen should also be mentioned. Attracted by the great possibilities of America, Christof de Graffenried (1661–1743),[35] Seigneur of Worb (Berne), founded in 1710 a colony of Bernese and German peasants between the Trent and the News in North Carolina. He called it New-Bern and became himself Landgrave of Carolina, Baron of Bernburg and honorary citizen of London. This agglomeration still exists and the American branch of the de Graffenried family is flourishing. In his turn, Jean Pierre de Pury (1673–1736), of Neuchâtel, arrived in South Carolina in 1730 and established there for George II a colony of Swiss and Neuchâtelois bearing the name of Purrysburg. His son Charles succeeded him as commander of this place.

VI

Eighteenth-century English diplomats of Swiss origin form the last group in this essay. English reluctance to accept appointments abroad, and the fact, moreover, that William III and his first

[34] R. L. de Roquebrune, 'Les Suisses au Canada', *Journal de Genève* (6 juin 1966).

[35] Thomas P. de Graffenried, *History of the de Graffenried Family* (New York 1925).

successors sought support for their policies from the Whigs, who were close to the City, but who did not, at first, have at their disposal enough diplomats of their own to defend the Crown's interests abroad, explain why they often had recourse to foreigners, including some Swiss Protestants.[36]

This was the case when George I sent as Ambassador to Schönbrunn (1718–27) General and Admiral François Louis de Pesme de St-Saphorin (1668–1737). Already knowing the Viennese Court very well, he was one of the diplomats best informed on European affairs, and was much sought after. In Holland he had made the acquaintance of Lord Townsend, the father-in-law of Robert Walpole and, like the latter, a leader of the Whig party, and it was Townsend and Walpole who proposed his name to the British sovereign. He being a foreigner and therefore incapable of becoming a British Ambassador, the difficulty was circumvented by giving him letters from the Hanoverian Chancellor.[37] After being considerably active in his new post, he had to leave it because George I had openly criticised the Pragmatic Sanction. He later attended the coronation of George II, when he also met Voltaire, whose *Henriade* he possessed. St-Saphorin being known for the inordinate length of his despatches, it became a joke to call any long official letter a 'St-Saphorin'.

King George I made use as well of the talents of another Swiss, Sir Luke Schaub[38] (1690–1758), of Basle, who became one of the best-known British diplomats of his day. He was sent first to Vienna and then to Madrid where he acted as an English agent. In Hanover he had to maintain friendly terms between the two Courts. Personal Secretary of the King, knighted in 1720, close friend of Lord Carteret, he took charge from 1721 to 1724, when he was 31, of the British Embassy in Paris with credentials as Ambassador (although he was an alien). After this and a short mission to Poland he continued to play a certain part in diplomatic affairs in London and became a favourite companion of George II.

Less spectacular were the activities of Kaspar Wettstein,[39] Lord Carteret's secretary and teacher of German during the war of the Austrian Succession (1743).

[36] D. B. Horn *The British Diplomatic Service 1689–1789* (Oxford 1961).

[37] D. B. Horn, *op. cit.*, pp. 113-114.

[38] D. B. Horn, *op. cit.*, p. 39. Rudolf Massini, *Sir Luke Schaub (1690–1758)* (Basel 1953).

[39] Andreas Staehelin, 'Der Englandbasler Kaspar Wettstein', *Basler Zeitschrift* (1959), lvii.

It is perhaps worth mentioning here, in addition, three distinguished families of British diplomats with Swiss origins: the Mallets, the Moriers and the de Salis, whose progenitors settled in England towards the end of the eighteenth century.

CONCLUSION

It was the London and the country houses of these diplomats, writers, bankers and patrons of the arts; the chambers of these scholars, scientists and philosophers; the studios, finally, of these Swiss artists, that Monsieur de Voltaire and his eighteenth-century contemporaries might have visited.

His presence there would no doubt have been warmly welcomed. His memory remains alive in one salon at least: that of the Bernese lady, Maria Grossholz, who became Madame Tussaud and who, in her famous museum in London, placed his wax effigy modelled from life[40] in the tableau of King Louis XVI and his family, where we can still contemplate his witty face and his searching gaze. One of his visitors there will surely have been Mr E. V. Rieu, of Geneva, Editor of the Penguin Classics in London, 1944–64, who is the great-great-grandson of Henri Rieu, of Geneva (1721–87), one of Voltaire's *confidents* and *agents d'affaires*.

Bibliography

BEER, SIR GAVIN DE: *Escape to Switzerland* (London 1945). *Travellers in Switzerland* (London 1949). *Speaking of Switzerland* (London 1952).

BONJOUR, EDGAR: 'Die Schweiz und England', *Die Schweiz und Europa* (Basel 1961), Bd ii.

BOOS, ERNST: *Die Schweizer Kolonie in England nach Berufsgruppen* (Bern 1966).

FUNKE, O.: *Die Schweiz und die englische Literatur* (Bern 1937).

HÄUSERMANN, H. W.: *The Genevese Background* (London 1952).

Historisch-Biograph. Lexicon der Schweiz: 'Grossbritannien' (Neuenburg 1926), iii. 758-768.

LÄTT, A.: 'Cultural Relations between Switzerland and England', *Journal of the Royal Society of Arts* (1946), xliv, 607-618. 'Schweizer in

[40] Information supplied by Madame Tussaud's.

England', *Schweizer im Ausland* (Genf 1931). 'Swiss Contributions to English Cultural Life', *Atlantis Sonderhaft/Englisch-schweizerische Beziehungen und das Schweizer Buch* (Zürich 1946).

LÖHRER, H.: *Die Schweiz im Spiegel englischer Literatur 1849–1875* (Zürich 1952).

LUNN, SIR ARNOLD: *Switzerland and the English* (London 1944). *Switzerland in English Prose and Poetry* (London 1947).

METTLER, ERIC: 'Switzerland and the English-Speaking World', *Switzerland Present and Future* (Berne 1961), 137-142.

SCHIRMER, GUSTAV: *Die Schweiz im Spiegel englischer und amerikanischer Literatur bis 1848* (Zürich 1929).

STRAUMANN, HEINRICH: *Switzerland and the English-Speaking World* (Berne 1961).

Swiss Bank Corporation: Swiss Merchant Bankers in London (London 1954).

VALLIÈRE, P. DE: *Honneur et Fidélité. Histoire des Suisses au service étranger* (Lausanne 1940).

WILDI, M.: 'Anglo-Zürich Annals 1500–1954, *Edwin Amet and others, The Book of Zürich* (Zürich 1959).

The Enlightenment as Medicine and as Cure

Peter Gay

The Enlightenment was a system of ideas securely grounded in the texture of eighteenth-century reality. Obviously, there were many reasons for the *philosophes*' appearance in their time and place, many links between their programme and the needs and possibilities of the age. Most significant, and most pervasive, was the spectacular career of the natural sciences; the impact of Newtonian modes of thinking both within the spheres of physics and astronomy and beyond them was so powerful that no historian of the Enlightenment can safely afford to neglect them. For the observant *philosophes*, however, the possibilities of an Enlightenment manifested themselves not so much in the theoretical formulations of physics or astronomy, nor even in their technological consequences, as in the achievements of medicine.

For the men of the Enlightenment, medicine—the most prosperous client that natural science recruited in the eighteenth century—was the most highly visible, and the most heartening, index to general progress: nothing after all was better calculated to buoy up men's feeling about life than growing hope for life itself. But beyond this, for the *philosophes* medicine had more than visceral, it had intellectual meaning. It was in medicine that the *philosophes* tested their philosophical positions; medicine was at once the model of their new philosophy and the guarantee of its efficacy. And beyond that, medicine allowed the *philosophes* to press as a realistic claim what projectors before them had only glimpsed as a shapeless, uncertain vision. 'I love life,' Diderot wrote to the famous surgeon Sauveur-François de Morand in 1748, 'hence I want to live, at least as long as I continue to be happy. But there is no true happiness for the man who is not in good health.'[1] This was an old idea, as old as Plato; what was new, and characteristic of the Enlightenment's hopes, was Diderot's insistence that he had a right to health and happiness together.

Modern medicine had been intimately linked to the scientific revolution—which was at bottom a philosophical revolution—from the beginning; the philosophical aims, the very rhetoric, of Bacon and Descartes make that perfectly plain. In his Utopian commonwealth, the New Atlantis, Bacon paid assiduous attention to the safeguarding of health and the cure of disease; and Descartes, extolling the new practical sciences of his day, ranked the preservation of good health as the highest of all values. After all, he argued, even the mind depends 'so much on the temper and disposition of the bodily organs that if one could only find some way of making men wiser and more competent than they have been hitherto, I think that it is in medicine that we must seek it.' In fact, Descartes' hopes for the new medicine were boundless: 'All that we know is practically nothing compared to what still remains to be known; we could be freed from innumerable ailments, of mind and body alike, and perhaps even from the infirmities of old age, if we had adequate knowledge of their causes, and of all the remedies that nature has provided for us.'[2] Here was a programme worthy of the ambitions of the new philosophy.

By the time of Locke, this confident claim—a brave hope disguised as a firm prediction—found echoes among practising scientists; gradually medicine was transforming itself from a medieval mystery, the furtive ally of alchemy and astrology, into a philosophical pursuit, and this—the association of the new philosophy with the art of healing—indicated to the thinkers of the day the strength of both. Leibniz forecast that new discoveries in natural philosophy, and new precision instruments, would above all result in 'advances in medicine', that 'important science'.[3] And John Locke experienced, and exhibited, the alliance of medicine and philosophy both in his life and in his thought. Locke was a physician

[1] (16 December 1748), Roth, i. 59.

[2] *Discours de la méthode*, *VI*^e^ *discours*, éd. Étienne Gilson (2nd ed., 1926), pp. 61-62.

[3] Quoted in Dr Cabanès, *L'Histoire éclairé par la clinique* (n.d. [*ca.* 1930]), p. 30.

before he was a philosopher, and a philosopher largely because he was a physician; medicine prompted his most philosophical reflections. 'I perfectly agree with you', he wrote to Molyneux, 'concerning general theories, the curse of the time and destructive not less of life than of science—they are for the most part but a sort of waking dream, with which when men have warmed their heads, they pass into unquestionable truths. This is beginning at the wrong end, men laying the foundations in their own fancies, and then suiting the phenomena of diseases and cure of them, to those fancies. I wonder, after the pattern Dr. Sydenham has set of a better way, men should return again to this romance way of physics. What we know of the works of nature, especially in the constitution of health and the operation of our own bodies, is only by the sensible effects, but not by any certainty we can have of the tools she uses or the way she works by.'[4] As his letter suggests, Thomas Sydenham was John Locke's hero. He was also Locke's friend. When Locke listed a select few 'master-builders', who had revolutionised the sciences, he included Sydenham, 'the English Hippocrates', and when he made 'experience' into the final court of appeal, he was generalising from his own, and from Sydenham's medical practice. In his turn, Sydenham collaborated with Locke and thought like him: the physician, he insisted, must avoid 'speculations', and devote himself to the 'industrious investigation of the history of diseases, and of the effects of remedies, as shown by the only teacher, experience.'[5] Sydenham taught medicine on philosophical, Locke taught philosophy on medical principles.

As in so much else, Locke in this too set the pattern for the eighteenth-century Enlightenment. The emotion the *philosophes* invested in medicine is as hard to appreciate today as their worship of Cicero, and just as revealing. A number of them were medical men: Daubenton and Quesnay were surgeons; Bernard Mandeville, who though not precisely a *philosophe* scandalised the same people the *philosophes* scandalised, was a practising physician. The chevalier de Jaucourt, Diderot's indispensable collaborator on the *Encyclopédie*, studied at Leyden under the incomparable Boerhaave and

[4] Quoted in G. S. Brett, *A History of Psychology* (1921), ii. 257.

[5] Locke on Sydenham: *Essay Concerning Human Understanding*, 'The Epistle to the Reader'; Sydenham on method: Maurice Cranston, *John Locke: A Biography* (1957), p. 92.

took his medical degree, although he seems to have neglected his practice for his philosophy. La Mettrie, another student of Boerhaave's, derived his philosophical materialism from medical principles and persistently alluded to his medical experience in his philosophical writings: the 'great art of healing', he insisted in *L'Homme machine*, was man's noblest activity.

Other *philosophes* were well-informed amateurs. As a young man of letters, Diderot had been among the translators of Robert James's bulky *Medicinal Dictionary*; as a mature philosopher, he reiterated his conviction that medical science was strategic to all true knowledge: 'It is very hard', he wrote, 'to think cogently about metaphysics or ethics without being an anatomist, a naturalist, a physiologist, and a physician.'[6] He secured more than twenty physicians to collaborate on his *Encyclopédie*, notably Théophile de Bordeu and Théodore Tronchin, minor *philosophes* in their own right, who were his friends. Bordeu, urbane, sceptical, a principled empiricist, was celebrated in his time for his brilliant polemical history of medicine as much as for his successful practice; he used his articles in the *Encyclopédie* to diffuse reliable medical information and unmask the pretensions of medical system-makers. Tronchin, the fashionable Genevan physician whose practice reached as far as Paris and who attended, among many other distinguished patients, Voltaire, contributed a vigorous article on inoculation in which he made propaganda for the new science and against medical superstitions.

The materialists among the *philosophes*, of course, had good reason to take medicine seriously: for them disease, including mental disease, was merely a disorder in the human machine. But the deists and sceptics had as much regard for medical science as the atheists. Hume was on intimate terms with the greatest in a great generation of British physicians, including Sir John Pringle, President of the Royal Society and a pioneer in military medicine, and William Hunter, the great anatomist. Adam Smith and Edward Gibbon attended Hunter's lectures on anatomy. Benjamin Franklin, who was interested in everything, was also interested in medicine, especially in the establishment of medical societies. Voltaire, who enjoyed ill health for eighty-four years and knew as much about medicine as he knew about everything else (which is to say, a good

[6] Quoted in Arthur M. Wilson, *Diderot: The Testing Years* (1957), p. 93.

deal), humorously distrusted but perpetually consulted physicians, and not as a patient alone. He went to Leyden to attend Boerhaave's lectures and discuss Newton's philosophy with s'Gravesande, and all his life he read widely on medical subjects—he had read as many books on medicine, he confessed, as Don Quixote had read on chivalry. He campaigned on behalf of inoculation and inveighed against quackery, ridiculed such craft mysteries as secret ingredients in drugs, urged the application of common sense in the compounding of prescriptions and the appointment of hospitals, and represented, in all he wrote on the subject, advanced and rational scientific opinion.

All these medical preoccupations were philosophical rather than hypochondriacal, and they enabled the *philosophes* to employ medical language in their polemics without any sense of strain. It is well known that the *philosophes* liked to argue that they must destroy in order to build: their military metaphors—metaphors of aggression—dramatise their destructive activities.[7] Their medical metaphors, in turn, justified their destructiveness: with monotonous reiterations, the *philosophes* represented their campaign against Christianity as a campaign against disease. Christianity, they wrote, was an infection, a malignant foreign body, a 'sacred contagion', a 'sick man's dream', a germ sometimes dormant but always dangerous, the source for epidemics of fanaticism and persecution. In the rhetoric of the Enlightenment, the conquest of nature and the conquest of revealed religion were one: a struggle for health. If the *philosophes* were missionaries, they were medical missionaries.

This rhetoric, like most rhetoric, was more than mere talk; it accurately reflects the *philosophes*' style of thinking, comically though it was sometimes expressed. In 1765, the Lombard *illuminista* Giuseppe Parini, a priest and radical satirist, wrote an ode to vaccination, and dedicated it to Giovammaria Bicetti, a prominent Italian physician. Ordinary minds, Parini wrote, always reject great new ideas, but an intrepid band of intellectuals in England, France —and Italy—were now standing bravely against the multitude; armed against murderous disease, they were protecting the lives of young children and defying relentless destiny with the healing art:

[7] On this point, see my discussion in *The Enlightenment: An Interpretation*, vol. i, 'The Rise of Modern Paganism', pp. 131-132.

Contro all' armi omicide
Non piu debole e nudo;
Ma sotto a certo scudo
Il tenero garzon cauto discese;
E il fato inesorabile sorprese.[8]

These lines may strike us as droll in their solemnity, and they are droll. But philosophic literature abounds in solemn claims for the affinity, the near equivalence, of modern medicine with modern philosophy. Perhaps the most striking of these claims came toward the end of the Enlightenment, in 1798, in an extraordinary essay on 'medical enlightenment' by the German physician Johann Karl Osterhausen. *Über medizinische Aufklärung*, in title and in content, is a deliberate imitation of Kant's *Was ist Aufklärung?* To make his imitation as unmistakable as possible, Osterhausen ostentatiously borrowed Kant's famous definition of Enlightenment for the medical profession: medical Enlightenment, he wrote, is 'man's emergence from his dependence in matters concerning his physical well-being.'[9] Nothing could be plainer than this: medicine was philosophy at work; philosophy was medicine for the individual and for society.

II

All this may sound extravagant, but it is a fact that by the end of the seventeenth century, the ideal of philosophical, modern medicine was beginning to invade the most progressive among the medical schools. Leyden, the best of them, was long dominated by Hermann Boerhaave, a philosophical physician of enormous range and energy. Boerhaave was clinician, methodologist, chemist, botanist, the most celebrated and influential medical teacher of his age: he lectured to generations of young physicians from all over the Western world including the American colonies, and left his mark on *philosophes* who came to listen even if they did not stay to matriculate. Boerhaave taught medical Newtonianism; he lectured on Newton and tried to embody Newton's empirical methods in his theoretical writings and clinical practice. His textbooks, promptly

[8] '*L'innesto del vaiuolo*', in Giuseppe Parini, *Poesie e prose* (ed. 1961), p. 197.

[9] Quoted in Alfons Fischer, *Geschichte des deutschen Gesundheitswesens* (1933), ii. 8.

and widely translated, were models of Newtonian reasoning; they acquired almost scriptural authority and reached the many who could not come to hear him. It is doubtless true that Boerhaave's ambitions outran his performance, and that his practice fell short of his preachments; he was more dogmatic than he knew. But his enlightened and enlightening precepts reverberated through Europe and America, while at home his colleagues and successors, s'Gravesande, Nieuwentyt and Musschenbroek, carried on his medical practice and his philosophical teachings. They went to England, sought out Newton, and kept in touch with British medicine and British science in general; when they came home to assume their chairs, they lectured, as Boerhaave had lectured before them, on Bacon and Locke, they warned their students against resorting to occult principles and exhorted them to eschew hypotheses, listen to phenomena, pay close attention to clinical experience, and design exact experiments. It was in gratitude to all this activity that eighteenth-century physicians named the age after its great Dutch preceptor. 'The age of Boerhaave', an English observer wrote in 1780, 'forms a memorable epoch in the history of physic. Theory, which before had been entirely conjectural, now assumed a more plausible and scientific appearance'—that is to say, a Newtonian appearance.[10] It was as a Newtonian that William Cullen, perhaps the most famous surgeon and physiologist in Britain, prided himself on having 'avoided hypothesis', and Cullen was typical, not exceptional.[11]

This stress on experience, clinical study, and experimentation, revolutionised medicine. Still, it is safe to speculate that in the eighteenth century a sick man who did not consult a physician had a better chance of surviving than one who did. There were troops of mountebanks who took their victims' money and shortened their lives; worse than that, responsible and knowledgeable physicians were often muddled and astonishingly ignorant. The medical guilds, crusty, doctrinaire, privileged and exclusive, resisted the influx of new ideas and the employment of new instruments; many drugs or surgical procedures reached the public from the hands of ill-trained but sensible and adventurous empirics—the bootleggers of

[10] Henry Manning, *Modern Improvements in the Practice of Physic*, 'Preface', quoted in Richard H. Shryock, *The Development of Modern Medicine* (1947), p. 74 n.

[11] Shryock, *Modern Medicine*, p. 37.

science—who were often humane healers. Instruments like the fever thermometer, or the machine for measuring blood pressure, were neglected by a profession far too much taken up with squabbles over precedence to attend to its proper business; the prevalence of quacks was more a criticism of professional conservatism than a measure of public gullibility. There was pressing and obvious need for renovating the medical profession; in France, the surgeons finally liberated themselves from the barbers' guild in 1731, and the English surgeons followed in 1745, but even after the reform, long overdue, surgeons and physicians continued to remain antagonistic: Diderot vividly caricatures these hostile factions as two professional men, standing over his sick body, ignoring his groans, and arguing with each other without paying the slightest attention to their suffering patient.

Diderot's satiric little drama displays a *philosophe* in a sceptical mood. Doctors have been the targets of wit ever since there have been patients, and the *philosophes* freely contributed to the treasury of caustic humour. Diderot put some rueful observations about the inefficacy of medical attention into the mouth of Dr Bordeu.[12] Voltaire scribbled into a notebook: 'Men must have a religion and not believe in priests, just as men must have a diet and not believe in physicians.'[13] David Hume warned one of his friends: 'I entreat you, if you tender your own Health or give any Attention to the Entreaties of those that love you, to pay no regard to Physicians: That is a considerable part of your Distemper. You cannot pay a moderate Regard to them; your only Safety is in neglecting them altogether.'[14]

There was real point to these sarcastic observations. Vital statistics were still scanty and unreliable, and what was reliably known was hardly reassuring. Rousseau could estimate on one page of *Émile* that half of all children died before their ninth year, and, only a few pages later, that about half reached adolescence—an indication not merely of continuing pessimism about life-expectancy, but of continuing uncertainty about the figures. In the late 1760s, Voltaire calculated that on the average men could expect to

[12] See *Rêve de d'Alembert*, *passim*.

[13] *Notebooks*, ed. Theodore Besterman (1952), ii. 352.

[14] Hume to John Crawford (20 July 1767), *New Letters of David Hume*, edd. Raymond Klibansky and Ernest C. Mossner (1954), p. 175.

live to the age of 22, and, a few years before, Diderot, writing to his mistress from his native town, pondered grimly the 'short existence of those who entered life at the same time we did'—most of his school-fellows were dead and he was only 46 at the time.[15] All the *philosophes* had oppressive memories of early death: when the aged Louis XIV was still on the throne—Voltaire was a young man then—nearly all the king's progeny died in rapid succession: his only son died in 1711, his eldest grandson the duc de Bourgogne, the duke's wife and eldest son all died in 1712, his youngest grandson the duc de Berry died in 1714. 'This time of desolation', Voltaire remembered, 'left so profound an impression on men's hearts that during the minority of Louis XV I saw numerous people who spoke of these losses only with tears.'[16]

Every eighteenth-century family had its own horror tale to tell. Goethe, recalling his childhood, could not remember just how many of his young siblings had died in infancy; Gibbon, recalling *his* childhood, coolly observed that 'the death of a new-born child before that of its parents may seem an unnatural, but it is strictly a probable event: since of any given number the greater part are extinguished before their ninth year'. His own infantile constitution, he added, had been so feeble, that 'in the baptism of my brothers, my father's prudence successively repeated the Christian name of Edward, that, in case of the departure of the eldest son, this patronymic appellation might still be perpetuated in the family'.[17] This story has been exploded as a trick of Gibbon's memory, but it stands as touching testimony to the overriding concern of the century, the omnipresent shadow of death.[18] Infanticide, organised cruelty to orphans or illegitimate children, epidemics, and above all destitution, remained ravenous killers: 'It is not uncommon, I have frequently been told,' Adam Smith soberly noted, 'in the

[15] Rousseau, *Émile*, Book I; Voltaire, 'A, B. C', in *Philosophical Dictionary*, transl. by Peter Gay (1962), ii. 590-591; Diderot to Sophie Volland (4 or 5 August 1759), Roth, ii. 202.

[16] Voltaire, *Siècle de Louis XIV*, chapter xxvii; in *Œuvres historiques*, ed. René Pomeau (1957), p. 944.

[17] Goethe, *Dichtung und Wahrheit*, in *Gedenkausgabe*, 24 vols (1948), xi. 44-45; Gibbon, *Autobiography*, ed. Dero A. Saunders (1961), p. 53.

[18] D. M. Low checked the parish registers at Putney Parish Church, and found that the seven Gibbon children included only one 'Edward' and one 'Edward James', and that the most cherished name in the family, in fact, was James, the name of Mrs Gibbon's father, which was repeated three times. See Low, *Gibbon's Journal to January 18th, 1763* (n.d.), xxix.

Highlands of Scotland for a mother who has borne twenty children not to have two alive.'[19] The poor died freely, in unrecorded numbers, but even persons of means and rank thought long life a stroke of unexpected luck.

III

But this was not all. Medicine was not merely the target of the *philosophes*' scorn and the centre of their pessimism, it was also the object of their admiration and the ground of their hopes. The *philosophes* could find cheer in signs of solid, often spectacular progress, and their confidence in progress still to come was even more exhilarating than their satisfaction with results already secure. It was gradually becoming obvious that the population of Europe was undergoing marked growth, and not among the Irish alone. In his essay 'On the Populousness of Ancient Nations', David Hume discredited the widespread view that modern Europe was less heavily populated than the Europe of classical antiquity: on the contrary, he argued, modern Europe supports more souls than ancient Europe ever dreamed of supporting; the three agents of wholesale destruction, 'war, pestilence, and famine', which had with hideous impartiality desolated royal houses, middle-class families, and ragged villages, were finally loosening their grip.[20]

Hume's case was reasonable: in England, the population grew from 6,500,000 in 1750 to 9,000,000 in 1800; in France, the population grew by four millions in the course of the eighteenth century; Sweden, the first country to develop a reliable system of vital statistics, reported a population increase of 70 per cent between 1720 and 1815. Malthus' very alarm at the population explosion was a backhanded tribute to it and—or so observers thought in the eighteenth century—to the progress of medicine.

Remarkable as it was, the history of medical progress in the eighteenth century is not without its irony. Down to about 1750, a whole tribe of would-be medical Newtons obstructed progress with their search for a single cause of disease or principle of cure, and it was not until mid-century, when the *philosophes* were at the

[19] *An Inquiry into the Nature and Causes of the Wealth of Nations* (Modern Library, ed. Edwin Cannan, 1937), p. 79.

[20] See Hume, *Works*, edd. T. H. Green and T. H. Grose (1882), iii. 383.

height of their influence, and partly as a result of their propaganda, that pluralistic empiricism changed the course of medical research. It continued to suffer setbacks: the eternal struggle between rigidity and flexibility, the desire to conserve and the need to innovate, went on. But the results remain impressive, and some statistics at least, especially in the last decades of the eighteenth century, gave solid cause for optimism. The British Lying-In Hospital reported that while, in the decade from 1749 to 1759, one baby in fifteen had died shortly after birth, by 1799 this dismal proportion had been reduced to one in 118. In the same period, in this hospital, the death rate for mothers declined from 26·7 to 2·4 per mill. Epidemic diseases like typhoid and smallpox almost disappeared, surgeons like John Hunter vastly improved surgical techniques, physiology made great strides, and so did obstetrics, *materia medica*, preventive medicine and anatomy. Enlightenment had turned out to be cure as well as medicine.

In consequence, enlightened men could look back upon the eighteenth century with sober pride, and claim with confidence that it was the ideas of the Enlightenment which had acted as a prime agent in the medical revolution, just as the medical revolution had acted as a prime agent in the efficacy of the Enlightenment. On 1 January 1801, on 'the first day of the nineteenth century', Dr David Ramsay, prominent American historian and leading American physician, could review the 'improvements, progress, and state of medicine in the eighteenth century' with undiluted optimism. The eighteenth century, he said, had witnessed the birth of rational medicine, based on the principles of Bacon, 'the father of all modern science', and on the teachings of Boerhaave. It had been an age of significant innovations in medical theory, astounding advances in anatomy, proper midwifery, brilliant experimentation, sensible classification of diseases, the professionalisation of surgery, improved understanding of the rôle that fresh air and sound food played in the preservation of health, and, perhaps best of all, of attacks on crippling superstitions: 'Many popular errors have been exploded; the common people have been accustomed to think and reason on medical subjects.' The results had been exhilarating: 'I appeal to those who can look back on thirty, forty, or fifty years, whether a great reformation in these particulars has not taken place within the sphere of their own observation; and whether in consequence of more judicious treatment there are not more women safely carried through the perilous periods of pregnancy and child-birth; and whether there are not fewer instances of deformity, and a greater proportion of children raised at the present time, than formerly. In the same number of families, where our ancestors counted four or five, we can now show seven or eight. Our schools, our streets and our houses are filled with straight, well-formed children, most of whom have happily got over the smallpox, without any of those marks of it, which deformed their grand-mother.'[21] The salutary effects of the Enlightenment were visible on men's very faces.

[21] David Ramsay, *A Review of the Improvements, Progress, and State of Medicine in the Eighteenth Century* (1801) *passim.* Significantly the little pamphlet is dedicated to 'Benjamin Rush, M.D.', the 'American Sydenham'.

'Patriote', 'patriotique', 'patriotisme' à la fin de l'Ancien Régime

Werner Krauss

Jusqu'aujourd'hui les historiens et les critiques de la littérature se sont passés, presque toujours, des services que la sémantique leur pouvait rendre. Il faut avouer, cependant, que voici la branche philologique la plus jeune, dont l'amplitude et l'efficacité n'a été découverte que par des investigations récentes, notamment celles de M. Georges Matoré. Il y a dix ans que celui-ci avait étudié les changements arrivés dans le champ notionel formant le noyau d'une époque nouvelle ou d'une génération nouvelle dont les mots-témoin ou mots-clef révèlent la nouveauté d'une mode linguistique correspondant aux découvertes d'une société renouvelée.

Il faut être conscient, pourtant, que l'apparition d'un mot-clef ne doit pas coïncider toujours avec le moment de sa création. Bien des néologies ne sont guère des néologies lexicales, mais tout simplement des nouveautés sémantiques. Le mot 'patriotique', par exemple, qui sera en vogue à partir du milieu du XVIIIe siècle, était une création de la fin du XVe siècle, sans qu'on pût soupçonner alors l'éclat futur de ce mot. Cette éclosion ne se révèle pas seulement par la fréquence et la position accentuée des citations, mais dans le plan sémantique par la création de mots-satellites. C'est ainsi que 'persiflage' et 'persifleur' ont surgi bientôt après la création du verbe 'persifler'. De la même façon le complexe de 'patriote' a été enrichi par l'invention d'un adjectif 'patriotique' et du substantif 'patriotisme'. La Révolution française a renouvelé l'essor des termes 'patriote', 'patriotisme', et c'est alors que surgissent de nombreuses dérivations. On parle des 'antipatriotes' et de 'l'antipatriotisme', ou bien d''impatriote' et d''impatriotisme', le verbe 'patriotiser' s'est formé sur le moule de 'fraterniser'. Louis-Sébastien Mercier, grand fauteur de néologies, a proposé la création de 'patriophobe' suivant exprès le mot et l'idée d''hydrophobie'. Il s'agit, bien sûr, de néologies lexicales, mais composées d'une racine et de désinances existantes. Au lieu de mots-satellites on pourrait les baptiser 'nouveautés morphologiques'.

Cependant, il ne faut jamais oublier, que toutes ces distinctions ne se réalisent que sur un plan purement philologique. Elles disparaissent en entrant dans le champ notionel. Pour un Français vivant vers 1770 le mot 'patriote' avait la même trempe d'actualité récente que les presque synonymes 'patriotisme' et 'civisme', c'est-à-dire que les nouveautés purement sémantiques ne se distinguaient guère des créations lexicales.

Tout ceci regarde la théorie de la sémantique. Quant au mot 'patriote', on peut prouver sa diffusion accrue et même multipliée au cours du XVIIIe siècle. Vers 1750 on peut constater l'apparition du mot 'patriotisme' témoignée par le mémorialiste d'Argenson qui subit, peut-être, l'influence du mot anglais. Un an après cette première citation le mot 'patriotisme' est répété par des 'Écrits pour et contre les immunités prétendues par le clergé de France'. On espère ou on feint d'espérer que le clergé sera assez patriote pour payer ses contributions comme l'immense majorité des citoyens. En vue de l'esprit foncièrement bourgeois de ce traité l'emploi de 'patriote' rapporté au clergé doit se considérer comme ironique, capable de démarquer l'égoïsme sacré des provilégiés. Déjà en 1757 l'adjectif 'patriotique' est accepté et reçu par le *Dictionnaire de l'Académie française*. La prédilection des Lumières pour la conception de 'patriote' est témoignée par une infinité de titres de livres parus à partir de l'année si décisive pour l'histoire du mot, c'est-à-dire à partir de 1750. Dans la même année parut le livre d'un certain Émilien Petit, *Le Patriote américain, ou Mémoires sur l'établissement de l'île de Saint-Domingue*. En 1751 le protestant Court de Gebelin publia *Le Patriote français et impartial*. En 1756 l'abbé Jean-Bernard Le Blanc donne à la publicité son livre *Le Patriote anglais*, camouflé comme traduction de l'anglais. En 1759 et en 1761 c'est le tour de la poésie, de s'emparer du mot 'patriotisme', titre d'un poème de Dujardin et encore d'une création de Colardeau, prudemmant dédié au duc de Choiseul, tout-puissant dans cette époque-là. En 1761 apparaît *Le Patriote artésien ou projet d'un établissement d'une académie d'agriculture, de commerce et des arts en la province d'Artois*, livre d'un auteur obscur, mais imbu de théories physiocrates. En 1766 nous avons *La Différence du patriotisme national chez les Français et chez les Anglais*: l'auteur, Basset de la Marelle, se révèle comme ennemi acharné des Lumières. Par contre, les Lumières se font jour dans un *Dictionnaire social et patriotique*, paru en 1770. Pendant la guerre d'Amérique on publia une ode 'Le patriotisme', composée par Duval-Sanadon. A la veille de la Révolution il y a deux titres curieux: *Le Patriotisme persécuté* par Sionneau-Duchesne et *Le Patriote ou Préservatif contre l'anglomanie* dont l'auteur était Bourdon, le futur jacobin.

Parallèlement à la révalorisation de 'patriote' le mot 'citoyen' acquiert une dignité nouvelle. De même 'civique', mot favori de Turgot, et le néologisme 'civisme' deviennent des mots-clefs, surtout auprès des physiocrates. 'Civisme' et 'patriotisme' sont des mots interchangeables, c'est-à-dire qu'il s'agit de véritables synonymes. Cependant, le mot et la notion de 'patriotisme' n'étaient point accueillis sans réserve. Montesquieu n'avait attribué qu'à la république la vertu civique, c'est-à-dire le patriotisme dans le sens le plus purifié de ce mot. Par contre la récompense en honneurs est le noyau du système monarchique, n'admettant guère des sentiments de patriotisme et de civisme. Seulement l'Angleterre, en tant que démocratie, devient le rempart du patriotisme véritable. C'est ainsi que le Marquis d'Argens dans ses *Lettres juives* de 1738 déclare, qu'en Angleterre même les courtisans ont le courage de s'opposer à leur maître. Selon d'Argens, chez les Français 'l'amour de la patrie n'est qu'une chimère ridicule. Que leur importe que tous leurs compatriotes soient malheureux, pourvu qu'ils aient le plaisir de s'élever et de posséder des charges'. (Éd. Lausanne 1750, v, p. 27.)

C'est l'abbé Coyer qui découvre la source de cette malaise. Selon lui, pour rehausser le sens et l'idée de 'Patrie', il faudrait: 'penser en commun. Si dans une nation on voyoit comme deux nations, on n'y entendait pas le mot "patrie" '. En 1759 Poinsinet de Sivry se demande pourquoi la patrie 'n'est plus qu'un nom chez nous' ('La Berlue', Londres, 1759, p. 70). Enfin, Holbach, dans son 'Éthéocratie', pose encore une fois la condition de tout patriotisme raisonnable: 'Le patriotisme véritable', dit-il, 'ne peut se trouver que dans les pays où les citoyens libres, et gouvernés par des lois équitables, sont bien unis et cherchent à mériter l'estime et l'affection de leurs concitoyens' (p. 288).

Jean-Jacques Rousseau, lui, est très certainement un partisan ardent du patriotisme. Dans le *Contrat social* les citoyens sont obligés à se donner sans réserve aux devoirs patriotiques. Cependant, Rousseau ne s'en doute que la théorie du *Contrat social* n'est point applicable aux grandes nations, occupant le centre de l'Europe et corrompues par leur commerce réciproque et leur contagion perpétuelle. Ce n'est qu'à la marge des grands États, en Pologne et en Corse, qu'on pourrait réaliser la théorie du *Contrat social.*

Les idées de Jean-Jacques sont reprises par le Bâlois Bridel, qui, dans ses *Délassements politiques* de 1788 s'exprime de la façon suivante: 'Mais l'état actuel de l'Europe et du monde littéraire rend l'originalité nationale aussi rare que difficile à saisir. L'esprit de sociabilité, qui est la vertu des siècles corrumpus, a rapproché les unes des autres toutes les nations policées. Le commerce, en les unissant par l'intérêt, les force journellement à se communiquer avec les productions de leurs climats, celles de leurs talents et de leur génie. Les voyages, qu'un caprice de la mode a rendus nécessaires, font circuler avec rapidité, d'Archangel à Cadix, les connaissances, les opinions, les préjugés et les vices des différents peuples. La lecture, encore plus contagieuse, ouvre aux désoeuvrés de tous les pays une école où souvent un seul maître dicte ses leçons, et inculque ses maximes à une foule innombrable de disciples. Dans cet échange et ce combat perpétuel d'idées, de principes, de vérités et d'erreurs, les formes nationales s'altèrent et disparaissent. Les esprits, emportés par un même mouvement et exposés aux mêmes chocs, s'arrondissent, si je puis m'exprimer ainsi, les uns par les autres, et perdent insensiblement les grands traits qui les avaient caractérisés. L'homme de lettres n'est plus Anglais, Français, Allemand. Cosmopolite nouveau, il fait sa récolte partout où il trouve de la culture, et s'enrichit des dépouilles de tout l'univers.'

Cependant toutes les discussions et résistances ne pouvaient pas empêcher les philosophes de rendre au patriotisme une signification entièrement nouvelle. Ce patriotisme ne saurait se fonder sur l'actualité française dominée par le système d'absolutisme avec tous ses méfaits. C'est un patriotisme orienté décidément vers l'avenir; à cette signification est rattachée la conception d'un renouvellement de tous les cadres et de la constitution française. Voici la signification révolutionnaire adoptée par les Français de bonne volonté, disposés à trancher le problème publique et à endurer les luttes acharnées de l'ancien régime avec les promoteurs de la réforme de l'Etat.

D'Alembert interrogé par le roi de Prusse, fait constater, que les encyclopédistes n'ont jamais désavoué leur attitude patriotique: 'Il se peut que quelque prétendu philosophe (car bien des faquins usurpent aujourd'hui ce nom) ait imprimé dans une brochure ignorée des sottises absurdes contre le patriotisme; mais croyez. Sire, que tous les philosophes vraiment dignes de ce nom désavoueraient cette brochure, s'ils la connaissaient, ou plutôt se rendraient assez de justice pour ne daigner pas même se justifier d'une imputation si injuste' (*Œuvres de Frédéric le Grand*, t.xxv).

Diderot avait encouragé l'abbé Coyer de rehausser l'idée du patriotisme dans l'Encyclopédie. Dans une lettre à Falconet il a résumé toute la pensée des philosophes en disant: 'Le sentiment patriotique qui embrasse le bonheur actuel et futur de la cité, la splendeur présente de la ville et sa longue durée, porte ses vues bien au-delà du présent' (5 août 1766). L'idée du patriotisme se rattache à la philosophie des Lumières. C'est ainsi que Mirabeau déclare en 1775: 'Il n'y a plus de patriotes parce qu'il n'y a plus d'hommes éclairés'. En réalité les patriotes sont tous ceux qui combattent les pouvoirs réactionnaires. Le titre de patriote est réclamé par les adversaires du chancelier Maupeou. Linguet oppose de même le patriotisme à l'argentisme des finances, et Helvétius écrit notamment: 'L'extrême avidité de l'or que ce grand commerce occasionne n'allume-t-elle pas ce foyer de corruption qu'entretiennent ceux qui gouvernent, pour perdre les mœurs, dénaturer le patriotisme . . .' (Helvétius à Laroche, 8 septembre 1768, *Œuvres complètes*, éd. Laroche, Paris 1795, xiv. 90).

Ces témoignages plutôt pessimistes révèlent cependant la pureté du patriotisme philosophique. M. Jean Fabre dans son introduction magistrale du *Neveu de Rameau* constate que Diderot, après avoir brandi le drapeau du patriotisme craignit qu'il ne se fût accroché à une pure illusion. L'ancien régime avait gagné deux batailles, en se délivrant de l'intromission jésuitique et en triomphant de l'opposition farouche des parlements jansénistes.

L'espoir revint pendant le ministère de Turgot et dans la crise qui aboutit à la Révolution française. Dix mois avant la prise de la Bastille le libraire Hardy fait la note suivante dans son Journal: 'Ce nouvel ordre des choses si justement et si fortement réclamé par 23 millions de patriotes . . . C'est presque la totalité des Français engagés dans la lutte contre les pouvoirs établis' (Carcassonne: *Montesquieu et le problème de la constitution française au XVIIIe siècle*, 1926, p. 635).

En constatant les rapports existants entre la philosophie des Lumières et le patriotisme on pourrait alléguer pourtant quelques textes qui semblent former une nette opposition à ce que nous venons de dire.

Il était inévitable que la réaction monarchique et cléricale s'emparât de la conception du patriotisme pour l'employer à contresens et l'appliquer à l'apogée de l'ancien régime. Les Palissot, les Moreau se présentent comme les véritables patriotes pendant que les philosophes seraient des êtres apatriotes et dévoués au cosmopolitisme le plus abstrait. La même défiguration de la pensée philosophique nous la trouvons dans l'œuvre de l'abbé Ansquer de Londres, qui dans ses *Variétés philosophiques et littéraires* (1762) répète les reproches adressés aux philosophes: 'En un mot, si pendant plus de treize siècles, l'éclat dont cette nation brilla en tout genre, ne fit que s'accroître; et si on l'a vu s'élever à un tel état de grandeur qu'on la soupçonnait de prétendre à la monarchie universelle; je le demande, ces prodiges ne furent-ils pas l'ouvrage de cet enthousiasme qui la transporta toujours lorsqu'il fallut agir ou combattre pour les intérêts de la patrie?—On prétend qu'une froideur apathique commence à s'introduire dans cette nation, sous le nom de *philosophie moderne*, et qu'elle succède à l'ardeur patriotique qui embrasait. A entendre ces nouveaux philosophes dont le nombre se multiplie, dit-on, de jour en jour, le sage ne doit pas proprement reconnaître de patrie; il doit s'afficher pour *cosmopolite*, c'est-à-dire que toutes ses pensées et ses affections doivent se borner à sa propre existence, que toute forme de gouvernement doit être pour lui un objet indifférent, et que les pertes, ou les avantages, les succès ou les revers que peut éprouver l'État qui l'a vu naître, ne le doivent nullement affecter.—Si les imputations n'étaient point chimériques; si cette façon de penser s'accréditait et s'était goûtée, il ne me resterait plus qu'une question à faire: la nation, ou la monarchie dont je parle, serait-elle encore bien éloignée du moment de sa chute?' (p. 152).

La confusion semée par l'attitude des réactionnaires monarchiques et cléricaux arrive au comble dans le livre de l'avocat Basset de la Marelle, qui, en 1766, publia *La différence du patriotisme national chez les Français et chez les Anglais*. Le patriotisme français y est opposé au patriotisme anglais de la façon suivante: 'L'amour de la patrie a constamment animé les Français depuis la fondation de cette monarchie. En Angleterre, l'amour de la patrie a fait aussi de grandes choses depuis la descente de Jules César sur les côtes britanniques, jusqu'à nos jours; mais comme les lois fondamentales de ces deux gouvernements sont tout-à-fait différentes entr'elles, le patriotisme doit nécessairement aussi être tout différent, soit en lui-même, soit dans ses effets, chez ces deux nations. L'amour de la patrie à Sparte n'avait rien de semblable au patriotisme des Athéniens, et cependant c'était le même sentiment qui animait ces deux peuples. L'amour des Français pour leur souverain est le plus ferme appui de l'État, la base inébranlable de la puissance et de la gloire de cette monarchie; c'est là le patriotisme français. L'Anglais plus attaché à ce qu'il nomme, bien ou mal à propos, sa liberté, ses droits, ses privilèges, qu'à la royauté, presque nulle à ses yeux, ne respire et ne forme des projets, ne tente des efforts que pour étendre encore ce fantôme de liberté, ces droits très-souvent chimériques, et ces privilèges abusifs; et cette ambition jalouse de balancer, ou même, pour si peu qu'on l'irrite, d'éclipser et d'humilier le pouvoir du souverain, de régner sur les mers, d'absorber les richesses, le commerce, et s'il se pouvait, les possessions du reste des nations, est le patriotisme, l'esprit, le sentiment qui fait tout dans la Grande Bretagne' (p. 9).

L'apparence d'une comparaison plus ou moins équitable des deux systèmes est dissipée par l'élévation du patriotisme français conçu comme fidélité inébranlable devant le maître, tandis que les intérêts particuliers seraient tout-puissants en Angleterre. Le *Journal encyclopédique*, dans sa critique du 1 janvier 1766 observe notamment: 'Mais les Anglais paraîtront peut-être un peu trop fortement maltraités par l'auteur; car qui croira que le patriotisme soit mal en Angleterre?'

Nous finirons par donner encore une preuve de l'abus systématique des idées des Lumières par la réaction cléricale. Cérutti, auteur de la dernière apologie de la Compagnie, dressait ce tableau édifiant en faveur des jésuites: '. . . aux autels un corps de ministres zélés, au trône un corps de sujets fidèles, à la patrie un corps de citoyens irréprochables . . .' (*Apologie générale de l'institut et de la doctrine des Jésuites*, Soleure 1763, p. 567).

Cependant la notion 'patriote', 'patriotisme' en passant en Espagne et en Allemagne, conservait la signification que les philosophes français lui avaient attribuée. Dans ce sens les mots 'patriota', 'patriotismo' sont employés par Cadalso et les autres promoteurs de l'*Illustration* espagnole. Le témoignage d'un certain Sotomayor confirme le rattachement de 'patriotismo' aux idées de progrès: 'Y yo soy algo curioso y buen patriota y como tal tengo especial complacencia en los progresos de la nación' (Don Joaquín de Amo y otros, *Dirección anatómica de tres monstruosos fetos literarios*, Madrid 1767, p. 1).

En Allemagne, dès le commencement du XVIIe siècle, on parlait de 'Reichspatriotismus', nanti des villes libres et faisant bientôt un amalgame avec la signification progressive du mot développée en France.[1]

La notion de 'patriotisme' qui atteignit le sommet dans la Révolution française, survécut l'époque de liquidation de toutes les valeurs progressives. Le mot fut encore employé par les instigateurs belliqueux de la première guerre mondiale. Mais à partir de cette date, tantôt en France qu'ailleurs, on abandonne la notion de 'patriotisme', usée et démodée, selon l'indiquaient des conceptions péjoratives comme 'le patriotisme de clocher' en France et le mot 'patriotero' extrêmement irrespectueux, lancé par les Espagnols. Même les mouvements nationalistes n'osaient reprendre un terme devenu vide et trivial. Cependant l'Union Soviétique ne s'est jamais lassée de parler du patriotisme communiste. Les autres pays socialistes adoptaient cet emploi du mot qui dans cette partie du monde allait recouvrer la signification d'une notion progressive créée jadis par les Lumières et la philosophie du XVIIIe siècle.

[1] Sur le mot 'patriotisme' voir Werner Krauss, *Studien zur deutschen und französischen Aufklärung* (Berlin 1963), p. 314 et suiv.

The Age of the Enlightenment

Robert Niklaus

Ernst Cassirer begins his study of the *Philosophy of the Enlightenment*[1] by quoting d'Alembert who stated in his *Essai sur les éléments de philosophie*:[2]

> Pour peu qu'on considère avec des yeux attentifs le milieu du siècle où nous vivons, les événements qui nous occupent, ou du moins qui nous agitent, nos mœurs, nos ouvrages, et jusqu'à nos entretiens, on aperçoit sans peine qu'il s'est fait à plusieurs égards un changement bien remarquable dans nos idées; changement qui par sa rapidité semble nous en promettre un plus grand encore. C'est au temps à fixer l'objet, la nature et les limites de cette révolution, dont notre postérité connaîtra mieux que nous les inconvénients et les avantages.
>
> Tout siècle qui pense bien ou mal, pourvu qu'il croie penser, et qu'il pense autrement que le siècle qui l'a précédé, se pare du titre de *philosophe*; comme on a souvent honoré de *sages* ceux qui n'ont eu d'autre mérite que de contredire leurs contemporains. Notre siècle s'est donc appelé par excellence *le siècle de la philosophie*; plusieurs écrivains lui en ont donné le nom, persuadés qu'il en rejaillirait quelqu'éclat sur eux; d'autres lui ont refusé cette gloire dans l'impuissance de la partager.
>
> Si on examine sans prévention l'état actuel de nos connaissances, on ne peut disconvenir des progrès de la philosophie parmi nous. La science de la nature acquiert de jour en jour de nouvelles richesses; la géométrie en reculant ses limites,

[1] 1951.
[2] Edd. R. N. Schwab, G. Olms (1965), pp. 8-12.

a porté son flambeau dans les parties de la physique qui se trouvaient le plus près d'elle; le vrai système du monde a été connu, développé et perfectionné; la même sagacité qui s'était assujetti les mouvements des corps célestes, s'est portée sur les corps qui nous environnent; en appliquant la géométrie à l'étude de ces corps, ou en essayant de l'y appliquer, on a su apercevoir et fixer les avantages et les abus de cet emploi; en un mot depuis la terre jusqu'à Saturne, depuis l'histoire des cieux jusqu'à celle des insectes, la physique a changé de face. Avec elle presque toutes les autres sciences ont pris une nouvelle forme, et elles le devaient en effet. Quelques réflexions vont nous en convaincre.

L'étude de la nature semble être par elle-même froide et tranquille, parce que la satisfaction qu'elle procure est un sentiment uniforme, continu et sans secousses, et que les plaisirs, pour être vifs, doivent être séparés par des intervalles et marqués par des accès. Néanmoins l'invention et l'usage d'une nouvelle méthode, de philosopher, l'espèce d'enthousiasme qui accompagne les découvertes, une certaine élévation d'idées que produit en nous le spectacle de l'univers; toutes ces causes ont dû exciter dans les esprits une fermentation vive; cette fermentation agissant en tout sens par sa nature, s'est portée avec une espèce de violence sur tout ce qui s'est offert à elle, comme un fleuve qui a brisé ses digues. Or les hommes ne reviennent guère sur un objet qu'ils avaient négligé depuis longtemps, que pour réformer bien ou mal les idées qu'ils s'en etaient faites. Plus ils sont lents à secouer le joug de l'opinion, plus aussi dès qu'ils l'ont brisé sur quelques points, ils sont portés à la briser sur tout le reste; car ils fuyent encore plus l'embarras d'examiner, qu'ils ne craignent de changer d'avis; et dès qu'ils ont pris une fois la peine de revenir sur leurs pas, ils regardent et reçoivent un nouveau système d'idées comme une sorte de récompense de leur courage et de leur travail. Ainsi depuis les principes des sciences profanes jusqu'aux fondements de la révélation, depuis la métaphysique jusqu'aux matières de goût, depuis la musique jusqu'à la morale, depuis les disputes scolastiques des théologiens jusqu'aux objets de commerce, depuis les droits des princes jusqu'à ceux des peuples, depuis la loi naturelle jusqu'aux lois arbitraires des nations, en un mot depuis les questions qui nous touchent davantage jusqu'à celles qui nous intéressent le plus faiblement, tout a été discuté, analysé, agité du moins. Une nouvelle lumière sur quelques objets, une nouvelle obscurité sur plusieurs, a été le fruit ou la suite de cette effervescence générale des esprits, comme l'effet du flux et reflux de l'océan est d'apporter sur le rivage quelques matières, et d'en éloigner les autres.

It would be difficult to find a more apposite expression of contemporary intellectual life. Thirst for knowledge and intellectual curiosity were directed to the external world. Awareness of the history, languages and religions of people from foreign countries; the new developments in science, especially physics, mathematics and the natural sciences and medicine, were changing the climate of opinion throughout the civilised world. Attention was drawn to the ethics, politics and economics of social man, but it centred on individual man, his nature, his happiness, his relationship to the cosmos, the very processes of his mind and their validity. The obvious parallel that can be established with the preoccupations of our own age has focussed interest once more on the intellectual contribution of the Enlightenment, and on the personality and thought of its leading figures. Many of the most significant critical studies on the eighteenth century seek to provide, more or less consciously, a key to the solution of some of our most pressing intellectual problems, or at least a clarification of certain burning issues. Herein lies their strength; for their preoccupations led reality and a sense of urgency to their argument: and also their weakness; for the authors, as their predecessors, can only speak for their own generation, and commonly only the fraction of their own generation to which they happen to belong.

Although many of the earlier critics of the Enlightenment have pertinent things to say on a wide variety of questions, few in fact have a substantial contribution to make for the serious student of today. L. G. Crocker in an important study[3] makes the point that before 1945 hardly any attempt was made to understand the Enlightenment as a whole, or to interpret its character and significance. He readily

[3] 'Recent Interpretations of the French Enlightenment', *Journal of World History* (1964), viii (3). 426-456, Edns. de la Baconnière, Neuchâtel.

concedes that books and articles of value were written on individual writers, and that specific questions were explored to good purpose—luxury (by A. Morize), primitivism and exoticism (by G. Chinard and others), the extraordinary journey (by G. Atkinson). But even studies on individual writers were expressions of personal opinion, condemnations or apologies. Irving Babbitt's *Rousseau and Romanticism* and L. I. Bredvold's *The Brave New World of the Enlightenment* are cited in evidence.

In his rapid survey of critical works published before the Second World War, L. G. Crocker praises wholeheartedly only R. Hubert's *Les Sciences sociales dans l'Encyclopédie* (1923) which remains a solid and impressive panorama of the various general problems which concerned the Encyclopædists. Kingsley Martin's *French liberal thought in the eighteenth century* (1929) is extolled for its analyses, but criticised for the limitations of its perspective, and for errors in interpretation of Rousseau and Helvetius. Carl Becker's *The heavenly city of the eighteenth-century philosophers* (1932) is described as a 'magnificent failure' since his thesis, which over-simplifies the facts, rests on an historical analogy between the Enlightenment and thirteenth-century christianity. R. R. Palmer's *Catholics and unbelievers in XVIIIth-century France* (1939) whilst providing us with a much-needed study of Jesuit and Jansenist thought, is tinged with prejudice and coloured by facile generalisations, and above all ignores the current of illuminists, theosophists and mystics who opposed rationalism and paved the way for the Romantic reaction against the Enlightenment. Even Daniel Mornet's monumental work on *Les Origines intellectuelles de la Révolution française* (1933) is now generally considered as little more than a reference work, a mine of information, a negative thesis, barren of ideas, failing to provide an evaluation of the problems and attempted solutions or of the various currents of thought indicated, and unable to show how the 'esprit de réforme' became between 1787 (Mornet's terminal point) and 1789 an 'esprit révolutionnaire'.[4] In practice only two pre-war publications stand out clearly as of intellectual significance: Ernst Cassirer, *Die Philosophie der Aufklärung* (1932), which was published in an English translation in 1951 under the title *The Philosophy of the Enlightenment* and was thereby given a new lease of life in all Anglo-Saxon countries: and

[4] See A. Meynial, rev. *Révolution Française* (1934), lxxxvi. 5-17.

Paul Hazard, *La Crise de la conscience européenne* (1935) completed in 1946 by *La Pensée européenne au XVIIIe siècle.*

Cassirer approached the Enlightenment as a philosopher and offered his readers a new and still valid perspective. Errors in detail may be forgiven since they can be corrected, and serious omissions such as ethics and social thought may be rectified by new studies; but his main fault lies in failure to take into account the true complexity of the Enlightenment because of his over-systematic approach, which involves a linear development of ideas leading up to Kant and to Goethe. He was certainly not equipped to deal with the protean quality of Diderot's thought.[5] Yet this work will continue to be studied for its informed philosophical approach, its clarity, the brilliance of the exposition, and for having singled out the truly important issues in our eyes. P. Hazard's finely written work has the merit of presenting a fuller panorama of eighteenth-century thought, embracing in his survey the lesser as well as the better-known figures, stressing very properly the part of christian forces which had been generally overlooked. It has been criticised for being descriptive rather than analytical, for neglecting socio-economic factors, e.g. the rise of the middle classes, and for failing to do justice to scientific development. Moreover, although P. Hazard deals intelligently with the intellectual crisis, which he placed between 1680 and 1715, he does not provide any data on the diffusion or the import of the new ideas. In his later work, whilst rightly stressing the search for happiness as the mainspring of eighteenth-century thought, he is too apt to oversimplify his vast canvass by spotlighting its most obvious stages. It is precisely this theme of happiness which gave R. Mauzi the title of his voluminous thesis: *L'Idée du bonheur au XVIIIe siècle* (1960). Mauzi's method of singling out one central theme around which to organise his material is fairly new in eighteenth-century studies, and foreshadows a number of works on similar lines.[6] L. G. Crocker has pointed out that invaluable as Mauzi's book is as a work of erudition, it fails somewhat as a general study because the conceptual unity provided leads to serious omissions. Since eighteenth-century

[5] See H. Dieckmann, review article, 'An interpretation of the eighteenth century', *Modern Language Quarterly* (1954), xv. 295-311.

[6] In this category may be placed: Jean Ehrard, *L'Idée de Nature en France dans la première moitié du XVIIIe siècle* (Paris, S.E.V.P.E.N., 1963), 2 vols.

thought and feeling involved more than happiness, R. Mauzi's perspective cannot be quite sound. His survey ignores the political antithesis of the age between three conflicting moral positions: religious, humanistic, anarchic. On the other hand Mauzi has brought out clearly one of the main *idées-forces* of the age, the search for absolutes, the hidden *malaise* and anguish. Preoccupation with ethics is also the main subject of L. G. Crocker, *An Age of crisis* (1959) and *Nature and culture: ethical thought in the French Enlightenment* (1963). In these vast works he shows how the concepts of morality develop and culminate in moral nihilism. His study is based on the examination of a large number of secondary as well as leading *philosophes*, christians and *anti-philosophes* in France, England and other countries. *An Age of crisis* deals with the metaphysical problem and the psychological conditions of ethical theory, bringing out the eighteenth-century conception of character and human motivation. It shows how the 'natural law of human behaviour', seen as the counterpart of the physical law of gravitation, evolved and led ultimately to a moral nihilism which the *philosophes* dreaded. They pinned their hopes on meliorism, i.e. the possibility that men could be made to obey moral laws despite contrary instincts, 'indeed, we may even say, because of them'. Crocker concludes *An Age of crisis* by surveying the nature of the impasse in which the analysis of human nature left ethics and the problem of values, and its significance for the present day. *Nature and culture* deals with ethical theory. After discussing Natural Law theory and the nature of moral experience, the author devotes a long section to the 'utilitarian synthesis' which leads ultimately to nihilism. The main theme in the exploration of human nature, social life and moral values is seen as the tension or polarity between nature and culture. This study brings out well the complexity and unity of the period, the nature of the ever present dialogue in the minds of the writers as well as between the thinkers themselves. Crocker sees the organic development of ideas not as linear but as concentric waves. He is quick to seize on factors which foreshadow nineteenth and twentieth-century developments from liberalism to totalitarianism. This may well be why he labours the rôle of authors such as Sade, which enable him to focus attention on the ultimate stage of nihilism rather than the in-between stage reached by some of the most inherently interesting thinkers he discusses. Mauzi in *L'Idée du bonheur* also touched on all the ethical theories of the age, showing the wide variety of sources from which they severally derive, noting the *philosophes'* effort rationally to deduce their ideas on happiness from a systematic knowledge of man, their awareness of the implications of *libertinage* and eroticism. Like H. Vyverberg who, in *Historical pessimism in the French Enlightenment*, attacked the notion that the *philosophes* were optimists imbued with a simple faith in progress, Mauzi sees in pessimism the main characteristic of this happiness-obsessed culture. The Christian way of life and *le bonheur mondain* impinge one on the other, and are to be distinguished from *le bonheur philosophique*. This approach leads him to emphasise the illusory nature of eighteenth-century relativism and the provisional nature of scepticism in face of what Crocker calls the real search for universals. But while searching for new certainties, many, like Voltaire, remain obstinately in the world of the relative, and do so with a kind of desperate intensity. The very notion of truth as a matter of degree of credibility, to which Voltaire clung, does in fact dominate his deism and sets his very real belief in God within the framework of the relative. Crocker is more illuminating than Mauzi in his own examination of the evolution from a feeling for the concrete and the individual to the unfolding of rationalistic programmes concerned with an abstract 'Man', 'general welfare', or public happiness, *la félicité publique*. Crocker, too, is more aware than Mauzi of the need to consider self-interest as part of the same complex, for *amour-propre* well understood can be seen as the source of all virtues. He is in my view close to the truth when he sees the eighteenth century as identifying virtue and happiness, and believing somewhat blindly that general welfare would also provide individual happiness. He has understood Sade and Laclos as products of an evolution, rather than as individual thinkers standing out of their context; just as elsewhere he has pinpointed Diderot's nihilism side by side with his defence of social morality. He would appear to believe that these attitudes are coherent, on the assumption that the demands of culture are more valid, more important than the demands of the rebellious individual bent on self-affirmation. But one may prefer to see here an ambivalence which is typical of Diderot, and which can be extended to other *philosophes*. The reconciliation of natural immorality with social morality presents the unbeliever and the determinist philosopher with a problem that is best solved in practice, i.e. by the consideration of individual cases on their merits, rather than by abstract philosophy. If this be so, we may then see the eighteenth century as at once social and anti-social, posing rather than resolving the problem of morality without God. We can understand better the anguish of Voltaire having to reject Providence and other *certitudes*, still clinging to God to avoid moral chaos, and making man's need a measure of the truth, i.e. the relative truth of an idea, as also Diderot's deep *malaise* in face of his own cherished materialism.

It is perhaps our better understanding of earlier writers such as Bayle and Fontenelle, and of the anonymous free-thinkers of clandestine literature, that is providing us with the necessary background to revaluations. The work of Mme Labrousse on Bayle, of I. O. Wade[7] and J. S. Spink,[8] on clandestine French literature bring out the manifold complexities of the earlier age, and the ferment of ideas inherited by the generation of *philosophes*. If we have learned to avoid facile generalisations, we can also note the general trend and the extraordinary impact of the great works which came at the right time, gave body to much needed reforms, data on which to plan for the future, vitality to inchoate ideas and style to formless notions. Work done on individual writers has provided a wealth of new material and interpretations which must lead to new and more accurate syntheses. New light has been shed on Voltaire by the publication of his Correspondence by Theodore Besterman, by R. Pomeau's fundamental contribution on Voltaire's religion, and by the *Studies on Voltaire and the* eighteenth *century*. On Rousseau, a new impetus has been given by the publication of his works in the *Pléiade* edition, and an earnest of his Correspondence edited by R. A. Leigh. There have also been important studies by J. Starobinski, M. Raymond, R. Grimsley and others, and in the *Annales J.-J. Rousseau*. On Diderot, we may give particular attention to the biography by A. Wilson and to the edition of many texts including the Correspondence as forerunners of a new general edition of his complete works. There are also the publications of H. Dieckmann, L. G. Crocker, G. May, J. Seznec and many others, as well as successive volumes of the *Diderot Studies*. On Montes-

[7] I. O. Wade, *The clandestine organisation and diffusion of philosophic ideas in France from 1700 to 1750* (Princeton, Univ. Press, 1938).

[8] J. S. Spink, *French free-thought from Gassendi to Voltaire* (1960).

quieu too, there have been considerable advances thanks to the work of J. Brethe de la Gressaye, A. Masson, R. Shackleton and P. Vernière. On d'Alembert (whose Correspondence needs to be published) valuable research has been done, as on d'Holbach, La Mettrie, Morelly, l'abbé Galiani and their contemporaries. As a result we are gathering a different and richer idea of intellectual life up to the time of the French Revolution.

From the historical standpoint, and for a general perspective, studies on the *Encyclopédie* and the Encyclopædists are of singular importance. J. Le Gras's brief *Diderot et l'Encyclopédie* (1928) has now little to offer; and P. Grosclaude's *Un Audacieux Message, l'Encyclopédie* (1951) restates the well-known facts. Arthur Wilson in *Diderot: the Testing Years, 1713–1759* (1957), has outlined the facts even more succinctly and satisfactorily, but for new information on the *Encyclopédie* itself, its contributors, their social background and the underlying political issues, we must turn to J. Proust, *Diderot et l'Encyclopédie* (1962). We can now see more clearly the rôle of the *Encyclopédie* and the Encyclopædists in the elaboration of political ideas and the shaping of events, in determining a new climate of opinion and in forming an *élite* as well as a public. This does not, however, invalidate the general view that ideological conflicts have their origin in economic and social pressures, and that revolutions are never more than partly due to intellectual causes. The *Encyclopédie* is important not because it was necessarily read by a large public, but because it was the epitome of the age. It synthesised the scientific knowledge of the period, rendering it accessible to the non-specialist but educated man: and this is of particular consequence to the historian of science of today. It formulated a number of new hypotheses to account for facts, suggested new techniques, and above all, because of this basic activity, it was an instrument of war against all the prejudices of the Ancien Régime. The growing daring of the contributors reflected the spirit of the times: yet they remained original interpreters of public opinion. They formed the most powerfully intellectual body of men, and their differences on many points merely serve to bring out the intensity of the conflicts which underlay society in their day. It is perhaps through a detailed study of the *Encyclopédie*, and the full career and works of the Encyclopædists that we shall get really close to the live forces of the age and understand better the complex originality of the five or six great French thinkers whose names stand out so clearly today.

The *Encyclopédie*, which underwent many vicissitudes from the time of its conception in 1746 to the appearance of the last volume some 25 years later, should be considered not only as an intellectual venture, but as a commercial enterprise involving the investment of very substantial capital and a great technical effort. In spite of what Proust has said in *Diderot et l'Encyclopédie*, it is fairly clear that the editors d'Alembert, and especially Diderot, were in fact responsible for the change in scope of the publication from the five volumes with 120 plates foreseen in 1745 to the ten volumes, two of which were to consist of 600 plates, as advertised in the 1750 Prospectus; and the 17 volumes, plus 11 volumes of plates, finally brought out. Proust has stressed the scope of the undertaking with its 150 contributors and 4,000 subscribers, and the attribution of many articles is still in dispute. He is right, however, in drawing our attention to the fact that the sheer business of finding contributors and subscribers, controlling the paper supply, the printing, the proof correcting, the binding and engraving of the volumes over a period of 25 years necessarily turned the publication from a relatively modest publishing venture into one of the most ambitious capitalist projects in the second half of the century. According to Voltaire, whose figures have been found remarkably accurate, there was a turnover of 7,650,000 *livres*, which eclipses that for the entire trade between the East and the West Indies and France. We are in fact confronted by a major concern with an expenditure of some 1,158,958 *livres* and an estimated profit for the publishers of 2,400,000 *livres*. Many of the contributors, some of whom were also subscribers, received no payment for their articles. It was the support of public opinion, and of certain vested interests in what became a national enterprise, that rendered publication possible and profitable. This fact must never be lost sight of in any close examination of the story of the publication of the *Encyclopédie*. For just as Government and official opposition were divided, so there was division on the other side. The interests of the rich capitalist publishers and their friends were not always identical with those of the editors; it is known that Le Breton deleted passages presumed too dangerous after the proofs had been corrected by Diderot. The threat to continue publication abroad disturbed officials in high quarters: and the necessary compromises and inevitable complications served to promote the liberalism enshrined in the *Encyclopédie*, which was also fostered in such supplements as the *Encyclopédie méthodique*, the *Journal encyclopédique* and the *Correspondance littéraire de Grimm*. For 25 critical years Le Breton's business house was the focal point of all information, of all literary, cultural, scientific, technological, political curiosity. The editors were in touch with writers, scientists, industrialists, technologists, artisans and artists, men of action; a bourgeois *élite* as attached to social order as to reform, preparing unwittingly the Revolution to come, deeply involved in the industrial rather than in the political transformation. It is this aspect of the history of the period which needs now to be examined; and individual studies of collaborators and others involved should follow Proust's more general survey. But we may already surmise what the editing of the *Encyclopédie* did for Diderot, the man and the thinker. It provided him with a first-class education in breadth and in depth, with connections of an exceptionally interesting kind; and left him with a determining political and intellectual rôle as the leader of the most enlightened part of the nation. He was also in the best position conceivable for effecting as a *philosophe* the vast synthesis of all knowledge, which d'Alembert in his *Discours préliminaire*, was also eager to promulgate for the greater benefit of mankind.

Following on the often biased studies of Soboul, Jean Luc, Momjian, Volguine and others concerned with the social background of the *Encyclopédie*, Proust points to the fundamental antagonism of the Encyclopædists and the Government, which is very often obscured by the turn of events, or persons involved in somewhat ambiguous attitudes. The contributors who were often privileged and endowed with private means belonged for the most part to the upper and midde bourgeoisie and the professional classes. They all had one thing in common: they were the intellectuals, part of an enlightened *élite*, well informed and bent on reform, liberal in outlook and involved in the elaboration of a new economic and social order. An enormous industrial and technological revolution was afoot, and the need to increase national productivity was seldom far from the minds of the chief contributors. Historically, this loosely formed group or party—which Voltaire appropriately termed 'la séquelle encyclopédique'—triumphed after the *neuf*

Thermidor, during the last period of the Convention, and under the Directoire, when the bourgeoisie turned away from the lower, popular classes, and assumed power on its own account. Most of the publishing houses were by then directed by former Encyclopædists. The Écoles Centrales, the École Normale Supérieure, the École Polytechnique and the Institut were established, and the Universities, as indeed all other grades of education, were reorganised on modern lines. Under the Convention, the Girondins were for the most part disciples of the Encyclopædists; and Diderot's writings were once again brought to public notice through the Naigeon edition of his works which appeared in 1798. A few former Encyclopædists achieved positions of distinction, others positions of importance to the State or in the corridors of power, but none of real political power. They remained, however, well placed for moulding opinion and upholding the Encyclopædist ideals. Daubenton, for example, the distinguished writer of articles on natural science, was appointed to a chair at the École Normale Supérieure; Deleyre was put in charge of the *écoles normales*; Desmarets was appointed to teach natural history at the École Normale de la Seine. All made their mark as teachers and administrators on the strength of their exceptional competence, and a careful study of the careers of those whom they taught might yield surprising results. One contributor is known to have been guillotined, and a number fled the country with the aristocrats.

Many misconceptions, due to prejudice, to the diverse attitudes taken up during and after the French Revolution, and to sheer ignorance, still need to be swept away. It is for instance no longer possible to make Diderot responsible, as contemporaries believed, for Babeuf and the abortive *babouviste* plot. For Babeuf was inspired in his Communist leanings by Morelly's *Code de la Nature*, wrongly attributed to Diderot, and included in the first volume of Diderot's *Œuvres philosophiques*, published at Amsterdam in 1773. Indeed, it was partly to rectify this and similar errors that in 1789 Naigeon undertook his monumental edition of Diderot's works. Men like Fontanes and La Harpe feared that the Encyclopædist policies would subvert the social order: and even in our time, Barrès and Maurras opposed the celebration of the bicentenary of Diderot's birth because of his alleged influence on the development of anarchist tendencies. The interpretation of history that is slowly unfolding pays particular attention to social and economic factors underlying political action. Proust has been in a position to show that the Encyclopædists were largely middle-class landowners of some substance, many of whom, like Buffon, d'Holbach, Quesnay, Rollier des Ormes the noted Parliamentarian, Voltaire and Diderot himself, enjoyed bourgeois comfort, and at times considerable wealth, from the exploitation of their properties, or through skilful modern investment in business and industrial or agricultural production. The purpose, policy and significance of Danton, who was more directly influenced by Diderot than he knew through the passages in Raynal that are in fact by Diderot, are more readily understood in this context. Even though Diderot chose his collaborators solely for their capacity, actual or potential, and their ability to play an active part in reviewing the economy of the nation, its ideology, its very structure, he was in his private life, class-conscious in modern terms, drawn to the hierarchy of wealth. It is significant that he married his daughter, whom he loved, to a man of substance from his own home town. There is a great difference between Voltaire with 200,000 *livres* income and the poorer Diderot, whom Rousseau however berates for having 'bons bas drapés, bons souliers, bonne camisole'. But, nevertheless, stress on intellectual activity as the main social activity of the Encyclopædists was necessary, if an editor like Diderot was to cut across the old social conventions and class distinctions, and this led him, at times, to cut across the new ones based on money, which were fast developing. Today, and since Proust's work, we are more concerned with a re-examination of the historical background to politics and thought than with a philosophical re-appraisal, and fresh information on matters of detail lead us to modify earlier generalisations.

The main contribution of French eighteenth-century thought to the history of ideas remains of course unchallenged. The *philosophes*' basic opposition to the fundamental conceptions underlying the dominant current of thought of the previous age, and indeed of earlier times, needs no emphasis. Their main theories were constantly reiterated: acceptance of nature, as opposed to asceticism; of reason, opposed to a naïve faith in the supernatural; and of tolerance opposed to religious persecution. Their vindication of the rights of man and the need to establish a better world on earth heralds the beginning of modern times. The age of the Enlightenment has been contrasted with that of the Crusades. If one accepts this basic contention, one may trace the development of eighteenth-century rationalism from the Renaissance, which rehabilitated Nature, dwelling on the part played by Rabelais, Erasmus and humanism, and stressing that of Montaigne who incarnated for many the new and essentially unchristian man of nature without the grace of God. Montaigne, although a believer, taught his disciples how to doubt, and perfected a technique, later adopted by Voltaire and others, of killing by ridicule, or leading the intelligent reader to deduce rationally the true implications of a statement. Thus when Montaigne writes: 'C'est un grand ouvrier de miracles que l'esprit humain', taking care not to say 'que l'esprit païen', he implicitly undermines belief in christian miracles themselves. And one may trace the development of the 'encyclopædic spirit' through Descartes, Fontenelle and Bayle to articles in the *Encyclopédie*. What, however, is holding the attention of contemporary critics are the modifications in this overall picture that need to be made in the light of what we now know about the minds of individual writers, and the continued effect of their upbringing on their mode of thought. We find in the case of many eighteenth-century advanced thinkers that what was true of Bayle is true of them: their knowledge of metaphysics, and their familiarity with metaphysical concepts remains great, and survives in the recesses of their mind even when they have discarded religious prejudice. A close study of the texts shows that they could not opt out of the prevailing climate of opinion of their day, nor eschew discussion with their adversaries, sometimes more present in their own minds than in the flesh. The religious issue, whether dealt with from the Protestant, the Catholic, the deist or the atheist standpoint, remained one of the most lively, as evidenced by the continued circulation of anonymous tracts by *colporteurs*, and by the considerable output of 'refutations' of works of alleged free-thinkers, such as the anonymously published *Pensées philosophiques* by Diderot.

In spite of research, and important publications, mostly centred around the more important figures, the polemical history of religious thought is still imperfectly known, but we can trace the survival of early preoccupations and interests in the mature thinking of writers such as Diderot. The detailed picture involves much shading of the overall picture, and the nuances now emphasised must in the end change our attitude. There is no doubt that when Vyverberg in his *Historical Pessimism in the French Enlightenment* attacks the notion that the *philosophes* were optimists imbued with a simple faith in progress, he overstates his case; but he is right in challenging our preconceptions, and in providing a needed corrective.

Uncertainty and conflicting viewpoints also face the contemporary critic when determining precisely the politics of the Encyclopædists, and their true rôle in foreshadowing the French Revolution, eighteenth-century liberalism and certain of the political assumptions, perhaps even myths, of our own age. It is agreed that for a long time the *philosophes* pinned their hopes of reform on an ideal Legislator, who would ensure happiness and virtue, then on an enlightened despot, and only reluctantly, at a late stage and out of despair, turning away from the monarchy to espouse Republican ideals that were often inspired by Rousseau, whom few really understood at the time. For the most part they were more concerned with practical reforms, affecting commerce and industry; and civil reforms, by which men would be allowed to do all that the laws were prepared to sanction. They did not ask for political freedom, as is clear from the perusal of the article 'liberté' in the *Encyclopédie*. They did not wish to see all forms of censorship abolished, but rather the appointment of censors favourable to their cause. They unfailingly attacked inequalities in the social system, and the idea of a social contract as the basis of society gained ground, with its implication that if the ruler breaks the tacit contract between himself and his subject, he may be removed. Rousseau's insistence on the need for popular consent provided a rational basis for a revolution that sprang from a multiplicity of causes, many of which were irrational. In the main, the peculiar contribution of eighteenth-century political thought can be summed up as follows: the conception of a state of nature which antedates organisation into society. The *philosophes*, especially Rousseau, presented an idyllic picture of primitive man, born innocent, that is to say neither good nor bad, that was not acceptable to all, witness Montesquieu's presentation of him in his *histoire des Troglodytes*; and Voltaire who in spite of the naïve Candide or the occasional *bon Huron* sees men essentially as 'des insectes se dévorant les uns les autres sur un petit tas de boue' (*Zadig*). But clearly the idea of natural man had the advantage of placing the responsibility for man's misery and crime on society itself, thereby justifying change. Man is more readily convinced of the truth of ideas that help him in his despair, even when they do not stand up to objective analysis. From the polemical point of view, the doctrine of the original goodness of man had the advantage of directly challenging a cardinal tenet of the Roman Catholic Church: original sin. Of course, in their analyses of natural man and social evolution, in their attitude to natural law (to which Rousseau is hostile and which Diderot favours) the *philosophes* held divergent views. This is one reason why Cobban's stimulating *In Search of Humanity* (1960) strikes many critics as old-fashioned and an oversimplification. It is in detailed studies of the writings of Voltaire, Rousseau, Montesquieu and Diderot that the political issues have been or will be most satisfactorily clarified. The bringing to light of new data on Diderot's political opinions is a case in point. Proust has shown that the political theory evolved by Diderot during the years 1750–65 was daring, but that Diderot remained timid and eclectic on the subject of political reform. He was opposed to the revolutionary theories of Rousseau, which he nevertheless always kept in mind. He advocated in the *Encyclopédie* an enlightened monarchy, which later he opposed. His theory, untrammelled by concern with its practical application, sprang logically from his materialistic monism, his determinism and his rationalism. His system of a democratic monarchy, politically absolutist, liberal in thought and economy, as expounded in the *Encyclopédie*, was well-suited to an elite of landowners seeking order and security, and to the Encyclopædist group as a whole. Historically, in spite of their obvious moderation, it is Diderot and his fellow materialists who attacked both the existing monarchy and the Church, whilst Voltaire and the deists wished to preserve the monarchy, and Rousseau wished to preserve religion. Diderot's rôle in the preparation of the Revolution is, therefore, the more comprehensive. Newer interpretations, based on greater knowledge of late writings, such as that outlined in the *Nouvelles Littéraires* of 19 December 1963, show that he was not a firm partisan of enlightened despotism, nor the dupe of Frederick II, nor the obsequious flatterer of Catherine the Great to whom he wrote: 'Il n'y a de vrai souverain que la nation', in a work which enshrined his claim that a monarch owed allegiance to the Constitution, and which Catherine II burnt in anger in 1784. He was not truly a Physiocrat. There is news of a thesis, which is nearing completion, in which it will be shown that Diderot's political ideas were taken over by the *idéologues* and the contributors to *La Décade*. In his *Mémoires*, addressed to Catherine, he outlined in eighteen points the reforms he thought that France required; and in the 1780 edition of Raynal's *Histoire des deux Indes*, under the title *Apostrophe à Louis XVI*, appears a passage which Raynal borrowed from Diderot, and which was published in the form of a tract in 1789. It is one of the first manifestoes of the Tiers État.

The new view of the eighteenth century comes therefore from detailed study of the social and political background of the age, a closer scrutiny of articles in the *Encyclopédie*, and of the works of the great and the minor writers. It comes too from our ability to cut across the divisions established by *genres* and disciplines. Thus Science, the history of science, and philosophy are now seen as enriching literature and the history of ideas; and the need is for the synthesizing of ever more complex data. Recently R. Mortier[9] has reminded us that we can no longer accept that rationalism and sensibility are exclusive—Diderot's and Rousseau's own works refute this. We no longer find it profitable to speak of pre-romanticism in connection with any author of the period. We are not so certain of the old, and indeed sometimes of the new generalisations. The works of Trahard, Monglond, Mornet, Van Tieghem, Hazard and even Cassirer are now being questioned on matters of principle as well as of detail. Critics such as Werner Krauss,[10] Yvon Belaval, J. Proust, R. Mauzi, L. G. Crocker, H. Dieckmann, R. Mortier envisage a broadening of the whole concept of the Enlightenment partly by placing it in its international context, relating for example a philosophical enthusiasm derived in some measure from Shaftesbury with the *Sturm-und-Drang* movement in Germany, so different from nineteenth-century romanticism which Mortier has described as 'idealistic, reactionary, fantastic and mystical'. He has reminded us that the eighteenth century was certainly interested in dreams: those of Diderot, and Rousseau, those of l'abbé de Saint-Pierre on everlasting peace, of Le Père Castel on the hidden relationship between the arts, of Restif de la Bretonne, etc. and with the possible

[9] 'Unité ou scission', *Studies on Voltaire and the Eighteenth Century* (1963), xxvi. 1207-1221.

[10] *Studien zur Deutschen und Französischen Aufklärung* (Berlin 1963).

exception of Rousseau and Diderot which Mortier has ignored in this connection, it was united in rejecting the supernatural, and all transcendental experience; but it was only towards the end of the century, with Sade and Bernardin de Saint-Pierre, that it dissociated the two dominant tendencies *reason* and *sensibility* which it had striven to harmonise into a coherent pattern. Certainly the capacity to receive emotions, the *uneasiness* of which Locke spoke and which Condillac translated into *inquiétude* and considered the basis of psychic life, is not opposed to reason and intelligence, but its live force.

Thus philosophy, the philosophical and critical spirit can no longer be separated from science, history, jurisprudence and politics, nor confined to the realm of abstract speculation. Reason and nature must go hand in hand since there is a close connection between the processes of the mind and the outside world it reflects: 'Le type de nos raisonnements les plus étendus', wrote Diderot, 'leur liaison, leur conséquence est nécessaire dans notre entendement comme l'enchaînement, la liaison des effets, des causes, des objets, des qualités des objets l'est dans la nature.'[11]

In the quest for happiness, sentiment and reason combine to reconcile anarchical man and social man. If the majority of the *philosophes* clung to the bourgeois dream of reconciling happiness and virtue, at least they recognised man as an authentic individual, as well as a social and political animal, conditioned by education, economic, social and political factors. It is the power of reason in individual man, whatever the nature of the factors that can lead it astray or distort it, that is the condition of his very real if limited freedom. For only the man who thinks can feel free and therefore be free.[12] And in spite of the determinist belief of many of the *philosophes* it is the constant awareness of this personal freedom so manifest in practice that enabled them to step into new pastures and to lay the foundations of much progressive thought in the nineteenth and twentieth centuries.

[11] AT., ix. 372.

[12] Cf. Voltaire, *Traité de métaphysique*, ed. H. Temple Patterson (Manchester Univ. Press, 1937), pp. 42-49.

The Idea of the Decline and Fall of the Roman Empire

H. R. Trevor-Roper

We all tend to simplify, perhaps to dramatise, our mental development. In retrospect, the slow processes of the mind are disguised, sometimes even obliterated, by the dramatic moment of discovery, or conversion. St Augustine's *tolle lege*, Newton's apple . . . intellectual history is full of such episodes which immortalise, though they may not explain, crucial stages in the transformation of thought. In the historical philosophy of the Enlightenment there is one such moment, and it too has been immortalised by retrospective isolation. 'It was at Rome, on 15th October 1764,' Gibbon wrote in his autobiography, 'as I sat musing amidst the ruins of the Capitol, while the barefooted friars were singing vespers in the Temple of Jupiter, that the idea of writing the decline and fall of the city first started to my mind . . .'

Those who (like myself) regard the *Decline and Fall of the Roman Empire* as the greatest historical work in our language must always be thankful for that dramatic moment. What would have happened, we may ask, if Gibbon had lacked that unforgettable experience? What would he then have written, if he had written any great work, in the next twenty years of his life? He himself has told us of his earlier projects: the projects which, up to that moment, had occupied his mind. He had conceived of English subjects—Richard Cœur de Lion, the baronial wars against Henry III, the life of Sir Philip Sidney, or of Sir Walter Ralegh. He had thought of Italian subjects too: of the French invasion of Italy in 1494 and the rule of the Medici in Renaissance Florence. He had also pondered long on another subject which fascinated him: the history of the liberty of the Swiss. How fortunate, we may now say, that he did not waste his genius on these subjects in which later scholarship would inevitably have overtaken him, as it has overtaken the historical works of Gibbon's revered contemporary masters, David Hume, the historian of England, and William Robertson, the historian of Scotland, of Charles V and of America! Who now reads those works, those 'well turned periods' of Robertson, those 'careless inimitable beauties' of Hume, which first inspired the young Gibbon with ambition, then caused him, as he tells us, 'to close the book with a mixed sensation of delight and despair'? And would not the same fate (we may ask), however unjust, have overtaken Gibbon too, had he confined himself to those medieval or modern subjects which had successively engaged his mind while he 'bumperised', in the barren years 1760–62, with his rural neighbours in the Hampshire militia?

Fortunately he did not. Early in 1763, while he was still beholding, 'in a dark and doubtful perspective', the 'splendid subject' of Medicean Florence, the affairs of Europe were suddenly transformed. The long war, the Seven Years War with France, was over; all America north of Mexico was British—for a time; and with the disbandment of the militia, temporary captain Gibbon could at last extract from his father, temporary major Gibbon, the fulfilment of that old promise: a tour of the Continent. With his mind still unsure, he crossed the Channel. He visited Paris and mixed, in the salons of the great, with the philosophers of the French Enlightenment—Diderot and d'Alembert, Helvétius and Holbach. He revisited Lausanne, the place of his education and there settled down, in more luxurious circumstances, for several months. At Lausanne he made two new friends. One was John Baker Holroyd, afterwards Lord Sheffield, whose 'long and active friendship', as he wrote in his will, he could never repay. Modern admirers of Gibbon may say the same; for it is to Lord Sheffield that we owe the preservation and publication of Gibbon's autobiography and other papers. The other was William Guise, the son of a Gloucestershire baronet. Afterwards Guise, Gibbon and Holroyd would all sit together in Parliament. And it was with Guise that Gibbon now completed his continental tour, going on from Switzerland into Savoy, over the Alps, to Austrian Milan, to Medicean Florence, to papal Rome.

With his mind still on the Medici, Gibbon lingered long in Florence. He visited the memorials of their rule and admired the products of their patronage. But then came Rome and that famous moment in the ruined Capitol. It was a moment of inspiration, never to be forgotten. Mr Arnold Toynbee, who, I fear, does not much like Gibbon or the Enlightenment in general, has described it rather grudgingly as the sole moment of inspiration ever experienced by Gibbon. This is one of the points—there are others—on which I venture to dissent from my distinguished compatriot. I believe that Gibbon's intellectual life was full of excitement, and that this experience in Rome, far from being a solitary flash, suddenly sparked off by an immediate occasion, was merely one episode in a long process of fermentation. In fact I suspect that Gibbon himself, in retrospect, may have dramatised that experience and, in so doing, over-simplified—at least to us who do not live in the eighteenth century or recognise all his allusions—the origin of his life's work. That work, I shall suggest, had deeper origins. It was not, I believe, merely the realisation of a sudden idea, of a momentary accidental inspiration. It was something far greater, and to his contemporaries far more significant, than that. It was the fulfilment of the historical ambitions and questionings of a whole generation.

But before coming to that general subject, let me dispose of a more immediate issue. The modern enemies of the Enlightenment sometimes represent its thinkers in general, and Gibbon in particular, as cold, unimaginative creatures. This view began, I suppose, with the Romantic movement. 'Gibbon's style is detestable,' wrote Coleridge sourly, 'but his style is not the worst thing about him', etc. etc.[1] But of course such a view is a travesty of the truth. Certainly Gibbon, and most of his friends, disapproved of public 'enthusiasm'. 'My temper,' he tells us, 'is not very susceptible of enthusiasm, and the enthusiasm which I do not feel I have ever scorned to affect. But'—he goes on (for the generalisation is only introduced to lead to the exception)—'at the distance of 25 years I can neither forget nor express the strong emotion which agitated my mind as I first approached and entered the eternal city. After a sleepless night, I trod, with a lofty step, the ruins of the Forum; each memorable spot where Romulus stood, or Tully spoke, or Caesar fell, was at once present to my eye; and several days of intoxication were lost

[1] S. T. Coleridge, *Table Talk*, ed. H. N. Coleridge, (New York, 1835) ii. 118.

or enjoyed before I could descend to a cool and minute investigation.' This is not the language of frigidity; nor is the excitement merely retrospective: Gibbon's letters to his father from Rome fully confirm the exaltation of that time. Nor indeed, is this the only evidence of such emotion. Again and again, whenever we look below the polished—the six times polished—surface of the *Autobiography*, or even below the august, coruscating prose of the *Decline and Fall*, we discover warmth and movement. 'I sighed as a lover, I obeyed as a son': how often has that phrase been quoted to indicate the low temperature of Gibbon's emotions! And yet, when we look at the raw material of the *Autobiography*, at the intimate papers which Lord Sheffield caused to be shut away from profane eyes for a whole century,[2] how different, how much more impassioned, the whole affair of Gibbon's romance with Suzanne Curchod appears! The man who, at the age of 16, had been swept from the tepid formalism of the established Anglican Church, the Church of Porteous and Hoadly, into the warm delusions of popery as seen through the golden prose of Bossuet and the majestic poetry of Dryden; the man who, re-converted, and faced by the marvellous, outrageous, newly re-built baroque abbey of Einsiedeln, flaunting its costly enchantments 'in the poorest corner of Europe', found himself animated by the spirit of the old Swiss reformers; the man whose humanity was revolted by being carried over the Alpine passes by human porters, '*mes semblables*', and who saw, in every gilded moulding in the palace of Turin, 'a village of Savoyards ready to die of hunger, cold and poverty';[3] the man who, in the last year of his life, when he could scarcely move without pain, hurried from Lausanne to London, skirting the armies of the French Revolution and the European coalition, within earshot of the French cannonade, in order to be with the suddenly widowed Lord Sheffield, was certainly not a cold, torpid soul; nor could I ever agree with Mr Toynbee in describing the eighteenth century, that century of new sensibility, and the Enlightenment, that movement of heightened

[2] Having edited and published the autobiography and the other miscellaneous works of Gibbon, Lord Sheffield placed the Gibbon MSS among his private papers and, by his will, instructed his heirs to keep them private. They became public in 1896 when the third (and last) Lord Sheffield sold them to the British Museum.

[3] *Gibbon's Journey from Geneva to Rome, His Journal from 20 April to 2 October 1764*, ed. Georges A. Bonnard (1961), pp. 6, 18.

humanity, as a mere 'weary lull' of exceptionally low temperature in the long, fevered decline of the West.

Gibbon's enthusiasm is, I believe, constantly discernible, even in his writings; and if we search more deeply in those writings, or more widely in the intellectual world around him, we can, I think, detect the successive stages of illumination which were brought together in the idea with which I am concerned: the idea of the *Decline and Fall.* The major stages, I shall suggest, were three. First, there was Gibbon's introduction to the new philosophy of the eighteenth century in Lausanne. Secondly, there was his discovery—an intoxicating discovery—of the great teacher of the new historians of the eighteenth century: Montesquieu. Thirdly, there was the general preoccupation of his age with the problem—'the great problem of the 18th century' as an Italian scholar has called it[4]—of the later Roman Empire and the Middle Ages. Only against this larger background, only as the culmination of this slower process, does Gibbon's Roman experience, I suggest, acquire its full significance.

For the first of these stages—for Gibbon's introduction to the new philosophy—we must go back eleven years, to his early exile from England: to that sudden, shameful removal from the premature liberty and laxity of unreformed Oxford to the straitened lodgings, mean diet and strict supervision of a Calvinist minister in Switzerland. How little Gibbon's father, that amiable, indolent, feckless tory squire, can have dreamed of the consequences of his impulsive act! A widower, without much interest in education, he had dumped his inconvenient son, out of 'perplexity rather than prudence', at Oxford. The result had been disastrous. The boy had become a papist. That, of course, was a fate worse than death, and it provoked Edward Gibbon senior into action. So, once more out of perplexity rather than prudence, he dumped his son elsewhere—further from temptation, further from popery, further from home. That done, he could return to Hampshire, mingle freely with the highest and lowest society, for which (as his son remarked) he was equally fitted, enter his horses for the local races, and sink, quiet and content, into the glutinous web of debt. And yet for the young Gibbon the consequences of this abrupt removal were enormous: how enormous

[4] G. Giarrizzo, *Edward Gibbon e la cultura europea del settecento* (Naples 1954), p. 194; cf. G. Falco, *La Polemica sul medioevo* (Turin 1933).

we can hardly envisage unless we compare the intellectual condition, in the 1750s, of England and Switzerland.

The European Enlightenment, admittedly, owes much to England. The Englishmen Bacon, Locke and Newton were its prophets; the English Revolution of 1688 was its political starting point; the English deists were its midwives. But in England itself, by 1750, these forces were spent. The great thinkers of the last century had become totem figures; the last of them, Newton, had died in majestic orthodoxy, carefully concealing his own heretical past. The whig revolutionaries had become a new establishment, an aristocracy fixed in complacent postures of ancester-worship. The deist controversy was played out. David Hume, in his letters, never ceased to lament the intellectual sterility of England in his time, 'so sunk in stupidity and barbarism and faction that you may as well think of Lapland for an author'. Only Scotland and America, he thought, produced writers of English; the only work of literature produced in England in the last generation, he wrote, was '*Tristram Shandy*, bad as it is'.

We may think this verdict unjust—Gibbon himself, that enthusiastic admirer of Fielding's *Tom Jones*, would certainly have thought it unjust—but there is no doubt that it was Hume's true opinion. When the first volume of the *Decline and Fall* broke the spell, Hume confessed to Gibbon his amazement. 'Your countrymen', he wrote, 'for almost a generation', had so given themselves up to 'barbarous and absurd faction', and so neglected all polite letters, that 'I no longer expected any valuable production ever to come from them'.[5] The English literary scene was dominated, in that generation, by Dr Johnson; and what Johnson and his obedient biographer thought of the Enlightenment we know. To them Voltaire was a coxcomb, Hume and Gibbon were poisonous infidels, Rousseau should be transported to the Plantations, Robertson was damned as a Presbyterian, and Adam Smith (according to that model of polite table-manners Dr Johnson) was not only as dull a dog as he had ever met but, 'a most disagreeable fellow' whose wine, at dinner-parties, 'bubbled in his mouth'.[6]

But if England, in those years, seemed to have lost touch with the

[5] See *The Letters of David Hume*, ed. J. Y. I. Greig (Oxford 1932), ii. 104, 208, 269, 310, etc.

[6] The last detail comes from Boswell's diary. See Boswell, *The Ominous Years 1774–6* (London 1963), pp. 264, 337.

Enlightenment which it had once inspired, how different was Switzerland! What Holland had been in the seventeenth century Switzerland had become in the eighteenth. It was the haven to which philosophy had fled from English indifference, French censorship, Italian persecution. Thither the greatest of eighteenth-century Italian historians, Pietro Giannone, had fled from the long arm of the Church—until that long arm hooked him out again and stuffed him into a Savoyard dungeon to languish and die. There Montesquieu had published his greatest work. There Voltaire had finished and published his most ambitious historical study, his *Essai sur les mœurs*. This vigorous intellectual life of Switzerland had its centre among the liberal 'Arminian' ministers of Geneva and Lausanne. After a long struggle, these liberals had defeated the old die-hards of the Word and inaugurated, with the new century, a new era of freedom. It was they who welcomed Giannone and corresponded with Voltaire. One of them, Jacob Vernet, a minister of Geneva, was a personal link between Giannone, Montesquieu and Voltaire. Another, Daniel Pavillard, a minister of Lausanne, was Gibbon's tutor. And it was through them and their philosophic teachers—Jean-Pierre de Crousaz, Jean Leclerc and Jean Barbeyrac—that Gibbon would find his way to the European, and even the English, writers who had never been commended to him in tory Oxford: to Grotius and Pufendorf, Chillingworth and Bayle, Locke and Tillotson. Through them also he would discover the great philosophic historians: read Giannone, devour Montesquieu, call on Voltaire.

Switzerland, it is not too much to say, introduced Gibbon to the eighteenth-century Enlightenment. It also introduced him to some of the great works of seventeenth-century scholarship which had equally been ignored in Oxford. For some of the best seventeenth-century scholars, those who had most influence on Gibbon, were either Swiss, like the legal historian Jacques Godefroy and the numismatist Ezechiel von Spanheim, or French Huguenots who belonged to the Calvinist International, whose capital was in Geneva, like Jacques Basnage, the historian of the Jews, and Isaac de Beausobre, the historian of the Manichees. He would say as much himself. 'Such as I am in genius or learning or manners,' he wrote, 'I owe my creation to Lausanne: it was in that school that the statue was discovered in the block of marble'; and again, 'if my childish revolt against the religion of my country had not stripped me in time of my academic gown, the five important years, so liberally improved in the studies and conversation of Lausanne, would have been steeped in port and prejudice among the monks of Oxford. Had the fatigue of idleness compelled me to read, the path of learning would not have been enlightened by a ray of philosophic freedom'—the philosophic freedom which, from Switzerland, had reanimated the subject which Gibbon, from his earliest years, had resolved to pursue: history.

Above all, at Lausanne Gibbon discovered Montesquieu. This was the second of the three great experiences I have mentioned. It was the greatest single inspiration of his years of study. Whenever Gibbon mentions Montesquieu, we sense the note of excitement. Above all other books, he tells us, 'my delight', in those Lausanne years, 'was in the frequent perusal of Montesquieu, whose energy of style and boldness of hypothesis were powerful to awaken and stimulate the genius of his age'. Before leaving Lausanne, Gibbon would begin his first published work, his *Essai sur l'étude de la littérature* (for all this time he preferred to write in French, not English), in which he would hail Montesquieu as the true guide (and Tacitus as the true example) for a philosophic historian. Even the style of that essay, he would afterwards write, was corrupted by the too faithful imitation of Montesquieu. And nearly thirty years later, in his last volume, he would pay a final tribute to that early master whose work, for the last forty years, he said, had been the greatest stimulus in historical enquiry.[7]

What was the lesson which Gibbon learned from Montesquieu? Briefly, it was that human history is not a mere pageant of dramatic (or undramatic) events, nor even a storehouse of noble (or deterrent) examples, but a process, and a process governed, in its detail, not by a divine plan, as the 'universal historians' of the past—the Protestant Ralegh, the Catholic Bossuet—had thought, but by a complex of social forces which a 'philosophic historian'—that is, an historian who looked behind mere events for fundamental ideas, causes and connexions, who saw 'the chief use of history' (in Hume's words) as the discovery of 'the constant and universal principles of human nature'—could isolate and describe. Geography, climate,

[7] E. Gibbon, *The Decline and Fall of the Roman Empire* (Everyman edition), vi. 91 n.

economic resources—these lay at the very base of history; institutions, laws, religion—these, conditioned by them but developing their own momentum, created in turn new and subtler forces to whose interwoven pattern human behaviour was subject. 'Men are governed by many things', wrote Montesquieu: 'climate, religion, laws, maxims of government, examples of things past, customs, manners; from all which is derived a general spirit'; and this 'general spirit' he strove to illustrate by thousands of examples, deductions, aphorisms in his great work, published in 1748, the work which we can see as the foundation of the modern science of sociology: *De l'Esprit des lois*.

Gibbon, of course, was not the first historian to read *L'Esprit des lois*. Already, in 1749, within a year of its publication, David Hume, passing through Savoy, had been captivated by it. He had at once opened a correspondence with Montesquieu; he had had part of Montesquieu's book published in Edinburgh; and he had decided to become an historian himself. Hume's *History*, which began to appear in 1754, was the application to English history of Montesquieu's principles. A few years later another Scotsman, William Robertson, applied them to Scottish history too. All the great Scotsmen of that generation—Adam Ferguson, Lord Kames, Adam Smith, John Millar—professed themselves disciples of Montesquieu, whose works were repeatedly reprinted in Scotland. For we are now in the great era of the Scottish Enlightenment: an enlightenment which, as in Switzerland, had followed the defeat of Calvinist bigotry. William Robertson himself, minister of the Kirk, Moderator of its General Assembly, friend of Hume, admirer of Voltaire, was the leader of the liberal clergy of Scotland, just as the clerical friends of Giannone and Voltaire—the Vernets, the Turrettini, the Tronchins—had led the liberal clergy of Switzerland. Thanks to such men Gibbon could refer to the 'strong ray of philosophic light' that has 'broke forth from Scotland in our own time', and could appreciate particularly those tributes which came to him, in London, from 'the northern part of our island, whither taste and philosophy seem to have retired from the smoke and hurry of this immense capital'.[8]

They had indeed. In those very years the 'immense capital' of

[8] *Decline and Fall*, vi. 297; *The Letters of Edward Gibbon*, ed. J. E. Norton (1956), ii. 100 (Gibbon to Adam Ferguson).

London bowed before the Great Cham of English literature, Dr Johnson: Johnson who did not look northwards to Scotland with veneration, but who, again unlike Gibbon, felt a comfortable glow on approaching the spired and cloistered orthodoxy of Oxford. It is interesting to observe Johnson's recorded remarks on history: they show that to him, and to his circle, the new 'philosophical history' which had triumphed in Scotland, meant absolutely nothing. History, to Johnson, was mere mechanical compilation in which 'there is but a shallow stream of thought' and 'all the greatest powers of the human mind are quiescent'. He never mentioned Montesquieu, boasted of having never read the 'infidel' Hume, put the hack-work of Goldsmith above 'the verbiage of Robertson', and praised as 'the first of historians' the now forgotten author of what Gibbon would call 'a partial and verbose compilation from Latin writers, 1300 folio pages of speeches and battles', devoid of any 'tincture of philosophy and criticism'.[9] 'The part of an historian', Gibbon once wrote, 'is as honourable as that of a mere chronicler or compiler of gazettes is contemptible.' It is obvious that to Johnson this distinction did not exist. However ennobled by dignity of language or moral commentary, history to him was essentially chronicles or gazettes.

But if Montesquieu had pointed the way, and Hume and Robertson had illustrated it, what subject should Gibbon, now that he had been inspired by these examples, choose for his own? Here let me interpose a general point. All great historians, whatever their subject, respond to some extent to the demands of their age. Many of them have been directly inspired by a present crisis. Such were Thucydides, Machiavelli, Guicciardini, Clarendon. Others have turned to a carefully chosen chapter of past history in order the better to interpret their own age. Thus Paolo Sarpi, the greatest of seventeenth-century historians—'that incomparable historian', as Gibbon called him—looked back to the Council of Trent in order to explain the resistance of Venice to papal aggression in his own time. Similarly the nineteenth-century English whigs—and their French disciples like Guizot—would see the justification of their present politics in the Glorious Revolution of England in 1688. It was this second category into which the 'philosophic historians' of

[9] Boswell, *Life of Johnson* (ed. 1826), i. 373, ii. 177, 217-218. Gibbon, *Decline and Fall*, vi. 293 note.

the eighteenth century fell. To interpret their own times, times not of crisis but of new Enlightenment, they looked back into previous centuries. They saw the history of humanity in a long perspective; and they asked themselves a series of questions about the past. Above all, they asked questions about the declining Roman Empire, the dark and middle ages of Europe.

Why did they ask these questions? Their predecessors of the seventeenth century did not. To their predecessors Antiquity and the Middle Ages had looked quite different. In the seventeenth century Antiquity, to Churchmen, was the age of pagan error from which Europe had not declined but risen; and if the humanists, as admirers of Greece and Rome, admitted the decline, they could not yet detect the signs of recovery. To them Antiquity was a heroic age which the degenerate modern could only admire, not judge. But with the eighteenth century, which began with the victory of the 'Moderns' over the 'Ancients', a new attitude was possible. A revolution had happened in the minds of men. Europe, they felt, had grown up; it was no longer in tutelage either to the Church or to the Ancients; and the Moderns, in Basil Willey's phrase, 'across the vast gulf of the monkish and deluded past', could 'salute the Ancients from an eminence perhaps as lofty as their own'. From such an eminence they could judge; over such a distance they could compare. They could measure progress in the past and infer progress to come. And why, they asked, had this progress happened? Why had it not been continuous? Why had the high civilisation of Antiquity not led directly to the high civilisation of modernity, but foundered in that dark, intermediary millennium? And finally, since that had happened once, might it perhaps happen again? Could the new Antonine age of the eighteenth century, this wonderful new century of 'light and freedom' so slowly and painfully achieved, also perhaps founder in a new age of monkish darkness and 'gothic' barbarism?

To answer these questions—even to pose them—would have been impossible in the seventeenth century; but they haunted the new 'philosophic historians' of the eighteenth. Listen to the earliest of them, Giannone—the great, unfortunate Giannone whose work so deeply influenced both Montesquieu and Gibbon. In his autobiography—which cannot have influenced either of them, since it only saw the light a century later—Giannone describes his preoccupation with this theme. As a young law student in Naples, he says, he studied the legal codes of Theodosius and Justinian—and of course, like Gibbon, he used and revered 'that stupendous work', the commentary on the Theodosian code by the Swiss Protestant Jacques Godefroy—'not as ends in themselves, but as effective means to understand the origins and changes of the Roman Empire, and how, from its ruins, there arose so many new rulers, laws, customs, kingdoms and republics in Europe'.[10] Later, the same question was posed by the English patron of the European philosophers, Lord Bolingbroke. 'Would you not be glad, my lord,' he wrote, in his fifth *Letter on the Study of History*, 'to see, in one stupendous draught, the whole progress of that government' (he was referring to the government of Rome) 'from liberty to servitude, the whole series of causes and effects, apparent and real, public and private . . . ? I am sorry to say it', added the fallen minister, who perhaps generalised too widely his own catastrophe, 'this part of the Roman history would be not only more curious and more authentic than the former, but of more immediate and more important application to the present state of Britain'.[11] Meanwhile one of Bolingbroke's French friends had already offered one answer to the problem. In his book *Considérations sur la grandeur des Romains et de leur décadence* Montesquieu gave his views on the subject; and Montesquieu's Scottish disciples all took up, in different ways, the same unsolved—still unsolved—problem. As one of them, Dugald Stewart, wrote, 'it was indeed a subject worthy of their genius; for in the whole history of human affairs no spectacle occurs so wonderful in itself, or so momentous in its effects, as the growth of that system which took its rise from the conquests of the barbarians. In consequence of these, the Western parts of Europe were overspread with a thick night of superstition and ignorance which lasted nearly a thousand years; yet this event, which had at first so unpromising an aspect, laid the foundation of a state of society far more favourable to the general and permanent happiness of the human race than any which the world has hitherto seen . . .'[12]

[10] Pietro Giannone, *Vita scritta da lui medesimo*, ed. Sergio Bertelli (Milan 1960), pp. 10-15.

[11] *Letters on the Use and Study of History* (Basel 1791), pp. 103-104, quoted by Bond, in *The Literary Art of Edward Gibbon*, p. 13. The preface to Bolingbroke's work is dated in France in 1735. Montesquieu's *Considerations* . . . were published in 1735.

[12] Dugald Stewart, 'Account of the Life and Writings of William Robertson',

That Gibbon, the greatest historical disciple of Montesquieu, should have taken up this challenge seems, in retrospect, almost inevitable. In his earliest work, his *Essai*, we see him groping towards it. Those modern themes which haunted his mind never caused him to suspend his classical studies. Indeed, it was while in camp with the Hampshire militia, and while thinking of modern topics, that he turned seriously to the study of Greek and made Homer 'the most intimate of my friends'. When he set out for Italy, still apparently intent on Medicean Florence, the books which he took with him were not Renaissance chronicles but ancient classics and modern antiquaries: books on the geography, the roads, the architecture, the coinage of Rome. Was this, we may ask, as we read the amazing catalogue of his travelling library, really the prospective chronicler of the Medici, or of the liberty of the Swiss, and not rather, even now, even before his Roman experience, the historian of the Decline and Fall of the Roman Empire?

And yet what historian could face, all at once, so huge a subject? Giannone had contented himself with a geographical fragment of it: he had studied the social consequences of the Church in the kingdom of Naples only. Hume had shown what could be done in one brilliant essay: his essay on the Populousness of Ancient Nations, which reversed the orthodoxy of the humanists and of Montesquieu himself, is a landmark in the new methods of history. Robertson had swept over the whole period from Antiquity to the Renaissance in two long, masterly sketches: his introductory chapters to the History of Charles V and of America. How much simpler it must have seemed to Gibbon to follow the example of these revered masters: to detach another manageable portion rather than tackle the whole gigantic problem! So, at first, he followed where they had led. His first subject, the French invasion of Italy, was inspired by Giannone;[13] the English subjects were suggested by Hume; Medicean Florence had been foreshadowed to him by those earlier masters, the Renaissance founders of 'philosophic history', Machiavelli and Guicciardini, who, as he would write, 'were justly esteemed

in *The Works of William Robertson D.D.* (1821), pp. 61-62.

[13] Giannone's direct influence has been shown by Signor Giarrizzo (*Edward Gibbon e la cultura europea del settecento*, Naples 1954), pp. 136, 209. For Gibbon's admiration for Giannone, see his *Autobiography*.

the first historians of modern languages till, in the present age, Scotland arose to dispute the prize with Italy herself'.[14]

And then there was that other tempting subject, the liberty of the Swiss. That too was a living issue, a chapter in the rise of Europe from feudal barbarism to modern enlightenment. Switzerland, like Holland afterwards, had broken away from the feudal and clerical domination of the Habsburgs and the Vatican. As a result, it had become the receptacle of all those European heretics who had challenged the tyranny of their native traditions: of Erasmus, of Calvin, of Bucer, of Castellio, of Sozzini, of the English republicans, of the French Huguenots, of the Vaudois of Savoy, of the philosophers of the eighteenth century. What a splendid subject for a 'philosophic historian' who himself owed his philosophy to Lausanne! In 1762 Gibbon wrote of it with enthusiasm, but then seemed to turn sadly away. 'The materials', he wrote, 'are inaccessible to me, fast locked in the obscurity of an old barbarous German language of which I am totally ignorant, and which I cannot resolve to learn for this sole and peculiar purpose.' Like his contemporary and supporter, the great Greek scholar, Richard Porson, Gibbon thought that life was too short to learn German—especially since he could read Mosheim in Latin and Winckelmann in French. It is never too short to learn Italian; so he turned back to Florence and the Medici and set out on his famous journey: the journey to which so many Northerners have owed their ultimate inspiration: the journey to Italy.

Thus all the subjects which in turn occupied Gibbon's mind can be seen as elements in the great problem which exercised the historians of the eighteenth century. Even in Rome, Gibbon's sudden vision was not of the whole problem, but of another element in it. What he saw was, as he makes quite clear, the decline and fall not of the empire but of the city of Rome. For if Medicean Florence was the patroness of the new ideas which would lead Europe out of gothic barbarism back to classical models and a new enlightenment, and if Swiss liberty was to provide the laboratory for the development of those ideas, could not the same long process be illustrated, perhaps more dramatically, in the medieval history of Rome itself, in the continuity and yet change of that eternal city, where the old temple of Jupiter had become the church of the Zoco-

[14] *Decline and Fall*, vi. 543 n.

lanti, where the mole of Hadrian had become the papal prison, and where the insolent palaces of Renaissance popes looked down upon the ruined Coliseum whence they had been quarried? To Gibbon's romantic—yes, romantic—spirit, those crumbling arches and grass-grown amphitheatres that we still see in the drawings of Piranesi presented an epitome of the whole process which so fascinated his contemporaries: the process which had since been reversed from such small beginnings as the merchant republic of Florence and the liberty of the Swiss.

So the seed of a new subject was planted in Gibbon's mind. And yet, when transferred to the cool climate of Hampshire, that seed somehow did not germinate. His mind returned to Switzerland, that Switzerland to which he owed so much: his intellectual formation, the friends of his life—Georges Deyverdun, Lord Sheffield, the de Severy family—and to which he himself would return to spend his later years. In 1767, after again considering Medicean Florence, he came to a decision. He would write the history of the liberty of the Swiss. In his friend Deyverdun he had a translator from the German; 'my judgment as well as my enthusiasm', he writes, 'was satisfied with the glorious theme'; he planned its range, wrote the first book, and submitted it to the historical master whom he most revered, David Hume.

Hume's only objection was that it was written in French. He assumed that Gibbon had chosen French as the international language of today; but what, he asked, about tomorrow? 'Let the French triumph in the present diffusion of their tongue' wrote the junior negotiator of the Treaty of Paris, the first Scotch founder of Canada. 'Our solid and increasing establishments in America, where we need less dread the inundations of barbarians, promise a superior stability and duration to the English language.' This answer of Hume clearly made a deep impression on Gibbon. As Mr Bond has pointed out, the ideas, even the phrases in it reappear in the *Decline and Fall*.[15] Perhaps it decided Gibbon to write his great work in English. But Gibbon's immediate reply is interesting for another reason. 'I write in French', he explained, 'because I think in French and, strange as it may seem, I can say, with some shame but with no affectation, that it would be a matter of difficulty to me to compose in my native language.' It is a reminder—one

[15] Bond *op. cit.*, pp. 19-20.

among many—that one of the greatest of English writers, though he 'gloried in the name of Englishman', though he described himself proudly as 'an Englishman and a whig', and though he sat in the English Parliament, was always, intellectually, not English but European.[16]

So three years after his experience in Rome, Gibbon was still thinking of old subjects. He had not yet envisaged the decline and fall of the Roman Empire. He had forgotten, or suspended, his project of the decline and fall—what fall anyway?—of the city. And meanwhile he was reading, as always, the Greek and Latin classics, studying, like Giannone and Montesquieu, the laws and institutions, the geography and topography and climate of the lower Empire, the Dark and Middle Ages, until gradually, fed by that copious nutriment, the buried seed grew into a new idea. He decided not merely to take another detail from the problem of his age, to cut off another manageable slice of it, but to seize, as none had yet dared to seize, the whole problem. The decline and fall of the city was transformed into the decline and fall of the empire. That vast subject, 'of whose limits and extent', as he admitted, 'I had yet a very inadequate notion', could be made to stretch from Antiquity to the Renaissance, from Europe through Arabia to China. It would subsume Gibbon's own early interest in the Middle and Far East, in the revolutions of China and Central Asia, Islam and India—an interest which links him, once again, with Montesquieu, and which caused Dr Johnson contemptuously to repeat the gossip that Gibbon, at Oxford, had been converted to Mohammedanism. It would extend Giannone's study of the social power of the Church from Naples to all Europe. It would apply the sociological ideas of

[16] This un-Englishness of Gibbon is brought out in many ways: his discomfort in the contemporary English literary world (as shown in Boswell's *Life of Johnson*); his complete independence of any English historical tradition; his apparently genuine failure to foresee the reaction in England to the *Decline and Fall*; his ultimate return—to the astonishment even of close friends like Lord Sheffield—to Lausanne. If he still thought in French in 1767, he was again thinking in French after 1783, and regrets, in his *Autobiography*, that the language of his last two volumes may have been invaded by 'Gallic idioms'. It is some reflection both on the fundamental cosmopolitanism of Gibbon and on the fundamental insularity of his fellow-Englishmen, that some of his best interpreters have been foreigners (I think of Georges A. Bonnard, G. Falco, E. Momigliano, G. Giarrizzo), while, as Signor Giarrizzo writes, 'nel mondo anglosassone e fuori, Gibbon è pretesto per le più banali esemplificazioni metodologiche e le chiacchierate più insulse'.

Montesquieu to the rise of Christianity. It would deepen the sketches of Robertson on the progress of medieval Europe, embrace the debates of Voltaire, Robertson and Hume on the character of feudalism, the transformation of society, the significance of the crusades.

Byzantine history, by itself, might seem to Gibbon—as modern Byzantists complain of him, a mean subject. But, as he observed, 'the fate of the Byzantine monarchy is passively connected with the most splendid and important revolutions which have changed the face of the world'—the revolutions which, together, raised Europe from barbarism to civility. In such a study, on such a scale, Gibbon could illuminate far more effectively than Montesquieu the great problem of the failure of Antiquity; in his 38th chapter, in his 'General Observations on the Fall of the Roman Empire in the West', he would face the troubling question whether modern civilisation too might fail; and in the last chapter of all he would fulfil his old ambition and finish his work with the history, over those 1300 years, of the city of Rome. Little had he thought in 1764, 'that this final chapter must be attained by the labour of six quartos and twenty years'. But now that it had been attained, his mind went back to that original impulse and ascribed to it, perhaps, a new clarity: 'it was among the ruins of the Capitol that I first conceived the idea of a work which has amused and exercised near twenty years of my life, and which, however inadequate to my own wishes, I finally deliver to the curiosity and candour of the public.'

With those words Gibbon, sitting, late at night, in his summer-house in Lausanne, ended his great work. Then—for how can one resist this final quotation from the *Autobiography*?—'after laying down my pen, I took several turns in a *berceau*, or covered walk of acacias, which commands a prospect of the country, the lake and the mountains. The air was temperate, the sky was serene, the silver orb of the moon was reflected from the waters, and all Nature was silent. I will not dissemble the first emotions of joy on recovery of my freedom and, perhaps, the establishment of my fame. But my pride was soon humbled, and a sober melancholy was spread over my mind, by the idea that I had taken an everlasting leave of an old and agreeable companion, and that whatsoever might be the future date of my history, the life of the historian must be short and precarious.' Short and precarious it might be; it had already been long enough to bring together and to answer, in one majestic work, the problems which had exercised all the greatest historical minds of that most inquisitive, most penetrating, most inspiring of generations, the generation of the Enlightenment.

Theodore Besterman, writer and editor: a bibliographical appreciation

Sir Frank Francis

Theodore Besterman is a man of varied gifts and wide interests. Given also that he has a ready pen, boundless energy and a vigorous urge to share his ideas and enthusiams with others, any attempt to provide a comprehensive bibliographical guide to his literary production would be a daunting task to a full-time bibliographer, and is I fear beyond the scope of what I can attempt to achieve. None the less, though I know that my puny efforts are a poor compliment to one who seems to be capable of endless multifarious achievement, I am glad to be able to participate in this tribute to a man whom I have known, admired and wondered at for something over thirty years. I remember in my fairly early days in the British Museum being struck by the familiar ease with which he associated with such heroic figures as Sir James George Frazer, whose bibliography he was compiling at the time. Throughout our friendship I have always been much encouraged, and helped, by Theodore's firm belief in and affection for the British Museum. Not that his attachment is sentimental or uncritical—it would not be worth as much as it is if it were!

For the student of Besterman's work who might easily be overwhelmed by its volume and variety, there is fortunately another quality which comes to the rescue: Besterman's capacity to throw himself wholeheartedly into his current activities. His publications seem to arrange themselves neatly into groups which correspond to his interests at various times. This is not to suggest that these interests are circumscribed at different times. Nothing could be further from the truth; but a pattern of activity emerges from a conspectus of his work which makes it easier to relate his written work to his other activities.

As I have already indicated, I have not been able to attempt a complete listing of Theodore Besterman's writings, desirable though this would be. This list is concerned almost entirely with separately published works such as can be found in the collection in the British Museum.

Theodore Besterman emerges into the full limelight of a productive literary career just under the age of twenty with a work on crystal-gazing, or scrying:

1. *Crystal-gazing: a study in the history, distribution, theory and practice of scrying.* By Theodore Besterman [quotation]. London, William Rider and Son, Ltd, 8 Paternoster Row, E.C.4. 1924.
   First published October 1924.
   pp. XIII +[1] 183 +[1].
   Dedication: 'To H.B.'

This work, which points in the direction in which Besterman's interests and activities were to develop during the next ten years, was by way of being a study of a neglected subject. 'Before Miss Goodrich-Freer's paper in the fifth volume (1888–9) of the *Proceedings of the Society for Psychical Research* nothing of any importance had been written about scrying,' he writes in his preface. 'It is my hope,' he continues, 'that the anthropologist and the folklorist as well as the psychical researcher and the scryer will find matter of interest in the following pages.' No doubt significantly, this, Besterman's earliest independent work, has a substantial bibliographical index.

In the same year, 1924, his interest in theosophy led him to compile a bibliography of Annie Besant, published by the Theosophical Society in a large paper edition, limited to 200 numbered copies, as well as an ordinary paper edition:

2. *A bibliography of Annie Besant.* By Theodore Besterman. [quotation] London, The Theosophical Society in England, 23 Bedford Square, W.C.1. 1924.
   pp. 114.
   Dedication: 'To Annie Besant. Exegi monumentum, etc.'
   Preface: 'This bibliography deals with the books and pamphlets of Annie Besant up to and including 1923.'

By the next year Besterman had joined the Society for Psychical

Research and had almost at once become an official of the Society, being in turn Honorary Librarian, Librarian and Editor, and finally Investigation Officer. Work for this Society and for the Theosophical Society occupied a very great deal of Besterman's time during the next ten years. This was a period of great activity, during which he wrote not only the independent works set out below, but undertook a considerable amount of practical work in the field of psychical investigation, and contributed largely to the *Proceedings of the Society for Psychical Research*, the *Theosophical Review*, the *Occult Review*, *Notes and Queries*, *Psychic Research* and *The Link* and also to *Folk-Lore, the journal of the Folk-Lore Society*, another of his active interests at this time (he was for a number of years a member of the Council of the Society and became its Hon. Treasurer in 1928 and 1929). It would have given me great satisfaction to have been able to include a full list of his contributions to these journals in this article, but alas! time has not permitted me to make the necessary searches. It should be stated, however, that many of his contributions are substantial: for example 'The belief in reincarnation' and 'The Witch of Endor' from the *Theosophical Review*, 'The belief in rebirth among the natives of Africa (including Madagascar)' from *Folk-Lore* and his 'Report of a four months' tour of psychical investigation' from the *Proceedings*. His contributions to *Notes and Queries* are typified by such notes as: 'A bibliography of Cleopatra' and 'A bibliography of Lord Macartney's embassy to China 1792–1794'. The latter contains an introductory note which begins 'This partial bibliography is intended as a specimen of a bibliography of voyages and travels, on which I have been long engaged, and the first part of which (1600–1800) is approaching completion.' This work never appeared.

The following separate publications appear during this period of Besterman's activity:

3. *In the way of heaven. Being the teaching of many sacred scriptures concerning the qualities necessary for progress on the path of attainment.* Edited by Theodore Besterman. Methuen & Co. Ltd, 36 Essex Street W.C. London.

First published in 1926.

pp. XVIII +[2] 183 +[1].

Dedication: 'To my wife.'

Preface: 'It is hoped that many students and aspirants will find it useful to have collected under one cover the principal passages in Buddhist, Christian, Confucian, Hindu, Jewish, Muslim, Taoist and Zoroastrian texts relating to the qualities that have to be cultivated in order to enable the individual to achieve spiritual progress.

The translations employed are without exception to be found in English and reasonably accessible works, so that no reader need be prevented from following up the references and studying in full the contexts from which the present passages have been extracted.'

4. *The divining-rod. An experimental and psychological investigation.* By Sir William Barrett, F.R.S. and Theodore Besterman. With 12 plates and 62 other illustrations. Methuen & Co. Ltd, 36 Essex Street W.C. London.

First published in 1926.

pp. XXIII +[1] 336; 8 pp. of advertisements.

Bibliography: pp. 293-311.

Preface: 'The object of this book is to investigate, by means of historical researches, by the collection and collation of large numbers of contemporary cases, by the carrying out of experiments, and by a discussion of the results thus obtained, the claims made on behalf of "water-divining." This investigation has involved a great deal of work, including a correspondence conducted by Sir William Barrett during the course of which he wrote some six to seven thousand letters, and including the examination of an almost equally large number of volumes of all kinds.

Every one must greatly regret that Sir William Barrett did not live to see this book published . . .' 'For the actual arrangement and writing of nearly the whole of the book I must take full responsibility.'

5. *The mystic rose. A study of primitive marriage and of primitive thought in its bearing on marriage.* By Ernest Crawley. A new editin, revised and greatly enlarged by Theodore Besterman. In two volumes. Vol. I (II). [quotation]. Methuen & Co. Ltd, 36 Essex Street W.C. London.

First published by Messrs. Macmillan & Co., Ltd, in 1902; first issued (Second Edition) by Methuen & Co., Ltd, in 1927.

2 vols. vol. I, pp. XX, 375 +[1]; vol. II, pp. VII +[1], 340; 4 pp. at end, with advert on [p. 1].

Bibliography: vol. II, pp. 263-304.

Dedication: p. [v] as in first edition, 'To Sir J. G. Frazer, O.M. in gratitude and admiration.'

Editor's preface: 'When I was invited to undertake this edition, I did not feel authorised to attempt any amendment of the theories herein expressed.

I have verified (few corrections were necessary) and reduced to order the references to authorities, striking out, together with the appropriate matter in the text, nearly all those taken at second-hand from such works as those of Featherman, Waitz-Gerland and Ploss-Bartels. Where I have been able . . . to trace such references to their sources, I have placed the new references within square brackets. A few paragraphs have been transposed . . . To these revisions affecting the text I have added a Bibliography and a new and more comprehensive Index.'

Several reprints of this work have appeared in various forms.

6. *A dictionary of theosophy*. By Theodore Besterman. The Theosophical Publishing House Limited, 38 Great Ormond Street, London, W.C.1.

Published in MCMXXVII.

pp. XVIII, 147 +3 pp. each headed 'Notes'.

Dedication: 'To the President, the Vice President and the General Secretaries of the forty-one national sections of the Theosophical Society in General Council assembled . . .'

Preface: 'I have attempted in this volume to fill a gap in Theosophical literature by supplying an up-to-date and, humanly speaking, complete dictionary of the technical terms current in that literature.'

7. *Mind and body. A criticism of psychophysical parallelism*. By Hans Driesch. Authorized translation with a bibliography of the author by Theodore Besterman. Methuen & Co. Ltd, 36 Essex Street W.C. London.

This translation first published in 1927.

pp. XVIII +[2], 163 +[1]; 8 pp. of advertisements.

Translator's note: 'The text is substantially that of the third German edition; but Dr Driesch has revised my translation and added a few passages, so that the present may in effect be regarded as a new edition. I am also indebted to Dr Driesch for checking the Bibliography and for sending me particulars of a few items overlooked by me.'

pp. 149-161. *A bibliography of Hans Driesch*. By Theodore Besterman. This bibliography was also issued separately.

8. *The mind of Annie Besant*. By Theodore Besterman. London, The Theosophical Publishing House Limited, 38 Great Ormond Street.

First published in MCMXXVII.

pp. XI +[1], 122 +[2].

Dedication: To C. Jinarājadāsa, Vice-President of the Theosophical Society.

Preface: 'This book is published in honour of Annie Besant's eightieth birthday, and is uniform with *The Annie Besant Calendar*, which is being issued simultaneously.

The present work is designed to give a systematic exposition of Annie Besant's attitude to some of the chief problems of man and the universe. This has been done as far as possible in Annie Besant's own words.

Each chapter also contains some account of Annie Besant's practical application of her views, together with references to the chief of her writings on each subject. Taken as a whole, therefore, the book is intended to give a picture of a mind, and of the reflection of that mind in teaching and in activity.

These two books are sent out not only as a token of great and widespread love and reverence, but in the belief that the example of such a life cannot fail to be an inspiration and a guide to all.'

9. *Annie Besant's geesteshouding*. Door Theodore Besterman. Vertaald uit het engelsch door Mr. J. D. Van Ketwich Verschuur. 1927, N.V. Theosofische Vereenigings Uitgevers My, Tolstraat 154, Amsterdam.

pp. XII, 128.

10. *The Annie Besant Calendar*. By Theodore Besterman. London, The Theosophical Publishing House Limited, 38 Great Ormond Street.

First published in MCMXXVII.

No pagination.

Preface: 'In another work (*The Mind of Annie Besant*) published simultaneously with this in honour of their subject's eightieth birthday, the attempt has been made to give a systematic survey of Annie Besant's outlook upon the chief problems of man and the universe. The aim of this *Calendar* is to give a portrait of the same mind by means of brief passages taken from her works and arranged under appropriate headings.'

11. *Library catalogue of the Society for Psychical Research*. Compiled by Theodore Besterman, Honorary Librarian. Printed for the Society by Robert MacLehose & Co. Ltd, The University Press, Glasgow, MCMXXVII.

pp. VIII, 367 + [1].

Published as Part 104, vol. xxxvii of *Proceedings* and also separately.

Preface: 'The Society's Library has been completely reorganised during the past year. The books have been arranged on the shelves by subject and date, many useless ones having been turned out; the important collection of pamphlets has been classified and bound, as have been several hundred books; new bookcases have been fitted; and, finally, the present catalogue has been compiled on a detailed and uniform plan.'

This catalogue was kept up-to-date by a series of supplements, each published in the *Proceedings* and separately.

12. *Library catalogue of the Society for Psychical Research.* (Supplement 1927–1928.) Compiled by Theodore Besterman, Honorary Librarian. Printed for the Society by Robert MacLehose & Co. Ltd, The University Press, Glasgow, MCMXXVIII.
No pagination.

13. *Library catalogue of the Society for Psychical Research.* (Supplement 1928–1929.) Compiled by Theodore Besterman, Librarian and Editor. Printed for the Society by Robert MacLehose & Co. Ltd, The University Press, Glasgow, MCMXXIX
No pagination.

14. *Library catalogue of the Society for Psychical Research.* (Supplement 1929–1930.) Compiled by Theodore Besterman, Librarian and Editor. The Society for Psychical Research, 31 Tavistock Square, London, W.C.1. Agents for America: The F. W. Faxon Co., 83 Francis Street, Boston, Mass.
pp. [2] +58.

15. *Library catalogue of the Society for Psychical Research.* (Supplement 1931–1933.) Compiled by Theodore Besterman. The Society for Psychical Research, 31 Tavistock Square, London, W.C.1. Agents for America: The F. W. Faxon Co., 83 Francis Street, Boston, Mass.
pp. [2] +47 +[1].

16. *Studies of savages and sex.* By Ernest Crawley. Edited by Theodore Besterman. Methuen & Co. Ltd, 36 Essex Street W.C. London.
First published in 1929.
pp. IX +[1], 300; 8 pp. of advertisements.
Editor's preface: 'The success of my revised edition of Mr Crawley's *The Mystic Rose* has encouraged me to bring together . . . some of his papers, previously unpublished in book-form.
I have allowed myself somewhat greater liberties in editing these studies. . . . That is, I have silently made a good many verbal alterations, omitted and added a few passages, and generally made slight adaptations to fit the papers for book-form.'

17. *Transactions of the Fourth International Congress for Psychical Research, Athens,* 1930. Edited by Theodore Besterman. The Society for Psychical Research, 31 Tavistock Square, London, W.C.1.
Published in 1930.
pp. 259.

18. *Some modern mediums*. By Theodore Besterman. With 4 plates and 20 diagrams. Methuen & Co. Ltd, 36 Essex Street W.C. London.
First published in 1930.
pp. XI + [1], 188 + [4].
Dedication: 'To Mrs Henry Sidgwick.'
Preface: 'In this book I discuss five of the most important and interesting living mediums. Some of them are surveyed from personal knowledge and investigation, others from a careful study of the available evidence.
To each chapter I have added a narrative survey of the literature on which it is based. And at the end of the book I have appended a very useful glossary, largely compiled by Mr. W. H. Salter, which is intended to form the basis of an international vocabulary of psychical research.
The Council of the Society for Psychical Research have not only given permission for the reprinting of various contributions of mine to its *Proceedings* and for the reproduction of a number of illustrations, but they have during the past few years given me valuable opportunities for study and investigation.'

19. *Dress, drinks, and drums. Further studies of savages and sex*. By Ernest Crawley. Edited by Theodore Besterman. Methuen & Co. Ltd, 36 Essex Street W.C. London.
First published in 1931.
pp. X + [2], 274 + [2]; 8 pp. advertisements.
Editor's preface: 'In *Studies of Savages and Sex* I brought together nine shorter essays. In the present volume are assembled three longer studies, the first of which, indeed, is long and important enough to have made a volume in itself. None of these twelve papers has been previously printed in book-form, and there still remains enough first-rate material to make a third and final volume of essays, should the publishers feel there is a sufficient demand for it.
As with *Studies of Savages and Sex* I have allowed myself somewhat greater freedom in editing than with *The Mystic Rose*. I have silently made a good many verbal alterations, omitted and added a number of passages, and generally made slight adaptations to fit the essays for book-form.'

20. *Psychical research. The science of the super-normal*. By Hans Driesch, Professor of Philosophy in the University of Leipzig. Authorised translation by Theodore Besterman, Investigation Officer of the Society for Psychical Research. London, G. Bell & Sons, Ltd, 1933.
pp. XVI. 176.
Foreword by Sir Oliver Lodge.
p. 62 'It seems to me that that praiseworthy "inexperienced

young man" in London, who is so little loved by the credulous, Mr. Besterman, holds quite similar views to my own in these matters: he is quite certainly not a negativist, but he is very critical.'

21. *Supernormal aspects of energy and matter*. By Eugène Osty, Director of the Institut Métapsychique, Paris. Translated by Theodore Besterman, Investigation Officer of the Society for Psychical Research. London, The Society for Psychical Research, 31 Tavistock Square, W.C.1.
No date [1933].
pp. [6], 39 +[1]; Diagram.
Half title: Supernormal aspects of energy and matter. Being the Frederic W. H. Myers Lecture, 1933.

22. *Men against women. A study of sexual relations*. By Theodore Besterman. With two illustrations. Methuen & Co. Ltd, 36 Essex Street W.C. London.
First published in 1934.
pp. IX +[1], 238.
Dedication: 'To Henrietta.'

23. The Thinker's Library, No. 40. *Oath, curse, and blessing, and other studies in origins*. By Ernest Crawley. Edited by Theodore Besterman. London: Watts & Co., 5 & 6 Johnson's Court, Fleet Street, E.C.4.
First published in the Thinker's Library, 1934.
pp. VII +[1], 152.
Foreword: 'Following on my revised edition of Ernest Crawley's masterpiece *The Mystic Rose* . . ., I edited two volumes of Crawley's shorter studies in social anthropology . . . The Rationalist Press Association have consequently thought it right to include in the Thinker's Library a selection of some of the best essays and studies in the two volumes just mentioned.'

24. *A bibliography of Sir James George Frazer*, O.M. Compiled by Theodore Besterman. With portraits and facsimiles and a note by Sir J. G. Frazer. 1934, Macmillan and Co. Ltd., St. Martin's Street, London.
pp. XXI +[1] 100; 2 portraits and one double page facsimile.
Preface: 'On 1 January 1934 Sir James George Frazer celebrates the eightieth anniversary of his birth, and in the same year falls the fiftieth anniversary of the publication of his first work . . . It was felt that such an occasion could not be allowed to pass by without being marked by some intimation to him of the regard and affection in which he is held.

The bibliography is arranged in as strict a chronological order as may be, irrespective of the dates shown on the title-pages, which are incorrect in a few cases. The month of publication is added wherever possible . . . With a single exception, every work has been described from personal inspection.'

Note by Sir James George Frazer: 'I thank the Folk-Lore Society for initiating the plan of this bibliography and Mr. Besterman for the diligence, patience, and skill with which he has executed it.'

25 *Mrs. Annie Besant. A modern prophet.* By Theodore Besterman. London, Kegan Paul, Trench, Trubner & Co., Ltd, Broadway House: 68-74 Carter Lane, E.C. 1934.

pp. XI +[1], 273 +[1]; 8 plates.

Dedication: 'To Gerald Heard.'

26. *Inquiry into the unknown.* A B.B.C. symposium, edited by Theodore Besterman. Methuen & Co. Ltd. London.

First published in 1934.

pp. [8], 141 +[1]; 8 pp. of advertisements.

Preface: 'Thanks to the enlightened policy of the B.B.C. it was recently possible for the first time to give the radio public a comprehensive statement of the aims and achievements of psychical research. The ten talks in which this was done were delivered in January to March 1934 and are printed in the following pages, for the most part in a thoroughly revised and much enlarged form.

The interest of the public was shown in no equivocal manner, the speakers receiving between them somewhere in the neighbourhood of 3,000 letters from listeners.'

27. *On dreams.* By William Archer. Edited by Theodore Besterman. With a preface by Professor Gilbert Murray. Methuen & Co. Ltd. 36 Essex Street W.C. London.

First published in 1935.

pp. XIV +[2], 218 +[2].

Editor's Preface: 'Mr. Archer left this book partly finished, partly in draft, and partly in the form of notes. Jn putting together this material I have tried to carry out his intentions as closely as possible, and I believe that the following pages pretty well represent the book as he would have wished it to appear.'

28. *A bibliography of Sir Oliver Lodge,* F.R.S. Compiled by Theodore Besterman. With a foreword by Sir Oliver Lodge and a portrait. Oxford University Press, London: Humphrey Milford, 1935.

pp. XIV, 219 +[1].

Preface: 'This bibliography celebrates the sixtieth anniversary of the publication of Sir Oliver Lodge's first work.

The order of arrangement is as strictly chronological as may be, considerable trouble having been taken to fix the month as well as the year of publication in every possible case.'

29. *The Druce-Portland Case.* By Theodore Besterman. Duckworth, 3 Henrietta Street, London, W.C.2.
First published in 1935.
pp. 308. Frontispiece and three plates.
Preface: 'The Druce-Portland case, in which the attempt was made to show that one of the first noblemen and wealthiest landowners in the country, was also, in secret, a London tradesman in a large way of business, strikes a rich vein of comedy.
In short, I do not hesitate to say that, from whatever point of view one looks at it, the Druce-Portland case is one of the most interesting on record.
It is an excellent tradition in books of this kind to leave the facts to speak for themselves.'

In 1931 Besterman began to lecture at the School of Librarianship at University College, London. Of his interest in bibliography throughout there is no doubt, but the 1930's show an increasing preoccupation with strictly bibliographical studies, though no. 34 below shows that he retained a deep interest in the studies with which he had previously been so closely concerned. Indeed, Besterman's *Collected papers on the paranormal* are now in the press.

In 1935 he became editor, in association with four other distinguished bibliographers, of the series, *Oxford Books on Bibliography*, and himself contributed, as the first volume, an outstanding study of the beginnings of bibliographical work:

30. *The beginnings of systematic bibliography.* By Theodore Besterman. MCMXXXV, Oxford University Press, London: Humphrey Milford.
pp. XI +[1], 81 +[3]. 12 plates.
Dedication: 'To W. H. and H. de G. Salter. Amicus certus in re incerta cernitur.'
Note: 'The bibliographies published to the end of the sixteenth century, hitherto almost wholly uncharted, are discussed in some detail in sections II-VII. The rest of Part I surveys in more summary form the bibliographies of the seventeenth century.
Certain of the following pages were delivered as a public lecture at University College, London, on 2 November 1932.'

This work went into a second edition in 1936. A revised French translation, forming a third edition, appeared in 1950:

31. *The beginnings of systematic bibliography.* By Theodore Besterman. Second edition, revised. Oxford University Press, London: Humphrey Milford.

Second edition, revised, April 1936.

pp. xi + [1], 81 + [1]. 12 plates.

Dedication as in the first edition.

Note to the second edition: 'The text has been revised and numerous minor changes have been made, together with a few additions and corrections.

I may be allowed to mention that I am making progress with an extensive bibliography of bibliographies, to which the present essay can be regarded as an introduction.'

32. *Theodore Besterman. Les débuts de la bibliographie méthodique.* Troisième édition revue. Traduit de l'anglais. La Palme, 1, rue Beaujon, Paris.

Copyright by La Palme 1950.

pp. 95 + [5]. 12 plates.

Dedication: 'A Julien Cain grand humaniste.'

Preface: 'Ce modeste ouvrage est né d'une conférence que je fis à Londres, à l'University College, le 2 novembre 1932. Mon texte, très augmenté, fut publié pour la première fois en 1935 par l'Oxford University Press dans la collection des *Oxford Books on Bibliography*, dont j'ai l'honneur d'être un des directeurs. Il en fut bientôt fait une seconde édition et j'eus un grand plaisir à le voir éveiller un renouveau d'intérêt pour l'histoire de la bibliographie et pour les bibliographies anciennes qui se manifesta par la publication d'intéressantes monographies.

Cette troisième édition est revue et augmentée sur la précédente.

Faut-il ajouter que ce livre n'est qu'un essai historique et non une bibliographie. Il forme, en quelque sorte, une introduction à ma bibliographie universelle des bibliographies (A World Bibliography of Bibliographies) dont la seconde édition fut publiée en 1947–1949, en trois volumes.'

The truly immense task of compiling the *World Bibliography of Bibliographies* referred to in these introductions was indeed occupying Besterman at this time. In June 1936 he read a paper on it at the annual conference of the Library Association:

33. *Introduction to a new bibliography of bibliographies.* By Theodore Besterman. London, 1936.

100 copies privately printed for the author by John Johnson, University Press, Oxford.

pp. 15 + [1].

Note: 'This paper is reprinted, by kind permission and with only trifling changes, from the *Library Association Record* for June, 1936.'

p. 7: 'But enough of these criticisms; it is all too easy to point to the errors of one's predecessors, though this is necessary if we are to learn the lessons these mistakes teach us and if we are to profit by them. I have tried to do so and I shall welcome criticism, in my turn, of the principles I am myself following in the bibliography of bibliographies on which I am working.'

p. 14: 'I am conscious that this whole enterprise will appear over-ambitious for one man to undertake single-handed.'

At the same time, and as an offshoot of his work on the *World Bibliography*, Besterman contributed to the *British Museum Quarterly* lists of 'Libri desiderati', short-title lists of bibliographies not in the British Museum Library; four such lists appeared in 1936, 37 and 38.

There was a slight reversion in 1938 when he published:

34. *Water-divining. New facts and theories.* By Theodore Besterman. With 2 plates and 7 plans and diagrams. Methuen & Co. Ltd. London, 36 Essex Street, Strand, W.C.2.

First published in 1938.

pp. IX +[3], 207 +[1].

Dedication: 'To the memory of Sir William Fletcher Barrett, F.R.S., whose courage and penetration added the facts of dowsing to the canon of scientific knowledge.'

Chapter One, Introduction: 'In *The Divining-Rod,* in which I had the honour of collaborating with the late Sir William Barrett, F.R.S., the whole field of dowsing was comprehensively surveyed, historically, factually and theoretically.

The present book, therefore, does not re-traverse any of the ground covered in *The Diving-Rod*; it makes no attempt again to establish the antiquity and historical respectability of the subject; it does not seek once more to recount the feats of the great British and foreign dowsers of the past generation and of previous centuries; it does not purpose to set out again a systematic description and analysis of the overwhelming evidence for the reality of the finding of water by some means the precise nature of which is as yet unknown; it merely proposes, in short, to *supplement* the previous volume.'

In the same year Besterman resumed his strictly bibliographical work with a second contribution to the series *Oxford Books on*

Bibliography, this time a documentary study of a well-known firm of publishers:

35. *The publishing firm of Cadell & Davies. Select correspondence and accounts 1793–1836.* Edited with an introduction and notes by Theodore Besterman. Oxford University Press, London: Humphrey Milford, 1938.

pp. xxxv +[1], 189 +[1].

Introduction: 'The *documents pour servir à l'histoire* brought together in this volume are derived, though not directly, from the actual files of Cadell & Davies. This firm had the very sensible habit of keeping copies, or making drafts or abstracts, of their letters on the second leaves or any other available blank spaces on the letters they were answering. The files thus created . . . found their way into the hands of various booksellers . . . from whom they were bought in recent years by Dr. John Johnson. . . . My debt to Dr. Johnson is, however, even greater, for to him I owe the suggestion that the present volume should be put together.

All these documents are printed here, so far as I know, for the first time. So far as typography permits, I have tried (apart from the long *s*, which I have dropped) to give a faithful representation of the original manuscripts in regard to spelling, punctuation, and kindred details. This has sometimes been regarded as pedantic, but such details are often highly informative to the expert.'

In the midst of his work on the *World Bibliography*, Besterman became interested in establishing and working a private press named after his house in Hampstead, Guyon House, and in editorial work connected with two books published by another 'private press', the Golden Cockerel. Besterman's own press was totally destroyed by bombing in 1940, its only productions being:

(i). *Magna carta and other charters of English liberties.* [device] The Guyon House Press.

The colophon reads: 'Magna carta . . . in a revised text and translation by Noel Denholm-Young and with head and tail-pieces by Berthold Wolpe has been printed and bound by Theodore Besterman assisted by V. H. Ridler and F. J. Coton . . . August-November 1938.'

250 numbered copies were printed on Batchelor hand-made paper and six copies on vellum, lettered A-F.

(ii). *This man. A sequence of wood-engravings* by Elizabeth Rivers. The Guyon House Press.

The colophon reads: 'This man . . . printed and bound by

Theodore Besterman assisted by V. H. Ridler and F. J. Coton . . . January to March 1939.'

200 numbered copies were printed on Corinthian Fine Text paper and five, lettered A-E, on vellum.

The sheets of a third publication, *The Dictionary of Love*, which were in process of binding, were completely destroyed.

The two books published by the Golden Cockerel Press were:

36. [DOUBLE SPREAD TITLE] *The travels & sufferings of Father Jean de Brébeuf among the Hurons of Canada as described by himself.* Edited & translated from the French and Latin by Theodore Besterman. The Golden Cockerel Press MCMXXXVIII.

pp. 196 +[4].

Colophon: 'This book has been printed and published by Christopher Sandford & Owen Rutter at the Golden Cockerel Press . . . and completed the 19th day of August, 1938. The two illustrations and the engraved titling on the title page are the work of Eric Gill. The edition is limited to 300 numbered copies.'

An edition of the original French text came out in 1957:

37. *Textes littéraires français. Saint Jean de Brébeuf, Les relations de ce qui s'est passé au pays des Hurons* (1635–1648). Publiées par Theodore Besterman. Librairie E. Droz, 8, rue Verdaine, Genève, 1957.

pp. XXVII +[1], 228 +[8].

Notice bibliographique: 'Le présent livre a déjà été publié, mais seulement en traduction anglaise.'

38. *The Pilgrim Fathers. A journal of their coming in the Mayflower to New England and their life and adventures there:* edited, with preface and notes, by Theodore Besterman: eight engravings by Geoffrey Wales. Reprinted, from the rare 1622 edition, at the Golden Cockerel Press: 1939.

pp. 87 +[1].

Edition limited to 300 numbered copies.

Preface: 'We must consider ourselves very fortunate that two or three of the Pilgrim Fathers had the wisdom, in the midst of their unceasing labours, to set down for posterity a detailed and accurate account of the events of those first months.

When the Journal was completed it was taken to England, in the Fortune, by Robert Cushman, who reached London in February 1622 . . . On 27 June we find it entered in the Stationers' Register under the provisional title of Newes from Newe England; and the book was published shortly after under the

> title shown on page 5 [A relation or Journall of the beginning and proceedings of the English Plantation setled at Plimoth in New England. . . .].
>
> The present reprint is a faithful reproduction of the British Museum copy, with the following exceptions: the long *s* and the frequent italics have been dropped, the marginal summaries and Biblical references have been omitted, the use of u–v and i–j has been modernized, obvious misprints have been corrected (though peculiarities of spelling have been retained), abbreviations have been expanded, and some of the longer passages have been broken up into paragraphs. Such notes as are necessary to make the text intelligible have been inserted in it, within square brackets.'

In 1939, 1940 the *World Bibliography* came out. In compiling it Besterman had examined personally between 80,000 and 100,000 volumes at the British Museum. It was 'compiled almost wholly at first hand; entries cited at second hand do not attain one per cent of the whole.' It was a magnificent personal and completely characteristic achievement; but, generous as always in acknowledging help from whatever quarter, he pays tribute to the assistance given by the British Museum and the National Central Library.

'I am conscious that this whole enterprise will appear over-ambitious for one man to have undertaken entirely single-handed, without any kind of subsidy, in his own time and at his own risk. I therefore think it well to make it clear that if the project has been carried through successfully this has been due mainly to two causes, which I take very great pleasure in acknowledging. The first is the ready help of the Keeper and the officers and staff of the Department of Printed Books at the British Museum. . . . The second cause to which I have referred is the equally generous help given to me by the Principal Librarian, . . . the Sub-Librarian . . . and the staff of the National Central Library.'

39. *A world bibliography of bibliographies*. By Theodore Besterman. Vol. I A-L (Vol. II M-Z, Index). Printed for the author at the University Press, Oxford, and published by him at 98 Heath Street, London, N.W.3. Sole agents for North and South America, The H. W. Wilson Company, 950–972 University Avenue, New York, N.Y. 1939 (1940).

2 vols. vol. I, pp. xxiv, 587 +[1].
vol. II, pp. [4], 641 +[3].

Dedication: 'This bibliography is dedicated to the Keeper, officers and staff of the Department of Printed Books in the British Museum with gratitude and admiration.'

Introduction: p. xxi. 'The bibliography has been carried systematically from the beginnings to the end of 1935, but also contains a large number of entries relating to works published up to the beginning of 1939.'

pp. xv, xvi. 'The question is . . . whether it is possible to give some indication of the degree of completeness of a bibliography without indulging in the annotation which is impossible in a work of the present scope and scale. It seemed to me that this could be achieved, to a considerable extent, by recording the approximate number of entries set out in it. This method if, of course, a rough-and-ready one, but experience shows that it is remarkably effective. And I trust that its novelty will not tell against it.'

Almost incredibly, Besterman was able to produce a second edition, ten years later, 'over 55 per centum bigger than the first', and including extensive changes in the transcription of titles. The number of volumes recorded and separately collated was 63,776 and the number of headings and sub-headings under which these volumes were set out was over 9,000.

40. *A world bibliography of bibliographies and of bibliographical catalogues, calendars, abstracts, digests, indexes, and the like.* By Theodore Besterman, Volume I A-H (Volume II I-Z; Volume III Index). Second edition revised and greatly enlarged throughout. Privately published by the author, Theodore Besterman, 16 Keats Grove, London, N.W.3., 1947 (1949).

Vol. I, pp. XXVIII, cols. 1-1450 +[1] p.
Vol. II, pp. [6], cols. 1451-3196 +[1] p.
Vol. III, pp. [6], cols. 3197-4111 +[1] p.
Dedication as in the first edition.

Preface to the second edition: 'This edition has been brought down to 1944—1945. Large parts of the field have been surveyed anew, the text has been minutely revised throughout, and very many changes and improvements have been made.'

Second impression, 1950.

A 'third and final' edition, produced, printed and published in Switzerland in 1955, 1956, at last acknowledges that 'the undertaking has in fact outstripped the capacity and resources of a single worker.' It would, I am sure, long since have outstripped the capacity and tenacity of any other single worker.

41. *A world bibliography of bibliographies and of bibliographical catalogues, calendars, abstracts, digests, indexes, and the like.* By

Theodore Besterman. Volume I, A-E (Volume II, F-N; Volume III, O-Z; Volume IV, Index). Third and final edition revised and greatly enlarged throughout. Societas bibliographica, 8 rue Verdaine, Genève.

Vol. I, February 1955; vol. II, February–November 1955; vol. III and IV, February 1955–June 1956.

Vol. I, pp. XXXIII +[2], cols. 1-1326 +[1] p.
Vol. II, pp. [4], cols. 1327-2858.
Vol. III, pp. [6], cols. 2859-4408 +[1] p.
Vol. IV, pp. [6], cols. 4409-5701 +[1] p.
Dedication as in the first edition.

Preface: 'This edition has been brought down to 1953, inclusive, and a good many bibliographies of later date are being inserted as the work passes through the press.... The number of cross-references has been multiplied. Most important, however, are the additional entries, of both old and new bibliographies, which make this edition twice as big as the first. The number of volumes recorded and separately collated is now about 80,000, arranged under about 12,000 headings and sub-headings.

The most important single improvement . . . results from a systematic search of the bibliographic collections of the Library of Congress. . . . Without this it would have been impossible to do justice to the greatly expanded bibliographic output of the Americas . . . and to record adequately the wartime and post-war publications of the European belligerents. I am much indebted to Unesco for a contribution towards the expenses of the journey: a grant the more appreciated in that it is the only financial help I have received throughout the twenty years during which the present bibliography has been a major preoccupation.

A special effort has also been made to improve still further the coverage of scientific bibliographies, and of those in slavonic languages.'

A world bibliography was reprinted in reduced facsimile by the Scarecrow Press, 1960.

42. *A world bibliography of bibliographies and of bibliographical catalogues, calendars, abstracts, digests, indexes, and the like.* By Theodore Besterman. Volume I, A-D (II, E-K; III, L-P; IV, Q-Z; V, Index). Fourth edition revised and greatly enlarged throughout. Societas Bibliographica, 7 rue de Genève, Lausanne.

T. p. verso of vol. V: Fourth edition March 1965–June 1966.

Numbered in one sequence throughout in columns, Vol. V, three columns to a page.
Printed in Switzerland.
Dedication as in the first edition.

Preface: 'When I published the third edition of this bibliography ten years ago I was firmly resolved that it should be the last. It seemed impossible to face once again the vast labour of bringing it up-to-date, to say nothing of the necessary revision, and in any case it was likely that another task would last out my time. However, that task has been completed, and the demand for a new edition of the present work has become insistent. So here is the fourth edition, this time really the last, of a work first undertaken thirty years ago.

This edition has been brought down to 1963, inclusive, and a good many bibliographies of later date are being recorded as the work passes through the press. Large parts of the field have been surveyed anew, the text has been minutely revised throughout, and very many changes and improvements have been made. In particular, the scientific, political and other developments of the post-war years have made necessary many additions to the subject-headings, and many changes.'

The preface to Vol. IV gives the number of volumes collated for this edition as 117, 187, and indicates that they are classified under 15,825 headings and sub-headings.

The 500th anniversary of the invention of printing, traditionally associated with the year 1440, was the occasion for the publication of a long planned bibliography of bibliographies of early printed books. 'As originally planned some years ago this book was to have been a fully annotated critical bibliography, accompanied by a lengthy introduction on the development of typographical bibliography, and clothed in type, paper and binding worthy of its purpose—the commemoration of the 500th anniversary of the Western invention of printing. The war has made this impossible, and perhaps it is just as well—for instead of a collector's piece the student is now offered the essential part of the project, the bare bones of the bibliography itself.'

43. *Early printed books to the end of the sixteenth century. A bibliography of bibliographies.* By Theodore Besterman. Bernard Quaritch Ltd, 11 Grafton Street, New Bond Street, London W.1.

Published in September 1940.

pp. 309 +[1].

Preface: 'I have persisted in the practice introduced in my *World Bibliography of Bibliographies*—that of showing in square brackets at the end of each entry the number of works set out in the bibliography to which it refers.'

A second edition, with the text 'revised and completed throughout, and brought up to date, the whole better arranged and indexed', came out in 1961:

44. *Early printed books to the end of the sixteenth century. A bibliography of bibliographies.* By Theodore Besterman. Second edition revised and much enlarged. Societas Bibliographica, 8 rue Verdaine, Genève, 1961.
pp. 344 +[4].
Printed in Switzerland. Typography by Theodore Besterman.

Long before Besterman became associated with Aslib—the Association of Special Libraries and Information Bureaux, established in 1926 to facilitate the co-ordination and systematic use of sources of knowledge and information in all public affairs and in industry and commerce and in all the arts and sciences. Connexion with Aslib eventually led to new, imaginative proposals:

45. *On a proposed union catalogue of periodicals.* By Theodore Besterman. Aslib offprint series No. 10. London, Association of Special Libraries and Information Bureaux, 31 Museum Street, W.C.1. 1943.
p. 8.
'This paper is based on one read to the seventeenth Aslib conference (1942) and printed in its *Report of proceedings* . . . some passages in it are revised from my article "Desiderata bibliographica", *Library Review* (Glasgow, 1942), No. 62.'

46. *On a bibliography of dictionaries.* By Theodore Besterman. From The Proceedings of the British Society for International Bibliography, IV, 63-73. One hundred copies privately printed for the author, 98 Heath Street, London, N.W.3. January 1943.
pp. 11 +[1].
'By a coincidence which I insist on taking as a happy omen, it is almost exactly ten years since I started to plan my *World bibliography of bibliographies.* I was fearful, I must confess, lest I had undertaken a task beyond the strength, to say nothing of the competence, of a single worker. Yet the doubts I then felt are as nothing compared to those I experience today; for I have now in hand a companion task, the difficulties of which on the whole exceed those of the *World bibliography*: nothing less, indeed, than a bibliography of dictionaries.'

The Union catalogue of periodicals eventually saw the light of day twelve years later, having been successively edited by Theodore Besterman, A. Loewenberg and James D. Stewart, under the title of *British union-catalogue of periodicals* (known for short as BUCOP), published by Butterworths Scientific Publications between 1955 and 1958. The bibliography of dictionaries has so far come to naught, but it is fitting to record that another, very useful suggestion from Besterman put forward a little later, while he was still associated with Aslib, came to fruition as the *British Union-Catalogue of Early Music* (1957). Besterman played no part in the compilation of this work, but it is right to recall his initial interest.

A third proposal, put forward at the September 1943 Conference of Aslib, 'Proposal for an international library clearing-house', which appeared in the Report of the Proceedings of this conference and was published separately as No. 12 of the Aslib offprint series, bore fruit in the Inter-Allied Book Centre which later became part of Unesco's International Clearing House for Publications.

There were also routine publications of a minor nature, such as:

47. Aslib Manuals. General editor: Theodore Besterman. Aslib (Association of Special Libraries and Information Bureaux), 52 Bloomsbury Street, London, W.C.1. 1945.

One Volume only published under Besterman's editorship:

Manual of special library technique. [By] J. E. Wright. A second edition came out in 1946.

Preface: 'The tasks and problems of the special librarian and information officer are many and varied. Some of them do not as yet form the subject-matter of formal teaching.

It is not in any sense a complete treatise on the subject: it is precisely what its title indicates, a manual of practice in technical special libraries. In short, it has the modest objective of helping the beginner in a hurry.

It is intended to publish further manuals on special parts of this wide field. Suggestions will be welcomed.'

48. *Select list of standard British scientific and technical books.* Compiled at the request of the British Council. Third edition revised and enlarged. Aslib (Association of Special Libraries and Information Bureaux), 52 Bloomsbury Street, London, W.C.1. 1946.

pp. 63 +[1].

Preface by Theodore Besterman: 'This list is not intended to be more than its title indicates, a select list of standard British scientific and technical books. . . . The list is . . . in principle limited to works in print, though under present conditions no assurance can be given on this point.

The general editorial work has been done in the Aslib office, largely by Miss Iris Lovatt, under my direction.'

The *Journal of Documentation* which Besterman founded in 1945 and edited from 1945 to 1947 is however a major achievement. It has now long been recognised as an important medium for the publication of authoritative studies in documentation and information work.

In his introductory note in the first number, which appeared in June, 1945 Besterman writes as follows: 'All, as opportunity serves, will receive attention in these pages. Nor will this attention be limited by national boundaries or by the artificial segregation of the sciences and humanities. Of all these things the present first number offers some testimony.'

49 *The journal of documentation. Devoted to the recording, organization and dissemination of specialized knowledge.* Aslib, 52 Bloomsbury Street, London, W.C.1.
Quarterly; edited 1945–1947 by Theodore Besterman; after June, 1947 by an Advisory Editorial Board.

The Chairman of the Aslib Council wrote as follows in the June 1947 number of the Journal: 'Mr. Besterman's term of office as Editor has been short, yet it has been long enough to establish the *Journal* as a publication with a definite character of its own and to set a high standard of production. Aslib will always be grateful to him for his energy and pertinacity in pressing forward against considerable difficulties.'

Besterman's work for Aslib was an appropriate training for the work in Unesco which now claimed his energies and initiative.

In 1946 he went over to Unesco to serve successively as Counsellor of the World Bibliographical and Library Centre, and Head of the Department for the Exchange of Information.

The desirability of better bibliographical access to books and periodicals has always been a dominating feature of Besterman's thought and a recurring theme of articles and papers. His *World Bibliography* and the *Union Catalogues* already mentioned provide clear indication, not only of his thoughts but also of his readiness to put his enormous energies to work to help in the creation of the much needed guides. He now had, it seemed, the chance to create the necessary instruments for the purpose on a world-wide basis. That his hopes were frustrated was perhaps inevitable in view of the magnitude of the tasks to be undertaken and the diversity of interests which Unesco had to serve. That he remained an enthusiast is shown by the book he published on Unesco in 1951:

50. *UNESCO. Peace in the minds of men.* By Theodore Besterman, lately Head of the Department for Exchange of Information, United Nations Educational, Scientific and Cultural Organization. Methuen & Co. Ltd, London, 36 Essex Street, Strand, W.C.2.
First published in 1951.
pp. XI +[1], 132 +[2]. Frontispiece and 11 plates.
Dedication: 'To Julian Huxley.'
In the preface to this work, he writes: 'Unesco is easy to criticize, even to mock. How could it be otherwise?
In this, the first book to be written about Unesco, I have resisted the temptation to pick holes—that would have been all too easy. Having at least had the advantage of occupying a central post in Unesco which brought me into contact with all its activities, I have tried instead to give an impartial exposisition of what Unesco has been established to do, what it has actually done, and what it hopes to do in the future.'

At this time also he produced a third edition of a guide to sources of information sponsored by Unesco and the International Federation for Documentation:

51. *Index bibliographicus. Directory of current periodical abstracts and bibliographies. Répertoire des revues courantes, de bibliographies analytiques et signalétiques.* Volume I: Science and technology. Sciences et technologie. Volume II: Social sciences, education, humanistic studies. Sciences sociales, éducation, sciences humaines. Compiled by, préparé par, Theodore Besterman. Unesco Paris, IFD. The Hague, FID La Haye.
Third edition, completely revised, March, May 1952.
2 vols. vol. I, pp. XI +[1], 52.
vol. II, pp. XI +[1], 72.
Publication No. 863 of Unesco; Publication No. 247 of the International Federation for Documentation.
Foreword: by Jaime Torres Bodet, Director general, Unesco:
'The first edition of the guide, edited by [Marcel] Godet, was published at Geneva in 1925. . . . In 1926 a supplement was published at Renaix, Belgium under the auspices of the International Institute for Bibliography, and a second edition of the Index as a whole was published in Berlin in 1931, jointly edited by Marcel Godet and Joris Vorstius of the Prussian State Library, Berlin.
The demand for a new directory was first brought to

Unesco's urgent attention by the International Conference on Science Abstracting, held in June 1949.

The present Index is in direct continuation of the earlier work, although the form and scope of the entries are somewhat changed.'

The Fourth edition compiled and published by F.I.D. in 1959, 1964.

But already a completely new development in Besterman's activities had taken place. He had long been a successful collector of the letters, manuscripts, books and portraits of Voltaire and had engaged in the preparation of a critical edition of his correspondence —a gigantic task, even for a Besterman. By 1952 he had engaged himself almost entirely to this task, giving his collection to the City of Geneva and becoming the Director of the Institut et Musée Voltaire, at Voltaire's old house, Les Délices. The first volumes of the Correspondence came from the press in 1953, but before this he had edited Voltaire's Notebooks. 'I have been preparing for a number of years,' he writes in the preface to this work, 'a critical edition of Voltaire's correspondence, and during the course of this work I have naturally come across a good many general manuscripts by and relating to Voltaire and to the French eighteenth century in general. Much of this material I hope to publish from time to time as the progress of the larger task permits. The present volumes form the first of these publications. I consider it a great privilege to have been able to put together for the first time so outstandingly important and exciting a publication as these notebooks which Voltaire kept throughout his life.'

52. *Voltaire's notebooks*. Edited, in large part for the first time, by Theodore Besterman. I (II). Institut et Musée Voltaire, Les Délices, Genève, 1952.

Printed in Great Britain at the University Press, Oxford, by Charles Batey, Printer to the University.

2 vols.: vol. I, pp. IX + [1], 240; vol. II, pp. [4], 241-506 + [2].

Dedication: 'To my wife. Quid faceret eruditio sine dilectione?'

Introduction: 'The editing of such notebooks as these is not without special problems. Voltaire, though highly fastidious about the presentation of his work in print, when writing was even more careless than most of his contemporaries in matters of spelling, punctuation, the use of capitals, and the like.

To reproduce in print the excitingly living feeling these notebooks give one is difficult and in some respects impossible: but it has been my aim to give the reader as near a sense of the original as is typographically practicable without making the reading of the text a constant struggle.

It is never possible completely to reproduce an informal manuscript in readable type, but I believe that the procedure here adopted has produced a text faithful enough to the original for all but the most minute diplomatic purposes.'

In 1953 the first volumes of what was later described as 'one of the most remarkable feats of scholarship of our lifetime' appeared, to be followed regularly each year by up to ten volumes!

53. *Voltaire's correspondence*. Edited by Theodore Besterman. Institut et Musée Voltaire, Les Délices, Genève 1953 (–1965). The half-title contains the words: Publications de l'Institut et Musée Voltaire. Sous la direction de Theodore Besterman.

General preface: 'Voltaire's correspondence superbly represents a critical period of history . . . it gives us a close-up of the society of an entire epoch, in all its nobility, grandeur and baseness.

The text has not been broken up, all notes being assembled at the end of each letter, and so arranged under four headings: Manuscripts, Editions, Textual notes, and Commentary, that the reader can go direct to the category of notes in which he is interested.'

Vol. I, 1953: 1704–1725; II, 1953: 1726–1732; III, 1953: 1733–1734; IV, 1954: 1735; V, 1954: 1736; VI, 1954: 1737; VII, 1954: Jan.–Nov. 1738; VIII, 1954: Dec. 1738–Feb. 1739; IX, 1954: Mar.–Dec. 1739; X, 1954: 1740; XI, 1955: 1741; XII, 1955: 1742–June 1743; XIII, 1955: July 1743–May 1744; XIV, 1956: 1744–1745; XV, 1956: 1746–1747; XVI, 1956: 1748; XVII, 1956: 1749; XVIII, 1956: 1750; XIX, 1956: Jan.–July 1751; XX, 1956: Aug. 1751–July 1752; XXI, 1957: Aug.–Dec. 1752; XXII, 1957: Jan.–June, 1753; XXIII, 1957: July–Dec. 1753; XXIV, 1957: Jan.–May 1754; XXV, 1957: June–Dec. 1754; XXVI, 1957: Jan.–April 1755; XXVII, 1957: May–Aug. 1755; XXVIII, 1957: Sept.–Dec. 1755; XXIX, 1957: Jan.–May 1756; XXX, 1958: June–Dec. 1756; XXXI, 1958: Jan.–July 1757; XXXII, 1958: Aug.–Dec. 1757; XXXIII, 1958: Jan.–June 1758; XXXIV, 1958: July–Dec. 1758; XXXV, 1958: Jan.–Mar. 1759; XXXVI, 1958: April–July 1759; XXXVII, 1958: Aug.–Nov. 1759; XXXVIII, 1958: Dec. 1759; XXXIX, 1960: Subject Index to Vols. I–XXXVIII, A-K; XL, 1960: Subject Index to Vols. I–XXXVIII, L-Z; XLI, 1958: Jan.–April 1760; XLII, 1959: May–July 1760; XLIII, 1959: Aug.–Sept. 1760; XLIV, 1959: Oct.–Dec. 1760; XLV, 1959: Jan.–April 1761; XLVI, 1959: May–

Aug. 1761; XLVII, 1959: Sept.–Dec. 1761; XLVIII, 1959: Jan.–May 1762; XLIX, 1959: June–Aug. 1762; L, 1959: Sept.–Dec. 1762; LI, 1959: Jan.–Mar. 1763; LII, 1960: April—Aug. 1763; LIII, 1960: Sept.–Dec. 1763; LIV, 1960: Jan.–April 1764; LV, 1960: May–Aug. 1764; LVI, 1960: Sept.–Dec. 1764; LVII, 1960: Jan.–Mar. 1765; LVIII, 1960, April–July 1765; LIX, 1960: Aug.–Dec. 1765; LX, 1961: Jan.–Mar. 1766; LXI, 1961: April–June 1766; LXII, 1961: July–Sept. 1766; LXIII, 1961: Oct.–Dec. 1766; LXIV, 1961: Jan.–Feb. 1767; LXV, 1961: Mar.–May 1767; LXVI, 1961: June–Aug. 1767; LXVII, 1961: Sept.–Dec. 1767; LXVIII, 1961: Jan.–Mar. 1768; LXIX, 1961: April–July 1768; LXX, 1962: Aug.–Dec. 1768; LXXI, 1962: Jan.–April 1769; LXXII, 1962: May–Aug. 1769; LXXIII, 1962: Sept.–Dec. 1769; LXXIV, 1962: Jan.–Mar. 1770; LXXV, 1962: April–June 1770; LXXVI, 1962: July–Sept. 1770; LXXVII, 1962: Oct.–Dec. 1770; LXXVIII, 1962: Jan.–Mar. 1771; LXXIX, 1962: April–July 1771; LXXX, 1963: Aug.–Dec. 1771; LXXXI, 1963: Jan.–April 1772; LXXXII, 1963: May–Aug. 1772; LXXXIII, 1963: Sept.–Dec. 1772; LXXXIV, 1963: Jan.–Mar. 1773; LXXXV, 1963: April–Aug. 1773; LXXXVI, 1963: Sept.–Dec. 1773; LXXXVII, 1963: Jan.–April 1774; LXXXVIII, 1963: May–Aug. 1774; LXXXIX, 1963: Sept.–Dec. 1774; XC, 1964: Jan.–April 1775; XCI, 1964: May–Aug. 1775; XCII, 1964: Sept.–Dec. 1775; XCIII 1964: Jan.–Mar. 1776; XCIV, 1964: April–July 1776; XCV, 1964: Aug.–Dec. 1776; XCVI, 1964: Jan.–June 1777; XCVII, 1964: July–Dec. 1777; XCVIII, 1964: Jan.–May 1778; XCIX, 1964: List of unidentifiable letters; List of appendixes; Keys to abbreviations and pseudonyms; Indexes of words, quotations and illustrations; Calendar of manuscripts; C, 1964: Bibliography of the correspondence; List of manuscripts quoted in the notes; CI, 1964: List of Works cited; CII, 1964: Concordance; List of letters by correspondents; CIII, 1965: General Index, A-C; CIV, 1965: General Index, D-F; CV, 1965: General Index, G-L; CVI, 1965: General Index, M-R; CVII, 1965: General Index, S-Z.

Besterman is also responsible for the abridged edition, with the notes in French, in the *Pléiade* series.

The Bestermans took up residence at Les Délices in 1953. The Institute was formally inaugurated in 1954 with an address by Besterman:

54. *Voltaire*. Discours prononcé par Theodore Besterman, à l'inauguration de l'Institut et Musée Voltaire. Institut et Musée Voltaire. Les Délices, Genève, 1954.

pp. 19 + [1].

The same year he contributed to *Genava* an article on early editions of Voltaire unknown to Bengesco: 'Quelques éditions anciennes de Voltaire inconnues à Bengesco.' After paying a tribute to the remarkable success of Bengesco's work, he goes on:

'Pourtant dans le monde de la bibliographie le dernier mot n'est jamais prononcé. En effet, parmi nos collections Voltairiennes (qui constituent actuellement la bibliothèque de l'Institut et Musée Voltaire) se trouve un assez grand nombre d'éditions inconnues à Bengesco. Il n'est pas question ici de refaire son travail dans le sens de la bibliographie technique, tâche entreprise par M. Desmond Flower, mais tout simplement de décrire les éditions manquant au Bengesco, en nous limitant à celles du dix-huitième siècle.'

He then amused himself by publishing, anonymously, in miniature form ($1\frac{3}{8}$ in. × 1 in.) an anthology of *Idle thoughts* (Geneva 1956).

Despite the work on the correspondence, Besterman was able also to prepare, and contribute largely to a series of studies on Voltaire:

55. *Travaux sur Voltaire et le dix-huitième siècle.* Sous la direction de Theodore Besterman. Institut et Musée Voltaire, Les Délices, Genève, 1955.

From vol. II (1956) the series appeared under the title: *Studies on Voltaire and the eighteenth century.*

Contributions to the series by Besterman himself include:

Tome I, 1955: Voltaire, discours inaugural; Voltaire jugé par Flaubert; Rousseau, conseiller familial: deux lettres; Voltaire's correspondence: additions I.

Tome II, 1956: Voltaire et le désastre de Lisbonne: ou, la mort de l'optimisme; Voltaire's commentary on Frederick's *L'art de la guerre*, edited by Theodore Besterman; Voltaire's correspondence: additions II.

Vol. IV, 1957: Voltaire's correspondence: additions III; Note on the authorship of the *Connaissance des beautés*; Review: René Pomeau, *La Religion de Voltaire.*

Vol. VI, 1958: Voltaire's correspondence, additions IV; The Manuscripts of the Institut et Musée Voltaire.

Vol. VIII, 1959: Some eighteenth-century Voltaire editions unknown to Bengesco.

Vol. X, 1959: Le Vrai Voltaire par ses lettres; Voltaire's correspondence: additions V.

Vol. XII, 1960: The terra-cotta statue of Voltaire made by Houdon for Beaumarchais; Voltaire's correspondence: additions VI.

Vol. XVIII, 1961: A provisional bibliography of Italian editions and translations of Voltaire.

Vol. XXXII, 1965: Voltaire, absolute monarchy, and the enlightened monarch.

At the time of writing, the Studies on Voltaire have reached vol. LI (1967).

From this time onwards, besides the volumes of these *Studies*, many works connected with Voltaire have appeared from Besterman's pen, separate publications noted below and articles such as: 'La terre cuite du "Voltaire assis" exécutée par Houdon pour Beaumarchais' in *Genava*, 1957 and 'Friedrich II an Voltaire. Neun bisher unveröffentlichte Briefe' in *Der Monat*, August 1958. He organised the First International Congress on the Enlightenment and edited its *Transactions* in four volumes (1963).

56. *Le goût des manuscrits*. Discours inaugural prononcé à Bâle le 28 juin 1956 par Theodore Besterman devant la Société Suisse d'amateurs d'autographes. Societas Bibliographica, 8 rue Verdaine, Genève.
Published in 1956.
pp. 45 +[3].

57. *Lettres d'amour de Voltaire à sa nièce*. Publiées pour la première fois par Theodore Besterman. 1957, Librairie Plon, 8 rue Garancière, Paris VIe.
pp. 207 +[3]. 4 plates.
Printed in Switzerland. 10 copies hors commerce, marked A-J; 100 on Rives paper watermarked Voltaire, numbered 1-100; 350 copies for the Fellows of the Pierpont Morgan Library.
Dedication: 'A Nancy Mitford.'
Notes préliminaires: 'Ces lettres composaient deux dossiers, . . . Le temps, heureusement, n'a pas trop amenuisé ces dossiers, de sorte que quand ils ont passé entre nos mains, ils contenaient encore 142 lettres sur 150. . . .'

58. *The love letters of Voltaire to his niece*. Edited and translated for first publication by Theodore Besterman. William Kimber, London.
First published in England in 1958.
pp. 158 +[2]. 3 plates.
Dedication: 'To Nancy Mitford.'

59. *Les lettres de la Marquise du Châtelet*. Publiées par Theodore Besterman. I lettres 1-231, 1733–1739 (II lettres 232-486, 1740–1749). Institut et Musée Voltaire, Les Délices, Genève, 1958.

2 vols. vol. I, pp. 389 +[1]. Frontispiece in colour.
vol. II, pp. 337 +[1]. Same „ „
The verso of the half-title bears the words:
Publications de l'Institut et Musée Voltaire. Sous la direction de Theodore Besterman. Série d'études III (IV).
Notes préliminaires: 'L'edition que nous donnons aujourd'hui de la correspondence de Mme du Châtelet est basée en grande partie sur les manuscrits eux-mêmes.
La présente édition . . . porte à 486 les lettres de la marquise, sans compter les nombreuses lettres à elle adressées.'

In 1958 Besterman contributed an *Index volume* (one of many indexes compiled by him) to A. U. Pope's *Survey of Persian Art*:

60. *A survey of Persian art from prehistoric times to the present.* Arthur Upham Pope, editor. Phyllis Ackermann, assistant editor. Index volume. Compiled by Theodore Besterman. Oxford University Press, London, New York, Toronto, 1958.
pp. [6] + 136.

61. *Voltaire essays and another.* Theodore Besterman. London, Oxford University Press, New York, Toronto, 1962.
Published in 1963.
p. [8], 181 +[1]. Six plates.
Preface: 'I am not at all sure that it is a good idea to give permanent life within the covers of a book to words written for delivery to a particular audience or on a special occasion. So far I have resisted the temptation, but recently a kindly critic wrote in the *Revue de littérature comparée* (1960), XXXIV, 293: "M. Besterman, trop absorbé par ses publications pour écrire beaucoup lui-même, prend volontiers la parole en des occasions solennelles; il s'efforce alors d'éviter l'académisme et parle volontiers en ami, voire en frère, toujours vigilant, du grand homme, dont il a choisi d'être en notre siècle, le porte-parole autant que l'éditeur." These words describe my intentions so exactly that they were irresistible, and here is the result.'

62. *Select letters of Voltaire.* Translated and edited by Theodore Besterman. Thomas Nelson and Sons Ltd, London [etc].
Published in 1963.
pp. XII, 180.
Preface: 'My edition of *Voltaire's Correspondence* will contain, when completed, about 20,000 letters addressed to over 1,200 correspondents. It is therefore impossible to give anything like a complete picture of this universal genius in a single volume. . . . An effort has nevertheless been made to give a glimpse of nearly every important aspect of Voltaire's long and varied life and activities.'

63. Gustave Flaubert, *Le Théâtre de Voltaire*. Published for the first time by Theodore Besterman. Studies on Voltaire and the eighteenth century, vols. L–LI. Institut et Musée Voltaire, Les Délices, Genève. 1967. pp. 722.

In concluding this list of Besterman's writings I can perhaps do nothing better than echo the words he used of Voltaire in the passage just quoted:

It is impossible to give anything like a complete bibliography of this universal genius in a single article.

Index